Visual QuickStart Guide

Illustrator CS2

for Windows and Macintosh

Elaine Weinmann
Peter Lourekas

Peachpit Press

For Simona

Visual QuickStart Guide
Illustrator CS2 for Windows and Macintosh
Elaine Weinmann and Peter Lourekas

Peachpit Press
1249 Eighth Street
Berkeley, CA 94710
510/524-2178
800/283-9444
510/524-2221 (fax)

Find us on the Web at: http://www.peachpit.com

Visual QuickStart Guide is a trademark of Peachpit Press, a division of Pearson Education

Cover design: Peachpit Press
Interior design: Elaine Weinmann
Production: Elaine Weinmann and Peter Lourekas
Illustrations: Elaine Weinmann and Peter Lourekas,
except as noted

Colophon
This book was created with QuarkXPress 6.5 on two Power Macintosh G5s. The fonts used are Sabon, Gill Sans, and Myriad from Adobe Systems, Inc.

ISBN 0-321-33656-9
9 8 7 6 5

Printed and bound in the United States of America

Our heartfelt thanks to

The creative and skilled *artists* whose work we're honored to feature in the color insert (for their contact information, see the following page). Special thanks to *Daniel Pelavin,* for his many illustrations that grace the text pages and the color insert.

Nancy Aldrich-Ruenzel, Publisher, Peachpit Press; *Nancy Davis,* Editor-in-Chief; *Marjorie Baer,* Senior Executive Editor; *Lisa Brazieal,* Production Editor; *Ellen Reilly,* cover production; *Gary-Paul Prince,* Promotions Manager; *Keasley Jones,* Associate Publisher; and the rest of the folks at Peachpit Press. They're a pleasure to work with.

Cary Norsworthy, our wonderful editor at Peachpit Press.

Victor Gavenda, clever and indispensible technical editor at Peachpit Press, for painstakingly testing the book in Windows.

Adobe Systems, Inc., for designing software that's fun to write about, and in particular to Anjali Ariathurai, Pre-Release Program Manager.

Malloy Lithographing, for a fine print job.

Mies Hora, of Ultimate Symbol, for the Design Elements CD (www.ultimatesymbol.com), a useful resource for vector graphics.

Nathan Olson and *Jeff Seaver,* for helping us revise some chapters.

Rebecca Pepper, copy editor, for her intelligent corrections and meticulous attention to detail.

Leona Benten, proofreader, for her grace under pressure.

Steve Rath, indexer, for his comprehensiveness (and last-minute adjustments).

Peter from *Elaine* and *Elaine* from *Peter*— nice to meet you!

DANIEL PELAVIN

Artist credits

Kenneth Batelman
kenneth@batelman.com
www.batelman.com
color section

Jeanne de la Houssaye
MardiDraw
mardidraw@hotmail.com
www.mardidraw.com
color section

Jib Hunt
Jib Hunt Illustration
jib@jibhunt.com
www.jibhunt.com
color section

Shane Kelley
Kelley Graphics
www.kelley-graphics.com
color section

Diane Margolin
dimargolin@ixpres.com
45, 136, 149, 156, 162, 170, 174, 175, 352, 353, 356, 367, 388, 390

Tom Nikosey
Nikosey Design, Inc.
www.tomnikosey.com
color section

Daniel Pelavin
daniel@pelavin.com
www.pelavin.com
ii, iii, iv, v, vii, xv, 33, 77, 78, 79, 80, 107, 108, 187, 190, 277, 369, 370, 377, 384, 391, 399, 545, 561, 563, 564, 584, color section

Nancy Stahl
www.nancystahl.com
481, color section

Mark Stein
Mark Stein Studios
steinstudios@att.net
www.marksteinstudios.com
288, color section

Carol Zuber-Mallison
Charts, maps, and informational graphics
carol@zmgraphics.com
www.zmgraphics.com
color section

Photo credits
PhotoDisc (Getty Images)
gettyimages.com
324, 341, 342, 349

Photospin
photospin.com
400; All rights reserved

DANIEL PELAVIN

Artists Directory

TABLE OF CONTENTS

DANIEL PELAVIN

AT A GLANCE

TOPICS IN DETAIL

Note: New or changed features are identified by this symbol: ✔

DANIEL PELAVIN

Table of Contents

Table of Contents

ix

Table of Contents

Table of Contents

Table of Contents

DANIEL PELAVIN

Table of Contents

ILLUSTRATOR INTERFACE

This chapter introduces Illustrator's tools, menus, palettes, and measurement systems.

Note: *If you'd like to glance onscreen at the features discussed in this chapter as you read, launch Illustrator and create a new document (see pages 39–41).*

Hide/show

Tab Hide/show all currently open palettes and tearoff toolbars, including the Toolbox.

Shift-Tab Hide/show all currently open palettes and tearoff toolbars, but not the Toolbox.

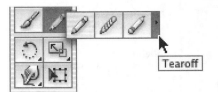

1 *Open a tearoff toolbar by choosing a* **tearoff** *bar.*

2 *A tearoff toolbar*

Tools

Using the Toolbox

The Toolbox contains **74 tools** that are used for object creation and editing. If the Toolbox is hidden, choose Window > Tools to show it. To move the Toolbox, drag its top bar. Click once on a visible tool to select it, or click and hold on a tool that has a tiny arrowhead to choose a related tool from a pop-out menu. Some tools have a related options dialog box; double-click the tool to open it.

To create a standalone **tearoff toolbar** **1**–**2**, release the mouse when it's over the vertical tearoff bar on the far right side of a tool pop-out menu. Move a tearoff toolbar by dragging its top bar. To restore a tearoff toolbar to the Toolbox, click its close box.

To access a tool quickly, use its letter **shortcut** (see the letters in parentheses on the next two pages). Some tools can be accessed temporarily via a toggle key (e.g., if the Pen tool is selected, pressing Cmd/Ctrl accesses the Selection tool). You'll learn more toggles later.

To turn tool pointers into a **crosshair** for precise positioning, go to Illustrator (Edit, in Windows) > Preferences > General and check Use Precise Cursors. Or press Caps Lock to turn the pointer into a crosshair temporarily.

➤ To allow an alert prompt to appear when a tool is used incorrectly, leave Disable Warnings unchecked in Preferences (Cmd-K/Ctrl-K) > General.

The Toolbox

Adobe Online access

(**V**) **Selection**
Selects entire objects

Direct Selection (**A**)
Selects parts of objects

(**Y**) **Magic Wand**
Selects objects by color

Lasso (**Q**)
Selects individual points and segments by marqueeing

(**P**) **Pen**
Draws paths with curved and/or straight segments

Type (**T**)
Creates and edits horizontal type

(\) **Line Segment**
Draws straight lines at any angle

Rectangle (**M**)
Draws rectangles and squares

(**B**) **Paintbrush**
Creates Calligraphic, Scatter, Art, and Pattern brush strokes

Pencil (**N**)
Creates freehand-style lines

(**R**) **Rotate**
Rotates objects

Scale (**S**)
Enlarges and shrinks objects

(**Shift-R**) **Warp**
Applies distortion

Free Transform (**E**)
Rotates, scales, reflects, shears, distorts, or applies perspective

(**Shift-S**) **Symbol Sprayer**
Sprays symbol instances

Column Graph (**J**)
Creates column graphs

(**U**) **Mesh**
Creates and edits multicolored mesh objects

Gradient (**G**)
Changes the direction of existing gradients

(**I**) **Eyedropper**
Samples paint and type attributes

Blend (**W**)
Creates shape and color blends between objects

NEW (**K**) **Live Paint Bucket**
Recolors faces and edges in a live paint group

Live Paint Selection (**Shift-L**)
Selects parts of a live paint group **NEW**

(**Shift-K**) **Slice**
Defines slice areas

Scissors (**C**)
Splits paths

(**H**) **Hand**
Moves the artboard in the document window

Zoom (**Z**)
Changes the zoom level of the document

(**X**) **Fill**
The color, gradient, or pattern that fills the inside of a path

Swap Fill and Stroke (**Shift-X**)

(**D**) **Default Fill and Stroke**
(white fill, 1 pt. black stroke)

Stroke (**X**)
The color that's applied to the edge of a path (click to activate)

(**>**) **Gradient**
Reapplies the last gradient fill

None (**/**)
Removes a stroke or a fill

(**<**) **Color**
Reapplies the last solid-color stroke or fill

Full Screen Mode (**F**)

(**F**) **Standard Screen Mode**

Full Screen Mode with Menu Bar (**F**)

Toolbox

The tearoff toolbars

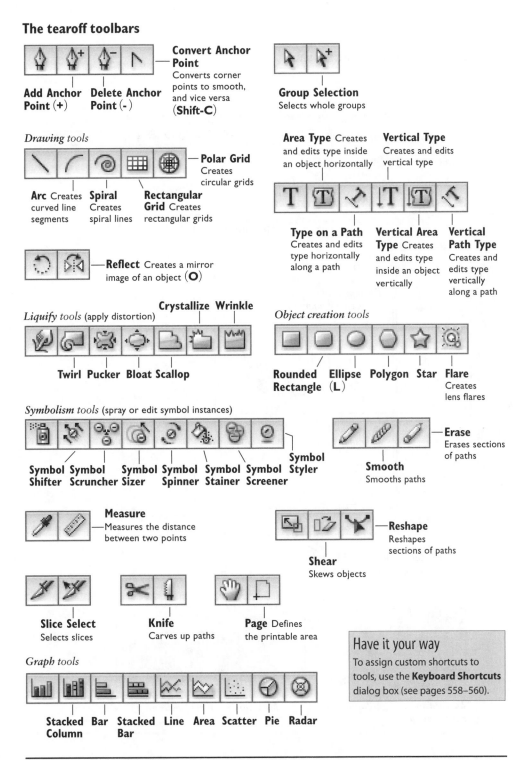

Add Anchor Point (+)

Delete Anchor Point (-)

Convert Anchor Point Converts corner points to smooth, and vice versa (**Shift-C**)

Group Selection Selects whole groups

Drawing tools

Polar Grid Creates circular grids

Arc Creates curved line segments

Spiral Creates spiral lines

Rectangular Grid Creates rectangular grids

Reflect Creates a mirror image of an object (**O**)

Area Type Creates and edits type inside an object horizontally

Vertical Type Creates and edits vertical type

Type on a Path Creates and edits type horizontally along a path

Vertical Area Type Creates and edits type inside an object vertically

Vertical Path Type Creates and edits type vertically along a path

Liquify tools (apply distortion)

Crystallize **Wrinkle**

Twirl **Pucker** **Bloat** **Scallop**

Object creation tools

Rounded Rectangle (L) **Ellipse** **Polygon** **Star** **Flare** Creates lens flares

Symbolism tools (spray or edit symbol instances)

Symbol Shifter **Symbol Scruncher** **Symbol Sizer** **Symbol Spinner** **Symbol Stainer** **Symbol Screener** **Symbol Styler**

Smooth Smooths paths

Erase Erases sections of paths

Measure —Measures the distance between two points

Shear Skews objects

Reshape Reshapes sections of paths

Slice Select Selects slices

Knife Carves up paths

Page Defines the printable area

> ### Have it your way
> To assign custom shortcuts to tools, use the **Keyboard Shortcuts** dialog box (see pages 558–560).

Graph tools

Stacked Column **Bar** **Stacked Bar** **Line** **Area** **Scatter** **Pie** **Radar**

Toolbox

On the screen

The Illustrator screen in Macintosh

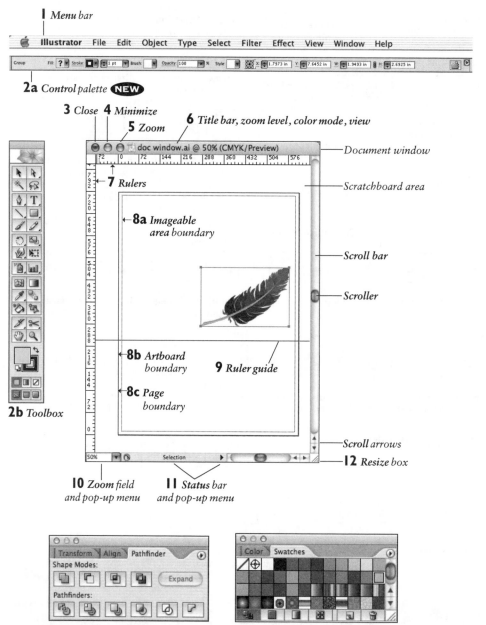

1 *Menu bar*

2a *Control palette* **NEW**

3 *Close* **4** *Minimize*

5 *Zoom*

6 *Title bar, zoom level, color mode, view*

— *Document window*

7 *Rulers*

— *Scratchboard area*

8a *Imageable area boundary*

— *Scroll bar*

— *Scroller*

8b *Artboard boundary*

9 *Ruler guide*

8c *Page boundary*

2b *Toolbox*

— *Scroll arrows*

12 *Resize box*

10 *Zoom field and pop-up menu*   **11** *Status bar and pop-up menu*

2c *Transform/Align/Pathfinder palette group*

2d *Color/Swatches palette group*

Key to the *Illustrator screen in Macintosh*

1 *Menu bar*
Use the menu bar to open dialog boxes or palettes or to choose commands.

2a–d *Palettes*
You can open any of the 32 movable palettes from the Window menu. The Control palette provides quick access to frequently used controls and temporary palettes; options vary depending on what type of object is selected. The Toolbox contains 74 (yes, 74!) drawing and editing tools, as well as color controls and screen mode buttons.

3 *Close button (red)*
To close a document or palette, click its close button.

4 *Minimize button (yellow)*
Click the minimize button to shrink the document window to an icon in the Dock; click the icon in the Dock to restore the document window to its former size.

5 *Zoom button (green)*
Click a document window zoom button to enlarge the window. (Click a palette zoom button to shrink the palette or to restore its previous size.)

6 *Title bar, zoom level, color mode, view*
The current document title, zoom level, color mode (CMYK or RGB), view (Preview, Outline, Pixel Preview, or Overprint Preview) are listed on the title bar, and if View > Proof Colors is on, the current proof profile is also listed.

7 *Rulers*
The current position of the pointer is marked by a dotted line on the horizontal and vertical rulers. Ruler increments can be displayed in points, picas, inches, millimeters, centimeters, or pixels.

8a–c *Imageable area, artboard, and page boundaries*
The imageable (printable) area within the margin guides is based on the media size currently selected in File > Print (General panel). The artboard is the user-defined work area and the largest possible printable area. The nonprinting page boundary matches the current paper size. Objects located in the area outside the artboard will save with the file, but won't print.

9 *Ruler guide*
Drag from the horizontal or vertical ruler to create a guide. Guides are used just for aligning objects; they don't print.

10 *Zoom field and pop-up menu*
Enter a new zoom percentage in this field or choose a preset zoom level from the pop-up menu.

11 *Status bar*
Depending on which category you choose from the Show submenu, the status bar displays the current tool name, date and time (from System Preferences), number of available undos, or document color profile. A Version Cue Status option will also be available if Enable Version Cue is checked in Preferences (Cmd-K) > File Handling & Clipboard. Option-click the status bar pop-up menu to access the moon phase, shopping days 'til Christmas, and other vital statistics via the Show pop-up menu.

12 *Resize box*
To resize a document window, drag its resize box diagonally.

Illustrator Screen in Macintosh

The Illustrator screen in Windows

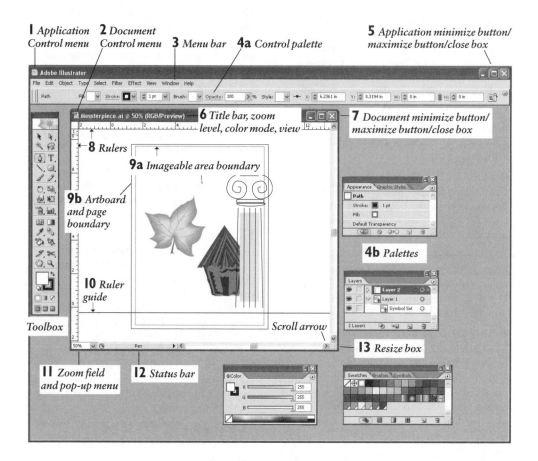

1 *Application Control menu* **2** *Document Control menu* **3** *Menu bar* **4a** *Control palette* **5** *Application minimize button/ maximize button/close box*

6 *Title bar, zoom level, color mode, view* **7** *Document minimize button/ maximize button/close box*

8 *Rulers*

9a *Imageable area boundary*

9b *Artboard and page boundary*

4b *Palettes*

10 *Ruler guide*

Toolbox

Scroll arrow

13 *Resize box*

11 *Zoom field and pop-up menu* **12** *Status bar*

Illustrator Screen in Windows

Key to the *Illustrator screen in Windows*

1 *Application Control menu*
The Application Control menu commands are Restore, Move, Size, Minimize, Maximize, and Close.

2 *Document Control menu*
The Document Control menu commands are Restore, Move, Size, Minimize, Maximize, Close, and Next.

3 *Menu bar*
Use the menu bar to open dialog boxes or palettes or to choose commands.

4a–b *Palettes*
You can open any of the 32 movable palettes from the Window menu. The Control palette provides quick access to frequently used controls and temporary palettes; options vary depending on what type of object is selected. The Toolbox contains 74 drawing and editing tools, as well as color controls and screen mode buttons.

5, 7 *Minimize, maximize/restore down buttons*
Click the document or application maximize button to enlarge either window to fill the available space completely. When a window is maximized, the button turns into a restore down button; click it to shrink the window to its former size.

Click the application minimize button to shrink the application to an icon on the taskbar; click the icon on the taskbar to restore the application window to its former size.

6 *Title bar, zoom level, color mode, view*
The current document title, zoom level, color mode (CMYK or RGB), view (Preview, Outline, Pixel Preview, or Overprint Preview) are listed on the title bar, and if View > Proof Colors is on, the current proof profile is also listed.

7 *Document minimize button, close box*
Click the document minimize button to shrink the document to an icon in the lower left corner of the application window. To restore the document to its previous size, click the icon or click the restore up button.

To close a document or a palette, click its close box.

8 *Rulers*
The current position of the pointer is marked by a dotted line on the horizontal and vertical rulers. Ruler increments can be displayed in points, picas, inches, millimeters, centimeters, or pixels.

9a–b *Imageable area, artboard, and page boundaries*
The imageable (printable) area is the area within the margin guides based on the media size currently selected in File > Print (General). The artboard is the user-defined work area and the largest possible printable area. The nonprinting page boundary matches the current paper size. Objects outside the artboard save with the file but don't print.

10 *Ruler guide*
Drag from the horizontal or vertical ruler to create a guide. Guides are used just for aligning objects; they don't print.

11 *Zoom field and pop-up menu*
Enter a new zoom percentage in this field, or choose a preset zoom level from the pop-up menu.

12 *Status bar*
Depending on which category you choose from the Show submenu, the status bar displays the current tool name, date and time from the computer's internal clock, number of available undos, or document color profile (RGB or CMYK). A Version Cue Status option will also be available if Enable Version Cue is checked in Preferences (Ctrl-K) > File Handling & Clipboard. Alt-click the status bar pop-up menu to access the moon phase, shopping days 'til Christmas, and other vital statistics via the Show pop-up menu.

13 *Resize box*
To resize a document window, drag its resize box diagonally or drag the edge of the window.

The Illustrator menus

Illustrator menu

Illustrator

About Illustrator...	
About Plug-ins...	
Preferences	▶
Services	▶
Hide Illustrator	
Hide Others	⌥⌘H
Show All	
Quit Illustrator	⌘Q

In Windows, there is no Illustrator menu; the Preferences command is on the Edit menu, and the Exit command is on the File menu.

File menu

File

New...	⌘N
New from Template...	⇧⌘N
Open...	⌘O
Open Recent Files	▶
Browse...	⌥⌘O
Close	⌘W
Save	⌘S
Save As...	⇧⌘S
Save a Copy...	⌥⌘S
Save as Template...	
Save a Version...	
Save for Web...	⌥⇧⌘S
Revert	F12
Place...	
Save for Microsoft Office...	
Export...	
Scripts	▶
Document Setup...	⌥⌘P
Document Color Mode	▶
File Info...	⌥⇧⌘I
Print...	⌘P

Edit menu

Edit

Undo Move	⌘Z
Redo Move	⇧⌘Z
Cut	⌘X
Copy	⌘C
Paste	⌘V
Paste in Front	⌘F
Paste in Back	⌘B
Clear	
Find and Replace...	
Find Next	
Check Spelling...	⌘I
Edit Custom Dictionary...	
Define Pattern...	
Edit Original	
Transparency Flattener Presets...	
Tracing Presets...	
Print Presets...	
Adobe PDF Presets...	
Color Settings...	⇧⌘K
Assign Profile...	
Keyboard Shortcuts...	⌥⇧⌘K

Object menu

Object

Transform	▶
Arrange	▶
Group	⌘G
Ungroup	⇧⌘G
Lock	▶
Unlock All	⌥⌘2
Hide	▶
Show All	⌥⌘3
Expand...	
Expand Appearance	
Flatten Transparency...	
Rasterize...	
Create Gradient Mesh...	
Slice	▶
Path	▶
Blend	▶
Envelope Distort	▶
Live Paint	▶
Live Trace	▶
Text Wrap	▶
Clipping Mask	▶
Compound Path	▶
Crop Area	▶
Graph	▶

Type menu

Type

Font	▶
Recent Fonts	▶
Size	▶
Glyphs	
Area Type Options...	
Type on a Path	▶
Threaded Text	▶
Fit Headline	
Create Outlines	⇧⌘O
Find Font...	
Change Case	▶
Smart Punctuation...	
Optical Margin Alignment	
Show Hidden Characters	⌥⌘I
Type Orientation	▶
Legacy Text	▶

Select menu

Select

All	⌘A
Deselect	⇧⌘A
Reselect	⌘6
Inverse	
Next Object Above	⌥⌘]
Next Object Below	⌥⌘[
Same	▶
Object	▶
Save Selection...	
Edit Selection...	

Filter menu

Filter

Apply Last Filter	⌘E
Last Filter	⌥⌘E

Illustrator Filters
- Colors ▶
- Create ▶
- Distort ▶
- Stylize ▶

Photoshop Filters
- Filter Gallery...
- Artistic ▶
- Blur ▶
- Brush Strokes ▶
- Distort ▶
- Pixelate ▶
- Sharpen ▶
- Sketch ▶
- Stylize ▶
- Texture ▶
- Video ▶

Window menu

Window

New Window	
Workspace	▶
Minimize Window	⌘M
Bring All To Front	
Actions	
Align	⇧F7
✓ Appearance	⇧F6
Attributes	⌘F11
Brushes	F5
Color	F6
✓ Control Palette	
Document Info	
Flattener Preview	
Gradient	⌘F9
✓ Graphic Styles	⇧F5
Info	F8
✓ Layers	F7
Links	
Magic Wand	
✓ Navigator	
✓ Pathfinder	⇧⌘F9
✓ Stroke	⌘F10
SVG Interactivity	
✓ Swatches	
Symbols	⇧⌘F11
✓ Tools	
Transform	⇧F8
Transparency	⇧⌘F10
Type	▶
Variables	
Brush Libraries	▶
Graphic Style Libraries	▶
Swatch Libraries	▶
Symbol Libraries	▶
✓ Untitled-2 @ 100% (CMYK/Preview)	

Effect menu

Effect

Apply Last Effect	⇧⌘E
Last Effect	⌥⇧⌘E
Document Raster Effects Settings...	

Illustrator Effects
- 3D ▶
- Convert to Shape ▶
- Distort & Transform ▶
- Path ▶
- Pathfinder ▶
- Rasterize...
- Stylize ▶
- SVG Filters ▶
- Warp ▶

Photoshop Effects
- Effect Gallery...
- Artistic ▶
- Blur ▶
- Brush Strokes ▶
- Distort ▶
- Pixelate ▶
- Sharpen ▶
- Sketch ▶
- Stylize ▶
- Texture ▶
- Video ▶

Help menu

Help

System Info...	
Illustrator Help...	F1
Registration...	
Welcome Screen...	
Updates...	
Activate...	
Transfer Activation...	

The **About Illustrator** and **About Plug-ins** commands are available on the Help menu in Windows.

In Windows, this menu contains **Cascade, Tile,** and **Arrange Icons** commands, but not the Minimize Window and Bring All To Front commands.

View menu

View

Outline	⌘Y
Overprint Preview	⌥⇧⌘Y
Pixel Preview	⌥⌘Y
Proof Setup	▶
Proof Colors	
Zoom In	⌘+
Zoom Out	⌘-
Fit in Window	⌘0
Actual Size	⌘1
Hide Edges	⌘H
Hide Artboard	
Show Page Tiling	
Show Slices	
Lock Slices	
Hide Template	⇧⌘W
Show Rulers	⌘R
Hide Bounding Box	⇧⌘B
Show Transparency Grid	⇧⌘D
Hide Text Threads	⇧⌘Y
Show Live Paint Gaps	
Guides	▶
Smart Guides	⌘U
Show Grid	⌘"
Snap to Grid	⇧⌘"
✓ Snap to Point	⌥⌘"
New View...	
Edit Views...	

➤ In Windows, to activate a menu, press Alt + the underlined letter in the menu name. (In Windows XP, press Alt to make the underlines appear first.) Then release Alt and press the underlined letter in the specific command you wish to use.

Menus

9

Using dialog boxes

Dialog boxes are like fill-in forms with multiple choices that open from the menu bar, from palette menus, or by using a shortcut. In some cases, clicking a button in a dialog box opens a related dialog box.

Settings are chosen by entering a number in an entry field; choosing from a list of options on a pop-up menu; clicking a check box on or off; or clicking a button. Many dialog boxes also have a **Preview** option that when checked lets you monitor changes in your document as you choose settings.

➤ Click near a check box to turn it on or off—you don't have to click right on it.

➤ Press **Tab** to apply the current value and highlight the next field in a dialog box; press **Shift-Tab** to highlight the previous field.

Click **OK** or press **Return/Enter** to apply the new settings and exit a dialog box. To cancel out of a dialog box, click Cancel or press Esc.

Illustrator dialog boxes, like all the other features in the program, function the same way in Mac as in Windows, though they differ slightly in appearance.

*In Windows, you can type an **underlined** letter to activate that field (e.g., type "U" for "Uniform"). If a field is already highlighted, type **Alt** plus the underlined letter. In Windows XP, you have to press Alt for the underlines to show up.*

*A dialog box in **Windows***

*Click **OK** or press **Return/Enter** to exit a dialog box and accept the new settings.*

*Type a number into a field. Press **Tab** to jump from one field to the next.*

*Click **Cancel** to exit a dialog box with no modifications taking effect.*

*Click a **check box** on or off.*

*Check **Preview** to preview new settings in your document while the dialog box is open.*

*A **dialog box** in Macintosh*

Using the palettes

Illustrator has 32 movable palettes, all of which can be opened from the **Window** menu. You can also show/hide some palettes via an assigned shortcut, and open temporary versions of some palettes via the Control **NEW** palette (see the sidebar on the next page). To save screen space, the palettes are organized into default **groups**, such as Swatches/Brushes/Symbols and Stroke/Gradient/Transparency.

You can compose your own palette groups. Move a palette **out** of its default group by dragging its tab (palette name) away from the group **1**–**2**, or **add** a palette to any group by dragging its tab over the group.

➤ When composing a palette group, start with one of the palette windows that's resizable.

To **dock** (hook up) one palette to the bottom of another palette or palette group, drag the tab to the bottom of the target palette, and release the mouse when the thick black line

appears **3**. To undock, drag a palette tab out of the dock group.

To **display** an open palette at the front of its group, click its tab. Palettes with an up/down arrowhead on the tab (such as the Color palette) contain more than one **panel**. Click the arrowhead or the tab name to cycle through the palette configurations: tab only, then two option panels, then one option panel. You can also display a full palette by choosing Show Options from the palette menu.

To **shrink** a palette group to tabs only, on the Mac, click the palette zoom button (green) in the upper left corner, or in Windows, click the minimize/maximize button. Click the button again to restore the palette's former size.

Palettes that are open when you quit/exit Illustrator will reappear in the same location when you relaunch the application. To restore the **default** palette setup, choose Window > Workspace > [Default].

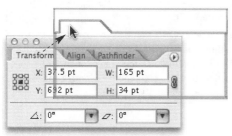

1 To *separate a palette from its group, drag the tab (palette name) out of the group.*

2 *Now the Transform palette is on its own.*

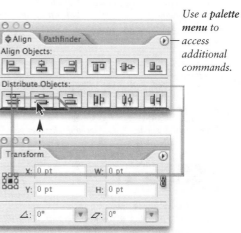

*Use a **palette menu** to access additional commands.*

3 To *dock palettes together, drag the tab name of one palette to the bottom of another palette, and release the mouse when the thick black line appears across the bottom of the target palette.*

Using the Palettes

(NEW) The palettes illustrated

Control palette

The Control palette houses many frequently used controls conveniently under one roof, and, as you can see from the screen shots on this page and the next, changes contextually depending on what type of object is selected. For example, you can use this palette to choose fill and stroke colors, change object opacity, change basic type attributes (font and point size), align and distribute multiple objects, change paragraph alignment, reposition an object, change document units, or embed or edit a linked image. The palette also incorporates a host of controls for the live trace and live paint features.

You can also use the Control palette to open a temporary Brushes, Character, Color, Graphic Styles, Paragraph, Stroke, Swatches, Transform, or Transparency palette (see the sidebar).

You can move the Control palette anywhere on your screen, or choose Dock to Top or Dock to Bottom from the palette menu on the right side of the palette to move it to the top or bottom, respectively, of your screen. Uncheck or check any of the items listed on the lower part of the palette menu to control which options display on the palette. To go to the Bridge application, click the Go to Bridge button 📷 at the far right side of the palette (see Chapter 4).

In the next program upgrade, we hope to see options for individual tools on the Control palette. Meanwhile, whether you're an Illustrator veteran or neophyte, it's well worth exploring.

Fast track to the palettes

Click a **blue underlined** word or letter on the Control palette to open a related palette. For example, click the word "Stroke" to open a temporary Stroke palette, or the word "Opacity" to open a temporary Transparency palette.

Other temporary palettes can be opened by clicking a **thumbnail** or **arrowhead.** For example, click the Brush thumbnail or arrowhead to open the Brushes palette or the Style thumbnail or arrowhead to open the Graphic Styles palette.

*Click the up or down **arrow** to change the value one increment at a time...* *...or enter a value in the field...* *...or choose a preset value from the pop-up menu.*

Click to open a temporary Swatches palette; Shift-click to open a temporary Color palette. *Click to open a temporary Stroke palette.* *Shift-click to open a temporary Color palette.* *Click the Brush thumbnail or arrowhead to open the Brushes palette.* *Reference point for a transformation* *Width of the selected object* *Maintain aspect ratio*

Stroke weight

The Control palette when a path, group, clipping mask, compound path, symbol, or symbol set is selected

Object opacity *Click the Style thumbnail or arrowhead to open the Graphic Styles palette.* *Horizontal location of the selected object, relative to the reference point* *Vertical location of the selected object, relative to the reference point* *Height of the selected object*

Click to open a temporary Paragraph palette. *Click the X, Y, W, or H to open a temporary Transform palette.*

Click to open a temporary Character palette. *Font* *Font style* *Point size* *Paragraph alignment*

The left side of the Control palette when type is selected

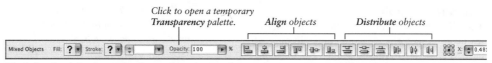

Click to open a temporary **Transparency** *palette.*   **Align** *objects*   **Distribute** *objects*

*The left side of the Control palette when objects of **more than one type** are selected*

*Click to access a pop-up menu for choosing **Relink, Go To Link, Update Link**, and other commands.*   **Embed** *a linked image into the file.*   **Edit** *a linked image in its **original** application.*   *Convert an image to a **live trace** object.*   **Tracing** *preset pop-up menu*

*The left side of the Control palette when a **linked, placed image** is selected*

Preset (settings) to be used for tracing   *Open* **Tracing Options** *dialog box*   **Threshold** *(for black and white images)*   **Min. Area** *(size of traceable area)*   **Raster** *view for image display*   **Vector** *view for tracing display*   **Expand** *live trace object into standard paths*   *Convert live trace object to **live paint group***

*The left side of the Control palette when a **live trace** object is selected*

Reference point for a transformation   **Width** *of the selected object*   **Maintain aspect ratio**

*The left side of the Control palette when a **mesh** or **envelope** is selected*   **Horizontal location** *of the selected object, relative to the reference point*   **Vertical location** *of the selected object, relative to the reference point*   **Height** *of the selected object*   *Click the X, Y, W, or H to open a temporary **Transform** palette.*

Add Paths *to live paint group*   **Expand** *live paint group into standard paths*   *Open **Gap Options** dialog box*   **Isolate** *selected group*

*The left side of the Control palette when a **live paint group** is selected*

Isolate Selected Group   **Reference point**

*The left side of the Control palette when a **blend** is selected*

Control Palette

13

The color controls

The fill is the solid color, gradient, or pattern inside an object; the stroke is the solid or dashed color on an object's edge. The current fill and stroke colors display in color squares on the Toolbox (shown at right) and on the Color palette. Use the Color palette to choose Web-safe colors or process colors, or to remix global process or spot color tints.

The **Stroke** palette displays the weight and style of the stroke in the currently selected object or objects, and can be used to change those attributes. If no objects are selected, changes made on the Color or Stroke palette apply to subsequently drawn objects.

Color palette (F6)

Use the Color palette to mix, choose, and switch between the fill and stroke colors. Choose a color model for the palette from the palette menu. Quick-select a color, black, white, or None from the spectrum bar at the bottom of the palette. To open a temporary Color palette, Shift-click the Fill or Stroke **NEW** thumbnail or arrowhead on the Control palette.

Whichever box (Fill or Stroke) is currently active (is in front on the Color palette and Toolbox) will be affected by changes made on the Color palette.

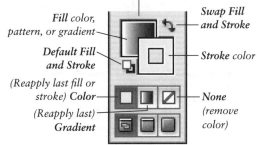

Fill color, pattern, or gradient

Default Fill and Stroke

Swap Fill and Stroke

Stroke color

(Reapply last fill or stroke) Color

(Reapply last) Gradient

None (remove color)

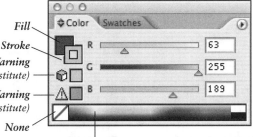

Fill

Stroke

Out of Web Color Warning (click box for Web-safe substitute)

Out of Gamut Warning (click box for printable substitute)

None

R	63
G	255
B	189

Spectrum bar

Stroke palette (Cmd-F10/Ctrl-F10)

Use the Stroke palette to edit the stroke weight, style, and alignment on selected objects, and to create dashed lines or frames. To open a temporary Stroke palette, click the blue underlined word "Stroke" on the **NEW** Control palette.

NEW *Align Stroke to Center, Align Stroke to Inside, and Align Stroke to Outside*

Dashed Line segment (dash) and gap lengths (spacing between dashes)

Stroke Weight (thickness)

Join (bend) styles

Cap (end) styles

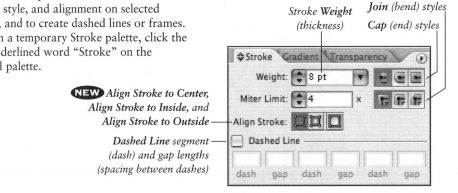

Weight: 8 pt

Miter Limit: 4 x

Align Stroke:

Dashed Line

| dash | gap | dash | gap | dash | gap |

Swatches palette

Use the Swatches palette to choose and store default and user-defined colors, patterns, and gradients. If you click a swatch, it becomes the current fill or stroke color, depending on whether the Fill or Stroke box is currently active on the Toolbox and Color palette.

Drag from the Fill or Stroke color box on the Toolbox or the Color palette to the Swatches palette to save that color as a swatch in the current file. Double-click a swatch to open the Swatch Options dialog box, where you can change the swatch name, type (global process, nonglobal process, or spot), or mode. Via the palette menu, you can merge swatches and perform other tasks.

To open a temporary Swatches palette, click the Fill or Stroke thumbnail or arrowhead **NEW** on the Control palette.

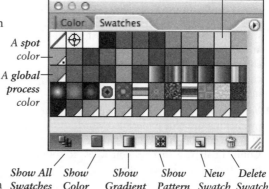

A nonglobal process color

A spot color

A global process color

Show All Swatches *Show Color Swatches* *Show Gradient Swatches* *Show Pattern Swatches* *New Swatch* *Delete Swatch*

Gradient palette (Cmd-F9/Ctrl-F9)

Use the Gradient palette to create new gradients and edit existing gradients. You can move a color by dragging its stop, choose a different color for a selected stop from the Color palette, click below the gradient slider to add new colors, move a midpoint diamond to adjust how adjacent colors are distributed, or change the gradient type (linear or radial) or angle.

Gradient Type: Linear or Radial

*The **Midpoint** diamond marks the point where two adjacent colors are at an equal, 50/50 mix.*

Gradient slider

Starting color stop *An added color stop* *Ending color stop*

Character palette (Cmd-T/Ctrl-T)

Use the Character palette to apply type attributes: font, font style, size, leading, kerning, tracking, horizontal scale, vertical scale, baseline shift, character rotation, underline, strikethrough, and a language for hyphenation. To edit an attribute for selected text, choose a value from the pop-up menu; or click the up or down arrow; or enter a value in the field and press Return/Enter.

NEW You can open a temporary Character palette by clicking the blue underlined word "Character" on the Control palette. The Control palette also gives you access to some basic type controls (see below).

Showing the type palettes

Except for the Control palette, the palettes that are used for formatting type are opened from the Window > **Type** submenu: Character, Character Styles, Glyphs, OpenType, Paragraph, Paragraph Styles, and Tabs. Four of these palettes have their own shortcut:

Character Cmd-T/Ctrl-T

OpenType Cmd-Option-Shift-T/
Ctrl-Alt-Shift-T

Paragraph Cmd-Option-T/Ctrl-Alt-T

Tabs Cmd-Shift-T/Ctrl-Shift-T

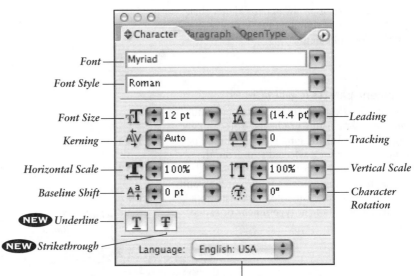

Hyphenation **Language** for the document

The **Control** palette when type or a type object is selected **NEW**

Character Styles palette

A **character** style is a collection of character attributes, such as font, font style, point size, leading, tracking, and kerning. Unlike paragraph styles, which affect whole paragraphs, character styles are applied to bits and pieces of type here and there, such as bullets, boldfaced words, italicized words, or large initial caps. When you edit a character style, the text that it's associated with updates accordingly. The Character Styles palette lets you create, apply, edit, store, duplicate, and delete styles.

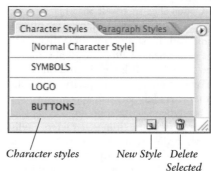

Character styles   *New Style*   *Delete Selected Styles*

Glyphs palette

Using the Glyphs palette, you can find out which character variations (alternate glyphs) are available for any given character in a specific OpenType font, and insert glyphs from any font into your text (including those that can't be inserted via the keyboard).

*Via the **Show** pop-up menu, you can control whether the palette displays glyphs in a specific category or for an entire font.*

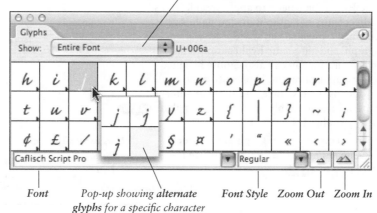

Font   *Pop-up showing **alternate** glyphs for a specific character*   *Font Style*   *Zoom Out*   *Zoom In*

OpenType palette

(Cmd-Option-Shift-T/Ctrl-Alt-Shift-T)

Amongst the 24 roman OpenType font families that ship with Illustrator, the fonts that contain a large assortment of alternate glyphs are labeled "Pro." By clicking a button on the OpenType palette, you can specify which alternate characters (glyphs) will appear in your text when you type the corresponding key(s), such as ligatures, swashes, titling characters, stylistic alternates, ordinals, and fractions. You can also use the palette to specify options for numerals, such as a style (e.g., tabular lining or oldstyle) and a position (e.g., numerator, denominator, superscript, or subscript).

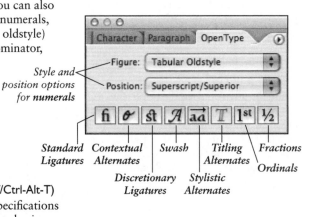

Style and position options for numerals

Standard Ligatures — Contextual Alternates — Swash — Titling Alternates — Fractions

Discretionary Ligatures — Stylistic Alternates — Ordinals

Paragraph palette (Cmd-Option-T/Ctrl-Alt-T)

Use the Paragraph palette to apply specifications that affect entire paragraphs, including horizontal alignment, indentation, space before/after paragraph, and automatic hyphenation. Via the palette menu, you can also choose hanging punctuation, justification, hyphenation, and composer options. Left, Center, and Right alignment buttons are also available on the Control palette 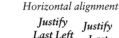 when a type object is selected.

To open a temporary Paragraph palette, click the blue underlined word "Paragraph" on the Control palette. **NEW**

Horizontal alignment

Left Center Right Justify Last Left Justify Last Center Justify Last Right Justify All

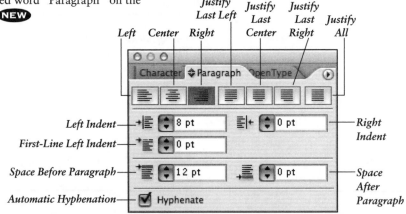

Left Indent
First-Line Left Indent
Space Before Paragraph
Automatic Hyphenation

Right Indent
Space After Paragraph

Paragraph Styles palette

A paragraph style is a collection of paragraph specifications (including horizontal alignment, indentation, space before paragraph, word spacing, letter spacing, hyphenation, and hanging punctuation) and character attributes, such as font and point size. When a paragraph style is applied, all currently selected paragraphs are reformatted according to the specifications in that style. When a paragraph style is edited, the text it's associated with updates accordingly. Using styles makes light work of formatting type and helps to ensure uniformity. You can create, apply, edit, store, duplicate, and delete paragraph styles by using the Paragraph palette.

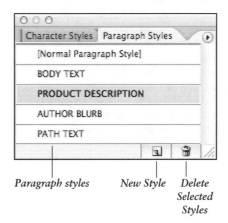

Paragraph styles   *New Style*   *Delete Selected Styles*

Tabs palette (Cmd-Shift-T/Ctrl-Shift-T)

If you want to create columns of text that align perfectly, you need to use tabs. Using the Tabs palette, you can insert, move, and change the alignment for custom tab markers (tab stops), as well as specify optional leader and align-on characters.

*Numeric **Location** of the currently selected tab marker*   *Optional **Leader** character*   *Optional character to **Align On***

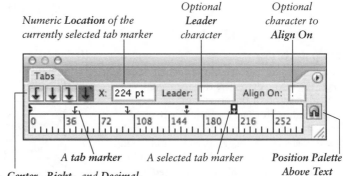

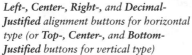

*A **tab marker***   *A selected tab marker*   *Position Palette Above Text*

Left-, Center-, Right-, and Decimal-Justified alignment buttons for horizontal type (or Top-, Center-, and Bottom-Justified buttons for vertical type)

Layers palette (F7)

Use the indispensable Layers palette to add and delete layers and sublayers from a document. You can also use this palette to select, restack, hide/show, lock/unlock, merge, change the view for, create a clipping set for, target, or dim a layer, sublayer, group, or individual object. When your artwork is finished, it can be flattened into one layer, or objects can be released to separate layers for export as a Flash animation.

*Click this icon to **target** an object or group to edit its appearances; drag the icon to **move** the object's appearance.*

Current Layer indicator

Selection square

*Click an **eye** icon to **hide/show** a layer, group, or object.*

*A **sublayer***

Lock a layer, sublayer, group, or object to make it uneditable.

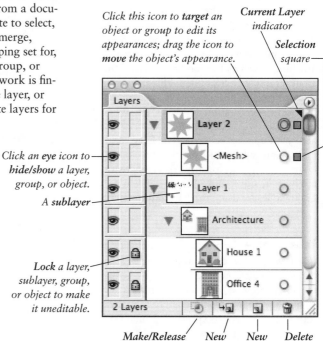

Make/Release Clipping Mask   *New Sublayer*   *New Layer*   *Delete Selection*

Info palette (F8)

If no objects are selected in the current document, the Info palette lists the horizontal and vertical location of the pointer in the document window (for most tools). When an object is selected, the palette lists the location of the object on the page, its width and height, and color data about its fill and stroke. When a type tool and type object are selected, the palette displays type specifications. The Info palette opens automatically when the Measure tool is used, and lists the distance and angle calculated by that tool.

*Horizontal (X) and **Vertical** (Y) location of the currently selected object*

*Object **Width** (W) and **Height** (H)*

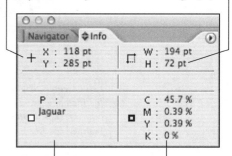

Fill info (color breakdown, or the pattern or gradient name)

Stroke info (color breakdown, or the pattern or gradient name)

Align palette (Shift-F7)

Buttons on the top two rows of the Align palette let you align and/or distribute two or more objects along their centers or along their top, left, right, or bottom edges. Buttons at the bottom of the palette let you equalize (redistribute) the spacing between three or more objects.

Align buttons also appear on the Control **NEW** *palette when multiple objects are selected.*

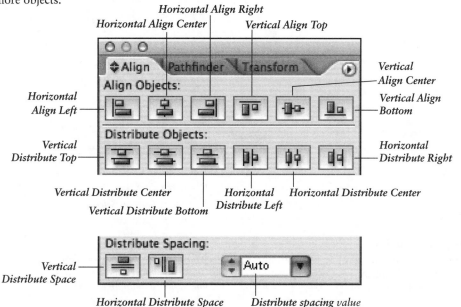

Horizontal Align Right
Horizontal Align Center
Vertical Align Top
Horizontal Align Left
Vertical Align Center
Vertical Align Bottom
Vertical Distribute Top
Horizontal Distribute Right
Vertical Distribute Center
Vertical Distribute Bottom
Horizontal Distribute Left
Horizontal Distribute Center
Vertical Distribute Space
Horizontal Distribute Space
Distribute spacing value

Transform palette (Shift-F8)

The Transform palette displays location, width, and height information for the currently selected object. You can also use the palette to move, scale, rotate, or shear a selected object or objects. To open a temporary Transform palette, click the blue underlined X, Y, W, or H on the Control palette. **NEW**

The reference point icon and X, Y, W, and H fields also appear on the Control palette when a path or paths are selected. **NEW**

The location of the currently selected object on the x and y axes. Change either or both of these values to move the object.

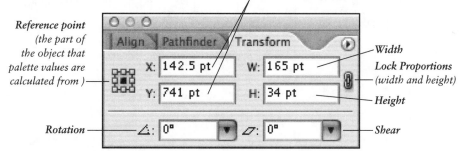

Reference point (the part of the object that palette values are calculated from)
Width
Lock Proportions (width and height)
Height
Rotation
Shear

Align Palette; Transform Palette

21

Actions palette

Actions let you automate commands and editing steps. As you create or edit a document, you record a series of commands or steps as an action. You can replay any action on an object, file, or batch (folder) of files.

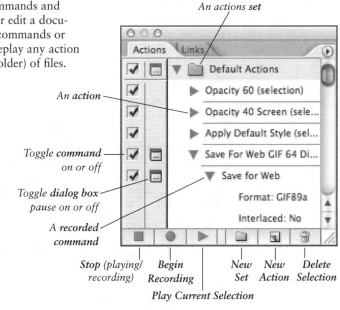

An actions set

An action

*Toggle **command** on or off*

*Toggle **dialog box** pause on or off*

*A **recorded** command*

Stop (playing/ recording)   Begin Recording   New Set   New Action   Delete Selection

Play Current Selection

Navigator palette

The Navigator palette lets you move an illustration in the document window and change the document zoom level.

*Drag the **view box** to **move** the illustration in the document window, or **click** the illustration **thumbnail** to move that part of the document into view.*

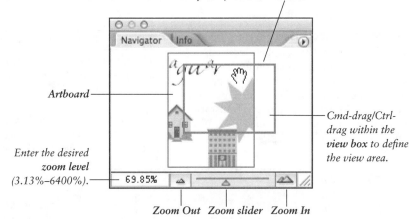

Artboard

*Enter the desired **zoom level** (3.13%–6400%).*

*Cmd-drag/Ctrl-drag within the **view box** to define the view area.*

Zoom Out   Zoom slider   Zoom In

Links palette

When you place an image into an Illustrator document, you can either embed the image into the file (and thereby increase the file size) or merely link the image to the file. The Links palette lets you keep track of and update linked images, modify a linked image in its original application, and convert linked images to embedded images. You can also embed a linked image by clicking the Embed **(NEW)** button on the Control palette, and edit it in its original application by clicking the Edit Original button.

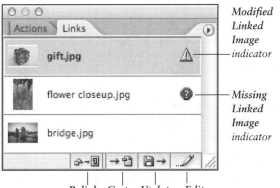

Modified Linked Image indicator

Missing Linked Image indicator

Relink Go to Link Update Link Edit Original

Pathfinder palette

(Cmd-Shift-F9/Ctrl-Shift-F9)

The shape mode buttons on the top row of the Pathfinder palette create new, editable, flexible compound shapes from multiple selected objects. The Expand button converts a compound shape into either a path or a compound path, depending on the way in which the original objects overlapped. The pathfinder buttons on the bottom row of the Pathfinder palette produce flattened, cut-up shapes from multiple selected objects.

Intersect Shape Areas   *Exclude Overlapping Shape Areas*

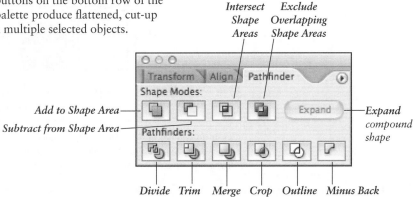

Add to Shape Area

Subtract from Shape Area

Expand compound shape

Divide Trim Merge Crop Outline Minus Back

Brushes palette (F5)

You can use any of the four varieties of brushes—Calligraphic, Scatter, Art, or Pattern—to apply decorative brush strokes to paths. You can do this either by choosing the Paintbrush tool and a brush and then drawing a shape or by applying a brush stroke to an existing path. To personalize your brush strokes, you can create and edit your own brushes. If you modify a brush that's been applied to paths in a document, you'll be given the option via an alert dialog box to update the paths with the revised brush. Brushes on the Brushes palette save with the current document.

To open a temporary Brushes palette, click the Brush thumbnail or arrowhead on the Control palette. **NEW**

Transparency palette
(Cmd-Shift-F10/Ctrl-Shift-F10)

You can use the Transparency palette to change the blending mode or opacity of any layer, group, or individual object. Via a Transparency palette menu command, you can generate an editable opacity mask from two or more selected objects. You can also change an object's opacity via the Control palette.

To open a temporary Transparency palette, **NEW** click the blue underlined word "Opacity" on the Control palette.

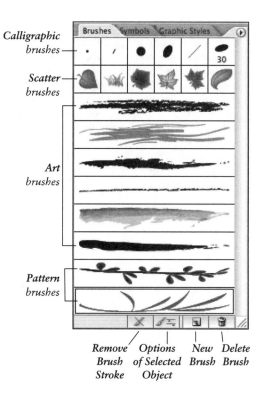

Calligraphic brushes

Scatter brushes

Art brushes

Pattern brushes

Remove Brush Stroke — *Options of Selected Object* — *New Brush* — *Delete Brush*

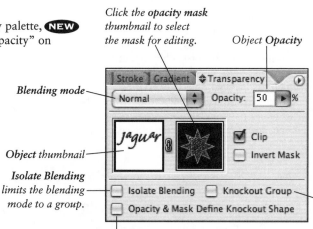

*Click the **opacity mask** thumbnail to select the mask for editing.*

*Object **Opacity***

Blending mode

Object thumbnail

Isolate Blending limits the blending mode to a group.

This option allows nested objects in a knockout group to show through transparent areas of an opacity mask.

***Knockout Group** prevents objects in a group from showing through one another.*

Graphic Styles palette (Shift-F5)

The Graphic Styles palette lets you store and apply collections of appearance attributes, such as multiple solid-color and pattern fills, multiple strokes, transparency and overprint settings, blending modes, brush strokes, and effects. Like character styles for type, graphic styles let you apply attributes quickly and with consistency.

To open a temporary Graphic Styles palette, click the Style thumbnail or arrowhead on the Control palette. **NEW**

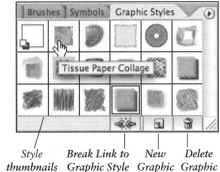

Style thumbnails   *Break Link to Graphic Style*   *New Graphic Style*   *Delete Graphic Style*

Appearance palette (Shift-F6)

The Appearance palette lists in minute detail the individual appearance attributes that are applied to the currently targeted layer(s), group(s), or object(s). You can use the palette to edit, add, or remove attributes, and to edit the attributes of a graphic style in conjunction with the Graphic Styles palette. You can also use this palette to apply and edit multiple fills and/or strokes on a layer, group, or object.

To edit an effect, click this icon (or the effect name).

New Art Has Basic Appearance   *Clear Appearance*   *Duplicate Selected Item*   *Delete Selected Item*

Reduce to Basic Appearance

Graphic Styles Palette; Appearance Palette

25

SVG Interactivity palette

You can use the SVG Interactivity palette to add interactivity to an Illustrator object for viewing in a Web browser. First you choose from a list of common JavaScript events on the Event pop-up menu. Then you add or enter a JavaScript command that will act on the object when that event occurs in the browser.

Attributes palette (Cmd-F11/Ctrl-F11)

The "catch-all" Attributes palette lets you choose overprint options for an object, show/hide an object's center point, reverse the fill of an object in a compound path, change an object's fill rule, choose a shape for an image map area, and enter a Web address for an object to designate it as a hot point on an image map. Click Browser to launch the currently installed Web browser.

Document Info palette

Like the Info palette, the Document Info palette is noninteractive. It simply lists information about the document, as per the category you choose from the palette menu, such as the current Selection Only, the whole Document, or individual Objects, Brushes, or Fonts.

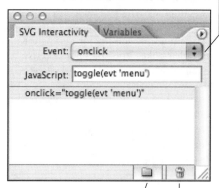

JavaScript Event pop-up menu

Link JavaScript Files — *Remove Selected Entry*

Use Even-Odd Fill Rule
Use Non-Zero Winding Fill Rule

Don't Show Center
Show Center

Reverse Path Direction Off *and* **Reverse Path Direction On** *buttons (switch the fill between color and transparency in a compound path)*

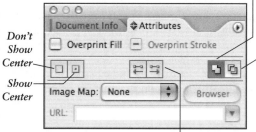

SVG Interactivity, Attributes, Doc Info Palettes

Magic Wand palette

The Magic Wand tool selects objects that have the same or similar fill color, stroke color, stroke weight, opacity, or blending mode as the currently selected object. Using the Magic Wand palette, you can choose parameters for the tool. The Tolerance is the range within which the tool selects objects with that attribute. For example, if you check Opacity, choose an opacity Tolerance of 10%, and then select an object that has an opacity of 50%, the tool will find and select all the objects in the document that have an opacity between 40% and 60%.

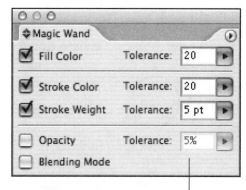

*The **Tolerance** is the range within which the **Magic Wand** will select objects with that attribute.*

Symbols palette

(Cmd-Shift-F11/Ctrl-Shift-F11)

Illustrator objects can be stored on the Symbols palette for use in any document. To create one instance of a symbol, you simply drag from the Symbols palette onto the artboard. To quickly create multiple instances, you can use the Symbol Sprayer tool.

With symbols, you can create complex art, such as a bank of trees or a group of clouds, quickly and easily. They're also useful for designing efficient Web pages, because a symbol image, even when used multiple times, has to download only once.

Using any of the other symbolism tools (Symbol Shifter, Scruncher, Sizer, Spinner, Stainer, Screener, or Styler), you can change the closeness (density), position, stacking order, size, rotation, transparency, color tint, or style of multiple symbol instances in a symbol set, while still maintaining the link to the original symbol. If you edit the original symbol, all instances of that symbol in the document update automatically.

Note: A brief description of the Variables palette appears on page 544, and a brief description of the Flattener Preview palette appears on page 496. For more information about these palettes, see Illustrator Help.

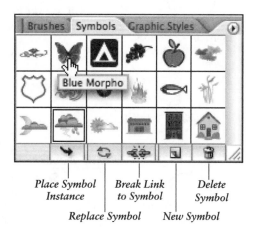

Place Symbol Instance   *Break Link to Symbol*   *Delete Symbol*

Replace Symbol   *New Symbol*

Mini-Glossary A brief introduction to some terms you'll encounter while reading this book.

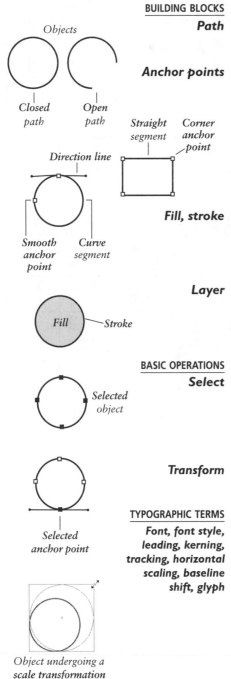

Objects

Closed path

Open path

Direction line

Smooth anchor point

Curve segment

Straight segment

Corner anchor point

Fill

Stroke

Selected object

Selected anchor point

Object undergoing a scale transformation

BUILDING BLOCKS

Path (Or "object") Any individual shape that's created in Illustrator. A path can be open (a line with two endpoints) or closed (no endpoints).

Anchor points Path segments are connected by smooth and/or corner anchor points. Smooth anchor points have a pair of direction lines that move in tandem and form a straight line; corner points can have no direction lines, one direction line, or a pair of direction lines that can be moved independently to reshape adjacent segments. A curve segment can join two smooth points, or a corner point and a smooth point. A straight segment always joins two corner points. You can reshape any path by modifying its anchor points and/or segments.

Fill, stroke A fill is the color, pattern, or gradient (transition between two or more colors) that you apply to the inside of an object. A stroke, which delineates the edge of an object, can be any solid color, can be of any width, and can be solid or dashed.

Layer A tier of a document that holds a stack of objects. A document can contain multiple top-level layers, sublayers, and groups. The "actual" objects in a document (paths, type, placed images, mesh objects, etc.) are nested within top-level layers, sublayers, or groups.

BASIC OPERATIONS

Select To highlight an object in the document window for editing. Only selected objects can be modified. When a whole path is selected, its anchor points are solid (not hollow). Selections can be made by using the Selection, Direct Selection, Group Selection, Lasso, or Magic Wand tool or via menu commands.

Transform To move, rotate, scale, reflect, or shear (slant) an object, apply distortion or perspective, or create a blend between two objects.

TYPOGRAPHIC TERMS

Font, font style, leading, kerning, tracking, horizontal scaling, baseline shift, glyph A font is the typeface that gives type its distinctive appearance; font style is the subcategory within a font (such as Myriad Bold in the Myriad font); leading is the spacing between lines of type; kerning is the adjustment of spacing between a pair of characters; tracking is the adjustment of spacing between three or more characters; horizontal scaling is the widening or narrowing of characters; baseline shift is the shifting of one or more characters upward or downward from the type baseline; and a glyph is a character variation.

Blend created using a circle and a star

Art brush stroke

Original objects | *Compound path made from the circle and star*

Original objects | *Compound shape made from the three objects*

Drop shadow effect

Envelope distortion

OTHER FEATURES

Action A recorded sequence of commands and edits that can be replayed on any object, file, or batch of files.

Appearances Editable and removable attributes, such as multiple fills, strokes, effects, blending modes, opacity settings, patterns, and brush strokes.

Blend A multistep color and shape progression between two or more objects. If you reshape, recolor, or move any of the individual objects in a blend or reshape, move, or transform the blend path (spine), the blend updates automatically.

Bridge **NEW** A standalone application that lets you locate, open, read info about, sort, rename, move, rotate, and delete files, edit metadata in a selected file, and choose global color settings for all the applications in the Adobe Creative Suite.

Brush A decorative Calligraphic, Art, Scatter, or Pattern stroke that's applied either to an existing path or via the Paintbrush tool.

Clipping set The reversible clipping of parts of overlapping objects that extend beyond an object's border to prevent them from displaying and printing.

Compound path Two or more objects combined into one via a reversible command. Where the original objects overlap, a transparent hole is created, through which shapes or patterns behind the compound object are revealed.

Compound shape An editable (and reversible) union of overlapping objects produced via the shape mode buttons on the Pathfinder palette. If individual objects within a compound shape are moved, restacked, or reshaped, the overall compound shape readjusts accordingly. Other commands on the Pathfinder palette determine where selected paths overlap and then divide, trim, merge, crop, outline, or subtract from them to produce nonoverlapping (flattened) closed paths.

Effects Commands on the Effect menu that change the appearance of an object without changing its actual path. Unlike filters, effects can be edited or removed via the Appearance palette.

Envelope A container used for applying distortion. When you reshape an envelope, all the objects in the envelope reshape accordingly. You can also apply distortion by pushing and pulling on an object's edges with a liquify tool (Warp, Twirl, Pucker, Bloat, Scallop, Crystallize, or Wrinkle), as you might

(Continued on the following page)

Mini-Glossary

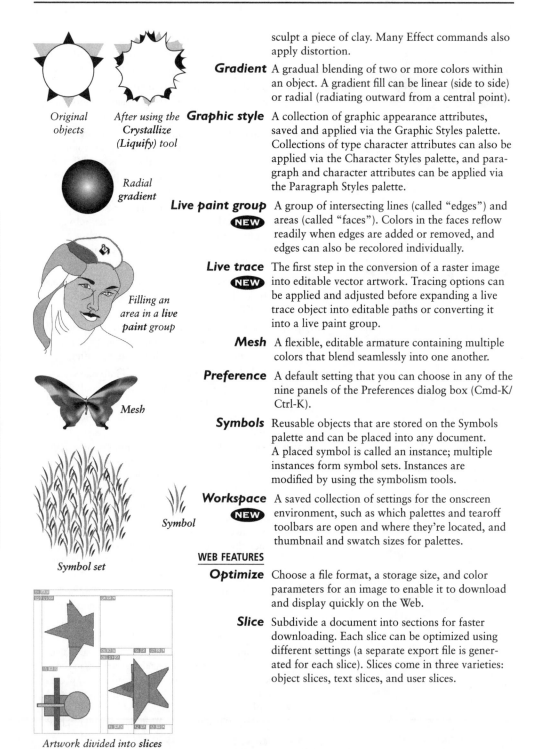

Original objects

After using the **Crystallize** (**Liquify**) tool

Radial gradient

Filling an area in a **live paint** group

Mesh

Symbol set

Symbol

Artwork divided into **slices**

sculpt a piece of clay. Many Effect commands also apply distortion.

Gradient A gradual blending of two or more colors within an object. A gradient fill can be linear (side to side) or radial (radiating outward from a central point).

Graphic style A collection of graphic appearance attributes, saved and applied via the Graphic Styles palette. Collections of type character attributes can also be applied via the Character Styles palette, and paragraph and character attributes can be applied via the Paragraph Styles palette.

Live paint group **NEW** A group of intersecting lines (called "edges") and areas (called "faces"). Colors in the faces reflow readily when edges are added or removed, and edges can also be recolored individually.

Live trace **NEW** The first step in the conversion of a raster image into editable vector artwork. Tracing options can be applied and adjusted before expanding a live trace object into editable paths or converting it into a live paint group.

Mesh A flexible, editable armature containing multiple colors that blend seamlessly into one another.

Preference A default setting that you can choose in any of the nine panels of the Preferences dialog box (Cmd-K/Ctrl-K).

Symbols Reusable objects that are stored on the Symbols palette and can be placed into any document. A placed symbol is called an instance; multiple instances form symbol sets. Instances are modified by using the symbolism tools.

Workspace **NEW** A saved collection of settings for the onscreen environment, such as which palettes and tearoff toolbars are open and where they're located, and thumbnail and swatch sizes for palettes.

WEB FEATURES

Optimize Choose a file format, a storage size, and color parameters for an image to enable it to download and display quickly on the Web.

Slice Subdivide a document into sections for faster downloading. Each slice can be optimized using different settings (a separate export file is generated for each slice). Slices come in three varieties: object slices, text slices, and user slices.

Division the easy way

Let's say you want to reduce an object's width by 25%. Select the object, highlight the entire W field on the Transform palette, type "75%", then press Return/Enter. The width will be reduced to three-quarters of its current value (e.g., 4p becomes 3p). You could also click to the right of the current entry, type an asterisk (*), type a percentage value, then press Return/Enter.

Symbols you can use

UNIT	SYMBOL
Picas	**p**
Points	**pt**
Inches	**" or in**
Millimeters	**mm**
Centimeters	**cm**
Q (a type unit)	**q**
Pixels	**px**

Points 'n' picas

12 pt = 1 pica
6 picas = 1 inch

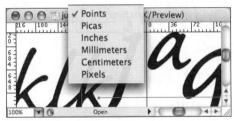

1 *You can choose **units** via a **context** menu in the document window...*

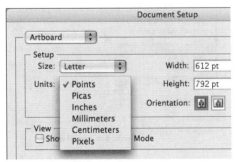

2 *...or from the **Units** pop-up menu in the **Document Setup** dialog box.*

Measuring up

The **measurement unit** that you choose for a document (see the instructions below) overrides the unit chosen for the application in Preferences (Cmd-K/Ctrl-K) > **Units & Display Performance.** The current unit is used in entry fields in most palettes and dialog boxes, and on the rulers in the document window.

You can enter values in dialog boxes and palettes using any of the units listed in the sidebar at left, regardless of the current default units. If you enter a value in a nondefault unit, it will be translated into the default unit when you press Tab or Return/Enter.

➤ If you enter the symbol for subtraction (-), addition (+), multiplication (*), division (/), or percent (%) after the current value in any field, Illustrator will do the math for you (see the sidebar).

➤ To enter a combination of picas and points, separate the two numbers with a "p". For example, 4p2 equals 4 picas plus 2 points, or 50 pt. (Be sure to highlight the entire contents of the field first.)

Follow the instructions below to change the **measurement units** just for the current **document.** Or go to Preferences (Cmd-K/Ctrl-K) > Units & Display Performance to choose a measurement unit for the current and future documents.

To change the units for the current document:

If the rulers aren't showing, choose View > **Show Rulers** (Cmd-R/Ctrl-R), then Control-click/right-click either **ruler** and choose a unit from the context menu **1**.
or
Choose File > **Document Setup** (Cmd-Option-P/Ctrl-Alt-P); choose Artboard from the pop-up menu; choose **Units: Points, Picas, Inches, Millimeters, Centimeters,** or Pixels **2**; then click OK.

➤ The current location of the pointer is marked by a dotted line on both rulers. The higher the zoom level, the finer the ruler increments.

Units of Measure

Undos and context menus

Multiple undos

To undo an operation, choose Edit > **Undo** (Cmd-Z/Ctrl-Z). To undo the second-to-last operation, choose Edit > Undo again, and so on. To reverse an undo, choose Edit > **Redo** (Cmd-Shift-Z/Ctrl-Shift-Z). You can also Control-click/right-click the artboard and choose either command from the context menu. You can undo or redo after saving your document, but not after you close and reopen it.

Context menus

A context menu (short for "contextual menu") lets you choose a command from an onscreen menu without having to mouse to the menu bar or even to a palette. We use them whenever we can. To open a context menu, **Control-click/right-click** the artboard.

Context menu offerings change depending on which tool is selected and whether any objects are selected in your document **1**–**3**. A command that's unavailable for the type of object currently selected will be dimmed on the context menu.

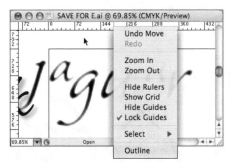

1 *Context menu when* **type** *is selected*

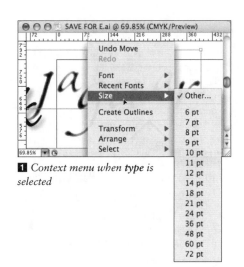

2 *Context menu when* **nothing** *is selected*

Don't overlook tool tips!

You can use **tool tips** to identify palette buttons, swatch names, tool names, tool shortcuts, and other application features. Simply rest the pointer (without clicking) on a button, swatch, or icon, and a tip will pop up onscreen **4**. (If the tool tips don't show up, go to Preferences [Cmd-K/Ctrl-K] > General, and check Show Tool Tips.)

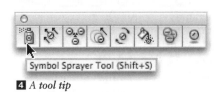

4 *A tool tip*

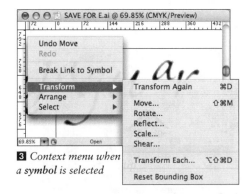

3 *Context menu when a symbol is selected*

HOW ILLUSTRATOR WORKS 2

In this chapter you'll learn the basic differences between object-oriented and bitmap applications and get a broad overview of how objects are created and edited in Illustrator.

1 *Object-oriented graphics, such as this compass by Daniel Pelavin, are defined mathematically. In Illustrator, you can create geometric shapes…*

2 *…or you can draw in a loose, freehand style (this is a live paint group).*

Vector or raster?

There are two main types of picture-making applications: bitmap (or "raster") and object-oriented (or "vector"), and each type has its strengths and weaknesses. Bitmap programs are best suited for creating soft, painterly images, such as photo-collages, whereas object-oriented programs are better suited for creating sharp, smooth shapes, such as mechanical illustrations, and typographic designs, such as logos.

Drawings created in **object-oriented** programs such as Adobe Illustrator, are composed of separate, distinct, mathematically defined objects or groups of objects. The vector objects that you create in Illustrator can be recolored, scaled, and reshaped without diminishing their sharpness or smoothness, and can be moved around or restacked onto other layers or sublayers independently of other objects.

Vector objects keep their smooth curves and sharp edges regardless of the size at which they're displayed or printed **1**–**2**. The higher the printer resolution, the sharper the print. Vector files usually have relatively small file sizes compared to bitmap files.

Images created in **bitmap** programs such as Photoshop, on the other hand, consist of one or more layers of tiny squares on a grid, called pixels. When you edit a bitmap image, pixels on just the currently selected layer are affected. You can isolate areas by using selections or masks, but you can't select objects, as you can in a vector program. If you zoom

(Continued on the following page)

way in on a bitmap image, you'll see the checkerboard of tiny squares **1**–**2**. Bitmap files tend to be large, and the quality of the print output varies depending on the image resolution. However, bitmap programs are ideal for creating digital paintings, montages, and photorealistic images, and for editing, correcting, and retouching photographs.

Although Illustrator images consist mostly of vector shapes, you can place or open bitmap images into an Illustrator document and apply some commands to them. You can also **rasterize** vector objects (convert them into bitmap images) and then apply filters to them.

Creating objects

The key building blocks that you'll be using to compose an illustration are Bézier objects and type. Bézier objects consist of **anchor points** connected by **curved** or **straight segments.** The edge that defines an object's shape is called its **path.** Paths can be open, with an endpoint at either end, or closed and continuous.

With some Illustrator tools—such as the **Rectangle, Ellipse, Polygon, Star, Polar Grid, Rectangular Grid,** and **Flare**—you produce closed paths simply by clicking on the artboard. You can use these tools to create simple geometric objects, such as polygons or circles, then reshape the results or combine them with other objects.

Other tools let you draw shapes "from scratch" by clicking or dragging. For example, you can draw open, freeform lines with the **Pencil** tool; Calligraphic, Scatter, Art, or Pattern strokes with the **Paintbrush** tool **3**; straight lines with the **Line Segment** tool; and smooth arcs with the **Arc Segment** tool.

If you enjoy sketching, you'll gravitate to Illustrator's **live paint** features. You start by converting a drawing that you create with the Pencil or another tool into a **live paint group.** Then using the Live Paint Bucket tool, you apply colors to faces, or areas where lines intersect. Because the object is "live," colors reflow instantly into any areas that you reshape.

1 A *bitmap image*

2 An extreme closeup of a *bitmap image,* showing individual *pixels*

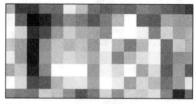

3 Strokes drawn with the **Paintbrush** tool using two different brushes

What Illustrator is used for

advertisements	maps
book jackets	menus
brochures	posters
business cards	postcards
CD/DVD covers, inserts	product packaging
editorial illustrations	shopping bags
fine art	signage
flyers	sketches
graphs and charts	stationery
hang tags	T-shirt graphics
invitations	technical drawings
labels and stickers	textile design
letterheads	Web graphics
logos	Web layouts

1 *Symbols applied via the **Symbol Sprayer** tool*

2 *Type on paths*

Using the **Pen** tool, you can create as many corner or curve anchor points as you need to form an object of virtually any shape.

If you want to use a scanned or digital image as a starting point, you can use the **live trace** feature to convert it into vector art. You can also build document layouts by using one of the **templates** that Illustrator supplies, or by creating your own.

Another way to build graphics efficiently is by using **symbols 1**. You use the Symbols palette or the Symbol Sprayer tool to place repetitive instances of a symbol into a document, then use other symbolism tools—the Shifter, Scruncher, Sizer, Spinner, Stainer, or Screener—to modify the instances.

To help you keep track of all the objects you've created, you'll use the **Layers** palette. It lists every top-level layer, sublayer, group, and object in an illustration, and also lets you select objects; target layers, groups, or objects for appearance changes; restack, move, and copy objects between layers; and turn lock, display, template, and print options on and off for individual layers, sublayers, groups, and objects.

Adding type

Illustrator offers a smorgasbord of features with which type can be created, styled, and formatted. Type can be freestanding (**point** type), it can flow along the edge of an object (**path** type) **2**, or it can be put inside an object of any shape (**area** type). Depending on the tool used to create it, type will flow (and be read) vertically or horizontally.

Once created or imported, type can be repositioned, edited, restyled, recolored, transformed, or warped. You can even design your own characters by converting standard type into **outlines** and then reshaping the outlines like standard paths.

Editing objects

Objects must be **selected** before they can be modified. There are five tools that let you do this mechanically (**Selection, Direct Selection, Group Selection, Lasso,** and **Magic Wand**) and a host of commands that let you select

(Continued on the following page)

objects by criteria such as color, style, or blending mode. You can also select objects by using the Layers palette.

Objects can be modified by using a wide assortment of menu commands, filters, dialog boxes, palettes, and tools (see Chapter 1 for a full rundown).

Reshaping objects

You can reshape an object's contour by moving its **anchor points** or **segments** 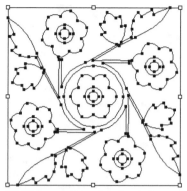 or by converting its curve anchor points into corner anchor points (or vice versa). To reshape segments, you can rotate, lengthen, or shorten the direction lines that stick out from the anchor points.

Among the tools that let you modify paths are the **Scissors** tool for splitting paths, the **Add Anchor Point** tool, the **Delete Anchor Point** tool, and the **Convert Anchor Point** tool, which converts corner points into curve points and vice versa. You can also transform an object by manipulating the handles on its bounding box.

Other tools are used like sculptors' utensils to change the contour of an object. The **Knife** tool carves out sections of an object; the **Smooth** tool removes points to create smoother curves; the **Erase** tool removes whole chunks of a path; and the **Pencil** and **Reshape** tools reshape an object as you push or pull on its contour.

You can also create new shapes by combining objects. For example, you could use the **Compound Path** command like a cookie cutter to cut a hole through an object to reveal underlying shapes, or use an object as a **clipping mask** to hide parts of other objects that extend beyond its edges. The **shape mode** buttons on the Pathfinder palette produce an editable compound shape from selected, overlapping objects, whereas the **Pathfinder** buttons on the same palette divide areas where objects overlap into new, separate objects.

Objects can also be **transformed** by using the **Scale** tool, **Rotate** tool, **Reflect** tool, and **Shear** tool, as well as the **Blend** tool – and command, which creates a series of

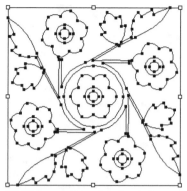

1 *Objects consist of* **anchor points** *and* **segments**.

2 *Two simple objects are selected...*

3 *...then made into a* **blend** *in one easy step.*

(side margin) **How Illustrator Works**

transitional shapes. Multiple transformations can be performed at once using the **Free Transform** tool, the **Transform Each** command, or the **Transform** palette.

To produce more extreme distortions, you can use the **Warp, Twirl, Pucker, Bloat, Scallop, Crystallize,** or **Wrinkle** tool to mold or twist objects, or put an object or objects (even type) into an **envelope** and then manipulate points in the envelope mesh to reshape the object(s) inside it.

If you hate having to repeat your steps, you can automate tasks by saving a series of editing steps and commands as an **action,** then replaying your action on one file or on a batch of files.

And finally, if you're the nervous type, relax —Illustrator has **multiple undos**!

Applying colors, patterns, transparency

Palettes such as **Color, Swatches, Gradient, Stroke,** and **Brushes** let you apply colors, patterns, and stroke attributes. You can **fill** the inside of any open or closed object with a **solid** color, a **gradient** (a smooth gradation between two or more colors), or a **pattern** of repeating tiles ∎. You can also apply a solid-color (plain or dashed) **stroke** or a **brush stroke** to the edge of any object. The stroke and fill colors that you apply to objects can be from a matching system, such as PANTONE, or you can mix your own CMYK, HSB, or RGB colors. You can even create your own patterns and gradients.

If you want a softer look, the **Transparency** palette lets you assign **opacity** levels to any type of object (even to placed raster images and type); apply **blending modes** to control how objects and layers interact; or use an object as an **opacity mask** to control the transparency of other objects.

And to create a naturalistic look or an illusion of volume, try creating a **mesh**. First you create a flexible, elastic armature, then you apply multiple colors. Colors blend smoothly and seamlessly from one area to the next.

Adding appearances

Appearance attributes—such as multiple fills and strokes, transparency settings, blending modes, brush strokes, and Effect menu commands—change an object's appearance without changing its actual path and, thankfully, can be reedited, restacked, or removed at any time. Many **Effect** menu commands, such as Feather, Drop Shadow, Inner Glow, Outer Glow, and the **3D** effects (Extrude & Bevel, Revolve, and Rotate), have counterparts on the **Filter** menu. The vector filters and effects distort an object's shape or modify its color, whereas the bitmap filters and effects add artistic, painterly touches or textures. The Filter menu commands permanently alter an object, whereas effects can be edited or removed from an object without causing the object to become permanently changed— only its appearance changes.

Whole collections of object attributes can be saved as graphic styles on the **Graphic Styles** palette, and then applied to any object in one fell swoop.

(Continued on the following page)

(Continued on the following page)

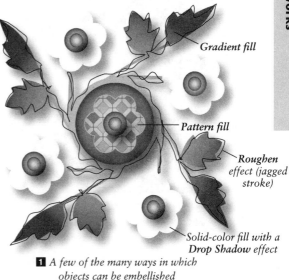

Gradient fill

Pattern fill

Roughen effect (jagged stroke)

Solid-color fill with a **Drop Shadow** *effect*

∎ *A few of the many ways in which objects can be embellished*

Using onscreen tools

You can position objects by eye or you can use a variety of Illustrator features to align them precisely, namely, **smart guides, ruler guides,** the **grid,** the **Measure** tool, the **Move** dialog box, the **Align** buttons, and the previously-mentioned transform commands and Transform palette.

To work effectively and to prevent eyestrain, you can easily change the **zoom level** of your document. Zoom to edit a small detail, then zoom back out to judge the overall effect—Illustrator does all but squint for you. If a drawing is magnified onscreen, you can move it around in the document window by using the **Hand** tool or the **Navigator** palette.

A document can be displayed and edited in **Preview** view **1**, in which all the fill and stroke colors are displayed; as simple wire-frame outlines in **Outline** view **2**; or in **Pixel preview** view, to see how it would look in rasterized form for the Web.

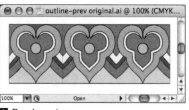

1 *Preview view*

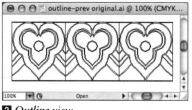

2 *Outline view*

Outputting your work

Many avenues are open for outputting your artwork **3**. It can be **color-separated** for off-set printing or **printed** on a composite color printer. Or you can save it in a file format (e.g., Photoshop, EPS, PDF, or TIFF) for export to a page layout application, such as QuarkXPress, InDesign, or Microsoft Office, or to an image-editing application, such as Photoshop.

Using the **Save for Web** dialog box, you can choose compression, transparency, and other options for a file, then save it in an appropriate format for Web output, such as GIF, JPEG, or PNG. Illustrator also lets you assign a **URL** to an object to create an image map, then export the file for use as a clickable element on a Web page, or you can use **slicing** tools to define slice areas in a document, then choose different optimization (compression) options for each slice.

Hopefully, this chapter has whetted your appetite—and not scared you away! Remember, unless you're very compulsive (or mistakenly signed up for a four-semester course), you don't have to master every Illustrator feature. Many features and commands let you reshape, recolor, embellish, transform, distort, and combine paths in just a few easy steps. Start by creating some simple shapes, then tackle more complex projects as your skill level and confidence grows. Enough said—it's time to start drawing!

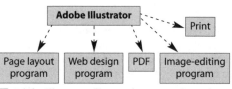

3 *Adobe Illustrator files can be **exported** to other software programs or **output** to a variety of media —from print to the Web.*

CREATE & SAVE FILES 3

In this chapter you'll learn how to launch Illustrator; create a new document; preview, open, and create templates; define the working and printable areas of a document; save a document in the Adobe Illustrator file format; save a copy of a document; close a document; and quit/exit Illustrator.

1 *Click the Adobe Illustrator CS2 application icon in the Dock.*

2 *In Illustrator, you can open (and save) a file in any of these formats.*

Launching Illustrator

A new document window doesn't appear automatically when you **launch Illustrator**. To create a new document after launching the application, see page 41.

To launch Illustrator in Macintosh:

On the startup drive, open the Applications > Adobe Illustrator CS2 folder, then double-click the **Adobe Illustrator CS2** program icon.
or
Click the Illustrator application icon in the **Dock 1**. (To create an icon, drag the application icon from the application folder to the Dock.)
or
Double-click any Illustrator **file icon**, or drag any Illustrator file icon over the application icon in the **Dock** to both launch Illustrator and open that file **2**.

By default, a welcome screen opens when Illustrator is launched **3**. If "Show this dialog at startup" was unchecked on the welcome screen to prevent it from appearing upon launching, you can make it reappear by choosing Help > **Welcome Screen**.

3 *The Illustrator CS2 welcome screen*

A new document window doesn't appear automatically when you **launch Illustrator.** To create a new document after launching the application, follow the instructions on the next page.

To launch Illustrator in Windows:

Open **My Computer,** double-click the hard drive icon where you installed Illustrator (the default is C:), follow the path Program Files/Adobe/Adobe Illustrator CS2, then double-click the **Adobe Illustrator CS2** icon.
or
Double-click an Illustrator **file icon** ❶ to both launch Illustrator and open that file.
or
Click the **Start** button on the taskbar, choose **All Programs,** then click **Adobe Illustrator CS2** ❷.

By default, a welcome screen opens when Illustrator is launched ❸. If someone unchecked "Show this dialog at startup" on the welcome screen to prevent it from appearing upon launching, you can make it reappear at any time by choosing Help > **Welcome Screen.**

❶ *Double-click an Illustrator* **file icon.**

❷ *Click the* **Start** *button, then locate and click the* **Adobe Illustrator CS2** *application.*

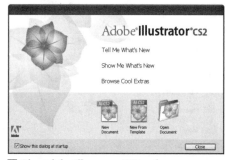

❸ *The Adobe Illustrator CS2* **welcome screen**

Launch Illustrator in Windows

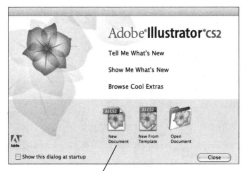

1 Click the **New Document** icon on the Adobe Illustrator CS2 welcome screen.

Creating new documents
To create a new document:

1. Choose File > New (Cmd-N/Ctrl-N).
   or
   If the Adobe Illustrator CS2 welcome screen is displaying, click the **New Document** icon **1**.

2. Type a **Name** for the new document **2**.

3. In the **Artboard Setup** area, choose dimensions for the document:

   From the **Size** pop-up menu, choose a preset size. For Web output, choose **640 x 480, 800 x 600,** or **468 x 60.** For print output, choose **Letter, Legal, Tabloid, A4, A3, B5,** or **B4.**
   or
   To enter custom dimensions, choose a measurement unit from the **Units** pop-up menu (use Pixels for Web output), then enter **Width** and **Height** values.

4. Click an **Orientation** button: **Portrait** (vertical) or **Landscape** (horizontal). This can be changed later.

5. Click a **Color Mode** for the document: **CMYK Color** for print output, or **RGB Color** for video or Web output.

6. Click OK. A new document window will open, at the maximum window size and zoom level for your display. You can resize the window by dragging the lower right corner.

New Document		
Name: Great Art		OK
Artboard Setup		Cancel
Size: Letter	Width: 612 pt	
Units: Points	Height: 792 pt	
	Orientation:	
Color Mode		
○ CMYK Color	● RGB Color	

2 In the **New Document** dialog box, type a name, choose dimensions for the artboard, and choose a color mode.

Create New Document

Using templates

Illustrator CS2 ships with **templates** that can be used as a starting point for creating industry-standard projects. The templates include layouts, crop marks, objects, styles, symbols, custom swatches, and more. To get an inkling of what the templates look like via PDF previews, follow these instructions. If you're new to Illustrator, this is a good way to see what the program can do. (To open an actual template file, follow the next set of instructions.)

NEW **To preview the Illustrator templates:**

1. Launch Bridge by clicking the **Go to Bridge** button 📷 at the far right side of the Control palette.

2. Click the Folders tab in the left panel, navigate to the Adobe Illustrator CS2/ Cool Extras/Templates folder, double-click any folder name, then browse through the images **1**.

The **New from Template** command opens a template file as a new, untitled document—content, specifications, and all—which can be edited like any other document; the original file is left intact.

You're not limited to using the templates that ship with Illustrator. You can open any existing Illustrator file as an untitled document via the New from Template command, using the instructions below. And on the following page, we show you how to save a file as a template.

To open a template or nontemplate file as an untitled document:

1. Choose File > **New from Template** (Cmd-Shift-N/Ctrl-Shift-N) or click **New From Template** on the Adobe Illustrator CS2 welcome screen.

2. To open an Illustrator template in Mac, go to Applications/Adobe Illustrator CS2/
NEW Cool Extras/Templates. In Windows, go to Program Files\Adobe\Adobe
NEW Illustrator CS2\Cool Extras\Templates.

   Click a folder in the **Templates** folder, click a template name, then click New.

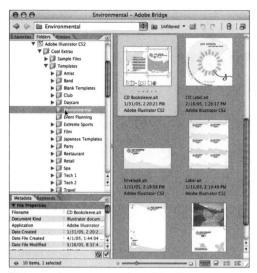

1 Use **Bridge** to preview the Adobe Illustrator CS2 templates.

Preview, Open File as Template

1 *A CD **template** in the **Band** folder*

2 *A **packaging template** in the Spa folder*

3 *A business card **template** in the **Club** folder*

The template will open in a new, untitled document window **1**–**3**.
or
Locate and select an existing Illustrator file, then click New to open the file as an untitled document.

3. Save the file.

You can go the extra mile and **save** any of **your own files** as a **template.** Regardless of what kind of project you're working on—CD label, business card, book cover, Web graphics—a template can serve as a useful labor- and time-saving foundation. In creating a template, you can choose settings and layout aids such as guides, zoom level, and artboard dimensions and also create actions, brushes, swatches, symbols, graphic styles, crop marks, and, of course, path objects.

To create a template:

1. Create a new file, then create any path objects, swatches, graphic styles, symbols, etc. that you want saved in the template. You can also choose specifications for the artboard; set a zoom level or custom views; create layers and guides; and define transparency flattener, PDF, or print presets. You can even create text boxes containing instructions for the lucky user of your template.

2. Save the file via File > **Save as Template** (leave the format as Illustrator Template (ait). That's all there is to it.

Create Template

Changing the document setup

In the center of every Illustrator document is one nonmovable **artboard** work area **1**. The dimensions of the artboard are chosen in the New Document dialog box.

The printable page size is the current Media (paper) Size chosen in File > Print > General. Letter size, for example, is 8½ x 11 inches. You're not limited to the default 8½ x 11 artboard or to the portrait format, though. That is, the artboard doesn't have to match the current media size or orientation.

To change the artboard dimensions or orientation:

1. Choose File > **Document Setup** (Cmd-Option-P/Ctrl-Alt-P).

2. Choose **Artboard** from the topmost pop-up menu.

3. From the **Setup: Size** pop-up menu, choose a preset size **2**. For Web output, choose 640 x 480, 800 x 600, or 468 x 60. For print output, choose **Letter, Legal, Tabloid, A4, A3, B5,** or **B4**.
   or
   To enter custom dimensions, choose a measurement unit from the **Units** pop-up menu (use Pixels for Web output), then enter **Width** and **Height** values. Custom will become the selection on the Size pop-up menu. The maximum work area is 228 x 228 inches. *Note:* For the current document, the Units chosen here override

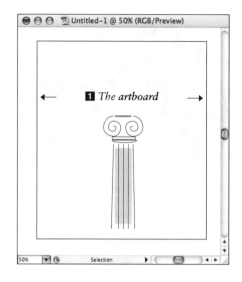

1 *The artboard*

the Units chosen in Preferences (Cmd-K/Ctrl-K) > Units & Display Performance.

4. Click a different **Orientation** icon, if desired (**1**, next page).

5. Click OK.

6. If you changed the artboard orientation, double-click the upper left corner of the document window to reset the ruler origin (the ruler origin is in the lower left corner).

➤ Objects (or parts of objects) outside the artboard will save with the illustration.

➤ Double-click the Hand tool to display the entire artboard in the document window.

2 *In the Document Setup dialog box, you can choose a preset Size or enter custom Width and Height values.*

Change Artboard Dimensions, Orientation

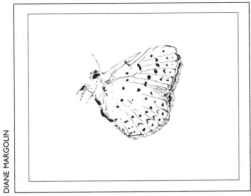

DIANE MARGOLIN

1 *The artboard in landscape orientation*

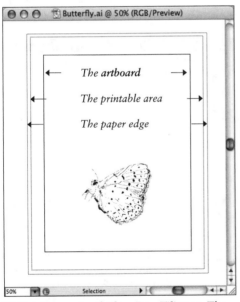

2 *The document with **Show Page Tiling** on. The size and orientation of the printable page doesn't necessarily match the size and orientation of the artboard.*

The artboard and printing

In the default setup for printing, only objects (or parts of objects) that are within the artboard area will print.

You can use the **Setup** panel in File > Print to reposition the printable page relative to the artboard. If the illustration is oversized, for example, in the Setup panel you can specify that it be tiled (subdivided) into a grid so it will print in sections on the paper size for your chosen printer (see pages 484–485).

To view the relationship between the current artboard and the paper size for the currently chosen printer, choose View > **Fit in Window** and View > **Show Page Tiling.** The outer dotted rectangle that you see onscreen represents the paper size; the inner dotted rectangle represents the actual printable area, which accounts for the printer's nonprintable margins on the edge of the paper **2**.

➤ You could use the Page tool to reposition the printable page relative to the artboard, but we prefer to do this via the Setup options in the Print dialog box.

For more information about printing files from Illustrator, see Chapter 32.

Artboard and Printing

Saving files

You can choose from six formats when **saving** an Illustrator file: Adobe Illustrator (ai), Illustrator EPS (eps), Illustrator Template (ait), Adobe PDF (pdf), SVG Compressed (svgz), and SVG (svg). Files in all of these formats can be reopened and edited in Illustrator.

If you're going to print your file directly from Illustrator, we suggest using the **NEW Adobe Illustrator Document** format (ai), or Illustrator format, for short.

If you're going to export your file to another application (e.g., a layout application for print or Web output), you'll need to choose one of the other formats, as not all applications can read native Illustrator (ai) files. The EPS format is discussed on pages 503–505, the PDF format on pages 506–510, and the SVG format on pages 539–541.

To save a file in the Illustrator format:

1. If the file has never been saved, choose File > **Save** (Cmd-S/Ctrl-S). If the file has already been saved in a different format, choose File > Save As.

2. Enter a name in the Save As (Mac) **1**/File Name (Win) field **2**. (The Save As dialog box in Mac OS X 10.4, Tiger, is shown in **1**, next page.)

3. Navigate to the desired folder or disk.

4. In Mac, choose **Format: Adobe Illustrator Document**.

   In Windows, choose **Save as type: Adobe Illustrator (*.AI)**.

5. Click **Save**. The Illustrator Options dialog box opens (**2**, next page). Leave Illustrator CS2 as the choice on the **Version** pop-up menu. (For the legacy formats, see the sidebar at right.)

6. Under **Fonts,** enter a percentage in the **Subset fonts when percent of characters used is less than** field to save fonts used in the illustration as part of the document. Characters in embedded fonts will display and print on any system, even where they aren't installed, but keep in mind that this

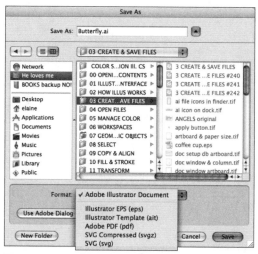

1 *The Save As dialog box in Mac OS X, Panther*

2 *The Save As dialog box in Windows*

Going back

To save a CS2 file in an earlier Illustrator format, in the Illustrator Options dialog box, choose the desired format under **Legacy Formats** on the **Version** pop-up menu. Bear in mind that "live" features from version CS2, such as effects, live paint groups, and transparency, won't be preserved in the legacy file. Also be sure to read the Warnings at the bottom of the Illustrator Options dialog box. If you need to save a file in Illustrator 8 format, please see page 503 for information about the transparency options.

Save in Illustrator (ai) Format

Shortcuts for saving files

	Mac	Windows
Save	Cmd-S	Ctrl-S
Save As	Cmd-Shift-S	Ctrl-Shift-S
Save a Copy	Cmd-Option-S	Ctrl-Alt-S

1 *The Save As dialog box in Mac OS X, Tiger*

2 *The **Illustrator Options** dialog box, showing options for the Illustrator CS2 format*

option increases the file storage size, depending on the specified percentage. At 100%, all font characters will be embedded.

If not all the characters in a particular font are used in your artwork, you can choose to embed just a subset of characters, as opposed to the whole font. This will help reduce the file size. For example, at a setting of 50%, the entire font will be embedded only if you use more than 50% of its characters in the file, and the Subset option will be used if you use fewer than 50% of its characters in the file.

7. Under **Options,** you can check:

   Create PDF Compatible File to save a PDF-compatible version of the file for use in other applications that support PDF. Checking this option increases the file storage size.

   Include Linked Files to save a copy of any linked files with the illustration. Read about linking on pages 282–286.

   If a profile was chosen in Edit > Assign Profile, check **Embed ICC Profiles** to embed those profiles in the file in order to color-manage the file.

   Use Compression to compress vector data and PDF data (if included) to help reduce the file storage size.

8. Click OK.

➤ If Enable Version Cue is checked in Preferences > File Handling & Clipboard, you can click the Use Adobe Dialog button in the Save dialog box to utilize the Version Cue file management features in the Adobe Creative Suite applications. Read about Version Cue in Illustrator Help.

Save in Illustrator (ai) Format

The prior version of a file is overwritten whenever the **Save** command is executed. Do yourself a favor and save often—don't be shy about it! And be sure to create backups of your work frequently, too.

To resave a file:

Choose File > **Save** (Cmd-S/Ctrl-S).

When you use the **Save a Copy** command, the original version of the file stays open onscreen, and a copy of it is saved to disk.

To save a copy of a file:

1. Choose File > **Save a Copy** (Cmd-Option-S/Ctrl-Alt-S).

2. To save the file in the Illustrator (ai) format, see pages 46–47; for the Adobe PDF format, see pages 506–510; for the Illustrator EPS format, see pages 503–505; and for the SVG format, see pages 539–541.

To revert to the last saved version:

1. Choose File > **Revert** (F12).

2. Click Revert.

Ending a work session

To close a file:

In Mac, click the **close** (red) button in the upper left corner of the document window (Cmd-W). In Windows, click the **close** box in the upper right corner of the document window (Ctrl-W).

If the file was modified since it was last saved, an alert dialog box will appear ■. Click Don't Save to close the file without saving; or click Save to save the file; or click Cancel to back out of the deal.

To quit/exit Illustrator:

In Mac, choose Illustrator > **Quit** Illustrator (Cmd-Q). In Windows, choose File > **Exit** (Ctrl-Q) or click the close box for the application window.

All open Illustrator files will close. If changes were made to any open files since they were last saved, an alert dialog box will appear. To save the file(s), click Save, or to quit/exit without saving, click Don't Save.

Save As or Save a Copy?

You can use the Save As or Save a Copy command to save an existing file in a different format, such as Illustrator AI, Adobe PDF, or Illustrator EPS. When you use **Save As** (discussed on the previous two pages), the new version of the file stays open onscreen, while the original file closes but is preserved on disk. With **Save a Copy,** discussed at left, the original version of the file stays open onscreen, and a copy of it is saved to disk.

Fast close

To close **all** open Illustrator files, **Option-click** one close button (Mac)/**Alt-click** one close box (Win).

> Save changes to the Adobe Illustrator document "Mosaic.eps" before closing?
> If you don't save, your changes will be lost.
>
> Don't Save   Cancel   Save

■ *If you try to close a file that was modified since it was last saved, this prompt will appear.*

Save; Save Copy; Revert; Close; Quit/Exit

OPEN FILES | 4

In this chapter you'll learn how to open files via the Open command and via Bridge, a standalone program that works with all the programs in the Adobe Creative Suite. You'll also learn how to use Bridge to label, sort, assign keywords to, find, rename, and delete files—among other tasks.

New chapter!

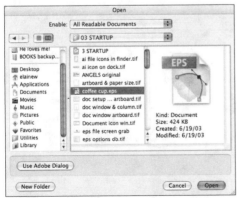

1 *The Open dialog box in Windows*

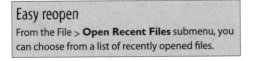

2 *The Open dialog box in Mac OS X, Panther*

Easy reopen

From the File > **Open Recent Files** submenu, you can choose from a list of recently opened files.

Opening files from Illustrator

You can follow the instructions on this page to open Illustrator (ai) files using the **Open** command in Illustrator. Or if you'd prefer to use the Bridge application to open files, as we do, read the next section. For instructions on opening files in other formats, such as EPS or PDF, see page 278.

To open a file from Illustrator:

1. Choose File > **Open** (Cmd-O/Ctrl-O).
   or
   Or if the Adobe Illustrator CS2 welcome screen is displaying onscreen, click the **Open Document** icon.

2. In Mac, to list files only in the formats Illustrator can read, choose **Enable: All Readable Documents.** In Windows, to list all files, readable or not, choose **Files of type: All Formats,** or choose a format.

3. Locate and highlight a file name **1**–**2**, then click **Open.** If an alert dialog box about a **missing profile** appears, see page 61; for the **Font Problems** dialog box, see the sidebar on page 54; and for an alert dialog box about a **linked** image file, see page 285. To learn about updating **legacy text** (text from earlier program versions), see pages 240–241.

To open a file from the Mac Desktop or from Windows Explorer:

Double-click an Illustrator file icon. In Mac, you can also open an file by dragging its icon over the Adobe Illustrator CS2 appplication icon on the Dock. Illustrator will launch if it isn't already running.

⟨NEW⟩ Using Bridge

Bridge is an independent application that functions as a feature-laden—yet easy to use—file browser for all the programs in the Adobe Creative Suite 2. We prefer to use it to open Illustrator files, as it lets us view and open Creative Suite files using thumbnails instead of just file names ⟨1⟩. (Those of you who used the File Browser in Photoshop CS will feel right at home here.)

You can also use Bridge to locate, read info about, sort, rename, move, rotate, and delete files; edit metadata in a selected file; and choose global color settings for all the Adobe Creative Suite applications. Don't be put off by our many pages of instructions for using this program. After launching Bridge, follow

the instructions on page 54 for opening files, then learn more about it as you see fit.

To launch Bridge:

In Illustrator CS2, at the far right side of the Control palette, click the **Go to Bridge** button.

or

Double-click the the **Adobe Bridge** application icon in the Applications folder in Mac, or in the Program Files\Adobe folder in Windows. In Mac, you could also click the Bridge icon on the Dock, if one was created.

or

Choose File > **Browse** (Cmd-Option-O/ Ctrl-Alt-O).

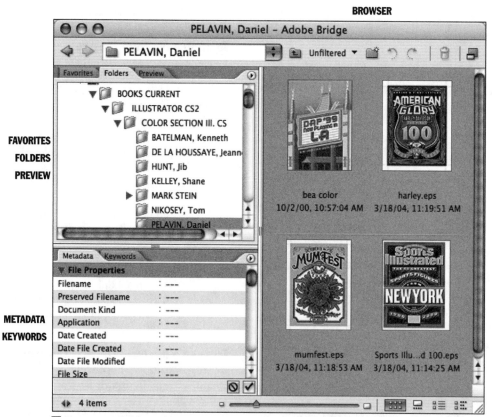

1 *You can use* **Bridge** *to locate, sort, open, move, rename, and delete files, among other tasks. In this screen shot, the* **Browser** *panel (on the right) is in* **Thumbnails** *view.*

The panels in Bridge

On the left side of the Bridge window, you'll see five panels, each with its own folder tab.

In the top portion of the **Favorites** panel, preset Bridge options are stored; in the lower section, you can select from a list of folders. To provide quick access to a folder, click its thumbnail in the Browser panel, then choose File > Add to Favorites to add the folder to the list in the Favorites panel. Choose File > Remove from Favorites to remove the currently selected favorites folder listing from this panel.

The **Folders** panel contains a scroll window with a hierarchical listing of the top-level and nested folders on your hard drive.

The **Preview** panel displays an enlargement of whichever file or folder is currently selected in the Browser panel on the right: a graphic if the file contains a preview that Illustrator can read, a generic icon if it doesn't, or a folder thumbnail.

The **Metadata** panel contains several sections. The File Properties section lists info about the currently selected file, such as the file name, kind (format), date created, date modified, and file size, and in some cases also the resolution, bit depth, and color mode.

The Document Title, Description, Author, Credit, Source, and other fields in the IPTC section are editable (note the pencil icon). If you click a listing, enter or modify the file description information, then click the Apply button, ✔ the new info will also appear in the Description and Origin panels of the File Info dialog box, and vice versa.

For more information about the Camera Data (Exif), Stock Photo Data 1, Stock Photo Data 2, and Stock Photos sections of the Metadata panel, see Bridge Help.

Using the **Keywords** panel, you can categorize images by assigning keywords to them, such as by event, name, location, or other criteria. This will enable you to find image thumbnails based on keyword searches. See pages 55–56 and Bridge Help.

Continuing our tour, on the right side of the Bridge window, in the **Browser** panel, you'll see either image thumbnails or folders that are nested within the currently selected folder.

➤ To shrink the entire Bridge window, click the Compact Mode button 🗗 in the upper right corner. In Mac, click the button again to restore the window to its previous size. In Windows, in Compact mode, you can click one button to return to Full mode or a second button to shrink the window to Ultra-Compact mode.

➤ In Thumbnails, Filmstrip, or Versions and Alternates view (see the following page), rest the pointer over a thumbnail or file name to learn more about the file. The tool tip **1** will list such information as the file's format, creator application, date created, date last modified, size, and dimensions.

To learn how to customize the panels, follow the instructions on the next page.

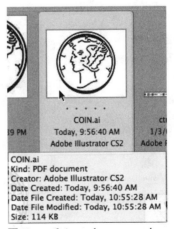

1 Use *tool tips* to learn more about a file.

You can **customize** the **panels** to your liking —a little more of this, a little less of that.

To customize the Bridge window:

Do any of the following:

➤ To make a panel **taller** or **shorter,** drag a horizontal bar; the other panels will resize automatically.

➤ To adjust the **width** of all the panels, drag the vertical bar to the left or right.

➤ To **hide** a panel, uncheck its name on the View menu.

➤ To change the arrangement of folders, drag any folder tab into another **group.**

➤ To have the Browser panel fill the entire window, click the **Show/Hide Panels** button ◀▶ in the lower-left corner of the Bridge window. Click the button again to redisplay the panels.

➤ To change the **size** of the **thumbnails** in the Browser panel, move the thumbnail size slider, located at the bottom of the window; or click the Smallest Thumbnail Size or Largest Thumbnail Size button. ▢

➤ To change the thumbnail layout, click one of the four **view** buttons in the lower right corner of the Bridge window (▦, ▦, ≣, or ▦) **1** or choose a view from the View menu.

➤ To toggle between the vertical and horizontal layouts for Filmstrip view, click the **Switch Filmstrip Orientation** button. ▣ To scroll through thumbnails in Filmstrip view, click either of these buttons. ◀ ▶

➤ To have images and folders display in the Browser panel, on the View menu, check **Show Folders**; or turn this option off to display image thumbnails but not folders. To reveal the contents of a nested folder, double-click its thumbnail.

(See also the sidebar on the following page.)

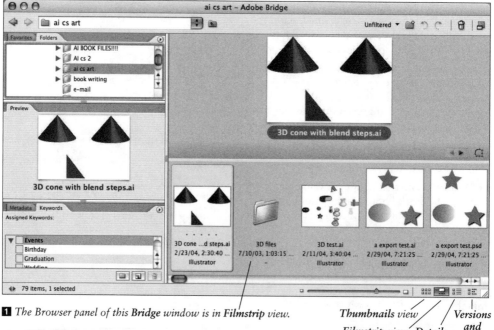

1 *The Browser panel of this **Bridge** window is in **Filmstrip** view.*

Thumbnails view
Filmstrip view Details view
Versions and Alternates view

Window dressing

The **Preferences** dialog box in Bridge ▮ lets you control a variety of default settings. Choose Bridge (Edit, in Windows) > Preferences, then click a panel name on the left side of the dialog box.

For example, in the **General** panel, you can move the Background slider to specify a gray value for the Browser panel, decide whether to Show Tooltips, and choose which types of data (called metadata) will display below each thumbnail. In the **Favorites Items** area, you can check which default items and folders you want listed in the Favorites panel.

For a brief description of the other panels in this dialog box, in Bridge, see Help > **Bridge Help.**

▮ *Use Bridge preferences to choose default settings for the application.*

▮ *Use the Save Workspace dialog box to assign a name and keyboard shortcut to a custom workspace.*

By **saving** your custom **workspaces** in Bridge, you won't have to set up your window configuration each time you use the application.

To save a workspace for Bridge:

1. Choose a size and location for the overall Bridge window, a size (and tab locations) for the panels, and a layout view for the Browser panel, then choose Window > Workspace > **Save Workspace.** The Save Workspace dialog box opens ▮.

2. Enter a name for the workspace, choose a shortcut (or choose None), check Save Window Location as Part of Workspace (optional), then click Save.

3. To choose any saved workspace, use the assigned shortcut or choose the workspace name from the Window > **Workspace** submenu. You can also choose from a list of preset workspaces (e.g., Filmstrip Focus) on this submenu.

The Bridge menus

Via the Bridge menu bar, you can use:

➤ **File** menu commands to open, delete, and access File Info for selected file(s). The Open With command lets you open a selected file, provided the required Adobe program is installed in your system.

➤ **Edit** menu commands to copy and paste a file into another folder, to quickly select labeled or unlabeled thumbnails, and to access the Find command to search for files.

➤ **Tools** menu commands to run scripts and automate commands, and to purge or export thumbnail cache files.

➤ **Label** menu commands to assign star ratings and color labels to files.

➤ **View** menu commands to choose a thumbnail view, control which panels display, sort thumbnails, control which file formats display, and refresh (update) the window display.

➤ **Window** menu commands to save or delete custom workspaces, restore the default workspace, and choose preset and user-created workspaces.

The number of Illustrator **documents** that can be **open** at the same time depends on currently available RAM and scratch disk space.

To open files via Bridge:

1. Locate a file by using the **Folders** panel. You can scroll upward or downward, expand or collapse any folder by using the arrowheads or by double-clicking, or open a folder by clicking its icon. You can also choose a **Favorites** or **Recent Folders** category from the pop-up menu at the top of the Bridge window.

   To move upward in the folder hierarchy, click the **Go Up** button 🗂 at the top of the window.

2. Click a thumbnail for an image file. A highlight frame will appear around it, a file preview will appear in the Preview panel, and file data will appear in the Metadata panel.
   or
   Cmd-click/Ctrl-click multiple non-consecutive thumbnails **1**. Or click the first thumbnail in a series of consecutive thumbnails, then Shift-click the last one.

3. Double-click a thumbnail (or one of several selected thumbnails).
   or
   Choose File > **Open** (Cmd-O/Ctrl-O).

4. If an alert dialog box about a **Missing Profile** appears, see page 61; for the **Font Problems** dialog box, see "Missing fonts?" in the sidebar at right; and for an alert dialog box about a **linked image** file, see page 285. To learn about updating **legacy text,** see pages 240–241.

   To activate a currently open window, you can either click in it or choose the document name from the list of open documents at the bottom of the Window menu.

➤ By default, the Bridge window stays open after you use it to open a file. To have the window close as a file is opened instead, hold down Option/Alt as you double-click a thumbnail.

For the [Converted]

By default, Illustrator CS2 automatically appends the word **[Converted]** to files from earlier versions of Illustrator that are opened in CS2. If you want to prevent this from happening, go to Preferences > General and uncheck Append [Converted] Upon Opening Legacy File. If you do uncheck this option, remember to rename the files yourself by using the Save As command. Don't open a legacy file for editing and use the Save command to save over the original!

Missing fonts?

If you open a file that uses a font that's unavailable to your system, the **Font Problems** dialog box will appear. Click Open to open the document as is, or click Cancel. If a missing font subsequently becomes available to the system, it will become available on Illustrator's font lists and the type will redisplay correctly without any action required on your part.

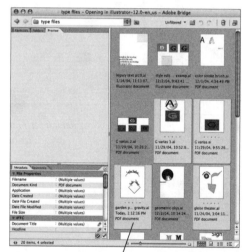

1 *Cmd-click/Ctrl-click to select multiple nonconsecutive thumbnails.*

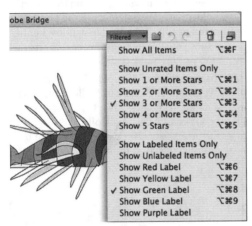

Label	
Rating	
No Rating	
*	⌘1
**	⌘2
✓ ***	⌘3
****	⌘4
*****	⌘5
Decrease Rating	⌘,
Increase Rating	⌘.
Label	
No Label	⌘0
Red	⌘6
✓ Yellow	⌘7
Green	⌘8
Blue	⌘9
Purple	

1 *Use the **Label** menu to assign a star Rating and/or color Label to selected thumbnails.*

obe Bridge

Filtered	
Show All Items	⌥⌘F
Show Unrated Items Only	
Show 1 or More Stars	⌥⌘1
Show 2 or More Stars	⌥⌘2
✓ Show 3 or More Stars	⌥⌘3
Show 4 or More Stars	⌥⌘4
Show 5 Stars	⌥⌘5
Show Labeled Items Only	
Show Unlabeled Items Only	
Show Red Label	⌥⌘6
Show Yellow Label	⌥⌘7
✓ Show Green Label	⌥⌘8
Show Blue Label	⌥⌘9
Show Purple Label	

2 *Use the **Unfiltered/Filtered** pop-up menu to control which thumbnail types display in the Browser panel, based on their star rating and/or color labels.*

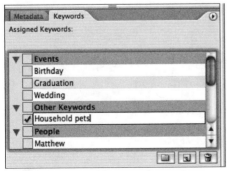

3 *A name is entered for a new **keyword**.*

By **assigning** star **ratings** and/or color **labels** to **files,** you'll be able to display them based on the presence or absence of labels and find them using the Find command.

To label and sort files via Bridge:

1. Select one or more thumbnails in the Browser panel. Ctrl-click/Cmd-click multiple nonconsecutive thumbnails, or click the first thumbnail in a series of consecutive thumbnails, then Shift-click the last.

2. From the Label menu **1**, choose a star **Rating** and/or a color **Label,** or press the assigned keyboard shortcut. To assign both a rating and a label to a file, you have to make two trips to the menu. If an alert dialog box appears, click OK.
   or
   Click the first, second, third, fourth, or fifth **dot** below a thumbnail. (To remove a star, click the star to its left; to remove the first star, click just to its left.)

3. On the **Unfiltered/Filtered** pop-up menu **2** above the Browser panel, check a rating and/or label category; only thumbnails that have been assigned that label will be displayed. To redisplay all thumbnails regardless of label, check **Show All Items** on the same pop-up menu.

Keywords are used by search utilities to locate files and by file management programs to organize them. In Bridge, you can create keywords and assign them to your files.

To assign keywords to files:

In the **Keywords** panel:

To create a **new keyword,** click the 🔳 button, then type a name **3**.

To create a new **keyword set,** click the 🔲 button, then type a name.

To **assign** a keyword to an image, click an image thumbnail or select multiple thumbnails (expand the desired category, if necessary), then click the box to the left of a keyword category to make a check mark appear.

To **rename** a category, Control-click/right-click it and choose Rename, then type a name.

To **remove** a category, Control-click/right-click it and choose Delete.

To search for files via Bridge:

1. In Bridge, choose Edit > Find (Cmd-F/ Ctrl-F). The Find dialog box opens **1**.

2. From the **Look in** pop-up menu, choose a folder to search through. If you need to select a different folder, click Browse, locate the folder, then click Choose.

3. Check **Include All Subfolders** to search through all subfolders within the designated folder, or uncheck this option to search through only the Look in folder. Keep **Find All Files** unchecked.

4. From the pop-up menus in the **Criteria** area, choose search criteria (e.g., file name, date created, label, or rating), and enter data in the adjoining field(s). If you need additional criteria fields in which to enter data, click the plus sign. ⊕

5. From the Match pop-up menu, choose **If any criteria are met** to find files based on one or more criteria, or choose **If all criteria are met** to narrow the selection to files that meet all the chosen criteria.

6. *Optional:* Check **Show find results in a new browser window** to display the results of the search in a new Bridge

---

Finding a file icon

To locate a file in the Finder/Explorer, click a thumbnail in Bridge, then choose File > **Reveal in Finder/Reveal in Explorer.** The file's folder will open as a window in Finder/Explorer, and the file icon will be highlighted.

---

window. If you don't want an additional Bridge window to be created, uncheck this option; the results will display in the current window instead.

7. Click **Find.** The results will display in Bridge in a temporary folder called Find Results, which will remain on the Recent Folders list (accessible from the pop-up menu at top of the Bridge window) until either you conduct another search operation or you quit/exit Bridge.

8. To save the find results to a permanent file group, click **Save as Collection,** enter a name, then click **Save.** Collections can be viewed by clicking Collections in the Favorites panel, then double-clicking the desired collection thumbnail.

1 *Use the **Find** dialog box to search for and locate files by various criteria.*

Find Files

View

Compact Mode ⌘↵
Slide Show ⌘L

✓ As Thumbnails
As Filmstrip
As Details
As Versions and Alternates

✓ Favorites Panel
✓ Folders Panel
✓ Preview Panel
✓ Metadata Panel
✓ Keywords Panel

Sort ▶ | ✓ Ascending Order

Show Thumbnail Only ⌘T | By Filename
| ✓ By Document Kind
Show Hidden Files | By Date Created
✓ Show Folders | By Date File Modified
| By File Size
✓ Show All Files | By Dimensions
Show Graphic Files Only | By Resolution
Show Camera Raw Files Only | By Color Profile
Show Vector Files Only | By Copyright
| By Label
Refresh F5 | By Rating
| By Purchase State
| By Version Cue Status

| Manually

1 *Choose a sorting method from the View > Sort submenu. This command merely changes the order in which thumbnails are displayed.*

Bouquet.TIF
3/29/04, 3:...

2 *Change the file name.*

Refresh yourself

If you move, add, or rename files in the Finder, the file and folder listings in the Bridge window will update the next time you make it the active window. You can also update the current listings at any time by choosing **Refresh** (F5) from the Folders panel menu or the View menu.

There are several ways that **thumbnails** can be sorted or **rearranged** in the Browser panel. This is important if you use batch or automate operations, as these commands process files based on the current order of thumbnails. First the straightforward, manual approach.

To rearrange thumbnails manually:

Drag a thumbnail (or thumbnails) to any new location. It will stay where you place it unless you perform a sorting operation.

By organizing your files in a **sorting** order (e.g., Date Created or Date Modified), you'll avoid having to fish through a lot of files to locate them.

To apply a sorting method:

From the View > **Sort** submenu, choose a sorting criterion for all the files in the current folder **1**. You can leave **Ascending Order** checked on this menu, or uncheck it to list files in descending order.

To rename a file via Bridge:

1. Click a **file name** below a thumbnail. The text to the left of the period will become highlighted automatically.

2. Type a new name **2**. Don't try to delete the extension (a warning prompt will appear if you do). To accept the entry, press Return/Enter or click outside the name field.

To create a folder via Bridge:

1. Via the Folders panel or via the pop-up menu at the top of the Bridge window, open the drive or folder that you want the new folder to appear in.

2. Click the **New Folder** button 🗁 at the top of the window, type a name in the highlighted field, then press Return/Enter.

➤ You can drag a file or folder thumbnail from the Browser panel into the Folders panel to relocate it to another folder or to the Desktop. Option-drag/Alt-drag a thumbnail to add a copy of the file or folder to another folder.

Arrange Thumbnails; Sort; Rename; Create Folder

To delete files via Bridge:

1. Click a thumbnail in the Browser panel, then click the **Delete File** 🗑 button at the top of the window. (Or to delete multiple files, Cmd-click/Ctrl-click multiple thumbnails first; or click the first in a series of thumbnails, then Shift-click the last in the series.)

2. Click **Yes.** *Note:* You can also delete a whole folder full of files, so be careful! To retrieve a deleted file or folder, double-click the system's Trash/Recycle icon to open its window, then drag the item back into the Bridge window. (Phew!)

When a folder is displayed in Bridge, the application creates a separate **cache** file containing information (e.g., thumbnail data, metadata, labeling) about all the files in that folder. Having the cache helps speed up the display of thumbnails in the Browser panel if you redisplay the same folder at a later time.

To export the cache for the current folder:

Choose Tools > Cache > **Export Cache.** Two cache files—named Adobe Bridge Cache.bc (metadata cache) and Adobe Bridge Cache.bct (thumbnail cache)—will be placed into the currently displayed folder.

Note: To display the cache files in Bridge, choose View > **Show Hidden Files.**

➤ When you copy image files to a removable disk or to a shared folder on a network, copy the cache files, too, to help speed up the display of thumbnails.

The **Purge** commands delete the ratings, labels, and thumbnail data that Bridge uses to generate image thumbnails. Use these commands to remove a damaged or problem cache.

To delete the cache files:

1. To remove the cache files from the current folder, choose Tools > Cache > **Purge Cache for This Folder.**
or
To remove all caches for all folders, choose Tools > Cache > **Purge Central Cache.**

2. Click OK.

MANAGE COLOR 5

In this chapter you'll learn how to manage and maintain color consistency between documents and output devices by using the Working Spaces, Color Management Policies, and Conversion options in the Color Settings dialog box; change document color profiles; and soft-proof your document colors.

Choosing color settings

Problems with color can creep up on you when various hardware devices and software packages you use treat color differently. If you open a file in several different imaging programs and in a Web browser, the colors in the image might look completely different in each case, and thus may not match the color of the picture you originally scanned in. Print the image, and you'll probably find that your results are different yet again. In some cases, you might find these differences to be slight and unobjectionable, but in other cases, such color changes can wreak havoc with your design and turn your project into a disaster.

A **color management system** can solve most of these problems by acting as a color interpreter. Such a system knows how each device and program understands color, and by using color profiles (mathematical descriptions of the color space of each device), adjusts colors so your images look the same as you move them from one program or device to another. Illustrator, Photoshop, and other Adobe programs use the standardized ICC (International Color Consortium) profiles to tell your color management system how specific devices use color. Whether you're planning a traditional print run or will be using the same graphic for multiple purposes (such as for Web and print), you'll benefit from using color management.

In Illustrator, you'll find most of the color management controls in Edit > **Color**

Settings. This dialog box gives you access to preset management settings for various publishing situations, including press and Web output, and also lets you choose custom settings. There are three main areas in the dialog box:

➤ The **Working Spaces** govern how RGB and CMYK colors are displayed in your document and provide a default color space for new Illustrator documents.

➤ The **Color Management Policies** for RGB and CMYK color files govern how the program deals with color when opening files that don't have an attached color profile, or whose profile doesn't match your document's current color settings.

➤ The **Conversion Options** control which color management engine is used for converting colors between color spaces.

Choosing the correct color settings will help keep your colors consistent from first document version to final output. The abundance of options may appear complex at first, but you and your documents will benefit if you take the time to learn about them.

➤ If you're planning to use a prepress service provider, ask them to recommend specific color management settings to ensure that your color management workflows run smoothly.

(Continued on the following page)

Monitor basics

Computer monitors come in two basic types: CRT (picture tube) and LCD (flat panel). CRTs fluctuate in display performance due to their analog technology and due to the fact that their display phosphors, which produce the glowing dots on the screen, tend to fade over time. Also, CRTs must be calibrated at least once a month using their built-in brightness and contrast controls. The calibration life span of a CRT monitor is only about 3 years; after that they can't be reliably calibrated.

LCDs use a grid of fixed-size liquid crystals that individually filter color coming from a backlight source. Although you can adjust only the brightness on an LCD (not the contrast), LCD technology achieves more reliable and consistent color output than a CRT, without the characteristic flickering of CRTs. The newest models provide good viewing angles, accurately display a neutral color and 6500K white balance, and are produced to tighter manufacturing standards than CRTs. The profile provided by the factory usually describes monitor characteristics accurately.

Calibrating your display

The first step toward achieving color consistency is to **calibrate your display** by adjusting the contrast and brightness, gamma, color balance, and white point. In Windows, the Adobe Gamma control panel is installed with Illustrator CS2, whereas the Mac version of Illustrator relies on the operating system's display calibration utility in the Displays panel (Color tab) in System Preferences.

Both Adobe Gamma and Displays generate an ICC profile that Illustrator can use as its working RGB space in order to display the colors in your artwork accurately. To generate a more complete profile, use a hardware calibrator. You have to calibrate your display and save the settings as an ICC profile just once; thereafter, the profile will be available to all applications. (For more information about calibrating a display, see Illustrator Help or our *Photoshop CS2: Visual QuickStart Guide.*)

To choose color settings:

Predefined color management settings

1. Choose Edit > Color Settings (Cmd-Shift-K/Ctrl-Shift-K).

2. Choose a preset from the **Settings** pop-up menu (**1**, page 63):

NEW **Monitor Color** uses the working space defined for your monitor. It's suitable for video output, but not for print (CMYK).

NEW **North America General Purpose 2** meets the requirements for screen and print output in the U.S. and Canada. All profile warnings are turned off.

NEW **North America Prepress 2** manages color based on common press conditions in the U.S. CMYK values are unchanged when documents are opened.

NEW **North America Web/Internet** is for Web output. All RGB images are converted to the sRGB working space.

(Choosing Emulate Adobe® Illustrator® 6.0 makes all the settings inaccessible and turns color management off.)

Checking **Advanced Mode** adds more configurations to the menu:

ColorSync Workflow (Mac only) manages color using the ColorSync color management system. Profiles are based on those in the ColorSync utility (including any monitor profile you may have created by using the Apple Display Calibrator utility). This setting is a good choice when you need to keep color consistent among Adobe and non-Adobe applications.

Emulate Acrobat 4 and **Emulate Photoshop 4** matches the color handling found in those two applications.

Europe/Japan General Purpose 2, Prepress 2, Web/Internet, etc. are equivalent to their American counterparts, but in each case the CMYK working space is changed to a standard press for that region.

Japan Color for Newspaper and **Japan Magazine Advertisement Color** use

CMYK working spaces that are suitable for periodical publishing in that country.

Photoshop 5 Default Spaces uses the same working spaces as the default settings found in Photoshop 5.

At this point you can click OK to accept the predefined settings or you can proceed with the remaining steps to choose custom settings.

3. The color **Working Spaces** define how RGB and CMYK colors are displayed in your document. For CMYK settings, you should ask your output service provider which working space to choose.

For **RGB,** choose one of the following:

Monitor RGB [current monitor name] sets the RGB working space to your monitor profile and is useful if you know that other applications you'll be using for your project don't support color management. Keep in mind, however, that if you share this working space with another user, that user's monitor profile will be used as the RGB working space, and color consistency may be undermined.

Adobe RGB (1998) produces a wide range of colors and is useful for converting RGB images to CMYK images, but not for Web work.

Apple RGB is useful for files that you plan to display on Mac displays, as it reflects the characteristics of the older standard Apple 13-inch displays. It's also a good choice for older files, such as Adobe Photoshop 4.0 files.

ColorMatch RGB produces a smaller range of colors than the Adobe RGB (1998) model. It matches the color space of Radius Pressview displays and is useful for print production.

sRGB IEC61966-2.1 is a good choice for Web work, as it reflects the settings on the average computer display. Many hardware and software manufacturers are using it as the default space for scanners, low-end printers, and software. Don't use it for prepress work (use Adobe RGB or ColorMatch RGB instead).

(Continued on the following page)

ColorSync RGB [current ColorSync default] (Mac only) matches the Illustrator RGB space to the space specified in Applications > Utilities > ColorSync Utility (which can be the profile you created using System Preferences > Displays). If you share this space with another user, it will utilize the ColorSync space specified by that user.

Color management policies

4. To choose a color management policy that will tell Illustrator how to deal with artwork that doesn't match your current color settings, from the **RGB** and **CMYK** pop-up menus in the **Color Management Policies** area:

Choose **Off** to prevent files from being color-managed when imported or opened.

Choose **Preserve Embedded Profiles** if you think you're going to be working with both color-managed and non-color-managed documents. This will tie each color file's profile to the individual file. Remember, in Illustrator, each open document can have its own profile.

Choose **Convert to Working Space** if you want all your documents to reflect the same color working space. This is usually the best choice for Web work.

For **Profile Mismatches,** check **Ask When Opening** to have Illustrator display a message if the color profile in a file you're opening doesn't match the program's working space. If you choose this option, you can override your color management policy when opening documents.

Check **Ask When Pasting** to have Illustrator display a message when color profile mismatches occur as you paste color images into your document. If you choose this option, you can override your color management policy when pasting.

For files with **Missing Profiles,** check **Ask When Opening** to have Illustrator display a message offering you the opportunity to assign a profile to the file you're opening.

Conversion options

5. To customize your conversion options, check **Advanced Mode,** then choose a color management **Engine** to be used for converting colors between color spaces: **Adobe (ACE)** uses the Adobe color management system and color engine; both **Apple ColorSync** and **Apple CMM** use the Apple color management system; and **Microsoft ICM** uses the system provided in Windows 2000 and Windows XP.

Next, choose a rendering **Intent** to govern how colors are changed as they're moved from one color space to another (differences between them are evident only on print output or a conversion to a different working space):

Perceptual changes color values in a way that seems natural to the human eye, and is a good choice for continuous-tone images.

Saturation changes colors and may compromise color accuracy as it attempts to preserve vivid colors, but is a good choice for charts and graphics that use a limited number of colors.

Absolute Colorimetric keeps colors that are inside the destination color gamut unchanged, but changes the relationships among colors outside that gamut in an attempt to maintain color accuracy.

Relative Colorimetric, the default intent for all predefined "General Purpose" settings, is the same as Absolute Colorimetric, except that it compares the white point (extreme highlight), of the source color space to the destination color space and shifts all colors accordingly. The accuracy of this intent depends on the accuracy of the white point information in the profile.

Check **Use Black Point Compensation** to allow adjustments to be made for differences in black points between color spaces. The full dynamic range of the source color space will be mapped to the full dynamic range of the destination color space. With this option off, blacks may appear as grays. Check this option for an RGB-to-CMYK conversion, but ask your commercial printer before checking it for a CMYK-to-CMYK conversion.

6. Click OK. *Optional:* To save your custom color settings for later use, click **Save.** To have your custom file name display on the Settings pop-up menu in Mac, save the file in Users/[CurrentUser]/Library/

Application Support/Adobe/Color/ Settings; in Windows, save it in the default location. To reuse your saved settings, choose the file name from the **Settings** pop-up menu. To load a settings file that wasn't saved in the Settings folder (and thus isn't on the Settings menu), click **Load** in the Color Settings dialog box.

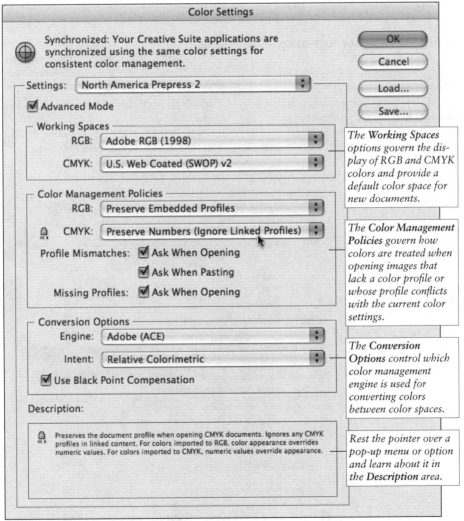

The *Working Spaces* options govern the display of RGB and CMYK colors and provide a default color space for new documents.

The *Color Management Policies* govern how colors are treated when opening images that lack a color profile or whose profile conflicts with the current color settings.

The *Conversion Options* control which color management engine is used for converting colors between color spaces.

Rest the pointer over a pop-up menu or option and learn about it in the *Description* area.

1 The *Color Settings* dialog box

Color Settings

Synchronizing color settings

If the color settings in another Adobe Creative Suite program (such as Photoshop CS2) don't match the current settings in Illustrator, an alert will display at the top of the Color Settings dialog box in Illustrator . If you don't own the complete Adobe Creative Suite, you'll have to start up the errant application and fix its color settings by hand. If you are lucky enough to have a copy of the whole suite installed, you can use the **Suite Color Settings** dialog box in **Bridge** to **synchronize** the color settings of all the programs in the suite.

*This alert tells us that our color settings aren't synchronized across our **Creative Suite** applications.*

NEW To synchronize color settings using Bridge:

1. In Bridge, choose Edit > **Creative Suite Color Settings** (Ctrl-Shift-K/Cmd-Shift-K). The Suite Color Settings dialog box opens **2**, with the same list of settings as found in the Color Settings dialog box when Advanced Mode is unchecked.

2. Click one of the settings to select it, then click **Apply.** Bridge will change (synchronize) the color settings of the other Adobe Creative Suite applications to match.

   Note: You can check Show Expanded List of Color Settings Files to display all your color settings on the list (the same list as in the Color Settings dialog box when Advanced Mode is checked).

2 *Use the **Suite Color Settings** dialog box to synchronize the color settings of the applications in the Adobe Creative Suite.*

Embedding profiles

When you use File > Save As to save a file in a format that supports embedded profiles, such as Adobe Illustrator Document or Adobe PDF (pdf), the **Illustrator Options** dialog box opens. There, you can check **Embed ICC Profiles** to embed a profile with the document, if one has been assigned.

Changing document profiles

You may need to change or remove a document's color profile to prep a document for a specific output device, or if you change your color management settings, or for some other reason. The **Assign Profile** command reinterprets the color data directly in the color space of the new profile (or lack thereof), and may cause visible color shifts.

To change or delete a file's color profile:

1. Choose Edit > **Assign Profile 1**.

2. Click **Don't Color Manage This Document** to remove the color profile.
   or
   Click **Working** (plus the document color mode and the name of the current working space) to assign that particular working space to a document that doesn't have an assigned profile or that uses a profile that's different from the current working space.
   or
   Click **Profile** to reassign a different profile to a color-managed document, then choose the desired profile from the pop-up menu.

3. Click OK.

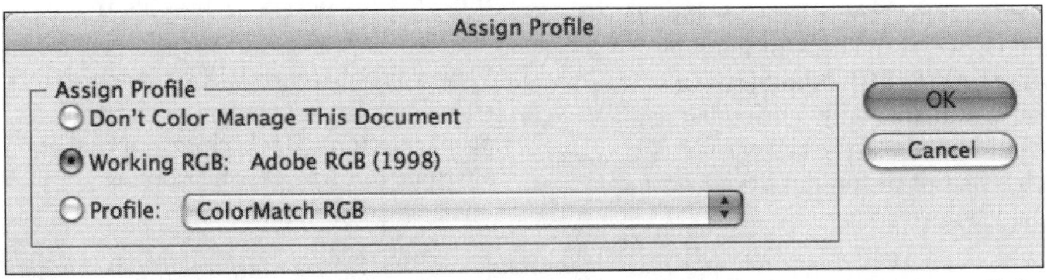

Assign Profile
Assign Profile
○ Don't Color Manage This Document
● Working RGB: Adobe RGB (1998)
○ Profile: ColorMatch RGB

OK
Cancel

1 *Use the* **Assign Profile** *dialog box to change a file's color profile. The Profile chosen here will also be listed as the Document Profile in the Color Management panel of the File > Print dialog box.*

Assign Profile

Soft-proofing a document

Specifying a color management setup is all well and good, but once you start creating some Illustrator files, you'll want to get an idea of how they're going to look in print or online. You can do this by **soft-proofing** your document. Although this method is less accurate than actually making a print or viewing your Web artwork on different displays, it can give you a general idea of how your work will look in different settings. You can choose either a preset soft-proof setup or custom settings.

To soft-proof a document:

1. From the View > **Proof Setup** submenu, choose an output display type to simulate:

    If your document is in CMYK Color mode, choose the **Working CMYK** profile.

    If your document is in RGB Color mode and you want to simulate colors using a Mac or Windows display profile as the proofing space, choose **Macintosh RGB** or **Windows RGB.** Or choose **Monitor RGB** to use your display profile as the proofing space.

    For either document color mode, you can choose **Customize** to create a proofing model for a specific output device. The Proof Setup dialog box opens **1**. From **NEW** the **Device to Simulate** pop-up menu, choose the color profile for your target output device, then check or uncheck **Preserve CMYK/RGB Numbers.** This option is available only when the document color mode of the current file matches that of the output device profile

currently chosen on the Device to Simulate pop-up menu (e.g., if the document color mode is RGB and the proofing profile is an RGB profile). With this option checked, colors will look as if they're not converted to the proofing space. With this option unchecked, Illustrator will simulate how colors will appear when converted, and you'll need to choose a **Rendering Intent** (see page 62). Click OK.

2. *Optional:* The Display Options (On-**NEW** Screen) are available for some profiles. Simulate Paper Color simulates the soft white of actual paper, based on the current proof profile. Simulate Black Ink simulates the dark gray that many printers produce when printing black.

3. View > **Proof Colors** will be checked automatically so you can see the soft proof onscreen. Uncheck this option at any time to turn off soft-proofing.

Proof Setup

Device to Simulate:	U.S. Sheetfed Coated v2
	☐ Preserve CMYK Numbers
Rendering Intent:	Perceptual
Display Options (On-Screen)	
☐ Simulate Paper Color	
☐ Simulate Black Ink	

OK Cancel ☐ Preview

1 *Use the **Proof Setup** dialog box to choose custom options for soft-proofing.*

WORKSPACE 6

In this chapter you'll learn how to change document zoom levels and document views (Preview, Outline, or Pixel Preview), save and choose custom view settings, display a document in more than one window, change screen display modes, move an illustration in its window, and save and manage custom workspace settings.

Changing zoom levels
To change zoom levels via the Navigator palette:

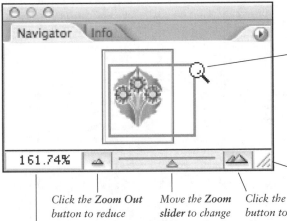

*Cmd-drag/Ctrl-drag in the view box to **define** the view area. The smaller the area you marquee, the greater the enlargement.*

Drag the resize box to scale the palette and thumbnail preview.

*Click the **Zoom Out** button to reduce the zoom level.*

*Move the **Zoom slider** to change the zoom level.*

*Click the **Zoom In** button to magnify the image.*

*Enter the desired **zoom percentage** between 3.13% and 6400%, then press Return/Enter. Or to zoom to a percentage and keep the field highlighted, press Shift-Return/Shift-Enter.*

➤ You can also change the zoom level by double-clicking the zoom field in the lower left corner of the document window, typing the desired zoom percentage (up to 6400%), and then pressing Return/Enter.

➤ To separate the Navigator palette from its group, drag its tab (palette name).

Zoom Levels via Navigator Palette

Preset Zoom Levels

Within the document window, you can display the entire artboard, an enlarged detail, or a zoom level in between. The **zoom level** (3.13%–6400%) is indicated as a percentage on the title bar and in the lower left corner of the document/application window. The zoom level has no impact on the output size.

To choose a preset zoom level:

Choose View > **Zoom In** (Cmd-+/Ctrl-+). Repeat to magnify further.
or
Choose View > **Zoom Out** (Cmd--/Ctrl--). Repeat, if desired.
or
Make sure no objects are selected, then Control-click/right-click the document and choose **Zoom In** or **Zoom Out 1**.
or
Choose a preset percentage from the **zoom pop-up menu** in the lower left corner of the document/application window **2**. Or choose **Fit On Screen** from the pop-up menu to make the artboard fit within the current document window size.
or
Double-click in the **zoom field** in the lower left corner of the document/application window, type in the desired magnification, then press Return/Enter.

➤ To display the entire artboard in the document window, choose View > Fit In Window (Cmd-0/Ctrl-0) or double-click the Hand tool.

➤ To apply a new zoom value without exiting the zoom field, press Shift-Return/ Shift-Enter.

1 *Make sure no objects are selected, then Control-click/right-click in the document window and choose Zoom In or Zoom Out from the context menu.*

2 *Choose a preset percentage from the zoom pop-up menu in the lower left corner of the document/ application window.*

Brush by Diane Margolin

1 *Drag with the Zoom tool.*

2 *The illustration is magnified.*

To change the zoom level with the Zoom tool:

1. Choose the **Zoom** tool (Z).

2. In the document window, click in the center of, or drag a marquee across, the area you want to **magnify 1–2**. The smaller the marquee, the greater the degree of magnification. (To move a magnified illustration in the document window, see pages 73–74.)

or

Option-click/Alt-click in the document window to **reduce** the zoom level.

or

Drag a marquee, and then, without releasing the mouse, press and hold down the Spacebar, **move** the **marquee** over the area you want to magnify, then release the mouse.

➤ To display an illustration at actual size (100%), double-click the Zoom tool or choose View > Actual Size (Cmd-1/Ctrl-1). *Note:* If you double-click the Zoom tool when your illustration is at a small zoom level, the white area around the artboard may appear in the document window instead of the illustration. Use the Navigator palette or the Hand tool to reposition the illustration in the window (see pages 73–74).

➤ You can click to change the zoom level while the screen is redrawing.

This **keyboard** is the fastest method for changing the **zoom level**, because you can do it with any tool selected.

To change the zoom level with any tool selected:

To **increase** the zoom level, Cmd-Spacebar-click/Ctrl-Spacebar-click or -drag in the document window.

or

To **reduce** the zoom level, Cmd-Option-Spacebar-click/Ctrl-Alt-Spacebar-click in the document window.

Zoom Tool; Zoom Shortcuts

Changing views

There are four views a document can be displayed and edited in: **Preview, Outline, Pixel Preview,** and **Overprint Preview.** In all views, the other View menu commands—Hide/Show Edges, Artboard, Page Tiling, Slices, Guides, and Grid—are accessible, and any selection tool can be used. (Overprint Preview view is discussed on page 489.)

To change the view:

From the View menu, choose **Preview** to display all the objects with their fill and stroke colors as well as all placed images, or choose **Outline** to display all the objects as wireframes with no fill or stroke colors. You can press Cmd-Y/Ctrl-Y to toggle between the two views. The screen redraws more quickly in Outline view.

or

Make sure no objects are selected (click a blank area of the artboard), then Control-click/right-click in the document window and choose **Outline** or **Preview** ■–■.

or

To turn on a 72 ppi preview for Web graphics, choose **Pixel Preview** (Cmd-Option-Y/Ctrl-Alt-Y toggles it on and off) ■, and also choose View > Actual Size. See also the sidebar.

➤ Let's say you've got a large file on a slow machine and you start to view it in all its glory in Preview view—nah, on second thought, you decide you'll preview it later. Press Esc to cancel the preview in progress.

➤ You won't learn much about layers until you get to Chapter 15, but just to give you a glimpse of what's to come, Cmd-click/Ctrl-click an eye icon for a layer (not an object) on the Layers palette to toggle between Preview and Outline views just for that layer.

It's a snap

When you choose **Pixel Preview** view (and View > Actual Size), you can get a good idea of what your vector graphics will look like when they're rasterized for the Web, but it's more than just a preview. When you choose this view, View > **Snap to Pixel** is turned on automatically, and edges of objects will snap to the nearest pixel edge as they're moved or reshaped. Snap to Pixel reduces the need for anti-aliasing and helps keep edges crisp. (Anti-aliasing adds pixels along the edges of objects to make them look smoother but can also diminish their crispness.)

■ *Deselect all objects, then choose **Outline** (or **Preview**) from the context menu. This is **Preview** view.*

■ *Outline view*

■ *Pixel Preview view*

New View

Name: [160% view, Preview]

OK
Cancel

1 *Type a Name for the view in the New View dialog box.*

View

Preview	⌘Y
Overprint Preview	⌥⇧⌘Y
Pixel Preview	⌥⌘Y
Proof Setup	▶
Proof Colors	
Zoom In	⌘+
Zoom Out	⌘-
Fit in Window	⌘0
Actual Size	⌘1
Hide Edges	⌘H
Hide Artboard	
Show Page Tiling	
Hide Slices	
Lock Slices	
Hide Template	⇧⌘W
Show Rulers	⌘R
Hide Bounding Box	⇧⌘B
Show Transparency Grid	⇧⌘D
Hide Text Threads	⇧⌘Y
Show Live Paint Gaps	
Guides	▶
Smart Guides	⌘U
Show Grid	⌘"
Snap to Grid	⇧⌘"
✓ Snap to Point	⌥⌘"
New View...	
Edit Views...	
225% view, Outline	
160% view, Preview	
175% view, Pixel Preview	

2 *Choose a custom view from the bottom of the View menu.*

Edit Views

225% view, Outline
160% view, Preview
175% view, Pixel Preview

OK
Cancel
Delete

Name: [160% view, Preview]

3 *In the Edit Views dialog box, highlight a view, then change the Name or click Delete.*

Creating custom views

For each **custom view** that you save, you can choose a zoom level, scroll bar positions, and a choice of Preview view or Outline view. You can save up to 25 custom views, and you can switch among them using either the View menu or assigned shortcuts.

To define a custom view:

1. Choose a zoom level for your illustration and choose scroll bar positions.

2. Put your illustration into Preview or Outline view (Cmd-Y/Ctrl-Y).

3. Choose View > **New View.**

4. Type a descriptive name for the new view in the **Name** field, as in "160% view" **1**.

5. Click OK. Choose the view name from the bottom of the View menu **2**.

➤ To assign a keyboard shortcut to up to 10 custom views, see pages 558–559 (in the Keyboard Shortcuts dialog box, look under Menu Commands > View).

➤ You can switch views at any time, even for a custom view. For example, if your illustration is at a custom view for which you chose Outline view, but you want to display your illustration in Preview view, choose View > Preview.

To rename or delete a custom view:

1. Choose View > **Edit Views.**

2. Click the name of the view you want to rename or delete **3**.

3. Change the name in the **Name** field.
   or
   Click **Delete** to delete the view.

4. Click OK. The View menu will update to reflect the changes.

➤ If you want to rename more than one view, you have to click OK and then reopen the dialog box for each one.

Custom Views

Creating new document windows

To facilitate editing, a **document** can be displayed simultaneously in **more than one window.** You could choose a high zoom level for one window (such as 200%) to edit small details and a lower zoom level for the other so you can see the whole illustration. Or in one window you could hide individual layers or display individual layers in Outline view and in another window you could preview all the layers together.

Note: The illustration in the window for which Preview view is selected will redraw each time you modify the illustration in a window for which Outline view is chosen. In this case, you won't save processing or redraw time by working in the latter window.

To create new document windows:

1. Open an illustration.

2. Choose Window > **New Window.** A new window of the same size will appear on top of the first one, bearing the same title, followed by ":2" **1**.

3. In Mac, reposition the new window by dragging its title bar so the original and new windows are side by side, and resize one or both of them.

    In Windows, you can choose any of these Window menu commands: **Cascade** arranges all currently open documents and windows in a stair-step configuration; **Tile** arranges them side by side; and **Arrange Icons** relocates any minimized windows to the bottom of the application window. (These commands arrange all windows, whether they're displaying one document or multiple documents.)

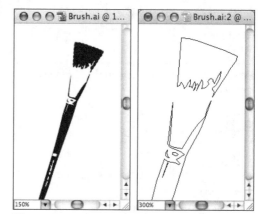

1 *One illustration displayed in **two windows***

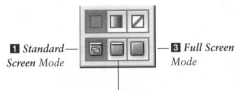

1 *Standard Screen Mode* — — **3** *Full Screen Mode*

2 *Full Screen Mode with Menu Bar*

4 *Spacebar-drag in the document window to move the illustration.*

Changing screen display modes
To change the screen display mode:
Click the **Standard Screen Mode** button at the bottom of the Toolbox **1** to display the artwork, menu bar, and scroll bars in the document window. This is the default mode.
or
Click the **Full Screen Mode with Menu Bar** (second) button **2** to display the illustration at full screen size with the menu bar visible and the scroll bars hidden.
or
Click the **Full Screen Mode** (third) button **3** to display the illustration at full screen size with the menu bar and scroll bars hidden.

➤ Press "F" to cycle through the three modes.

➤ Press Tab to hide (or show) all currently open palettes, including the Toolbox; press Shift-Tab to hide (or show) all the palettes, leaving the Toolbox.

Moving the illustration
To move the illustration with the Hand tool:
Choose the **Hand** tool (H) 🖐 (or hold down the Spacebar to turn any other tool into a temporary Hand tool), then drag the illustration to the desired position **4**.

➤ Double-click the Hand tool to fit the entire artboard in the document window.

➤ You can also move the illustration by clicking any of the scroll arrows at the edge of the document window.

Screen Modes; Move Illustration

73

To move the illustration via the Navigator palette:

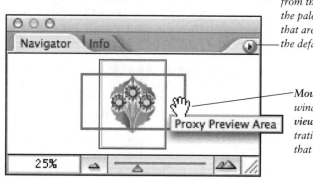

*Choose **View Artboard Only** from the palette menu to have the palette display only objects that are on the artboard (within the default printable area).*

*__Move__ the illustration in its window by dragging the **view box**, or click the illustration thumbnail to display that area of the illustration.*

➤ To change the color of the view box frame from its default light red, choose Palette Options from the Navigator palette menu, then choose a preset color from the Color pop-up menu, or double-click the color swatch and choose a color from the system Color palette. Check "Draw dashed lines as solid lines" to have dashed lines display as solid lines on the palette.

➤ The proportions of the view box match the proportions of the document window. Resize the document window and you'll see what we mean.

➤ The Navigator palette will display multiple pages, if any, and tiling of the imageable area.

Back to basics

To restore the default workspace, choose Window > Workspace > **[Default].** Or if you're using a laptop or a Tablet PC, choose Window > Workspace > **Minimal.**

1 *Type a **Name** for the workspace in the Save Workspace dialog box.*

Creating workspaces

In previous versions of Illustrator, each time you started a work session you had to set up your workspace anew, deciding which palettes you wanted open and where. You turned your back for one minute and returned to discover that your partner had rearranged everything onscreen. Now you can have it both ways because you can each **save** your own **workspace settings.** Then, when you sit down to work, all you have to do is choose that setting name from the Window > Workspace submenu. (Now you'll have to look for something else to argue about!)

To save a workspace: NEW

1. Do any or all of the following:

   Position all the palettes where you want them, including the Toolbox and any library palettes, in the desired palette groups. (Illustrator remembers where you last positioned the palettes, even if they're not open when you save your workspace.)

   Open any **tearoff toolbars.**

   Resize any palettes, including any that open from the Control palette.

   Choose a **thumbnail** or **swatch size** from any palette menu, including any that open from the Control palette. For example, you can choose a different swatch size for the Swatches palette that opens from the Control palette than for the Swatches palette that opens from the Window menu.

   Open the palettes that you use frequently and **close** the ones you rarely use.

2. Choose Window > Workspace > **Save Workspace.**

3. Enter a **Name** for the workspace (we suggest using your own name) **1**.

4. Click OK. You can choose any workspace name from the Window > Workspace submenu at any time.

➤ The arrangement of palettes on a computer with dual displays will be saved as one workspace. You could put all the palettes in one display, or put the ones you use most often in one display and the ones you use less often in the other.

Save Workspace

NEW **To rename, delete, or duplicate a workspace:**

1. Choose Window > Workspace > **Manage Workspaces.**

2. Do any of the following:

   To **rename** a workspace, click the workspace name, then type the desired name in the field **1**.

   To delete a workspace, click the workspace name, then click the **Delete Workspace** button. 🗑

   To duplicate a workspace, click an existing workspace, then click the **New Workspace** button. ⬛

3. Click OK.

➤ If no workspaces are selected in the Manage Workspaces dialog box and you click the New Workspace button, the new workspace will be based on the current state of your display, palettes, etc.

➤ If you want to edit an existing workspace, follow the instructions on the previous page, entering the same name in the Save Workspace dialog box. When the alert dialog box appears **2**, click Yes.

1 *Use the Manage Workspaces dialog box to rename and delete workspaces.*

The specified workspace name is already in use.
Would you like to overwrite the existing workspace?

No   Yes

2 *This prompt will appear if you try to save a new workspace using the same name as an existing one.*

Rename, Delete, Duplicate Workspace

GEOMETRIC OBJECTS 7

Paths (objects) that you create in Illustrator consist of anchor points connected by straight and/or curved line segments. You can create closed paths, such as polygons and ovals, or open paths, such as arcs or straight lines. In this chapter, you're going to be creating a lot of objects, so we'll start off by telling you how you can get rid of the ones you don't need. Then you'll learn how to create geometric objects quickly and easily by using the Rectangle, Rounded Rectangle, Ellipse, Polygon, Star, Flare, Line Segment, Arc, Spiral, Rectangular Grid, and Polar Grid tools. Once you've learned the basics in this chapter, your next step is to learn how to select paths for editing (Chapter 8), copy and align them (Chapter 9), apply colors to them (Chapter 10), and reshape them (Chapters 11 and 12).

Danny Pelavin builds crisp, effective illustrations using basic geometric shapes.

Deleting objects

You'll be creating lots of different shapes in this chapter, and your artboard may start to get crowded with junk. To remove an object you've just created, choose Edit > Undo (Cmd-Z/Ctrl-Z). To **remove** an **object** that's been lying around, follow these instructions.

To delete objects:

1. Choose the **Selection** tool (V), ▸ then click the object you want to delete or drag a marquee around multiple objects (other methods for selecting multiple objects are described in the next chapter).

2. Press **Delete/Backspace** or **Del.**

➤ If you're using the Direct Selection tool and only some of the object's points are selected, press Delete/Backspace or Del twice to delete the whole object.

Creating rectangles and ellipses

To create a rectangle or an ellipse by dragging:

1. Choose the **Rectangle** tool (M) ▣ or the **Ellipse** tool (L). ⬤

2. Drag diagonally ◼1. As you drag, you'll see a wireframe representation of the rectangle or oval. When you release the mouse, the rectangle or oval will be selected, and it will be painted with the current fill and stroke settings (Preview view).

   You can also use these modifiers:

   To draw the object from its **center**, Option-drag/Alt-drag.

   To **move** the rectangle or ellipse as you draw it, Spacebar-drag.

   To draw a **square** with the Rectangle tool or a **circle** with the Ellipse tool, Shift-drag.

➤ To create a series of perfectly aligned, equal-size rectangles, create or select a rectangle, then use Object > Path > Split Into Grid (see page 457).

To create a rectangle or an ellipse by specifying dimensions:

1. Choose the **Rectangle** tool (M) ▣ or the **Ellipse** tool (L). ⬤

2. Click on the artboard where you want the object to appear. The Rectangle or Ellipse dialog box opens ◼2.

3. Enter **Width** and **Height** values. To create a circle or a square, enter a value in the Width field, then click the word Height (or vice versa)—the value in one field will copy to the other field.

4. Click OK.

➤ Values in dialog boxes in the current document display in the measurement units currently chosen on the Units pop-up menu in File > Document Setup > Artboard.

➤ The last-used dimensions display when the Rectangle or Ellipse dialog box is opened.

Recoloring: a sneak preview

You'll learn all about Illustrator's fill and stroke controls in Chapter 10, but here's a sneak preview. Select an object, click the **Fill** or **Stroke** thumbnail or arrowhead on the **Control** palette, then click a **NEW** swatch on the **Swatches** palette. You could also Shift-click the thumbnail, then click the color bar on the **Color** palette.

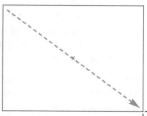

◼1 *With the **Rectangle** (or Ellipse) tool, drag diagonally.*

◼2 *Enter Width and Height values in the **Rectangle** (or Ellipse) dialog box.*

Ellipses and rectangles

Rectangle, Ellipse Tools

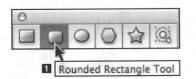

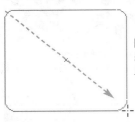

Rounded Rectangle Tool

To create a rounded rectangle:

1. Choose the **Rounded Rectangle tool** .

2. Drag diagonally. As you drag, you'll see a wireframe representation of the rounded rectangle **2**. When you release the mouse, the rounded rectangle will be selected and painted with the current fill and stroke settings (Preview view) **3**.

2 *Drag diagonally with the **Rounded Rectangle** tool.*

➤ As you create an object with the Rounded Rectangle tool, keep the mouse button down and keep pressing the up arrow to make the corners more round, or the down arrow to make them more square. Press (don't hold) the left or right arrow to toggle between square and round corners.

➤ To draw a rounded rectangle of a specific size, choose the Rounded Rectangle tool, click on the artboard, then enter Width, Height, and Corner Radius values. The Corner Radius value (0–8192 pt), which controls the degree of curvature in the corners of rounded rectangles, can also be specified in Preferences (Cmd-K/Ctrl-K) > General. When this value is changed in one location, it updates automatically in the other.

3 *The rectangle is automatically painted with the current fill and stroke colors (see Chapter 10).*

Rounded Rectangle Tool

DANIEL PELAVIN

DANIEL PELAVIN

*Great uses for **rounded rectangles!***

Here's a quick introduction to one of the many Illustrator filters: **Round Corners**.

To round the corners of an existing object:

1. Select an object.

2. Choose **Filter** > Stylize > **Round Corners** (on the top portion of the Filters menu).
   or
   Choose **Effect** > Stylize > **Round Corners** to create an editable appearance (not a permanent change to the object). To learn about effects and filters, see Chapter 20.

3. Enter a **Radius** value (the radius of the curve, in points). When using an effect, you can check Preview, then make adjustments before closing the dialog box.

4. Click OK **1**.

Creating polygons

There are a number of tools, such as **Polygon, Star**, and **Spiral**, that make light work of drawing geometric objects. All you have to do is draw a marquee in the artboard or enter values in a dialog box. As you can see from the wonderful graphics by Daniel Pelavin in this chapter, you can create illustrations using basic geometric objects as building blocks.

To create a polygon by clicking:

1. Choose the **Polygon** tool **2**. ⬡

2. Click where you want the center of the polygon to be. The Polygon dialog box opens **3**.

3. Enter a **Radius** value (0–8192 pt) for the distance from the center of the object to the corner points.

4. Choose a number of **Sides** for the polygon by clicking the up or down arrow or by entering a number (3–1000). The sides will be of equal length.

5. Click OK **4**. A polygon will appear where you clicked on the artboard; the current fill and stroke settings are applied automatically (see Chapter 10).

1 *Top row: the original objects; second row: after applying the* **Round Corners** *filter (30 pt)*

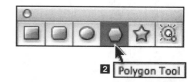

2 Polygon Tool

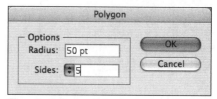

3 *In the* **Polygon** *dialog box, enter a Radius distance and choose a number of Sides.*

4 *A polygon drawn with the* **Polygon** *tool*

DANIEL PELAVIN

Polygons, ellipses, and rectangles

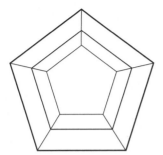

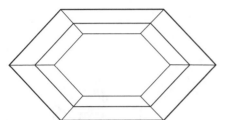

1 *To create these gemstones, we started with a* **polygon,** *created copies with the Scale tool, then added connecting lines with the Line Segment tool.*

Star	
Options	OK
Radius 1: 24 pt	Cancel
Radius 2: 49 pt	
Points: 5	

2 *Enter/choose Radius 1, Radius 2, and Points values in the Star dialog box.*

3 *A classic five-pointed* **star**

4 *After putting circles on top of the points, then clicking the Add to Shape Area button on the Pathfinder palette to unite the shapes*

To create a polygon by dragging:

1. Choose the **Polygon** tool.
2. Drag on the artboard, starting from where you want the center of the polygon to be.

   While dragging, do any of the following:

   To **scale** the polygon, drag away from or toward the center.

   To **rotate** the polygon, drag in a circular direction.

   To **constrain** the bottom side of the polygon to the horizontal axis, hold down Shift.

   To **add sides** to or **delete sides** from the polygon, press or hold down the up or down arrow key.

   To **move** the polygon (without scaling it), hold down the Spacebar.

3. When you release the mouse, the polygon will be selected, and it will be painted with the current fill and stroke settings **1**.

➤ To align a new object with an existing object as you draw it, use smart guides (see pages 100–101).

Creating stars

To create a star by clicking:

1. Choose the **Star** tool.
2. Click where you want the center of the star to be. The Star dialog box opens **2**.
3. Enter **Radius 1** and **Radius 2** values (0–8192 pt). The higher value is the distance from the center of the star to its outermost points; the lower value is the distance from the center of the star to the innermost points. The greater the difference between the two values, the thinner the arms of the star.
4. Choose a number of **Points** for the star by clicking the up or down arrow or by entering a number (3–1000).
5. Click OK **3–4**.

➤ To rotate the completed star, use its bounding box (see page 139).

Polygon, Star Tools

To create a star by dragging:

1. Choose the **Star** tool. ☆

2. Drag on the artboard, starting from where you want the center of the star to be **1**.

   While dragging, do any of the following:

   To **scale** the star, drag away from or toward its center.

   To **rotate** the star, drag in a circular direction.

   To **constrain** two points to the horizontal axis, hold down Shift.

   To **add points** to or **delete points** from the star, press the up or down arrow key.

   To **move** the star, hold down the Spacebar.

   To make pairs of shoulders (opposite segments) **parallel** to each other, hold down Option/Alt **2**.

   To increase/decrease the **length** of the **arms** of the star while keeping the inner radius points constant, hold down Cmd/Ctrl and drag away from/toward the center.

3. When you release the mouse, the star will be selected and it will be painted with the current fill and stroke settings **3**–**4**.

➤ Hold down ~ (tilde) while dragging quickly with the Star or Polygon tool to create progressively larger copies of the shape **5**. You can apply stroke colors and settings to the copies afterward.

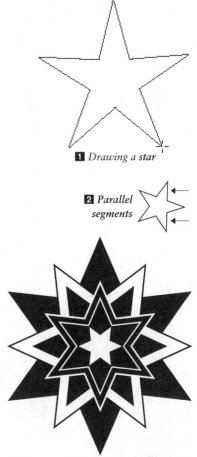

1 *Drawing a star*

2 *Parallel segments*

3 *Stars scaled and copied via the Scale tool dialog box and rotated via the Rotate tool dialog box—no drawing required!*

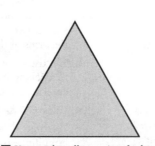

4 *You might call it a* ***triangle,*** *but actually it's a three-pointed* ***star.***

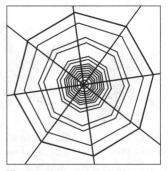

5 ***Multiple*** *polygons drawn with the* ***Polygon*** *tool with ~ held down*

Star Tool

Rays

Halo

End handle

Rings

Center handle

 A selected flare

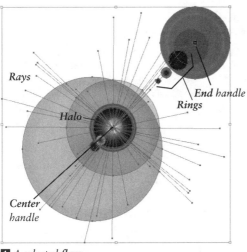

2 Choose Center, Halo, Rays, and Rings options for a flare in the **Flare Tool Options** dialog box.

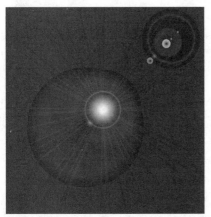

3 Flares don't print well in this type of book.

Creating flares

The **Flare** tool creates soft glow circles, like a camera lens flare, consisting of four components: a center, a halo, rays, and rings **1**. The components are filled automatically with the current fill color at various opacity settings. You may not use this tool very often, but the instructions are here should you ever need them.

To create a flare by entering values:

1. Choose the **Flare** tool 🔆 (the last tool on the Rectangle tool pop-out menu).

2. Click on the artboard where you want the flare to appear. The Flare Tool Options dialog box opens **2**.

3. For the **Center** portion (inner circle) of the flare, choose the **Diameter** (0–1000 pt), **Opacity**, and **Brightness** values.

4. For the **Halo**, choose the **Growth** (radius) as a percentage of the overall size, and choose or enter a **Fuzziness** value.

5. *Optional:* Check **Rays**, then specify the **Number** of rays (0–50), the length of the **Longest** ray as a percentage of the average ray, and the **Fuzziness** of the rays.

6. *Optional:* Check **Rings**, then specify the overall length of the flare **Path** (0–1000 pt), the **Number** of rings (0–50), the **Largest** ring as a percentage of the average ring, and the **Direction** (angle) of the rings. The Rings feature produces randomized results.

7. Click OK. The flare may show up better if you move it on top of a dark object (use the Selection tool to do this) **3**.

To create a flare using the current Flare tool settings:

1. Choose the **Flare** tool. 🔆

2. Option-click/Alt-click where you want the flare to appear (no dialog box will open).

Flare Tool

To create a flare by dragging:

1. Choose the **Flare** tool 🔘 (the last tool on the Rectangle tool pop-out menu).

2. Drag on the artboard to create the flare. The farther you drag, the larger the center and halo.

   Before releasing the mouse, you can do any of the following:

   To **scale** the flare without rotating it, drag horizontally.

   To **constrain** the rays to the nearest 45° angle, press Shift.

   To **add** rays, press the up arrow key.

   To **remove** rays, press the down arrow key.

   To **rearrange** the rings **randomly,** press ~ (tilde).

   To **scale** the flare without scaling the center halo, Cmd-drag/Ctrl-drag.

3. Release the mouse, but don't deselect the flare. Click (and drag, if necessary) in another spot to position the end handle and add rings. Deselect, then choose another tool.

To edit a flare:

To change the **length** or **direction** of the rays on a flare and move its rings, choose the Selection tool, click the flare, choose the **Flare** tool, 🔘 Cmd-Spacebar-drag/Ctrl-Spacebar-drag to zoom in, click the exact center point of the center or end handle of the flare **1** (arrowheads will appear in the flare pointer), then drag the handle.
or
To edit any of the components of a flare using its **options** dialog box, select the flare, double-click the **Flare** tool on the Toolbox, then change any of the settings in the Flare Tool Options dialog box (see the previous page). The Preview option will be checked.
or
To edit the **individual components** of a flare, expand it into individual objects first (you won't be able to edit it with the Flare Tool Options dialog box). Choose the Selection tool, select the flare, choose Object > **Expand,** check all three Expand boxes, check Specify, ignore the Objects value, and click OK.

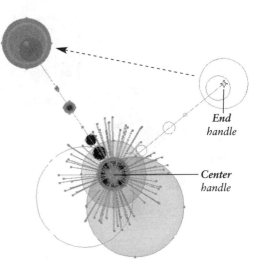

End handle

Center handle

1 Drag the **center** handle to move the rays and large circles, or the **end** handle to change the overall length of the flare and move the rings.

1 *The Line Segment tool and its related tools on the tearoff toolbar*

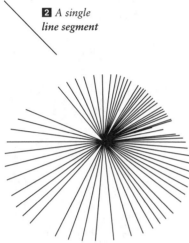

2 *A single line segment*

3 *Lines drawn with the Line Segment tool with ~ (tilde) held down*

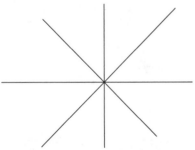

4 *Lines drawn with the Line Segment tool with Shift-~ (tilde) held down*

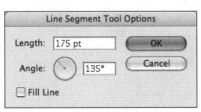

5 *Choose settings for the Line Segment tool in its options dialog box.*

The **Line Segment, Arc, Spiral, Rectangular Grid,** and **Polar Grid** tools **1** on the Line Segment tool pop-out menu create independent objects or groups of objects.

Creating line segments

The **Line Segment** tool (and the Arc tool, which is discussed on the next page), create either one line or multiple separate lines. Each time you drag with either tool, a new, separate path is created.

To draw a line segment by dragging:

1. Choose the **Line Segment** tool.

2. Drag to draw a line **2**. As you drag, you can do any of the following:

   To **extend** the line outward from both sides of the origin point, press Option/Alt.

   To **constrain** the line to the nearest 45° increment, press Shift.

   To **move** the line, press the Spacebar.

   To create **multiple** lines of **varied** lengths from the same center point, at any angle, press ~ (tilde) **3**. Move the mouse quickly to spread the lines apart.

   To create **multiple** lines at 45° increments, press Shift-~ (tilde) **4**.

To draw a line segment by entering values:

1. Choose the **Line Segment** tool.

2. Click where you want the segment to begin. The Line Segment Tool Options dialog box opens **5**.

3. Enter the desired line **Length.**

4. Enter an **Angle** or move the dial.

5. *Optional:* Check **Fill Line** to assign the current fill color to the line (see Chapter 10). If the line is subsequently joined to another line or segment, that color will be used as the fill. With this option unchecked, the line will have a fill of None, which can be changed later.

6. Click OK.

➤ Normally, the last used values display in the Line Segment Tool Options dialog box when it's opened. To restore the default values, Option/Alt-click Reset.

Line Segment Tool

Creating arcs

The **Arc** tool creates perfectly smooth arcs.

To draw arcs by dragging:

1. Choose the Arc tool.
2. Drag to create arcs **1**. As you drag, you can do any of the following:

   To toggle between an **open** and **closed** arc, press C.

   To **flip** the arc while keeping the origin point constant, press F.

   To increase or decrease the **angle** of the arc, press (or press and hold) the up arrow or down arrow key.

   To **extend** the **arc** outward from both sides of the origin point, press Option/Alt.

   To **move** the arc, press the Spacebar.

   To create **multiple** arc segments from the same origin point, press ~ (tilde).

   To toggle between a **concave** and **convex** arc, press and release X.

To draw arcs by entering values:

1. Choose the Arc tool.
2. Click where you want the arc segment to begin. The Arc Segment Tool Options dialog box opens **2**.
3. Enter a **Length X-Axis** value for the width of the arc and a **Length Y-Axis** value for the height of the arc. (If desired, click a new point on the reference point locator.)
4. From the **Type** pop-up menu, choose whether the arc will be Opened or Closed.
5. From the **Base Along** pop-up menu, choose whether the arc will be measured from the X Axis or the Y Axis.
6. Move the **Slope** slider or enter a value for the steepness of the curve.
7. Leave **Fill Arc** unchecked for no fill, or check this option to fill the arc with the current fill color.
8. Click OK.

➤ To restore the default values to the Arc Segment Tool Options dialog box, hold down Option/Alt and click Reset (Cancel becomes Reset).

Using arc segments

In Chapter 14 you'll learn how to draw curves "from scratch" with the **Pen** tool. You can use the Join command (see page 165) to combine **pen** and **arc** segments into a single object, or you can add segments to an arc using the Pen tool.

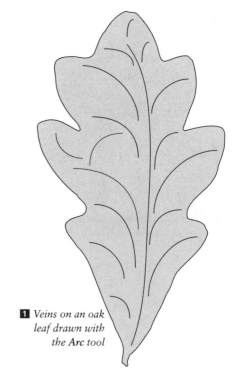

1 *Veins on an oak leaf drawn with the Arc tool*

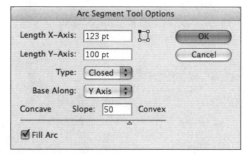

2 *Choose options for the Arc tool in its options dialog box.*

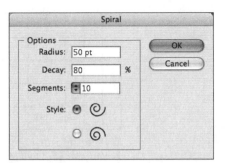

1 In the **Spiral** dialog box, enter Radius and Decay values, choose a number of Segments, and click either Style button.

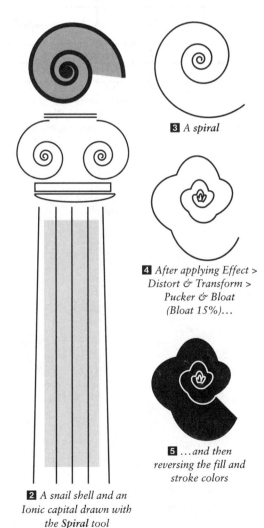

3 A spiral

4 After applying Effect > Distort & Transform > Pucker & Bloat (Bloat 15%)...

5 ...and then reversing the fill and stroke colors

2 A snail shell and an Ionic capital drawn with the **Spiral** tool

Creating spirals

To create a spiral by entering values:

1. Choose the **Spiral** tool.
2. Click roughly where you want the center of the spiral to be. The Spiral dialog box opens **1**.
3. Enter a **Radius** value (1–1892 pt) for the distance from the center of the spiral to the outermost point.
4. Enter a **Decay** percentage (5–150) to control how tightly the spiral winds.
5. Choose or enter the number of **Segments** (quarter revolutions around the center point) for the spiral (2–1000).
6. Click a **Style** button for the direction the spiral will wind from the center point.
7. Click OK **2**.
8. Apply stroke attributes to the spiral (see page 113 and 118).

To create a spiral by dragging:

1. Choose the **Spiral** tool.
2. Drag in the document window, starting from where you want the center of the spiral to be.
3. While dragging, do any of the following:

   To **resize** the spiral, drag away from or toward the center.

   To control how **tightly** the spiral winds (the Decay value), Cmd-drag/Ctrl-drag slowly away from or toward the center.

   To **add** segments to or **delete** segments from the center of the spiral, press the up or down arrow key.

   To **rotate** the spiral, drag in a circular direction.

   To **constrain** the rotation of the entire spiral to an increment of 45°, hold down Shift.

   To **move** the spiral, hold down the Spacebar.

4. When you release the mouse, the spiral will be selected and it will be painted with the current fill and stroke settings **3**–**5**.

Spiral Tool

Creating rectangular grids

A **rectangular grid** can be created by dragging (instructions on this page) or by entering values in a dialog box (instructions on the following page). The grid is composed of a group of separate lines and a rectangle. You can't put anything into it, but you can put it on its own layer (lock it to make it uneditable), and then create objects or type on a layer above it (see Chapter 15).

To create a rectangular grid by dragging:

1. Choose the **Rectangular Grid** tool (it's on the Line Segment tool pop-out menu). ⊞

2. Drag diagonally. After you start dragging, you can press any of the following keys:

   Shift to **constrain** the grid to a square **1**.

   Option/Alt to draw the grid from the **center.**

   Shift-Option/Shift-Alt to draw a **square** grid from the **center.**

   Spacebar to **move** the grid as you draw.

   To adjust the grid **dividers,** press:

   Up arrow or down arrow to **add** or **remove horizontal** dividers.

   Right arrow or left arrow to **add** or **remove vertical dividers.**

   X to **skew** the **vertical** dividers to the **left** by increments of 10% **2** or C to **skew** the vertical dividers to the **right** (the dividers will be progressively closer together).

   F to **skew** the **horizontal** dividers to the **bottom** by increments of 10% or V to skew the horizontal dividers to the **top.**

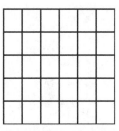

1 *Shift-drag with the **Rectangular Grid** tool to draw a square grid.*

2 *Press X after you start dragging the **Rectangular Grid** tool to skew the vertical dividers to the left.*

Rectangular Grid Tool Options

Default Size
Width: 100 pt
Height: 100 pt

OK
Cancel

Horizontal Dividers
Number: 5
Bottom   Skew: 0%   Top

Vertical Dividers
Number: 5
Left   Skew: 0%   Right

☑ Use Outside Rectangle As Frame
☐ Fill Grid

1 *Choose parameters for the **Rectangular Grid** tool in its options dialog box.*

2 *Use Outside Rectangle As Frame on: The outer segment is a single rectangle.*

3 *Use Outside Rectangle As Frame off: Each of the four outer segments is a separate object.*

4 *A polar grid*

To create a rectangular grid by entering values:

1. Choose the **Rectangular Grid** tool (it's on the Line Segment tool pop-out menu). ⊞

2. Click in the document window to establish an origin point for the grid. The Rectangular Grid Tool Options dialog box opens **1**.

3. In the **Default Size** area, enter Width and Height values for the overall grid, and to specify the point from which the grid will be drawn, click a corner on the reference point locator.

4. Enter the Number of **Horizontal Dividers** to be inserted between the top and bottom edges of the grid. *Optional:* Choose a Skew value above or below 0 to cluster the dividers toward the bottom or top.

5. Enter the number of **Vertical Dividers** to be inserted between the left and right edges of the grid. *Optional:* Choose a Skew value above or below 0 to cluster the dividers toward the right or left.

6. *Optional:* Check **Use Outside Rectangle As Frame** to have the top, bottom, left, and right segments be a separate rectangular object instead of a line **2**–**3**.

7. *Optional:* Check **Fill Grid** to fill the grid with the current fill color.

8. Click OK.

➤ Hold down Option/Alt and click Reset to restore the tool's default values.

Creating polar grids

You can draw a **polar** (elliptical) **grid** by dragging (instructions on this page) or via a dialog box (instructions on the next page).

To create a polar grid by dragging:

1. Choose the **Polar Grid** tool (it's on the Line Segment tool pop-out menu). ◉

2. Choose fill and stroke colors (see Chapter 10), then drag diagonally **4**. As you drag, you can do any of the following:

   To **constrain** the grid to a circle, press Shift.

   To **resize** the grid from **all** sides of the origin point, press Option/Alt.

(Continued on the following page)

Rectangular Grid, Polar Grid Tools

To **move** the grid, press the Spacebar.

3. To adjust the grid dividers, do any of the following as you drag:

To **add** or **remove concentric circles,** press the up arrow or down arrow key.

To **add** or **remove radial lines,** press the right arrow or left arrow key.

To **skew** the **concentric dividers** toward the **center,** press X.

To **skew** the **concentric dividers** toward the outer **edge,** press C.

To **skew** the **radial dividers counterclockwise,** press V; or to skew them **clockwise,** press F.

To create a polar grid by entering values:

1. Choose fill and stroke colors (see Chapter 10).

2. Choose the **Polar Grid** tool, ⊕ then click to establish a reference point for the grid. The Polar Grid Tool Options dialog box opens **1**.

3. In the **Default Size** area, enter Width and Height values for the overall grid, and to choose which corner the grid will be drawn from, click a corner on the reference point locator.

4. Enter the Number of curved **Concentric Dividers** to appear inside the grid **2**. *Optional:* Choose a Skew value above (or below) 0 to cluster the concentric dividers toward the edge (or center) of the grid **3**.

5. Enter the number of straight-line **Radial Dividers** to appear in the grid. *Optional:* Choose a Skew value above (or below) 0 to cluster the straight dividers in a clockwise (or counterclockwise) direction around the grid **4**.

6. *Optional:* Check **Create Compound Path From Ellipses** to convert each concentric circle into a separate compound path.

7. *Optional:* Click **Fill Grid** to fill the whole grid with the current fill color. If Create Compound Path From Ellipses is checked, alternating circles will be filled **5**.

8. Click OK.

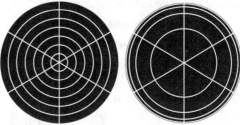

1 *The Polar Grid Tool Options dialog box*

2 *Both Skew values at zero*   **3** *Concentric Dividers: Skew 120%*

4 *Radial Dividers: Skew -128%*   **5** *Create Compound Path From Ellipses and Fill Grid on: The white rings are see-through. The fill color is applied to the opaque rings automatically, and the stroke color to the dividers.*

SELECT 8

In this chapter, you'll learn many methods for selecting objects for editing, including five tools, a host of Select menu commands, and the Layers palette. Once you master these fundamental skills, you'll be ready to learn how to copy and align objects (next chapter), and from there you can plunge into all the fun stuff—recoloring, transforming, reshaping, applying effects, etc.

A few pointers

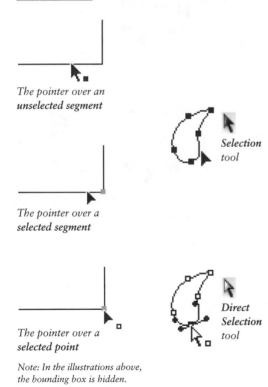

The pointer over an
unselected segment

The pointer over a
selected segment

The pointer over a
selected point

Note: In the illustrations above,
the bounding box is hidden.

Selection
tool

Direct
Selection
tool

Selection tools

Only selected objects can be modified, so before learning how to modify objects you have to know how to select and deselect them.

The five selection tools

This description of the basic functions of the selection tools will help prepare you for the step-by-step instructions that follow.

Use the **Selection** tool (**V**) to select or move whole paths (or to scale or rotate a path via its bounding box). If you click the edge of an object with the Selection tool, all the points on the object will become selected. You can also select an object with this tool by clicking its fill (if it has one), provided Object Selection by Path Only is unchecked (the default setting) in Preferences (Cmd-K/ Ctrl-K) > General and the document is in Preview view.

Use the **Direct Selection** tool (**A**) to select one or more individual anchor points or segments of a path. If you click a curve segment with the Direct Selection tool, that segment's direction lines and anchor points will become visible. (Straight segments don't have direction lines—they only have anchor points.) If Object Selection by Path Only is unchecked in Preferences > General and you click an object's fill (solid color, gradient, or pattern) in Preview view using this tool, all the points on the object will become selected.

(Continued on the following page)

Although the **Group Selection** tool can be used to select all the anchor points on a single path, its primary purpose is selecting groups of objects that are nested inside larger groups. Click once with this tool to select an object; click twice to select that object's group; click three times to select the next group that was added to the larger group, and so on 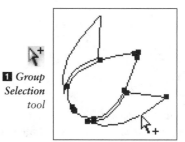.

➤ The easiest way to access the Group Selection tool is by holding down Option/Alt when the Direct Selection tool is active (note the plus sign in the pointer).

1 *Group Selection tool*

Another way to work with a group is to **isolate** it. If you double-click it with the Selection tool, a double gray rectangle will appear around the whole group. Objects within an isolated group can be selected with the Selection tool; individual path components can be selected with the Direct Selection tool. When you're done, double-click outside the gray rectangle. To learn more about groups, see page 199 and pages 203–207.

2 *Lasso tool*

Use the **Lasso** tool (**Q**) to select path points and segments by dragging a freeform marquee around them .

The **Magic Wand** tool (**Y**) selects objects of the same or a similar fill color, stroke color, stroke weight, opacity, or blending mode as those of the object you click on, depending on which of those options are chosen for the tool on the Magic Wand palette 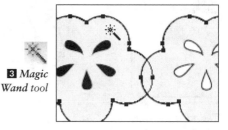.

3 *Magic Wand tool*

➤ If Use Precise Cursors is checked in Preferences > General, you'll see a crosshair pointer onscreen -¦- instead of an icon for the current tool.

Object selection by path only

With **Object Selection by Path Only** unchecked in Preferences > General, you can select an object in Preview view by clicking with a selection tool anywhere within the object's bounding box. When this option is checked, with the Selection, Direct Selection, or Magic Wand tool, you must click a path segment or anchor point in order to select an object.

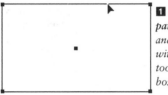

1 *Selecting a path (and all its anchor points) with the Selection tool (bounding box hidden)*

Using the Selection tool
To select an object or objects:
1. Choose the Selection tool (V). ⬈
2. Click the **edge** of the path **1**.
   or
   If the path has a color fill, your document is in Preview view, and the Object Selection by Path Only option is off (see the sidebar), click the **fill**.
   or
   Position the pointer outside the path(s) you want to select, then drag a **marquee** across all or part of it **2**. The whole path will be selected, even if you marquee just a portion of it. (If the document is in Outline view, use this marquee technique or click the edge of the path.)

You can **add** or **subtract** whole objects from a selection with the Selection tool.

To add or subtract objects from a selection:
Choose the Selection tool (V), ⬈ then Shift-click or Shift-drag (marquee) any unselected objects to add them to the selection, or do the same for any selected objects to deselect them **3**–**4**.

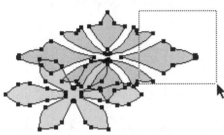

2 *Marqueeing two paths with the Selection tool*

3 *Marqueeing one of two selected objects with the Selection tool in order to deselect it*

4 *One path is deselected.*

Using the Direct Selection tool

You will learn how to reshape objects in Chapter 12. But before you can begin reshaping, you have to know how to **select** individual **points** and **segments**. It's important to be precise about which components you select.

To select/deselect anchor points or segments with the Direct Selection tool:

1. Choose the **Direct Selection** tool (A).

2. Click the edge of the path (not the fill). A **segment** will become selected. If you click a curve segment, the direction lines for that segment will become visible.
   or
   If the path isn't selected, click the edge of the path (not the fill), then click an **anchor point** **1**–**2**.
   or
   Position the pointer outside the object or objects whose **anchor points** you want to select, then drag a marquee across them (a dotted marquee will define the area as you drag over it). Only the points you marquee will become selected **3**–**4**.

3. To select additional anchor points or segments or to deselect selected anchor points or segments individually, Shift-click or Shift-marquee those points or segments with the Direct Selection tool.

➤ To access the last-used selection tool (Selection or Direct Selection) temporarily when using a nonselection tool, hold down Cmd/Ctrl (note the pointer icon).

Selecting via a command

The **Select commands** select objects whose characteristics are similar to those of the last or currently selected object. Each command is aptly named for the attributes it searches for.

To select objects via a command:

Do any of the following:

Select an object to base the search on, or deselect all objects to base the search on the

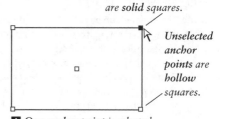

Selected anchor points are solid squares.

Unselected anchor points are hollow squares.

1 *One anchor point is selected with the Direct Selection tool (shown in Outline view).*

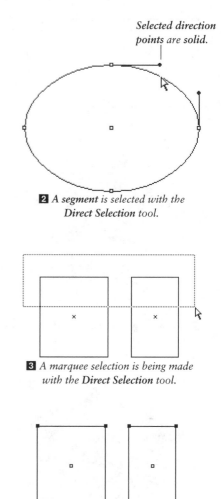

Selected direction points are solid.

2 *A segment is selected with the Direct Selection tool.*

3 *A marquee selection is being made with the Direct Selection tool.*

4 *Only the four points within the marquee become selected.*

Reselect

Let's say you just used a Select > **Same** submenu command and you love it so much you want to choose it again. Just press **Cmd-6/Ctrl-6.** Unlike the Undo command, this command doesn't have to be executed right away; you can perform other edits, and Illustrator will remember which Select > Same submenu command was last used. Watch out, though. You may get unexpected results, depending on what type of object is selected.

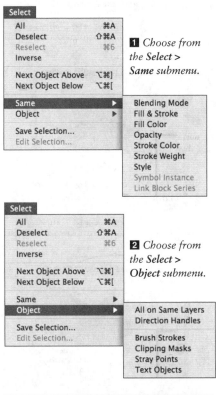

1 *Choose from the Select > Same submenu.*

2 *Choose from the Select > Object submenu.*

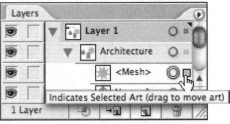

3 *Click the selection area for an object on the Layers palette.*

last object that was selected. Then from the Select > **Same** submenu **1**, choose **Blending Mode, Fill & Stroke, Fill Color, Opacity, Stroke Color, Stroke Weight, Style, Symbol Instance,** or **Link Block Series.**

or

Select an object or objects, then from the Select > **Object** submenu **2**, choose **All on Same Layers** to select all the objects on the layer the object resides on (or layers, if objects from more than one layer are selected), or choose **Direction Handles** to select all the direction lines on the currently selected object or objects.

or

With or without an object selected, from the Select > **Object** submenu, choose **Brush Strokes** to select objects that have the same brush strokes; **Clipping Masks** to select masking objects (helpful for getting the edges of a masking object to display on screen); **Stray Points** to select lone points that aren't part of any path (so they can be deleted easily); or **Text Objects** to select all the text objects in the document.

Selecting via the Layers palette

You'll learn more about the Layers palette in Chapter 15.

To select an object via the Layers palette:

1. On the **Layers** palette, click the expand/collapse triangle for any top-level layer, sublayer, or group list so the name of the object that you want to select is visible.

2. At the far right side of the Layers palette, click the **selection area** for the object you want to select (a colored square will appear) **3**. (Or to select all the objects on a layer or sublayer, click the selection area for the layer.) See also pages 202–205.

Select via Layers Palette

Using the Lasso tool

Let's say you need to select a few points on one path and a couple of points on a nearby path. You could grab the Direct Selection tool and click the points individually (tedious) or you could marquee them (works only if the points in question fall conveniently within the rectangular marquee). With the **Lasso** tool, you can weave an irregular pathway around just the points and segments you want to select, and it's especially helpful for creating selections among overlapping paths. Don't try to use it to select whole paths.

1 *Wend your way around parts of objects with the **Lasso** tool.*

To select/deselect points or segments with the Lasso tool:

1. Deselect (click a blank area of the artboard).

2. Choose the **Lasso** tool (Q), then drag to encircle the segments or points you want to select **1**–**2**. You can drag right across a path. You don't need to "close" the lasso path; simply release the mouse when the desired points have been lassoed.

3. *Optional:* Shift-drag around any unselected points or segments anywhere in the document window to add them to the selection, or Option-drag/Alt-drag around any selected points or segments to deselect them.

2 *Only the **points** and **segments** you marquee will become selected.*

Saving selections

Via the **Save Selection** command, you can save any selection under a custom name, then reselect those objects quickly by choosing that name from the Select menu.

To save a selection:

1. Select the objects you want to save as a selection; deselect all others.

2. Choose Select > **Save Selection.**

3. Enter a descriptive name.

4. Click OK. To reselect those objects at any time, choose the selection name from the bottom of the **Select** menu **3**.

➤ To rename or delete a saved selection, choose Edit Selection. Click a selection, then change the name or click Delete **4**.

3 *To reselect a saved selection, choose the selection name from the bottom of the **Select** menu.*

Select	
All	⌘A
Deselect	⇧⌘A
Reselect	⌘6
Inverse	
Next Object Above	⌥⌘]
Next Object Below	⌥⌘[
Same	▶
Object	▶
Save Selection...	
Edit Selection...	
Tree Image	
House symbols	
Logo	
Fish	

Edit Selection

Tree Image
House symbols
Logo
Fish

OK
Cancel
Delete

Name: Sugar maple

4 *You can use the **Edit Selection** dialog box to rename or delete a saved selection.*

1 *The Magic Wand palette*

Using the Magic Wand tool

The Magic Wand tool selects all the objects in a document that have the same or a similar fill color, stroke color, stroke weight, opacity, or blending mode as those of the object you click on, depending on which options you choose on the **Magic Wand palette.** To use the Magic Wand tool, follow the instructions on the next page.

To choose options for the Magic Wand tool:

1. To open the **Magic Wand** palette, double-click the **Magic Wand** tool ✴ or choose Window > **Magic Wand.**

   If the three panels aren't showing (as shown in **1**), click the up/down arrowhead on the palette tab until they're all visible, or choose Show Stroke Options and Show Transparency Options from the palette menu.

2. On the left side of the palette, check the attributes you want the tool to select: **Fill Color, Stroke Color, Stroke Weight, Opacity,** or **Blending Mode.**

3. For each option you checked in the previous step, except Blending Mode, choose a **Tolerance** range. Choose a low value to select only colors, weights, or opacities that match or are very similar to the area you'll click; or choose a high value to allow the tool to select a broader range of colors, weights, or opacities. For Fill Color or Stroke Color, choose a specific color value (the range is 0–255 for RGB or 0–100 for CMYK, depending on the document color mode); for Stroke Weight, choose a width Tolerance (0–1000 pt); and for Opacity, choose a percentage (0–100).

4. To permit the Magic Wand tool to select objects on all layers, make sure **Use All Layers** on the palette menu has a check mark, or to allow the tool to select objects on only the current layer, leave this option unchecked.

➤ The Reset command on the palette menu resets all fields on the Magic Wand palette to their default values and unchecks all the attributes except Fill Color.

Magic Wand Palette

To use the Magic Wand tool:

I. Choose the **Magic Wand** tool (Y).

2. To create a **new** selection, click an object color in the document window. Depending on which options are checked on the Magic Wand palette, other objects with the same or a similar fill color, stroke color, stroke weight, opacity, or blending mode may become selected **1**–**2**.

3. To **add** to the selection, Shift-click another object.

To **subtract** from the selection, Option-click/Alt-click a selected object.

Selecting/deselecting all objects

To select all the objects in a document:

Choose Select > **All** (Cmd-A/Ctrl-A). All unlocked objects in your document will be selected, whether they're on the artboard or on the scratch area. Hidden or locked objects or objects on hidden layers (eye icon off on the Layers palette) won't become selected.

➤ If the text cursor is flashing in a text block when the Select > All command is executed, all the text in the block will become selected—not all the objects in the document.

To prevent objects from being modified, you must **deselect** them.

To deselect all objects:

Choose Select > **Deselect** (Cmd-Shift-A/ Ctrl-Shift-A).
or
Choose any selection tool, then click a blank area of the artboard.

➤ To deselect an individual object within a multiple-object selection, Shift-click it with the Selection tool. To deselect an object within a group, Shift-click it with the Direct Selection tool (for more about groups, see pages 203–207).

The **Inverse** command deselects all selected objects and selects all unselected objects.

To inverse a selection:

Choose Select > **Inverse**.

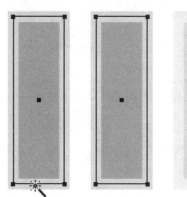

1 *These objects have the same* **stroke** *color, but the rectangle on the far right has a lower* **opacity** *(50%). The* **Opacity** *option is* **on** *for the Magic Wand tool, and the tool is clicked on the stroke of the leftmost object. Only the objects with the same stroke color* **and opacity** *become selected.*

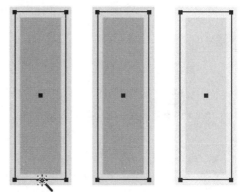

2 *This time the Magic Wand tool is used with the* **Opacity** *option* **off**. *All three objects become selected, and* **opacity** *is* **ignored** *as a factor.*

MOVE, COPY & ALIGN 9

In this chapter you'll learn how to move objects; use smart guides to align them; duplicate objects by dragging or by using the Clipboard or the Offset Path command; and align and distribute objects via palette buttons.

1 *You can drag the **edge** of an object with the Selection tool.*

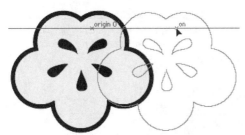

2 *If the object contains a fill, the document is in Preview view, and the **Object Selection by Path Only** preference is off, you can drag the object's fill. Here, **smart guides** are being used to move an object along the horizontal axis.*

Moving objects

Below, we discuss the simplest and most direct method for **moving objects**: by **dragging**. In conjunction with a great feature called smart guides (see the next page), dragging can easily take care of most of your moving needs. To learn other techniques for moving objects, such as the Control palette, Transform palette, and Move dialog box, see Chapter 11; to use ruler guides, object guides, and the grid as alignment tools, see Chapter 29.

To move an object by dragging:

1. Choose the **Selection** tool (V).

2. Drag the object's **edge** (you can do this in Outline or Preview view) **1**.
   or
   If the document is in Preview view, the object has a fill, and Object Selection by Path Only is off in Preferences > General, you can drag the object's **fill** **2**. This can also be done with the Direct Selection tool.

➤ If View > Snap To Point is on (Cmd-Option-"/Ctrl-Alt-") and there are ruler guides on your artboard, the part of an object that's directly underneath the pointer will snap to a guide if it comes within 2 pixels of it (the pointer becomes hollow when it's over a guide). The pointer will also become hollow and snap to any anchor point it passes over.

➤ Hold down Shift while dragging an object to constrain the movement to either a multiple of 45° or the current Constrain Angle in Preferences > General, if the latter value isn't 0.

Using smart guides

Smart guides are temporary guides that appear when you draw, move, duplicate, transform, or move the pointer over an object. They're designed to help you align objects with one another or along a particular axis. Smart guides also have magnetism: Drag an object near one, and the pointer snaps to it. You'll understand pretty quickly how smart guides work once you start working with them—they're easier done than said. To start with, try using smart guides to move an object along an axis or to align one object with points on another object. Here's how it works.

To use smart guides to align objects:

1. Make sure View > **Smart Guides** (Cmd-U/ Ctrl-U) is on (has a check mark), and make sure View > Snap to Grid is off.

2. Choose Preferences > (Cmd-K/Ctrl-K) **Smart Guides & Slices** 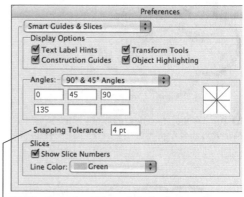. For Display Options, check **Text Label Hints** 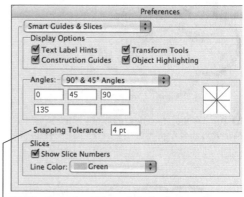, **Transform Tools,** and **Object Highlighting** 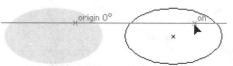, then click OK. (Construction Guides, Transform Tools, and other smart guides options are also discussed on page 475.)

3. Choose the **Selection** tool (V).

4. Do any of the following:

   To use **angle guides** to position an object, start dragging the object—guides will appear as you move it (e.g., at 0°, 45°, 90°). Release the mouse any time the word "**on**" appears next to the pointer, to position the object on that angle. You don't need to hold down Shift to constrain the movement—that's the whole point!

   To align **one object to another,** as you drag an object, position the pointer over the edge (path) of another object, and release the mouse when the word "**anchor**" or "**path**" appears next to the pointer (**1**, next page). You can also drag an object over a point on another object to "pick up" an **angle guide,** then drag along that guide. Or align an object's **center** point or path to the center point or

Use them for finding

Smart guides aren't just used for aligning objects. With **Text Label Hints** checked in Preferences > Smart Guides & Slices, you can use smart guides to help you locate individual points on any object, whether the object is selected or not. With **Object Highlighting** checked, you can use smart guides to locate the edges of objects (e.g., irregularly shaped objects, objects in a group, or objects in a mesh). Object Highlighting works even when View > Hide Edges is chosen.

1 *The **Snapping Tolerance** is the farthest distance the pointer can be from an object for the snap function to work.*

2 *Text label hints and angle guides display when an object is moved along an axis.*

3 *The edge of an object highlights when the pointer is moved over it (mouse button up).*

Interesting angle

You can specify the angles for smart guides in Preferences > **Smart Guides & Slices.** You can choose a predefined **Angles** set from the pop-up menu or you can enter custom angles. If you switch from Custom Angles to a predefined set and then switch back to Custom Angles at a later time, the last-used custom settings will be reinstated.

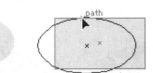

1 *As an ellipse is dragged over the edge of a rectangle, the word "**path**" appears on the unselected object.*

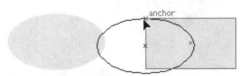

2 *An ellipse is dragged by an anchor point and is aligned with an anchor point on the rectangle (as indicated by the word "**anchor**") on the rectangle.*

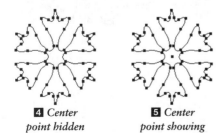

3 *The **Don't Show Center** and **Show Center** buttons on the Attributes palette*

4 *Center point hidden*

5 *Center point showing*

path of another object; the word "center" will appear. *Note:* In order for the center point to show up as a smart guide, the object's center point must be visible (see the next set of instructions).

To align objects by **anchor points,** make sure the object you want to move isn't selected, then position the pointer over one of its anchor points (the word "**anchor**" will appear). Drag the object over an anchor point on another object and release the mouse when the word "anchor" appears on the second object **2**.

You can also align a path of one object to an anchor point or the center point on another object, or align an anchor point of one object to the path of another object.

➤ You can't lock smart guides—they vanish as quickly as they appear. To create guides that stay onscreen, drag from the horizontal or vertical ruler into the artboard (see page 454).

➤ Smart guides display in the same color as Guides, and the color can be changed in Preferences > Guides & Grid.

You drag an object by its center point, and you can also align objects via their center points with the assistance of smart guides. In order to do so, however, the **center point**(s) must be **visible.**

To hide/show an object's center point:

1. Select an object (or objects). Or to show or hide the center point for all the objects in the document, choose Select > All (Cmd-A/Ctrl-A).

2. Show the **Attributes** palette (Cmd-F11/ Ctrl-F11) **3**. **NEW**

3. If the Show Center options aren't visible on the palette, choose **Show All** from the palette menu or click the up/down arrowhead on the palette tab.

4. Click the **Don't Show Center** button **4**.
   or
   Click the **Show Center** button **5**.

5. Deselect the object(s).

Duplicating objects

To **duplicate** objects, you can use any of the following techniques:

➤ **Drag-duplicate** (this page)

➤ The **Clipboard** (page 103)

➤ The **Offset Path** command (page 104)

➤ A **transform** tool (Chapter 11)

➤ The **Layers** palette (page 210)

➤ The **Move** dialog box (page 150)

➤ **Nudging** (sidebar at right)

To drag-duplicate an object:

1. Choose the **Selection** tool (V).

2. Option-drag/Alt-drag the fill or edge of an object (not the bounding box) **1**–**2**. You can release the mouse in the same document or in another document window. The pointer will turn into a double arrowhead. Release the mouse before releasing Option/Alt.

    or

    To constrain the position of the copy to the horizontal or vertical axis (or to the current Constrain Angle in Preferences > General), start dragging the object, then hold down Option-Shift/Alt-Shift and continue to drag. You can also use smart guides for positioning.

➤ To repeat the last transformation (such as drag-duplicate), press Cmd-D/Ctrl-D as many times as you like. To copy and transform an object, see pages 138 and 147.

➤ If you drag-duplicate an object in a group (start dragging with the Direct Selection tool, then continue dragging with Option/Alt held down), the copy will be a member of that group. If you use the Clipboard to copy and paste an object in a group (see page 103), the object will paste outside the group. The Group command is discussed on page 199.

Give it a nudge

Choose the Selection tool, select an object, then press Option-arrow/Alt-arrow to copy the object and move the copy by the current **Keyboard Increment** in Preferences > General. The default increment is 1 pt. To copy the object and move the copy by 10 times the current increment Press Option-Shift-arrow/Alt-Shift-arrow. The arrow key you press determines the direction of the move.

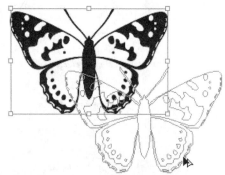

1 *To copy an object,* **Option-drag/Alt-drag** *it. Note the double-arrowhead pointer.*

2 *A copy is made.*

Remembering layers

If you want to paste an object to the top of its own layer or sublayer rather than to a different layer, turn the **Paste Remembers Layers** option on via the Layers palette menu. If this option is on and the original layer is deleted after the object is copied but before the Paste command is used, the object(s) will paste onto a brand new layer.

Hiding the box

On page 139, you'll learn how to transform an object via its bounding box **1**–**2**. In the meantime, if you want to hide (or show) all bounding boxes, choose View > **Hide Bounding Box** (or Show Bounding Box) or press Cmd-Shift-B/Ctrl-Shift-B.

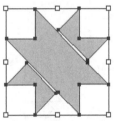 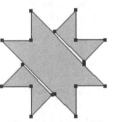

1 *Bounding box on*   **2** *Bounding box off*

If you select an object or a group and then choose the **Cut** or **Copy** command, the object or group will be placed onto the **Clipboard,** a temporary storage area in memory. The previous contents of the Clipboard are replaced each time you choose Cut or Copy.

The **Paste** command places the current Clipboard contents in the center of the active layer in the currently active document window. The **Paste in Front** and **Paste in Back** commands paste an object in its original *x/y* location in front of or behind the current selection; these commands are handy for positioning the Clipboard contents in a particular stacking position.

Objects are copied to the Clipboard in the PDF and/or AICB format, depending on the options currently chosen in Preferences > File Handling & Clipboard (see page 478). The same Clipboard contents can be pasted an unlimited number of times.

To duplicate or move objects between documents via the Clipboard:

1. Open two documents.

2. Select the object or group that you want to copy or move.

3. To place a copy of the object or group on the Clipboard, leaving the original in the current document, choose Edit > **Copy** (Cmd-C/Ctrl-C).
   or
   To move the object or group, deleting it from the current document, choose Edit > **Cut** (Cmd-X/Ctrl-X).

4. Click in the target document, then click a layer name on the Layers palette (see Chapter 15).

5. *Optional:* Select an object to paste the copied object in front of or behind.

6. Choose Edit > **Paste** (Cmd-V/Ctrl-V).
   or
   If you selected an object in the target document, you can choose Edit > **Paste in Front** (Cmd-F/Ctrl-F) or **Paste in Back** (Cmd-B/Ctrl-B).

➤ To copy objects between documents by drag-duplicating, see the previous page.

Duplicate/Move Objects via Clipboard

The **Offset Path** command duplicates a path and offsets the duplicate around or inside the original path by a specified distance. The duplicate is also reshaped automatically so it fits nicely around the original path. The fill and stroke attributes of the duplicate will match those of the original.

To offset a duplicate of a path:

1. Select an object **1**. For your first try, we recommend using a path that has a stroke color and a fill of None.

2. Choose Object > Path > **Offset Path**. The Offset Path dialog box opens **2**.

3. In the **Offset** field, enter the distance you want the duplicate path to be offset from the original path. Be sure your Offset value is larger or smaller than the stroke weight of the original path so the duplicates will be visible. A positive value will create a path that's larger than the original; a negative value will create a smaller path.

4. Choose a **Joins** (bend) style: **Miter** (pointed) **3**, **Round** (semicircular) **4**, or **Bevel** (square-cornered) for the shape of the joints in the duplicate.

5. *Optional:* Change the Miter limit (1–500) value for the point at which a miter (pointed) corner becomes a bevel corner. A high Miter limit creates long, pointy corners; a low Miter limit creates bevel joins.

6. Click OK **5**. The offset path will be a separate path from, and stacked behind or in front of, the original path. And regardless of whether the original object was open or closed, the offset path will be closed.

➤ The Offset Path command can also be applied as an editable effect via Effect > Path > Offset Path (for more about effects, see page 310).

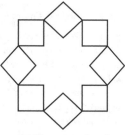

1 *The original path*

2 *In the **Offest Path** dialog box, choose Offset, Joins, and Miter limit options.*

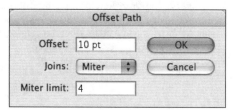

3 *After applying the **Offset Path** with the Joins: **Miter** option*

4 *After applying the **Offset Path** command with the Joins: **Round** option*

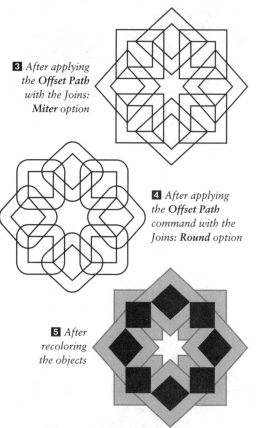

5 *After recoloring the objects*

Offset Path

Aligning and distributing objects

Buttons, point type blocks—anything that's lined up in a row or column—will require aligning and distributing in order to look neat and tidy. With commands on the **Align** ❶ **NEW** and **Control** palettes, it's easy to do.

To align or distribute objects:

1. To align, select two or more objects or groups; to distribute, select three or more objects. Display the **Align** palette (Shift-F7) or the **Control** palette.

2. Turn **Use Preview Bounds** on from the Align palette menu or in Preferences > General to have Illustrator factor in an object's stroke weight and any effects when calculating the alignment or distribution. Turn this option off to have Illustrator ignore the stroke weight and any effects. The stroke straddles the edge of the path, halfway inside and halfway outside.

3. *For occasional use:* Choose **Align to Artboard** from the palette menu to align the objects along the top, right, bottom, or left edge of the artboard, depending

(Continued on the following page)

Align and Distribute

Horizontal Align Right
Horizontal Align Center
Vertical Align Top
Vertical Align Center

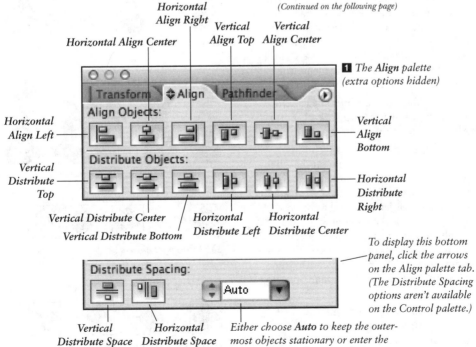

❶ *The Align palette (extra options hidden)*

Horizontal Align Left
Vertical Align Bottom
Vertical Distribute Top
Horizontal Distribute Right

Vertical Distribute Center
Vertical Distribute Bottom
Horizontal Distribute Left
Horizontal Distribute Center

To display this bottom panel, click the arrows on the Align palette tab. (The Distribute Spacing options aren't available on the Control palette.)

Vertical Distribute Space
Horizontal Distribute Space
*Either choose **Auto** to keep the outermost objects stationary or enter the desired distance between objects.*

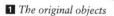

1 *The original objects* ***Vertical Align Center*** **Horizontal Align Center**

on which Align Objects button you click. If Align to Artboard is on and objects are distributed vertically, the topmost object will move to the top edge of the artboard, the bottommost object will move to the bottom edge of the artboard, and the remaining objects will be distributed between them. If objects are distributed horizontally with this option on, objects will be aligned between the leftmost and rightmost edges of the artboard.

4. *Optional:* By default (with Align to Artboard off), and depending on which Align Objects button you click, the topmost, bottommost, leftmost, or rightmost object will remain stationary. To choose a nondefault object to remain stationary, click that selected object now (that is, after all the objects are selected and before you click an align button). To go back to the default object, choose **Cancel Key Object** from the palette menu (the command will become dimmed).

5. Click an **Align Objects** button **1** and/or a **Distribute Objects** button **2**–**4** on the Align palette or the Control palette.

   Or for **Distribute Spacing 5**, choose Auto from the pop-up menu on the Align palette to keep the two objects that are farthest apart stationary (the topmost and bottommost or leftmost and rightmost) and redistribute the remaining objects evenly between them, or enter the exact desired distance between objects (the outermost objects will probably move); then click either of the two Distribute Spacing buttons.

➤ If you change your mind and want to apply a different Align palette option, Undo the last one first.

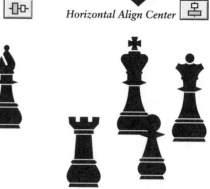

2 *The original objects*

3 *After clicking **Vertical Align Bottom**…*

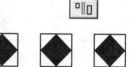

4 *…and then clicking **Horizontal Distribute Center***

5 *The original objects*

Horizontal Distribute Space

In this chapter you'll learn to fill the inside or stroke the edge of an object with a solid color or pattern and choose stroke attributes, such as dashes and joins. You'll also learn how to change a document's color mode; mix and choose colors for print or Web output; save, copy, edit, load, replace, delete, merge, move, and duplicate color swatches; select objects for recoloring; globally replace and edit colors; sample colors using the Eyedropper tool; blend fill colors between objects; invert, adjust, convert, and saturate/desaturate colors; colorize images; and finally, create and modify fill patterns.

Opening the palettes **NEW**

Color palette — Shift-click the Fill or Stroke thumbnail or arrowhead on the Control palette* or press F6

Stroke palette — Click the word "Stroke" on the Control palette* or press Cmd-F10/Ctrl-F10

Swatches palette — Click the Fill or Stroke thumbnail or arrowhead on the Control palette* or choose Window > Swatches

*When opened from the Control palette, these palettes stay open only temporarily.

Related topics

Live paint groups, Chapter 13

Graphic styles and appearances, Chapter 19

Gradients, Chapter 24

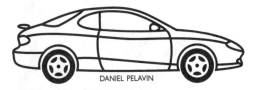
DANIEL PELAVIN

Fill and stroke defined

A **solid color, pattern,** or **gradient** that's applied to the inside of a closed or open path is called the **fill.** The **stroke**—the color that's applied to the edge of a closed or open path —can be a **solid color** (or None), a **dashed** line (Stroke palette), or a scatter, calligraphic, art, or pattern **brush stroke** (Brushes palette). You can't apply a gradient as a stroke.

Colors and patterns can be applied via the **Color** or **Swatches** palette, via buttons on the **Toolbox,** or, as you'll see in Chapter 13, via the **Live Paint Bucket** tool. Using the **Stroke** palette, you can change the stroke thickness (weight), style (dashed or solid), alignment (position on the path), and endcaps.

When an object is selected, its color attributes display on the Toolbox and on the Color, Control, and Appearance palettes. The current fill and stroke colors are automatically applied to any new object you create, and can be stored on the Swatches palette for later use.

Note: Before applying colors, be sure to calibrate your display (see page 60 and Illustrator Help). Also, choose Preview view for your document so you can see colors onscreen as you apply them!

Applying colors quickly

Here are two **quick** methods for **applying color,** just to get the ball rolling. The beauty of Method 1 is that you don't need to choose any particular tool or select any objects.

To apply a solid color via the Color bar on the Color palette:

Method 1 (drag)

1. Click the **Fill** box **1** or **Stroke** box **2** on the **Toolbox** or the **Color** palette. (To display the full Color palette, click the double arrowhead on the palette tab.)

2. Click a color on the **color bar** at the bottom of the Color palette **3**.

3. Drag from the **Fill** or **Stroke** box (whichever box you clicked in step 1) over an object. The object doesn't have to be selected. If an object is already selected, simply clicking a color swatch or a color on the color bar will automatically change its fill or stroke, depending on whether the Fill or Stroke box is active.

➤ Shift-drag to apply a stroke color if the Fill box is active, or to apply a fill color if the Stroke box is active.

➤ You can also apply a color by dragging a swatch from the Swatches palette over an object.

Method 2 (objects selected)

1. Choose the **Selection** tool (V), then select one or more objects.

NEW 2. Shift-click the **Fill** or **Stroke** thumbnail or arrowhead on the **Control** palette **5** to open the Color palette, then click a color on the color bar at the bottom of the palette.

To apply a black or white fill or stroke:

1. Select an object or objects.

2. Click the **Fill** or **Stroke** box on the **Color** palette **1**–**2**, then click the white or black selector at the right end of the color bar on the palette **4** or click the white or black swatch on the **Swatches** palette **6**–**7**.
or
To apply a white fill and a 1-pt. black stroke, click the **Default Fill and Stroke** button (D) on the Toolbox.

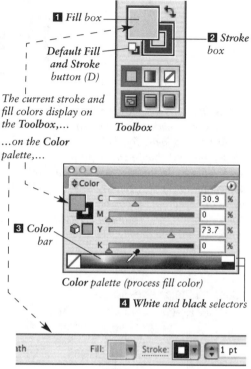

1 *Fill box*

2 *Stroke box*

Default Fill and Stroke button (D)

The current stroke and fill colors display on the Toolbox,...

Toolbox

...on the Color palette,...

3 *Color bar*

C		30.9 %
M		0 %
Y		73.7 %
K		0 %

Color palette (process fill color)

4 *White and black selectors*

Fill: | Stroke: | 1 pt

5 *...and on the Control palette.*

White swatch   *Black swatch*

Swatches   Brushes   Symbols

White

6 *Swatches palette*

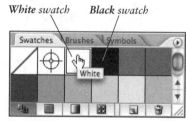

7 *White fill, black stroke, full moon?*

DANIEL PELAVIN

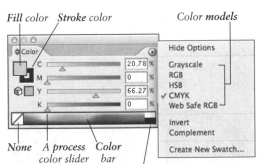

Fill color   Stroke color   Color models

None   A process   Color   Black/white selectors
        color slider bar

1 Color palette features

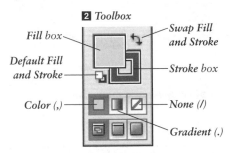

2 Toolbox

Fill box   Swap Fill
                                    and Stroke

Default Fill
and Stroke   Stroke box

Color (,)   None (/)

                                    Gradient (.)

A global process
color has a white   A nonglobal
corner and no dot.   process color   A spot color
                     (see page 112)   has a dot.

None

Show   Show   Show   Show   A gradient
All   Colors Gradients Patterns

A pattern

3 The Swatches palette

Palettes used for applying color

Color palette

The **Color** palette **1**, accessible as a stand-alone palette or via the Control palette, is used for mixing and choosing solid colors. The Fill and Stroke color boxes on the palette display the colors of the current, or most recently selected, object (or new colors chosen when no objects are selected). You can click a color on the color bar or mix a process color by choosing or entering exact percentages. Palette options change depending on whether the Grayscale, RGB, HSB, CMYK, or Web Safe RGB color model is chosen from the palette menu. The color model on the palette can be different from the document color mode (see page 114).

Toolbox

The Fill and Stroke boxes on the **Toolbox** **2**, like those on the Color palette, update whenever the current fill or stroke color is changed (see also page 116).

Swatches palette

The **Swatches** palette, also accessible as a standalone palette or via the Control palette, is used for storing and applying RGB or CMYK process colors (depending on the current document color mode), spot colors, patterns, and gradients **3**. To the default swatches on the palette, you can append additional swatches from other libraries, such as PANTONE. You can also create your own swatches, which save with the current file. Click a swatch to apply that color to all currently selected objects.

Back to nothing

To **remove** a **color, pattern, gradient,** or **stroke** from an object, select the object, click the Fill or Stroke thumbnail or arrowhead on the Control **NEW** palette, then click the **None** button ☑ on the Swatches palette. (Or select an object, click the Fill or Stroke box on the Color palette or Toolbox, then click the None button on either palette.)

Color Palette; Toolbox; Swatches Palette

NEW **Basic coloring steps**

1. Select the objects whose color attributes you want to change **1**.

2. Click the **Fill** or **Stroke** thumbnail or arrowhead on the **Control** palette, or the **Fill** or **Stroke** box on the **Color** palette.

3. Click a color, pattern, or gradient swatch on the **Swatches** palette.
   or
   Choose a color model from the **Color** palette menu, then click the color bar on the palette or choose/enter color percentages.

   (You can also drag a swatch over an unselected object.)

4. Click the word "**Stroke**" on the Control palette, then adjust the stroke weight and other attributes (see pages 118–120).

5. *Optional:* To save the current color as a swatch, follow the instructions below.

Saving colors as swatches

Swatches that are **stored** on the **Swatches** palette save only with the current file.

To save the current fill or stroke color as a swatch:

Drag the **Fill** or **Stroke** box from the Color palette or the Toolbox to an empty area of the Swatches palette to make it the last swatch, or release the mouse between two colors **2** to insert the new color between them.
or
On the Color palette, activate whichever box (Fill or Stroke) contains the color you want to save as a swatch, then click the **New Swatch** button □ on the Swatches palette.
or
To choose options for the new swatch as you save it, Option-click/Alt-click the **New Swatch** button, □ type a Swatch Name, choose a Color Type (Process Color or Spot Color), check or uncheck Global, leave the Color Mode as is, then click OK.
or
To save the color as a **spot** color, Cmd-click/Ctrl-click the New Swatch button, or Cmd-drag/Ctrl-drag from the Fill or Stroke box to the Swatches palette.

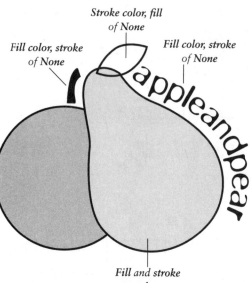

Stroke color, fill of None

Fill color, stroke of None

Fill color, stroke of None

Fill and stroke colors

1 *Fill and stroke combinations*

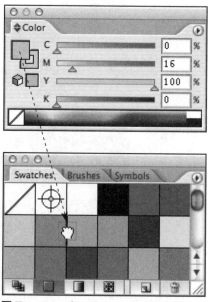

2 *To save a color as a **swatch**, drag it from the Color palette onto the Swatches palette.*

Don't be fooled

Illustrator's **Color Settings** command works with the system's color management software to ensure accurate color matching between CMYK or RGB colors as displayed onscreen and when printed (see Chapter 5). Utilizing monitor and printer device profiles and output intents chosen by the user, this command translates color between specific devices. The profiles can't produce a perfectly reliable onscreen proof, though, so for print output, don't mix or choose process colors or choose spot colors (e.g., PANTONE) based on how they look onscreen, no matter how seductive they appear. Rather, use a **matching system book** to choose spot colors or mix process colors, and run a color **proof** (or two, or even three) of your document.

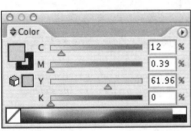

1 *Use the CMYK process color model for print output.*

2 *The "[Registration]" color appears on every plate when a file is color-separated.*

Spot color   Global process color

Color types
Colors for print

Spot colors are used for offset printing; each spot color appears on its own plate after color separation. On rare occasions you might mix a spot color yourself, but normally you'll pick a named, numbered, premixed spot color from a matching system book (e.g., PANTONE). You can use spot colors exclusively if your document doesn't contain any continuous-tone (raster) images—as many spot colors as your budget permits.

➤ If you mix your own spot color, to ensure that it color-separates onto its own plate, double-click the swatch for the color on the Swatches palette, choose Color Type: **Spot Color,** then click OK.

➤ You can achieve a pleasing range of tints using a black plate and a single spot color plate by applying an assortment of tint percentages of the spot color throughout your document.

Process colors are printed from four separate plates: cyan (C), magenta (M), yellow (Y), and black (K). You can enter process color percentages yourself **1** or you can choose premixed process colors from a matching system, such as TRUMATCH or PANTONE Process. (FOCOLTONE, DIC Color, and Toyo aren't commonly used in the United States.)

Process printing must be used for any document that contains continuous-tone images, because it's the only way a range of graduated tones can be printed. Budget permitting, you could use four-color process printing and a spot color plate or two, say, for a logo.

➤ The "[Registration]" color is used for crop marks and the like **2**. If you need to change it (say your artwork is very dark and you need white registration marks), click the Registration swatch, then adjust the sliders on the Color palette.

➤ Double-click a spot color swatch to display its process color breakdown.

Note: By default, Illustrator converts all spot colors into process colors during color separation. To ensure that your spot colors

(Continued on the following page)

Colors for Print

separate properly to their own plates, choose File > Print, click Output on the left-hand side, choose a Separations option from the Mode pop-up menu, and leave **Convert All Spot Colors to Process** unchecked.

To define a swatch on the Swatches palette as process or spot, double-click it, choose **Color Type: Process Color** or **Spot Color,** check or uncheck **Global,** choose a **Color Mode,** then click OK (see the sidebar on page 114).

➤ The Info palette displays the color break-downs for the currently selected object: for the current fill color on the left and for the current stroke color on the right **1**. (If the bottom portion of the palette is hidden, click the double arrowhead on the palette tab.) If two or more objects with different color values are currently selected, no color readouts will appear on the palette.

Global colors

If a process color is **global** (that is, the Global option is checked for that color in the Swatch Options dialog box) and you modify its swatch, the color will update on all objects to which it is currently applied. If you modify a **nonglobal** color (Global box unchecked), that color will update only on currently selected objects. See page 128.

Colors for the Web

For Web viewers whose monitors display millions of colors, you can choose colors freely, with confidence that they'll display accurately. If you must cater to the handful of viewers who still have 8-bit monitors, on the other hand, choose colors using the **Web Safe RGB** color model on the Color palette **2**. Web-safe colors won't shift (substitutes won't be chosen for them) when viewed in a browser. When this model is chosen, the sliders align with the vertical notches.

If you mix an RGB color that isn't Web-safe, the **Out of Web Color Warning** button 🔲 will appear on the palette, and the closest Web-safe version of that color will appear in the little adjacent swatch. You can click the cube or the swatch to convert the color to its closest Web-safe cousin.

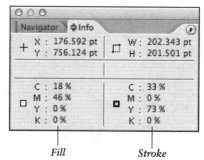

Fill   *Stroke*
1 *Color breakdowns on the Info palette*

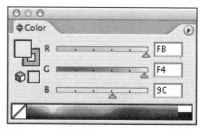

2 *Use the **Web Safe RGB** color model for Web graphics. In this model, **notches** mark the available positions for the sliders.*

Selecting type for recoloring

➤ To recolor **all** the type in a block, highlight it with the Selection tool.

➤ To recolor only a **portion** of a type block, select it with a Type tool.

➤ To recolor a **type object** (not the type), click its edge or fill with the Direct Selection tool. See pages 237 and 239.

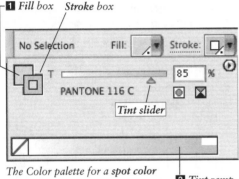

1 *Fill box*   *Stroke box*

The Color palette for a spot color   **2** *Tint ramp*

Tint slider

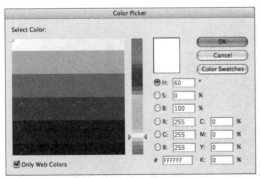

3 *In the* **Color Picker,** *you can enter HSB, RGB, or CMYK percentages. Check* **Only Web Colors** *to choose Web-safe colors.*

Painting paths

To apply a fill or stroke color to an existing path:

1. Select an object.

2. Click the Fill box **1** on the **Color** palette.
   or
   Click the **Fill** thumbnail or arrowhead on the **Control** palette to open the Swatches **NEW** palette; or Shift-click the thumbnail or arrowhead to open the Color palette.

3. Click a color or pattern swatch on the **Swatches** palette. If it's a spot color or global process color swatch, you can move the tint (T) slider on the Color palette or click or drag inside the tint ramp to adjust the percentage of that color **2**.
   or
   Choose a color model from the **Color** palette menu, then move the sliders or enter percentage values (the models are discussed on page 115, step 3).
   or
   Double-click the Fill box on the Color palette, then mix a color using the **Color Picker 3**.

   To choose a color from a matching system, such as PANTONE, see page 117.

4. To apply a stroke color, click the **Stroke** thumbnail on the Control palette, then click a color; or Shift-click the Stroke thumbnail and mix a color. Click the up or down **Stroke Weight** arrow on the Control palette to choose a weight.

To choose a fill or stroke color before drawing:

Deselect all objects, follow the instructions above, then choose a drawing tool and draw. The current Color and Stroke palette attributes will be applied as you use the tool.

➤ You can apply a pattern as a fill or stroke to any object, using a pattern supplied by Illustrator or a pattern that you create (see pages 134–136). (Don't apply a path pattern as a fill, though—it won't look right.) Gradients can't be applied as stroke colors (to work around this limitation, see page 395).

Choose Fill or Stroke Color

Changing the document color mode

When you created your new document, you had the option to choose a Color Mode: CMYK or RGB. The current **document color mode** displays in the document title bar. Any colors you mix or choose in a document automatically conform to that mode.

When you change the color mode, all the colors in the document convert to the new mode. Color shifts may occur, particularly when converting from RGB to CMYK, so we suggest you make a copy of your file first. If you need two versions of a document, one in RGB mode for Web output and one in CMYK mode for print output, copy the file, then change the color mode for the copy.

Note: To reverse a document mode change, don't rechoose the prior color mode. Instead, to restore the original colors, use Edit > Undo.

To change a document's color mode:

1. Use File > **Save As** to create a copy of your file (Cmd-Shift-S/Ctrl-Shift-S).

2. Choose File > Document Color Mode > **CMYK Color** or **RGB Color.**

In the mode

➤ Any process colors you create in a document will conform to the current **document color mode,** regardless of which mode you choose from the Color Mode pop-up menu in the Swatch Options dialog box (see page 133). You can create process CMYK or process RGB colors in a document, but not both.

➤ The Swatches palette displays process and global **swatches** for the current document color mode only.

➤ **Blend** and **gradient** colors conform automatically to the current document color mode.

➤ Placed and pasted **images,** linked or embedded, are converted to the current document color mode automatically.

➤ In the **Rasterize** dialog box, available color mode options will vary depending on the current document color mode.

➤ When a **spot** color is displayed on the Color palette, a current document color mode indicator ⊠ ▯ also displays on the palette. The color mode of a spot color is independent from the document color mode (e.g., you can apply a CMYK spot color in an RGB document).

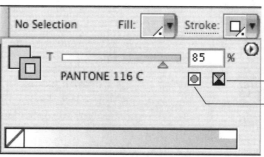

1 *Document color mode indicator (for CMYK, in this case)*

Color type indicator: A circle appears for a spot color (a solid gray square would appear for a global process color).

You can click either of the two indicators on the Color palette to convert a spot or global process color in a selected object to the current **document color mode** (both buttons produce the same result).

1 *If the fill or stroke colors differ among currently selected objects, a **question mark** will appear in the corresponding Fill or Stroke box on the Toolbox, Color palette, and Control palette, but you can go ahead and apply a new fill and/or stroke color to all the selected objects.*

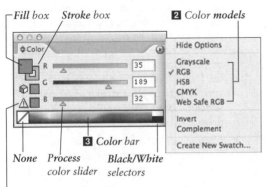

Fill box   Stroke box   **2** *Color models*

3 *Color bar*

None   Process   Black/White
       color slider   selectors

4 *An **exclamation point** will appear if you mix a color that's outside the printable **gamut**.*

What's the gamut?

If an exclamation point appears below the Color boxes on the Color palette **4**, it means the current RGB or HSB color has no **CMYK** equivalent, and thus **isn't printable** on a four-color press. If you click the exclamation point, Illustrator will substitute the closest CMYK (printable) equivalent.

Mixing process colors

Follow these instructions to **mix** your own **process color.** (To apply a color from a color matching system, such as TRUMATCH or FOCOLTONE, see page 117.)

To mix a process color:

I. **Select** the object or objects you want to recolor **1**.
   or
   To choose a color for an object you're about to draw, **deselect** all objects.

2. On the **Color** palette (F6), click the **Fill** or **Stroke** box.
   or
   On the **Control** palette, Shift-click the **Fill** or **Stroke** thumbnail. **NEW**

3. Choose a color model from the Color palette menu **2**:

   Grayscale to convert colors in any selected objects to grayscale, or to choose a gray shade.

   RGB to mix colors for video or Web output.

   HSB to adjust a color's hue (location on the color wheel), saturation (purity), and brightness values.

   CMYK to create process colors for output on a four-color printing press.

   Web Safe RGB to choose colors for Web output.

4. If you don't need to be precise about your color choice, click a color on the color bar at the bottom of the Color palette **3**.
   and/or
   To mix a color using specific color values, move the available sliders (0–255 for RGB; 0–100 for CMYK; 0, 33, 66, CC, or FF for Web). For a CMYK color for print, use values from a matching system book!

5. *Optional:* To save the newly mixed color as a swatch, click the New Swatch button **5** on the Swatches palette.

➤ Grayscale, global, and spot colors that are applied to objects remain associated with their color model. If you click a swatch or an object to which such a color is applied, the Color palette will reset to that color's model.

Mix Process Color

Using color editing shortcuts

➤ To open the standalone Color palette, press **F6**; to open the Stroke palette, press **Cmd-F10/Ctrl-F10** or click "Stroke" on the Control palette. There is no default shortcut for opening the Swatches palette.

➤ To open the Color palette from the Control palette, Shift-click the **Fill** or **Stroke** thumbnail or arrowhead.

➤ Shift-click the color bar on the Color palette to cycle through the color **models.** Or to display the color values for the current color in a different model, choose that model from the palette menu.

➤ To toggle between the Fill and Stroke boxes on the Toolbox and the Color palette, press **X.**

➤ To make the fill color the same as the stroke color, or vice versa, drag one box **over** the other on the Toolbox or the Color palette.

➤ To swap the fill and stroke colors, press **Shift-X** or click the **Swap Fill and Stroke** button on the Toolbox.

➤ To apply a white fill and 1-pt. black stroke, press **D** or click the **Default Fill and Stroke** button on the Toolbox.

➤ If you apply a fill or stroke of None to a path and then decide you want to reapply the last color, click the **Last Color** button on the Color palette.

➤ To invert the current color (produce its opposite on the color scale), choose **Invert** from the Color palette menu; or to convert the current color to its complement within the same color model, choose **Complement.**

➤ If you **Shift-drag** an RGB or a CMYK **slider** on the Color palette, the other sliders will readjust automatically.

➤ To modify the stroke while the Fill box is active, or vice versa, **Option-drag/ Alt-drag** in the **color bar.**

➤ To **select** objects bearing the same paint attributes via a **command,** see page 127.

➤ If the Fill box is active, you can click the **Color** button (<) on the Toolbox **1** to reselect the last chosen solid color; or click the **Gradient** button (>) to reselect the last chosen gradient ; or click the **None** button (/) to apply a fill of None. *Note:* If the Stroke box is active, don't click the Gradient button.

If an object is selected and you click any of the above-mentioned buttons, the last fill or stroke color that was applied to that object will be reapplied (or if you click the None button, the current color will be removed). For example, let's say the Fill box on the Toolbox is active and you want to apply a stroke of None to a selected object. You would press X, then press /.

➤ If you click the Color button on the Toolbox, the Color palette and any other palettes that it's grouped or docked with will display.

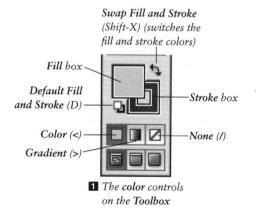

Swap Fill and Stroke (Shift-X) (switches the fill and stroke colors)

Fill box

Default Fill and Stroke (D)

Stroke box

Color (<)

None (/)

Gradient (>)

1 *The color controls on the Toolbox*

Save that color

If you apply a color to a path directly from a library palette that contains colors in a matching system (e.g., PANTONE), the color will be added to the current document's Swatches palette automatically. To save a color from another type of swatch library, such as Pastels or Web, apply it to an object, select the object (at this point the library doesn't have to be open), then drag the **Fill** or **Stroke** box from the **Color** palette to the **Swatches** palette.

Color libraries for print

ANPA colors are used for newspaper printing.

DIC Color Guide and **TOYO Color Finder** colors are used in Japan.

FOCOLTONE is a process color system developed in the U.K to help prevent registration problems.

HKS process colors and HKS spot colors (no "Process" in the name) are used in Europe.

PANTONE process colors and PANTONE spot colors (no "Process" in the name) are used widely in the U.S.

TRUMATCH is a process color system, organized differently from PANTONE colors.

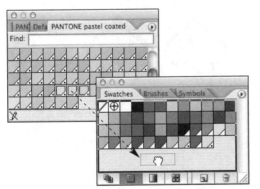

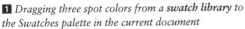
1 *Dragging three spot colors from a swatch library to the Swatches palette in the current document*

Using matching system and Web colors

You can add colors from a **matching system**, such as PANTONE or TRUMATCH, or from the Web palette, to your document's **Swatches** palette. It will be converted to the current document color mode. The Web palette contains 216 Web-safe RGB colors.

To add matching system or Web colors to the Swatches palette:

1. Display the Swatches palette.

2. From either the **Open Swatch Library** submenu on the Swatches palette menu or the Window > **Swatch Libraries** submenu, choose a color matching system (see the sidebar).

3. For some types of libraries, all you have to do is **click** a swatch, and that color will appear on your document's Swatches palette. If this isn't the case with the library you've opened, do one of the following:

   Click a swatch on the library palette (scroll downward or expand the palette, if necessary), then choose **Add to Swatches** from the library palette menu. Or to add multiple swatches, Cmd-click/ Ctrl-click them individually or click, then Shift-click a contiguous series of them, then choose **Add to Swatches.**
   or
   Drag any swatch (or multiple swatches) from the library palette onto your document's Swatches palette **1**.

➤ If multiple swatch libraries are grouped in the same palette and you want to close one of them, drag its tab out of the palette, then click its close box.

➤ You can't modify swatches on a library palette (note the non-edit icon in the palette's lower left corner); the Swatch Options dialog box won't be available. However, you can edit any swatch once it's been added to the Swatches palette.

Changing stroke attributes

Next, you'll learn to change a **stroke's weight** (width), **position** on the path, and **style** (dashed or solid, rounded or sharp corners, flat or rounded ends). First, the width.

To change the width of a stroke:

1. Select one or more objects.

2. On the **Stroke** palette (Cmd-F10/ **NEW** Ctrl-F10) **1** or the **Control** palette **2**:

   Click the **Weight** up or down arrow to widen or narrow the stroke by one unit at a time, or Shift-click either arrow to change the weight by a larger interval.
   or
   Choose a preset value from the **Weight** pop-up menu.
   or
   Enter a **Weight** value (.01 to 1000 pt). *Note:* A stroke narrower than .25 pt. may not print. A weight of 0 produces a stroke of None **3**.

➤ Don't apply a wide stroke to small type —it will distort the letterforms.

➤ You can enter a stroke weight in points (pt), picas (p), inches (in), millimeters (mm), centimeters (cm), or pixels (px). When you click Return/ Enter or Tab, the value will be converted automatically to the Stroke unit currently chosen in Preferences (Cmd-K/Ctrl-K) > Units & Display Performance.

➤ User-defined values remain in effect on the Stroke palette until you either change them or quit/exit Illustrator.

Remember, you can open the Stroke palette by clicking "Stroke" on the Control palette.

NEW To change the position of a stroke on a closed path:

1. Select one or more closed objects.

2. On the **Stroke** palette, click the **Align Stroke to Center** ◻, **Align Stroke to Inside** ◻, or **Align Stroke to Outside** button ◻ **4**–**6**. *Note:* If the buttons aren't visible, choose Show Options from the palette menu.

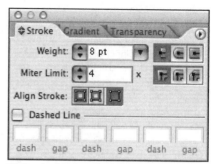

1 *On the **Stroke** palette, enter a stroke **Weight** value, or click the up or down arrow, or choose from the pop-up menu...*

2 *...or do the same thing on the **Control** palette.*

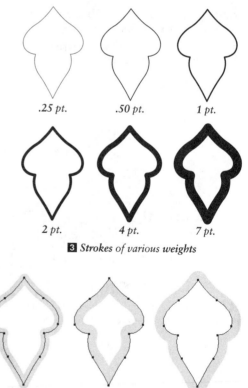

.25 pt.   .50 pt.   1 pt.

2 pt.   4 pt.   7 pt.

3 *Strokes of various weights*

4 *Align Stroke to Center*   **5** *Align Stroke to Inside*   **6** *Align Stroke to Outside*

Stroke Width, Position

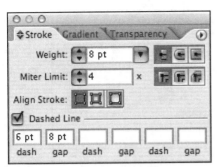

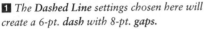

1 The *Dashed Line settings chosen here will create a 6-pt. dash with 8-pt. gaps.*

Weight .6,
dash 8.75,
gap .5, Butt cap

Weight 1.25, dash 5,
gap 10, dash 10,
gap 3.75, Butt cap

Weight 2.5,
dash 15, gap 5,
Round cap

Weight 1.25, dash 0,
gap 3.75, Round
cap and join

Weight 2, dash .5,
gap 12, dash 6,
gap 5, dash 5, gap 3,
Round cap

An appearance with a weight of 3, dash 2.5, gap 3.75, Butt cap; also a separate path with a gray stroke, 3 pt.

Using the **Dashed Line** feature, you can easily create dashed strokes.

To create a dashed stroke:

1. Select an object. Make sure it has a stroke color and its stroke is wider than zero.

2. Display the **Stroke** palette (press Cmd-F10/Ctrl-F10 or click "Stroke" on the **NEW** Control palette). If all the options aren't visible, choose Show Options from the palette menu.

3. Click a **Cap** button for the dash shape (see the following page) **1**.

4. Check **Dashed Line.**

5. Enter a value in the first **dash** field (the length of the first dash, in points), then press Tab to proceed to the next field. If you don't enter values in any other dash fields, the first dash value will be used for all the dashes **2**.

6. *Optional:* Enter a value in the first gap field (the length of the first gap after the first dash), then press Tab to proceed to the next field or press Return/Enter to exit the palette. If you don't enter a gap value, the dash value will also be used as the gap value.

7. *Optional:* To create dashes (or gaps) of varying lengths, enter values in the other dash (or gap) fields. The more different values you enter, the more irregular the dashes or gaps.

➤ To create a dotted line, click the second Cap button, enter 0 for the dash value, and enter a gap value greater than or equal to the stroke Weight.

➤ You can enter a dash or gap value in points (pt), picas (p), inches (in), millimeters (mm), centimeters (cm), or pixels (px). The number will be converted automatically to the Stroke unit currently chosen in Preferences > Units & Display Performance.

Dashed Stroke

To modify stroke caps or joins:

1. Select an object. Make sure it has a stroke color and its stroke is wider than zero.

2. Display the **Stroke** palette (press Cmd-F10/Ctrl-F10 or click "Stroke" on the Control palette). If all the Cap and Join buttons aren't visible, choose Show Options from the palette menu **1**–**2**.

3. To modify the endpoints of a solid line or all the dashes in a dashed line **3**:

   Click the **Butt** (left) **Cap** button to create square-cornered ends in which the stroke stops at the endpoints, or to create thin rectangular dashes. Use this option if you need to align your paths very precisely.

   Click the **Round** (middle) **Cap** button to create semicircular ends or dashes that end in a semicircle.

   Click the **Projecting** (right) **Cap** button to create square-cornered ends in which the stroke extends beyond the endpoints, or to create rectangular dashes.

4. To modify the bends on corner points (not curve points) of the path:

   Click the **Miter** (left) **Join** button to produce pointed bends (miter joins).

   Click the **Round** (middle) **Join** button to produce semicircular bends (round joins).

   Click the **Bevel** (right) **Join** button to produce square-cornered bends (bevel joins). The sharper the angle, the wider the bevel.

5. *Optional:* Change the Miter Limit (1–500) value for the point at which a miter (pointed) corner becomes a bevel corner. When the measurement from the inside to the outside of the corner point becomes greater than the miter limit value times the stroke weight, the miter corner is replaced with a bevel corner. Incomprehensible? Don't worry about how it works; just use a high Miter Limit to create long, pointy corners or a low Miter Limit to create bevel join corners.

➤ Hot tip: You can save a dashed stroke by dragging a path to which the stroke is applied onto the Graphic Styles palette (see pages 300–301).

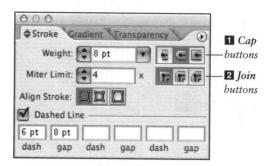

1 *Cap buttons*

2 *Join buttons*

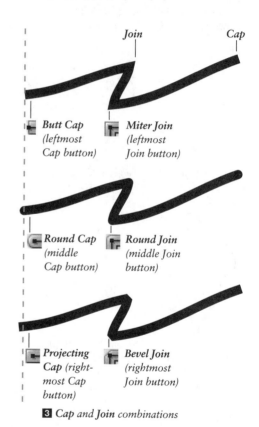

Butt Cap *(leftmost Cap button)*

Miter Join *(leftmost Join button)*

Round Cap *(middle Cap button)*

Round Join *(middle Join button)*

Projecting Cap *(rightmost Cap button)*

Bevel Join *(rightmost Join button)*

3 *Cap and Join combinations*

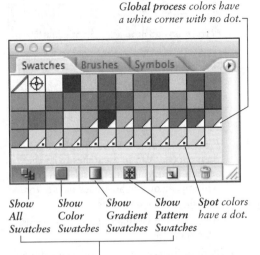

Global process colors have a white corner with no dot.

Show All Swatches · Show Color Swatches · Show Gradient Swatches · Show Pattern Swatches · *Spot colors have a dot.*

1 *Use the "Show" buttons on the Swatches palette to control which categories of swatches are displayed on the palette (here, only the solid-color swatches are displayed).*

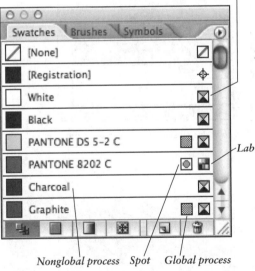

CMYK document color mode

Lab

Nonglobal process   Spot   Global process

2 *The Swatches palette in List view*

Using the Swatches palette

You can control whether the **Swatches palette displays** all types of swatches or only a few categories of swatches, and also whether the swatches are large or small. To show the Swatches palette, click the Fill or Stroke **NEW** thumbnail or arrowhead on the Control palette or choose Window > Swatches.

To choose swatch display options:

1. To control which category of swatches is displayed, at the bottom of the Swatches palette, click one of these buttons **1**: **Show All Swatches** for all types (solid colors, gradients, and patterns); **Show Color Swatches** for solid colors only; **Show Gradient Swatches** for gradients only; or **Show Pattern Swatches** for patterns only.

2. From the palette menu, choose a view for the currently chosen category of swatches: **Small Thumbnail View, Large Thumbnail View,** or **List View.** In List view **2**, the palette also displays an icon for the color's color model.

   ➤ Choose Large Thumbnail View for gradients and patterns, to help you identify them more easily.

3. From the palette menu, choose **Sort by Name** to sort the swatches alphabetically by name.
   or
   Choose **Sort by Kind** to sort swatches into solid-color, then gradient, then pattern groups (use when all the categories of swatches are displayed).

   ➤ To choose a swatch by typing, choose Show Find Field from the palette menu, click in the field, then start typing. A matching swatch, if found, will become selected.

   ➤ If you've chosen different views for the different categories of swatches (solid colors, gradients, and patterns) and you want to force all the categories of swatches to display in the same view, hold down Option/Alt as you choose **NEW** Small Thumbnail View, Large Thumbnail View, or List View from the palette menu.

Whatever swatches you **load** onto the Swatches palette will save with the current file. (To load matching system colors, see page 117.)

To copy swatches between Illustrator files:

1. Open the file that you want to load swatches into, then from the Swatches palette menu, choose Open Swatch Library > **Other Library.**

2. Locate the Illustrator file you want to copy swatches from, then click Open. A swatch library will appear onscreen, bearing the name of the source file.

3. Drag a swatch from the newly opened swatch library into the current document's Swatches palette **1.** To load multiple swatches, before dragging, Cmd/Ctrl click them individually or click, then Shift-click, a contiguous series of them. *or*

Auto copy

If you **drag and drop** an object from one file to another, any global or spot color swatches that are applied to that object will also appear in the target file.

Click the swatch(es) you want to load, then choose **Add to Swatches** from the swatch library menu. The selected color will appear on the Swatches palette for the current document **2.**

If the Swatch Conflict dialog box opens, see page 126.

➤ Pattern library files are stored in Adobe Illustrator CS2/Presets/Patterns; gradients are stored in Illustrator CS2/Presets/Gradients.

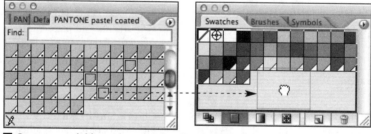

1 *Open a swatch library from another file, then* **drag** *a swatch or swatches from one swatch palette to another.*

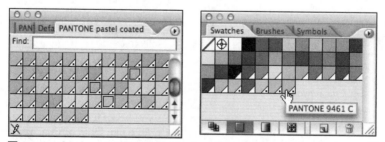

2 *A* **copy** *of each swatch appears on the* **Swatches** *palette.*

Swatches at launch time

If you want to control which colors appear on the Swatches palette when the application is launched, add those colors to the **Startup** file (see page 469).

If you enable the **Persistent** command on a swatch library palette menu, that swatch library palette will reopen automatically when you relaunch Illustrator.

There's no simple, one-step method for restoring the **default swatches** to the Swatches palette. You have to manually drag swatches from either of the two default library palettes.

To restore default swatches to the Swatches palette:

1. *Optional:* To clear unused swatches from your document's Swatches palette before refilling it with the default swatches, choose Select All Unused from the palette menu, click the Delete Swatch button, 🗑 then click Yes.

2. From the Swatches palette menu, choose Open Swatch Library > **Default_CMYK** or **Default_RGB** (depending on the current document color mode).

3. On the Default_CMYK or Default_RGB palette that you just opened, select the swatches you want to restore to your document (click, then Shift-click to select contiguous swatches or Cmd-click/Ctrl-click to select multiple individual swatches).

4. Choose **Add to Swatches** from the library palette menu **1**–**2**.
   or
   Drag the selected swatches to your document's **Swatches** palette.

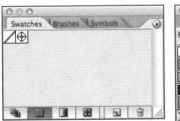

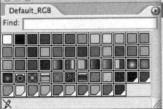

1 *All the Default_RGB swatches are selected, then Add to Swatches is chosen from the palette menu.*

2 *The Default_RGB swatches appear on the current document's Swatches palette.*

To delete swatches:

1. Click the swatch you want to delete. Or click, then Shift-click a series of contiguous swatches or Cmd-click/Ctrl-click individual swatches.

or

To select only the swatches that aren't currently applied to objects in your document, choose **Select All Unused** from the Swatches palette menu. To limit the selection to a particular category (e.g., patterns or gradients), make sure only those swatches are displayed on the palette before choosing Select All Unused.

2. Click the **Delete Swatch** button 🗑 at the bottom of the Swatches palette, then click **Yes 1**.

or

To bypass the alert dialog box, Option-click/Alt-click the **Delete Swatch** button.

or

Drag the swatch(es) you want to delete over the **Delete Swatch** button (you won't get a prompt with this method, either).

➤ If you delete a global process color or a spot color that's currently applied to an object or objects, the nonglobal process color equivalent of the deleted color will be applied to those objects.

➤ To restore a deleted swatch or swatches, choose Undo right away. To restore swatches from a default library or any other library, follow the instructions on the previous page.

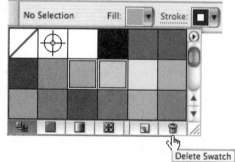

Quick rescue

If you inadvertently delete a solid color, gradient, or pattern swatch that was applied to an object in the current file, you can retrieve it by selecting the object and then dragging the **Fill** box from the Toolbox or the Color palette onto the **Swatches** palette.

1 *Select the swatch or swatches that you want to delete from the Swatches palette, then click or Option-click/Alt-click the* **Delete Swatch** *button.*

Delete Swatches

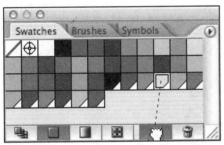

1 *Two swatches are selected, then moved to a new location on the palette.*

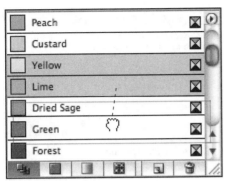

2 *Drag the swatch you want to duplicate to the New Swatch button.*

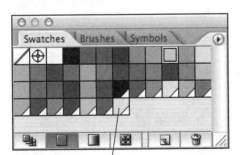

3 *The duplicate appears on the palette.*

To rearrange swatches:

Drag a swatch to a new location on the palette **1**. A dark vertical line will show the swatch location as you drag it. (To move multiple swatches, click, then Shift-click to select contiguous swatches or Cmd-click/Ctrl-click to select noncontiguous swatches, then drag.)

To duplicate a swatch:

Click the swatch you want to duplicate, then click the **New Swatch** button **▣** (or choose Duplicate Swatch from the Swatches palette menu). The duplicate swatch will appear next to the last swatch on the palette.
or
Drag the swatch to be duplicated over the **New Swatch** button **2**–**3**.

➤ If no swatch is selected when you click the New Swatch button, a new swatch will be created for the current fill or stroke color, depending on which box is currently active on the Color palette.

➤ Option-drag/Alt-drag one swatch over another to replace the existing swatch with the one you're dragging.

Rearrange, Duplicate Swatches

If you copy and paste or drag and drop an object from one document window to another, the object's colors will appear as swatches on the target document's Swatches palette. If a global process or spot color on the copied object contains the same name but different color percentages as an existing swatch in the target document, the **Swatch Conflict** dialog box will open **1**. This dialog box will also appear if a conflict arises when you append swatches from one library palette to another between documents.

To resolve swatch conflicts:

In the Swatch Conflict dialog box:

Click **Merge swatches** to apply the swatch of the same name in the target document to the copied objects. Or click **Add swatches** to add the new swatch to the Swatches palette in the target document; a number will be appended to the swatch name (choosing this option will prevent colors in the copied objects from changing).

Check **Apply to all** to have the current Options setting apply to any other name conflicts that crop up. This will prevent the alert dialog box from opening repeatedly.

Normally, if spot colors have the same color percentages but different names, Illustrator will color-separate each color to a separate sheet of film. You can use the **Merge Swatches** command to selectively merge colors into a chosen swatch so it will print from one plate.

To merge spot color swatches:

1. The **first** swatch you select will replace all the other selected swatches, regardless of its location on the Swatches palette. Take a minute to strategize, then select the spot color swatches to be merged. Click, then Shift-click to select contiguous swatches or Cmd-click/Ctrl-click to select noncontiguous swatches **2**.

2. Choose **Merge Swatches** from the Swatches palette menu **3**. If any of the merged swatches were applied to objects in the file, the first swatch you selected for merging will be applied to those objects.

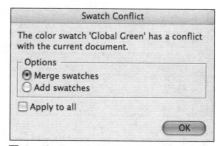

1 *Use the Swatch Conflict dialog box to resolve name conflicts.*

2 *Select the spot colors to be merged.*

3 *The Merge Swatches command merged the selected swatches into the first swatch that we selected.*

Select or ignore tints

If **Select Same Tint %** is checked in Preferences > General, the Select > Same > **Fill Color** and **Stroke Color** commands will select only colors that have the same tint (spot color) percentage as the selected object. With this option unchecked, a spot color in varying tint percentages will be treated as the same color.

1 *Choose from the Select > Same submenu.*

Select	
All	⌘A
Deselect	⇧⌘A
Reselect	⌘6
Inverse	
Next Object Above	⌥⌘]
Next Object Below	⌥⌘[
Same	▶
Object	▶
Save Selection...	
Edit Selection...	

Blending Mode	
Fill & Stroke	
Fill Color	
Opacity	
Stroke Color	
Stroke Weight	
Style	
Symbol Instance	
Link Block Series	

2 *The original group of objects*

3 *All the colors inverted*

Selecting objects by color

To select objects based on their color attributes:

1. Select an object whose paint or other attributes you want to change.
   or
   With no object selected, choose the attributes that you want to search for from the Swatches palette, the Color palette, or the Stroke palette.

2. Choose Select > Same > **Fill & Stroke, Fill Color, Opacity, Stroke Color,** or **Stroke Weight** to select objects with the same paint attributes as you chose in the previous step **1**. All objects with those paint attributes will now be selected. Read the sidebar on this page regarding tint percentages.

3. Now that the objects are selected, you can mix a new color using the Color palette, click a new swatch on the Swatches palette, choose a new Weight or other attributes from the Stroke palette, or perform other edits.

➤ To globally change a spot color or global process color by replacing its swatch, see the next page.

Inverting colors

The **Invert Colors** filter converts multiple nonglobal process colors (but no other color types) in selected objects to their respective color negatives, whereas the **Invert** command converts all color types in selected objects to the inverse of the last chosen fill or stroke color.

To invert colors:

To invert **multiple nonglobal process colors** (fill and stroke), select an object or objects, then choose Filter > Colors > Invert Colors **2**–**3**. The filter doesn't convert spot colors, global process colors, gradients, or patterns.
or
To invert a **single solid color**—spot, global process, or nonglobal process—click an object, click the Fill or Stroke box on the Color palette, then choose **Invert** from the Color palette menu. If you select more than one object, all objects will acquire the inverse of the last chosen fill or stroke color.

Making global color changes

If you need to change a color that's being used on multiple objects, instead of recoloring one object at a time, you can do it globally by replacing the color swatch. When you **replace** one **spot** or **global process color** swatch with another, the color automatically updates in all the objects where it's being used. Tint percentages are preserved.

To replace a swatch globally:

1. Deselect all objects.

2. On the **Color** palette, mix a brand new color (not merely a tint variation of the global process or spot color you want to replace). Then Option-drag/Alt-drag the Fill or Stroke box from the Color palette over the swatch on the **Swatches** palette you want to replace 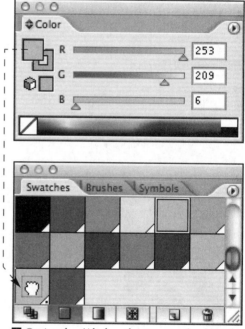.
   or
   On the **Swatches** palette, Option-drag/Alt-drag one swatch over another swatch.
   or
   To edit a **gradient** swatch, use the Gradient palette (see pages 380–381). To edit a **pattern** swatch, follow the instructions on page 135.

When you edit (change the percentages for) a nonglobal process color swatch, the color updates only on selected objects where it's being used. When you **edit** a **global process color,** as in the instructions below, the color updates in all the objects where it's being used, whether they're selected or not. This method also preserves tint percentages.

To edit a color globally:

1. Double-click a global **process** swatch on the Swatches palette. The Swatch Options dialog box opens. Check Preview.

2. Modify the color via the Color Type menu or the Color Mode menu, or by moving the sliders, then click OK. The color will update in all objects where it's being used.

> ### Change without changing
> Sometimes replacing a swatch is just too drastic a step. To globally change a color without changing the swatch from which it originated, use a command on the Select > **Same** submenu to select all the objects that contain that color (see the previous page), then click a new swatch or mix a new color for the selected objects.

1 *Option-drag/Alt-drag the current color from the Fill or Stroke box over the spot or global process swatch you want to replace. The color will update in objects where the color is being used.*

Replace, Edit Colors Globally

Adding color to grayscale

To colorize a grayscale image that you've imported into Illustrator, you can either apply the **Adjust Colors** filter to it, as per the instructions on this page (convert the image to CMYK or RGB), or apply a **fill** color to it (see page 133).

1 Use the **Adjust Colors** filter to adjust solid colors in any kind of object.

Adjusting and converting colors

Use the **Adjust Colors** filter to adjust color percentages or convert color modes in one or more selected path objects; type objects; or opened or placed Photoshop TIFF, EPS, PDF, JPEG, or PSD images—but not in gradients or patterns. To adjust individual PSD layers, convert them into separate Illustrator objects first (see pages 280–281).

To adjust or convert colors:

1. Select the object or objects that contain the colors you want to adjust or convert.

2. Choose Filter > Colors > **Adjust Colors.** The Adjust Colors dialog box opens **1**. Check Preview.

3. Check **Adjust Options: Fill** and/or **Stroke** to adjust one or both of those attributes.

4. If the selected objects contain colors in more than one mode, the sliders will represent the first **mode** that's present, in the following order: Global mode, then either CMYK or RGB mode, then Grayscale mode. Make sure Convert is unchecked, then to **adjust** the colors, move the sliders or enter new percentages in the fields. Only colors in that mode will be adjusted. After you adjust colors in one mode, you can choose another mode and continue adjusting colors. Only color modes that are present in the selected objects will be available on the pop-up menu.
   or
   To **convert** all the currently selected objects to the same color mode regardless of their original mode, check Convert, choose the desired Color Mode from the pop-up menu, then move the sliders.

5. Click OK.

To convert object colors to grayscale mode:

1. Select the object or objects that contain the colors you want to convert.

2. Choose Filter > Colors > **Convert to Grayscale.**

Using the Eyedropper tool

The Eyedropper tool picks up paint attributes from anywhere onscreen. Before using the tool (instructions on the following page), you'll use the **Eyedropper Options** dialog box to control which paint attributes the Eyedropper picks up.

To choose Eyedropper options:

1. Double-click the **Eyedropper** tool. The Eyedropper Options dialog box opens.

2. Expand the **Appearance** list **1**, if necessary, as well as the **Focal Fill** and **Focal Stroke** lists. Check the paint attributes you want the Eyedropper tool to pick up, and uncheck the attributes you want the tool to ignore.

3. Choose a **Raster Sample Size** for the size of the area you'll allow the tool to sample from: **Point Sample, 3 x 3 Average,** or **5 x 5 Average.**

4. Click OK.

Grab a color from another application

In Mac, open the application that you want to sample colors from. Move the window or palette from which you want to sample over to one side of the screen, and move the Illustrator document window so you can see the other application window behind it. Choose the **Eyedropper** tool (I), drag from the Illustrator document window over to a color in another application window or to the Desktop, then release the mouse. The color will appear on the Illustrator Toolbox and Color palette. Save the color as a swatch. Repeat for any other colors. (This technique doesn't work in Windows.)

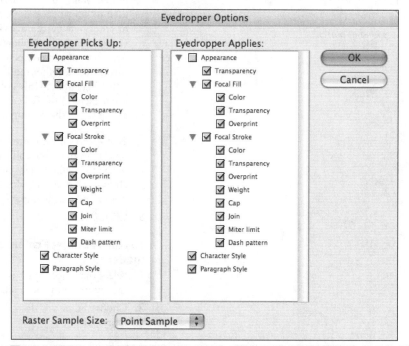

1 *You can customize the* **Eyedropper** *tool via its* **options** *dialog box.*

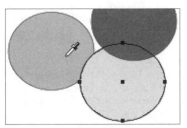

1 *Click with the* **Eyedropper** *tool on the color attributes you want to* **sample.**

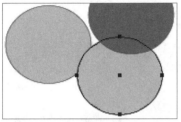

2 *The sampled attributes are* **applied** *to the currently* **selected** *object.*

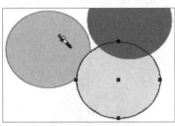

3 *Or* **Option-click/Alt-click** *with the Eyedropper tool to apply attributes* **from** *the currently* **selected** *object to the one you* **click** *on.*

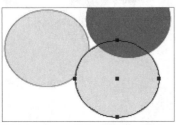

4 *After Option/Alt-clicking with the* **Eyedropper** *tool*

When you click a path or a placed image with the **Eyedropper** tool, it samples the object's paint attributes (not graphic styles), displays them on the Color and Stroke palettes, and applies them to any currently selected objects—all in one step. To control which attributes the tool picks up, follow the instructions on the previous page.

To use the Eyedropper tool:

1. *Optional:* Select an object or objects if you want them to be recolored immediately with the attributes you pick up with the Eyedropper, and also click the Fill or Stroke box on the Toolbox or Color palette.

2. Choose the **Eyedropper** tool (I).

3. Do any of the following:

   Click an object in any open Illustrator window that contains the attributes you want to **sample** **1**. The object doesn't have to be selected.

   To have the Eyedropper tool pick up only the **color** it clicks on (not other attributes, such as the presence or absence of a stroke color) within a gradient, pattern, mesh object, or placed image, **Shift-click** the color.

   If you **selected** any objects before using the Eyedropper tool, the color attributes of the object you Shift-click with the tool will be applied to the fill or stroke of the selected objects immediately **2**, depending on whether the Fill or Stroke box is active on the Toolbox and Color palette.

   Option-click/Alt-click any objects to do **NEW** the opposite of the above: Apply color attributes from the currently selected object to the object you click **3**–**4** (this replaces the defunct Paint Bucket tool).

   ➤ To preserve a sampled color to use again, drag the Fill or Stroke box from the Toolbox or the Color palette onto the Swatches palette.

Eyedropper Tool

Using the Saturate filter

The **Saturate** filter deepens or fades colors in selected objects or placed images by a relative percentage.

To saturate or desaturate colors:

1. Select an object or objects.

2. Choose Filter > Colors > **Saturate**. The Saturate dialog box opens. Check Preview.

3. Move the **Intensity** slider or enter a percentage for the amount you want the color(s) to intensify or fade 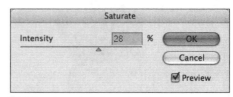. A 100% tint can't be further saturated.

4. Click OK.

Blending fill colors

To blend fill colors between objects:

1. Select **three** or more objects that contain a fill color. Objects with a fill of None won't be recolored. The more objects you use, the more gradual the blend.

   Note: The two objects that are farthest apart (or are frontmost and backmost) can't contain gradients, patterns, global colors, or different spot colors, but they may contain different tints of the same spot color. Objects will stay on their respective layers.

2. From the Filter > **Colors** submenu, choose:

   Blend Front to Back to create a color blend using the fill colors of the frontmost and backmost objects as the starting and ending colors.

   Blend Horizontally to create a color blend using the fill colors of the leftmost and rightmost objects as the starting and ending colors.

   Blend Vertically to create a color blend using the fill colors of the topmost and bottommost objects as the starting and ending colors **2**–**3**.

   Any selected objects that are stacked between the frontmost and backmost objects (or between the leftmost and rightmost or topmost and bottommost objects) will be assigned intermediate blend colors. Stroke colors won't change.

1 *Change a color's intensity via the Saturate dialog box.*

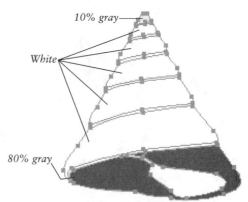

2 *Seven objects are selected.*

3 *After applying the Blend Vertically filter*

Saturate/Desaturate; Blend Fill Colors

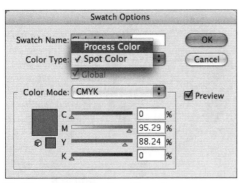

1 *Choose* **Swatch Options.** *Note: For a process color, regardless of whether CMYK or RGB is chosen from the Color Mode pop-up menu, only the option that matches the document's current color mode will be applied when you click OK.*

Quick conversion

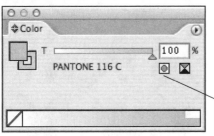

Click this button to convert the spot color on the currently selected **object** *to the current document color mode (CMYK or RGB). The original spot swatch won't change.*

Transparent backgrounds

If you want the background of a grayscale image to be transparent (not opaque white), do the following. Create a layered grayscale image in Photoshop that contains transparent pixels on top of a white Background, and save it in the Photoshop (PSD) format. In Illustrator, use File > Place to import the PSD file, clicking **Convert Photoshop layers to objects** in the Photoshop Import Options dialog box. On the Layers palette, hide the Background object in the newly placed group, then apply a spot color to the selected object.

Converting colors

To convert a process color to a spot color or vice versa:

1. **Deselect** all objects, then mix a color on the Color palette.
   or
   Select the object that contains the color you want to convert.

2. If the color isn't already on the Swatches palette, click the **New Swatch** button ⬛ on the Swatches palette.

3. Double-click the swatch to open the Swatch Options dialog box.

4. Choose **Color Type: Process Color** or **Spot Color 1**, and rename the color, if desired.

5. For a process color, check or uncheck **Global.** If you edit a global process color that's been applied to objects in a file, the color will update on those objects; not so for a nonglobal color.

6. Choose **Color Mode: Grayscale, RGB, HSB, CMYK, Lab,** or **Web Safe RGB.**

7. Click OK.

➤ By default, spot colors are converted to process colors during color separation. To prevent this from occurring, uncheck Convert All Spot Colors to Process in File > Print (Output panel).

Colorizing images

You can **colorize grayscale** EPS, JPEG, PCX, (NEW) PDF, PSD, or TIFF **images** that you open or place in an Illustrator document. Shades of gray will be recolored, and white background areas will remain opaque white (see the sidebar at left).

To colorize a grayscale image:

1. Using File > **Open** or File > **Place,** embed or link a grayscale image, and keep it selected.

2. Apply a **fill** color (not a stroke color) via the Color palette. You can apply a spot color; it will color-separate correctly (see page 111).

➤ You can't colorize a linked EPS image or a grayscale image that's been dragged and dropped into Illustrator.

Creating fill patterns

To create a fill pattern:

1. Draw an object or objects to be used as a pattern 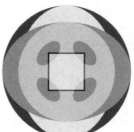. The objects can contain brush strokes or a gradient, mask, blend, mesh, or bitmap image, but keep in mind that simple shapes are less apt to cause printing errors.

2. *Strictly optional:* Apply Filter > Distort > Roughen or Effect > Distort & Transform > Roughen at a low setting to give the shapes a hand-drawn look.

3. Marquee all the objects with the Selection tool (V).

4. Choose Edit > **Define Pattern.**
   or
   Drag the selection onto the **Swatches** palette, deselect the objects, then double-click the new swatch.

5. Type a name in the **Swatch Name** field.

6. Click OK **2**–**3**. You can now apply the pattern to any object's fill or stroke.

You can use a **rectangle** to control the amount of white space around a **pattern** or to crop parts of the objects that you want to eliminate from a pattern.

To use a rectangle to define a fill pattern:

1. Draw objects to be used as the pattern.

2. Choose the **Rectangle** tool (M).

3. Drag a rectangle or Shift-drag a half-inch to 1-inch square around the objects (use the Info palette to check the dimensions). Fit the rectangle closely around the objects if you don't want any blank space to be part of the pattern (use smart guides to assist you) **4**. If the pattern is complex, keeping the rectangle small will help prevent printing errors.

4. On the Layers palette, drag the rectangle path below the pattern objects.

5. Apply a fill and stroke of None to the rectangle if you don't want it to become part of the pattern, or apply a fill color to the rectangle if you do.

1 *Select one or more objects. You can use anything from geometric objects to freehand lines, but from an output standpoint, the simpler, the better.*

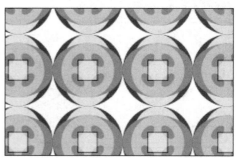

2 *After dragging the selected objects onto the Swatches palette*

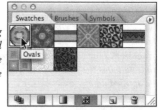

3 *An object is filled with the pattern from figure* **1**.

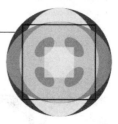

4 *Draw a rectangle around the objects, then send the rectangle to the back.*

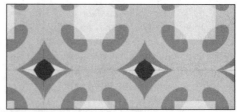

5 *An object is filled with the pattern from the previous figure.*

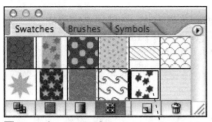

1 Drag the pattern that you want to modify out of the Swatches palette.

2 The original pattern swatch

3 The pattern is modified (then selected and dragged back over the original swatch).

4 The modified pattern, used as a fill

6. Follow steps 3–6 in the previous set of instructions (**5**, previous page).

You can **edit** any **pattern,** including any pattern that's supplied with Illustrator. To change an existing pattern, you first have to drag its swatch back into a document.

Note: Patterns are fun, patterns are beautiful, patterns choke printers. Try to keep it simple.

To edit a fill pattern:

1. Display a blank area in your document window, then drag the pattern swatch out of the Swatches palette **1**. It will consist of a group with a bounding rectangle (with a fill and stroke of None) as the bottommost layer in the group **2**.

2. Modify the pattern objects. Use the **Direct Selection** tool (A) to select individual components **3**. The pattern will be listed as one or more nested groups on the Layers palette.

3. Choose the **Selection** tool (V).

4. Click any object in the pattern; the whole group will become selected.

5. Option-drag/Alt-drag the selected pattern shapes over the original pattern swatch. The pattern will update in any objects where it's already being used **4**.

Note: If you don't want to save over the original pattern, drag the selection onto the Swatches palette without holding down Option/Alt, then double-click the new swatch to rename it. The original swatch won't change, and the pattern won't update in any objects.

➤ Read about transforming patterns on pages 138 and 147.

Edit Fill Pattern

To create a geometric fill pattern:

1. Create a symmetrical arrangement of geometric objects  using the Rectangle, Ellipse, Polygon, Spiral, Star, or any other tool (see Chapter 7).

   To copy an object, Option-drag/Alt-drag it, using a selection tool. Add Shift to constrain the movement horizontally or vertically. Position objects so they abut each other, using the grid, smart guides (see pages 100–101), or the Align buttons (see pages 105–106) to assist you.

2. *Optional:* Apply assorted fill and stroke colors to add variety to the pattern.

3. Choose the **Rectangle** tool (M).

4. Choose a fill and stroke of None, then carefully draw a rectangle around the objects, preserving the symmetry so the pattern will repeat properly ◼.

5. On the **Layers** palette, drag the rectangle listing below the pattern object listings.

6. Marquee all the objects with the Selection tool (V), then drag the selection onto the **Swatches** palette. The pattern can now be applied to any object ◼.

➤ For instructions and pointers on how to create a pattern that repeats seamlessly, see Illustrator Help.

To expand a pattern fill or stroke into individual objects:

1. Select an object that contains a pattern ⑤–⑥.

2. Choose Object > **Expand.**

3. Check **Fill** and/or **Stroke,** then click OK ⑦. The pattern will be divided into the original shapes that made up the pattern tile, and will be nested as groups inside a clipping mask. You can release the mask (it's listed on the Layers palette as <clipping path>), change the mask shape, or delete it altogether.

Shifting patterns

To **reposition** the **pattern** fill or stroke in an object without moving the object itself, hold down ~ (tilde) and drag inside it with the Selection tool.

1 *Draw geometric objects.*

2 *Copy the object(s) and arrange the copies symmetrically.*

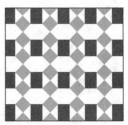

3 *Draw a rectangle, and position it so it will create symmetry in the pattern tile.*

4 *The **geometric** pattern being used as a fill*

DIANE MARGOLIN

5 *The original pattern*

6 *A detail of the pattern expanded (Outline view)*

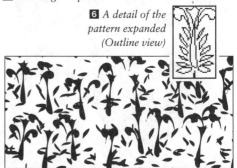

7 *After applying the **Expand** command, releasing the mask, and applying Effect > Distort & Transform > Roughen at low settings*

TRANSFORM

In this chapter, you'll learn a variety of methods for transforming objects, including manipulating an object's bounding box, using the Free Transform tool, using the four individual transformation tools (Rotate, Reflect, Scale, and Shear), using the Transform and Control palettes, and using the Transform Each, Transform Effect, and Move commands.

Transformation tools and commands

The **Rotate** tool rotates an object around its center or around another specified reference point.

The **Reflect** tool creates a mirror image of an object across a specified axis.

The **Scale** tool enlarges or reduces the size of an object proportionally or nonproportionally.

The **Shear** tool slants an object at a specified angle.

The multipurpose **Free Transform** tool rotates, scales, reflects, or shears an object, or applies perspective or distortion.

In addition to the tools listed above, you can also transform an object by dragging the handles on its **bounding box,** or by entering values in the **Transform palette, Transform Each** dialog box, or **Move** dialog box.

Transforming by dragging

The most natural and intuitive method for transforming an object is by dragging with one of the five **transformation tools,** or by dragging the handles on an object's **bounding box.** An advantage to these methods is that you see the results onscreen immediately. Later in this chapter you'll learn how to transform objects by entering numbers on the Transform palette or in the dialog box for each of the individual transformation tools.

The basic method, when dragging with a transformation tool, is as follows: Select the whole object; choose the **Rotate, Reflect, Scale, Shear,** or **Free Transform** tool; position the pointer outside the object; then drag. In this basic scenario, the object will be transformed from its **center** as the reference point.

These are some pointers to keep in mind:

➤ To **move** the **reference point** from which an object is transformed, select the object, choose any transformation tool except Free Transform, drag the reference point **1**, reposition the mouse **2**, then drag to transform the object **3**.

➤ For finer control over the transformation, move the pointer **far away** from the reference point before dragging. You can use **smart guides** (Cmd-U/Ctrl-U) to help you position the pointer on a chosen axis. Try it!

➤ To transform a **copy** of an object, with any transformation tool except Free Transform, start dragging, then hold down **Option/Alt** and continue to drag.

➤ If you transform an object that contains a pattern fill or stroke and **Transform Pattern Tiles** is checked in Preferences (Cmd-K/Ctrl-K) > General, the pattern will also transform. (*Note:* Checking or unchecking this option in the dialog box for a transformation tool automatically resets the preference, and vice versa.)

➤ To transform a **pattern** but **not** the object, with any individual transformation tool chosen except Free Transform, select the object, click to establish the reference point, then hold down ~ (tilde) and drag.

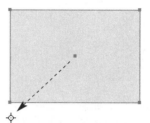

1 *Drag the reference point, if desired, from the center of the object to another location.*

2 *Reposition the mouse.*

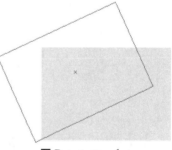

3 *Drag to transform.*

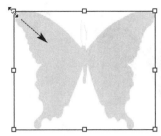

1 *Option-drag/ Alt-drag to* **scale** *an object from its center.*

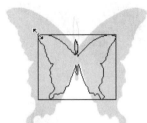

2 *The object is scaled down.*

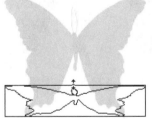

3 *To* **reflect** *an object, drag a bounding box handle all the way across it.*

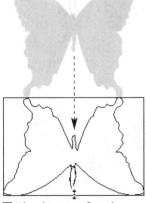

4 *The object is* **reflected.**

One of the fastest ways to **transform** an object is by using its **bounding box.** With this method, though, you can't copy an object or move the reference point.

To transform an object via its bounding box:

1. If bounding boxes are currently hidden, choose View > **Show Bounding Box** (Cmd-Shift-B/Ctrl-Shift-B).

2. Select an object (or objects) using the Selection tool. A rectangular bounding box with eight handles will surround the object(s).

3. To **scale** the object(s) along two axes, drag a corner handle; to scale it along one axis, drag a side handle. Or Shift-drag to resize the object proportionally; or Option-drag/Alt-drag to scale it from its center **1**–**2**; or Option-Shift-drag/Alt-Shift-drag to scale the object proportionally from its center.
or
To create a **reflection** (mirror image) of the object, drag a side handle all the way across it **3**–**4**.
or
To **rotate** the object, move the pointer slightly outside of a corner handle (the pointer will be a curved double arrow), then drag in a circular direction.
or
To **rotate** the object 180°, drag a corner handle all the way across the object (we recommend using smart guides for this).

After you rotate an object by using a tool or by dragging the corner of its bounding box, the bounding box will no longer align with the *x/y* axes of the page. The **Reset Bounding Box** command resets the orientation of the bounding box but not the orientation of the object. It's not always necessary to do this, but it's handy to know how to do it.

To square off the bounding box:

With the object selected, Control-click/right-click and choose Transform > **Reset Bounding Box,** or choose Object > Transform > **Reset Bounding Box.**

The **Free Transform** tool does everything the transformation tools do, plus it also can be used to apply distortion or perspective. However, unlike the other transformation tools, you can't use the Free Transform tool to move the reference point or make copies.

To use the Free Transform tool:

1. Select one or more objects or a group. The Free Transform tool won't make a clone, so copy the object now if you want to transform a copy of it.

2. Choose the **Free Transform** tool (E).

3. To **scale** the object(s) along two axes, drag a corner handle; to scale it along one axis, drag a side handle. Shift-drag to scale the object proportionally; Option-drag/ Alt-drag to scale it from its center; or Option-Shift-drag/Alt-Shift-drag to scale it proportionally from its center.

   To **rotate** the object, position the pointer outside it, then drag in a circular direction. Shift-drag to rotate in 45° increments.

   To **shear** the object, drag a side handle then hold down Cmd/Ctrl and continue to drag **1**–**2**. To constrain the movement, drag a side handle, then Cmd-Shift-drag/Ctrl-Shift-drag. To shear the object from its center, start dragging, then hold down Cmd-Option/Ctrl-Alt and continue to drag.

   To **reflect** the object, drag a side handle all the way across the object. To rotate the object **180°**, drag a corner handle all the way across it. To reflect or rotate it from its center, Option-drag/Alt-drag a side or corner handle. To reflect or rotate proportionally, Shift-drag a corner handle.

   To **distort** the object, drag a corner handle, then hold down Cmd/Ctrl and continue to drag **3**–**4**. *Note:* You can't apply distortion to editable type.

   To apply **perspective** to the object, drag a corner handle, then hold down Cmd-Option-Shift/Ctrl-Alt-Shift and continue to drag **5**–**6**. The perspective will occur along the x or y axis, depending on which direction you drag. *Note:* You can't apply perspective to editable type.

1 *Shearing*

2 *The sheared object*

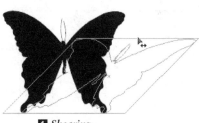

3 *Distorting*   **4** *The object distorted*

5 *Applying perspective*

6 *After applying perspective*

Free Transform Tool

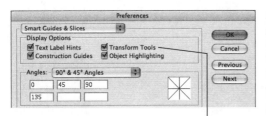

1 *Check Transform Tools in Preferences > Smart Guides & Slices.*

2 *Using smart guides with the Reflect tool*

3 *Using smart guides with the Scale tool*

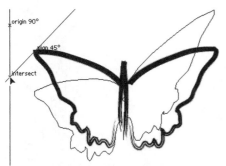

4 *Using smart guides with the Shear tool*

As we showed you in Chapter 9, **smart guides** can be a great help when aligning objects or points onscreen. In these instructions, you'll use them as you **transform** an object.

To use smart guides as you transform an object:

1. In Preferences (Cmd-K/Ctrl-K) > Smart Guides & Slices, make sure **Transform Tools** is checked **1**. You can also choose a different Angles set or enter custom angles, if you like.

2. Make sure View > **Smart Guides** is on (Cmd-U/Ctrl-U).

3. Select the object(s) or group to be transformed.

4. Choose the **Rotate** (R), ⟳ **Reflect** (O), ▨ **Scale** (S), ▦ **Shear**, ▱ or **Free Transform** ▥ tool.

5. As you drag the mouse to transform the object, smart guides will appear onscreen temporarily **2**–**4**. Move the pointer along a smart guide to apply the transformation on that axis (read more about smart guides on pages 100–101).

➤ The rotate angle and other readouts appear on the Info palette as you transform an object.

To rotate, reflect, scale, or shear an object by dragging:

1. Select an object(s) or group.

2. Choose the **Rotate** (R), ⟳ **Reflect** (O), ⧆ **Scale** (S), ⬚ or **Shear** ⬧ tool.

3. Do any of the following:

   To transform the object from its **center,** move the mouse (button up) far away from the center for better control, then drag. To **scale** the object, drag away from or toward it; to **rotate** the object, drag around it; or to **shear** the object **1**–**2**, drag away from it. Use smart guides!

   To transform from a **reference point** of your **choosing,** click near the object (the pointer will turn into an arrowhead), move the mouse (button up) away from the reference point for better control, then drag (**1**–**2**, next page).

   For **reflect,** click to establish a reference point, then click again to define the axis of reflection (or Shift-click to place the second point along the nearest 45° angle) (**3**–**4**, next page).

   To transform a **copy** of the object, start dragging, then hold down Option/Alt and continue to drag (release the mouse first).

   To transform the object along a multiple of **45°** or to **scale** it **proportionally,** start dragging, then hold down Shift and continue to drag (release the mouse button first)(**5**, next page).

   To transform a **copy** of the object along a multiple of **45°,** or to **copy** and **scale** it **proportionally,** start dragging, then hold down Option-Shift/Alt-Shift and continue to drag.

   To **flip** and **scale** the object simultaneously, drag completely across it with the Scale tool.

➤ The **Scale** tool scales an object's stroke weight if Scale Strokes & Effects is checked in Preferences > General, the Scale tool dialog box, or the Transform palette. Checking/unchecking this option in one location resets it automatically in the other locations.

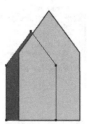

1 *The shadow object is selected.*

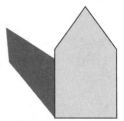

2 *The shadow object **sheared** along the horizontal axis*

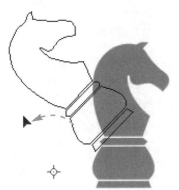

1 *After clicking a point of origin with the **Rotate** tool, the mouse is repositioned, then dragged in a circular direction.*

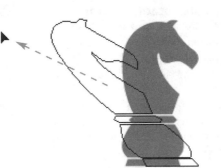

2 *After clicking a point of origin with the **Shear** tool, the mouse is repositioned, then dragged to the left.*

3 *A point of origin is clicked with the **Reflect** tool...*

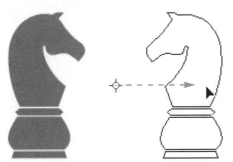

4 *...then the mouse is Option-Shift/Alt-shift dragged to the right.*

5 *After clicking a point of origin with the **Scale** tool, the mouse is repositioned, then Shift-dragged to the upper right.*

Transforming via a palette

Use the **Transform** palette to move, scale, rotate, or shear objects based on exact values or percentages.

To move, scale, rotate, or shear objects via the Transform palette:

1. Select one or more objects or a group.

2. Show the **Transform** palette (press Shift-F8 or click the blue underlined X, Y, W, **NEW** or H on the Control palette).

3. Choose a reference point for the transformation by clicking a handle on the **reference point locator** on the left side of the palette **1**.

4. From the Transform palette menu, choose **Transform Object Only, Transform Pattern Only,** or **Transform Both** (to transform objects and patterns).

5. If you're going to scale the object(s), decide whether you want the **Scale Strokes & Effects** option to be on or off (palette menu). With this option on, the object's stroke and appearances will scale proportionally. This option can also be turned on or off in Preferences (Cmd-K/Ctrl-K) > General.

6. Enter or choose a value as per the instructions below, then apply it by using one of the shortcuts listed in the sidebar on this page.

   To **move** the object **horizontally,** enter a new **X** position. Enter a higher value to move the object to the right, or a lower value to move it to the left.

   To **move** the object **vertically,** enter a new **Y** position. Enter a higher value to move the object upward, or a lower value to move it downward.

   To **scale** the object, enter new **width** and/or **height** values. You can enter a percentage instead of an absolute value. To scale the object **proportionally,** first click the **Constrain Proportions** button 🔒 (a bracket will appear next to the button).

   Enter a positive **Rotate** value to **rotate** the object counterclockwise, or a negative

Applying Transform palette values

Exit the palette	Return/Enter
Apply a value entered in a field and highlight the **next** field	Tab
Apply a value and **rehighlight** the same field	Shift-Return/ Shift-Enter
Clone the object and **exit** the palette	Option-Return/ Alt-Enter
Clone the object and highlight the **next** field (Mac only)	Option-Tab
Repeat the last transformation (after exiting the palette)	Cmd-D/Ctrl-D

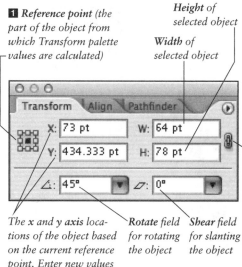

1 *Reference point (the part of the object from which Transform palette values are calculated)*

Height of selected object

Width of selected object

The x and y axis locations of the object based on the current reference point. Enter new values to position the object's reference point at that value on the x or y axis.

Rotate field for rotating the object

Shear field for slanting the object

Constrain Proportions button for scaling objects proportionally

Let the palette do the math

In the W or H field on the **Transform palette,** you can perform simple math to scale an object. Try using any of the following methods:

➤ After the current number, type an asterisk ***** and then a **percentage** value or whole number. For example, to reduce an object's scale by half, click to the right of the current value, then type "*50%" (e.g., 4p would become 2p).

➤ Replace the entire field with a **percentage.** Enter "75%," for example, to reduce the W or H to three-quarters of its current value (e.g., 4p becomes 3p).

➤ Enter a **positive** or **negative** value to the right of the current number, as in "+2" or "-2," to increase or decrease the current value, respectively, by that amount.

Press **Tab** to apply the math and advance to the next field, or press **Return/Enter** to apply the math and exit the palette.

value to rotate it clockwise. Or choose a preset rotation angle from the pop-up menu.

To shear (slant) the object to the right, enter or choose a positive **Shear** value. To shear an object to the left, enter or choose a negative Shear value.

7. From the palette menu, you can also choose **Flip Horizontal** or **Flip Vertical.**

➤ To apply a transformation as an editable and removable effect, see page 149.

➤ If Use Preview Bounds is checked in Preferences (Cmd-K/Ctrl-K) > General, the full dimensions of an object, including its stroke and any effects, will be listed in the Width and Height fields on the Transform, Control, and Info palettes.

To move an object or group via the (NEW) Control palette:

1. Select an object or group.

2. In the X (horizontal) and or Y (vertical) field on the Control palette **1**, enter the desired axis locations for the object.

Repeating a transformation

Once you've applied a transformation to an object by any method, via the **Transform Again** command you can quickly apply the same transformation (using the last-used values) to any selected object. Note that if you copy an object while transforming it and then choose Transform Again, the result will be a transformed copy.

To repeat a transformation:

1. Select one or more objects or a group, then transform it via a tool, a palette, or by dragging **2**.

2. Keep the object selected, or select another object or group.

3. Control-click/right-click and choose Transform > **Transform Again** (Cmd-D/Ctrl-D) **3**.

➤ To apply transformations at a custom angle, enter a Constrain Angle in Preferences (Cmd-K/Ctrl-K) > General.

X: ▲▼ 200 pt   Y: ▲▼ 180.4258 p   W: ▲▼ 380

1 On the **Control** palette, enter the desired X and/or Y location for an object or group.

2 An object is copy-rotated...

3 ...and then the Transform Again command is applied twice (Cmd-D/Ctrl-D).

Transforming via a dialog box

An advantage to using a dialog box to transform an object versus using a tool is that you can enter values and/or copy the object as it's transformed. The **Rotate, Reflect, Scale,** and **Shear** tools each have their own **dialog box.** (For the Move dialog box, see page 150.)

To rotate, reflect, scale, or shear an object via a dialog box:

1. Select one or more objects or a group.

2. To transform the object from its center, double-click the **Rotate,** ⟳ **Reflect** (on the Rotate tool pop-out menu), ⟲ **Scale,** ⬚ or **Shear** ⬚ tool. The default reference point at the object's center will now be visible.

   or

   To transform the object from its center, Control-click/right-click in the document window and choose **Rotate, Scale, Reflect,** or **Shear** from the Transform submenu on the context menu.

   or

   To transform the object from a reference point of your choosing, choose the **Rotate, Reflect** (O), **Scale** (S), or **Shear** tool, then Option-click/Alt-click on or near the object.

3. A dialog box will open. Check Preview.

4. For **Rotate** **1**, enter a positive **Angle** (then press Tab) to rotate the object counterclockwise or a negative Angle to rotate it clockwise (−360 to 360).

   For **Reflect** **2**, click Axis: **Horizontal** or **Vertical** (the axis the mirror image will flip across). Or enter an **Angle** (360 to −360) for the object to flip over, then press Tab. A positive value is measured counterclockwise from the horizontal *(x)* axis; a negative value is measured clockwise from the horizontal axis.

   For **Scale** **3**, to scale the object proportionally, click **Uniform,** enter a Scale percentage (−20000 to 20000!), then press Tab to apply. Or to scale the object nonproportionally, click **Non-Uniform,**

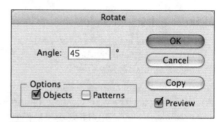

1 *Enter an **Angle** in the **Rotate** dialog box.*

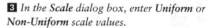

2 *In the **Reflect** dialog box, click **Horizontal** or **Vertical** or enter an **Angle.***

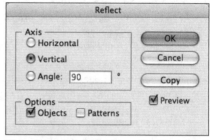

3 *In the **Scale** dialog box, enter **Uniform** or **Non-Uniform** scale values.*

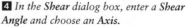

4 *In the **Shear** dialog box, enter a **Shear Angle** and choose an **Axis.***

Get the numbers

A transformation dialog box will continue to display the **last-used** values for that type of transformation—whether a tool or a dialog box was used—until the values are changed or you quit/exit Illustrator.

Get an angle on it

When transforming objects, the default **Horizontal** angle is **0°** and the default **Vertical** angle is **90°**. The default starting point for measuring the degree of an angle is the horizontal *(x)* axis (the three o'clock position). You can enter a custom **Constrain Angle** in Preferences > General.

1 *The original object*

2 *The object scaled **uniformly**, Patterns box **checked***

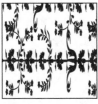 

3 *The original object scaled **non-uniformly**, Patterns box **checked***

4 *The original object scaled **non-uniformly**, Patterns box **unchecked***

enter Horizontal and Vertical percentages, then press Tab to apply. *Note:* Enter 100 to leave a dimension unchanged. *Optional:* Check **Scale Strokes & Effects** to also scale the stroke width(s) and any effects applied via the Effects menu by the same percentage. (This option can also be chosen in Preferences > General and on the Transform palette menu; checking or unchecking this option in one location automatically resets it in the others.)

For **Shear** (**4**, previous page), enter a Shear Angle (360 to −360), then press Tab. Next, click Axis: **Horizontal** or **Vertical** (the axis along which the object will be sheared, or slanted); or click Axis: **Angle,** enter an Angle value, then press Tab. The angle will be calculated clockwise relative to the horizontal *(x)* axis.

5. *Optional:* Check **Patterns** if the object contains a pattern fill and/or stroke and you want the pattern(s) to scale with the object **1**–**4**, or uncheck **Objects** to scale only the pattern and not the object.

6. Click **Copy** to transform a copy of the object (not the original object).
or
Click OK to transform the **original** object.

➤ If you clicked Copy in a transformation tool dialog box, you can Control-click/right-click and choose Transform > Transform Again (Cmd-D/Ctrl-D) as many times as you like to create more transformed copies of the original object(s), or of any other selected objects, using the last-used values for that type of transformation. See page 145.

The Transform Each command modifies one or more selected objects relative to their individual center points. The transformation tools, by contrast, transform multiple objects relative to a single, common reference point **1**. To make your artwork look less regular and more hand-drawn, apply the Transform Each command to a bunch of objects with the Random option checked.

The original formation

The formation rotated 15° via the Rotate tool

To perform multiple transformations via the Transform Each command:

1. Select one or more objects (preferably two or more). Objects in a group can't be transformed individually.

2. Control-click/right-click and choose Transform > **Transform Each** (Cmd-Option-Shift-D/Ctrl-Alt-Shift-D), or choose Object > Transform > **Transform Each.**

The formation rotated 15° via the **Transform Each** command with the **Random** option **unchecked**

1 The Transform Each command vs. the Rotate tool

3. Check Preview, and move the dialog box out of the way, if necessary.

4. Do any of the following **2**:

   Move the Horizontal or Vertical **Scale** slider (or enter a percentage then press Tab) to scale the objects horizontally and/or vertically from their reference points.

   Choose a higher Horizontal **Move** value to move the objects to the right or a lower value to move them to the left; and/or choose a higher Vertical Move value to move the objects upward, or vice versa.

   Enter a **Rotate: Angle** value and press Tab, or rotate the dial.

   Check the **Reflect X** or **Reflect Y** box to create a mirror reflection of the objects.

   Check **Random** to have Illustrator apply random transformations within the range of the values that you've chosen for Scale, Move, or Rotate. For example, at a Rotate Angle of 35°, a different angle between 0° and 35° will be used for each selected object. Uncheck and recheck Preview to get different random effects.

   Click a different **reference point** (the point transformations are calculated from).

5. Click OK or Copy (**1**–**2**, next page).

2 The Transform Each dialog box

Reference point

Transform Each

1 *The original objects*

2 *After applying the* **Transform Each** *command using these values: Horizontal Scale 120, Vertical Scale 80 (note the nonmatching Horizontal and Vertical Scale values), Horizontal Move 13, Vertical Move –13, and Rotate 17°.*

Transform Effect

Scale
Horizontal: `130` %
Vertical: `100` %

OK
Cancel

`5` copies

Move
Horizontal: `–24 pt`
Vertical: `0 pt`

☐ Reflect X
☐ Reflect Y

Rotate
Angle: `54` °

☐ Random
☑ Preview

3 *Use the* **Transform Effect** *dialog box to apply editable effects.*

Appearance | Graphic Styles

▣ Path

Stroke: ▣ 1 pt
Fill: ▣

Transform
Default Tran: Double–click to edit effect

4 *To edit a transform effect, double-click the* **Transform** *listing on the* **Appearance** *palette.*

If you apply transformations via the **Transform Effect** dialog box, you will be able to edit (not just undo) those transformations long after you've closed the dialog box, and even after you close and reopen the file!

To use the Transform Effect command to apply editable effects:

1. Select one or more objects.

2. Choose Effect > Distort & Transform > **Transform**.

3. The Transform Effect dialog box looks and behaves just like the Transform Each dialog box, with one exception: In the Transform Effect dialog box, you can specify how many copies you want **3**. Follow the instructions for the Transform Each dialog box on the previous page.

4. To edit the transformation after you click OK, select the object, then double-click Transform on the Appearance palette **4** to reopen the Transform Effect dialog box. This is a sneak preview of what's to come in Chapter 19, Appearances & Styles.

You can precisely reposition an object by entering values in the **Move** dialog box. Move dialog box settings remain the same until you change them, move an object using the mouse, or use the Measure tool, so you can repeat the same move as many times as you like using the Transform Again shortcut (Cmd-D/Ctrl-D)—even on another object.

To move an object via a dialog box:

1. *Optional:* Choose a lower zoom level for your document so the object won't disappear from view when it's moved.

2. Choose the **Selection** tool (V).

3. Select the object you want to move.

4. Double-click the **Selection** or **Direct Selection** tool.
   or
   Control-click/right-click and choose Transform > **Move** from the context menu 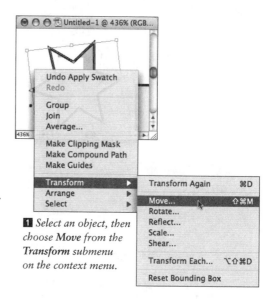.
   or
   Choose Object > Transform > **Move** (Cmd-Shift-M/Ctrl-Shift-M).

5. In the Move dialog box, check Preview 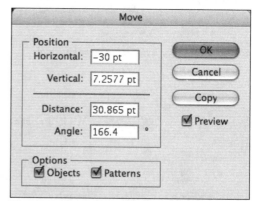.

6. Press Tab to preview these changes:

   Enter positive **Horizontal** and **Vertical** values to move the object to the right and upward, respectively; enter negative values to move the object to the left or downward; or enter a combination of positive and negative values. Enter 0 in either field to prevent the object from moving along that axis. You can use any of these units of measure: p, pt, in, mm, q, or cm.
   or
   Enter a positive **Distance** and a positive **Angle** between 0 and 180 to move the object upward; enter a positive Distance and a negative Angle between 0 and –180 to move the object downward. The other fields will change automatically. (Angle values don't cause rotation.)

7. *Optional:* Click Copy to close the dialog box and move a copy of the object (not the object itself). For the Options, see the sidebar on this page.

8. Click OK.

Shifting patterns

If you move an object that contains a pattern fill manually or by using the Move dialog box, and **Patterns** is unchecked in the Move dialog box, the object will move but not the pattern. If Patterns is checked but **Objects** is not and you use the Move command, the pattern position will shift but not the object.

1 *Select an object, then choose* **Move** *from the* **Transform** *submenu on the context menu.*

2 *In the* **Move** *dialog box, enter Horizontal and Vertical values or enter the Distance and Angle you want the object to move.*

RESHAPE 12

In Chapter 7 you learned how to draw closed and open geometric paths without thinking about their individual components. In this important chapter, you'll learn how to reshape paths by manipulating the nuts and bolts that all paths are composed of: direction lines, direction points, anchor points, and segments. Once you learn how to alter the profile of an object by changing the number, position, or type (smooth or corner) of anchor points on its path, you'll be able to create just about any shape imaginable.

In addition, you'll also learn how to quickly reshape all or part of a path with the Erase, Pencil, Paintbrush, Smooth, and Reshape tools; average anchor points; join endpoints; combine paths; split paths; cut paths using the Divide Objects Below command; and carve away parts of a path using the Knife tool. We've also included three practice exercises.

The path building blocks

Paths can be open or closed, and consist of anchor points connected by straight and/or curved **segments** **1**. **Smooth** anchor points have a pair of direction lines that move in tandem; **corner** anchor points have no direction lines, one direction line, or a pair of direction lines that move independently. At the end of each **direction line** is a **direction point** that controls the shape of the curve **2**–**3**.

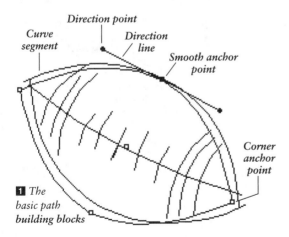

Direction point

Curve segment

Direction line

Smooth anchor point

Corner anchor point

1 The basic path building blocks

2 The **angle** of a direction line affects the **slope** of the curve into the anchor point.

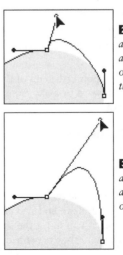

3 The **length** of a direction line affects the **height** of the curve.

Moving points and segments

If you **move** an **anchor point,** the segments that are connected to it will reshape. If you move a **curve segment,** the curve will reshape but the connecting anchor points will remain stationary. And if you move a **straight segment,** connecting anchor points will also move.

To move an anchor point or a segment:

1. Choose the **Direct Selection** tool (A).
   Note: You can move more than one point at a time, even if they're on different paths. To select them, Shift-click them individually or drag a marquee around them.

2. **Drag** an anchor **point** **1**; or **drag** the middle of a **segment** **2**; or **click** an anchor **point** or **segment,** then press an arrow key. You can use smart guides for positioning.

➤ To constrain the movement to a multiple of 45°, click an anchor point or segment, then Shift-drag.

➤ If all the anchor points on a path are selected, you won't be able to move any individual points or segments. Deselect the object, then try again.

Reshaping curves

In the instructions above, you learned that you can drag a curve segment or an anchor point to reshape a curve. A more precise way to **reshape** a **curve** is to lengthen, shorten, or change the angle of its direction lines.

To reshape a curve segment:

1. Choose the **Direct Selection** tool (A).

2. Click an anchor point or a curve segment **3**.

3. **Drag** a **direction point** (the end of the direction line) toward or away from the anchor point **4**.
   or
   Rotate the **direction point** around the anchor point. You can use Shift to constrain the angle, or use smart guides for positioning.

➤ Direction line antennae on a smooth point always rotate in tandem, and stay in a straight line even if you move the segment or anchor point they're connected to.

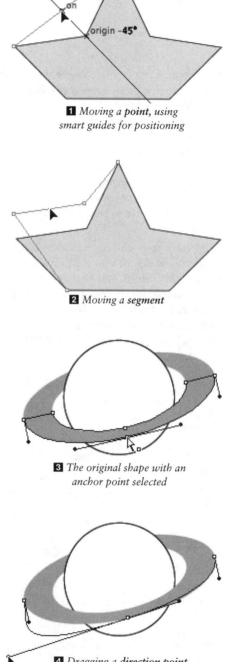

1 *Moving a point, using smart guides for positioning*

2 *Moving a segment*

3 *The original shape with an anchor point selected*

4 *Dragging a direction point away from its anchor point*

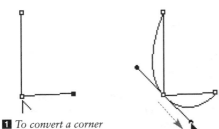

1 *To convert a corner point into a smooth point, click with the* **Convert Anchor Point** *tool on the anchor point...*

2 *...then drag away from the point.*

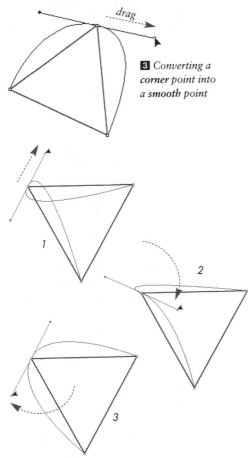

drag

3 *Converting a* **corner** *point into a* **smooth** *point*

1

2

3

4 *If the curve twists around the anchor point, rotate the direction line to untwist it.*

Converting points

To convert a corner anchor point into a smooth anchor point:

1. Choose the **Convert Anchor Point** tool. It's on the Pen tool pop-out menu. (Shift-C is the shortcut, but it works better for right-handed mousers than left-handed mousers—grrr...).
   or
   Choose the **Pen** tool (P).

2. Cmd-click/Ctrl-click the edge of the object to display its anchor points.

3. If you're using the Convert Anchor Point tool, click, then drag away from an anchor point **1**–**2**. Direction lines will appear as you drag. If you're using the Pen tool, do the same thing with Option/Alt held down. You can use smart guides to help you align direction lines.

4. *Optional:* To further modify the curve, choose the Direct Selection tool (A), then drag the anchor point or either of its direction lines **3**.

   Note: If the new curve segment twists around the anchor point as you drag, keep the mouse button down, rotate the direction line back around the anchor point to undo the twist, then drag in the desired direction **4**.

➤ To reshape paths by using a vector filter, try Filter > Stylize > Round Corners, or to reshape paths by using a removable effect, try Effect > Stylize > Round Corners (to remove the rounded corners, remove the effect).

Tearoff toolbar

While you're practicing the techniques in this chapter, we recommend tearing off the toolbar for the **Pen** tool **5** so the Pen and its related tools are visible and easily accessible. Once you memorize the shortcuts for accessing these tools, you won't need to use the toolbar.

5 *Tearoff toolbar for the* **Pen** *tool*

Convert Corner Point to Smooth

To convert a smooth anchor point into a corner anchor point:

1. Choose the **Convert Anchor Point** tool (Shift-C).

   or

   Choose the **Pen** tool (P).

2. Cmd-click/Ctrl-click the edge of an object to display its anchor points.

3. If you're using the Convert Anchor Point tool, click a smooth point—don't drag! Its direction lines will disappear **1**–**2**. If you're using the Pen tool, do the same thing with Option/Alt held down.

In these instructions, you'll learn how to convert a point so its **direction lines,** instead of remaining in a straight line, can be **rotated independently** of each other.

To rotate direction lines independently:

1. Choose the **Direct Selection** tool (A).

2. Click the edge of an object to display its anchor points, then click a point **3**.

3. Choose the **Convert Anchor Point** tool (Shift-C).

   or

   Choose the **Pen** tool (P) and hold down Option/Alt.

4. Drag a direction point at the end of one of the direction lines. The curve segment will reshape as you drag **4**. Release Option/Alt, if it's pressed down.

5. Choose the Direct Selection tool (if it's not already chosen), click the anchor point, then drag the other direction line for that anchor point **5**.

➤ To restore independently rotating direction line antennae back to their original straight-line alignment and produce a smooth, unpinched curve segment, choose the Convert Anchor Point tool, then click and drag away from the anchor point (if you just click on it instead, you'll create a corner).

1 *Click with the* **Convert Anchor Point** *tool on a smooth point...*

2 *...to convert it into a corner point.*

3 *A point is selected on an object.*

4 *A* **direction line** *is moved independently using the* **Convert Anchor Point** *tool.*

5 *The second* **direction line** *is moved.*

Nice curves

It's hard to get a symmetrical curve if you place points at the high point of a curve.

*You'll get a more symmetrical curve by placing points only at the **ends**.*

1 *Click a segment to **add a new point**...*

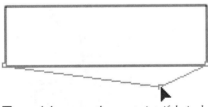

2 *...and then **move** the new point, if desired.*

Adding points

Another way to reshape a path is by manually **adding anchor points** to or **deleting anchor points** from it. A closed path will stay closed.

To add anchor points to a path manually:

1. Choose the **Selection** tool (V), then select the object you want to add a point or points to.

2. Choose the **Add Anchor Point** tool (+). It's on the Pen tool pop-out menu.
   or
   Choose the **Pen** tool (P). Also make sure Disable Auto Add/Delete is unchecked in Preferences > General.

3. Click the edge of the object. A new, selected anchor point will appear **1**. Repeat, if desired, to add more points.

   An anchor point that's added to a curve segment will be a smooth point with direction lines; an anchor point that's added to a straight segment will be a corner point.

4. *Optional:* Use the Direct Selection tool (A) to move the new anchor point or its direction lines **2**.

➤ If you don't click precisely on a segment with the Add Anchor Point tool, an alert dialog box may appear. Click OK, then try again.

➤ Hold down Option/Alt to use the Delete Anchor Point tool when the Add Anchor Point tool is selected, and vice versa.

Add Anchor Points

The **Add Anchor Points** command inserts one point midway between every pair of existing anchor points in a selected object.

To add anchor points to a path via a command:

1. Choose the **Selection** tool (V), then select the object or objects that you want to add points to.

2. Choose Object > Path > **Add Anchor Points** . Repeat, if desired.

1 *The original object*

Handy shortcuts

Pen tool	P
Add Anchor Point tool	+
Delete Anchor Point tool	-
Convert Anchor Point tool	Shift-C
Pencil tool	N
Paintbrush tool	B
Scissors tool	C
Lasso tool	Q
Pen tool to Convert Anchor Point tool	Option/Alt
Disable Auto Add/Delete function of Pen tool	Shift
Pen tool to last-used selection tool	Cmd/Ctrl
Add Anchor Point tool to Delete Anchor Point tool, and vice versa	Option/Alt
Pencil or Paintbrush tool to Smooth tool	Option/Alt
Average endpoints	Cmd-Option-J/ Ctrl-Alt-J
Join endpoints	Cmd-J/Ctrl-J
Average and join endpoints	Cmd-Option-Shift-J/ Ctrl-Alt-Shift-J

2 *After applying the **Add Anchor Points** command to the original object and then applying Filter > Distort > Pucker & Bloat (Pucker –70%)*

DIANE MARGOLIN

3 *After reapplying the **Add Anchor Points** command, and applying the Pucker & Bloat filter (Bloat 70%)*

1 *The Paintbrush pointer is positioned over an endpoint of an arc.*

2 *An addition to the path is made.*

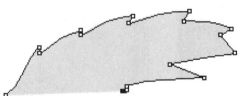

3 *The pointer is positioned over an endpoint. Note the slash next to the pen icon.*

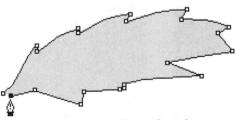

4 *After the endpoint is clicked, it becomes solid.*

5 *New points are then added to the path.*

You can use the **Pencil** to **add** to any **open** **NEW** **path,** regardless of which tool was used to draw the path initially; the path can have an applied brush stroke. Alternatively, you can use the **Paintbrush** tool to add to any path that has an applied brush stroke. An addition made with either tool will automatically adopt the attributes of the existing path.

To add to an open path with the Pencil or Paintbrush tool:

1. Choose the **Selection** tool (V), then select an open path.

2. Choose the **Pencil** tool (N), or if the path has a brush stroke, you can choose the **Paintbrush** tool (B).

3. Position the pointer directly over an endpoint, then draw an addition to it **1**. When you release the mouse, the path will remain selected **2**.

➤ If you end up with a separate path instead of an addition to an existing path, delete the new path and try again.

To add to an open path with the Pen tool:

1. Choose the **Pen** tool (P).

2. Position the pointer over the **endpoint** of the path that you want to add a segment to (the path doesn't have to be selected). A slash will appear next to the Pen pointer when the tool is positioned correctly **3** (use smart guides!).

3. Click the endpoint to make it a corner point or drag from it to make it a smooth point. The point will become solid **4**.

4. Position the pointer where you want the additional anchor point to appear.

5. If desired, continue to click to create more corner points or drag to create more smooth points **5**. Choose another tool when you're done.

➤ To use the Pen tool to close a path or join two separate paths, see page 166.

Add to Path with Pencil, Paintbrush, Pen

Deleting points

To delete anchor points from a path:

1. Choose the **Delete Anchor Point** tool (-). It's on the Pen tool pop-out menu.

   or

   Choose the **Pen** tool (P). Also make sure Disable Auto Add/Delete is unchecked in Preferences > General.

2. Cmd-click/Ctrl-click the edge of the object that you want to delete anchor points from.

3. Click an anchor point (don't press Delete!). The point will be deleted **1**–**2**. Repeat to delete other anchor points, if desired.

➤ Hold down Shift to disable the add/delete function of the Pen tool. Release Shift before releasing the mouse button.

➤ If you don't click precisely on an anchor point with the Delete Anchor Point tool, an alert dialog box will appear. Click OK and try again. If you want to use smart guides to help you find anchor points, check Text Label Hints in Preferences > Smart Guides & Slices, under Display Options.

1 *Click an anchor point with the Delete Anchor Point tool (or the Pen tool).*

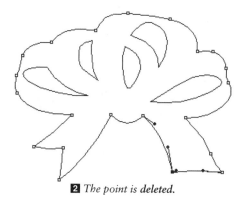

2 *The point is deleted.*

1 *The original objects*

2 *Using the Erase tool to erase points*

3 *Reshaping a path with the Pencil tool. (To get a crosshair pointer, check Use Precise Cursors in Preferences > General, or press Caps Lock.)*

4 *The reshaped path*

Quick reshaping

The **Erase** tool deletes points, too—but you don't have to click on them individually.

To erase part of a path with the Erase tool:

1. Choose the **Erase** tool. It's the last tool on the Pencil tool pop-out menu.

2. Cmd-click/Ctrl-click an object to select it (not a mesh or a type path).

3. Position the eraser tip of the pencil pointer directly over the area that you want to remove points from, then drag once across that area **1**–**2**. If you erase points from a closed path, you'll end up with an open path. If you erase points from an open path (not endpoints), you'll end up with two separate paths.

Next, we'll show you how use the **Pencil** and **Paintbrush** tools to quickly reshape an existing path.

To reshape a path with the Pencil or Paintbrush tool:

1. To reshape a path that doesn't have a brush stroke, choose the **Pencil** tool (N).
   or
   To reshape a path that does have a brush stroke, choose the **Pencil** tool (N) or the **Paintbrush** tool (B).

2. Cmd-click/Ctrl-click a path to select it.

3. Position the pointer **directly** over the edge of the path, then start dragging **3**. The path will reshape instantly **4**. *Note:* Be sure to position the pointer precisely on the edge of the path. If you don't, you'll create a new path instead of reshaping the existing one.

➤ Press Caps Lock to turn the pointer into a Precise Cursor (crosshair). Press Caps Lock again to restore the default cursors.

➤ To add to an open path using the Pencil or Paintbrush tool, see page 157.

Erase Tool; Reshape Using Pencil, Paintbrush

To smooth part of a path:

1. Choose the **Selection** tool (V), select an open or closed path, then choose the **Smooth** tool  (it's on the Pencil tool pop-out menu).
or
If the **Pencil** or **Paintbrush** tool is currently chosen, Cmd-click/Ctrl-click an open or closed path to select it, then hold down Option/Alt to access a temporary Smooth tool.

2. Drag along the path. Any bumps on the path will be smoothed out **1**. Some anchor points may be removed. Next, read about the Smooth Tool preferences, which affect how drastic an effect this tool may have on a path.

1 *Using the Smooth tool*

To choose settings for the Smooth tool:

1. Double-click the **Smooth** tool **2**.

2. Choose a **Fidelity** value (0.5–20) **3**–**4**. The higher the Fidelity, the more anchor points will be removed.

3. Choose a **Smoothness** value (0–100%). The higher the Smoothness value, logically, the greater the amount of smoothing; the lower the Smoothness, the less drastic the reshaping.

4. Click OK.

➤ Click Reset in the Smooth Tool Preferences dialog box to restore the default settings.

2 *The Smooth Tool Preferences dialog box*

3 *The Smooth tool used with **high Fidelity** and **Smoothness** settings*

4 *The Smooth tool used on the original object with **moderate Fidelity** and **Smoothness** settings*

Smooth Tool

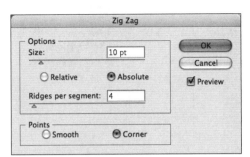

1 The Zig Zag dialog box

Some of the Illustrator filters and effects can be used to explode a simple shape into a more complex shape in one fell swoop. The **Zig Zag** filter, for example, adds anchor points to a path and then moves those points to produce waves or zigzags. The version on the Effect menu applies the Zig Zag effect without actually altering the path. Effect menu commands are reeditable; Filter menu commands are not. Read more about effects and filters in Chapter 20.

To apply the Zig Zag effect:

1. Select a path.

2. Choose Effect > Distort & Transform (upper part of the menu) > **Zig Zag.** The Zig Zag dialog box opens **1**.

3. Check Preview.

4. Click Points: **Smooth** (bottom of the dialog box) to make curvy waves, or **Corner** to create sharp-cornered zigzags.

5. To move the added points by a percentage of the size of the object, click **Relative,** then choose a Size percentage (0–100).
   or
   To move the added points by a specified distance, click **Absolute,** then choose or enter that distance (0–100 pt) via the **Size** slider or field.

6. Choose a number of **Ridges** per segment (0–100) for the number of anchor points to be added between existing points. If you enter a number, press Tab to preview.

7. Click OK **2–5**.

2 The original star

3 After applying the Zig Zag effect (Size 45, Ridges 4, Smooth)

4 The original circle

5 After applying the Zig Zag effect (Size 24, Ridges 20, Corner)

Zig Zag Effect

The **Reshape** tool is hard to describe in words. It's the best tool for gentle reshaping because it causes the least amount of distortion. Our favorite way to use this tool is to select a handful of points with it, then drag. That portion of the path will keep its overall contour while it elongates or contracts, and the rest of the path will stay put.

To use the Reshape tool:

1. Choose the **Direct Selection** tool (A), then click the edge of a path. Only one point or segment should be selected.

2. Choose the **Reshape** tool 🖌 (it's on the Scale tool pop-out menu).

3. Drag any visible **point.** A square border will display around the point when you release the mouse.
   or
   Drag any **segment** of the path. A new square border point will be created.
   or
   Try this: Shift-click or marquee **multiple** points on the path using the Reshape tool (squares will display around these points), then drag one of the square points. For smooth reshaping, let the unselected points on the path (the ones without a square around them) serve as anchors for the shape **1**–**2**.

➤ Option-drag/Alt-drag with the Reshape tool to make a copy of the object as it's reshaped.

➤ Choose Edit > Undo to undo the last Reshape edit(s).

➤ To reshape multiple paths at a time, select some points on each path.

➤ Compare the Reshape tool, which adds one new point a time, with the liquify tools (especially the Warp tool), which add many new points as they produce more drastic reshaping (see Chapter 28).

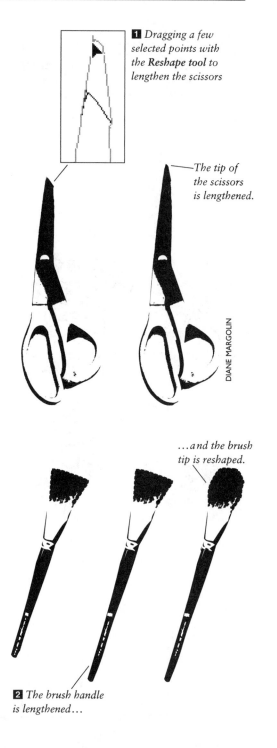

1 *Dragging a few selected points with the **Reshape tool** to lengthen the scissors*

The tip of the scissors is lengthened.

DIANE MARGOLIN

...and the brush tip is reshaped.

2 *The brush handle is lengthened...*

Reshape Tool

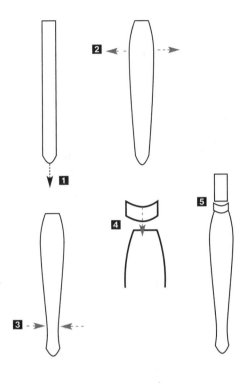

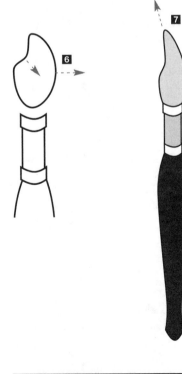

Exercise
Draw a paintbrush with the Reshape tool

1. Using the **Rectangle** tool, draw a narrow vertical rectangle. Give it a white fill and a black stroke (press D).

2. Choose the **Direct Selection** tool (A), deselect the path, then click on its edge.

3. With the **Reshape** tool, drag downward from the center of the bottom segment **1**.

4. Drag the upper middle of the right vertical segment slightly outward, and drag the central upper part of the left vertical segment outward the same distance **2**.

5. Drag each side of the bottom vertical segments inward to pinch the stem **3**.

6. Using the **Rectangle** tool, draw a small horizontal rectangle. Choose the **Direct Selection** tool, deselect the rectangle, then click its edge.

7. Choose the **Reshape** tool again, click the middle of the top segment, Shift-click the middle of the bottom segment, then drag downward **4**.

8. Choose the **Selection** tool (V), move the rectangle over the top of the brush stem, and scale it to fit.

9. Draw a slightly thinner vertical rectangle above the horizontal rectangle. Then, on the Layers palette, drag the new path below the curved rectangular path **5**.

10. Using the **Selection** tool, Option-Shift/Alt-Shift drag the horizontal rectangle up to the top of the vertical rectangle.

11. Using the **Ellipse** tool (L), draw an oval for the brush tip. Choose the **Direct Selection** tool (A), deselect the oval, then click the edge of the oval path.

12. Choose the **Reshape** tool, drag the right middle point outward, drag the upper left segment inward **6**, and drag the top point upward to lengthen the tip **7**.

13. With the **Selection** tool (V), move the brush tip over the brush stem, then Control-click/right-click and choose Arrange > Send to Back.

Averaging points

The **Average** command reshapes one or more paths by precisely realigning their endpoints or anchor points along the horizontal and/or vertical axis. It's like an align command for points.

To average points:

1. Choose the **Direct Selection** tool (A) or the **Lasso** tool (Q).

2. Shift-click or marquee two or more anchor points **1**. They can be on the same path or on different paths.

3. Control-click/right-click the artboard and choose **Average** from the contextual menu.
   or
   Choose Object > Path > **Average** (Cmd-Option-J/Ctrl-Alt-J).

4. Click **Horizontal** to align the points along the horizontal (*x*) axis **2**. Points will move vertically.
   or
   Click **Vertical** to align the points along the vertical (*y*) axis. Points will move horizontally.
   or
   Click **Both** to overlap the points along both the horizontal and vertical axes. Choose this option if you're planning to join them into one point (instructions on the following page).

5. Click OK **3**.

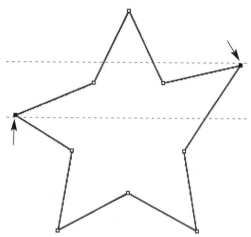

1 *Two anchor points are selected.*

2 *Click an Axis button in the Average dialog box.*

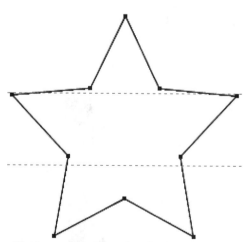

3 *After averaging the selected points, using Axis: Horizontal, the points are now aligned horizontally.*

Average Anchor Points

164

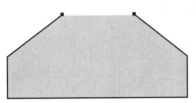

1 *Two endpoints are selected.*

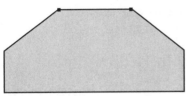

2 *The* Join *command joins the endpoints and adds a segment between them.*

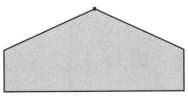

3 *If you choose the Join command when one selected endpoint is right on top of another, the* Join *dialog box will open.*

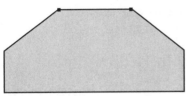

4 *This is figure* **1** *after the two endpoints were averaged and then joined into one point.*

Joining endpoints

If you align one endpoint on top of another, select the endpoints, and then apply the **Join** command, they'll be combined into one anchor point (that's method 1, below). If the endpoints aren't right on top of each other, the command will create a new straight segment between them. The Join command won't add direction lines to the new anchor point.

Note: The endpoints you join can be on separate open paths or on one open path. If you join an open path with a path in a group that's on a lower layer, the resulting path will appear on the upper of the two layers.

To join two endpoints:

Method 1 (Join command)

1. Choose the **Direct Selection** tool (A) or the **Lasso** tool (Q).

2. *Optional:* If you want to combine two endpoints into one, move one endpoint on top of the other manually, or use the Average command (Axis: Both) to align them (instructions on the previous page).

3. Marquee two endpoints **1**.

4. Control-click/right-click the artboard and choose **Join** from the context menu, or choose Object > Path > **Join** (Cmd-J/Ctrl-J). If one endpoint *isn't* on top of the other, the Join command will connect them with a straight segment **2**.

   If one endpoint *is* right on top of the other, the Join dialog box will open **3**. In the Join dialog box:

   Click **Corner** to join corner points into one corner point with no direction lines; or to connect two smooth points into one smooth point with independently moving direction lines; or to connect a corner point and a smooth point into a smooth point with one direction line.
   or
   Click **Smooth** to connect two smooth points into a smooth point with direction lines that move in tandem.

5. Click OK **4**.

(Continued on the following page)

Join Endpoints

Method 2 (Pen tool)

1. Choose the **Pen** tool (P).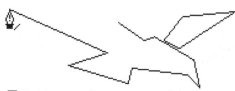

2. Position the pointer over the endpoint of one of the paths you want to join. A small slash will appear next to the Pen pointer when the tool is positioned correctly **1** —and also the word "anchor," if you're using smart guides and Text Label Hints is checked in Preferences > Smart Guides & Slices.

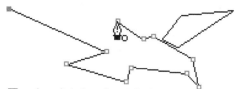

1 To join two endpoints, position the **Pen** over one **endpoint** and click...

3. Click the endpoint.

4. Position the pointer over the other endpoint of the same path (a small hollow circle will appear next to the Pen pointer) or over an endpoint on another path (a small square with a line behind it will appear next to the pointer) **2**.

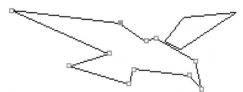

2 ...then click the other **endpoint**.

5. Click the second endpoint. A new segment will appear between the two points you clicked **3**.

➤ If the path has an effect applied to it that's making it hard to locate its endpoints, try using smart guides to locate them.

3 The two points are joined by a **new segment**.

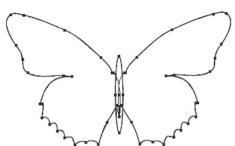

1 *Arrange two or more objects so they overlap, and then select them.*

2 *Clicking the Add to Shape Area button on the Pathfinder palette unites the individual shapes into a single shape.*

3 *The original objects*   **4** *After applying the Add to Shape Area command*

5 *The original objects*   **6** *After applying the Add to Shape Area command*

Combining objects via a command

Using the tools that create shapes, such as the Rectangle, Ellipse, Star, or even the Pencil or Paintbrush, together with the reshaping functions covered in this chapter and occasionally some of the **Pathfinder** palette commands that are discussed in Chapter 25, you can create complex objects without having to draw with the Pen tool.

Rather than joining individual points, the **Shape Mode** commands on the Pathfinder palette combine whole objects. Here's an introduction to one of the most straightforward and useful of the Shape Mode commands: **Add to Shape Area**.

To combine objects using a command:

1. Position two or more objects so they overlap at least partially **1**.

2. Choose any selection tool.

3. Marquee at least some portion of all the objects.

4. Display the **Pathfinder** palette (Cmd-Shift-F9/Ctrl-Shift-F9). **NEW**

5. Click the **Add to Shape Area** (first) button on the palette. The individual objects will combine into one closed compound shape **2**–**6** and will be painted with the attributes of the topmost object. To learn more about compound shapes, see Chapter 25.

   Note: If you apply a stroke color to the new object, it will appear only on the perimeter of the overall combined shape, not on the interior segments. The interior segments are editable, but you can't apply a stroke color to them. If you want to delete those interior segments, select the object, then click Expand on the Pathfinder palette.

➤ Although you can't use multiple objects as a mask, you can use a closed object that the Add to Shape Area command produces as a masking object.

Add to Shape Area Command

Slicing and dicing

The **Scissors** tool can be used either to open a closed path or to split an open path into two paths. A path can be split either at an anchor point or in the middle of a segment.

To split a path with the Scissors tool:

1. Choose any selection tool.

2. Click an object to display its points. *Note:* You can split a closed path that contains type (area type), but not an open path that has type on or inside it.

3. Choose the **Scissors** tool (C).

4. Click the object's path **1**: If you click once on a **closed** path, it will turn into a single, open path; if you click **two** different spots on a closed path, the object will be split into two open paths; or if you click once on an **open** path, it will split into two paths.

   If you click a **segment,** two new endpoints will appear, one on top of the other. If you click an anchor **point,** a new anchor point will appear on top of the existing one, and it will be selected.

5. To move the two new endpoints apart, choose the **Direct Selection** tool (A), then drag the selected point away to reveal the other one below it **2**. (To move the bottom endpoint instead, marquee both endpoints, Shift-click the top one, then press and hold an arrow key.)

The method for **splitting a path** described below is quick, but the results are not as controllable as in the method described above. If you delete a point from a closed path, the adjacent segments will be deleted; if you delete an endpoint from an open path, the adjacent segment will be deleted; and if you delete a point or segment from within an open path, it will split into two shorter paths.

To split a path by deleting a point or a segment:

1. Deselect the object you want to split.

2. Choose the **Direct Selection** tool (A).

3. Click an anchor point or segment.

4. Press **Delete/Backspace.**

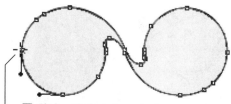

1 *Click with the Scissors tool on an anchor point or a segment.*

There is no segment, and thus no stroke, between the endpoints.

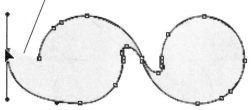

2 *After moving the new **endpoint**. If you apply a stroke color to an open path, you'll be able to see where the missing segment is. An open path can contain a fill.*

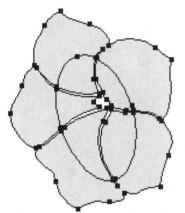

1 *The white oval is the cutting object.*

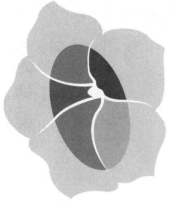

2 *After **Divide Objects Below** is chosen, all the resulting objects become selected.*

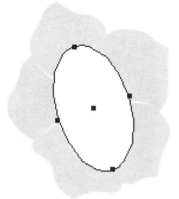

3 *After recoloring the five separate paths that originally formed an oval*

The **Divide Objects Below** command uses an object like a cookie cutter to cut the objects underneath it, and then deletes the cutting object.

To cut objects via the Divide Objects Below command:

1. Create or select an object that contains a solid-color fill and/or stroke (not a group or live paint group) to be used as a cutting shape. The Slice command will cause this object to be deleted, so make a copy of it now if you want to preserve it.

2. Place the cutting object on top of the filled object(s) you want to cut **1**.

3. Make sure only the cutting object is selected.

4. Choose Object > Path > **Divide Objects Below.** The topmost shape (cutting object) will be deleted automatically and the underlying objects will be cut into separate paths where they meet the edge of the cutting object **2**–**3**. All the objects will become selected, and you can move them with the Selection tool. Any objects that were in a group will remain grouped.

➤ To prevent an object below the cutting shape from being affected by the Divide Objects Below command, hide or lock it (see pages 214–215).

Divide, or Divide Objects Below?

Compare the Divide Objects Below command, discussed on this page, with the Divide button on the Pathfinder palette, which is discussed on pages 393–394. **Divide Objects Below** deletes the top cutting object and leaves the resulting objects ungrouped, whereas **Divide** preserves the paint attributes of all the objects, including the topmost object, and groups the resulting paths. You usually end up with smaller pieces with Divide than with Divide Objects Below.

And don't forget **live paint groups,** to which you can add/delete and paint faces and edges. See Chapter 13.

Divide Objects Below

The **Knife** tool reshapes paths as a carving knife would, and is a wonderful tool for artists who like to draw in a freehand style.

To cut an object into separate shapes:

1. *Optional:* If you select an object (or objects) before using the Knife tool, the tool won't cut any of the unselected objects. This is useful if there are many objects close together in the artwork and you don't want them all to be cut. If you don't select any objects first, any object the Knife passes across is fair game.

   Note: The Knife tool works on a closed path or a filled, open path, but not on an unfilled open path or a live paint group. To carve up type, you must convert it to outlines first (select it, then choose Type > Create Outlines).

2. Choose the **Knife** tool ▯ (it's on the Scissors tool pop-out menu). Don't confuse it with the Slice tool!

3. Starting from outside the object(s), drag completely across it to divide it in two, or carve off a chunk of it **1**–**3**.
   or
   Option-drag/Alt-drag to cut in a straight line. (Press and hold Option/Alt before dragging.) Option-Shift-drag/Alt-Shift-drag to constrain the cutting strokes to an increment of 45°.

➤ If you make a "closed" cut (drag back over the starting point) with the Knife tool completely inside an object, you'll create a new, separate object. You can move the new object with the Direct Selection tool to expose the hole.

➤ Choose Object > Group to group the newly separated shapes together, then use the Direct Selection tool if you need to select individual shapes within the group.

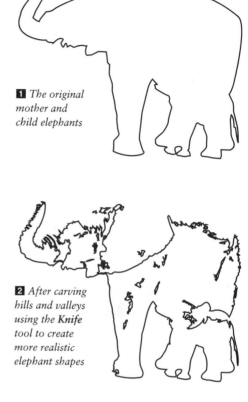

1 *The original mother and child elephants*

2 *After carving hills and valleys using the* **Knife** *tool to create more realistic elephant shapes*

3 *The final image, after applying a black fill*

DIANE MARGOLIN

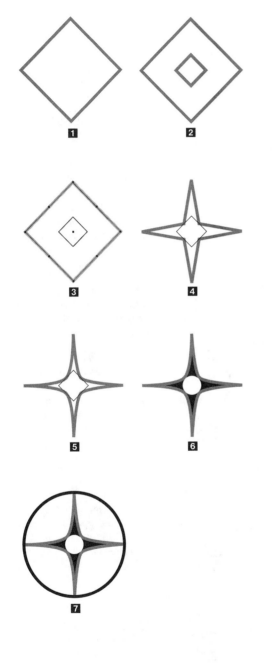

Exercise

Change a square into a star

1. Choose the **Rectangle** tool (M). Choose a fill of None and a 2-pt. stroke (see Chapter 10).

2. Click on the artboard. The Rectangle dialog box opens.

3. Enter 2" in the Width field, click the word Height, then click OK.

4. Double-click the **Rotate** tool, enter 45 in the Angle field, then click OK **1**.

5. Double-click the **Scale** tool, enter 30 in the **Uniform Scale** field, then click Copy **2**.

6. Choose View > Guides > **Make Guides** (Cmd-5/Ctrl-5) to turn the small diamond into a guide.

7. Choose the **Selection** tool (V), then select the large diamond shape. Choose Object > Path > **Add Anchor Points 3**.

8. Choose the **Direct Selection** tool (A). Deselect, then click on the edge of the diamond.

9. Drag each of the new midpoints inward until it touches the guide shape. Use smart guides to align the points at a 45° angle **4**.

10. Choose the **Convert Anchor Point** tool (Shift-C), and drag each of the inner midpoints to create a curve. Drag clockwise and along the edge of the guide shape **5**.

11. Choose the **Ellipse** tool (L), position the pointer over the center point of the star shape, then Option-Shift-drag/Alt-Shift-drag until the circle touches the curves of the star.

12. To the circle, apply a white fill and a stroke of None; to the star shape, apply a black or dark fill and a lighter stroke **6**.

13. *Optional*: Select the circle. Choose the Scale tool (S). Start dragging, hold down Option-Shift/Alt-Shift, and continue to drag until the copy of the circle touches the outer tips of the star. Fill the large circle with None, and apply a 2-pt. stroke **7**.

Exercise
Draw a light bulb

I. *Draw a **circle** about 1 inch in diameter and a **rectangle** about .5 inch square. Apply a fill of None and a 3-pt. black stroke to both objects.*

2. *Choose the **Direct Selection** tool (A), select the bottom point of the circle, then drag the point downward. Using the **Selection** tool (V), select **both** objects.*

3. *Option-click/Alt-click the **Add to Shape Area** button on the Pathfinder palette. Use the **Add Anchor Point** tool (+) to add a point on the bottommost segment (1), then use the **Direct Selection** tool to drag the new point downward.*

(1)

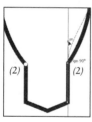

(2)   (2)

4. *Click on each point where the curve meets the straight segment (2). Using **smart guides** to assist you, rotate the direction line upward to 90° vertical.*

5. *Apply a fill of white to the bulb.*

6. *Create a rounded rectangle or an oval that's wider than the base of the bulb. With the **Selection** tool, drag outside a corner of the bounding box to rotate the rectangle, then Option-Shift-drag/Alt-Shift-drag a copy downward. Repeat to create another copy.*

7. *Apply a fill color and a stroke of None to the ovals, and place them on the bottom part of the bulb.*

8. *Use the **Star** tool to create a 20-point star (Radius 1: .4", Radius 2: .69"). Apply a light fill color and a stroke of None. Scale the star, if necessary, so it's larger than the bulb.*

9. *Position the star over the bulb. On the **Layers** palette, drag the star object below the bulb object.*

10. *Select the star. Apply Effect > Distort & Transform > **Roughen** (Size: 2, Relative, Detail: 8). Deselect.*

11. *Choose the **Pencil** tool (N), a fill of None, a black stroke, and a stroke weight of 1–2 pt. Draw a filament line inside the bulb. It should be the topmost object on the Layers palette.*

12. *Select the bulb. On the **Transparency** palette, set the Opacity slider to 60–70%, Normal mode.*

13. *Select the bulb, star, and filament. Apply Effect > Stylize > **Drop Shadow** (Opacity 50–60%, Blur 1–3 pt).*

LIVE PAINT | 13

In this chapter, first you'll learn to draw in a freehand style using the Pencil tool. Then you'll learn how to convert objects to a live paint group, apply colors to faces and edges in the group, reshape the group, and finally, expand it into standard paths. At the end of the chapter you'll find a practice exercise.

New chapter!

1 *A pencil sketch, converted to a **live paint group***

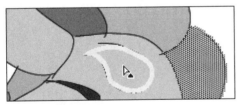

2 *A **face** being selected*

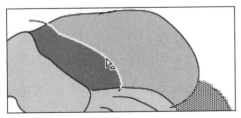

3 *An **edge** being selected*

What is a live paint group? NEW

The live paint features offer a novel method for filling in sketches and are a boon to Illustrator users who like to draw in a freehand style. First you create some open or closed paths with the Pencil tool or another drawing tool, then you convert the whole drawing into a **live paint group** **1**. With the **Live Paint Bucket** tool, you simply click any area formed by intersecting lines (called a **face**), and the current paint attributes are applied **2**. Add to and reshape the live paint objects at any time, and the fill color flows into the new shape.

One of the unique features of live paint groups is that you can also recolor (or leave unpainted) individual line segments, called **edges** **3**, instead of whole paths.

This method of recoloring sketches is quick and exceedingly flexible. Creating similar kinds of filled shapes in prior versions of Illustrator was very time-consuming. You had to create closed paths, select them, apply fill and stroke colors, then use Pathfinder commands to split overlapping objects into flat, separate objects—and even then, there was no live paint flow.

When you're done using the "live" aspect of a live paint group, you can expand it into normal Illustrator objects (a group of strokes and a group of closed fill paths).

Before delving into the live paint features, though, we'll explore the Pencil tool, the ultimate electronic sketching tool.

Using the Pencil tool

If you enjoy sketching objects by hand, you'll gravitate to the **Pencil** tool, especially if you own a pressure-sensitive tablet. This tool has three distinct functions. If you drag in an empty area of the artboard with it, you'll create a new, open path. If you drag along the edge of an existing, selected path (open or closed), the tool will reshape the path (see page 159). And if you drag from an endpoint of an existing open path, you'll add a new segment to the path (see page 157). Paths drawn with this tool can be reshaped like any other paths (see Chapter 12).

Note: If you want to draw straight lines or smooth curves, you'll go mad trying to do it with the Pencil tool; use the Line Segment, Arc, or Pen tool instead.

To draw with the Pencil tool:

1. Choose the **Pencil** tool (N).

NEW 2. On the Control palette, click the **Stroke** color box, then choose a stroke color. Also click the word **Stroke** on the palette, then choose stroke attributes (see pages 118–120).

3. Draw a line. A dotted line will appear as you draw. When you release the mouse, in Preview view, the line will be colored with the current stroke settings and its anchor points will be selected 1. In Outline view, you'll see just a wireframe representation of the line 2. The lines may or may not have a fill, depending on the current Pencil tool preferences, which are discussed on the next page.

   Continue to draw as many lines as you like.

➤ To create a closed path with the Pencil tool, start drawing with the tool, then hold down Option/Alt and continue dragging.

➤ To close an existing Pencil line, choose the Selection tool (V), select the line, then choose Object > Path > Join (Cmd-J/ Ctrl-J). The two endpoints will be joined by a straight segment.

1 *A blue-footed booby, drawn with the* **Pencil** *tool*

2 *The booby in* **Outline** *view*

DIANE MARGOLIN

Pencil Tool

1 *The Pencil tool has its own Preferences dialog box.*

2 *A line drawn with a high Fidelity value*

3 *A line drawn with a low Fidelity value*

4 *An illustration by Diane Margolin, drawn with the Pencil tool*

Use the **Pencil Tool Preferences** dialog box to customize the Pencil tool. If you change these settings, only subsequently drawn lines will be affected—not existing lines.

To choose Pencil tool preferences:

1. Double-click the **Pencil** tool ✏ (or press N to choose the tool, then press Return/ Enter). The Pencil Tool Preferences dialog box opens **1**.

2. For **Tolerances:**

   Choose a **Fidelity** value (.5–20) **2**–**3**. The lower the Fidelity value, the more closely the line will follow the movement of the mouse and the more anchor points will be created. The higher the Fidelity value, the fewer the anchor points and the smoother the path.

   Choose a **Smoothness** value (0–100). The higher the Smoothness value, the smoother the curves; the lower the Smoothness value, the more bends and twists in the path.

3. *Check any of the following options:*

   Fill new pencil strokes to apply the **(NEW)** current fill color to new paths (open or closed) that are drawn with the tool.

   Keep selected to have Pencil paths remain selected after they're created. This is handy if you tend to add to your paths right after drawing them.

   Edit selected paths to activate the reshaping function of the Pencil tool (see page 159). The Within: [ ] pixels value (2–20) is the minimum distance the pointer must be from a path in order for the tool to affect it. Uncheck this option if you want to be able to draw multiple Pencil lines near one another without reshaping any existing selected paths.

4. Click OK **4**.

➤ Click Reset in the Pencil Tool Preferences dialog box to restore the tool's default settings.

➤ To smooth an existing path, use the Smooth tool (see page 160).

NEW Creating live paint groups

To **create** a live **paint group**, you click some existing paths with the Live Paint Bucket tool or choose the Live Paint command. To draw paths for a live paint group, we like to use the Pencil tool, but you can use any drawing tool. The important thing is to draw lines that intersect, because the Live Paint Bucket tool, which you'll also use for coloring, detects and fills only faces (areas) that are formed by intersecting lines.

When converting path objects into a live paint group, keep the following in mind:

➤ All attributes are removed except the fill and stroke settings.

➤ To make a live paint group from a symbol or blend, apply Object > Expand first. To use a clipping set in a live paint group, release the set first. To create a live paint group from type, convert it to outlines via Type > Create Outlines first.

➤ To convert a bitmap image into a live paint group, instead of following the instructions below, choose Object > Live Trace > Make and Convert to Live Paint.

All the faces and edges of a live paint group stay on one level; they're not stacked from front to back, as paths are. When you apply fill or stroke attributes to a live paint group, you're recoloring faces or edges—not the actual paths. If you reshape the group in any way, such as by editing the paths, colors will flow instantly into the new faces.

To create a live paint group:

1. Draw some open or closed paths using any tool, such as the **Pencil, Paintbrush, Pen, Arc, Line Segment,** or **Ellipse,** and apply some initial stroke colors and weights **1**. As you create your sketch, be sure to create intersecting areas.

2. Select all the paths manually or via the Layers palette.

3. Choose the **Live Paint Bucket** tool (K), then click any of the selected objects **2**–**3**.
   or
   Choose Object > Live Paint > **Make** (Cmd-Option-X/Ctrl-Alt-X).

Choose colors quickly

Click the **Fill** or **Stroke** thumbnail or arrowhead on the Control palette to open a temporary **Swatches** palette, or Shift-click the Fill or Stroke thumbnail or arrowhead to open a temporary **Color** palette. To choose a **Stroke Weight,** click the up/down arrowhead, or enter a number in the field, or choose from the drop-down menu.

1 *Draw pencil lines, then convert them to a live paint group.*

2 *With the **Live Paint Bucket** tool, click the faces you want to apply color to.*

3 *Our finished sketch*

Create Live Paint Group

1 *A live paint group, consisting of lines created with the **Pencil** tool*

2 *If you click with the **Live Paint Bucket** tool on a face (an area where paths intersect), the current fill color is applied.*

If an alert prompt appears, give it a read, then click OK. On the Layers palette, note that the paths are now nested in a live paint group.

➤ Some Illustrator commands aren't available for live paint groups, such as the clipping mask, mesh, pathfinder, and Select > Same commands.

Using the Live Paint Bucket tool

Here's the fun part—applying colors to a live paint group. In these instructions, you'll recolor faces with the Live Paint Bucket tool.

To recolor faces with the Live Paint Bucket tool:

1. Have a live paint group at the ready, **1** and choose the Live Paint Bucket tool (K). *(The Paint Bucket tool is gone.)

2. Choose a fill color, gradient, or pattern (via the Control palette, if desired). You don't need to select anything in the document window.

3. Move the pointer over any **face** area where two or more paths intersect (the face will become highlighted), then click **2**. *or*
   Drag across **multiple faces**.

   Note: If the tool doesn't behave as described above, try Shift-clicking with the tool instead, and also read about the tool options on the following page.

➤ Double-click a face to flood-fill, that is, fill adjacent faces across unstroked edges. Triple-click a face to recolor all faces that have the same color as the one you click, adjacent or not.

➤ Transparency settings, brush strokes, and effects can be applied to an entire live paint group but not to individual faces or edges. *Note:* To apply a brush stroke, drag the brush over the group.

➤ Hold down Option/Alt to turn the Live Paint Bucket tool into a temporary Eyedropper tool, then use it to sample fill colors from anywhere in the document window.

To choose Live Paint Bucket tool options:

1. Double-click the **Live Paint Bucket** tool. 🖱️
   or
   Click the **Live Paint Bucket** tool (K), then press Return/Enter.

   The Live Paint Bucket Options dialog box opens **1**.

2. For Options, click **Paint Fills** and/or **Paint Strokes,** depending on the desired default behavior.

   When using the Live Paint Bucket tool, you can hold down **Shift** to switch its function from painting fills (faces) to applying stroke (edge) colors and attributes.

3. *Optional:* Check **Highlight** (if unchecked), then, from the **Color** pop-up menu, choose a different highlight color for faces and edges the tool passes over, or click the color swatch and choose a color from the Colors dialog box. Also change the highlight **Width,** if desired.

4. Click OK.

Live paint and trace

The **live trace** feature converts bitmap images into vector shapes. You can convert the vector shapes into a **live paint group** (see page 348), then repaint and reshape the resulting areas and segments to further enhance the vector image.

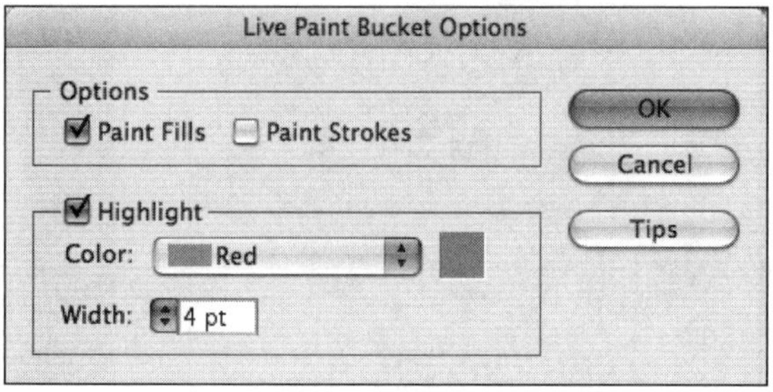

1 Use the **Live Paint Bucket Options** dialog box to specify default behavior for the tool, including a highlight color.

1 *You can use the **Live Paint Bucket** tool to apply stroke attributes to edges.*

2 *Paths were drawn on the neck, lips, and face to create fillable faces.*

3 *The **Live Paint Bucket** tool was used to fill the new faces and to apply a stroke of None to edges on the neck, cheeks, and forehead.*

You can also use the **Live Paint Bucket** tool to apply **stroke** colors and/or line **weights**. Only the edges you click will be modified, not the whole path. Each edge in a path can have a different color, weight, and other stroke attributes—or a stroke color of None!

To modify live paint edges with the Live Paint Bucket tool:

1. Double-click the **Live Paint Bucket** tool, check **Paint Strokes** in the Live Paint Bucket Options dialog box, then click OK (see the previous page).

2. Choose a stroke color, and choose a stroke weight and other attributes via the Stroke palette (access via the Control palette, if desired). To remove colors from edges, choose a color of None.

3. Click any **edges** in a live paint group **1**–**3**.
   or
   Drag across **multiple edges.**
   or
   Double-click an edge to **flood-stroke—**apply the current stroke attributes to all contiguous edges that have the same color and weight.

➤ Triple-click an edge to apply the current stroke color and Stroke palette attributes to all edges—contiguous or not—that have the same attributes as the one you click.

Using the Live Paint Selection tool

The **Live Paint Selection** tool lets you select edges and/or faces in a live paint group. But you need to choose options for the tool.

To choose Live Paint Selection tool options:

1. Double-click the **Live Paint Selection** tool.

   or

   Click the **Live Paint Selection** tool (Shift-L), then press Return/Enter.

   The Live Paint Selection Options dialog box opens 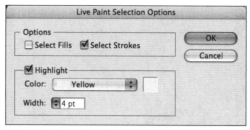.

2. Check **Select Fills** and/or **Select Strokes,** (and choose a different Highlight Color and/or Width for selections, if desired), then click OK.

➤ To avoid confusion, use different highlight colors for the Live Paint Bucket and Live Paint Selection tools.

To use the Live Paint Selection tool:

1. Choose the **Live Paint Selection** tool (Shift-L), and choose options for the tool as per the instructions above.

2. Click an edge or face in a live paint group, then Shift-click additional edges or faces . (Shift-click to deselect individual edges or faces.) The selections display as a gray pattern.

3. Do any of the following:

   For the **fill,** choose a solid color , gradient, or pattern. You can use the Gradient tool to modify a gradient fill (see page 382).

   Change the **stroke color, weight,** or other stroke attributes. Apply a stroke of None to any edges that you want to hide.

   Press **Delete/Backspace** to remove selected edges or faces.

4. When you're done making changes, click outside the live paint group to deselect it.

➤ To see your color changes more clearly, hide the selection pattern by choosing View > Hide Edges (Cmd-H/Ctrl-H).

1 *Use the* **Live Paint Selection Options** *dialog box to specify default behavior for the tool, and to choose a highlight color for selections.*

2 *Three areas of the woman's hair are being selected with the* **Live Paint Selection** *tool.*

3 *A new fill color is applied to the selected faces.*

Live Paint Selection Tool

1 *A path is selected in a live paint group with the Selection tool and lengthened until it crosses another path, thereby creating a new face.*

2 *The new face (behind the neck) is filled using the Live Paint Bucket tool.*

Reshaping live paint groups

If you **isolate** a **live paint group,** you can transform or move whole paths in the group, manipulate points on a path, and add new faces.

To reshape or move paths in a live paint group:

1. Choose the **Selection** tool (V).

2. To isolate a live paint group:

   Double-click a path or face in the group.
   or
   Click a path or area in the group, then click the **Isolate selected group** button on the Control palette.

   A gray rectangle will display around the live paint group.

3. To select a whole path in the group, choose the **Selection** tool, then click a face that contains a fill color or click a path. A bounding box with star-filled selection handles will display. Drag the path to **move** it; drag a handle to **transform** it **1**–**2**.
   or
   To reshape a path, choose the **Direct Selection** tool (A), then click the edge of a path to make its anchor points and direction points visible (see page 94).

   Fill colors will reflow automatically into any areas you reshape. You can also change the stroke color and/or weight for any selected path.

4. When you're done, click the **Exit selected group** button on the Control palette; or with a selection tool, double-click outside the group.

Modify Live Paint Paths

Adding paths to a live paint group

Here are three methods for **adding paths** to an existing **live paint group**.

To add paths to a live paint group:

Method 1 (Layers palette)

Draw the path you want to add, then on the **Layers** palette, drag the new path into the live paint group.

Method 2 (isolate group)

1. Choose the **Selection** tool (V), then double-click the live paint group to isolate it.

2. Draw the path you want to add **1**–**2**. The new path will be part of the live paint group.

3. Double-click outside the group.

Method 3 (Add Paths button)

1. Deselect the live paint group, then draw a new path or paths on the same layer or on a new layer.

2. Choose the **Selection** tool (V), then select both the new paths and the live paint group.

3. Click the **Add Paths** button on the Control palette.

➤ The Align Stroke buttons aren't available for edges in a live paint group.

Live paint rules

➤ Faces in a live paint group are repainted instantly when an edge is **reshaped** or **deleted** or when a closed path in the group is **moved** over a face.

➤ When an edge is deleted from between two faces, the fill color from the **larger** of the two faces is usually applied—but not always!

➤ When a **closed** path is **moved** over filled faces, **anything** may happen! The fill from the closed path may impose its color on the face(s), or a large face may impose its color on the path you're moving. Be ready to use Undo if you don't like the results.

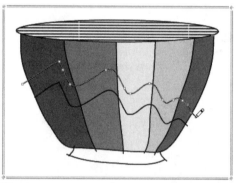

1 *A live paint group is* **isolated***, then two new paths are drawn across existing edges to create new faces.*

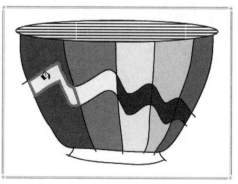

2 *With the* **Live Paint Bucket** *tool, fill colors are applied to the new faces.*

Add Path to Live Paint Group

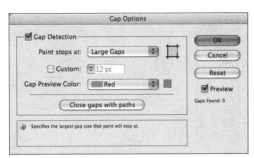

1 *Choose* **Gap Options** *to control color leakage in your live paint groups.*

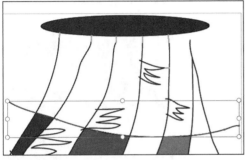

2 *We chose the* **Paint stops at: Large Gaps** *option. The gaps preview in light gray (in this case, they're just below the dark ellipse).*

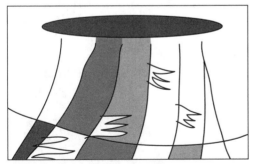

3 *With the* **Large Gaps** *option chosen, open areas with small- to medium-sized gaps can be filled.*

Minimize the gap

The more you allow lines to **intersect** in the original objects, the fewer the gaps in the live paint group. As shown in step 11 on page 186, you can **delete** or apply a stroke of **None** to any overhanging edges.

Choosing gap options

If you reshape an edge so as to create a gap in a formerly closed area (face), any fill color in that face will disappear because in the world of live paint, fills can't be applied to areas that have large gaps. Via the **Gap Options** dialog box, you can specify a gap size to stop fill colors from leaking. Gap options are chosen separately for each live paint group.

To choose gap options for a live paint group:

1. Choose the **Selection** tool (V), then click a live paint group.

2. Click the **Gap Options** button ▦ on the Control palette. The Gap Options dialog box opens **1**.

3. Check Preview, then do any of the following:

   Make sure **Gap Detection** is checked, then from the **Paint stops at** pop-up menu, choose a gap size that colors can't flow through, or check **Custom** and enter a specific gap size (.01–72 pt). We like to set our pop-up menu to Large Gaps **2** so we can draw lines freely yet still be able to fill faces.

   Choose a preview color from the **Gap Preview Color** pop-up menu for the invisible (nonprinting) gap "lines" that stop paint leakage. You can also click the color swatch and choose a color from the Colors dialog box. Gap lines display onscreen while the Gap Options dialog box is open or when View > **Show Live Paint Gaps** is on.

   Click the **Close gaps with paths** button to have Illustrator close up any existing gaps with actual unpainted edge segments. This can improve image processing time.

4. Click OK. If you increased the gap size, try using the Live Paint Bucket tool to fill areas that couldn't be filled before **3**. Colors will still leak from gaps larger than the specified gap size.

➤ Use tool tips in the Gap Options dialog box to learn about the various options.

Expanding and releasing live paint groups

When you're done editing a live paint group, you can **expand** or **release** the paths into normal Illustrator objects, at which point, of course, they'll cease to be live.

To expand or release a live paint group:

1. Using the Selection tool or the Layers palette, select a live paint group.

2. On the Control palette, do either of the following:

   Click the **Expand** button to convert the live paint group into two nested groups on the same layer 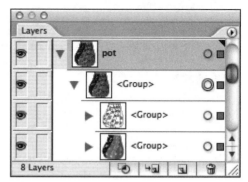. The former faces will become filled paths in one group, and the former edges will become paths with strokes in the other group **2**.

   or

   Choose Object > Live Paint > **Release** to convert the live paint group into separate paths with a .5-pt. black stroke and no fill (not in a group). Use this option, say, if you want to remove the fill colors and start your sketch over with just linework.

➤ After applying the Expand command, you can easily apply stroke or fill attributes en masse to each group (e.g., apply a brush stroke or effect) **3**. To create traps for printing, set the path (strokes) group to overprint.

1 *After* **expanding** *a live paint group, two nested groups appear on the Layers palette.*

2 *For illustration purposes, we moved the closed, filled objects apart in this former live paint group, and hid the group layer that contains the stroked paths.*

3 *We applied the Roughen and Drop Shadow effects to the former edges group to add depth to the line work.*

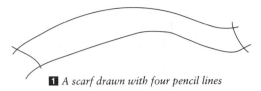

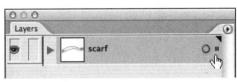

1 *A scarf drawn with four pencil lines*

2 *Click the selection area for the scarf layer.*

3 *Click with the **Live Paint Bucket** tool to apply a fill color to the scarf face.*

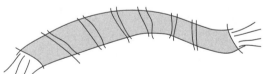

4 *Draw stripes with the **Pencil** tool.*

5 *Click with the **Live Paint Bucket** tool to fill the stripes.*

Exercise

In this exercise,, you'll use the live paint feature to create a loosely drawn sketch of a striped scarf.

Sketch a scarf

1. Create a new layer on the Layers palette. Double-click the layer name, enter the name "scarf," then click OK.

2. Choose a black stroke of 1 pt. Double-click the **Pencil** tool, 🖉 make sure **Fill new pencil strokes** is unchecked, **Edit selected paths** is checked, and the Within value is set to around 3 pixels, then click OK.

3. Draw one edge of a scarf, draw the other edge of the scarf, then draw a line at each end of the scarf shape to connect the two longer lines **1**. Make sure your new strokes cross over the existing ones.

4. On the Layers palette, click the selection area for the scarf layer (far right) to select all the objects on that layer **2**, then choose Object > Live Paint > **Make** (Cmd-Option-X/Ctrl-Alt-X).

5. Choose the **Selection** tool (V), then double-click any path in the live paint group to isolate the group. A gray rectangle displays.

6. Choose a fill color for the background of the scarf. Double-click the **Live Paint Bucket** tool, check **Paint Fills** and **Paint Strokes,** then click OK (now the tool can be used to recolor faces and edges). Click inside the scarf face **3**.

7. Choose a stroke color. Choose the **Pencil** tool (N). Draw lines for stripes across the scarf, making sure your new lines cross over the existing edges **4**, and deselect the last line.

8. Choose the **Live Paint Bucket** tool (K), 🖑 choose a fill color, then click within each stripe area **5**. Zoom in, if necessary, to help you click precisely on the correct faces.

(Continued on the following page)

9. On the Control palette, click the **Exit Isolated Group** button, ⊟ then save your document **1**.

10. *Optional:* For a more hand-drawn look, on the Layers palette, click the circle for the live paint group to target the group. Choose Effect > Distort & Transform > Roughen, check Preview, click Absolute, move the Size slider to around 4 and the Detail slider to around 4, click Smooth, then click OK **2**.

11. *Optional:* To hide the scraggly lines on the scarf, choose the Live Paint Selection tool (Shift-L) and zoom in on the scarf. Click one of the edges that juts out from the scarf, Shift-click the others, then choose a stroke of None (or press Delete/Backspace to delete them) **3**. If you applied the Roughen effect, it will update automatically.

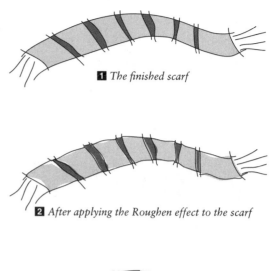

1 *The finished scarf*

2 *After applying the Roughen effect to the scarf*

3 *After applying a stroke of None to the edges that jut out from the scarf*

PEN 14

Mastering the Pen tool—Illustrator's most difficult tool—requires patience and practice. Once you become comfortable using this tool, refer to Chapter 12 to learn how to reshape the resulting paths. If you find the Pen to be too difficult to use, remember that you can create shapes using other methods. For example, you can draw simple geometric shapes (Chapter 7) and then combine them (Chapter 25), or if you prefer to draw in a freehand style, use the Pencil along with the Live Paint Bucket tool (Chapter 13).

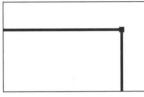

1 This **corner** point joins two **straight** segments, and has **no** direction lines.

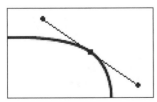

3 This **corner** point has direction lines that move **independently**. This is a nonsmooth curve.

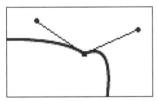

2 A **smooth** point always has a pair of direction lines that move in **tandem**. This is a smooth curve.

Drawing with the Pen tool

The **Pen** tool creates precise curved and straight segments connected by anchor points. If you click with the Pen tool, you'll create corner points and straight segments *without* direction lines **1**. If you drag with the Pen tool, you'll create smooth points and curve segments *with* direction lines **2**–**3**. The distance and direction in which you drag the mouse determine the shape of the curve segment.

In the instructions on the following pages, you'll learn how to draw straight segments, smooth curves, and nonsmooth curves. Once you master all three techniques, you'll naturally combine them without really thinking about it as you draw your artwork. Drag-drag-click, drag, click-click-drag…

DANIEL PELAVIN

Click with the **Pen** tool to create an open or closed **straight-sided** polygon.

To draw a straight-sided object with the Pen tool:

1. If a solid color, gradient, or pattern (not None) is chosen as the fill (look at the Fill box on the Control palette), the Pen path will be filled as soon as you create your first three points. You'll see this only in Preview view, of course. To create segments that appear as lines only, choose a stroke color and a fill of None now or at any time while drawing a path.

2. Choose the **Pen** tool (P).

3. **Click** to create an anchor point.

4. Click to create a second anchor point. A straight segment will now connect the two points.

5. Click to create additional anchor points. They will be also be connected by straight segments.

6. To complete the shape as an **open** path:

   Click the Pen tool or any other **tool** on the Toolbox.
   or
   Cmd-click/Ctrl-click outside the new shape to deselect it.
   or
   Choose Select > **Deselect** (Cmd-Shift-A/ Ctrl-Shift-A).

   Or to complete the shape as a **closed** path, position the Pen pointer over the **starting point** (a small circle will appear next to the pointer), and click on it 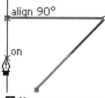.

➤ Hold down Shift while clicking with the Pen tool to constrain a segment to an increment of 45°.

➤ Use smart guides to help you align points and segments (see pages 100–101) .

➤ If the artboard starts to fill up with extraneous points, use the Object > Path > Clean Up command with only the Delete: Stray Points option checked.

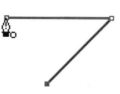

1 *The **Pen** tool pointer is positioned over the starting point to close the new shape.*

2 *You can use **smart guides** to align points as you create them.*

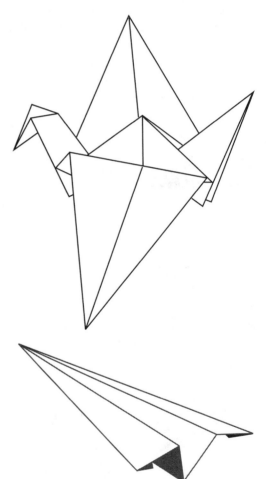

1 *Drag to create the first anchor point.*

2 *Release and reposition the mouse, then drag in the direction you want the curve to follow.*

3 *Continue to reposition and drag the mouse.*

4 *Continue to reposition and drag.*

Follow these instructions to create **smooth curves** with the **Pen** tool. The anchor points that connect smooth curve segments have a pair of direction lines that move in tandem. The longer the direction lines, the steeper or wider the curves. You can practice drawing curves by tracing over a placed image that contains curved shapes (see page 217) or by converting curved objects into guides and then tracing the guide lines (see page 455).

To draw smooth curves with the Pen tool:

1. Choose the **Pen** tool (P). 🖋 *Optional:* Turn on Smart Guides (Cmd-U/Ctrl-U toggle).

2. **Drag** to create the first anchor point **1**. The angle of the pair of direction lines that you create will be determined by the direction you drag.

3. **Release** the mouse, **move** it away from the last anchor point, then drag a short distance in the direction you want the curve to follow to create a second anchor point **2**. A curve segment will connect the first and second anchor points, and a second pair of direction lines will be created. The shape of the curve segment will be defined by the length and direction in which you drag the mouse.

   Remember, you can always reshape the curves later (see Chapter 12). When you drag a direction line after it's drawn, only one of the curves that the smooth point connects will be reshaped.

4. Drag to create additional anchor points and direction lines **3**–**4**. The points will be connected by curve segments.

   (Continued on the following page)

Smooth Curves with Pen Tool

5. To complete the object as an **open** path:

Choose a different **tool.**
or
Cmd-click/Ctrl-click away from the new object to deselect it.
or
Choose Select > **Deselect** (Cmd-Shift-A/ Ctrl-Shift-A).

Or to complete the object as a **closed** path, position the Pen pointer over the **starting point**. A small loop will appear next to the pointer, and if Text Label Hints is on in Preferences (Cmd-K/ Ctrl-K) > Smart Guides & Slices, the word "anchor" will also appear. Drag, then release the mouse.

➤ The fewer the anchor points, the smoother the shape. Too many anchor points will produce bumpy curves, and also may cause printing errors. Try to make your direction lines relatively short at first—you can always lengthen them later.

Adjust as you go

➤ If the last-created anchor point was a **smooth** point and you want to convert it to a **corner** point, click it with the Pen tool, release and move the mouse, then continue to draw. One direction line from that point will disappear.

➤ If the last point you created was a **corner** point and you want to add a direction line to it, position the Pen tool pointer over it, then drag. One direction line will appear. Continue to draw.

➤ To move a point as it's being created, keep the mouse button down, hold down the **Spacebar,** and drag the point.

Be smart with your pen

To display temporary angle lines that align to existing points as you click or drag with the Pen tool **1**, check **Construction Guides** in Illustrator (Edit, in Windows) > Preferences > Smart Guides & Slices and turn on **Smart Guides** (Cmd-U/Ctrl-U).

Favorite toggles (Pen tool selected)

Convert Anchor Point tool   Option/Alt

Last-used **selection** tool   Cmd/Ctrl

DANIEL PELAVIN

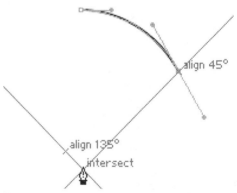

1 *Use* ***smart guides*** *to help you align new anchor points with existing, unselected anchor points.*

1 *Drag to create the first anchor point.*

Release the mouse, reposition it, then drag to create a second anchor point.

3 *Option-drag/Alt-drag from the last anchor point in the direction you want the new curve to follow. The direction lines are on the same side of the curve segment.*

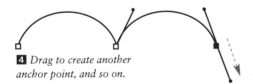

4 *Drag to create another anchor point, and so on.*

Converting points

You can use the Pen tool to create corner points that join nonsmooth curves, which are segments that curve on the same side of an anchor point. (Segments curve on both sides of a smooth anchor point.) If you move one direction line from a corner point, only the curve on that side of the point will change shape. Smooth points and corner points can be combined in the same path, of course. You can **convert smooth points** into **corner points** (or vice versa) as you draw them (instructions on this page) or after you draw them (instructions on the next page).

To convert smooth points into corner points as you draw them:

1. Choose the **Pen** tool (P). 🖋

2. **Drag** to create the first anchor point **1**.

3. **Release** the mouse, **move** it away from the last anchor point, then drag to create a second anchor point **2**. A curve segment will connect the first and second anchor points, and a second pair of direction lines will be created. The shape of the curve segment will be determined by the length and direction you drag.

4. Position the pointer over the last anchor point, **Option-drag/Alt-drag** from that point to create a new direction line (the kind that can be moved independently), then drag in the direction you want the curve to follow **3**.
   or
   Click the **last** anchor point to remove one of the direction lines from that point.

5. Repeat steps 3 and 4 to draw more anchor points and curves **4**.

6. To close the shape:
   Drag on the starting point to keep it as a **smooth** point.
   or
   To **convert** the starting point to a corner, **click** on it.

This is a recap of the various ways to use the **Convert Anchor Point** tool. These techniques were covered in three separate sets of instructions in Chapter 12.

To convert points on an existing path:

1. Choose the **Direct Selection** tool (A).

2. Click on a path.

3. Choose the **Convert Anchor Point** tool (Shift-C).
   or
   Choose the **Pen** tool (P), then hold down Option/Alt.

4. Drag new direction lines from a **corner point** to convert it into a smooth point 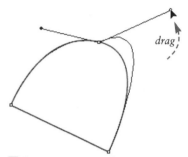.
   or
   To convert a **smooth point** into a corner point with a nonsmooth curve, rotate a **direction line** from the point so it forms a V shape with the other direction line **2**.
   or
   Click a **smooth point** to convert it into a corner point with no direction lines **3**–**4**.

5. Repeat step 4 to convert other anchor points.

1 *Converting a **corner** point into a **smooth** point*

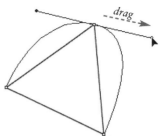

2 *Converting a **smooth** point into a **corner** point (creating a **nonsmooth** curve)*

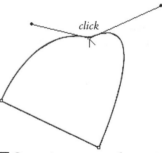

3 *Converting a **nonsmooth** curve into a **corner** point with **no direction lines***

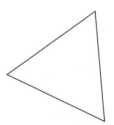

4 *Back to the original triangle*

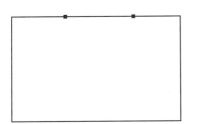

1 *Click to add two anchor points along the top segment, dividing it into thirds.*

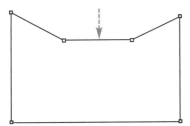

2 *Drag the middle segment downward.*

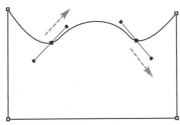

3 *Convert each new point into a smooth point.*

Exercise

Convert a rectangle into a costume mask

The outer part of the face mask

1. Choose the **Rectangle** tool, ▥ choose a fill of None and a 1-pt. black stroke, then draw a rectangle.

2. Choose the **Direct Selection** tool (A), ▸ then select the rectangle.

3. Choose the **Pen** tool (P), ✎ and make sure Disable Auto Add/Delete is unchecked in Preferences (Cmd-K/Ctrl-K) > General.

4. Click to add two anchor points at the points along the top segment of the rectangle, dividing it into thirds **1**.

5. Cmd-drag/Ctrl-drag the segment between the new points downward **2**.

6. Option-drag/Alt-drag the new point on the left upward and to the right to convert it into a smooth point, and Option-drag/Alt-drag the new point on the right downward and to the right **3**.

7. Option-drag/Alt-drag the bottom left corner point upward and to the left and the bottom right corner point downward and to the left **4**.

8. Release Option/Alt, then click to add a point in the middle of the bottommost segment.

9. Hold down Cmd/Ctrl, click the new center point, then drag it slightly upward **5**.

(Continued on the following page)

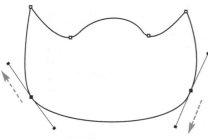

4 *Convert the bottom corner points into smooth points.*

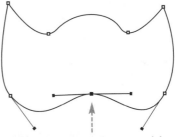

5 *Add a point in the center of the bottom segment, then drag the new point upward.*

The eye holes

1. Choose the **Ellipse** tool (L), move the pointer inside the existing shape, then draw a small ellipse for an eye hole **1**.

2. Choose the **Direct Selection** tool (A). Deselect, click the leftmost anchor point of the ellipse, then drag it upward to form an eye shape **2**.

3. Click the bottommost anchor point of the ellipse, then drag the left handle of that point to the left to widen the bottom segment **3**.

4. Click the top middle point of the ellipse, then drag the right handle (direction point) of that point upward and to the right to widen the top right segment **4**.

5. Choose the **Selection** tool (V), then move the ellipse to the left side of the mask shape.

6. Choose the **Reflect** tool (O).

7. Option-click/Alt-click the center of the face mask. In the dialog box, check Preview, click Vertical, enter "90" in the Angle field, then click Copy **5**.

8. Use the **Selection** tool to marquee all three shapes, and fill the shapes with a color. Leave them selected.

9. To create a compound shape, choose Object > Compound Path > **Make** (Cmd-8/Ctrl-8) or click the **Subtract from Shape Area** button on the Pathfinder palette. The eye holes, which now cut through the face mask **6**, can be modified with the Direct Selection tool.

1 Create a small ellipse for the eye holes.

2 Drag the leftmost anchor point upward with the Direct Selection tool.

3 Drag the left direction handle of the bottommost anchor point to the left.

4 Drag the right handle of the top middle anchor point upward and to the right.

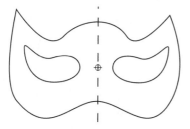

5 To create the second eye hole, Option-click/Alt-click in the center of the mask shape with the Reflect tool. Check Preview, click Vertical, enter "90" in the Angle field, then click Copy.

6 All the shapes are selected and made into a compound shape, and a fill color is applied to the compound shape. A gray rectangle is visible behind the mask, proving that the eye holes are transparent.

LAYERS 15

In this comprehensive and important chapter you'll learn how to create
top-level layers and sublayers; create and edit groups; highlight layers;
select objects using the Layers palette; restack, duplicate, and delete layers
and objects; choose layer options such as hide/show, lock/unlock, view, and
print; collect objects onto a new layer; and finally, merge and flatten layers.

Show/hide *Lock/unlock* *Target* object or
layer, sublayer, layer, sublayer, group to edit
or object group, or object its appearances

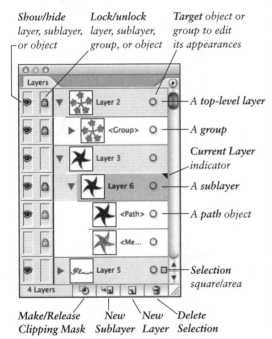

— A *top-level layer*

— A *group*

Current Layer
indicator

— A *sublayer*

— A *path* object

— *Selection*
square/area

Make/Release *New* *New* *Delete*
Clipping Mask *Sublayer* *Layer* *Selection*

1 The objects (paths, type, images,
meshes, etc.) in this document are
nested within top-level layers and
sublayers at various stacking levels.

2 The Layers
palette for this
artwork is
shown above.

The Layers palette
What the palette is used for

Until now (unless you snuck ahead to this
chapter!), you've been creating objects on a
single, default layer that was created automatically when you created your document,
with each new path stacked above the last.

Now it's time to get acquainted with the feature that allows you to change the stacking
order of objects—the Layers palette. To
show (or hide) the palette, press F7. With a
document open, click the Layer 1 arrowhead
on the Layers palette to reveal the list of
objects on that layer. Layer 1 is called a **top-
level layer,** meaning it's not nested within
another layer **1**–**2**.

You can add as many layers as you like to
a document, available memory permitting,
and you can also create **sublayers** (indented
layers) within any top-level layer. The actual
objects that make up your artwork—paths,
text, images, etc.—are nested within one or
more top-level layers, or on sublayers within
top-level layers.

By default, each object is nested automatically within whichever layer was highlighted
when the object was created. Objects can be
moved to different layers at any time, either
individually or by restacking the whole layer
or sublayer the objects reside in.

The Layers palette has other important functions beyond restacking! You can also use it
to highlight, select, target (for appearance
changes), show/hide, or lock/unlock any
layer, sublayer, group, or individual object.
(Continued on the following page)

Layers Palette

Object names on the Layers palette

By default, each new vector object you create is listed as **<Path>**; each placed raster image or rasterized object is listed as **<Image>**; each mesh object is listed as **<Mesh>**; each **symbol** is listed by the name of that symbol (e.g., "Button"); and each **text** object is listed by the first few characters in that object (e.g., "The planting season has begun" might be shortened to "The plan"). Similarly, object groups are listed by such names as Live Paint, Compound Path, Blend, etc.

➤ Double-click an object or layer name to assign a custom name to it. We suggest you leave the word "group" or "path" in the name to help you identify it later.

You may say "Whoa!" when you first see the long list of names on the Layers palette. Once you get used to working with it, though, you may become enamored with its clean, logical design, as we are, and you'll enjoy how easy it makes even simple tasks, such as selecting objects.

➤ Layers and sublayers are numbered in the order in which they are created, regardless of their position in the stacking order or how far in they're indented.

You can choose different **Layers palette options** for each document.

To choose Layers palette options:

1. Choose **Palette Options** from the bottom of the Layers palette menu.

2. Do any of the following **1**–**2**:

   Check **Show Layers Only** to have the palette list only top-level layers and sublayers—not individual objects.

   For the layer and object thumbnail size, click a **Row Size:** Small (12 pixels), Medium (20 pixels), or Large (32 pixels). Or click Other and enter a custom size (12–100 pixels).

   Check which **Thumbnails** to display: Layers, Groups, or Objects. For the Layers option, check Top Level Only to have thumbnails display for top-level layers but not for sublayers.

3. Click OK.

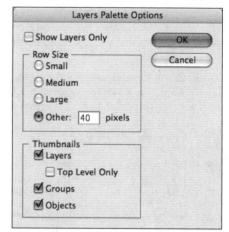

1 *You can customize the Layers palette for each file.*

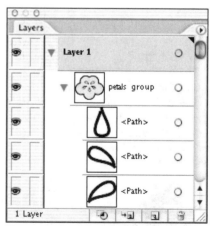

2 *For this document, we chose a large, custom Row Size (Other: 40 pixels), and turned Thumbnails off for Layers.*

Quick layer

To insert a new top-level layer in the topmost position on the palette, regardless of which layer is currently highlighted, **Cmd-click/Ctrl-click** the **New Layer** button at the bottom of the Layers palette. ▣

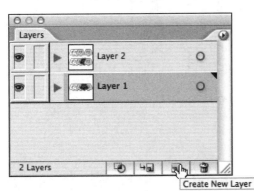

1 *Option-click/Alt-click the **New Layer** button on the **Layers** palette to choose options for or rename a new layer as you create it.*

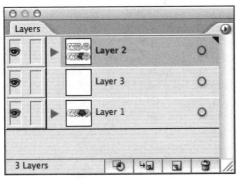

2 *The new Layer 3 appears above Layer 1.*

Creating layers

In these instructions, you'll learn how to create the granddaddy of layers—**top-level layers**.

To create a new top-level layer:

Method 1 (quick, no options)

1. On the Layers palette (F7), click the name of the top-level layer that you want the new layer to appear above.

2. To create a layer without choosing options for it, click the **New Layer** button. ▣ Illustrator will assign to the new layer the next number in order and the next available color, as listed on the Color pop-up menu in the Layer Options dialog box.

Method 2 (choose options)

1. On the Layers palette (F7), click the name of the top-level layer that you want the new layer to appear above.

2. Option-click/Alt-click the **New Layer** button ▣ **1**–**2** (or choose **New Layer** from the Layers palette menu).

3. Do any of the following:

   Change the layer **Name.**

   Choose a different selection border color for objects on the layer via the **Color** pop-up menu. The various selection colors are there to help you identify which layer or sublayer a selected object resides in. Colors are assigned to new layers in the order in which they appear on this pop-up menu. If the fill or stroke colors of objects on the layer are similar to the selection border colors, and it's hard to figure out which is which, try choosing a different selection color.

   Choose other layer options (for information about these options, see pages 212–213).

4. Click OK.

➤ A group or object will always be nested within a top-level layer or sublayer—it can't float around aimlessly by itself.

Create Top-Level Layer

Once you become accustomed to adding and using top-level layers, you're ready for the next level of intricacy: **sublayers.** Each sublayer is nested within (indented under) either a top-level layer or another sublayer, and layer options can be chosen separately for each individual sublayer. If you create a new object or group of objects while a sublayer is selected, the new object or group will be nested within that sublayer.

By default, every sublayer has the same generic name: "Layer." You can rename your layers and sublayers to make it easier to identify them (e.g., "inner pieces" or "order form" or "tyrannosaurus").

To create a sublayer:

Method 1 (quick, no options)

1. On the Layers palette (F7), click the top-level layer (or sublayer) name that you want the new sublayer to appear in.

2. To create a new layer without choosing options for it, click the **New Sublayer** button **1**–**2**.

Method 2 (choose options)

1. On the Layers palette (F7), click the top-level layer (or sublayer) that you want the new sublayer to appear in.

2. To create a new sublayer and choose options for it, Option-click/Alt-click the **New Sublayer** button or choose **New Sublayer** from the Layers palette menu.

3. Enter a **Name** for the new sublayer.

4. *Optional:* Change the selection Color for the sublayer, and check or uncheck Template, Show, Preview, Lock, Print, or "Dim Images to" (see pages 212–213).

5. Click OK.

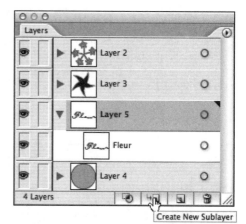

1 *Highlight a layer name, then click the* **New Sublayer** *button.*

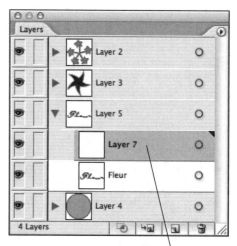

2 *A new sublayer name (in this case, Layer 7) appears within Layer 5.*

Create Sublayer

1 *First, select the objects to be grouped. You can draw a marquee around them...*

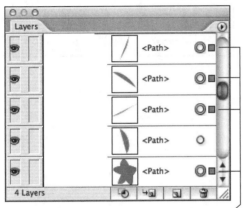

2 *...or Shift-click the selection area on the Layers palette for each object.*

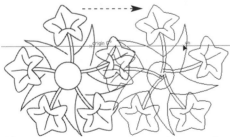

3 *If you move a group using the Selection tool, all the objects in the group will move in unison.*

Creating groups

If you **group objects** together, you can easily select, isolate, cut, copy, paste, transform, recolor, or move them as a unit. When objects are grouped, they're automatically placed on the same top-level layer (the top-level layer of the frontmost object in the group) and are assigned the same selection color. You can group any types of objects together (e.g., type objects with placed images) and you can select and edit individual objects in a group without having to ungroup them first.

To create a group:

1. Choose the **Selection** tool (V). Then, in the document window, Shift-click or marquee all the objects to be grouped **1**.
   or
   Shift-click the **selection area** or the **target circle** ○ at the far right side of the Layers palette for each object you want to be part of the group. A selection square will appear for each of those objects **2**. (You'll learn more about the selection squares later in this chapter.)

2. Choose Object > **Group** (Cmd-G/ Ctrl-G) **3**.
   or
   Control-click/right-click in the document window and choose **Group** from the context menu.

Create Group

Highlighting layers and objects

If you want to control where a new (or pasted) object will be positioned within the overall stacking order of a document, you need to **highlight** (click the name of) a **top-level layer, sublayer, group,** or **object** on the Layers palette before you start pasting or drawing.

Highlighting a top-level layer or sublayer doesn't cause objects on that layer to become selected. Selecting objects via the Layers palette is a separate step, and targeting items for appearance attributes is yet another step (see the sidebar on the next page). Think of highlighting as a layer management technique, and selecting as an essential first step when editing objects. To learn how to select objects by using the Layers palette, see pages 202–205.

➤ If you click a **top-level** layer but not a sublayer or group, and then create or place an object, the new object (e.g., <Path> or <Mesh>) will be listed at the top of the top-level layer.

➤ If you click a **sublayer** without selecting any objects, and then create or place an object, the new object will appear on that sublayer. Or if you click a **group,** the new object will appear above the group.

➤ If you select an **object** and then create or place an object, the new object will appear in the same layer or sublayer as the selected object, outside any group.

Note: What we call highlighting (for the sake of brevity) Adobe calls "selecting a layer listing."

To highlight a layer, sublayer, group, or object:

Click a top-level layer, sublayer, group, or object **name**—not the selection area at the far right side of the palette. The **Current Layer** indicator (black triangle) ◼ will appear at the far right side of the palette for the top-level layer that contains the layer you clicked. (To highlight multiple layers, groups, or objects, follow the instructions on the next page.)

◼ *The **Current Layer** indicator appears when you highlight a layer, sublayer, group, or object.*

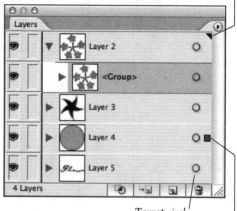

Target circle

Selection square/area

Circles and squares

The column of little circles on the right side of the Layers palette is used for **targeting** an object, group, or layer when applying appearance attributes (read about appearances in Chapter 19).

When you click the **target** circle or the **selection area** at the far right side of the palette for a group or object, the object or group becomes **selected** and becomes a listing on the Appearance palette (you'll learn more about selection methods beginning on the next page).

For a top-level layer or sublayer, it's a different story. To select all the objects on a top-level layer or sublayer, click the selection area. To target a top-level layer or sublayer and have it become a listing on the Appearance palette, click the target circle. You can't target a top-level layer or sublayer via its selection area.

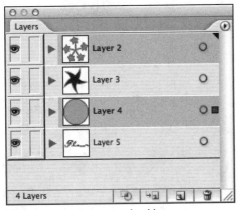

1 *Two noncontiguous top-level layers are highlighted.*

When **more than one layer,** sublayer, or object is **highlighted,** they can be restacked on the palette en masse and the same layer options can be applied to them.

First, a few rules:

➤ You can highlight more than one **sublayer** within the same top-level layer, provided they're at the same nesting level, but you can't highlight sublayers on different top-level layers.

➤ You can highlight more than one item of the same **category** (e.g., multiple top-level layers), but you can't highlight items on different nesting levels at the same time (e.g., not top-level layers with sublayers).

➤ You can highlight multiple **objects** (e.g., paths) in the same top-level layer, but you can't highlight objects on different top-level layers.

Note that highlighting and selecting serve different functions. When objects are selected, their anchor points and segments become visible in the document window and they're ready for editing. When an object is selected, its top-level layer or sublayer becomes highlighted automatically, but simply clicking a name on the Layers palette won't cause any objects to become selected.

To highlight multiple items:

1. On the **Layers** palette (F7), click a top-level layer, sublayer, or object **name.**

2. Shift-click another layer, sublayer, or object name. The items you clicked and all items between them of a similar kind will become highlighted.
   or
   Cmd-click/Ctrl-click noncontiguous top-level layer, sublayer, or object names **1**.

   Note that although you can activate any number of layers, only one top-level layer or sublayer can have a Current Layer indicator (little black triangle).

➤ Cmd-click/Ctrl-click to unhighlight any individual items when multiple items are highlighted.

Selecting objects

As we explored in Chapter 8, objects can be selected in the document window by using a variety of selection tools and Select menu commands. We also like to use the **Layers palette** to **select** paths or groups. Here, we're talking about selecting for the purpose of editing or reshaping—selection handles and all—not just highlighting, which we showed you how to do on the previous two pages.

To select all the objects in a layer:

Click the **selection area** for a top-level layer or sublayer at the far right side of the Layers palette. A colored selection square will appear for every sublayer, group, and object on that layer; every object on the layer, regardless of its indent level, will become selected in the document window; and the target circle for each path and group will also become selected (a double ring), unless the items are within a group **1**–**2**.

➤ To deselect any individual selected object when a whole layer is selected, expand the object's top-level layer or sublayer list, then Shift-click the object's selection square.

➤ To learn about the target circle on the Layers palette, see page 290.

To deselect all the objects in a layer:

Shift-click a layer's **target circle** or **selection square** twice. All the objects in the layer will be deselected, including any objects in any sublayers or groups on the layer.

To select one object:

1. On the Layers palette, expand any top-level layer, sublayer, or group list, if necessary, so the name of the object that you want to select is visible.

2. At the far right side of the palette, click the **selection area** or **target circle** for the object you want to select **3**.

   To select multiple objects on different layers, follow the instructions on the next page.

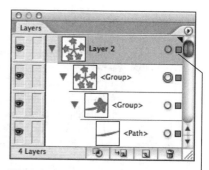

1 *Click the* **selection area** *for a layer to select all the paths and groups on that layer.*

2 *All the paths and path groups on our "flowers" layer became selected in the document window.*

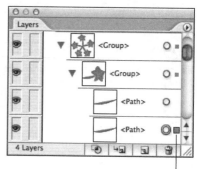

3 *One object is* **selected.**

Select, Deselect Objects

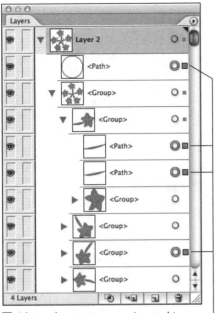

1 *Objects from **nonconsecutive** stacking levels are **selected** (note the selection squares).*

Using the **Layers** palette, you can **select multiple groups** or **objects** on different— even nonconsecutive—top-level layers or sublayers.

To select multiple objects on different layers:

Method 1 (Shift-clicking)

Expand any layer or group lists so the names of all the nested objects that you want to select are visible. Click the **selection area** or **target circle** for any object, then Shift-click any other individual groups or objects that you want to add to the selection **1**. They don't have to be listed consecutively.

Method 2 (dragging)

Option-drag/Alt-drag upward or downward through a series of consecutive top-level or sublayer **names** (not the selection areas) to select all the objects on those layers.

➤ To deselect any selected object individually, Shift-click its selection square or target circle.

Working with groups

To select all the objects in a group:

Method 1 (Layers palette)

1. Expand a top-level layer on the palette that contains a nested group.

2. To select all the objects in a group, (including any groups that may be nested inside it), click the group's **selection area** or **target circle** at the far right side of the Layers palette **2**.
   or
   To select all the objects in a group that's nested inside another group, expand the list for the larger group, then click the **selection area** for just the nested group.

(To learn how to create a group, see page 199.)

(Method 2 is on the following page.)

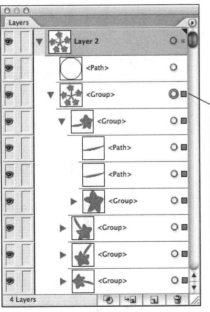

2 *If you click the selection area for a **group**, all the objects in the group will become selected.*

Select Multiple Objects; Select Grouped Objects

Method 2 (document window)

To select an entire group, click any item in the group with the **Selection** tool (V).

or

To select an object in a group—or individual anchor points or segments on an object in a group—click the object, point, or segment with the **Direct Selection** tool (A).

or

To select a group that's nested within a larger, parent group, you can either use the **Direct Selection** tool while holding down Option/Alt or use the **Group Selection** tool (on the Direct Selection tool pop-out menu). Click once to select an object in a group **1**; click the same object again to select the whole group the object is part of **2**; click a third time on the object to select the next larger group that the newly selected group is a part of **3**, and so on.

➤ To display the bounding box around a selection, choose View > Show Bounding Box (if it says Hide Bounding Box, the feature is on; don't choose it), keep the object(s) selected, and choose the Selection tool.

NEW If you **isolate a group,** you'll then be able to select any object in the group with the Selection tool.

To isolate a group:

1. Choose the **Selection** tool.

2. Double-click a group in the document window.

or

Click the **Isolate Selected Group** button on the Control palette.

A gray rectangle will appear around the group. You can now use the Selection or Direct Selection tool to select, move, transform, or reshape any object in the group.

3. When you're done, double-click outside the gray rectangle or click the **Exit Isolated Group** button on the Control palette.

1 *Click once to select an object in a group (in this case, the topmost flower).*

2 *Click again to select the remaining objects in the same group.*

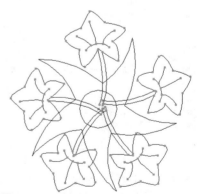

3 *Continue clicking to select other groups, if any, that are nested inside the larger group.*

Isolate Group

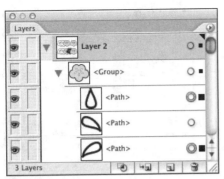

1 To *select multiple objects in a group, expand the group list, then Shift-click the* **selection area** *for each object. A* **selection square** *will appear for each object. (To deselect an object in a group, Shift-click its selection square.)*

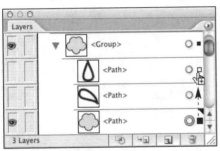

2 To *copy an object in a group, Option-drag/ Alt-drag its selection square upward or downward (note the plus sign).*

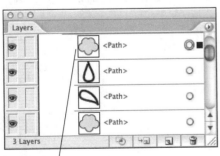

3 *The duplicate appears.*

To select some objects in a group:

1. Deselect all (Cmd-Shift-A/Ctrl-Shift-A).

2. Expand the group list on the **Layers** palette, then Shift-click the selection area or target circle at the far right side of the palette for each object in the group that you want to select **1**.
   or
   Choose the **Selection** tool, then double-click the group to isolate it. Click, then Shift-click the objects you want to select.

To deselect an object in a selected group:

On the Layers palette, expand the group list, then Shift-click the **selection square** or **target circle** for an object in the group.
or
Choose the **Direct Selection** tool (A), ▶ then Shift-click an object in the document window.

To copy an object in a group:
Method 1 (Layers palette)

1. Expand the group list.

2. Click the selection area for the object you want to copy.

3. Option-drag/Alt-drag the selection square upward or downward, then release the mouse when the little outline square is at the desired stacking position, either inside the same group or in another sub-layer or top-level layer **2**–**3**.

Method 2 (document window)

1. Choose the **Direct Selection** tool (A), ▶ then select the object you want to copy.

2. To keep the copy **inside** the group, Option-drag/Alt-drag the object.
   or
   To have the copy appear **outside** the group, copy the object (Cmd-C/Ctrl-C), deselect, click the layer that you want the object to appear on, then paste (Cmd-V/Ctrl-V).

Follow these instructions to **add** an existing object to a **group.** The object will stay in its original *x/y* position.

To move an object (or group) into a group:

1. Make sure the name of the object you want to add to the group is visible on the Layers palette.

2. Drag the object name upward or downward in the palette, and release the mouse when the large, black arrowheads point to the desired group **1**–**2**.

➤ You can also move an object into a group by selecting it in the document window, choosing Edit > Cut (Cmd-X/Ctrl-X), double-clicking the group with the Selection tool to isolate it, then choosing Edit > Paste (Cmd-V/Ctrl-V).

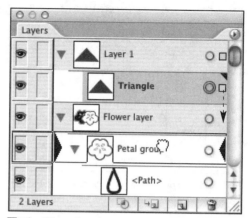

1 *The "Triangle"* **object** *is dragged downward into the "Petal group."*

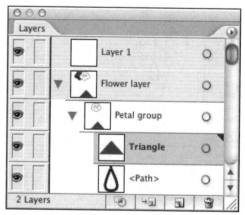

2 *With the "Petal group" expanded, you can see the "Triangle" object on the list.*

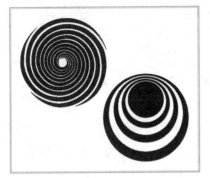

1 *A group is isolated.*

2 *Two new objects are added to the isolated group.*

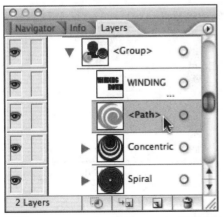

3 *The new type and path are nested within the same group on the Layers palette.*

Before creating an object or placing an image into an Illustrator document, you can **choose which group** you want it to belong to.

To add a new object to a group:

1. Choose the **Selection** tool (V), ▸ then double-click a group to isolate it **1**.

2. Draw a new object or objects **2**. A listing for each new object will appear at the top of the nested group **3**.

3. *Optional:* On the Layers palette, expand the group that you added an object to, then drag the new object name to any other position in the group list.

There comes a time when a group has to be disbanded—**ungrouped,** that is.

To ungroup a group:

1. If the group isn't already selected:
   Choose the **Selection** tool (V), ▸ then click the group in the document window.
   or
   Click the selection area or target circle for the group on the Layers palette.

2. Choose Object > **Ungroup** (Cmd-Shift-G/ Ctrl-Shift-G).
   or
   Control-click/right-click the artboard and choose **Ungroup** from the context menu. If the command isn't available, it means no group is selected.

   The "group" listing will disappear from the Layers palette.

➤ Keep choosing the same command again to ungroup nested groups.

Restacking objects and layers

The order of objects and layers on the Layers palette matches the front-to-back order of objects (and layers) in the artwork. To change how your artwork looks, you can move a group or object to a different stacking position within the same layer, move a group or object to a different top-level layer or sublayer, or even move a whole top-level layer or sublayer upward or downward on the list. We'll show you several methods for **restacking objects** and **layers,** starting with the **Layers** palette.

To restack a layer, group, or object:

Drag a top-level layer, sublayer, group, or object name upward or downward on the Layers palette (the pointer will turn into a hand icon). Release the mouse between layers or objects to keep the object at the same indent level (say, to keep a path within a group) **1**–**2**. Or to move the object to a new group or layer, release the mouse when the large black arrowheads point to the desired group or layer **3**–**4**. The document will redraw with the objects in their new stacking position.

Beware! If you move an object that's part of a group or clipping mask to a different top-level layer, the object will be released from the group or mask.

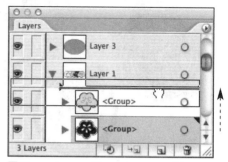

1 *Drag a layer, sublayer, group, or object name upward or downward on the list. Here the mouse is released at the **same indent level.***

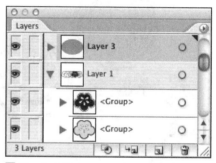

2 *The dark flower group is restacked.*

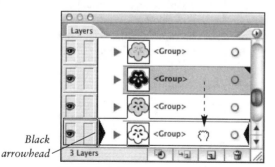

Black arrowhead

3 *The dark flower group is moved into a **different group.***

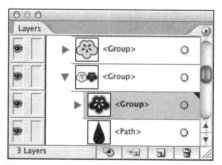

4 *The dark flower group is in a **new group** and **indent level.***

(side margin) **Restack Layers or Objects**

Upside down

To reverse the order of sublayers, groups, and objects in a layer, on the Layers palette, highlight (don't select) all the items that you want to reverse. To highlight noncontiguous items, Cmd-click/Ctrl-click them; to highlight contiguous items, click the first and then Shift-click the last. Then choose **Reverse Order** from the Layers palette menu.

Remembering layers

If you want to paste an object to the top of its own layer or sublayer rather than to a different layer, turn the **Paste Remembers Layers** option on via the Layers palette menu. If this option is on and the original layer is deleted after the object is copied, but before the Paste command is used, the objects will paste into a brand new layer.

1 *Select the object that you want to restack, then choose Edit > Cut.*

2 *Select the object that you want to paste directly in front of or directly behind.*

3 *Choose Edit > Paste in Front or Paste in Back (we chose Paste in Back.)*

This method for **restacking** objects uses both the **Layers palette** and a **command.**

To move an object to a different layer:

1. Choose the **Selection** tool (V), ▶ then select one or more objects.
2. On the Layers palette, click the layer you want to move the selected object(s) to.
3. Right-click/Ctrl-click in the document window and choose Arrange > **Send to Current Layer** (or choose the command from the Object > Arrange submenu).

The **Paste in Front** and **Paste in Back** commands paste the Clipboard contents directly in front of or directly behind the currently selected object within the selected object's layer, in the same horizontal and vertical (x/y) position from which it was cut.

To restack an object in front of or behind another object:

1. Choose the Selection tool (V), ▶ then select an object **1**.
2. Choose Edit > **Cut** (Cmd-X/Ctrl-X).
3. Select the object (in the same document or a different document) that you want to paste directly in front of or directly behind **2**. If you don't select an object, the Clipboard contents will be pasted to the top or bottom of the currently highlighted top-level layer.
4. Choose Edit > **Paste in Front** (Cmd-F/Ctrl-F).
   or
   Choose Edit > **Paste in Back** (Cmd-B/Ctrl-B) **3**.

   Note: If you paste in front or in back of an object in a group, the object you paste will be added to the group.

Restack Objects

Duplicating layers and objects

If you **duplicate** an entire **top-level layer**, all the sublayers and objects in that layer will also appear in the duplicate. The duplicate layer will be stacked directly above the original from which it was made.

To duplicate a layer, sublayer, or object:

On the Layers palette, highlight the layer, sublayer, or object that you want to duplicate, then choose **Duplicate** "[layer or object name]" from the Layers palette menu.
or
Drag a layer, sublayer, or object name over the **New Layer** button 🔲 **1**–**2**. If you duplicate a top-level layer or sublayer, the word "copy" will appear in the duplicate name.

Follow these instructions to **copy** all the **objects** from a **top-level layer,** and any sublayers or groups that it contains, to an existing layer or sublayer of your choice. (In the previous set of instructions, the duplicate objects appeared in a new layer.)

To copy objects between layers:

1. Click the selection area for a top-level layer, sublayer, group, or object.

2. Option-drag/Alt-drag the selection square for the layer, sublayer, group, or object upward or downward on the list. Release the mouse when the selection square is in the desired location **3**–**4**. The duplicate objects will appear in the same *x/y* location as the original objects.

➤ If you Option-drag/Alt-drag a <clipping path> (a mask) into a different top-level layer, the mask copy won't clip any objects below it. It will be a basic path with a fill and stroke of None.

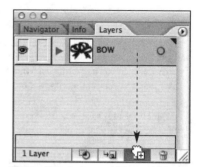

1 *Duplicate a layer, sublayer, group, or object by dragging it over the* **New Layer** *button (note the plus sign).*

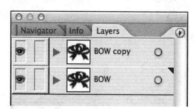

2 *A copy of the BOW layer is made.*

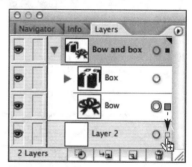

3 *To copy an object, Option-drag/Alt-drag its selection square.*

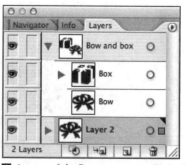

4 *A copy of the Bow appears on Layer 2.*

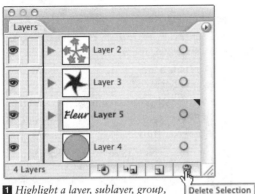

1 *Highlight a layer, sublayer, group, or object, then click the* ***Delete Selection*** *button.*

Deleting layers

You know how to make 'em. Now you need to learn how to **get rid of 'em.**

Beware! If you delete a top-level layer or sublayer, any and all objects on that layer will be removed from the document.

To delete a layer, sublayer, group, or object:

1. On the Layers palette, highlight all the layers, sublayers, groups, and objects that you want to delete (Cmd-click/Ctrl-click to highlight more than one). Remember, you can highlight multiple items at the same indent level (e.g., all top-level layers), but not items from different indent levels (e.g., not a top-level layer and objects from a different top-level layer).

2. Choose **Delete** "[layer or object name]" from the Layers palette menu or click the **Delete Selection** button ⬚ at the bottom of the palette **1**. If there are any objects on a layer or sublayer that you're deleting, an alert dialog box will appear. Click Yes.

   or

   To bypass the prompt, drag the highlighted layers or objects over the **Delete Selection** button.⬚

➤ To retrieve a deleted layer and the objects it contained, choose Edit > Undo Deletion (Cmd-Z/Ctrl-Z) immediately.

Choosing layer and object options

To choose multiple options (e.g., color, lock, show/hide, and print) for a layer or object from one central dialog box, use the Layer Options dialog box, as per the instructions below (one-stop shopping). To choose individual options for a layer or an object (e.g., hide a layer or change its view mode), see pages 214–216.

If you choose **Layer Options** for a top-level layer, those options will apply to all the sublayers, groups, and objects within that layer. You can also choose options for a sublayer, group, or individual object.

To choose layer or object options:

1. Double-click a layer, sublayer, group, or object on the Layers palette.
   or
   Highlight a layer, sublayer, group, or object on the Layers palette, then choose **Options for "[   ]"** from the palette menu.
   or
   Highlight more than one layer, sublayer, group, or object, then choose **Options for Selection** from the palette menu.

2. For the highlighted layer, sublayer, group, or object, do any of the following **1**–**2**:

   Type a different **Name** for the layer, sublayer, group, or object.

   Check **Show** to display that object or all the objects on the layer or sublayer; uncheck to hide the object or objects. Hidden layers won't print.

   Check **Lock** to prevent that object or all the objects on that layer or sublayer from being edited; uncheck to allow the objects to be edited.

   ➤ For quicker ways to lock layers and sublayers, see page 214; to quickly hide/show layers, see page 215.

   For a layer or sublayer, do any of the following:

   Choose a different **Color** for the object's selection border in the artwork and for its selection square on the Layers palette.

Making layers nonprintable

There are three ways to make a layer nonprintable, and there are significant differences among them:

➤ If you **hide** a layer, the layer can't be printed, exported, or edited.

➤ If you turn a layer into a **template,** it can't be printed or exported, but it can be edited and will be visible (images on the layer can be dimmed).

➤ If you turn off the **Print** option in the Layer Options dialog box, the layer won't print, but it can be exported and edited, and it will be visible.

1 *The Layer Options dialog box for a layer*

2 *The Options dialog box for a path*

(Note: Sublayers have a different color than their top-level layer.) If the current selection color is similar to colors in the artwork, you may want to choose a selection color that stands out more. Choose a preset color from the pop-up menu; or choose Other, mix a color using the Colors dialog box, then click OK.

Click **Template** to convert the layer or sublayer into a nonprintable tracing layer. The layer will be locked and its name will be listed in italics. By default, when you convert a layer into a template, any placed images and rasterized objects on the layer are dimmed automatically by 50%.

Check **Preview** to have the layer display in Preview view; uncheck it to have the layer display in Outline view.

➤ To switch views for a layer without opening the Layer Options dialog box, see "To change the view for a top-level layer" on page 216.

Check **Print** to make the layer printable; uncheck it to prevent all the objects on that layer from printing (see the sidebar on the previous page). Nonprintable layers are listed in italics.

➤ Another way to make a layer non-printable is by hiding it (click the eye icon on the Layers palette).

If you want to dim any placed images or rasterized objects on the layer or change the "dimming" percentage for a template layer, check **Dim Images to** and enter a percentage. With Template unchecked, images on the layer will be fully editable and print normally, regardless of the "Dim Images to" percentage.

Choose Layer/Object Options

Locking layers and objects

Locked objects can't be selected or modified, but they do remain visible unless you also hide them. When a whole layer is locked, none of the objects on that layer are editable. If you save, close, and reopen a file that contains locked objects, they'll remain locked. You can't lock (or hide) part of a path.

In these instructions, we list a number of ways to **lock layers and objects**. Personally, we use just the first three.

To lock/unlock layers or objects:

On the Layers palette, click in the **edit** (second) column for a layer **1**, sublayer, group, or object **2**. The padlock icon 🔒 will appear. Click the padlock icon to unlock.
or
To lock multiple layers, sublayers, groups, or objects, drag upward or downward in the **edit** column. Drag back over the padlock icons to unlock.
or
Option-click/Alt-click in the **edit** column for a top-level layer to lock or unlock all the other top-level layers except the one you're clicking on.
or
Highlight the layer(s) that you want to keep unlocked, then to lock all the unhighlighted layers, choose **Lock Others** from the Layers palette menu.

Note: Let's say you lock an object and then lock its top-level layer. If you later want to unlock the object, you first have to unlock the top-level layer.

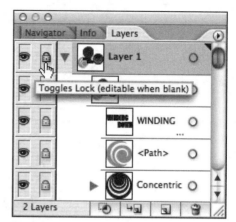

1 *If you lock an entire layer, none of the objects on that layer will be editable.*

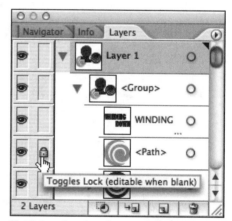

2 *Click in the edit column to lock a layer, group, or object (the padlock icon will appear).*

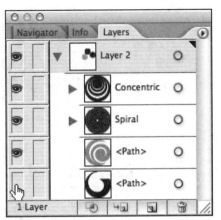

1 *You can hide/show individual* **objects** *or* *groups...*

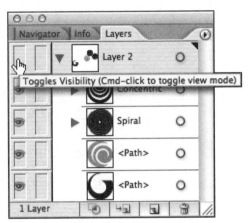

2 *...and you can hide whole* **layers.**

Hiding layers and objects

What have you got to hide? If your artwork tends to be complex, you'll find the ability to **hide objects** to be useful both for isolating the objects you want to work on and for boosting the screen redraw speed. You can hide a top-level layer and all its nested layers, hide a group, or hide an individual object. Hidden objects don't print and are invisible in both Outline and Preview views. When you save, close, and reopen your file, hidden objects remain hidden.

To hide/show layers or objects:

Note: If you want to show an object, but its top-level layer is hidden, you must show its top-level layer first.

Click the **eye** icon 👁 (in the first column) for a top-level layer, sublayer, group, or object **1**–**2**. If you hide a top-level layer or sublayer, any objects nested within that layer or sublayer will be hidden, whether they're selected or not. To redisplay what was hidden, click where the eye icon was.

or

Drag upward or downward in the **eye** column to hide multiple, consecutive top-level layers, sublayers, groups, or objects. To redisplay what was hidden, drag again.

or

Option-click/Alt-click the **eye** column 👁 to hide/show all the top-level layers except the one you're clicking on.

or

Make sure all the layers are visible (choose **Show All Layers** from the Layers palette menu if they're not), highlight the top-level layer or layers that you want to keep visible, then choose **Hide Others** from the Layers palette menu.

Hide Layer or Object

Changing layer views

If you change the **view** for a top-level layer, all nested layers and objects within it will display in that view.

To change the view for a top-level layer:

To display a top-level layer in **Outline** view when the document is in **Preview** view, Cmd-click/Ctrl-click the eye icon 👁 for that layer. The eyeball will become hollow **1**.
To redisplay the layer in **Preview** view, Cmd-click/Ctrl-click the eye icon again.
or
Double-click the layer name, then check or uncheck **Preview**.

To display all top-level layers in Outline view except one:

Cmd-Option-click/Ctrl-Alt-click a top-level layer eye icon 👁 to display all layers and sublayers in **Outline** view except the one you're clicking on. Repeat to redisplay all layers in Preview view.
or
Click the top-level layer that you want to display in **Preview** view, then choose **Outline Others** from the Layers palette menu.

➤ To display all layers in Preview view, choose Preview All Layers from the Layers palette menu.

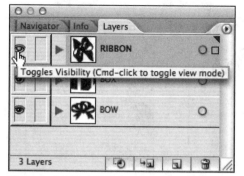

1 *Cmd-click/Ctrl-click the eye icon to toggle between* **Outline** *and* **Preview** *views for that top-level layer.*

(sidebar) Change View for Layer

Show or hide 'em

To **show/hide** all **template layers** in a document, press Cmd-Shift-W/Ctrl-Shift-W.

1 *Template layers have this icon;
the template layer name is in italics.*

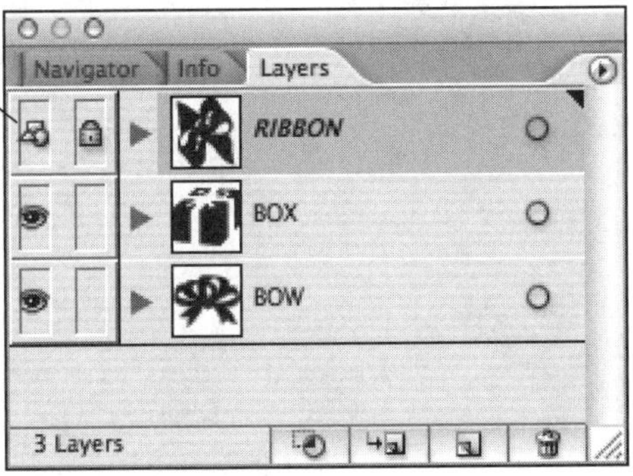

Creating template layers

Objects on a **template layer** are locked, non-printable, and nonexportable, and images on a template layer are also dimmed. However, you can create a new layer above a template layer, then use the objects or images on the template layer as a guide as you draw with the Pen, Pencil, or any other drawing tool. Be sure to also read about the live trace features in Chapter 21.

To create a template layer:

Method 1 (choose options)

1. Double-click an existing top-level layer name.
   or
   To create a new top-level template layer, Option-click/Alt-click the **New Layer** button at the bottom of the Layers palette.

2. Check **Template.**

3. Choose a **Dim Images to** percentage for any placed images or rasterized objects on the template layer.

4. Click OK. A template icon will appear in the eye icon slot for the layer, and any nested layers or objects in that layer will now be locked **1**.

➤ You can unlock a template layer via the Layers palette, then selectively lock/unlock objects on that layer.

Method 2 (quick)

1. Click an existing layer.

2. Choose **Template** from the Layers palette menu.

Method 3 (as an image is placed)

To create a template layer for an image as you place it into Illustrator, in the File > Place dialog box, check **Template.** To place an image on an existing template layer, you have to convert it back into a nontemplate layer first.

Locating objects

When the list of layers and objects on the Layers palette is long, sometimes it's hard to find things on the palette. The **Locate Object** command can help.

To locate an object on the Layers palette:

1. Choose the **Selection** tool (V).

2. Select the object in the document window that you want to locate on the Layers palette. You can select more than one object; they'll all be found. (To select an object in a group, use the Direct Selection or Group Selection tool.)

3. Choose **Locate Object** from the Layers palette menu. The list for the layer containing the topmost selected object will expand, if it's not already expanded.

➤ If "Locate Layer" appears on the palette menu instead of "Locate Object," choose Palette Options from the palette menu and uncheck the Show Layers Only option. The Locate Object command will then become available.

Locate Object

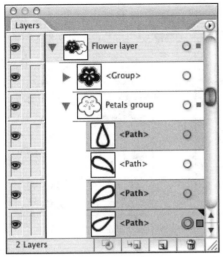

1 *Three paths are highlighted.*

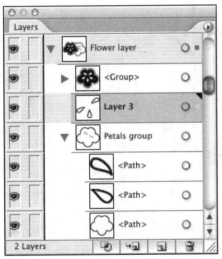

2 *The Collect in New Layer command gathered the three highlighted paths into a new sublayer (Layer 3, in this case).*

Collecting objects in a new layer

The **Collect in New Layer** command moves all the currently highlighted top-level layers, sublayers, groups, or objects into a brand new layer.

To move layers, sublayers, groups, or objects to a new layer:

1. Cmd-click/Ctrl-click the layer, group, or object names that you want to gather together **1**. They must all be at the same indent level (e.g., all objects from the same sublayer or on consecutive sublayers). Don't click the selection area.

2. From the Layers palette menu, choose **Collect in New Layer**. Sublayers, groups, or objects will be nested inside a new sublayer within the same top-level layer **2**, and top-level layers will be nested as sublayers within a new top-level layer. (Bug: To make the expand triangle appear for the new layer, you have to click the selection area.)

Releasing objects to layers

The **Release to Layers** command disperses all objects or groups that are nested within the currently highlighted layer onto new, separate layers within that layer.

If you're planning to export your Illustrator file to an animation program to use as the contents of an object or frame animation, you'll first need to release any groups and expand any appearances or blends in the file, and then use the Release to Layers command to release the objects to individual layers (nested within a top-level layer). In the animation program, you'll then be able to convert the layers from the placed file into separate objects or into a sequence. See pages 512–513.

Read step 2 carefully before deciding which of the two commands you're going to use.

To move objects to new, separate layers:

1. On the Layers palette, highlight or select a top-level layer, sublayer, or group (not an object)(**1**, next page).

(Continued on the following page)

2. From the Layers palette menu, choose:

Release to Layers (Sequence) ▇2. Each object in the highlighted layer or group will be nested in its own new layer within the original layer. The objects' original stacking order will be preserved.

or

If you want to build a cumulative animation sequence, choose **Release to Layers (Build)** ▇3. The bottommost layer will contain only the bottommost object; the next layer above that will contain the bottommost object plus the next object above it; the next layer above that will contain the two previous objects plus the next object above, and so on. Choose this option if you're going to use another application to create a frame animation in which objects are added in succession.

➤ If you release a layer or sublayer that contains a clipping mask that was created using the Layers palette, the mask will still clip the objects within the same layer or sublayer.

➤ If you release a layer or group that contains a scatter brush, the brush object will remain as a single <Path>. If, on the other hand, you highlight only the brush object and release to layers, each object in the scatter brush will be moved to a separate layer; the original scatter brush path will be preserved.

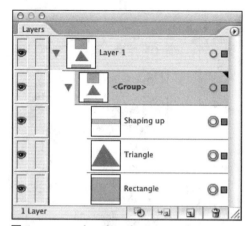

▇1 A *group* is selected on the Layers palette.

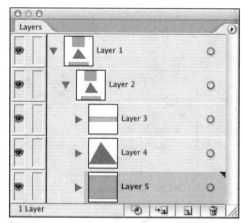

▇2 After choosing **Release to Layers (Sequence)**

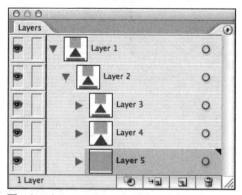

▇3 After choosing **Release to Layers (Build)**

Release to Layers

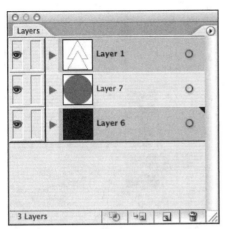

1 *Highlight the layers, sublayers, groups, or objects that you want to merge together.*

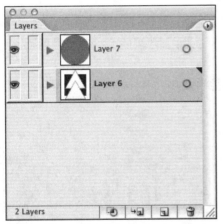

2 *After Merge Selected is chosen, the two highlighted layers are merged into one.*

Merging layers and groups

Warning! If there's a chance you're going to want to work with any individual layers in your file again, save a copy of the file by using File > Save As before applying the **Merge Selected** or **Flatten Artwork** command.

If you have more layers and sublayers on the Layers palette than you can comfortably handle, you can consolidate the list at any time by **merging** some of them together.

You can also merge two or more groups, or merge a group with a sublayer. In the latter case, the individual object(s) on the sublayer will become part of the group. You can't merge one individual object with another.

To merge layers, sublayers, or groups:

1. Highlight two or more layers, sublayers, or groups. Cmd-click/Ctrl-click to highlight noncontiguous top-level layers or sublayers. Click the layer, sublayer, or group that you want the selected items to be merged into last; that item will have the **Current Layer** indicator (the little black triangle at the far right side of the Layers palette) **1**. You can merge locked and/or hidden layers.

2. Choose **Merge Selected** from the Layers palette menu **2**.

➤ If you've created a clipping mask for a layer via the Layers palette that you want to preserve, select that layer last and merge the other layers into it.

Merge Layers or Groups

Flattening layers

Warning! The **Flatten Artwork** command **discards** hidden top-level layers (read that again) and flattens **all** layers in the file into **one top-level layer,** with any sublayers and groups nested within it. Actually, you'll get an alert dialog box that will give you the option to keep the hidden artwork when layers are flattened, but you still need to think ahead.

The Flatten Artwork command doesn't change how the artwork looks, and objects remain fully editable. If you flatten the artwork into a highlighted layer that has appearances attached to it, those appearances will be applied to all the objects.

To flatten artwork:

1. Redisplay any hidden top-level layers that you want to keep **1**.

2. By default, if no layers are highlighted, the Flatten Artwork command merges all the currently visible layers into whichever top-level layer is displaying the Current Layer indicator. To flatten into a layer of your choice, highlight it now.

3. Choose **Flatten Artwork** from the Layers palette menu. If there are any hidden layers that contain artwork, an alert dialog box will appear **2**–**3**. Click Yes to discard the hidden artwork or click No to preserve the artwork in the flattened document. You can choose Undo right away, if need be.

   Note: If you try to flatten artwork into a hidden, locked, or template layer, Illustrator will flatten all the layers into the topmost top-level layer that isn't hidden, locked, or a template.

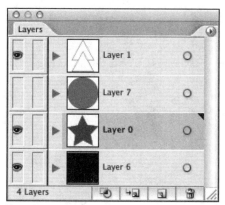

1 *In this original four-layer document, at least one layer is hidden and contains artwork (Layer 7), so an alert dialog box will appear when the **Flatten Artwork** command is chosen.*

2 *It's always nice to get a second chance.*

3 *The **Flatten Artwork** command flattened all the layers into the currently highlighted layer (Layer 0, in this case).*

Flatten Layers

This chapter is an introduction to Illustrator's type tools. First you'll learn how to create point type, type in a rectangle, type inside an object, and type along a path. Then you'll learn how to import type from another application, thread type between objects, copy type and a type object, and convert type into graphic outlines. In the next chapter, you'll learn how to select type and change its typographic attributes via the Character, Paragraph, Character Styles, Paragraph Styles, Control, Glyphs, OpenType, and Tabs palettes.

The Type tool creates point type or type inside a rectangle.

1 *Type tool*

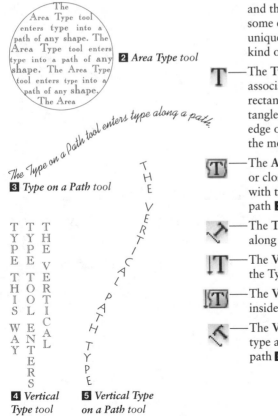

2 *Area Type tool*

3 *Type on a Path tool*

4 *Vertical Type tool*

5 *Vertical Type on a Path tool*

Type tools

There are three **horizontal** type tools: the Type tool, the Area Type tool, and the Type on a Path tool; and three equivalent **vertical** type tools: the Vertical Type tool, the Vertical Area Type tool, and the Vertical Type on a Path tool. Although some of their functions overlap, each tool has unique characteristics for producing a particular kind of type object.

The **Type** tool creates a block of type that isn't associated with a path **1**. You can also draw a rectangle with it and enter type inside the rectangle, or you can use it to enter type along the edge of an open path or inside a closed path. It's the most versatile of all the type tools.

The **Area Type** tool creates type inside an open or closed path. Lines of type that are created with this tool automatically wrap inside the path **2**.

The **Type on a Path** tool creates a line of type along the outer edge of an open or closed path **3**.

The **Vertical Type** tool has the same function as the Type tool, except it creates vertical type **4**.

The **Vertical Area Type** tool creates vertical type inside an open or closed path.

The **Vertical Type on a Path** tool creates vertical type along the outer edge of an open or closed path **5**.

Creating point type

Point type stands by itself—it's neither inside an object nor along a path. This kind of type is appropriate for small amounts of text that stand independently, such as headlines, titles, and button names.

To create point type:

1. Choose the **Type** tool (T) **T** or **Vertical Type** tool. **ĮT**

2. Click a blank area of the artboard where you want the type to start (don't click an object). A flashing insertion marker will appear.

3. Enter type. Press Return/Enter each time you want to start a new line **1**.

4. Choose a **selection** tool on the Toolbox (don't use a keyboard shortcut to select the tool), then click outside the type block to deselect it.
   or
   Click the **type** tool again to complete the type block and start a new one.

➤ To align separate blocks of point type, use the align buttons on the Control palette or the Align palette (see pages 105–106).

➤ If you open a file containing text from a non-CS version of Illustrator into CS2, an alert dialog box will appear, offering you choices for updating the older, legacy text (see pages 240–241).

Choose type attributes first?

If you want to choose character and paragraph attributes for your type before creating it, you can choose from a variety of settings on the **Character** and **Paragraph** palettes; or choose font, point size, and paragraph alignment settings from the **Control** palette; or even click a paragraph style on the **Paragraph Styles** palette. You'll learn about these palettes in depth in the next chapter.

Recolor after?

When you enter type inside an object or on a path, a fill and stroke of None is applied to the object automatically. After entering type, if you want to apply fill and/or stroke colors to the **type object,** deselect it, click the edge of the object with the Direct Selection tool, then choose a color. To recolor the **type** itself, first select it using a type tool or a selection tool (methods for selecting type are discussed in the next chapter).

I DON'T KNOW THE KEY TO SUCCESS, BUT THE

KEY TO FAILURE IS TRYING TO PLEASE EVERYBODY.

Bill Cosby

1 *Point type created with the Type tool*

Point Type

No going back

Once you place type inside or along a graphic object, it becomes a **type object,** and it can be converted back into a graphic object only via the Undo command. To preserve the original graphic object, Option-drag/Alt-drag it to copy it, then use the copy as a type object. You can't enter type into a compound path, a mask object, a mesh object, or a blend, nor can you make a compound path from a type object. If you create type on a path that has a brush stroke, the brush stroke will be removed.

'It spoils people's clothes to squeeze under a gate; the proper way to get in, is to climb down a pear tree.'

1 *Drag with the* **Type** *tool to create a rectangle, then enter type. To see the edges of the rectangle, choose Outline view or use smart guides with Object Highlighting.*

2 *Drag with the* **Vertical Type** *tool, then enter type. Type flows from top to bottom and from right to left.*

A P E A R　T R E E

C L I M B　D O W N

:　:　:

'It spoils people's clothes to squeeze under a gate; the proper way to get in, is to climb down a pear tree.'

3 *After reshaping a type rectangle using the* **Direct Selection** *tool*

Creating type in a rectangle

On this page are instructions for drawing a **type rectangle** before entering type. On the next page, you'll learn how to enter type inside an existing object of any shape.

To create type in a rectangle:

1. Choose the **Type** tool (T) **T** or the **Vertical** Type tool. |T

2. Drag to create a rectangle. When you release the mouse, a flashing insertion marker will appear.

   ➤ To draw a square, start dragging, then hold down Shift and continue to drag.

   ➤ To create vertical type with the Type tool or horizontal type with the Vertical Type tool, hold down Shift, start dragging, release Shift, then continue dragging.

3. Enter type **1**–**2**. The type will wrap automatically to fit into the rectangle. Press Return/Enter only when you need to create a new paragraph.

4. Choose a **selection** tool on the Toolbox (don't use a keyboard shortcut to select the tool), then click outside the type block to deselect it.
   or
   To keep the **type** tool selected so as to create another, separate type rectangle, press Cmd/Ctrl to temporarily access the last-used selection tool, then click outside the type block to deselect it. Release Cmd/Ctrl, then click again to start the new type block. (You can also complete a type object by clicking the type tool.)

   Note: If the overflow symbol appears on the edge of the rectangle (a tiny red cross in a square) and you want to reveal the hidden type, deselect the rectangle, then reshape it using the Direct Selection tool. You can use smart guides (with Object Highlighting) to locate the edge of the rectangle. The type will reflow to fit the new shape **3**. Another option is to thread the overflow type into another object, which we show you how to do on page 231.

Type Rectangle

225

Creating area type

Use the **Area Type** or **Vertical Area Type** tool to place type inside a path of any shape, or onto an open path. The object will be converted into a type path.

To enter type inside an object:

1. *Optional:* Drag-copy the object to preserve the original.

2. If the object is a closed path, choose the **Area Type** tool 🔳, **Vertical Area Type** tool 🔳, or either one of the **Type** tools (**T** or **|T**). If it's an open path, choose either one of the Area Type tools.

3. Click precisely on the edge of the path. A flashing insertion marker will appear, and any fill or stroke on the object will be removed. The object will now be listed as <Type> (not <Path>) on the Layers palette.

4. Enter type in the path, or copy and paste text from a text-editing application into the path. The text will stay inside the object and conform to its shape **1**–**2**. Vertical area type flows from top to bottom and from right to left.

   ➤ To make type fit better inside an object, choose a small point size, click a Justify alignment button on the Control palette, and turn on hyphenation.

5. Choose a **selection** tool, then click outside the type object to deselect it.
   or
   To keep the **type** tool selected so as to enter type in another object, press Cmd/Ctrl to temporarily access the last-used selection tool, click away from the type block to deselect it, release Cmd/Ctrl, then click the next type object. You could also click again on the tool you used to create the type object.

   ➤ The Area Type Options, which control the position of type inside a type object, are discussed on pages 268–269.

Switcheroo

To rotate vertical area type characters, highlight only the characters that you want to convert. On the Control palette, click the word Character, then from the Character palette menu, choose **Standard Vertical Roman Alignment** to uncheck that option. To rotate horizontal or vertical type characters on a custom angle, see page 229.

This is text in a copy of a light bulb shape. You can use the Area Type tool to place type into any shape you can create. When fitting type into a round shape, place small words at the top and the bottom. This is text in a copy of a light bulb shape. You can use the Area Type tool to place type into any

1 *Area type*

The kiss of memory made pictures of love and light against the wall. Here was peace. She pulled in her horizon like a great fish-net. Pulled it from around the waist of the world and draped it over her shoulder. So much of life in its meshes! She called in her soul to come and see.

ZORA NEALE HURSTON

2 *Type in a circle*

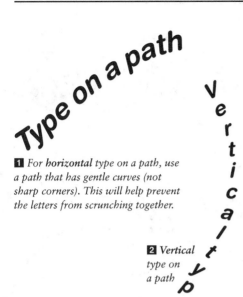

1 For *horizontal type on a path*, use a path that has gentle curves (not sharp corners). This will help prevent the letters from scrunching together.

2 *Vertical type on a path*

These icons will appear next to the pointer when it's moved over a bracket on a selected type path: **NEW**

Left bracket   Center bracket   Right bracket

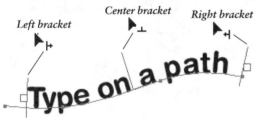

3 The left, center, or right brackets are visible when *path type* is selected with the **Selection** or **Direct Selection** tool.

4 The *left bracket* is dragged to the right.

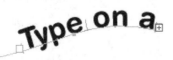

5 After moving the *left bracket* to the right

Creating path type

Use the **Type on a Path** tool to place type on the inner or outer edge of a path. Type can't be placed on both sides of the same path, but it can be moved from one side to the other after it's created.

To place type along an object's path:

1. Choose the **Type on a Path** or **Vertical Type on a Path** tool, then click the edge of a closed path. Or choose the **Type T** or **Vertical Type IT** tool, then click an open path. The path can be selected, but it doesn't have to be.

2. When the flashing insertion marker appears, enter type. Don't press Return/Enter. The type will appear along the edge of the object, and the object will now have a fill and stroke of None **1**–**2**.

3. Choose a **selection** tool (or hold down Cmd/Ctrl), then click outside the type object to deselect it.
   or
   If you want to create a new type block, click the **type** tool again.

To reposition type on a path:

1. Choose the **Selection** tool (V) or **Direct Selection** tool (A).

2. Click on the type. Center, left, and right brackets will appear **3**.

3. As you do any of the following, be sure to drag the bracket (the vertical bar)—not the little square! If your tool switches to a type tool, choose a selection tool and try again.

   Drag the **center** bracket to the left or right to reposition the type block along the path.

   Drag the **left** bracket **4**–**5** to reposition the starting point of the type on the path. Or drag the **right** bracket back across the existing type; this will shorten the amount of type that's visible on the path and may produce a type overflow. (For right-aligned type, do the opposite of the above.)

   To **flip** the type to the other side of an open path, drag the center bracket across to the other side of the path.

Type on Path

227

You can change the orientation of type on a path by choosing from an assortment of distortion, alignment, and letterspacing options in the **Type on a Path Options** dialog box. These settings can be changed at any time.

To apply options to path type:

1. Choose the **Selection** tool, then click type on a path.
2. Choose Type > Type on a Path > **Type on a Path Options.** The Type on a Path Options dialog box opens (■, next page).
3. Check Preview.
4. Do any of the following:

   From the **Effect** pop-up menu, choose **Rainbow, Skew, 3D Ribbon, Stair Step,** or **Gravity** ■.

   Choose **Align to Path: Ascender, Descender, Center,** or **Baseline** to specify which part of the text will touch the path (■, next page).

   Check (or uncheck) **Flip.**

   Choose or enter a new letter **Spacing** value (–36 to 36).
5. Click OK. If you want to change or reverse any of the settings you've chosen, reselect the object and reopen the dialog box.

➤ Individual type effects can also be applied via the Type > Type on a Path submenu.

■ *Type on a Path effects*

Rainbow effect

Skew effect

3D Ribbon effect

Stair Step effect

Gravity effect

1 Use the **Type on a Path Options** dialog box to choose effect, alignment, orientation, and spacing options for type on a path.

2 **Align to Path** options

3 The original type

4 After **rotating** some of the characters by differing amounts

5 After adjusting the kerning

Rotating type

To rotate type characters on a custom angle:

1. Select the type object with the Selection tool, or select a type character or characters with a type tool.

2. On the Character palette, choose or enter a positive or negative **Character Rotation** value **3**–**4**.

➤ After rotating type, you may need to adjust its kerning values **5** (see pages 246–247).

To make a whole horizontal type block vertical, or vice versa:

1. Choose the **Selection** tool, then click a type block.

2. Choose Type > Type Orientation > **Horizontal** or **Vertical.**

Rotate Type

Importing text

Using the **Place** command, you can **import text files** in the Microsoft Word (doc), Microsoft RTF (rtf, short for rich text format), or plain (ASCII) text format into an Illustrator document. The text will appear in a new rectangle.

Note: To place text onto or into a custom path, first place it by following the instructions on this page, then copy and paste it onto or into the path (see "To move type from one object to another" on page 233).

To import text:

1. Choose File > **Place**.

2. Locate and click the text file that you want to import.

3. Click **Place**.

4. For a Microsoft Word (doc) or Microsoft RTF (rtf) file, the Microsoft Word Options dialog box will open ■. For a plain text format file, the Text Import Options dialog box will open ■.

   Decide which options you want to include. For Microsoft Word or Microsoft RTF text, if you want to preserve text formatting, be sure to leave Remove Text Formatting unchecked. The plain text format (called Text Only, in Microsoft Word) removes formatting and styling.

5. Click OK. The imported text will appear in a rectangle ■. Be sure to learn about threading type, starting on the next page.

➤ To export text from Illustrator, see page 233 and the sidebar on page 516.

➤ To create columns and rows of type, see pages 268–269.

■ *For text in Microsoft Word or Microsoft RTF, choose settings in the* **Microsoft Word Options** *dialog box.*

■ *For text in the ASCII (plain text) format, choose settings in the* **Text Import Options** *dialog box.*

May the day come (soon perhaps) when I'll flee to the woods on an island in Oceania, there to live on ecstasy, calm, and art. With a new family by my side, far from this European scramble for money. There, in Tahiti, in the silence of the beautiful tropical nights, I will be able to listen to the soft murmuring music of the movements of my heart in amorous harmony with the mysterious beings around me. Free at last, without financial worries and able to love, sing, and die.
Paul Gauguin

■ *Placed text appears in a rectangle.*

Import Text

In port

Here was peace. She pulled in her horizon like
a great fish-net. Pulled it from around the
waist of the world and draped it over her

Out port

1 *To thread text, first click the **Out** port*
with the Selection tool...

Here was peace. She pulled in her horizon like
a great fish-net. Pulled it from around the
waist of the world and draped it over her

2 *...then drag (or click) elsewhere*
*with the **Loaded Text** pointer.*

Here was peace. She pulled in her horizon like
a great fish-net. Pulled it from around the
waist of the world and draped it over her

shoulder. So much of life in its
meshes! She called in her soul
to come and see.

Zora Neale Hurston

3 *The overflow type spills from the first*
object into the second, in the direction
*shown by the **thread** arrowheads.*

Not all is copied

If you click to create a **duplicate** of a type object
(step 4 on this page), only the object's shape will
be copied, not its fill and stroke attributes or Area
Type Options. To copy the attributes afterward,
choose the Direct Selection tool, click the edge of
the duplicate object, choose the Eyedropper tool
(I), then click the background of the original text
object (before you click with the Eyedropper, make
sure the pointer doesn't have a little "t").

Threading type

Before we explore threading, the process of
linking overflow text between text objects,
consider this simple solution: If your type
object is almost—but not quite—large
enough to display all the type on or inside
it, you can enlarge the object to reveal the
hidden type by using one of these methods:

➤ Click the type block with the **Selection**
tool, then drag a handle on its **bounding
box** (choose View > Show Bounding Box
if the box isn't visible).

➤ Select only the rectangle—not the type—
with the **Direct Selection** tool (turn on
Smart Guides with Object Highlighting
or go to Outline view to locate the
rectangle), then **Shift-drag** a **segment.**

If your type overfloweth, you can spill, or
thread, it into a different object or into a
copy of the same object. Text can be threaded
between path objects or area type objects, or
between an area type object and a path object.

To thread overflow type to another object:

1. Choose the **Selection** tool (V).

2. Select the original type object.

3. Click the **Out** port ⊞ on the selected
object. The pointer will turn into a
Loaded Text pointer ⌸ **1**.

4. To create a **new** object for the overflow
text, either click where you want a duplicate of the **currently selected** text object
to appear, or drag to create a **rectangular**
type object **2**–**3**.
or
Position the pointer over an **existing**
object—the pointer will change to ⌸—
then click the object's path. A fill and
stroke of None will be applied to the path.

Overflow type from the first object will
flow into the second one.

5. Deselect the objects.

➤ If you double-click an Out port with the
Selection tool, a linked copy of the text
object will be created automatically.

Thread Type

If you're curious to see what's threaded to what, you can **display** the **text threads**.

To display text threads:

Select a linked type object. If the threads aren't showing, choose View > **Show Text Threads** (Cmd-Shift-Y/Ctrl-Shift-Y). *Note:* The stacking order of type objects on the Layers palette has no impact on how text flows from one object to another.

When you **unthread two objects**, you break the chain and the overflow text gets sucked back into the first object of the two. Both objects are preserved.

To unthread two type objects:

1. Choose the **Selection** tool (V), then click a threaded type object.

2. Double-click the object's **In** port or **Out** port **1**–**2**.
   or
   Click an **In** port or **Out** port, ▶ move the pointer slightly (the Unthread cursor 🐾 displays), then click the port again to cut the thread.

Follow these instructions if you want to keep the remaining links intact as you **release one object** from a **thread**. The type will reflow.

To release an object from a thread and preserve the remaining threads:

1. Choose the **Selection** tool (V), then click the type object to be released **3**.

2. To unthread the object but also preserve it, choose Type > Threaded Text > **Release Selection 4**.
   or
   To unthread the type object by deleting it, press **Delete/Backspace**.

And finally, follow these instructions if you want to **disconnect threaded objects** from one another but keep the type where it is.

To remove all threading between objects and leave the type in place:

1. Choose the **Selection** tool (V), then click a threaded type object.

2. Choose Type > Threaded Text > **Remove Threading**.

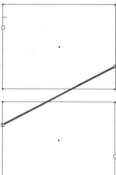

1 *An Out port is double-clicked,...*

2 *...causing the first type object to become* **unthreaded.**

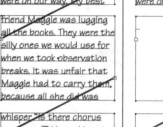

3 *The middle type object is selected...*

4 *...and then* **released** *from the thread.*

Unthread; Release, Remove Threading

Moving type

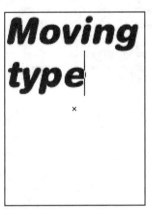

1 *Point type is highlighted, put on the Clipboard via Edit > **Cut**...*

Moving type|

×

2 *...and then **pasted** into a rectangle.*

Copying and moving type

To **copy** or **move type** with or without its object, you can use the Clipboard, a temporary storage area in memory. The Clipboard commands are Cut, Copy, and Paste. You could also use the drag-and-drop method to move a whole type object (see pages 287-288). You can copy type between Illustrator files, or from an Illustrator file to a Photoshop file.

To copy type and its object between files:

1. Choose the **Selection** tool (V).
2. Click the type you want to copy, or click the edge or baseline.
3. Choose Edit > **Copy** (Cmd-C/Ctrl-C).
4. Click in another Illustrator document window, then choose Edit > **Paste** (Cmd-V/Ctrl-V). The type and its object will appear.
    or
    Click in a Photoshop document window, choose Edit > **Paste** (Cmd-V/Ctrl-V), click **Pixels,** then click OK. The type and object will appear as imagery on a new layer.

➤ If you copy a threaded text object, only that object and the text it contains will be copied.

To move type from one object to another:

1. Choose the **Type** tool **T** or **Vertical Type** tool. **IT**
2. Select (drag across) the type that you want to move **1**. Or to move all the text in a thread, click in one of the objects, then choose Select > **All** (Cmd-A/Ctrl-A).
3. Choose Edit > **Cut** (Cmd-X/Ctrl-X). The object you cut the type from will remain a type object.
4. Cmd-click/Ctrl-click the object you want to paste into, then click the edge of that object. A blinking insertion marker will appear. (To create path type, Option-click/Alt-click the object).
    or
    Drag to create a type rectangle.
5. Choose Edit > **Paste** (Cmd-V/Ctrl-V) **2**.

Creating type outlines

The **Create Outlines** command converts each character in a type object into a separate graphic object. As outlines, the paths can then be reshaped, used in a compound or as a mask, or filled with a gradient or mesh, as nontype objects can.

Before proceeding, a word of caution: once type is converted into outlines, unless you undo the conversion immediately, you won't be able to change fonts, apply other typographic attributes, or convert the outlines back into type. For this reason, consider converting a duplicate of a type object instead of the original.

To create type outlines:

1. Create type using any type tool. All the characters in the type object or on the path will be converted, so enter only the text that you want to convert.

2. Choose the **Selection** tool (V).

3. If the type isn't already selected, click a character or the baseline.

4. Choose Type > **Create Outlines** (Cmd-Shift-O/Ctrl-Shift-O) **1**–**3**.
   or
   Control-click/right-click and choose **Create Outlines** from the context menu.

   The fill and stroke attributes and any appearances from the original characters will be applied to the outlines. If the type was on or in an object, the object will be preserved, unless it had no stroke or fill, in which case it will be deleted.

   The points and segments on each object can now be reshaped (see Chapter 12).

➤ Type characters become separate compound paths when converted to outlines. If any of the characters you converted had an interior shape (known as a "counter")—as in an "A" or a "P"—those outer and inner shapes will also form a compound path. To release the compound into separate objects, choose Object > Compound Path > Release, then choose Object > Ungroup. To reassemble the parts at any time into a compound, select them, then choose Object > Compound Path > Make.

Converter beware

For creating **custom characters,** such as logos, the Create Outlines command is invaluable; plus, outlines can be printed from any application without printer fonts. However, we don't recommend converting small type to outlines, for the following reasons: the command removes the hinting information that preserves character shapes in printing; outline shapes are slightly heavier than their nonoutline counterparts, and thus are less legible (especially if a stroke color is applied to them); and outlines use more file storage space than type characters.

1 *The original type*

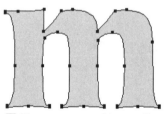

2 *The type converted into* **outlines**

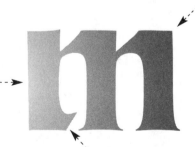

3 *The outlines were reshaped in the areas indicated by the arrows, and filled with a gradient.*

Don't space out!

If you press the Spacebar to access the Hand tool when your cursor is in a type block, you'll end up adding spaces to your text instead of moving the artwork in the window. Worse yet, if type is selected, you'll end up replacing your text with spaces. Instead, to acccess a temporary **Hand** tool, press **Cmd-Spacebar/Ctrl-Spacebar,** then **release Cmd/Ctrl.** This may take some getting used to.

And another thing: keep an eye on your pointer. If it's in a palette field, you'll edit palette values instead of your type!

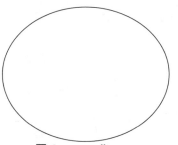

1 *Create an ellipse.*

2 *Create path type at the top of the inner ellipse. The ellipse will have a stroke of None.*

Exercise

Putting type on both sides of an ellipse, and having all of it read vertically, requires creating two ellipses.

Type on an ellipse

Type on the top

1. Choose File > Document Setup > **Artboard** (Cmd-Option-P/Ctrl-Alt-P), choose Units: **Inches,** then click OK.
2. Using the Control palette, make the fill color None and the stroke color black.
3. Choose the **Ellipse** tool (L), ⬭ then click on the artboard (don't drag).
4. Enter "3.6" in the **Width** field, enter "2.8" in the **Height** field, then click OK **1**.
5. Double-click the **Scale** tool. Enter "70" in the **Uniform: Scale** field, then click **Copy.** Deselect.
6. Choose the **Type on a Path** tool.
7. On the Control palette, click **Character** to open the Character palette, enter "24" in the **Size** field and "150" in the **Horizontal Scale** field, and choose a font.
8. Click the top of the inner ellipse, then type the desired text (*"type on top,"* in our example) **2**.
9. Choose the **Selection** tool, then drag the center bracket (it's near the bottom of the circle) along the outside of the ellipse to reposition the type. Be aware that the left and right brackets are practically on top of each other near the starting point of the type. Don't move the left bracket over the right bracket, as you may cause a text overflow. If you like, you can move the right bracket all the way around, close to where the type characters end.

Type on the bottom

1. With the inner ellipse selected, double-click the **Selection** tool. In the Move dialog box, enter "0" in the Horizontal field and "−0.1" in the **Vertical** field, then click **Copy.**

(Continued on the following page)

2. Drag the center bracket into the copy of the ellipse (which should still be selected). The type will now be positioned on the inside of the ellipse **1**.

3. Double-click the bottom type with the Selection tool (the Type tool will be chosen automatically), select the type, type the desired text, then click the Selection tool.

Click the type on the bottom to reveal the center bracket, then move the center bracket to center the type **2**.

4. On the **Layers** palette (F7), click and then Shift-click the selection area of each type object to select both of them.

5. *Optional:* To recolor the type, apply a fill color and a stroke of None to the selected type objects.

6. Choose Type > Type on a Path > **Gravity** to slant the type for better orientation on the ellipse. (The default Rainbow path orientation would work better on a circle.)

7. Choose Object > **Group** (Cmd-G/Ctrl-G). (To recolor either ellipse path now, you would need to select it first with the Direct Selection tool.)

8. *Optional:* To produce the artwork as shown in **3**, choose the **Ellipse** tool (L), click to the left of center of the current type objects, enter "1" for the Width and ".75" for the Height, then click OK. Choose the **Selection** tool (V), then drag the new ellipse into the center of the type objects. On the Control palette, click the **Style** thumbnail, then on the palette, click the Neon Type graphic style. Other graphic style libraries can be opened via the Open Graphic Style Library submenu on the palette menu (see Chapter 19).

➤ Set the Horizontal Scale field back to zero (with no type selected) to prevent the scale value from being applied to any subsequently created type.

➤ To select either one of the type blocks, click its selection area on the Layers palette, or do it manually, using smart guides (Cmd-U/Ctrl-U) to assist you.

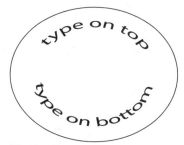

1 *Use the Move dialog box to copy the type object, then drag the center bracket into the ellipse.*

2 *Select the type on the bottom of the ellipse and type the words that you want to appear there. Center the type at the bottom of its ellipse.*

3 *For the inner circle, we created another ellipse and applied the Neon Type graphic style. You could create a graphic or import an image instead.*

STYLE & EDIT TYPE

In this chapter, you'll first learn how to select type for editing and updating legacy text. Then you'll learn how to use the Character and Control palettes to apply typographic attributes, such as point size and leading; the Glyphs and OpenType palettes to insert special characters; the Paragraph palette to apply paragraph formats, such as alignment and indentation; the Paragraph Styles and Character Styles palettes to quickly apply whole collections of attributes; and word processing features to check spelling and replace text. At the end of the chapter, you'll choose area type options, set tabs, wrap type around an object, create type with a shadow, create slanted type, and perform a few practice exercises.

Selecting type

Before you can modify type, you must select it. The **Selection** tool selects both the type and its object **1**; the **Direct Selection** tool selects the type object alone or the type object and the type **2**; and the **type** tools select only the type itself, not the type object **3**.

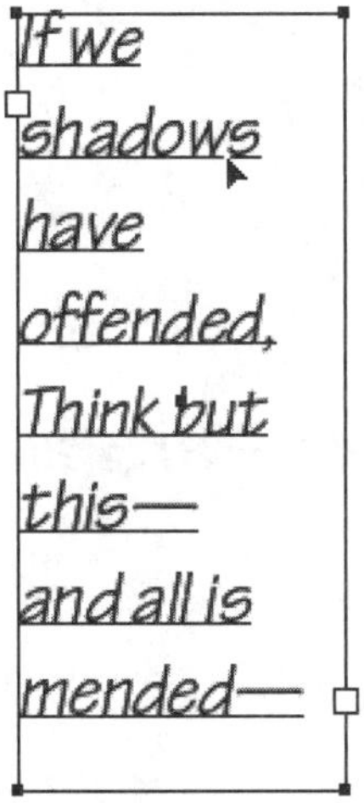

If we
shadows
have
offended,
Think but
this—
and all is
mended—

1 *Type and type object selected with the* **Selection** *tool*

If we
shadows
have
offended,
Think but
this—
and all is
mended—

2 *Type object selected with the* **Direct Selection** *tool*

If we
shadows
have
offended,
Think but
this—
and all is
mended—

William Shakespeare

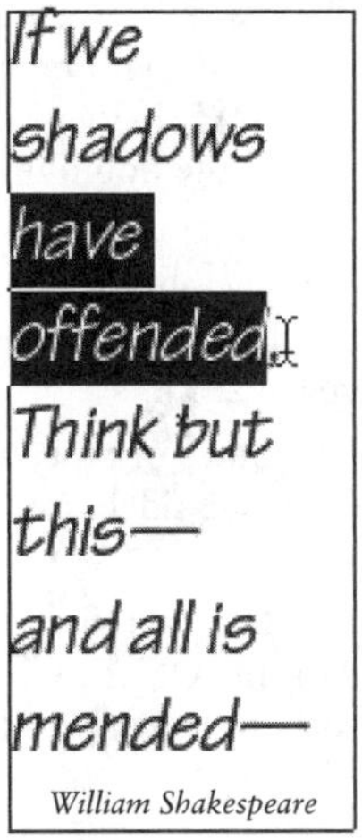

3 *Type (not the object) selected with the* **Type** *tool*

Use the **selection** method described here if you're going to move, transform, restyle, or recolor **all the type** in or on a type object. To reshape or recolor a type object (not the type), use the first selection method on the next page instead. Or to edit, restyle, or recolor just some of the type in a block, use the second selection method on the next page.

To select type and its object:

1. Choose the **Selection** tool (V).

2. Turn on **smart guides** (Cmd-U/Ctrl-U), with Object Highlighting on in Preferences > Smart Guides & Slices.

3. For **area** type (inside an object):

   If Type Object Selection by Path Only is checked in Preferences > Type & Auto Tracing, you must click either the baseline of the type **1** or the edge of the object. If this option is unchecked and the object has a fill other than None, you can click anywhere on the object (the fill, a character, the baseline, or the outer path). With smart guides with Object Highlighting on, the baseline and path are easy to locate **2**–**3**.

   For **point** or **path** type:

   Click the type baseline, or, for path type, you can also click the path **4**. If View > Show Bounding Box is on, the bounding box will also display.

➤ If you select a threaded type object, all the other objects in the thread will also become selected (see page 231).

➤ To modify the paint attributes of type, use the Color palette (see the sidebar on page 224).

➤ To move, scale, rotate, shear, or reflect type, use a command on the Object > Transform submenu or a transform tool.

Hot tip

If you double-click a type character in a type object with the Selection or Direct Selection tool, the **Type tool** (or Vertical Type tool) will become selected automatically and an insertion point will appear where you clicked.

Appearances and type

The relationship between type color and appearances may be confusing at first. If you select a type object with the **Selection** tool, "Type" will be listed at the top of the Appearance palette and "Characters" will be listed among the attributes.

If you highlight text characters using a **type** tool or if you double-click the word **"Characters"** on the Appearance palette, the Stroke and Fill attributes for those characters will be listed on the palette. If you want to redisplay the type object's attributes, click the word **"Type."** To learn more about the Appearance palette, see Chapter 19. To work with type color and appearances, see pages 291–292, and also page 408.

---

1 *To select type and its object, click the type...*

2 *...or click the type object's path (smart guides is on, in this case).*

3 *The type and type object are selected.*

4 *Point type is selected.*

Insert or delete

To **add** characters to an existing type block, choose a type tool, click to create an insertion point, then start typing.

To **delete** one character at a time, choose a type tool, click to the right of the character you want to delete, then press Delete/Backspace. Or to delete multiple characters, select them with a type tool, then press Delete/Backspace.

Think but this—and all is mended—

1 *The type object is selected; the type is not.*

Think but this— and all is mended—

2 *The type object is reshaped and recolored.*

My line drawing is the purest and most direct translation of my emotion.

Henri Matisse

3 *Two words are selected.*

Use this **selection** method if you want to reshape a **type object** (and thus allow the type to reflow) or recolor the object.

To select a type object but not the type:

1. Choose the **Direct Selection** tool (A).
2. Click the **edge** of an area or path type object **1**. Use smart guides (with Object Highlighting on) to assist you. Now modifications you make will affect only the type object—not the type **2**.

Use this selection method to **select only** the type—not the object—so you can edit the text or change its character, paragraph, or paint attributes.

To select type but not its object:

1. Choose any **type** tool.
2. For horizontal type, drag horizontally with the I-beam cursor to select and highlight a **word** or a **line** of type **3**. For vertical type, drag vertically.
   or
   For horizontal type, drag vertically to select whole **lines** of type. For vertical type, drag horizontally to select lines.
   or
   Double-click to select a **word.**
   or
   Triple-click to select a **paragraph.**
   or
   Click in the text block, then choose Select > **All** (Cmd-A/Ctrl-A) to select all the type in the block or on the path, plus any other type it's threaded to.
   or
   Click to start a **selection,** then Shift-click where you want it to stop (Shift-click again, if desired, to extend the selection).
3. After modifying the type:
   Click **in** the type block to create a new insertion point for further editing.
   or
   Cmd-click/Ctrl-click **outside** the type object to deselect it.

➤ If you recolor type with smart guides on and text characters highlighted, choose a selection tool afterward so you can see how the new color looks.

Select Type Object; Select Type

Updating legacy text

The Illustrator text engine allows text to be formatted with OpenType fonts, composition commands, and character and paragraph styles. If you open a file from Illustrator 10 or earlier into Illustrator CS2, any text in the file from the earlier version must be updated before it can be edited ■. Nonupdated text is called **legacy** text.

Updating may change text as follows:

➤ Line and character **spacing,** such as leading, tracking, and kerning, may be altered.

➤ Words may **wrap** to the next line.

➤ Text may **overflow** in an area type object, or words may flow into the next threaded type object.

If you **open** a file that contains **legacy text,** an alert dialog box will appear. You can update all the legacy text right away, or you can do it after opening the file at any time, either one object at a time or all at once.

To respond to a legacy text warning:

1. Using File > Open, open a file from an earlier version of Illustrator. An alert dialog box will appear ■.

2. As explained in the dialog box, you can:

   Click **Update** to update all legacy text now.
   or
   Click **OK** to update the legacy text later.
   or
   Click **Cancel** to cancel opening of the file.

■ *Selected legacy text objects have an X across the box.*

■ *This alert dialog box displays if you open a file that contains text from an older version of Illustrator.*

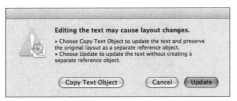

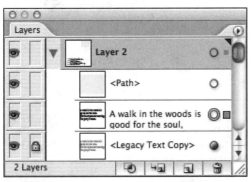

1 *This alert dialog box appears if you double-click a **legacy** text object.*

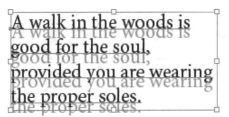

2 *After you click **Copy Text Object**, the updated text displays at its original opacity and the legacy text copy displays below it at 40% opacity. (We moved the updated text object upward a bit.)*

3 *On the Layers palette, the updated text layer is directly above the **Legacy Text Copy** layer. The Legacy Text Copy layer is locked automatically.*

Find 'em or get rid of 'em

To select and unlock all copies of legacy text objects, choose Type > Legacy Text > **Select Copies.**

To delete all copies of legacy text objects (they don't have to be selected), choose Type > Legacy Text > **Delete Copies.**

You can **update legacy text objects** after opening a file, either individually or en masse. For individual objects, you can update either a copy of the legacy text object or the original. If you elect to update a copy, the legacy text will be placed on its own locked layer (with an opacity of 40%) below the updated copy so you can compare the two for any threading or wrapping changes.

To update legacy text objects:

1. Open a file that contains text from an earlier version of Illustrator.

2. Do one of the following:

   Choose the Selection tool or a type tool, double-click a legacy text object (or select more than one object, then double-click one of them). An alert dialog box will appear **1**. Click **Copy Text Object** or **Update.** If you click Copy Text Object, a copy of the legacy text will appear on its own layer, directly below the updated object **2**; choose the Selection tool, move the updated text object upward a bit, and compare it with the legacy text. If you click Update, the legacy text will be updated without a copy being made.
   or
   To update all the legacy text in the file (with no copies being made), choose Type > Legacy Text > **Update All Legacy Text.** You don't have to select anything.
   or
   Choose the Selection tool (V), click a legacy text object in the document window (or multiple-select more than one legacy object), then choose Type > Legacy Text > **Update Selected Legacy Text.** No copy will be made in this case, either.

➤ On the Layers palette, legacy text objects are listed as <Legacy Text>, and the copies are listed as <Legacy Text Copy> **3**. *Note:* You can't specify an opacity value for the legacy copies ahead of time.

The Character, Paragraph, and Control palettes

In this section, we'll show you how to use the Character, Paragraph, and Control palettes to apply type attributes. Later in this chapter we'll show you how to use the Character Styles and Paragraph Styles palettes to apply attributes collectively.

To modify font, style, point size, kerning, leading, and tracking values for one or more highlighted text characters, use the **Character** palette **1**. To show it, press **Cmd-T/Ctrl-T**, or with a type tool chosen, click **Character** on the **Control** palette. To access horizontal scale, baseline shift, vertical scale, character rotation, and language options, choose Show Options from the palette menu or click the up/down arrow ⬍ on the palette tab twice.

To modify paragraph attributes, such as alignment and indentation, use the **Paragraph** palette **2**. To show it, press **Cmd-Option-T/Ctrl-Alt-T**, or with a type tool chosen, click **Paragraph** on the **Control** palette. To access the Space Before Paragraph, Space After Paragraph, and hyphenation options, choose Show Options from the palette menu or click the up/down arrow. ⬍

You can also use the **Control palette** to change fonts, point sizes, and alignment.

As we explained on pages 238–239, to change the paragraph attributes of all the text in a type object or on a path, select the object or path with the Selection tool; or to isolate a paragraph or series of paragraphs, select just those paragraphs with a type tool.

➤ A paragraph is created whenever the Return/Enter key is pressed within a type block. To reveal the symbols for line breaks and spaces, choose Type > Show Hidden Characters (Cmd-Option-I/Ctrl-Alt-I).

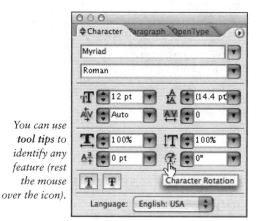

You can use **tool tips** *to identify any feature (rest the mouse over the icon).*

1 *The Character palette*

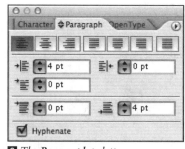

2 *The Paragraph palette*

12 pt Myriad–Roman
0 /1000 em

3 *The Info palette when the Type tool is selected*

Fast info

The point size, font, and tracking info for selected type are listed on the **Info** palette **3**.

Palette shortcuts

When entering values on the Character and Paragraph palettes:

Apply value and highlight **next** field	Tab
Apply value and highlight **previous** field	Shift-Tab
Apply value and **exit** palette	Return/Enter
Highlight the **Font** field on the Character palette	Cmd-Option-Shift-M/Ctrl-Alt-Shift-M

1 *Select the type you want to modify...*

Font cha

| Undo Apply Swatch |
| Redo Typing |
| Font ▶ |
| Recent Fonts ▶ |

O Bernhard Modern Std	▶
A Birch	
O Birch Std	
A **Blackoak**	
A Bauer Bodoni	▶
A Bodoni	▶	Roman
A BodoniHighlightICG		Italic
O Brush Script Std Medium		Bold
A ΦΦΦ⊡⊠Φ⊡ ΦⰟ	▶	Poster
A BurweedICG-Thorny	
A Coptish Script	▶
A Compostland Soft	
A Caslon 3	▶
A Caslon 540	▶
A Caslon Open Face	
O Adobe Caslon Pro	▶
O Century Old Style Std	▶

*...then choose a font from the **context menu**.*

Font change

2 *The **font** and **font style** are changed from Gill Sans Bold to Bodoni Poster.*

| ◇ Character | Paragraph | OpenType | ▶ |

| Tekton | ▼ |
| Oblique | ▼ |

🔠 ⬍ 12 pt ▼	A⬍ (14.4 pt) ▼
A⬍V Auto ▼	AV 0 ▼
T 100% ▼	IT 100% ▼
A³ 0 pt ▼	0° ▼

| **T** | **T** |

Underline   Strikethrough

3 *The Font and Font Style pop-up menus on the Character palette.*

| Character: Myriad ▼ | Italic ▼ | 18 pt ▼ | Para |

4 *Font and Font Style options on the Control palette*

> You must learn to be ~~still~~ **still** in the midst of activity and to be vibrantly ~~alive~~ in repose.
> —*Indira Gandhi*

5 *Underline and strikethrough type styling*

Changing fonts

To change fonts:

1. Choose any **type** tool, then select the type you want to modify.
   or
   Choose the **Selection** tool, then click the type object.

2. Control-click/right-click the type and choose a font from the **Font** submenu **1**–**2** or **Recent Fonts** submenu on the context menu.
   or
   On the **Character** palette **3** or **Control** 🆕 palette **4**, choose a font from the **Font** pop-up menu and a style from the **Font Style** pop-up menu.

➤ To choose a font by typing a name, in Mac, double-click the Font field on the Character palette; in Windows, just click the Font field. Then start typing the first few characters of the desired font name. When the name appears, press Tab. In addition, for a style other than Roman (or Regular), start typing the style name in the next field, then press Return/Enter. The name or style with the closest spelling match will appear in the field.

➤ To have font families display in the actual typeface (WYSIWYG) on the Character palette and Type > Font submenu in Mac, the Type > Font submenu in Windows, and the Font submenu on the context menu in both platforms, in Preferences > Type & Auto Tracing, check Font Preview Size and choose a font preview size (Small, Medium, or Large).

If you create Web page mock-ups, you might find a use for the **underline** feature.

To apply underline or strikethrough 🆕 styling:

1. Choose a **type** tool, then select the type you want to apply the underline or strikethrough styling to.

2. On the Character palette, for **underlining**, click the **T** button **3**, or for **strikethrough**, click the **T** button (click the button again to remove the styling) **5**.

Changing the point size

To change the point size:

1. Choose any **type** tool, then highlight the type you want to modify.
   or
   Choose the **Selection** tool (V), then click the type object.

2. ***Character palette*** (Cmd-T/Ctrl-T) or
   NEW ***Control palette***

   Enter a point size in the **Font Size** field (.1–1296 pt). You don't need to reenter the unit of measure. If you're using the Character palette, you can press Return/Enter to apply the new value and exit the palette, or press Tab to apply the value and highlight the next field **2**.

   ➤ If the selected type contains more than one point size, the Font Size field will be blank, but the new size you enter will apply to all selected type.
   or
   Choose a preset size from the **Font Size** pop-up menu or click the up or down arrow. Or click in the Font Size field, then press the up or down arrow on the keyboard.

   ### *Keyboard*
   Hold down Cmd-Shift/Ctrl-Shift and press > to enlarge or < to reduce the point size **3**. The type will scale according to the current Size/Leading value in Preferences > Type & Auto Tracing (the default increment is 2 pt). Hold Cmd-Option-Shift/Ctrl-Alt-Shift and press > or < to change the point size by five times the current Size/Leading value.

   ### *Context menu*
   Control-click/right-click the type and choose a preset size from the context menu. Choosing Other from the context menu highlights the Font Size field on the Character palette.

Scale type interactively
To scale point or path type by dragging, select it using the Selection tool, then drag a handle on its **bounding box** (press Cmd-Shift-B/Ctrl-Shift-B if the box isn't visible). You can also scale type with the **Scale** tool. Shift-drag to scale type proportionally using either tool **1**.

1 *Shift-drag a handle on the bounding box for a type object to scale the type proportionally.*

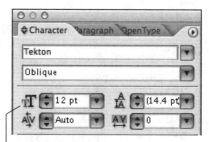

2 *On the **Character** palette (or Control palette), enter a **Font Size**, or click the up or down arrow, or choose a preset size from the pop-up menu.*

3 *You can also scale type by using a keyboard shortcut.*

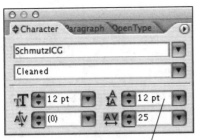

1 On the **Character** palette, enter a **Leading** value, or click the up or down arrow, or choose a preset value from the drop-down menu.

> How can one conceive
> of a one-party system in a
> country that has over 200
> varieties of cheese?
> — *Charles de Gaulle*

2 *12-pt. type, 18-pt. "loose" leading*

> How can one conceive
> of a one-party system in a
> country that has over 200
> varieties of cheese?
> — *Charles de Gaulle*

3 *12-pt. type; 13-pt. "tight" leading*

Changing leading

Leading, the distance from baseline to baseline between lines of type, is traditionally measured in points. Each line of type can have a different leading value. (To adjust the spacing between paragraphs, see page 256.)

Note: To change the vertical spacing in vertical type, change the horizontal tracking (see the next page). In vertical type, leading controls the horizontal spacing between vertical columns.

To change leading via the Character palette:

1. Select horizontal type:

   Click anywhere in a type block with the Selection tool to change the leading of the entire **block.**
   or
   Highlight an entire paragraph with a type tool (triple-click anywhere in the paragraph) to change the leading of all the lines in that **paragraph.**
   or
   Highlight (drag across) an entire line with a type tool, including any spaces at the end, to change the leading of just that **line.**

2. On the **Character** palette (Cmd-T/Ctrl-T), enter a **Leading** value (press Return/Enter or Tab to apply) **1–3**; or choose a preset leading value from the Leading pop-up menu; or click the up or down arrow. If you choose Auto from the pop-up menu, the leading will be the percentage of the largest type size on each line specified in the Auto Leading field in the Justification dialog box (the default is 120%), which opens from the Paragraph palette menu.

To change leading via the keyboard:

1. Select the type you want to modify as per step 1, above.

2. Option-press/Alt-press the **up arrow** on the keyboard to decrease the leading or the **down arrow** to increase the leading by the Size/Leading increment specified in Preferences > Type.

   Hold down Cmd-Option/Ctrl-Alt as you press an arrow to change leading by five times the current Size/Leading increment.

Change Leading

Applying kerning and tracking

Kerning is the addition or removal of space between **pairs** of adjacent characters. Kerning values for specific character pairs (e.g., an uppercase "T" next to a lowercase "a") are built into all fonts. The built-in kerning values are adequate for small text, such as body type, but not for large type, such as headlines and logos. You can remedy awkward spacing in large type by applying manual kerning. To kern a pair of characters, first insert the cursor between them.

Note: Built-in kerning can be turned on or off for individual groups of characters. Before kerning text manually, turn built-in kerning off for your selected type by choosing Auto from the Kerning pop-up menu on the Character palette **1**, then choosing or entering zero.

Tracking is the simultaneous adjustment of the space between each of **three or more characters.** Normally, it's applied to a whole line of type, occasionally to a whole paragraph. To apply tracking, you'll first highlight some type using a type tool or select an entire type block with a selection tool.

To apply kerning or tracking:

1. Zoom in on the type that you want to apply kerning or tracking to. Choose a **type** tool, then click to create an insertion point between two characters for kerning, or highlight a range of text for tracking.
   or
   To track all the type in an object, choose the **Selection** tool, then click the object.

2. In the **Kerning** or **Tracking** area on the **Character** palette (Cmd-Option-K/ Ctrl-Alt-K), enter a positive value (up to 10000) to add space between the characters or a negative value (down to –1000) to remove space, then press Return/Enter or Tab to apply **2**–**4**; or choose a preset kerning or tracking amount from the pop-up menu; or click the up or down arrow.
   or

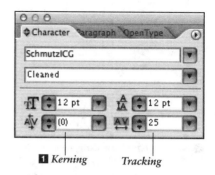

1 *Kerning*   *Tracking*

2 *Normal type*

3 *After adding space between the first two characters via* **kerning**

4 *After removing space from between the last five characters via* **tracking**

You can choose from two different types of automatic (nonmanual) kerning in Illustrator. The "all-purpose" default method, **Auto** kerning (or "metrics" kerning), is applied to new or imported text based on the information for kern pairs (e.g., To, Ta, We, Wo, Yo) that's included with each font.

For fonts that have less than adequate or no built-in kerning, or for a line that contains multiple type-faces or point sizes, you can give **Optical** kerning a try: Choose Optical for the type from the Kerning pop-up menu on the Character palette. Illustrator will adjust the spacing between adjacent characters as it sees fit. See if you like it.

1 *The original, selected characters*

Fit Headline

2 *The* **Fit Headline** *command added space* ***between*** *characters to fit the type object.*

Hold down Option/Alt and press the right arrow on the keyboard to add space between letters or the left arrow to remove space. Space will be added or subtracted by the current Tracking value in Preferences > Type. To kern or track in larger increments, hold down Cmd-Option/Ctrl-Alt and press an arrow.
or
Press Cmd-Shift-[or]/Ctrl-Shift-[or].

➤ Tracking/kerning changes the vertical spacing of characters in vertical type.

➤ To adjust the overall word or letter spacing in a text block, use the Word Spacing and Letter Spacing fields on the Paragraph palette (see the sidebar on page 256).

The **Fit Headline** command uses tracking to fit a one-line paragraph of horizontal or vertical area type to the edges of its container.

To fit type to its container:

1. Choose any type tool.

2. Highlight or click in a one-line paragraph (not a line in a larger paragraph; we're talking about a line by itself).

3. Choose Type > Fit Headline **1**–**2**.

Horizontal scaling

You can use the **Horizontal Scale** command to either extend type (make it wider) or condense type (make it narrower). The **Vertical Scale** command makes type taller or shorter. The default scale for both is 100%.

Note: In typefaces that are narrow or wide by design (e.g., Helvetica Narrow or Univers Extended), the weight, proportions, and counters (interior spaces) are adjusted along with the width. For this reason, they look better than Regular or Roman style characters that are extended or narrowed via Illustrator's Horizontal or Vertical Scale command. That being said...

To scale type horizontally and/or vertically:

Make sure the full **Character** palette is displayed (click the up/down arrow ⇕ on the palette tab, if necessary). Select the type that you want to modify, change the **Horizontal** or **Vertical Scale** value (1–10,000%!), then press Return/ Enter or Tab to apply **1**–**2**. You could also choose a preset value from the pop-up menu or click the up or down arrow.
or
To scale point or path type manually **3**, select it using the **Selection** tool (V), then drag a side handle of the bounding box without holding down Shift.
or
To scale a selected type block by a percentage, double-click the Scale tool, change the **Non-Uniform: Horizontal** or **Vertical** value, then click OK.

Back we go!

To restore normal scaling:

1. Select the type you want to restore normal scaling to.

2. Press Cmd-Shift-X/Ctrl-Shift-X.
or
Choose 100% from the **Horizontal Scale** and **Vertical Scale** pop-up menus on the **Character** palette. *Note:* If you applied scaling via an object's bounding box or via the Scale tool, restoring normal scaling to the type won't restore the object's original dimensions.

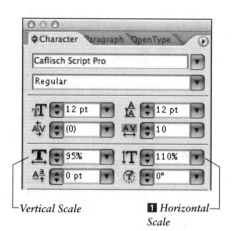

Vertical Scale   **1** *Horizontal Scale*

DANIELLA
Normal type (no scaling)

DANIELLA
75% horizontal scale

DANIELLA
125% horizontal scale

2 *Various horizontal scale values*

3 *You can scale path type by dragging a handle on its bounding box.*

Scale Type

Dialog box option	Keyboard	Smart punctuation
ff, fi, ffi Ligatures	ff, fi, ffi	ff, fi, ffi
ff, fl, ffl Ligatures	ff, fl, ffl	ff, fl, ffl
Smart Quotes	' "	' " " '
Smart Spaces (one space after a period)	. T	. T
En (dashes)	--	–
Em Dashes	---	—
Ellipses	...	...
Expert Fractions	1/2	½

1 *Check* **Replace Punctuation** *options in the* **Smart Punctuation** *dialog box.*

Using smart punctuation

The **Smart Punctuation** command converts text to professional typesetting characters (not for OpenType fonts).

To create smart punctuation:

1. *Optional:* Select text with a type tool to smart-punctuate just that text. Otherwise, the command will affect all the type in the document.
2. Choose Type > **Smart Punctuation**.
3. Check any of the **Replace Punctuation** boxes **1** (see also the sidebar).
4. Click **Replace In: Selected Text Only** if you selected text for step 1; otherwise click **Entire Document**.
5. *Optional:* Check Report Results to have a list of your changes appear onscreen after you click OK.
6. Click OK **2**–**3**.

To specify a quotation marks style for future type:

1. Choose File > **Document Setup** (Cmd-Option-P/Ctrl-Alt-P).
2. Display the Type panel, choose a **Double Quotes** style and a **Single Quotes** style, and check **Use Typographers Quotes**. You can also choose an alternate **Language**, if desired.
3. Click OK.

Smart Punctuation

"We are living in a world today where lemonade is made from artificial flavors and furniture polish is made from real lemons."

--Alfred E. Newman

2 *Dumb punctuation: Straight quotation marks, two hyphens, and no ligatures.*

"We are living in a world today where lemonade is made from artificial flavors and furniture polish is made from real lemons."

–Alfred E. Newman

3 *Smart punctuation: Smart quotation marks, a single dash, and ligatures (note the "fi" in "artificial and the "fl" in "flavors").*

Inserting alternate glyphs

Fonts in the **OpenType** format, which was developed jointly by Adobe and Microsoft, can be used both in Mac and Windows to prevent font substitution and text reflow problems when transferring files between platforms. Illustrator CS2 supplies you with over 100 OpenType font families. The ones with extra characters have a "Pro" in the name **1**.

The OpenType format also allows for a broad range in the number of stylistic variations available for any given character in a specific font. These character variations are called **glyphs** (sounds like something out of *The Hobbit*). For each individual character in an OpenType font, an assortment of glyphs may be substituted, such as ligatures, swashes, titling characters, stylistic alternates, ordinals, and fractions. **Alternate glyphs** can be **inserted manually** by using the **Glyphs** palette (see below), or automatically by using the OpenType palette (see the next page). The Glyphs palette isn't just used for OpenType fonts, though—you can use this palette to locate and insert characters in any font.

To replace a character with an alternate glyph manually:

1. Using a type tool, select a character or character pair in your text.

2. To open the **Glyphs** palette, choose Glyphs from the Type menu or the Window > Type submenu. The character you selected will be highlighted on the palette. You can choose a font from the bottom of the palette.

3. Choose Show: **Alternates for Current Selection 2**, then double-click the glyph that you want the selected character to be replaced with. Or choose Show: **Entire Font 3**, and if the square containing the currently highlighted glyph has a triangle in the lower right corner, click the triangle and choose from the pop-up menu.

Spot the impostors!
To highlight any substituted glyphs in the current document, choose File > Document Setup, display the Type panel, then check **Highlight: Substituted Glyphs;** to highlight any font substitutions (due to a missing font), check **Substituted Fonts.**

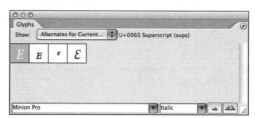

1 *When the font submenus are set to display font families in the actual font face (WYSIWYG), OpenType ("Pro") fonts are identified by this symbol. O*

2 *The Glyphs palette with the letter "e" highlighted and **Alternates for Current Selection** chosen from the Show pop-up menu*

3 *The Glyphs palette displaying the pop-up menu of alternates for a highlighted glyph*

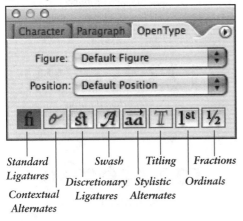

1 *The Show pop-up menu on the Glyphs palette*

2 *The OpenType palette*

Standard
Ligatures

Swash

Titling

Fractions

Contextual
Alternates

Discretionary
Ligatures

Stylistic
Alternates

Ordinals

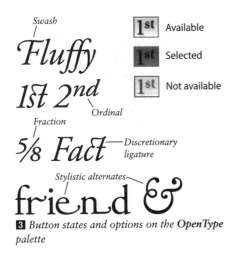

Swash

Fluffy

1st 2nd

Ordinal

Fraction

⅝ Fact

Discretionary
ligature

Stylistic alternates

friend &

1st Available

1st Selected

1st Not available

3 *Button states and options on the OpenType palette*

To insert a glyph into text manually:

1. Choose a **type** tool, then click in the text to position the text insertion marker.

2. From the **Show** pop-up menu on the **Glyphs** palette **1**, choose a category of glyphs to be displayed on the palette (choices vary depending on the current font).

   You can also choose a **font** from the pop-up menu at the bottom of the palette, and a type **style** from the pop-up menu to its right.

3. Double-click the desired glyph, or click a mini arrowhead and choose a glyph from the pop-up menu. It will appear in the text.

➤ Click the Zoom Out or Zoom In button in the lower right corner of the Glyphs palette to change the display size of the glyphs on the palette.

Using the OpenType palette, you can decide ahead of time or for existing text whether **alternate glyphs** will be inserted **automatically** in lieu of standard characters, based on the context of the text situation. For example, you can choose to have a glyph for a properly formatted fraction be inserted automatically whenever you type 1/2 or 1/4. Other available options, as shown on the Open Type palette **2**, include ligature glyphs for specific letter pairs (e.g., ff, ffl, and st) and swash, titling, and other special characters.

To specify or insert alternate glyphs automatically:

1. Display the **OpenType** palette (Cmd-Option-Shift-T/Ctrl-Alt-Shift-T).

2. To change **existing** text, either select a text object to change all appropriate text occurrences in the object, or select specific text to limit the change to that text.
   or
   To specify alternate glyph options for **future** text to be entered in an OpenType font, deselect all type.

3. Click any of the available buttons on the palette **3**.

Insert Glyph; OpenType Palette

Some **OpenType** fonts also contain **alternate glyphs** for **numerals.** From the Figure pop-up menu on the Open Type palette, you can choose a style for numeral glyphs for existing or future text; or from the Position pop-up menu, you can choose a position for numeral glyphs relative to the baseline.

Note: If the currently chosen font contains numeral glyphs, such categories as Denominators, Numerators, Oldstyle Figures, Tabular Figures, etc. will be listed on the Show menu on the Glyphs palette.

To choose an alternate numeral style:

1. Do one of the following:

Select a **type object,** to change all the appropriate numerals in that object.

Select specific **text** that contains numerals, to change just that text.

Deselect all, to specify numeral options for future text.

2. On the **OpenType** palette, choose from the **Figure** pop-up menu **1**–**2**:

Default Figure to keep (or revert to) the selected font's default numeral style.

Tabular Lining to create full-height numerals of equal width. This is a good option when creating tables, as these numerals can be lined up in columns.

Proportional Lining to create full-height numerals of different widths. This choice is appropriate if you want numerals that are the same height as all-caps text.

Proportional Oldstyle to create old-fashioned numerals of non-uniform heights and widths. It is beautiful for formal invitations and the like.

Tabular Oldstyle to create old-fashioned, varying-height numerals, but in uniform widths so they can be lined up in columns.

3. To choose whether the numerals can be raised or lowered relative to the baseline, choose an option from the **Position** pop-up menu (**1**–**2**, next page):

Default Position to use the font's default position for numerals.

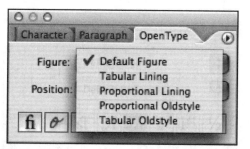

1 The **Figure** *pop-up menu on the* **OpenType** *palette*

Default Figure or Tabular Lining

123456789

Proportional Lining

Proportional Oldstyle

Tabular Oldstyle

2 *Tabular glyphs are wider than proportional glyphs; some* **oldstyle** *numerals sit below the baseline (this is the Adobe Caslon Pro font).*

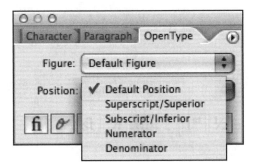

1 *The* **Position** *choices on the* **OpenType** *palette*

123456789
Default Position (on baseline)

123456789
Superscript/Superior

1̶2̶3̶4̶5̶6̶7̶8̶9̶
Subscript/Inferior

123456789
Numerator

123456789
Denominator

2 *Position options for numerals in an OpenType font*

1/2 4/5 | **3** *Standard numerals, entered with slashes in the Adobe Garamond Pro font*

½ ⅘ | **4** *The numerals and slashes reformatted as proper fractions—much better!*

Superscript/Superior to use glyphs that sit above the baseline.

Subscript/Inferior to use glyphs that sit below the baseline.

Numerator or **Denominator** to use small numerals that are raised or lowered relative to adjacent characters/numerals.

If you selected numerals in step 1 in a font that contains the alternate numeral glyphs that you chose from the Figure and/or Position pop-up menus, the new glyphs will appear in your selected text.

To produce fractions:

1. Select a type object to change all appropriate numerals (e.g., 1/2, 2/3, 3/4) in the object.
or
Select specific text that contains numerals, to limit the change to just that text.

In either case, make sure an OpenType font is chosen for the numerals you want to restyle.

2. Click the **Fractions** button ½ on the **OpenType** palette. If the font used in the selected text contains glyphs for numerators, superscripts, denominators, or subscripts, the proper number glyphs will appear in your text **3**–**4**.

The **Change Case** commands change selected text to all UPPERCASE, lowercase, Title Case, or Sentence case.

To change case:

1. With a type tool, highlight the text you want to modify.

2. Choose Type > Change Case > **UPPERCASE; lowercase; Title Case** (the first character in each word is uppercase, the other characters are lowercase); or **Sentence case** (only the first character in each sentence is uppercase).

➤ Some fonts, such as Lithos and Castellar, don't contain any lowercase characters.

Fractions; Change Case

Paragraph Alignment

Changing paragraph alignment

Alignment and indentation values affect whole paragraphs. But before you learn how to apply paragraph formatting, you need to know what a paragraph is, at least as far as Illustrator is concerned.

➤ To create a new paragraph (hard return) in a text block, press **Return/Enter.** The type that precedes a return or that wraps automatically belongs to one paragraph; the type that follows a return belongs to the next paragraph.

➤ To create a line break (soft return) within a paragraph in nontabular text, press **Shift-Return.**

To change paragraph alignment:

1. Choose a **type** tool, then click in a paragraph or drag through a series of paragraphs.
   or
   Choose a **selection** tool, then select a type object.

2. Show the **Paragraph** palette (Cmd-Option-T/Ctrl-Alt-T or click Paragraph on the Control palette), then click an **alignment** button **1**–**2**. The first three alignment options (Align left, Align center, and Align right) are also available as **(NEW)** buttons on the **Control** palette.
   or
   Use one of the keyboard shortcuts listed in the sidebar on this page.

➤ Don't bother applying any of the justify alignment options to point type (type that's not in an object or block). Such objects don't have edges, so there's nothing to justify the type to.

➤ To move path type along its path, see page 227.

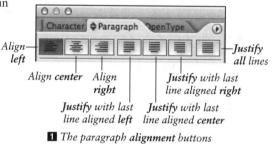

Paragraph alignment shortcuts

Align left	Cmd-Shift-L/Ctrl-Shift-L
Align center	Cmd-Shift-C/Ctrl-Shift-C
Align right	Cmd-Shift-R/Ctrl-Shift-R
Justify with last line aligned left	Cmd-Shift-J/Ctrl-Shift-J
Justify all lines	Cmd-Shift-F/Ctrl-Shift-F

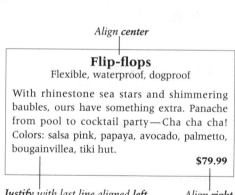

Align left — *Justify all lines*

Align center — *Align right*

Justify with last line aligned right

Justify with last line aligned left — *Justify with last line aligned center*

1 *The paragraph alignment buttons*

Align center

Flip-flops
Flexible, waterproof, dogproof

With rhinestone sea stars and shimmering baubles, ours have something extra. Panache from pool to cocktail party—Cha cha cha! Colors: salsa pink, papaya, avocado, palmetto, bougainvillea, tiki hut.

$79.99

Justify with last line aligned left   *Align right*

2 *A few paragraph alignment options*

What to select

If you want to change paragraph attributes for all the text in a type object or on a path, select the object or path with the **Selection** tool.

To edit a paragraph or series of paragraphs, select just those paragraphs with a **type** tool.

Left Indent

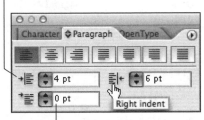

First-Line Left Indent

1 *If you forget which Indent field on the Paragraph palette is which, rest the mouse over an icon—the tool tip will remind you.*

The Mock Turtle sighed deeply, and began, in a voice choked with sobs, to sing this:—

    Beautiful Soup, so rich and green,
    Waiting in a hot tureen!
    Who for such dainties would not stoop?
    Soup of the evening, beautiful Soup!
    Soup of the evening, beautiful Soup!
        Beau—ootiful Soo-oop!
        Beau—ootiful Soo-oop!
    Soo—oop of the e—e—evening,
    Beautiful, beautiful Soup!

              — *Lewis Carroll*

2 *Left indentation*

Changing paragraph indentation

You can apply **left** and/or **right indent** values to area type, but only left indent values to point type.

To change paragraph indentation:

1. Choose a **type** tool, then select the paragraph(s) you want to modify or click to create an insertion point in a single paragraph.
or
Choose a **selection** tool, then select a type object.

2. On the **Paragraph** palette (Cmd-Option-T/Ctrl-Alt-T or click Paragraph on the Control palette):

Change the **Left** and/or **Right Indent** value, then press Return/Enter or Tab to apply **1**–**2**, or click the up or down arrow. Note that these values also affect any lines that follow a soft return.
or
To indent only the first line of each paragraph, enter a positive **First-Line Left Indent** value.

➤ To create a hanging indent **3**, enter a negative value in the First-Line Left Indent field.

CHAPTER 1: What am I becoming? So you know who I am now, a traitor to my friends, and my new friends. I wish everyone could get off my back and let me live, I mean really it is kind of MY life. Everyone wants me to go their way; independent, popular, regular, brilliant. But what about me, I don't want to set out my future, I just want to live life the way it's set out for me.

3 *A hanging indent*

Inter-paragraph spacing

Use the **Space Before Paragraph** field or the **Space After Paragraph** field on the Paragraph palette to add or subtract space between paragraphs. To adjust the spacing between lines of type within a paragraph, use leading (see page 245).

To adjust inter-paragraph spacing:

1. Select the type you want to modify. To modify the space before only one paragraph in a type block, select the paragraph with a **type** tool. To change all the type in an object, select the object with the **Selection** tool.

2. In the **Space Before Paragraph** or **Space After Paragraph** field on the Paragraph palette **1**, enter a positive value to move paragraphs apart or a negative value to move them closer together (press Return/Enter or Tab to apply) **2**, or click the up or down arrow.

➤ Keep in mind that the space before a paragraph is combined with the spacing from the paragraph above it, so you could end up with more space between paragraphs than you intend.

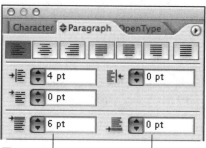

1 *Space Before Paragraph*   *Space After Paragraph*

DEM DAR
BEVERLY HILLS

DIRTY LITTLE SOCKS

DON'T PLUNK MY
HEART STRINGS

COOL, CALM,
COLLECTIBLES

BEHIND THESE
HAZY EYES

LOSE CONTROL…
AND WEIGHT, TOO!

2 *The Space Before Paragraph values were increased for these paragraphs to add space above them.*

Spacing and scaling defaults

To change the horizontal word or letter spacing for justified paragraphs, choose **Justification** from the Paragraph palette menu, then in the Justification dialog box, change the Minimum, Desired, or Maximum **Word Spacing** or **Letter Spacing** values **3**–**5**. Desired is the only setting that affects nonjustified paragraphs. (Tip: try reducing the word spacing for large type.) The **Glyph Scaling** (50%–200%) affects the width of all characters.

OCEAN
Body more immaculate than a wave,
salt washing away its own line,
and the brilliant bird
flying without ground roots.
Pablo Neruda

3 *Normal **word** and **letter** spacing*

OCEAN
Body more immaculate than a wave,
salt washing away its own line,
and the brilliant bird
flying without ground roots.

4 *Loose **letter** spacing*

OCEAN
Body more immaculate than a wave,
salt washing away its own line,
and the brilliant bird
flying without ground roots.

5 *Tight **word** spacing*

Inter-Paragraph Spacing

Your favorite composer

On the Paragraph palette menu, you have a choice of two line-composer options for selected type:

Adobe Every-line Composer examines all the lines within a paragraph first, and then arranges line lengths and endings in order to optimize the appearance of the overall paragraph.

Adobe Single-line Composer examines and arranges text and hyphenation one line at a time without regard to other lines.

Gimme no break

To prevent a word from breaking, such as a compound word or proper name, select it, then choose **No Break** from the Character palette menu.

1 *Use the **Hyphenation** dialog box to set parameters for auto hyphenation.*

```
AN
OVER-
ABUN-
DANCE
OF HY-
PHENS
MAKES  2
FOR
TIR-
ING
READ-
ING.
```

Hyphenation

To choose hyphenation options:

1. Auto hyphenation affects only currently selected or subsequently created text. If you want to hyphenate existing text, select it with a type tool or selection tool now.

2. On the **Paragraph** palette, check **Hyphenate** to enable hyphenation. (If this option isn't visible, choose Show Options from the palette menu.)

3. To choose hyphenation options, choose **Hyphenation** from the **Paragraph** palette menu.

4. In the **Words Longer Than** [ ] **letters** field, enter the minimum number of characters a word must contain in order to be hyphenated (3–25) **1**.

   In the **After First** [ ] **letters** field, enter the minimum number of characters that can precede a hyphen (we use a value of 3).

   In the **Before Last** [ ] **letters** field, enter the minimum number of characters that can be carried over onto the next line following a hyphen.

   In the **Hyphen Limit** field, enter the maximum allowable number of end-of-line hyphens in a row (0–25). More than two hyphens in a row makes type hard to read, and looks ugly to boot **2**.

   When using Adobe Single-line Composer (see the sidebar), you can enter a value in the **Hyphenation Zone** field to specify the distance from the right margin within which hyphenation can't occur.

   Decide whether you want to permit the program to **Hyphenate Capitalized Words.**

5. Click OK. Look over the newly hyphenated text, and correct any awkward breaks manually.

➤ In Preferences > Hyphenation, you can enter hyphenation exceptions, specify how particular words are to be hyphenated, and confirm the default language for hyphenation (see page 476).

The **Roman Hanging Punctuation** command, mimicking a traditional typesetting technique, forces punctuation marks that fall at the beginning and/or end of a line of type in an area type block to hang slightly outside the block—period, comma, quotation mark, apostrophe, hyphen, dash, colon, semicolon. Why? It looks better!

To hang punctuation:

1. With a **type** tool, select a paragraph in an area type object; or with a **selection** tool, select the whole object.

2. From the **Paragraph** palette menu, choose **Roman Hanging Punctuation** **1**.

➤ For a more pleasing alignment of letters, such as the letter W, O, or A (not punctuation), at the beginning and/or end of lines in a whole type object, choose Type > **Optical Margin Alignment.** Some characters may shift slightly outside the block.

Character and paragraph styles

Now that you know how to style type manually by using the Character and Paragraph palettes, you're ready to learn how to create and apply character and paragraph styles, which accomplish the same thing with much less sweat.

Paragraph **2** styles include paragraph formats, such as leading and indentation, and character attributes, such as font and point size. When a paragraph style is applied, all currently selected paragraphs are reformatted.

Character styles contain only character attributes, and are applied to selectively highlighted text within a paragraph (such as bullets, or boldfaced or italicized words), not to whole paragraphs **3**. Character styles should be applied in addition to paragraph styles—they're the icing on the cake.

Not only do styles make light work of typesetting, they also help to ensure consistency within a document and among related documents. Styles are created, modified, and applied by using the **Character Styles** and **Paragraph Styles** palettes (open both palettes from the Window > Type submenu) **4**.

"Dining is and always was a great artistic opportunity."

—*Frank Lloyd Wright*

1 *Let it hang out, with* **Roman Hanging Punctuation**

This **ahimsa** is the basis of the search for truth. § I am realizing every day that the search is vain unless it is founded on **ahimsa** as the basis. § It is quite proper to resist and attack a system, but to resist and attack its author is tantamount to resisting and attacking **oneself.** § For we are all tarred with the same brush, and are children of one and the same Creator, and as such the divine powers within us are infinite. § To slight a single human being is to slight those divine powers, and thus to harm not only that being but with him the whole **world.** §

Mohandas K. Gandhi

2 *Paragraph style*   **3** *Character styles*

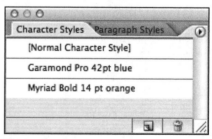

4 *The* **Character Styles** *and* **Paragraph Styles** *palette group*

To create or modify a character or paragraph style:

1. Choose Window > Type > **Character Styles** or **Paragraph Styles.**

2. To create a **new** style, we suggest you use a type tool to select some text in your document that contains the attributes you want saved in the style. Next, Option-click/Alt-click the **New Style** button ⬛ at the bottom of the Character or Paragraph Styles palette. If this is your first foray into styles, we recommend creating a paragraph style first.

   or

   To **edit** an existing style, deselect all, then double-click a style name on the palette. (Or if text is selected, Cmd-Option/Ctrl-Alt double-click a style **name.** These modifier keys will prevent the style from being applied to any text.)

3. An options dialog box will open for the chosen style type. Change the default **Style Name** to a more descriptive name for the type of formatting that it contains (such as "Subheads").

4. The options dialog box has several panels, which you can access by clicking a category on the left side. If text was selected in step 2, some panels will already contain information. Display any panel to choose attributes for the style.

Check **Preview** to preview the chosen options in any currently selected text.

Click **General** to display a list of the current settings for all the categories ⬛.

Click **Basic Character Formats** to choose basic character attributes, such as font, point size, kerning, leading, and tracking.

Click **Advanced Character Formats** to choose scaling, baseline shift, and rotation values.

Click **Character Color,** click the Fill or Stroke square, then choose a fill and/or stroke color for the type. Colors from the Swatches palette will be listed here (non-global colors first, then global colors). For a stroke, you can also choose a Weight.

Click **OpenType Features** to choose options to be applied when OpenType fonts are used (⬛, next page).

5. In the Paragraph Style Options dialog box, you can also choose settings in the **Indents and Spacing** (⬛, next page), **Tabs, Composition** (Composer), **Hyphenation,** and **Justification** panels.

6. Click OK. To apply styles, see page 261.

(Continued on the following page)

Create, Modify Character or Paragraph Style

Paragraph Style Options

Style Name: Ad copy

General	
General	General
Basic Character Formats	
Advanced Character Formats	
Indents and Spacing	Style Settings: [Normal Paragraph Style] +
Tabs	
Composition	▼ Basic Character Formats
Hyphenation	Size:58.2 pt
Justification	▼ Advanced Character Formats
Character Color	Horizontal Scale:100%
OpenType Features	Baseline Shift:0 pt
	▼ Indents and Spacing
	Left Indent:4 pt
	Right Indent:6 pt

☑ Preview   Reset Panel   Cancel   OK

⬛ *The **General** panel of the **Paragraph Style Options** dialog box*

1 *Checking an option in the* **OpenType Features** *panel of the* **Character Style Options** *dialog box is equivalent to clicking a button on the OpenType palette.*

2 *The* **Indents and Spacing** *panel of the* **Paragraph Style Options** *dialog box*

➤ Click Reset Panel at any time to clear all settings in the currently displayed panel. Some individual nonnumeric options can be reset to a blank state (no value or effect) by choosing (Ignore) from the pop-up menu.

➤ You can also create a new style by duplicating an existing style and then changing attributes in the duplicate. To duplicate a style, click the style name, then choose Duplicate Character Style or Paragraph Style from the respective palette menu; or drag the style that you want to copy over

the New Style button. You can't duplicate the Normal styles.

➤ You can also open the Paragraph or Character Style Options dialog box by clicking a style name and then choosing Paragraph or Character Style Options from the palette menu.

➤ A dash/green check mark in an option check box means that option won't override any attributes that were applied manually to the text.

What if...

If you inadvertently apply a character style to a whole type object and then apply a paragraph style, only the paragraph style's formats will be applied, not its character attributes, and the paragraph style name won't display a "+." To force a paragraph style to completely override a character style, select the type object, then click **[Normal Character Style]** on the Character Styles palette.

Removing overrides

Option-clicking/Alt-clicking a paragraph style removes **manual** overrides from the paragraph style, but doesn't remove character styling. To remove overrides from a character style, you have to Option-click/Alt-click that style, too. Overrides are removed either from selected characters or from the whole object, if no characters are selected.

GEORGES BRAQUE (1882–1963)

THERE IS ONLY ONE VALUABLE THING IN ART: THE THING YOU CANNOT EXPLAIN.

REPORTED IN **SATURDAY REVIEW**, MAY 28, 1966

1 *Type styled with paragraph styles* *Type styled with character styles*

GEORGES BRAQUE (1882–1963)

THERE IS ONLY ONE **VALUABLE** THING IN ART: THE THING YOU CANNOT EXPLAIN.

REPORTED IN **SATURDAY REVIEW**, MAY 28, 1966

2 *The boldfacing in the word "valuable" was applied manually, so is considered an* **override.**

GEORGES BRAQUE (1882–1963)

THERE IS ONLY ONE VALUABLE THING IN ART: THE THING YOU CANNOT EXPLAIN.

REPORTED IN **SATURDAY REVIEW**, MAY 28, 1966

3 *Option-clicking/Alt-clicking the paragraph style for the main paragraph on the Paragraph Styles palette* **removed** *the boldfacing (override).*

To apply a type style:

1. For **paragraph** styling, select a type object, or select some paragraphs in a type object.

   For **character** styling, select some text (not a whole object).

2. Click a style name on the **Paragraph Styles** or **Character Styles** palette **1**.

   Note: If the text doesn't adopt the attributes of the style sheet, follow the next set of instructions.

➤ To choose a style for text before you type it, deselect all, click a style name on the Paragraph palette, then create your text.

A + (plus) sign after a style name signifies that some text in the selected type was styled **manually** using the Character or Paragraph palette after a style was assigned to it; that is, the text attributes no longer exactly match the attributes as defined in the applied style. Adobe calls this situation an **override.**

Follow these instructions if you need to **clear** any **overrides** in your text. The text will readopt the character attributes as defined in the style.

To remove overrides from styled text:

1. Select the characters or paragraphs that contain overrides to be removed **2**–**3**. Or to "fix" the whole object, select the object but not any characters.

2. Option-click/Alt-click a name on the Character Styles or Paragraph Styles palette. The manually applied attributes in your text will disappear, and the "+" sign will disappear from the style name on the palette (see also the sidebar at left).

To redefine a type style:

1. Select the characters or paragraphs that are assigned the style you want to edit and have the desired style changes. (The style name will become selected on the palette.)

2. Choose **Redefine Character Style** from the Character Styles palette menu, or choose **Redefine Paragraph Style** from the Paragraph Styles palette menu. The style will be modified to reflect the custom styling in the selected text.

When you **delete** a **paragraph** or **character style,** the text attributes don't change in the document—the text merely ceases to be associated with a style name.

To delete a character or paragraph style:

1. Deselect all.

2. Click a style name (or Cmd-click/Ctrl-click multiple style names) on the Character Styles or Paragraph Styles palette, then click the **Delete Selected Styles** button 🗑 (or choose Delete Character Style or Paragraph Style from the palette menu).
or
Drag a style name over the **Delete Selected Styles** button. If the style is currently applied to text in your document, an alert dialog box will appear; click Yes.

➤ You can't delete the Normal paragraph or character style.

➤ To delete all unused styles in the current document (styles that aren't currently applied to any text in your document), choose Select All Unused from the palette menu, then click the Delete Selected Styles button.

When **loading paragraph** or **character styles** from another Illustrator file, an incoming style will overwrite any style that bears a matching name in the current document, and type styled with the original style will adopt the attributes of the incoming style.

To load type styles from another Illustrator document:

1. From the Character Styles or Paragraph Styles palette menu, choose one of the following:

Load Character Styles.

Load Paragraph Styles.

Load All Styles to load both character and paragraph styles from another document.

2. Locate the desired Illustrator document name, then click Open; or simply double-click the document name.

Finding and replacing text

You can use the **Find and Replace** command to search for and replace type characters (not attributes).

To find and replace text:

1. *Optional:* Click with a type tool to create an insertion point from which to start the search. If you don't do this, the search will begin from the most recently created object.

2. Choose Edit > **Find and Replace.**

3. Enter a word or phrase to search for in the **Find** field ◼, or choose a special character from the adjacent pop-up menu.

4. Enter a replacement word or phrase in the **Replace With** field ◼; or choose a character from the adjacent pop-up menu; or leave the field blank to delete instances of the Find text altogether.

5. *Check any of these optional boxes:*

   Match Case to find only those instances that match the exact uppercase/lowercase configuration of the Find text. With this box unchecked, case will be ignored as a criterion.

   Find Whole Word to find only instances of the complete Find text by itself, not instances in which the characters may

be embedded within a larger word (e.g., "go" but not "going").

Search Backwards to search from the bottom to the top of the stacking order.

Check Hidden Layers to search hidden layers.

Check Locked Layers to search locked layers.

6. Click **Find** to search for the first instance of the Find word or phrase.

7. Do any of the following:

   Click **Replace** to replace only the currently found instance of the Find text, then click **Find Next** to search for the next instance.

   Click **Replace & Find** to replace the current instance and search for the next instance in one step.

   Click **Replace All** to replace all instances at once without pausing.

8. Click Done (Return/Enter or Esc).

◼ *In the Find field, enter the text to be searched for.* ◼ *In the Replace With field, enter the replacement text.*

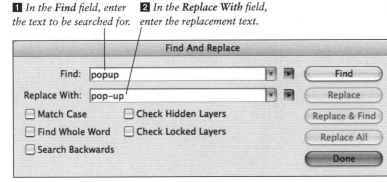

*Use the **Find And Replace** dialog box to find and change text characters.*

Checking spelling

The **Check Spelling** command checks spelling in an entire document, using a built-in dictionary and a user dictionary.

To check spelling:

1. Choose Edit > **Check Spelling** (Cmd-I/Ctrl-I). If you want to see the spelling corrections being made, change zoom levels or move all the text into view in the document window. You don't need to select anything in your document.

2. In the Check Spelling dialog box, click **Start**. The first word that isn't found in the application or user dictionary will appear in the Word Not Found window (**1**, next page), and will also be highlighted in the document window.

3. *Optional:* To refine the search, click the Options arrowhead to access Find and Ignore options for numerals, capitalization, and repeated words (two or more instances of the same word side by side).

4. Do any of the following:

   If the correctly spelled word appears—highlighted or not—on the **Suggestions** list, double-click it. This will fix just the current instance of the word.

   To change all instances of the misspelled word, click the correctly spelled word, then click **Change All.** The next misspelled word (if there is one) will now become highlighted.

If the correct word doesn't appear on the list, or if no words appear there at all (because no similar words were found in either dictionary), start typing the correctly spelled word. Your typing entry will replace the highlighted word in the Word Not Found window. Then click **Change** to change only the first instance of the highlighted misspelled word, or click **Change All** to change all instances of the misspelled word.

For any word, you can click **Ignore** to leave the current instance of the word as is (no change), or click **Ignore All** to leave all instances of the current word as is.

Click **Add** to add the currently highlighted word (from the Word Not Found window) to the user dictionary, leaving the word unchanged in the document, and move on to the next misspelled word. Clicking this button will create a user dictionary, if none already exists for this document.

5. Click Done (Return/Enter or Esc) when no more mispelled words are found, or at any time to end the spell check.

Check Spelling

1 The **Check Spelling** dialog box, with the **Options** panel displayed

To edit the custom dictionary:

1. Choose Edit > **Edit Custom Dictionary.** The Edit Custom Dictionary dialog box opens **2**.

2. Do any of the following:

   Click a word in the list, correct it in the Entry field at the top of the dialog box, then click **Change.**

   Click a word, then click **Delete.**

   Type a new word in the Entry field at the top of the dialog box, then click **Add.** Hyphenated words, such as "pop-up," are permitted.

3. Click Done.

Click a word, retype it in the Entry field, then click Change.

Or type a new word in the Entry field, then click Add.

Or click a word, then click Delete.

2 Using the **Edit Custom Dictionary** dialog box, you can create your own word list or edit any words that were added to the list.

Finding and replacing fonts

The **Find Font** command can be used either to generate a list of the fonts currently being used in a document or to replace fonts (not characters). When fonts are replaced, the type color, kerning, tracking, and other attributes are retained.

To find and replace a font:

1. Choose Type > **Find Font.**

2. Check any of the boxes in the **Include in List** area at the bottom of the dialog box (OpenType, Type 1, TrueType, Roman, CID, Multiple Master, or Standard) to have fonts of just those types appear on the Replace With Font From scroll list.

3. To display a list of fonts of the types checked in the previous step, on the **Replace With Font From** pop-up menu:

   To list only fonts that are currently being used in your document, leave the choice as **Document.**
   or
   To list fonts that are currently available in your system, choose **System** (**1**, next page). If you choose this option, be patient while the list updates (take a catnap, call a friend).

4. On the **Fonts in Document** scroll list, click a font to search for. The first instance of that font will be highlighted automatically in your document.

5. Click a replacement font on the replacement font scroll list.

6. Click one of the following:

   Change to change only the current instance of the currently highlighted font.

   Change All to change all instances of the currently highlighted font. Once all the instances of a font are replaced, that font will disappear from the Fonts in Document list.

   Find to search for the next instance of the currently highlighted font, or click the font name on the Fonts in Document list again.

7. *Optional:* To save a list of the fonts currently being used in the file as a text document, click Save List, enter a name, choose a location in which to save the file, then click Save. The text document can later be opened directly from the Desktop or it can be imported into a text editing or layout application.

8. Click **Done.**

1 *Choose* **System** *from the* **Replace With Font From** *pop-up menu to display on the replacement font list all available fonts in the system of the types checked, or choose* **Document** *to list only the fonts being used in your document.*

Click a font to be searched for on the **Fonts in Document** *scroll list.*

Click **Change All**; *or click* **Change,** *then click* **Find.**

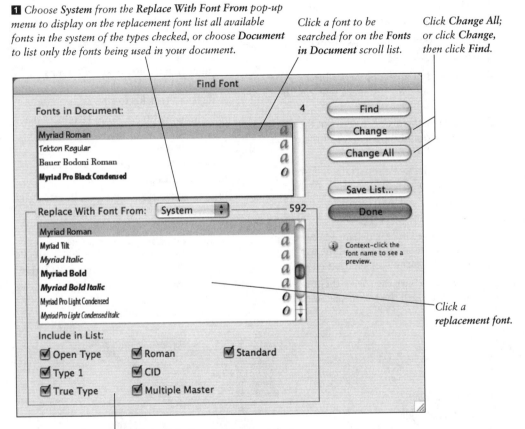

Click a replacement font.

Uncheck any **font types** *to narrow the list of replacement fonts.*

Choosing area type options

Using the **Area Type Options** dialog box, you can change the inset spacing between area type and the edge of its type object, or reposition the first line of type in a type object, or divide a type block into columns and/or rows.

To choose area type options:

1. Select an area type object with a selection tool or type tool **1**.

2. Choose Type > **Area Type Options**.

3. Check Preview **2**.

4. In the Offset area, choose an **Inset Spacing** value for the space between the type and the type object.

5. To control the distance between the first line of text and the top edge of the object, choose a **First Baseline** option:

   Ascent to have the top of the tallest characters touch the top of the object.

   Cap Height to have uppercase letters touch the top of the object.

   Leading to make the distance between the first baseline of the text and the top of the object be equal to the leading value.

   x Height to have the top of the font's "x" character touch the top of the object.

Em Box Height to have the top of the em box in Asian fonts touch the top of the object.

Fixed, then enter a Min value for the location of the baseline of the first line.

Legacy to use the method from previous versions of Illustrator.

Enter a minimum baseline offset value in the **Min** field. Illustrator will use either this minimum value or the **First Baseline** option value, whichever is greater.

6. To arrange text in linked rows and/or columns, in the **Rows** and **Columns** areas, click an up or down arrow or enter values in the fields to choose:

The total **Width** and total **Height** of the entire type object (read about the Fixed option, below).

The total **Number** of rows and columns to be produced.

The **Span** for the height of each row and the width of each column. With **Fixed** checked, if you scale the type object, columns will be added or deleted as needed, but the row or column span won't change. With this option unchecked, the row or column span will change to fit the newly scaled object, but no new rows or columns will be added.

Hey! diddle, diddle,
The cat and the Fiddle,
The cow jumped over the moon;
The little dog laugh'd
To see such sport,
And the dish ran away with the spoon.

1 *The original text object*

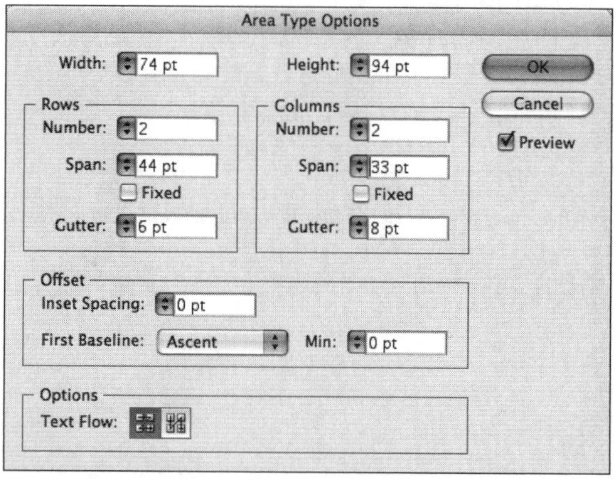

2 *Use the **Area Type Options** dialog box to position type within an object and to arrange type into columns and/or rows.*

Area Type Options (vertical sidebar text)

Hey! diddle, diddle, | The cow jumped
The cat and the | over the moon;
Fiddle, | The little dog

laugh'd | away with the
To see such sport, | spoon.
And the dish ran

1 *The object converted into two **rows** and two **columns**. The arrows show the direction of the text flow.*

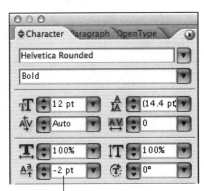

2 *Path type, Baseline Shift 0*

3 *Baseline Shift*

4 *Path type, negative Baseline Shift value*

𝒜lice

5 *The "A" has a Baseline Shift value of –9 pt.*

The **Gutter** (space) between the rows and the columns. If Fixed is checked when the Gutter value is changed, the overall Width or Height will change but not the span; if Fixed is unchecked when the Gutter value is changed, the span will change but not the width or height.

7. Click one of the two **Text Flow** buttons to control the direction of the text flow—from row to row or from column to column.

8. Click OK **1**.

➤ If you select the type object and then reopen the Area Type Options dialog box, the current settings for that type object will be displayed.

Baseline-shifting type (NEW)

By adjusting the **Baseline Shift** value, you can shift characters upward or downward from the baseline, or offset type from a path.

To baseline-shift type:

1. Select the type you want to shift **2**.

2. Click **Character** on the **Control** palette, then enter a positive **Baseline Shift** value to shift characters upward or a negative value to shift them downward **3**–**5**; or choose a preset value from the pop-up menu; or click the up or down arrow.

   Note: If you're not using the Control palette to access the Character palette and the Baseline Shift area isn't visible on the palette, click the up/down arrow ⬍ on the palette tab twice.
   or
   Option-Shift-press/Alt-Shift-press the **up arrow** on the keyboard to shift the characters upward or the **down arrow** to shift them downward as per the current Baseline Shift increment in Preferences > Type & Auto Tracing. Cmd-Option-Shift-press/Ctrl-Alt-Shift-press an arrow to shift by five times the above-mentioned increment.

➤ To insert superscript and subscript characters in OpenType fonts, use the OpenType palette.

Setting tabs

To align columns of text correctly, you must use **tabs**—not spaces. The default tab stops are half an inch apart. You can use the Tabs palette to set custom left-, center-, right-, and decimal-justified tabs in horizontal type, or top-, center-, bottom-, and decimal-justified tabs in vertical type.

To insert tabs into text:

Press Tab **once** as you input copy before typing each new column. The cursor will jump to the next default tab stop.

or

To **add** a tab to existing text, click just to the left of the text that is to start a new column, then press Tab. The text will move to the next default tab stop.

To set custom tab stops, see the next page.

Out of hiding

To display the tab characters that are hidden in your text, along with other nonprinting characters, such as paragraph returns, soft returns, and spaces, choose Type > **Show Hidden Characters** (Cmd-Option-I/Ctrl-Alt-I). Tab characters display as right-pointing arrows. The nonprinting characters display in the color that's assigned to the layer the objects reside in ■. Choose the command again at any time to turn off the display.

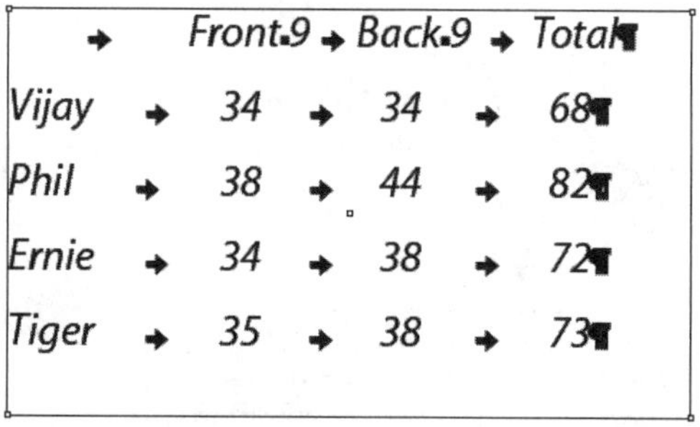

■ *Text aligned using **custom tab stops**, with hidden characters displayed*

Insert Tabs

To set or modify custom tab stops:

1. Choose the **Selection** tool, then click a text object.
   or
   Choose a **type** tool and select some text.

2. Choose Window > Type > **Tabs** (Cmd-Shift-T/Ctrl-Shift-T) to display the Tabs palette.

3. *Optional:* Choose **Snap to Unit** from the palette menu to have tab markers snap to the nearest ruler tick mark as you insert or move them.

4. Do any of the following:

   Click just above the Tabs palette ruler to **insert** a new marker (the selected text will align to that stop) **1**, then click a tab **alignment** button in the top left corner of the palette. Repeat to insert more markers. You can change the alignment of any marker at any time; simply Option-click/Alt-click a tab marker to cycle through the alignment types.

   To **delete** a marker, drag it off the ruler. Cmd-drag/Ctrl-drag to delete a marker and all markers to its right.

   To **move** a tab marker, drag it to the left or right, or enter an exact location in the X field for horizontal type, the Y field for vertical type. Cmd-drag/Ctrl-drag a marker to move all the markers to its right by the same distance. Shift-drag a marker to turn the snap feature on/off

temporarily (the opposite of the current Snap to Unit state).

5. *Optional:* Click a tab marker in the ruler, then enter a character (up to 8 characters, actually) in the **Leader** field to have that character be repeated between tab stops **2**. The style of the leader characters can only be changed manually (use a character style!).

6. *Optional:* For the Decimal-Justified tab alignment option, you can enter a character for numerals to align on in the **Align On** field **3**. For this to work, the tabbed text must contain that character.

➤ If you move the Tabs palette, you can click the Position Palette Above Text button 🔒 to realign the tab ruler with the left and right margins of the selected text for horizontal type, or the top and bottom margins for vertical type.

➤ To create a series of tab stops that are equidistant from one another, click one marker, then choose Repeat Tab from the palette menu. Beware! This command deletes all existing markers to the right of the one you clicked.

➤ The Tabs palette ruler units display in the increment currently chosen in File > Document Setup (Artboard: Units).

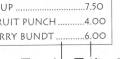

```
SCRUFFY SLAW..........................8.95
SLURPY SOUP ............................7.50
PASSIONFRUIT PUNCH...........4.00
BOYSENBERRY BUNDT............6.00
```

2 *Leader* **3** *Align On*
character *character*

Left-, Center-, Right-, and Decimal-Justified alignment buttons (or Top-, Center-, Bottom-, and Decimal-Justified buttons for vertical type)

Numeric location of the currently selected tab marker

Optional Leader character

Optional Align On character

Position Palette Above Text button

1 *The Tabs palette*

A left-justified tab marker   *A selected decimal-justified tab marker*   *Resize box (drag to widen or shorten the ruler)*

Tabs

X: 172 pt   Leader: Align On:

0   36   72   108   144   180   216   252

Creating special effects with type

Type can **wrap** around an Illustrator path, Illustrator type, or a placed bitmap image.

To wrap type around an object:

1. Create area type (type inside an object).

2. Choose the **Selection** tool (V).

3. Follow this instruction carefully, or the wrap won't work: Make sure the object that the type is going to wrap around (the "wrap object") is in **front** of the type that you want to wrap around it, in the **same** top-level layer, sublayer, or group. You can use the Layers palette to restack the wrap object, if necessary. It can be a vector object or a bitmap (placed) image.

4. Select the wrap object **1** (click its selection area on the Layers palette).

5. Choose Object > Text Wrap > **Make.** If an alert dialog box appears, click OK.

6. Choose Object > Text Wrap > **Text Wrap Options.** In the dialog box **2**, click Preview, then enter or choose an Offset value (–100 to 100 pt) for the distance between the wrap object and any type that wraps around it. If the wrap object is a placed image, the type will wrap around opaque or partially opaque pixels in the image.

   Optional: To entertain yourself on a rainy day, check Invert Wrap. This option will force the text to wrap inside the path instead of outside it.

7. Click OK **3**.

➤ To prevent a text object from being affected by the wrap object, via the Layers palette, move it above the wrap object or to a different top-level layer.

➤ To modify the options for an existing wrap object, select it, then choose Object > Wrap > Text Wrap Options. The dialog box reopens.

To release a text wrap:

1. Select the wrap object (not the type).

2. Choose Object > Text Wrap > **Release.**

1 *Select the object that the type is going to wrap around.*

2 *In the Text Wrap Options dialog box, enter an Offset value and check Preview.*

3 *The type is **wrapping** around the palm tree.*

Text Wrap

Another idea

Use the Layers palette to select the shadow object, choose the **Free Transform** tool, then vertically scale or shear the object by moving its top center handle. Or to reflect the shadow block with the same tool, drag the top center handle downward all the way across the object.

1 *Create the shadow and send it to the back.*

2 *Shorten the shadow by dragging the top center handle on its bounding box.*

3 *Slant the shadow using the **Shear** tool.*

4 *Reflect the shadow using the **Reflect** tool.*

A **drop shadow** created using the following method (unlike the Effect > Drop Shadow command) is an independent vector object that can be modified with effects, the transform tools, and other techniques.

To create a shadow for point type:

1. Create **point** type (see page 224).

2. *Optional:* Select the type, then apply positive tracking (Option-right arrow/ Alt-right arrow).

3. With the **Selection** tool, select the type.

4. Apply a dark fill color, stroke of None.

5. Option-drag/Alt-drag the type block slightly to the right and downward. Release the mouse, then Option/Alt.

6. With the copy of the type block still selected, lighten its shade.

7. On the **Layers** palette, drag the copy of the type below the original **1**, and make sure it still has a selection square.

8. Choose Effect > Stylize (on the upper part of the menu) > **Feather,** check Preview, choose a Radius value (try a low value), click OK, and then, via the **Transparency** palette, lower the transparency.

Slant the shadow

1. Select the shadow object, using the Layers palette.

2. Choose the **Selection** tool. Drag the top center handle downward a bit to shorten the type **2**.

3. With the shadow type still selected, double-click the **Shear** tool (it's on the Scale tool pop-out menu).

4. Enter "45" in the **Shear Angle** field, click **Axis: Horizontal,** then click OK.

5. Use the arrow keys to move the baseline of the shadow text so it aligns with the baseline of the original text **3**.

Reflect the shadow

1. Select the shadow type.

2. Double-click the **Reflect** tool (it's on the Rotate tool pop-out menu), click **Axis: Horizontal,** then click OK.

3. Move the two blocks of type together so their baselines meet **4**.

To slant a type block:

1. Choose the **Rectangle** tool (M), ▭ then draw a rectangle. Choose the **Area Type** tool, ⊤ click the edge of the rectangle, then enter some type **2**.
   or
   Choose the **Type** tool, draw a rectangle, then enter some type.

2. With the rectangle still selected, double-click the **Rotate** tool. ↻

3. Enter "30" in the **Angle** field, then click OK **3**.

4. Make sure Smart Guides are on (Cmd-U/Ctrl-U) with Object Highlighting (Preferences > Smart Guides & Slices).

5. Choose the **Direct Selection** tool (A), ▷ deselect the object, then Shift-drag the top segment diagonally to the right until the side segments are vertical **4**–**5**.

6. *Optional:* Drag the right segment of the rectangle a little to the right to enlarge the object and reflow the type.

➤ To rotate just the type characters but not slant the whole baseline as in the steps above, select the type object, then choose or enter a positive or negative Character Rotation value ♔ on the Character palette.

Use the shears

You can use the **Shear** tool ↗ (on the Scale tool pop-out menu) to slant type along its baseline or along a vertical axis **1**.

1 *Select the type, click with the **Shear** tool on the left edge of the type, then drag upward or downward from the edge of the type block. (Shift-drag to constrain the shear to the vertical or horizontal axis.)*

2 *The original type object*

3 *The type rotated 30°*

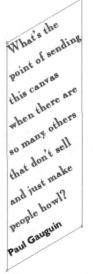

4 *The top segment dragged diagonally to the right*

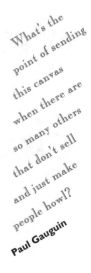

5 *The final type object in Preview view*

Slant Type

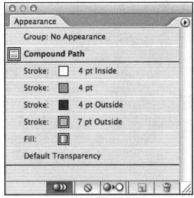

1 *Use the **Align Stroke** buttons on the **Stroke** palette to reposition the stroke on the path.*

2 *The Appearance palette, listing 4 strokes that were applied to a type object*

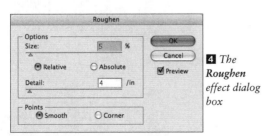

Exercises

Three different ways to embellish type.

Add multiple strokes to a character

1. Create a type character in a font of your choosing, about 180 points in size.

2. Click the type object with the Selection tool (V) and choose Type > **Create Outlines** (Cmd-Shift-O/Ctrl-Shift-O). Leave the object selected.

3. On the Appearance palette, double-click Contents, click the **Fill** listing, then apply a gradient fill.

4. Click the **Stroke** listing. On the Control palette, click the Stroke thumbnail and apply a stroke color. Click "Stroke," choose a Weight of 4 pt, then click the **Align Stroke: to Inside** button **1**. [■]

5. From the Appearance palette menu, choose **Duplicate Item** to duplicate the Stroke, then apply a new color to the duplicate (the lower listing). On the Stroke palette, click the **Align Stroke: to Center** button. [■]

6. Duplicate the Stroke again, apply a new stroke color, then click the **Align Stroke: to Outside** button. [□]

7. Finally, duplicate the Stroke once more, then apply a new stroke color, 7 pt. in width **2**.

8. Choose the **Gradient** tool [■] and drag vertically to position the gradient within the type shape **3**.

Create type with a rough fill area

1. Create a type character, about 180 points in size. On the **Layers** palette, click the target circle to target the type object.

2. On the **Appearance** palette, choose **Add New Fill** from the palette menu. Both a new Stroke and Fill listing will now display on the palette.

3. Click the **Fill** listing. Choose Effect > Distort & Transform > **Roughen**. Click Relative, set the Size to 5, Detail to 4, then click OK **4**.

(Continued on the following page)

3 *The finished type object*

4 *The **Roughen** effect dialog box*

4. On the Appearance palette, click the **Stroke** listing. Via the Control palette, apply a 1-pt. stroke and choose a light stroke color.

5. Duplicate the **Stroke** listing, then to the copy (the lower listing), apply a new stroke color, 7 pt. in width.

6. Double-click the **Characters** listing on the palette, then set both the Stroke and Fill listings to None .

7. Click the **Type** listing at the top of the Appearance palette to view appearance attributes for the type object.

8. Click the Fill listing and change its blend mode to **Overlay** by using the **Transparency** palette; repeat for the wider **Stroke** . This will make the fill and stroke color blend with any underlying objects .

1 *The Appearance palette with Characters selected*   **2** *The Appearance palette for the finished type object*

Create an embossed letter

1. Create a type character, about 180 points in size. Click the type object with the Selection tool and choose Type > **Create Outlines** (Cmd-Shift-O/Ctrl-Shift-O).

2. Apply a fill color to the selected object.

3. Choose the **Rectangle** tool (M) and create a shape that covers the type object (it should have the same fill color).

4. On the Layers palette, drag the rectangle Path below the Group listing for the type outline, and expand the group listing.

5. Click the **Compound Path** name and choose **Duplicate "<Compound Path>"** from the palette menu. Repeat to create another duplicate 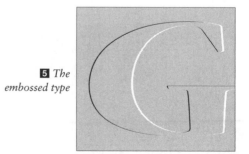.

6. Click the selection area for the bottommost **Compound Path,** then apply a dark fill color. Press the left arrow on the keyboard three times to move the object.

7. Click the selection area for the middle **Compound Path,** then apply a white fill color. Press the right arrow on the keyboard three times to move the object.

The dark and white type shapes should now appear as dark and light edges behind the topmost type shape 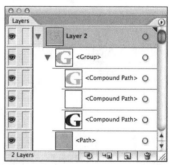.

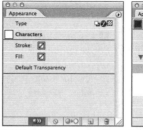

3 *The "loose" fill*

4 *The Layers palette showing three objects used for the embossed type*

5 *The embossed type*

Exercise: Embossed Type

ACQUIRE 18

In this chapter you'll learn how to get images into Illustrator via the Open and Place commands; learn how to work with the Links palette and the Control palette to edit, replace, locate, update, relink, and convert linked images; and learn how to duplicate images between files by using the drag-and-drop method.

DANIEL PELAVIN

Acquiring images

In Illustrator, you can open or import objects or images from other applications in a variety of formats and incorporate them into your overall design. For instance, you could layer path type over a bitmap image for a book jacket or poster, or use a graphic as part of a logo or product label.

Methods for acquiring images from other applications include the Open command, the Place command, and drag-and-drop. Your method of choice will depend on which file formats are available for saving the file in its original application and how you're planning to use the imagery in Illustrator.

If you open a document from another drawing (vector) application by using the **Open** command, a new Illustrator file will be created, and the acquired objects can then be manipulated using Illustrator tools and commands. If you open a bitmap image by using the Open command, the image won't be converted into separate vector objects, but rather will stay as one object in its own box.

Via the **Place** command, you can link or embed images into your Illustrator file. For

print output, the recommended formats for linked images—EPS, TIFF, and PDF—preserve the color, detail, and resolution of the original image. If you place a layered Photoshop (PSD) file in Illustrator, you can have it appear either as a single flattened object or as separate objects on separate layers.

You can also acquire images quickly by using the **drag-and-drop** method: simply drag an image from one Illustrator window into another or from a window in another application, such as Photoshop, into your Illustrator document, and a duplicate appears automatically.

A bitmap image that's acquired in Illustrator via the Open, Place, or drag-and-drop method can be moved, placed on a different layer, masked, modified using any transformation tool, or modified using color and raster (bitmap) filters. All three methods preserve the resolution of the original image.

(The Clipboard commands—Cut, Copy, and Paste—are covered on page 103. To learn how to trace images, see Chapter 21.)

Using the Open command

A list of file formats that you can **open** in Illustrator appears in the sidebar at right.

To use the Open command:

1. In Illustrator, choose File > **Open** (Cmd-O/Ctrl-O). The Open dialog box opens. In Mac, choose **Enable: All Documents** to list files in all formats, or choose **All Readable Documents** to dim the files in formats that Illustrator can't read. In Windows, you can filter out files via the **Files of Type** pop-up menu, or choose **All Formats** (the default setting) to display files in all formats. Double-click a file name, or locate and highlight a file name and click Open.

   or

   NEW In Bridge, click a thumbnail, then choose File > Open With > **Adobe Illustrator CS2**.

   Note: If you get an alert dialog box concerning a linked file, see page 285.

2. If you're opening a multipage PDF, the Open PDF dialog box will open **1**. Check Preview, click an arrow to locate the desired page (or enter the desired page number in the field), then click OK. If an alert dialog box appears, read it, then click OK to proceed.

   If you're opening a Photoshop file that contains layers or layer comps, the **Photoshop Import Options** dialog box will open. See pages 280–281.

➤ If you open an EPS file that contains a clipping path, the image will be nested in a group on the Layers palette, with the path directly above it. If the clipping path consists of several paths, they'll be listed separately on the Layers palette. To move or reshape one, click the path listing and use the Direct Selection tool. If you delete or hide the selected clipping path, the entire image will become visible. To release the clipping path ("clipping mask," in Illustrator) at any time, click the Make/Release Clipping Mask button on the Layers palette.

File formats

File formats that you can open in Illustrator

Illustrator formats: Illustrator (ai) versions 1.0 through CS2, Illustrator .ait, Illustrator EPS and PDF.

File formats you can open or place in Illustrator

Raster (bitmap) formats: BMP, GIF, JPEG, JPEG2000, Kodak PhotoCD, PCX, PIXAR, PNG, Photoshop, TGA, and TIFF.

Vector formats: CorelDRAW versions 5 through 10.

Graphics (vector) formats: CGM; DWG (AutoCAD drawing and export); FreeHand (up to version 9); PICT; SVG and SVGZ; EMF; and WMF. Illustrator can't open Macromedia Flash SWF files.

Text formats: Plain text (ASCII), Unicode, RTF, and MS Word (up to version 2004 in Mac and version 2002 in Windows).

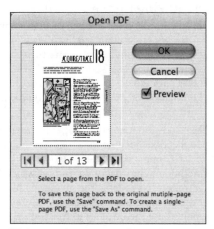

1 *For a **multipage** PDF, choose the page you want to open.*

1 *A selected linked, placed image in Preview view*

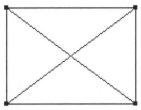

2 *A placed (linked or embedded) bitmap image in Outline view, with Show Images In Outline Mode unchecked*

3 *A placed (linked or embedded) image in Outline view, with Show Images In Outline Mode checked, showing a posterized, grayscale preview*

Over the edge

If the current layer in a Photoshop file contains pixels that extend outside the **live canvas area,** those pixels won't appear in the Illustrator file, no matter which method you use to acquire it—drag-and-drop, place, or open. Before acquiring the image, in Photoshop make sure the pixels that you want to import are within the live canvas area!

Resolution changes

Reduce the scale of an opened or placed TIFF or EPS image, and its resolution increases accordingly. Enlarge it, and its resolution decreases.

Using the Place command

A file that you **place** into an Illustrator document can be moved to a different *x/y* location, restacked within the same layer, moved to a different layer, masked, transformed, or modified using effects or filters, and you can also change its opacity and blending mode. For a list of "place-able" file formats, see the sidebar on the previous page.

To place an image into an Illustrator document:

1. Open an Illustrator file, and click the layer you want the image to appear on.

2. In **Illustrator,** choose File > **Place,** then click a file to be placed. Check **Link** to place a screen version of the image into your Illustrator document, with a link to the original image file; Illustrator won't color-manage the image. The original image file won't be affected by your edits in Illustrator, but in order for it to print properly, it must be available on your hard disk (read more about linking in the next section). Or uncheck Link to **embed** the actual image into the Illustrator file, in which case Illustrator will color-manage the image. Embedding increases the storage size of the Illustrator file. Click **Place.**
    or
    In **Bridge,** click a thumbnail, then choose File > Place > **In Illustrator.** The image will be linked.

    If you're placing a Photoshop file that contains multiple layers, the Photoshop Import Options dialog box will open. See the next page.

    In Preview view, selected linked image boxes have an X **1**. In Outline view, if View: Show Images In Outline Mode is checked in File > Document Setup (Artboard panel), placed images have a low-resolution preview; with this option off, placed image boxes are blank **2**–**3**.

➤ To choose preferences for placed or opened images, see page 478.

➤ Check Template in the Place dialog box to place a dimmed version of the image on a template layer for tracing.

Place Command

NEW Choosing Photoshop import options

If you import a single-layer Photoshop image with **Link** checked in the Place dialog box, it will appear on the Layers palette as an image nested inside the currently active layer —not in a group—and no dialog box will open. No clipping mask will be generated by Illustrator, but any Photoshop clipping path will remain in effect and will be listed as a clipping mask. If you embed a single-layer Photoshop image (uncheck the Link option), it will appear within a group on the current layer.

If you use the Place command (with Link unchecked) or the Open command to import a Photoshop file, if the file contains layers or layer comps, the **Photoshop Import Options** dialog box will open **1**. Choose from the following settings:

Check **Show Preview** to display a thumbnail preview of the image.

Choose from the **Layer Comp** pop-up menu to import a layer comp. Any comments entered in Photoshop for the chosen comp will display in the **Comments** window. (The Layer Comp pop-up menu will be blank if the Photoshop file does't contain any layer comps.) If you need to import additional layer comps from the same Photoshop image, you have to choose the Place command again for each one.

When placing an image that contains layer comps, if you checked Link in the Place dialog box, you can choose **When Updating Link: Keep Layer Visibility Overrides** to preserve the layer visibility (hide/show) state the layers were in when you originally placed the image, and ignore any visibility changes made in Photoshop; or choose **Use Photoshop's Layer Visibility** to apply any layer visibility changes made in Photoshop.

If you placed the file with the Link option unchecked, you have the option to keep or flatten the layers. If you click **Convert Photoshop layers to objects,** each object will be nested within an image group within the current layer **2**. Transparency levels,

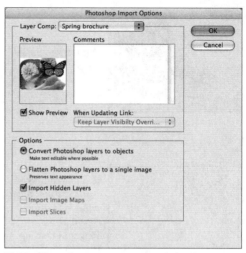

1 *The Photoshop Import Options dialog box opens if you place a Photoshop image with the Link option unchecked.*

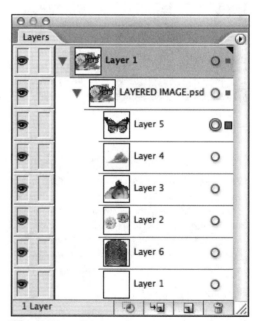

2 *Each Photoshop layer becomes a separate Illustrator object, nested within the image group layer.*

blending modes, layer masks, and vector masks will be preserved, will be listed as editable appearances (see page 293), and will be targeted to the appropriate converted object in Illustrator. Layer sets will be preserved; any clipping path that was saved with the Photoshop file will remain in effect and will be listed as a clipping mask at the top of the stack of objects in the group; and type will remain editable, when possible (see the last paragraph on this page). Each converted layer from the Photoshop file will be listed as a separate item on the Links palette, but any imagery outside the original canvas area will be trimmed.

If you click **Flatten Photoshop layers to a single image,** a flattened version of the image will be nested within the current layer. All transparency levels, blending modes, and layer mask effects will be applied to the flattened image, but those attributes won't be listed as editable appearances in Illustrator. Any clipping path saved with the Photoshop file will remain in effect and will be listed as a clipping mask above the nested image within a group.

Check **Import Hidden Layers, Import Image Maps,** and/or **Import Slices,** if available, to import those elements with the file.

Linked files are flattened automatically (the "Convert Photoshop layers to objects" option will be dimmed).

➤ If a layered Photoshop image is opened in Illustrator or placed with the Link option unchecked and you click "Convert Photoshop layers to objects" in the Photoshop Import Options dialog box, the Background from the Photoshop file will become one of the nested objects within Illustrator, and will be opaque (you can change its opacity). You can delete or hide the background via the Layers palette in Illustrator.

Placing adjustment layers

In Photoshop, the position of adjustment layers in the layer stack affects how image layers are converted into objects when the file is placed and embedded (not linked) into Illustrator. Any layers above an adjustment layer in the Photoshop file will be converted into separate objects in Illustrator. Any layers below an adjustment layer in the Photoshop file will be flattened along with the adjustment layer into one object in Illustrator. You can delete or hide adjustment layers in Photoshop before placing the image into Illustrator.

EPS versus PSD

When placing or opening a Photoshop EPS file, any Photoshop shape layers will become a clipping set in Illustrator, editable text will become a compound path, and all other Photoshop layers will be flattened into one object below the shape layer(s).

In contrast, each layer from a Photoshop PSD file will be converted to a separate object layer.

Placing Photoshop text

If you place a Photoshop file that contains editable type into Illustrator (Link option unchecked) and click the Convert Photoshop layers to objects button, the type objects will remain editable, provided the type layer in Photoshop was neither warped nor had any effects applied to it. If you want to import a type layer as vector outlines instead, in Photoshop, use Layer > Type > Convert to Shape, save the file, then open the file in Illustrator via the Open or Place command.

Photoshop Import Options

Working with linked images

To keep your Illustrator file from becoming too large, you can link imported images (e.g., BMP, EPS, GIF, JPEG, PICT, PNG, PSD, or TIFF files) to the file instead of embedding them. A screen version of each image will act as a placeholder in your document, but the actual image will remain separate from the Illustrator file. Unlike embedded images, linked images can be revised via the **Edit Original** button and updated in the Illustrator document.

To link a file, use the File > Place command with the Link option checked (see page 279). The **Links** palette **1** helps you and your output service provider keep track of linked files. It lists all the linked and embedded files in your Illustrator document and puts a number of useful controls at your fingertips.

Photoshop filters (Filter menu) can be applied to embedded images. Photoshop effects (Effect menu) can be applied to both linked and embedded images, and will remain editable. Linked images can be transformed (moved, rotated, sheared, or reflected).

To convert a linked file into an embedded file, see page 286. The Object > Rasterize command automatically embeds linked images, whereas the Effect > Rasterize command does not.

To edit a linked image in its original application:

1. On the Links palette, click the image name, then click the **Edit Original** button.
   or

   NEW Click the image in the document window, then click **Edit Original** on the **Control** palette.

   The application in which the linked image was created will launch, if it isn't already open, and the image will open.

2. Make your edits, resave the file, then return to Illustrator. If a warning dialog box appears, click Yes (see the sidebar) **2**. The linked image will update onscreen.

Update options

Via the **Update Links** pop-up menu in Preferences (Cmd-K/Ctrl-K) > File Handling & Clipboard, you can specify whether linked images are updated when they're modifed in their original application. Choose from these options:

Automatically: Linked images are updated automatically when the original files are modified.

Manually: Linked images aren't updated automatically when the original files are modified. You can use the Links palette at any time to update the links.

Ask When Modified: A dialog box will appear if the original files are modified and you either return to Illustrator or reopen the file (click Yes or No to update the files or not).

Missing Linked Image indicator *Modified Linked Image indicator*

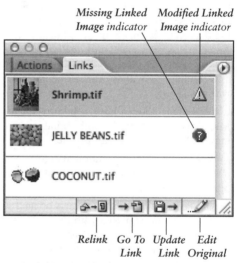

Relink Go To Link Update Link Edit Original

1 *The Links palette lets you keep track of, replace, and embed linked files.*

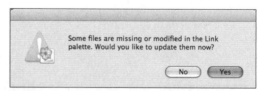

2 *This prompt appears if you edit a linked file in its original application via the Edit Original button.*

Linked versus embedded

A **linked** image will be listed on the Layers palette as <Linked File> (or, for a PSD file, as the file name) within the currently active layer. Any clipping path in the original file will be applied, but it won't have a listing on the palette. You can apply opacity and blending modes, the Feather command, and some Effect menu filters (they'll be listed as appearances) to linked images.

An **embedded** image will be listed on the Layers palette as a nested image object within a group sublayer on the current layer. If a clipping path is included, it will be active and will be listed on the Layers palette as a clipping path within the group sublayer, stacked above the image object.

1 *Click the linked image that you want to replace, then click the* **Relink** *button.*

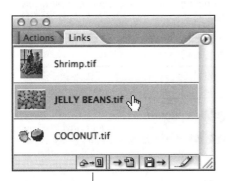

2 *The linked image is* **replaced.**

If you **replace** one **placed image** with another, any transformations that were applied to the image in Illustrator, such as scaling or rotation, will be applied to the replacement. The following instructions apply to both linked and embedded images.

To replace a linked image or an embedded TIFF or JPEG:

1. On the **Links** palette, click the name of the file that you want to replace **1**.
2. Click the **Relink** button 🔄 (new icon) **NEW** at the bottom of the Links palette.
   or
   Click the image in the document window, then click the image name on the Control **NEW** palette and choose **Relink.**
3. Locate the replacement file, then click **Place 2**.

➤ To replace a placed image another way, select it in the document window, choose File > Place, locate the replacement image, check Replace, then click Place.

The **Go To Link** command locates a placed image for you, and selects and centers it in the document window.

To select a linked image or an embedded TIFF or JPEG:

1. On the **Links** palette, click an image name.
2. Click the **Go To Link** button ➡️ at the bottom of the palette.
   or
   Click the image in the document window, then click the image name on the Control **NEW** palette and choose **Go To Link.**

➤ To locate a linked image in Bridge, click **NEW** the image name on the Links palette, then choose Reveal in Bridge from the palette menu.

Replace, Select Images

To view file information for a file:

I. On the **Links** palette, double-click the listing for a linked or embedded file.

or

NEW Click the image in the document window, then click the image name on the **Control** palette and choose **Link Information** 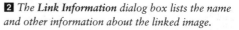.

A dialog box listing information about the image, such as its file format, location, size, modifications, and transform information, will appear **2**.

2. Click OK.

NEW ➤ To see keywords, view camera, IPTC Contact, Content, Image, or Status info, or view other data about a placed file, click the file on the Links palette, then choose Link File Info from the palette menu.

To choose Links palette display options:

To change the size of the thumbnail images on the Links palette, choose **Palette Options** from the Links palette menu, click the preferred size, then click OK. To display just the file icons without the thumbnails, click None.

To change the order of links on the palette, from the Links palette menu, choose **Sort by Name** (alphabetical order), **Sort by Kind** (file format), or **Sort by Status** (missing, then modified, then embedded, then fully linked) **3**. To sort only selected links, first click, then Shift-click consecutive names, or Cmd-click/Ctrl-click nonconsecutive names.

To control which types of links display on the palette, choose **Show All, Show Missing, Show Modified,** or **Show Embedded** from the Links palette menu.

If an exclamation mark icon appears to the right of an image name on the Links palette, it means the original file has been **modified** and the link is outdated. To **update** a linked file that's been modified, follow the first set of instructions on the next page.

If you've edited your linked image via the Edit Original button and if Manually is chosen from the Update Links pop-up menu in Preferences > File Handling & Clipboard, you'll need to update the image as per the

1 *To access these options, select a linked image in the document window, then click the file name on the Control palette.*

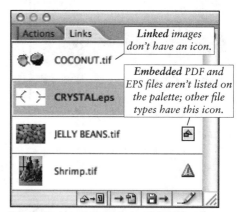

2 *The **Link Information** dialog box lists the name and other information about the linked image.*

3 *The Links palette with the Show All and Sort by Name display options chosen*

Sidebar: File Information; Links Palette Display

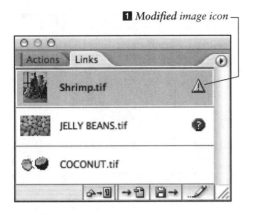

1 *Modified image icon*

following instructions. If the setting is Automatically, the image will be updated automatically; if the setting is Ask When Modified, you'll get an alert prompt for updating the file or not.

To update a modified linked image:

I. Click the name of the modified image on the Links palette **1**.

2. Click the **Update Link** button 🖫→ at the bottom of the palette.
   or
   Click the image in the document window, then click the image name on the Control **NEW** palette and choose **Update Link**.

To locate or replace images upon opening a file:

If you move a linked image file from its original location after saving the Illustrator file into which it was placed, you'll be prompted to relink it when you reopen the Illustrator file **2**. Do one of the following:

To locate the missing image, click **Repair,** **NEW** locate the file, then click Replace.

To substitute another file for the missing one, click **Replace,** locate a replacement file, then click Replace.

If you click **Ignore,** the linked image won't display, but a question mark icon will display near the file name on the Links palette and its bounding box will still be visible in the Illustrator file in Outline view or, if Smart Guides are on, when the cursor passes over the bounding box. To completely break the link and prevent any alert prompts from appearing in the future, delete the bounding box and resave the file.

Optional: Check Apply to All to have the **NEW** button you click apply to all missing images.

Could not find the linked file "JELLY BEANS.tif". Choose Repair to locate the missing file, Replace to select another file, or Ignore to leave the link unchanged.

☐ Apply to All ⟨ Repair ⟩ ⟨ Replace ⟩ ⟨ Ignore ⟩ ⟨ Cancel ⟩

2 *If a linked file is **missing**, Illustrator will alert you via this dialog box when you open the document.*

Update Modified Linked Image; Replace Image

Via the **Placement Options** dialog box, you can control how any replacement image will fit into the same bounding box.

To choose placement options for a linked image:

1. Click a linked image in the document window, then on the **Control** palette, click the file name and choose **Placement Options**.

   or

   On the **Links** palette, click a linked image, then choose **Placement Options** from the palette menu.

   The Placement Options dialog box opens **1**.

2. Choose a **Preserve** option, then study the thumbnails and read the description to learn how the image will be affected.

3. For an option other than Transforms or Bounds, you can click a point on the **Alignment** icon from which you want to align the artwork relative to the bounding box. Or to prevent the artwork from overlapping the bounding box, check **Clip To Bounding Box.**

4. Click OK.

The **Embed Image** command changes a file's status from linked to embedded (and also increases the file size).

To change a file's status from linked to embedded:

On the **Links** palette list, click the name of the image that you want to embed **2**, then choose **Embed Image** from the Links palette menu **3**.

or

Click the image in the document window, then click **Embed** on the **Control** palette.

If the file is a multilayer Photoshop image, the Photoshop Import Options dialog box will open. See pages 280–281.

➤ You can't convert an embedded image into a linked one, but you can choose Undo immediately after using the Place command, or at any time you can use the Relink button or Relink command on the Links palette menu to replace an embedded image with a linked one.

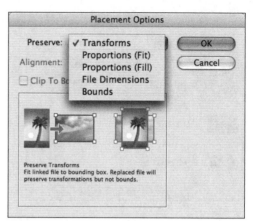

1 *Use the* **Placement Options** *dialog box to choose options for a placed image.*

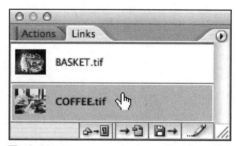

2 *Click an image name on the Links palette, then choose* **Embed Image** *from the palette menu.*

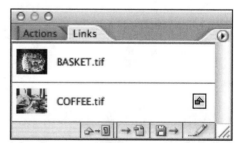

3 *The* **embedded** *image icon appears. The file name is preserved for TIFF, GIF, JPEG, or flattened PSD images when such files are embedded.*

Paste options

If you copy a path from Photoshop and paste it into Illustrator, the **Paste Options** dialog box opens **1**. Choose **Paste As: Compound Shape (fully editable)** or **Compound Path (faster).** We recommend the first option for multiple or overlapping paths.

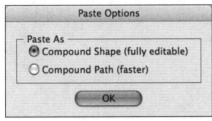

1 *If you paste a path from Photoshop to Illustrator, the* ***Paste Options*** *dialog box opens.*

Using drag-and-drop

Drag-and-drop is a quick method for duplicating images between applications or files (the copy is made automatically for you). You can drag and drop objects between Illustrator documents or between Illustrator and Adobe GoLive, Adobe InDesign, or any other drag-aware application, and you can drag and drop a selection or layer from Photoshop to Illustrator (see below). The drag-and-drop method doesn't use the Clipboard; whatever is currently on the Clipboard is preserved.

Note: To acquire a Photoshop image for print output, instead of using the drag-and-drop method as outlined below, we would convert the image to CMYK Color mode in Photoshop, save it as a Photoshop PSD, then acquire it via the Place command in Illustrator. Just our humble opinion.

Whatever you drag and drop from Photoshop with the Move tool gets rasterized, if it isn't already (type, a shape layer, etc.). To keep a path as a path, see the last tip on the next page.

To drag and drop from Photoshop to Illustrator:

1. In Photoshop, select some pixels or click a layer.

2. Open an Illustrator file.

3. Choose the **Move** tool in Photoshop, then drag the selection or layer into the target Illustrator document window. The target window will become active and a copy of the image pixels will appear inside it. The selection or layer will be embedded at the resolution of the original image and will adopt the document color mode of the Illustrator file. Any clipping paths in the Photoshop file will be ignored.

In Mac, the image will be nested within a new <Group> layer within the currently active layer. In Windows, the image will be listed as <Image>.

(Continued on the following page)

CHAPTER 18

Drag-and-Drop

The following may also occur, depending on what you drag and drop:

➤ You can create your own clipping mask in Illustrator if you want to further mask the acquired image.

➤ The opacity of the Photoshop selection or layer will become 100%, regardless of its original opacity (it may appear lighter if its original opacity was below 100%). You can lower the transparency in Illustrator, if desired.

➤ Photoshop blending modes will be ignored.

➤ Layer masks and vector masks from Photoshop will be applied to the image (meaning the image will be clipped), and then will be discarded.

➤ In Mac, a generic clipping path (based on the dimensions of the Photoshop selection or layer) will appear within the image group; it can be deleted without affecting the image.

➤ In Mac, if you drag an Illustrator object to the Desktop, a Picture Clipping file will be created, and it will be stored in PICT format. The files can then be dragged back into any Illustrator file (with paths intact) or into any drag-aware application.

➤ You can also drag and drop a selected path or vector mask from Photoshop to Illustrator with the Path Selection tool. The path will become a compound path in Illustrator, and won't be rasterized.

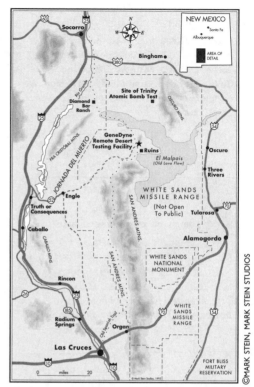

The background topography is a bitmap image that was placed into an Illustrator file; the other elements were created in Illustrator.

Drag-and-Drop from Photoshop

APPEARANCES & GRAPHIC STYLES

19

Appearance attributes are editable settings, such as stroke, fill, effect, and transparency. In this chapter you'll learn how to apply, edit, restack, duplicate, modify, and remove appearance attributes; use the Graphic Styles palette to save appearance attributes collectively as graphic styles; apply graphic styles to an object, group, or layer; edit, duplicate, move, unlink from, merge, expand, and delete graphic styles; and create graphic style libraries.

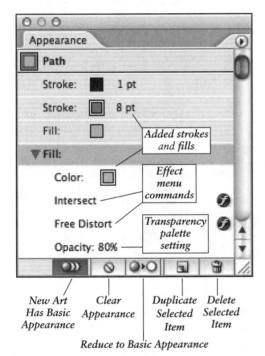

New Art
Has Basic
Appearance

Clear
Appearance

Duplicate
Selected
Item

Delete
Selected
Item

Reduce to Basic Appearance

1 *Use the Appearance palette to apply, restack, and remove appearance attributes in layers, sublayers, groups, objects, and graphic styles. This screen shot shows the appearance attributes for an object.*

Using the Appearance palette

Using the **Appearance** palette **1**, you can apply multiple fills and strokes to the same object, and to each stroke or fill you can apply a different opacity level, blending mode, or Effect menu command. Furthermore, although appearance attributes change how an object looks, they don't actually alter its underlying path. Appearance attributes add flexibility—and also some complexity—to object editing.

Because appearance attributes change only an object's appearance, not its actual underlying path, you can save, close, and reopen a document, and you'll still be able to reedit or remove appearance attributes in the saved file. When an object is selected, its appearance attributes are listed on the Appearance palette. You can also use the palette to reedit, restack, and remove appearance attributes.

Note: After learning how to use the Appearance palette, be sure to read about effects in the next chapter.

Appearance attributes and layers

Any attributes that are applied to an object beyond the run-of-the-mill stroke and fill are called **appearance attributes.** When an object contains appearance attributes, its listing has a gray **target circle** on the Layers palette **1**.

You can either apply appearance attributes to individual objects one by one or you can target a whole top-level layer or group for appearance changes. In the latter case, the appearance attributes that you choose will apply to all the objects nested within the targeted layer or group. For example, if you target a layer and then modify its opacity or blending mode, all objects nested within that layer will adopt that opacity or blending mode. To edit the attribute at any time, simply retarget the layer.

These are the basic techniques:

➤ To **select** an **object** or **group,** click the **selection area** or **target circle** on the Layers palette. Clicking either of these icons will also cause that object or group to be targeted for appearance attributes.

➤ To **select** (but not target) a **layer,** click the **selection** area. To **target** a **layer,** click the **target** circle (see the sidebar on this page).

➤ To **view** and **modify** the existing **appearance attributes** for an object, group, or layer, click the gray target circle; Shift-click the gray circle to deselect that object, group, or layer.

To target appearance attributes to a layer:

To **target** appearance attributes to a whole top-level layer, click its target circle on the Layers palette. A ring will appear around the circle, indicating an active target, and all the objects on the layer will become selected in the document. Also, the word "Layer" will appear at the top of the Appearance palette. (Shift-click the ring to untarget.)

Layers and appearances

Although selecting and targeting both cause objects to become selected in your document, they're not interchangeable operations when you're working with whole layers. If you **target** a top-level layer by clicking its target circle and then apply appearance attributes (e.g., fill color, Effect menu commands, Transparency palette settings), those attributes will be applied to, and listed on the Appearance palette for, the layer as a whole.

If you click the **selection** area for a top-level layer instead of the target circle, and then apply appearance attributes, those attributes will be applied separately to each object or group in that layer, not to the layer as a whole. In this case, you won't see an itemized list of appearance attributes on the Appearance palette; you'll just see the generic words "mixed appearances" at the top of the palette. Nor will they be listed if you subsequently target the layer.

*This layer is **active** but **not targeted,** and it doesn't contain appearance attributes.*

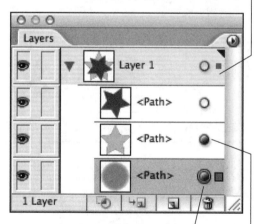

*This object is **targeted,** and it already contains appearance attributes.*

1 *This path object contains **appearance attributes,** but it's not currently targeted.*

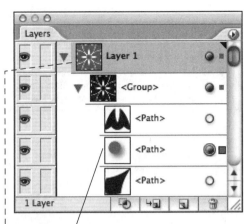

1 This *targeted* object is nested within a group and a layer.

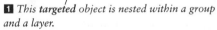

The palette is currently listing the attributes for a targeted *path*. (The layer and group the path resides in have their own appearance attributes, which aren't currently listed.)

Appearance palette icons

Depending on whether an object, group, or layer is currently targeted and what attributes are applied to them, you may see one or more of these icons in the upper portion of the Appearance palette:

➤ 🗗 Additional **stroke** and/or **fill** attributes are applied

➤ 🌀 **Effects** are applied

➤ ▨ **Transparency** settings are applied

The generic name for the currently targeted item (e.g., Layer, Group, or Path) is listed in boldface at the top of the Appearance palette. If an object is targeted and that object is nested within a layer and/or group to which appearance attributes have been applied, the word(s) "Layer" and/or "Group" will also appear above the word "Path" at the top of the palette **1**.

If the selected object is a mesh, the word "Mesh" will appear instead of the word "Path." The same holds true for type ("Type"), an image ("Image"), a symbol ("Symbol"), an envelope ("Envelope"), a compound shape ("Compound Shape")—you get the idea.

Applying appearance attributes

When you **apply appearance attributes,** your object adopts a new look that can be modified or removed at any time, even after the file is saved, closed, and reopened.

To apply appearance attributes:

I. In the document window, select the object you want to apply appearance attributes to.
   or
   On the Layers palette, click the circle for a layer, group, or object to target that item for appearance changes.

(Continued on the following page)

2. Show the **Appearance** palette (Shift-F6) **1**, then do any of the following:

   Click **Stroke,** then modify the stroke color via the Color or Swatches palette; or modify the stroke width or other settings via the Stroke palette; or modify the brush stroke (if the path has one) via the Brushes palette; or modify stroke and brush attributes via the Control palette.

   Click **Fill,** then modify the fill via the Color, Swatches, Control, Gradient, or Transparency palette.

   Double-click **Default Transparency** (or the current transparency appearance attribute) to show the Transparency palette, then modify the Opacity value and/or change the blending mode.

   Choose a command from a submenu on the **Effect** menu (for starters, try applying an effect from the Distort & Transform or Stylize submenu), modify the dialog box settings, then click OK. The Effect command will be listed in the attributes area of the palette. (Read more about effects in Chapter 20.)

   Note: Remember to choose appearance commands from the Effect menu, not the Filter menu. Filter menu commands will permanently alter an object, whereas Effect menu commands, because they're vector effects, can be reedited or removed at any time without permanently changing the object. The Photoshop filters are illustrated on pages 324–332. The Photoshop effects, under the Effect menu, produce equivalent results.

➤ Copy an object several times, then experiment with different appearance attributes and variations for each copy. No commitment, no obligation.

➤ To copy or move multiple attributes from one object or layer to another, see page 299.

Working with attributes

If a layer or group is targeted, the word **Contents** will appear on the attributes list on the Appearance palette; if an individual type object is targeted, you'll see the word **Characters;** if an object with a mesh fill is targeted, you'll see the words **Mesh Points.**

*The item that the appearance attributes are being targeted to is listed in boldface (e.g., **Layer, Group,** or **Path**).*

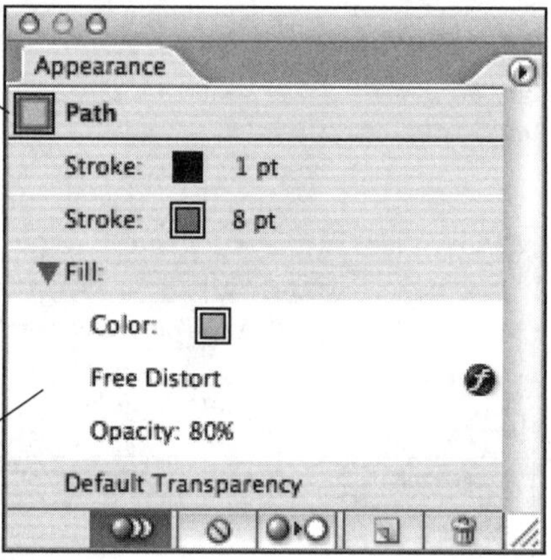

1 ***Appearance attributes*** *are listed in this part of the palette.*

Apply Appearance Attributes

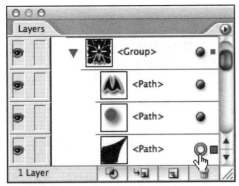

1 *A path is targeted on the Layers palette.*

2 *The Fill attribute is clicked on the Appearance palette.*

3 *When Appearance attributes are applied to the fill, the Fill list expands automatically.*

Editing and restacking attributes

Aside from merely listing appearance attributes, the Appearance palette can also be used to open palettes and dialog boxes for previously applied appearance **attributes** (e.g., effects, strokes, fills) in order to **edit** them.

To edit or restack appearance attributes:

1. In the document window, select the **object** whose appearance attributes you want to modify.
   or
   On the Layers palette, click the gray **target** circle for a layer, group, or object.

2. On the **Appearance** palette:

   Double-click any appearance attribute to open its dialog box or show its related palette, and make modifications.
   and/or
   Drag any appearance attribute (except Opacity) upward or downward on the list. Its location will change on the list, thus changing how the object looks. For example, if you drag a stroke below a fill attribute and then lower the opacity of the fill attribute, the stroke will show through the fill.

To edit a stroke or fill attribute:

1. Target an object **1**. (To apply a stroke or fill to a layer or group, see the next page.)

2. On the Appearance palette, click **Stroke** or **Fill 2**.

3. Change the opacity or blending mode using the **Transparency** palette, and/or apply an **Effect** menu command. These attributes will apply only to the selected stroke or fill—not to the whole object. The list for the attribute you're modifying will expand automatically **3**. You can click the expand/collapse arrowhead at any time to collapse the list.

   Apply a **brush stroke.** The brush name will appear next to the Stroke attribute on the Appearance palette. Double-click the brush name to open the Stroke Options dialog box.

Edit, Restack Appearance Attributes

To remove a brush stroke from a stroke attribute:

1. Target a layer, group, or object.

2. Show the Brushes palette (F5), then click the **Remove Brush Stroke** button ✕ at the bottom of the palette. Any prior stroke will be restored.

   or

   Click the **Stroke** attribute on the Appearance palette, then click the **Delete Selected Item** button 🗑 at the bottom of the palette. The stroke becomes None.

To apply multiple stroke or fill attributes:

1. Target a layer, group, or object **1**.

2. From the Appearance palette menu, choose **Add New Fill** (Cmd-/; Ctrl-/) or **Add New Stroke** (Cmd-Option-/; Ctrl-Alt-/).

   or

   Click an existing Stroke or Fill listing on the Appearance palette, then click the **Duplicate Selected Item** button 🔲 at the bottom of the palette **2** (or drag the Stroke or Fill icon over the button).

   Note: For text (as in our example), choose Add New Stroke, adjust the stroke width and color, then either add another stroke attribute or duplicate the first one.

3. A second Stroke or Fill attribute will appear on the palette **3**–**4**. Now modify its attributes so it's different from the original.

➤ Make sure narrower strokes are stacked above wider strokes on the palette list. If the narrower strokes are on the bottom, you won't see them. Similarly, apply opacity and blending modes to the upper fill attributes, not the lower ones.

➤ If a layer, group, or object has multiple fills or strokes, be sure to click the attribute you want to modify.

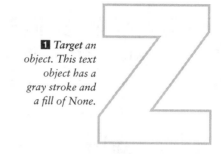

1 *Target an object. This text object has a gray stroke and a fill of None.*

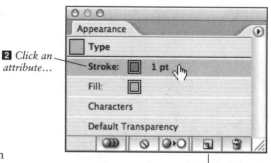

2 *Click an attribute...*

*...then click the **Duplicate Selected Item** button.*

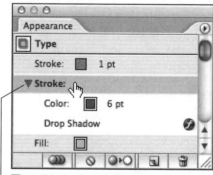

3 *Modify the **duplicate** stroke.*

4 *After **duplicating** the stroke, increasing the width of the duplicate, and applying the Drop Shadow effect to the duplicate*

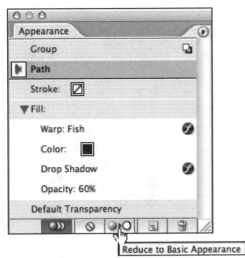

1 *Target a layer, group, or object, then click the **Reduce to Basic Appearance** button at the bottom of the Appearance palette.*

2 *All appearance attributes are **removed** from the targeted entity.*

Duplicating attributes

To duplicate an appearance attribute:

1. Target a layer, group, or object.

2. Click an attribute, then choose **Duplicate Item** from the Appearance palette menu.
or
Click an attribute, then click the **Duplicate Selected Item** button at the bottom of the palette. (Or drag an attribute over that button.)

Removing attributes

To remove an appearance attribute:

1. Target a layer, group, or object.

2. On the Appearance palette, click the attribute you want to remove.

3. Click the **Delete Selected Item** button at the bottom of the palette (or drag the attribute over the button).

➤ The sole remaining Fill and Stroke appearance attributes can't be removed. Clicking the Delete Selected Item button for either of these appearance attributes will produce a fill or stroke of None.

To remove all appearance attributes from an item:

1. Target an object, layer, sublayer, or group.

2. To remove **all** the appearance attributes and apply a stroke and fill of **None,** click the **Clear Appearance** button at the bottom of the Appearance palette (for type, the fill color will be preserved).
or
To remove all the appearance attributes except **one stroke** and **one fill** listing, click the **Reduce to Basic Appearance** button at the bottom of the Appearance palette **1**–**2**.

➤ If you target a layer or group, any appearance attributes that were applied directly to nested paths within that layer or group won't be removed by the commands used in the instructions above. To remove individual appearance attributes from a nested path, you need to target that path, not its layer or group.

Duplicate, Remove Appearance Attributes

Choosing options for future objects

To choose appearance options for future objects:

If the **New Art Has Basic Appearance** command on the Appearance palette menu has a check mark or you click the **New Art Has Basic Appearance** button  at the bottom of the palette, subsequently created objects will have only one fill and one stroke. With this option unchecked in either location, the currently displayed appearance attributes will apply automatically to new objects.

Blends and appearances

If you blend objects that contain different **appearance** attributes (e.g., effects, fills, or strokes), those appearance attributes will be in full force in the original objects and will have sequentially less intensity in the intermediate blend steps **1**. The Object > Blend > Make command automatically nests blend objects on a **Blend** sublayer.

If you blend objects that contain different **blending modes,** the blending mode for the topmost object will be applied to all the intermediate blend steps.

On the Layers palette, <Blend> sublayers have a gray target circle, indicating that an appearance attribute is applied to the objects. Also, the **Knockout Group** option will be checked on the Transparency palette by default to prevent the blend steps from blending with or showing through each other when a blend object has an opacity below 100% or has a blending mode other than Normal. Uncheck Knockout Group if you want the blend steps to show through or blend with one another. Whether Knockout Group is on or off, though, objects behind the blend will be visible if the blend objects have an opacity below 100% or a blending mode other than Normal.

To attach appearance attributes to, and view the Transparency palette options for, an entire blend, first click the target circle for the <Blend> sublayer on the Layers palette, or select the blend in the document window with the Selection tool.

1 *The **Drop Shadow** effect was applied to just the bottommost horse, so the drop shadow fades gradually in the intermediate objects.*

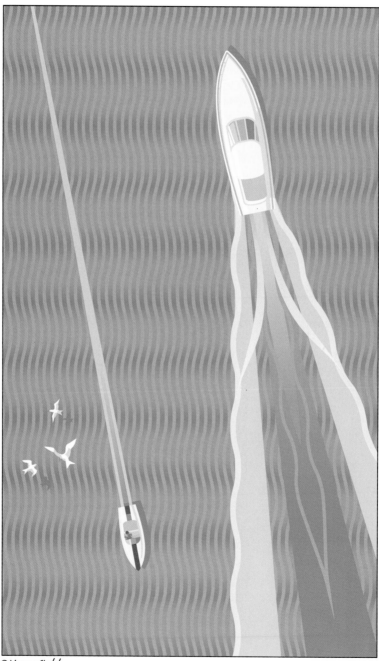

©Nancy Stahl (texture added in Photoshop)

Nancy Stahl

-THE ORIGINAL-

PUBHOUSE

BEER BATTERED

CHICKEN

-AND OTHER FINE FARE-

Tyson Foods, Inc.; art director, Steve Pope; design and illustration ©Tom Nikosey

Tom Nikosey

©Tom Nikosey

Thelma's Lemonades; art director, Chris Bohlin, Latitude;
design and illustration ©Tom Nikosey

©Telecom; art director, Julie Albin/
Townsend Agency; illustration, Tom Nikosey

Paramount Farms/California; art director, Brad Donenfeld; design and illustration ©Tom Nikosey

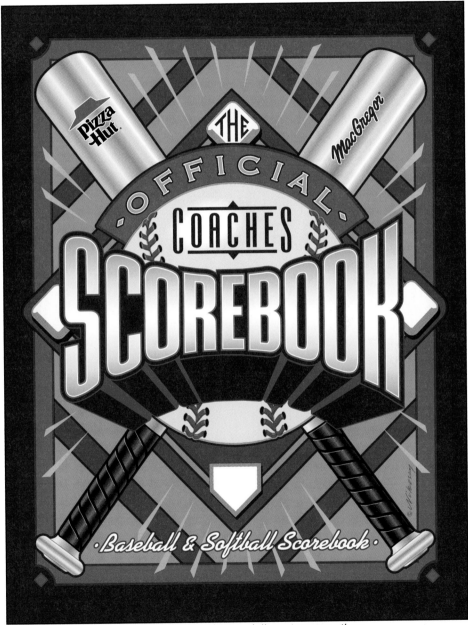

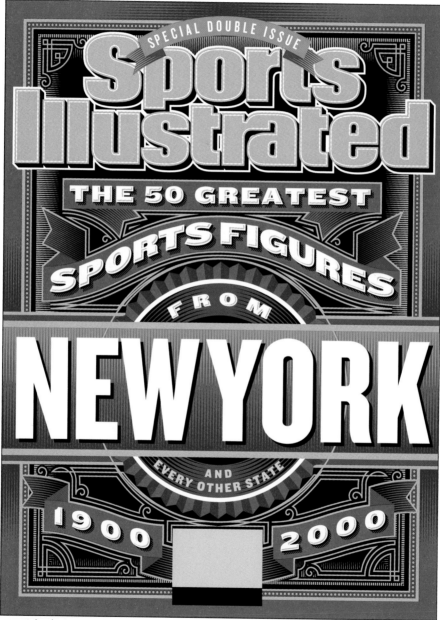

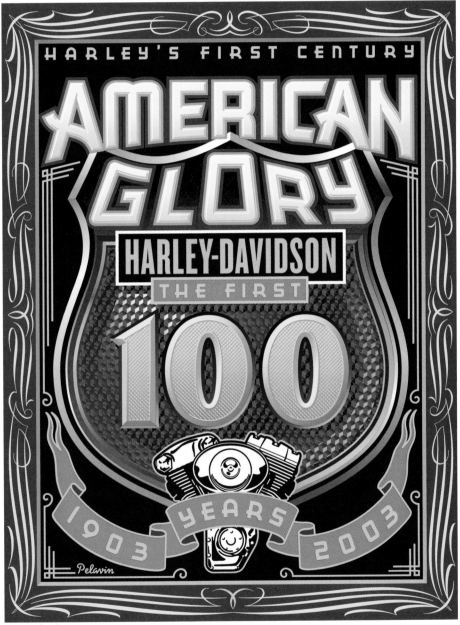

©Dynamic Graphics, illustration by Jeanne de la Houssaye

Jeanne de la Houssaye

©Dynamic Graphics, illustration by Jeanne de la Houssaye

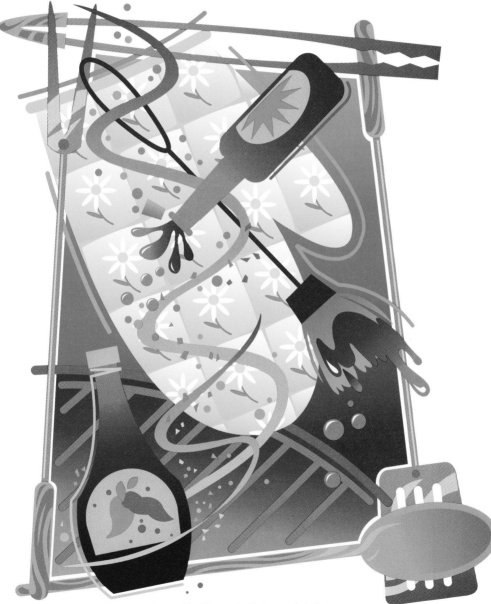

The American West

As settlers moved west, they came into conflict with American Indians. After the last armed Indian resistance was defeated, the U.S. government moved many tribes to reservations.

The completion of the transcontinental railroad in 1868 opened the West to more settlement. Gold and silver strikes also drew people hoping to get rich.

The railroads helped make the rise of the Cattle Kingdom possible. Cowboys drove huge herds of cattle from ranches to railway stations to be shipped East.

Farmers settled the Great Plains in large numbers. They overcame great hardships to make the Plains the breadbasket of America.

©*Kenneth Batelman*

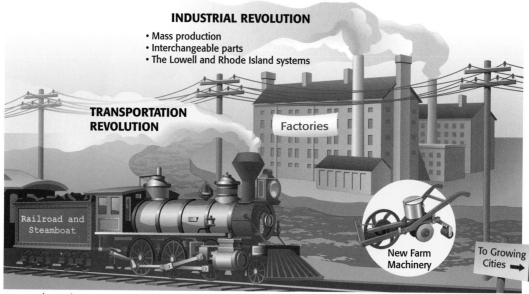

INDUSTRIAL REVOLUTION
• Mass production
• Interchangeable parts
• The Lowell and Rhode Island systems

TRANSPORTATION REVOLUTION

Factories

Railroad and Steamboat

New Farm Machinery

To Growing Cities →

©*Kenneth Batelman*

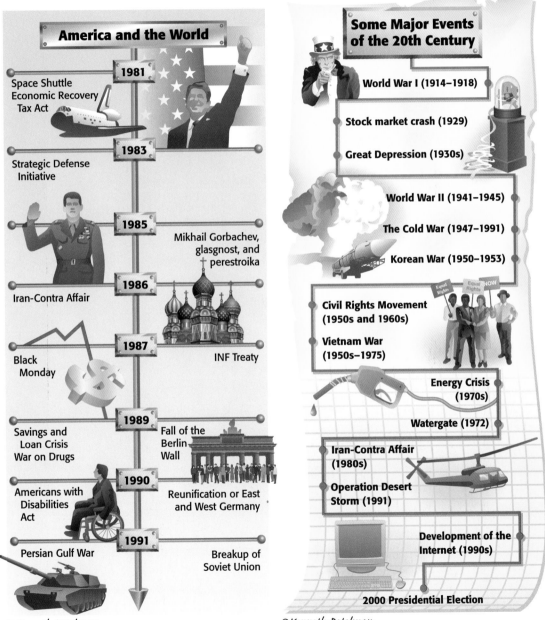

Kenneth Batelman

America and the World

1981
Space Shuttle
Economic Recovery
Tax Act

1983
Strategic Defense
Initiative

1985
Mikhail Gorbachev,
glasgnost, and
perestroika

1986
Iran-Contra Affair

1987
Black
Monday
INF Treaty

1989
Savings and
Loan Crisis
War on Drugs
Fall of the
Berlin
Wall

1990
Americans with
Disabilities
Act
Reunification or East
and West Germany

1991
Persian Gulf War
Breakup of
Soviet Union

©Kenneth Batelman

Some Major Events of the 20th Century

World War I (1914–1918)

Stock market crash (1929)

Great Depression (1930s)

World War II (1941–1945)

The Cold War (1947–1991)

Korean War (1950–1953)

Civil Rights Movement
(1950s and 1960s)

Vietnam War
(1950s–1975)

Energy Crisis
(1970s)

Watergate (1972)

Iran-Contra Affair
(1980s)

Operation Desert
Storm (1991)

Development of the
Internet (1990s)

2000 Presidential Election

©Kenneth Batelman

Kenneth Batelman

©Kenneth Batelman

©Kenneth Batelman

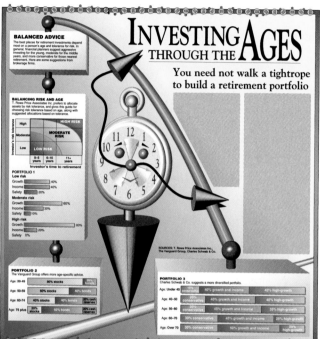

©Carol Zuber-Mallison

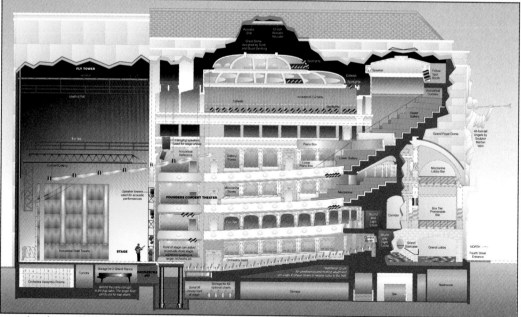

©Carol Zuber-Mallison

Fulton Saratoga
Montgomery Schenectady **VERMONT**
Albany Rensselaer
Otsego Schoharie Columbia **MASSACHUSETTS**
Delaware **Jansen Site**
Greene **Van Rensselaer Site**
Tinklepaugh Site
Ulster Litchfield Hartford **CONNECTICUT**
NEW YORK Dutchess
Hallan Site
New Haven
Orange Putnam West-chester Fairfield
Suffolk
Nassau

— Iroquois Pipeline
⬛ Historic Site Location

N

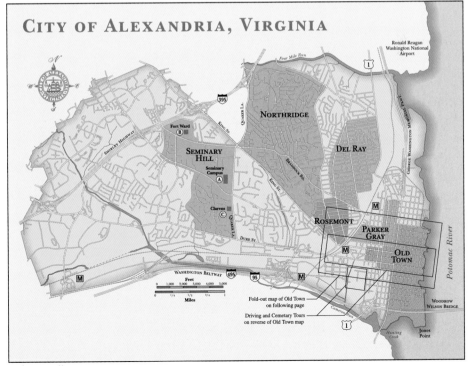

CITY OF ALEXANDRIA, VIRGINIA

Ronald Reagan Washington National Airport

Four Mile Run

395

NORTHRIDGE

Fort Ward Ⓑ

SEMINARY HILL

Seminary Campus Ⓐ

Clarens Ⓒ

DEL RAY

ROSEMONT

PARKER GRAY

OLD TOWN

Potomac River

Shirley Highway

King St.

Quaker La.

Duke St.

Washington Beltway

495

95

Feet
0 1,000 2,000 3,000 4,000 5,000

Miles
0 1/4 1/2 3/4 1

Fold-out map of Old Town on following page

Driving and Cemetary Tours on reverse of Old Town map

WOODROW WILSON BRIDGE

Jones Point

Hunting Creek

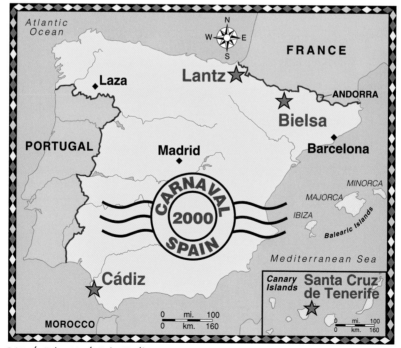

©*Mark Stein, Mark Stein Studios*

Mark Stein

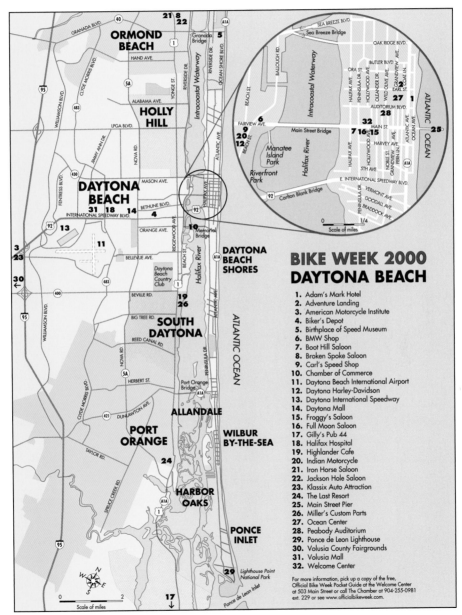

BIKE WEEK 2000
DAYTONA BEACH

1. Adam's Mark Hotel
2. Adventure Landing
3. American Motorcycle Institute
4. Biker's Depot
5. Birthplace of Speed Museum
6. BMW Shop
7. Boot Hill Saloon
8. Broken Spoke Saloon
9. Carl's Speed Shop
10. Chamber of Commerce
11. Daytona Beach International Airport
12. Daytona Harley-Davidson
13. Daytona International Speedway
14. Daytona Mall
15. Froggy's Saloon
16. Full Moon Saloon
17. Gilly's Pub 44
18. Halifax Hospital
19. Highlander Cafe
20. Indian Motorcycle
21. Iron Horse Saloon
22. Jackson Hole Saloon
23. Klassix Auto Attraction
24. The Last Resort
25. Main Street Pier
26. Miller's Custom Parts
27. Ocean Center
28. Peabody Auditorium
29. Ponce de Leon Lighthouse
30. Volusia County Fairgrounds
31. Volusia Mall
32. Welcome Center

For more information, pick up a copy of the free,
Official Bike Week Pocket Guide at the Welcome Center
at 503 Main Street or call The Chamber at 904-255-0981
ext. 229 or see www.officialbikeweek.com.

©Mark Stein, Mark Stein Studios

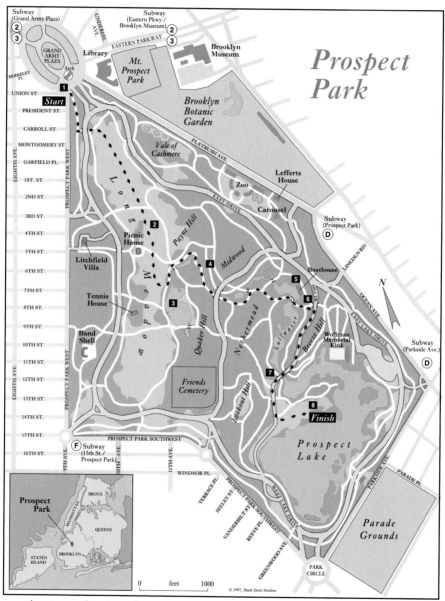

Prospect Park

©Mark Stein, Mark Stein Studios

Mark Stein

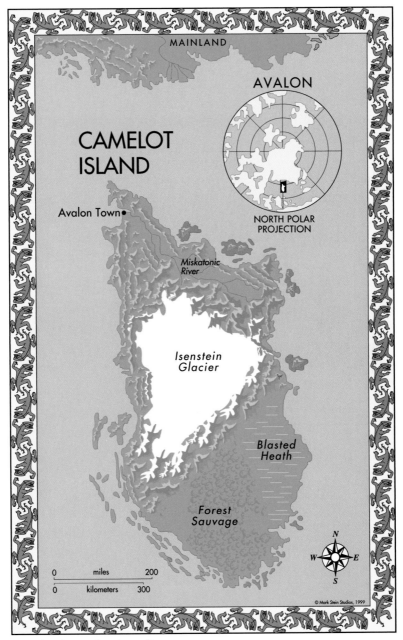

MAINLAND

AVALON

CAMELOT
ISLAND

Avalon Town•

NORTH POLAR
PROJECTION

Miskatonic
River

Isenstein
Glacier

Blasted
Heath

Forest
Sauvage

0   miles   200
0   kilometers   300

© Mark Stein Studios, 1999

©Mark Stein, Mark Stein Studios

Mark Stein

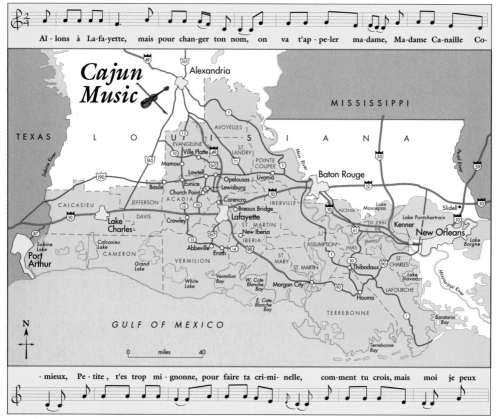

Graphic   Break Link to   New   Delete
styles   Graphic Style Graphic Graphic
                          Style   Style

1 *The Graphic Styles palette*

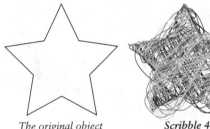

The original object   *Scribble 4*

RGB Denim   *Motion Trail Long*

RGB Cartoon Shading   *Scribble 6*

2 *We applied a few Illustrator **graphic styles** to a star, just to give you an inkling of what styles can do.*

Applying graphic styles

A **graphic style** is a collection of appearance attributes that can be applied to objects, groups, or layers. Any appearance attributes that can be applied to an object can also be saved in a graphic style, such as solid colors, gradients, patterns (stroke and fill), stroke attributes (weight, dash pattern, etc.), blending modes, transparency settings, effects—even Attribute palette overprint options.

Graphic styles are created, saved, and applied via the **Graphic Styles** palette (Shift-F5 or click the style thumbnail or arrowhead on **NEW** the Control palette) **1**–**2**. Each graphic style's individual attributes, however, are listed on the Appearance palette, and the Appearance palette is also used for creating or modifying those attributes.

There are several compelling reasons to work with graphic styles:

➤ By applying a graphic style, you can apply many attributes at once with the click of a button.

➤ Like appearance attributes, graphic styles change the way an object looks without changing its underlying path. A graphic style can be turned on or off easily, and a different one can be applied at any time.

➤ If you edit a graphic style, the style will update on any objects to which it's already linked—a workflow bonus.

Graphic styles differ from paragraph and character styles (see pages 258–262) in one significant respect. If you modify an attribute directly on an object that a graphic style is linked to, that modification breaks the link between the object and the style. In other words, if you subsequently edit that graphic style, it won't update on the object.

There are a couple of rules to keep in mind when applying and creating graphic styles:

➤ Graphic styles can be applied to layers, sublayers, groups, or objects. When applied to a layer or group, a graphic style will be linked to all the objects in that layer or group, as well as any objects that you may subsequently add to it.

(Continued on the following page)

Apply Graphic Styles

➤ A layer, sublayer, group, or object can be linked to only one graphic style at a time.

Graphic styles remain associated with the objects to which they're applied, unless you break that link (as per the instructions on page 300). If you **apply** a **graphic style** to a layer or group, that style will be applied to all the current and subsequently created objects in that layer or group.

To apply a graphic style:

1. Choose the **Selection** tool (V), then select an object or objects in the document window.
   or
   On the **Layers** palette, click the target circle for an object, layer, sublayer, or group **1**–**2**.

   Remember, for a top-level layer, selecting and targeting have different functions! See page 290.

2. Display the **Graphic Styles** palette (Shift-F5 or click the Style arrowhead on the **NEW** Control palette).

3. Click a style name or thumbnail on the palette **3**–**4** or drag a style name or thumbnail from the palette over a group or object in the document window. You don't have to select the object first. (See also **1**, next page.)

➤ To open other Illustrator graphic style libraries, choose from the Open Graphic Style Library submenu on the Graphic Styles palette menu.

➤ To choose a different view for the Graphic Styles palette, from the palette menu, choose Thumbnail View, Small List View, or Large List View.

➤ The name of the graphic style that's linked to the currently selected object is listed at the top of the Appearance palette.

➤ Graphic styles can also be applied to symbol instances by using the Symbol Styler tool (see pages 434–435).

1 *The original text object*

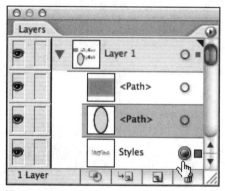

2 *We **targeted** the text object for an appearance change on the **Layers** palette…*

3 *…then clicked our custom Powder puff **swatch** (here, the palette is being accessed via the Control palette).*

4 *The graphic style appears on the **object**.*

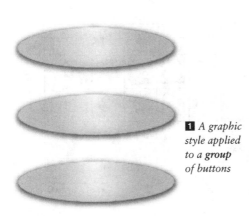

1 *A graphic style applied to a* **group** *of buttons*

Copying and moving attributes

To copy or move appearance attributes from one object or layer to another:

Method 1 (dragging)

To **copy** appearance attributes, Option-drag/ Alt-drag the target circle from the item that you want to copy onto the target circle for another layer, group, or object. Pause for the attributes to copy.

or

To **move** appearance attributes from one item to another, drag a target circle from one layer, group, or object to another without holding down any keys **2**. The appearance attributes will be removed from the original layer, group, or object.

Method 2 (Appearance palette)

1. Choose the **Selection** tool (V), then click an object whose graphic style or appearance attributes you want to **copy.**

2. Drag the square thumbnail from the upper left corner of the **Appearance** palette over an unselected object **3**.

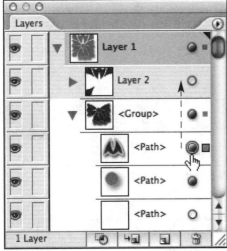

2 *Moving existing appearance attributes from a path to a sublayer (to Layer 2, in this case)*

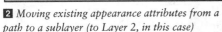

3 *Drag the thumbnail from the* **Appearance** *palette over an object.*

Copy, Move Attributes

Breaking the link to a style

If you **break the link** between an object and a graphic style and then subsequently edit the style, the style won't update on that object.

To break the link to a graphic style:

1. Choose the **Selection** tool (V), then select an object or objects in the document window, or click the target circle for an object on the Layers palette.
   or
   If the style was applied to a group or layer, click the **target** circle for a layer, sublayer, or group on the **Layers** palette.

2. Click the **Break Link to Graphic Style** button ![icon] at the bottom of the Graphic Styles palette **1**.
   or
   Change any appearance attribute for the selected item or items (e.g., apply a different fill color, stroke settings, pattern, gradient, transparency settings, or effect).

   The graphic style name will no longer be listed at the top of the Appearance palette for the selected item.

Creating graphic styles

Next, we offer two methods for creating a **new graphic style**. First you'll learn how to create a style from an object. This method will probably feel the most natural and intuitive, especially if you're going to experiment with various settings for the new style. To create a new graphic style by duplicating and then altering an existing one, follow the instructions on the next page instead.

To create a graphic style from an object:

1. Target an object that has the attributes you want to save as a graphic style. If desired, use the Appearance palette to apply other attributes you want the style to have **2**.

2. On the **Graphic Styles** palette, Option-click/Alt-click the **New Graphic Style** button, ![icon] enter a name for the style, then click OK **3**. The new style will appear as the last listing or thumbnail on the palette **4**.

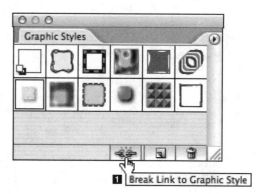

1 Break Link to Graphic Style

2 *Click the object whose attributes you want saved as a graphic style.*

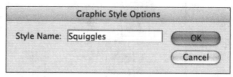

3 *Give the new graphic style a* **name**.

4 *The new* **graphic style swatch** *appears at the bottom of the Graphic Styles palette.*

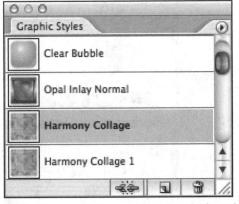

1 *The Harmony Collage graphic style is duplicated.*

or

Drag the thumbnail from the top of the Appearance palette onto the Graphic Styles palette, or drag the object onto the Graphic Styles palette. Double-click the new style swatch, type a name for it, then click OK.

To duplicate a graphic style:

1. On the Graphic Styles palette, **click** the style swatch or name that you want to duplicate, then click the **New Graphic Style** button.

   or

   Or **drag** a swatch over the **New Graphic Style** button.

   The number "1" will be appended to the existing style name **1**.

2. Double-click the duplicate style, type a style name, then click OK.

3. Click the duplicate graphic style swatch or name, then view a listing of its appearance attributes on the Appearance palette **2**.

2 *The **duplicate** style is renamed, and then its attributes are edited via the Appearance palette. The graphic style name is listed at the top of the palette.*

Editing graphic styles

Beware! If you **edit** a **graphic style,** the style will update on any objects that it's linked to. If you don't want this to happen, duplicate the style instead (follow the instructions on the previous page), then edit the duplicate.

To edit a graphic style:

1. Apply the graphic style to be edited to an object so you'll be able to preview your edits **1**.

2. Via the **Appearance** palette (Shift-F6), edit or restack the existing appearance attributes or add new attributes **2**.

3. Choose **Redefine Graphic Style "[style name]"** from the Appearance palette menu.
   or
   Option-drag/Alt-drag the object thumbnail from the top left corner of the **Appearance** palette over the original style swatch on the **Graphic Styles** palette.

   Regardless of which method you use, the style swatch will update to reflect the modifications **3**, and any objects to which the style is linked will update automatically **4**.

➤ While editing a graphic style, don't click other styled objects or style swatches, or you'll lose your current appearance attributes settings.

1 *Start by applying the graphic style that you want to edit to an object.*

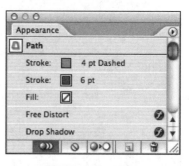

2 *Edit the style on the object, via the Appearance palette.*

3 *The style is replaced on the Graphic Styles palette.*

4 *The graphic style also updates automatically on any other objects it's linked to.*

Edit Graphic Style

What stays, what goes

Attributes are listed on the Appearance palette in the order in which they're applied. When graphic styles are merged, the final **order of fill attributes** on the Appearance palette follows the top-to-bottom order of the styles that were selected for merging on the Graphic Styles palette. The fill of the topmost selected style on the palette will be listed above other fills on the Apperance palette in the merged style. Of course, if you merge graphic styles that contain fully opaque fills, only the topmost fill will be visible. To achieve different results using the same fills, edit their opacity and/or blending modes or restack them on the Appearance palette (and thus change the order in which they're applied).

1 *Click two styles, then choose **Merge Graphic Styles** from the palette menu.*

2 *The merged style is **renamed.***

3 *The newly **merged style** appears on the Graphic Styles palette.*

Merging graphic styles

If you have **two graphic styles** whose attributes you want to combine, you can **merge** them into one new (additional) style without changing the original swatches. Before proceeding, please read the sidebar at left.

To merge graphic styles:

1. Cmd-click/Ctrl-click two or more style swatches or names on the Graphic Styles palette **1**.
2. Choose **Merge Graphic Styles** from the Graphic Styles palette menu. The Graphic Style Options dialog box opens **2**.
3. Enter a name for the new merged style, then click OK. The new style will appear as the last listing or thumbnail on the palette **3**.

Deleting graphic styles

If you **delete** a **graphic style** that's linked to any objects in your document, the object's appearance attributes will remain, but the objects will no longer be linked to the style, logically, since it no longer exists.

To delete a style from the Graphic Styles palette:

1. On the Graphic Styles palette (Shift-F5), click the style you want to remove, or Cmd-click/Ctrl-click multiple styles.
2. Click the **Delete Graphic Style** button on the palette.
   or
   Choose **Delete Graphic Style** from the Graphic Styles palette menu.
3. Click **Yes**.
➤ Oops! Change your mind? Choose Undo.

Using graphic style libraries

Graphic styles can't be deleted or edited from a library, but you can **copy** them to the **Graphic Styles** palette in your document and then edit them. You can also copy (and then edit) styles from other Illustrator files.

To copy graphic styles from a library or file to the Graphic Styles palette:

1. Open the **Graphic Styles** palette (Shift-F5).

2. If the library you want to copy graphic styles from is in the Adobe Illustrator CS2/Presets/Graphic Styles folder (the default location), choose from the **Open Graphic Style Library** submenu on the palette menu **1**–**4**.
   or
   If the library you want to copy graphic styles from isn't in the Graphic Styles folder, from the palette menu choose Open Graphic Style Library > **Other Library,** locate the library, then click Open. You can also use this command to open any Illustrator file and then use the file's Graphic Styles palette as a library.

3. To add a graphic style by styling an object, **select** an **object,** then click a style thumbnail in the library. Or drag a style thumbnail from the library over any object, selected or not. In either case, the new style will appear on the Graphic Styles palette.
   or
   To add a style to the Graphic Styles palette without styling an object, **deselect** all, then click a style thumbnail in the library.
   or
   To add **multiple** styles, click, then Shift-click consecutive styles or Cmd-click/Ctrl-click individual styles on the library palette, then drag the selected styles onto the Graphic Styles palette or choose **Add to Graphic Styles** from the library palette menu.

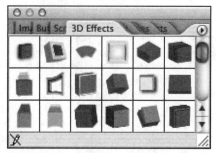

4 *Illustrator's **Buttons and Rollovers** style library*

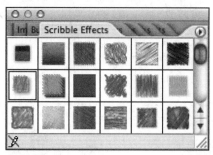

3 *Illustrator's **Type Effects** style library*

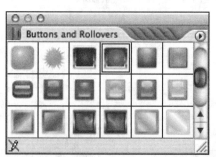

2 *Illustrator's **Scribble Effects** style library*

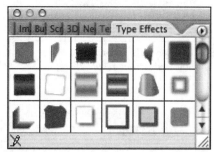

1 *Illustrator's **3D Effects** style library*

Back to the defaults

To restore the default graphic styles to the Graphic Styles palette, from the palette menu, choose Open Graphic Style Library > **Default_RGB** or **Default_CMYK.** A library palette opens. Click the first thumbnail in the library, Shift-click the last thumbnail, then choose **Add to Graphic Styles** from the library palette menu. If you want to clear out the Graphic Styles palette before restoring the default styles, click the second style name or thumbnail, Shift-click the last style, click the **Delete Graphic Style** button, then proceed as above.

By **saving graphic styles** to **custom libraries,** you'll be able to load them easily onto the Graphic Styles palette and use them in any document. You can organize and name a graphic styles library in any way that's useful to you, such as by theme or by client name.

To create a graphic styles library:

1. In an Illustrator document, create and/or copy the graphic styles that you want saved in a library. All the styles currently on the Graphic Styles palette will be saved in the new library.

2. *Optional:* To remove all the styles from the Graphic Styles palette that aren't currently being used in the document, choose Select All Unused from the Graphic Styles palette menu, click the Delete Graphic Style button 🗑 on the palette, then click Yes.

3. From the Graphic Styles palette menu, choose **Save Graphic Style Library,** enter a name for the library file (the Presets/ Graphic Styles folder in the application folder will be chosen automatically as the location), then click Save.

4. Quit/exit Illustrator, then relaunch. The new style library will be listed on, and can be opened from, the Open Graphic Style Library submenu on the palette menu.

➤ Any brush used in a style from a graphic style library that isn't present on the document's Brushes palette will be added to the document's Brushes palette if the style is applied to an object in the document.

Create Graphic Style Library

Expanding attributes

When you **expand** an object's **appearance attributes,** the paths that were used to create the attributes become (dozens of) separate objects and can be edited individually. This command comes in handy when you need to export files to other applications that can't read appearance attributes per se.

To expand an object's appearance attributes:

1. Select an object that contains the appearance attributes (or graphic style) that you want to expand **1**–**2**.

2. Choose Object > **Expand Appearance.** On the Layers palette, you'll see a new group (or a nested series of groups) containing the original object and the effects and appearance attributes, which will be listed either as paths or images **3**–**4**.

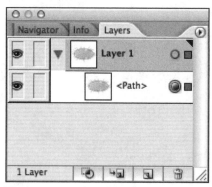

1 *Select an object that contains appearance attributes.*

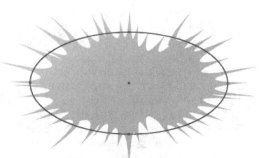

2 *The Layers palette for the original object*

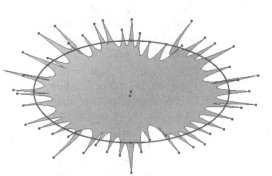

3 *After expanding the object's appearances*

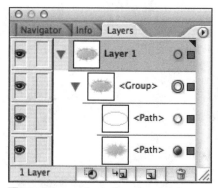

4 *The Layers palette after choosing the Expand Appearance command*

Expand Appearance Attributes

EFFECTS & FILTERS 20

In this chapter, after learning the differences between filters and effects, you'll learn how to apply a few of them specifically, add effects to a graphic style, rasterize a path to prep an object for applying filters, and use the Filter Gallery and Effects Gallery. You can also browse through our compendium of Photoshop filters and follow our detailed instructions for applying the 3D effects.

Overview of Effects and Filters

Effect	
Apply Sumi-e	⇧⌘E
Sumi-e...	⌥⇧⌘E
Document Raster Effects Settings...	
Illustrator Effects	
3D	▶
Convert to Shape	▶
Distort & Transform	▶
Path	▶
Pathfinder	▶
Rasterize...	
Stylize	▶
SVG Filters	▶
Warp	▶
Photoshop Effects	
Effect Gallery...	
Artistic	▶
Blur	▶
Brush Strokes	▶
Distort	▶
Pixelate	▶
Sharpen	▶
Sketch	▶
Stylize	▶
Texture	▶
Video	▶

1 *The Effect menu has two sections: **Illustrator Effects** (vector effects plus a few raster effects) on the top, and **Photoshop Effects** (raster effects) on the bottom.*

Effects and filters: An overview

Effects and filters apply distortion, texture, color adjustment, 3D, artistic, shape, and stylistic changes to objects and images, with results ranging from subtle to marked. Many of the filters on the Filter menu have matching counterparts on the Effect menu **1**. In fact, the Filter and Effect menus are so interdependent that settings used for a command on one menu become the settings for its counterpart on the other menu.

There are significant differences between effects and filters, however, in terms of the kind of objects they can be applied to and whether the results are editable after the command is applied. We'll address some of those differences next.

Using effects...

Filter menu commands change the path of the underlying object and aren't reeditable, whereas **effects** change only the **appearance** of an object—not its underlying path—and are fully **editable**. Because they can be edited or deleted at any time without permanently affecting the object they're applied to (and even without affecting other effects or appearance attributes on the same object), effects lend themselves to experimentation. What's more, if you reshape the underlying object's path, the effects adjust accordingly. In other words, effects are live.

(Continued on the following page)

All the **Illustrator effects** (on the top part of the Effect menu) are vector, meaning they output as vectors—except for Drop Shadow, Inner Glow, Outer Glow, and Feather on the Effect > Stylize submenu, which are rasterized (converted from vector to raster) on output. Some Illustrator effects have counterparts on the Filter menu, such as Drop Shadow and Roughen, but many are exclusive to the Effect menu, such as Feather and Convert to Shape.

All the **Photoshop effects** (bottom part of the Effect menu) are raster, meaning they're rasterized on output even when exported to a vector format such as SWF. All the Photoshop effects have counterparts on the Filter menu.

Both Illustrator effects and Photoshop effects can be applied to editable type (you don't have to convert it to outlines), and the type will remain editable.

Like object attributes, effects are listed on the **Appearance** palette for each object they're applied to **1**. Effects that are applied to a **targeted** layer, sublayer, or group are applied automatically to all the current and future objects on the layer, sublayer, or group.

Furthermore, because effects are appearance attributes (display on the Appearance palette) they can be saved in and applied via a **graphic style,** and edited at any time (see page 311).

➤ To intensify the results of a Photoshop effect on a vector object, apply an effect such as Feather or Inner or Outer Glow first to add variation to the fill color.

...versus using filters

Unlike effects, Filter menu commands (**1**, next page) alter an object's actual path. Vector filters for path objects are found in the Illustrator Filters (upper) portion of the menu.

Photoshop filters for embedded bitmap images and rasterized objects are on the bottom portion of the Filter menu. Some of them introduce randomness or distortion; others, such as the Artistic, Brush Strokes,

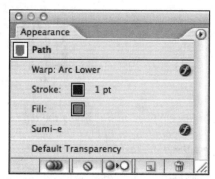

1 *The Warp and Sumi-e effects were applied to a path, as listed on the* **Appearance** *palette.*

Choosing raster settings

All the Photoshop Effects, along with the Stylize > Drop Shadow, Inner Glow, Outer Glow, and Feather effects, are rasterized upon output. But how do you control the rasterization process? Choose Effect > **Document Raster Effects Settings,** then choose Color Model, Resolution, Background treatment, and other options **2**. These settings also control how a raster efffect looks in the Illustrator document. For a more detailed explanation of these settings, see page 501.

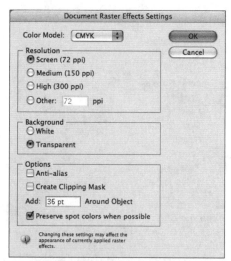

2 *Choose* **Document Raster Effects Settings** *to control how effects are rasterized upon output.*

Quick reapply

Reapply **last effect** using the same settings (no dialog box opens)	Cmd-Shift-E/ Ctrl-Shift-E
Reopen **Effect Gallery** or last effects dialog box	Cmd-Option-Shift-E/ Ctrl-Alt-Shift-E
Reapply **last filter** using the same settings (no dialog box opens)	Cmd-E/Ctrl-E
Reopen **Filter Gallery** or last filter dialog box	Cmd-Option-E/ Ctrl-Alt-E

Filter

Apply Last Filter ⌘E
Last Filter ⌥⌘E

Illustrator Filters
  Colors ▶   *Illustrator*
  Create ▶   *Filters*
  Distort ▶
  Stylize ▶

Photoshop Filters
  Filter Gallery...
  Artistic ▶
  Blur ▶
  Brush Strokes ▶
  Distort ▶
  Pixelate ▶   *Photoshop*
  Sharpen ▶   *Filters*
  Sketch ▶
  Stylize ▶
  Texture ▶
  Video ▶

1 *The Filter menu*

Roughen

Options
Size: [25] %
  ◉ Relative   ○ Absolute
Detail: [10] /in

Points
○ Smooth   ◉ Corner

OK
Cancel
☑ Preview

2 *To monitor changes in the document window, check Preview (if available) in an effect or filter dialog box.*

Sketch, and Texture filters, give an image a hand-rendered look.

Applying filters and effects

To apply a filter or an effect, target a layer, group, or object, then choose a command from a submenu on the Filter or Effect menu. For the **Illustrator filters** and **Illustrator effects** and the **Photoshop filters** and **Photoshop effects** on the **Blur, Pixelate, Sharpen,** and **Video** submenus, an **individual** dialog box opens. To learn more about applying Illustrator effects, see the next page.

When you choose any other **Photoshop filter** **NEW** or **Photoshop effect,** the **Filter Gallery** or **Effect Gallery** opens, respectively. You can also choose Filter > Filter Gallery or Effect > Effect Gallery to open that gallery (see pages 322–323).

Note: To access any Photoshop filters or the effects on the Artistic, Brush Strokes, Distort, Sketch, Stylize, Texture, or Video submenus, your document must be in RGB Color mode.

Many vector filter and effect dialog boxes have a **Preview** option **2** that lets you preview the results in your document as you choose settings. If you enter a value in a field, press **Tab** to update the preview.

You can apply **filters** to embedded bitmap images, but not to linked images. You can apply **effects** to embedded bitmap images, or to the embedded preview of a linked image (not to the linked image itself).

➤ For memory-intensive filters, lowering the settings or choosing different settings can help speed up processing.

➤ You can install and use plug-in filters from third-party developers in Illustrator.

➤ For page locations of filters or effects that are discussed in other chapters, look under "Filters" or "Effects" in the index.

Applying Illustrator effects

In the instructions below, you'll **apply** an **Illustrator effect** directly to a layer, sublayer, group, or object. In the instructions on the following page, you'll learn how to add to, or edit an effect in, a graphic style.

To apply an effect:

1. On the Layers palette (F7), click the **target** circle for a layer, sublayer, group, or object **1**. The target circle should have a double border.
   or
   To limit an effect to just an object's stroke or fill, select the object, then click the **Stroke** or **Fill** listing on the Appearance palette.

2. Choose an **Illustrator effect** from the top portion of the Effect menu.

3. Check Preview (if available) to preview the effect as you choose options, then choose options **2**.

4. Click OK **3**. If you applied the effect to just a stroke or fill, the effect will be nested within the Stroke or Fill listing on the Appearance palette.

To edit an applied effect:

1. On the Layers palette (F7), **target** the layer, sublayer, group, or object that the effect you want to edit is applied to.
   or
   If the effect was applied to just an object's stroke or fill, select the object, then expand the **Stroke** or **Fill** listing on the Appearance palette.

2. Double-click the effect name or icon *ƒ* on the **Appearance** palette **4**. The effect dialog box will reopen.

3. Make the desired adjustments, then click OK.

1 *The original object*

2 *A value is chosen in the effect dialog box.*

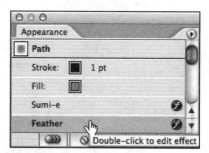

3 *The Feather effect is applied.*

4 *Double-click an effect name or icon on the Appearance palette to edit that attribute.*

Apply, Edit Effect

1 *Click a style on the Graphic Styles palette.*

2 *To edit an effect, double-click the effect name or icon on the Appearance palette.*

From effect to graphic style

To save all the attributes currently listed on the Appearance palette as a graphic style, click the **New Graphic Style** button on the **Graphic Styles** palette, or drag the square thumbnail from the upper left corner of the Appearance palette to the Graphic Styles palette. See pages 300–301.

Using effects in graphic styles

Graphic styles let you apply multiple attributes en masse, including effects. You can edit any effect used in a style, and also **add effects to a style**. To learn more about styles and appearances, see Chapter 19.

To add an effect to or edit an effect in a graphic style:

1. Click a style name or swatch on the Graphic Styles palette (access it via the **NEW** Control palette, if you wish) **1**, or select an object that uses that style so you can preview your edits. The style name will appear at the top of the Appearance palette.

2. To **add** an effect, choose an Illustrator effect from the Effect menu, choose options (check Preview if you selected an object in the previous step), then click OK.
   or
   To **edit** an existing effect, double-click the effect name or icon on the Appearance palette, choose options, then click OK **2**.

3. From the Appearance palette menu, choose **Redefine Graphic Style "[style name]"** to update the style.

You can **remove** an effect from a layer, object, or style as easily as you can add one.

To remove an effect from a layer, object, or graphic style:

1. On the **Layers** palette, target the layer, sublayer, group, or object that contains the effect you want to remove.
   or
   On the **Graphic Styles** palette, click the graphic style name or swatch that contains the effect you want to remove.

2. On the Appearance palette, click the effect name or icon, then click the **Delete Selected Item** button 🗑 on the Appearance palette (or drag the effect name over the button).

3. If you're removing an effect from a style, choose **Redefine Graphic Style "[style name]"** from the Appearance palette menu to update the style.

Effects in Graphic Styles

A few Illustrator effects up close

The effects discussed in this section are found only on the upper part of the Effects menu; they don't have counterparts on the Filter menu.

To apply Pathfinder effects

The commands on the **Effect > Pathfinder** submenu are similar to the commands on the Pathfinder palette (see pages 393–394), with these important differences **1**:

➤ The effects modify an object's appearance but not its actual path.

➤ You can delete a Pathfinder appearance attribute at any time.

➤ The effects don't create compound shapes.

➤ The Divide, Trim, and Merge effects don't break up overlapping areas into separate objects.

Next, a few **guidelines** for **applying Pathfinder effects:**

➤ Before applying a Pathfinder effect, collect the objects to which you want to apply the effect into a **sublayer** or **group,** then target the sublayer (that's target—not select), or select or target the group.

➤ Via the Layers palette, you can **move** objects into or out of a group that a Pathfinder effect is applied to.

➤ Pathfinder effects can be included in a **graphic style** (see the previous page).

➤ Pathfinder effects can be **removed** at any time (see the previous page).

➤ To **change** which Pathfinder effect is applied to the currently targeted group (with a convenient preview), double-click a Pathfinder effect listing on the Appearance palette to open the Pathfinder Options dialog box, then choose a Pathfinder option from the Operation pop-up menu.

➤ If you **expand** a Pathfinder effect by choosing Object > Expand Appearance, the result will be a path shape, a compound path, or an image.

Effect	
Apply Feather	⇧⌘E
Feather...	⌥⇧⌘E
Document Raster Effects Settings...	
Illustrator Effects	
3D	▶
Convert to Shape	▶
Distort & Transform	▶
Path	▶
Pathfinder	▶
Rasterize...	
Stylize	▶
SVG Filters	▶
Warp	▶
Photoshop Effects	
Effect Gallery...	
Artistic	▶
Blur	▶
Brush Strokes	▶
Distort	▶
Pixelate	▶
Sharpen	▶
Sketch	▶
Stylize	▶
Texture	▶
Video	▶

Pathfinder submenu:
Add
Intersect
Exclude
Subtract
Minus Back
Divide
Trim
Merge
Crop
Outline
Hard Mix
Soft Mix...
Trap...

1 *The **Pathfinder** commands can be applied as effects via the **Effect** menu.*

It's a hard mix

To simulate overprinting, target a group or layer that contains two or more objects that overlap one another at least partially (they can be type objects), then choose Effect > **Pathfinder** > **Hard Mix.** The highest C, M, Y, and K, or R, G, and B values from the objects will be mixed in areas where they overlap. The greater the difference between the original colors, the more marked the resulting effect.

1 *The original object*

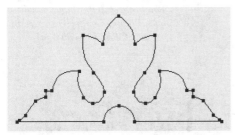

2 *Choose shape and scaling options in the Shape Options dialog box.*

3 *The Convert to Shape > Rectangle effect was applied to the object, but it didn't change the underlying path.*

4 *Rectangle is listed as an effect on the Appearance palette.*

In these instructions, you'll use a **Convert to Shape** effect to change an object's silhouette to a rectangle, rounded rectangle, or ellipse without altering the actual underlying path.

To apply a Convert to Shape effect:

1. Select or target an object or objects in the document window or via the Layers palette **1**.

2. Choose Effect > Convert to Shape > **Rectangle, Rounded Rectangle,** or **Ellipse.** The Shape Options dialog box opens **2**. *Note:* Any of the three options can also be chosen from the Shape pop-up menu once the dialog box is open.

3. Check Preview.

4. Click **Absolute,** then enter the total desired **Width** and **Height** values for the shape's appearance.
   or
   Click **Relative,** then enter the **Extra Width** or **Extra Height** if you want the shape to be larger or smaller than the actual path (enter a positive or negative value).

5. For the Rounded Rectangle shape, you can also change the **Corner Radius** value.

6. Click OK **3**–**4**.

   For an exercise using the Convert to Shape effects, see the following page.

➤ To simply round off sharp corners on an object without converting its shape, use Effect > Stylize > Round Corners.

Convert to Shape Effect

313

Exercise

Next we'll show you how to use the **"live"** aspect of **effects,** using type as an example. You could use this technique to create buttons for a Web page.

Use live shapes with type

1. Select a type block with the Selection tool ■.
2. Choose **Add New Fill** from the Appearance palette menu.
3. Click **Fill** on the Appearance palette, choose a color from the Color or Swatches palette, and leave the Fill listing selected.
4. Click the **Duplicate Selected Item** button ■ at the bottom of the Appearance palette.
5. Click the lower of the two **Fill** listings on the Appearance palette, then choose a different color for it ■.
6. Apply an effect from the Effect > **Convert to Shape** submenu to the new Fill listing, using the Relative option ■.
7. To see how the live effect works, add or delete some type characters or resize the type. The new fill shape will resize accordingly ■.

1 *The original text*

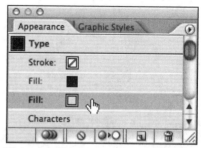

2 *A new Fill listing is created and duplicated, and a different color is chosen for it.*

3 *After applying the **Convert to Shape** effect to the duplicate Fill (Shape: Ellipse; Relative: Extra Width 13 pt, Extra Height 3 pt)*

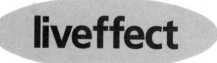

4 *Here's the point: When more characters are added to the text, the shape **scales automatically** to accommodate it.*

Keeping up with appearances

Appearances, such as effects or extra fill attributes, can be applied to a whole type object but not to individual type characters. That's why the Appearance palette displays one list of attributes when a whole type object is selected, and the original fill and stroke colors if you double-click the "Characters" listing on the palette or select the type with a type tool.

Confusing? Just keep track of the name next to the image thumbnail at the top of the Appearance palette. If it says **Characters,** your edits will affect type **characters;** if it says **Type,** your edits will affect the whole **type object.**

1 *The original group of objects*

2 *Choose options in the Inner Glow dialog box.*

3 *After applying the Inner Glow effect*

The **Inner Glow** effect spreads a color on the interior of an object; the **Outer Glow** effect spreads a color from the edge of an object outward.

To apply the Inner Glow or Outer Glow effect:

1. Select or target a layer, sublayer, group, or object **1**.

2. Choose Effect > Stylize > **Inner Glow** or **Outer Glow**.

3. Check Preview **2**.

4. Do any of the following:

   Click the **Color** square next to the Mode pop-up menu, then choose a different glow color (it can be a spot color). **NEW**

   Choose a blending **Mode** for the glow color.

   Choose an **Opacity** for the glow color.

   Click the **Blur** arrowhead, then move the slider to adjust how far the glow extends inward or outward. The higher the Blur value, the wider the glow.

   For the Inner Glow effect, click **Center** to have the glow spread outward from the object's center, or **Edge** to have the glow spread inward from the object's edge toward its center.

5. Click OK **3**–**5**.

4 *After applying the Outer Glow effect*

5 *Both Glow effects applied*

Inner Glow, Outer Glow Effects

Scribble Effect

The **Scribble** effect makes an object's fill and stroke look as though it was drawn with a felt-tip marker or pen.

To apply the Scribble effect:

1. Select a path object or objects, or type **1**.

2. Choose Effect > Stylize > **Scribble.** The Scribble Options dialog box opens **2**.

3. Check Preview. As a start, choose a preset from the **Settings** pop-up menu. Follow the remaining steps if you want to choose custom settings for the preset; otherwise, click OK.

4. Enter an **Angle** value or rotate the dial to change the angle of the sketch lines.

5. Choose a positive **Path Overlap** value to allow the sketch lines to extend beyond the edge of the path, or a negative value to keep them inside the path. Choose a high **Variation** value to produce random variations in line lengths and a wilder, more haphazard look, or a low Variation for more uniform lengths.

6. For **Line Options,** do any of the following:

   Choose a **Stroke Width** for the lines.

   Choose a **Curviness** value to control whether the lines angle more sharply or loop more loosely where they change direction. The **Variation** slider controls the degree of random variation in these direction changes.

   Choose a **Spacing** value to cluster sketch lines more tightly or to spread them apart. The **Variation** slider controls how much random variation occurs in the spacing.

7. Click OK **3**–**4**. Scribble will become an effect listing on the Appearance palette. Double-click the listing at any time to edit the effect.

➤ If you make Scribble setting changes and then choose a preset from the Settings pop-up menu, your custom settings will be deleted. As of yet, you can't save your settings as a preset.

1 *The original object*

2 *Choose Scribble Options.*

3 *Scribble filter, Settings: Moiré*

4 *Scribble filter, Settings: Sketch*

*1 Sometimes we're satisfied with the default settings in the **Drop Shadow** dialog box, as shown here; at other times we might change the opacity or blur value.*

SHADOW

*2 The **Drop Shadow** effect applied to editable type*

*3 **Drop Shadow** effect (and Feather effect)*

Two Illustrator filters/effects up close

The **Drop Shadow** command creates soft, naturalistic shadows and can be applied as a filter or an effect. The filter creates a new shadow image, separate from the original object, and has a Create Separate Shadows option that nests the object and the shadow image into a new group on the Layers palette.

Unlike the filter, the Drop Shadow effect has a Preview option and becomes an appearance on the original object. You can double-click the Drop Shadow listing on the Appearance palette and change the settings, including the shadow color, at any time.

To create a drop shadow:

1. Select one or more path objects or editable type.

2. Choose **Filter > Stylize > Drop Shadow** or **Effect > Stylize > Drop Shadow.** The Drop Shadow dialog box opens **1**. If you chose the command from the Effect menu, check Preview.

3. Do the following:

   Choose a blending **Mode**.

   Choose an **Opacity** value for the shadow.

   Enter an **X Offset** for the horizontal distance between the object and shadow and a **Y Offset** for the vertical distance between the object and shadow.

   Enter a **Blur** value (0–144 pt) for the width of the shadow.

   Optional: Click Color, click the color square, then choose a different shadow color from the Color Picker (it can be **NEW** a spot color), then click OK. Or click Darkness, then enter a percentage of black to be added to the shadow.

4. *Optional:* If you're using the filter (not the effect), you can check Create Separate Shadows to keep the shadow separate from the image. The image and shadow will be nested in a new group.

5. Click OK **2**–**3**.

Drop Shadow

The **Roughen** filter or effect adds anchor points and then moves them, making an object look more hand-drawn.

To apply the Roughen effect or filter:

1. Select a path object or objects 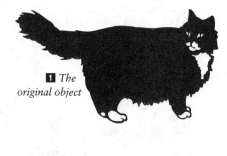, and also choose View > Hide Edges (Cmd-H/Ctrl-H) if you like, to make previewing easier.

2. Choose Effect > Distort & Transform > **Roughen,** or Filter > Distort > **Roughen.**

3. Check Preview 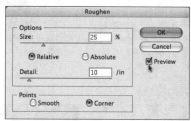.

4. Click **Relative** to move points by a percentage of the object's size, or **Absolute** to move points by a specific amount. Then choose a **Size** amount to specify how far the object's anchor points may move. To preserve the object's overall shape, choose a very low Size amount.

5. Choose a **Detail** amount for the number of points to be added to each inch of the path segments.

6. Click **Smooth** to produce curves, or click **Corner** to produce pointy angles.

7. Click OK **3**.

The **Twist** effect or filter twists an object's outer shape but not its fill. You can twist a single object or multiple objects together.

To apply the Twist effect or filter:

1. Select a path object or objects **4**. If you select two or more objects, they'll be twirled together.

2. Choose Effect > Distort & Transform > **Twist,** or Filter > Distort > **Twist.**

3. Enter a positive **Angle** to twirl the path(s) clockwise or a negative value to twirl it counterclockwise (–360 to 360).

4. Click OK **5**.

➤ For comparison, try using the Twirl tool (see page 442).

1 *The original object*

2 *The Roughen dialog box*

3 *After applying the Roughen filter (or eyeing a dog?)*

4 *The original object*   **5** *After applying the Twist effect*

Rasterizing objects

The **Rasterize** command converts vector objects into bitmap images. If you choose the RGB Color Model in the Rasterize dialog box, you'll be able to apply any of the Photoshop filters to the resulting object. (Photoshop effects can be applied to vector objects, so there's no need to rasterize them —at least for that reason).

To rasterize a path object:

1. Select a path object or objects, or target them on the Layers palette.

2. Choose Object > **Rasterize** or Effect > **Rasterize.** The effect is reversible and editable, whereas the Object menu command is permanent. If you're going to apply Photoshop filters, you must use the Object command, not the effect.

3. Choose a **Color Model** for the object **1**. Depending on the current document color mode, you can choose **CMYK** for print output (few Photoshop filters and effects will be available for the object); **RGB** for video or onscreen output (all

(Continued on the following page)

1 *Choose a Color Model in the **Rasterize** dialog box.*

Photoshop filters and effects will be available); **Grayscale** (if you're using Object > Rasterize, all Photoshop filters and effects will be available; if you're using Effect > Rasterize, no Photoshop filters will be available); or **Bitmap** for only black-and-white or black-and-transparent (no Photoshop filters or effects will be available).

4. For **Resolution,** choose **Screen** for Web or video output, **Medium** for desktop printers, or **High** for imagesetter output; or enter a resolution in the **Other** field; or click **Use Document Raster Effects Resolution** to use the global resolution settings as specified in Effect > Document Raster Effects Settings.

5. Click **Background: White** to make the transparent areas in the object opaque white, or **Transparent** to make the background transparent (see the sidebar).

6. For **Options:**

   Choose **Anti-aliasing: Art Optimized (Supersampling)** to have Illustrator soften the edges of the rasterized shape; this option may make type or thin lines look blurry. **Type Optimized (Hinted)** is recommended for type objects. If you choose **None,** edges will be jagged.

   Optional: If you clicked Background: White and you check Create Clipping Mask, Illustrator will generate a clipping mask for the shape to make its background transparent (see the sidebar).

   To add pixels around the object for padding (the bounding box will become larger), enter an **Add [ ] Around Object** value.

7. Click OK.

➤ Once an object is rasterized, you can change its solid color fill only via Filter > Colors > Adjust Colors.

➤ If you rasterize an object that contains a pattern fill and you want to preserve any transparency in the pattern in the Rasterize dialog box, click Background: Transparent and choose Anti-aliasing: Art Optimized.

Transparent versus clipping mask

Both the **Background: Transparent** and **Create Clipping Mask** options in the Object > Rasterize dialog box remove an object's background. The **Transparent** option creates an alpha channel in order to remove the background, and the resulting image stays as an individual listing on the Layers palette. Transparency (blending mode and opacity) settings are removed, but the object keeps any transparency appearances. Transparency settings can be applied to the targeted image at any time, and will be preserved if the file is exported to Photoshop.

The **Create Clipping Mask** option produces a nested group containing a clipping path and the image, and the clipping path preserves any existing appearance attributes, but not any transparency settings. Transparency settings for the object can be adjusted for the targeted image, but not for the clipping path. If you click the Transparent option, you don't need to create a clipping mask.

The Effect > Rasterize command and the SVG format preserve the appearance of blending and opacity, whereas the SWF format preserves only the appearance of opacity.

1 *The original image*

2 *The Object Mosaic dialog box*

3 *The Object Mosaic filter applied*

4 *The Object Mosaic filter applied to the original image, this time with spacing between the tiles*

An Illustrator filter up close

The **Object Mosaic** filter breaks up a raster image into a grid of little squares; each square is a separate object that can be moved or recolored individually. (There's no effect version of this filter.)

To apply the Object Mosaic filter:

1. Select a rasterized object or an embedded bitmap image **1**.

2. Choose Filter > Create > **Object Mosaic.**

3. *Do either of the following optional steps:*

   Change the **New Size: Width** and/or **Height** values **2**. (The Current Size area lists the current width and height of the image.) If you want to enter dimensions in percentages relative to the original, check Resize using Percentages at the bottom of the dialog box; the Width and Height fields will switch to percentage values.

   or

   Enter a **New Size: Width** (or **Height**), click Constrain Ratio: Width (or Height) under Options to lock in that dimension, then click Use Ratio to have Illustrator automatically calculate the second dimension proportionate to the object's original dimensions.

4. Enter the desired **Number of Tiles** to fill the **Width** and **Height** dimensions. *Note:* If you clicked Use Ratio, the Number of Tiles will be calculated automatically.

5. *Optional:* To add spacing between the tiles, enter Tile Spacing: Width and Height values.

6. *Optional:* Illustrator will apply the Object Mosaic filter to a copy of a bitmap image (on top of the original). Check Delete Raster to delete the original image; uncheck to keep it.

7. Click **Result: Color** or **Gray.**

8. Click OK **3**–**4**. The mosaic object will be listed as a group on the Layers palette.

Object Mosaic Filter

NEW Using the Filter or Effect Gallery

Using the **Filter Gallery** or **Effect Gallery**, you can access all the Photoshop filters or Photoshop effects under one roof.

In the Filter Gallery (not the Effect Gallery), you can also preview multiple filters, show/hide individual previews, and change the sequence in which they're applied. As you try out multiple filters—whether solo or in combination—let your creative juices flow!

To use the Filter or Effect Gallery:

1. Select a rasterized object, embedded image, or editable or outline type, and make sure your document is in RGB Color mode so all the Photoshop filters and effects will be available.

2. Choose Filter > **Filter Gallery** or Effect > **Effect Gallery** or choose an individual Photoshop filter or Photoshop effect from either menu (but not a filter or effect on the Pixelate, Blur, Sharpen, or Video sub-menu). The gallery will open (**1**, next page).

3. If you chose an individual filter or effect, that effect thumbnail will be highlighted in the dialog box. To choose a different filter or effect in the dialog box, in the middle panel, click an arrowhead/chevron to expand one of the six categories, then click a thumbnail.

4. Choose settings for the chosen filter or effect in the right panel. You can change the zoom level for the preview via the zoom buttons or pop-up menu, or move the preview in the window.

5. *In the Filter Gallery, you can do any of the following:*

   To apply an additional filter, click the **New Effect Layer** button, ⬛ click another filter thumbnail in any category (or choose from the pop-up menu on the right side of the dialog box), then choose settings. The previewed filters are listed in the bottom right of the dialog box, with the most recently chosen filter at the top of the list.

   To **replace** a filter, leave the existing name selected on the scroll list, click a new thumbnail, and choose settings.

   To **hide** a filter, on the scroll list, click the eye icon (click again to redisplay it).

   To change the **sequence** in which the filters are applied, drag an effect name upward or downward on the list. Each sequence variation produces a different result in the document.

   To **remove** the currently selected filter from the list, click the Delete Effect Layer button. 🗑

6. For some effects and filters, such as Rough Pastels and Underpainting, you can choose a texture type from the **Texture** pop-up menu (**2**–**3**, next page). Move the Scaling slider to scale the pattern, and move the Relief slider, if there is one, to adjust the depth and prominence of the texture on the surface of the image.

7. Click OK.

➤ Hold down Cmd/Ctrl and click Default (the Cancel button becomes a Default button) to remove all filters from the scroll list. Hold down Option/Alt and click Reset to restore the last-used settings.

➤ In addition to the Photoshop filters, you can apply the following Illustrator filters to a raster object: Colors submenu > Adjust Colors, Convert to Grayscale, Convert to CMYK, and Convert to RGB (depending on the current document color mode), Invert Colors, and Saturate; also Stylize > Drop Shadow.

To **move** the image in the **preview** window, use the scroll bars or arrows or drag in the preview.

Click the arrowhead/chevron to hide the **middle panel** and expand the preview window to two panels wide; click it again to redisplay the middle panel.

Choose **settings** for the selected filter or effect.

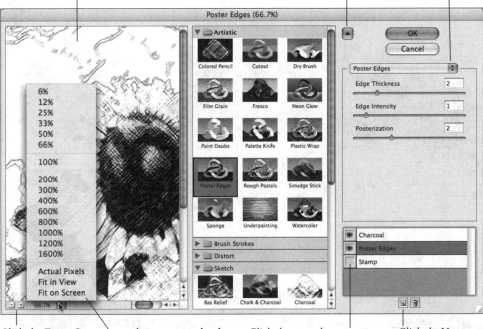

Poster Edges (66.7%)

6%
12%
25%
33%
50%
66%

100%

200%
300%
400%
600%
800%
1000%
1200%
1600%

Actual Pixels
Fit in View
Fit on Screen

▼ Artistic

Colored Pencil   Cutout   Dry Brush
Film Grain   Fresco   Neon Glow
Paint Daubs   Palette Knife   Plastic Wrap
Poster Edges   Rough Pastels   Smudge Stick
Sponge   Underpainting   Watercolor

▶ Brush Strokes
▶ Distort
▼ Sketch

Bas Relief   Chalk & Charcoal   Charcoal

OK
Cancel

Poster Edges

Edge Thickness   2
Edge Intensity   1
Posterization   2

Charcoal
Poster Edges
Stamp

Click the **Zoom Out** or **Zoom In** button...   ...or choose a **zoom level** from the pop-up menu.

Click the eye column to **hide/show** a filter preview.

Click the **New Effect Layer** button to preview additional filters.

1 The **Filter Gallery** has three panels: an image **preview** on the left; **categories** with filter thumbnails in the middle; and settings and a list of previewed filters on the right.

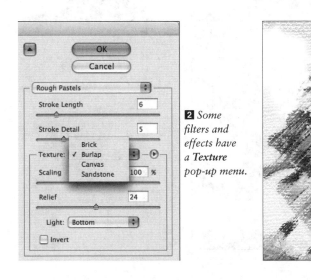

OK
Cancel

Rough Pastels

Stroke Length   6
Stroke Detail   5

Texture: ✓ Burlap   Brick   Canvas   Sandstone
Scaling   100   %
Relief   24
Light: Bottom
☐ Invert

2 Some filters and effects have a **Texture** pop-up menu.

3 The Rough Pastels filter/ effect, with the Burlap **Texture** chosen

The Photoshop Filters illustrated
Artistic filters

Artistic Filters

ORIGINAL IMAGE © PHOTODISC

Original image

Colored Pencil

Cutout

Dry Brush

Film Grain

Fresco

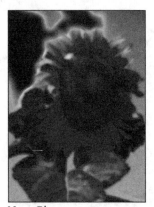

Neon Glow

Paint Daubs

Palette Knife

Artistic filters *(continued)*

Original image

Plastic Wrap

Poster Edges

Rough Pastels

Smudge Stick

Sponge

Underpainting

Watercolor

Artistic Filters

Blur filters

Original image

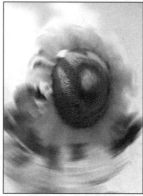

Radial Blur

Gaussian Blur (or Smart Blur)

Brush Strokes filters

Original image

Accented Edges

Angled Strokes

Crosshatch

Dark Strokes

Ink Outlines

Brush Strokes filters *(continued)*

Spatter

Sprayed Strokes

Sumi-e

Distort filters

Original image

Diffuse Glow

Glass (Blocks)

Ocean Ripple

Brush Strokes Filters; Distort Filters

Pixelate filters

Original image

Color Halftone

Crystallize

Mezzotint (Short Strokes)

Mezzotint (Medium Dots)

Pointillize

To learn about the Unsharp Mask filter, see our Visual QuickStart Guide to Photoshop CS2!

Sketch filters

Original image

Bas Relief

Chalk & Charcoal

Charcoal

Chrome

Conté Crayon

Graphic Pen

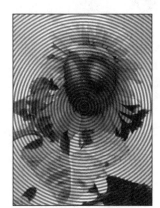

Halftone Pattern (Circle)

Halftone Pattern (Dot)

Sketch Filters

Sketch filters *(continued)*

Original image

Note Paper

Photocopy

Plaster

Reticulation

Stamp

Torn Edges

Water Paper

Sketch Filters

Stylize filter

Original image

Glowing Edges

Texture filters

Original image

Craquelure

Grain (Enlarged)

Grain (Horizontal)

Mosaic Tiles

Patchwork

Texture filters *(continued)*

Original image

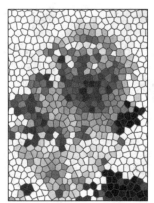

Stained Glass

Texturizer

Texture Filters

1 *The original 2D object*

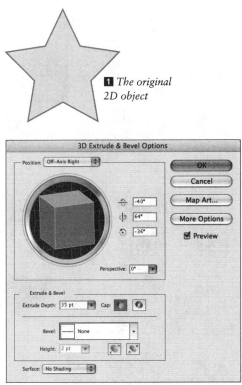

2 *Use the 3D Extrude & Bevel Options dialog box to choose depth, position, and perspective options; add beveling; and, after clicking More Options, choose Surface and Lighting options.*

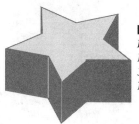

3 *Position: Off-Axis Right, Extrude Depth 35 pt, Surface: No Shading*

4 *Position: Isometric Top, Extrude Depth 35 pt, Surface: No Shading*

With very little effort, the **Extrude & Bevel, Revolve,** and **Rotate** effects on the Effect > 3D submenu let you make 2D (two-dimensional) objects, even type, look 3D (three-dimensional). You can bevel edges; change the perspective, lighting, surface reflectivity, and shadow color; and even map artwork onto your 3D objects.

Once applied, 3D effects are listed on the Appearance palette and can be edited or saved as styles for use with other objects, and removed at any time. To learn how to create and edit effects by using the Appearance palette, see pages 289–295.

Applying the Extrude & Bevel effect

The **Extrude & Bevel** effect makes an object look three-dimensional by adding depth along its z-axis (the axis that's perpendicular to the object's front surface). A solid (or hollow) appearance is achieved by capping (or uncapping) extruded objects. Bevels can be used to reshape an object's edges and to add facets.

To apply the Extrude & Bevel effect:

1. Select an object or editable type **1**.

2. Choose Effect > 3D > **Extrude & Bevel.** The 3D Extrude & Bevel Options dialog box opens **2**. Check Preview (this will prolong the rendering times between steps, but you can't judge the outcome otherwise).

3. *Optional:* Choose a preset from the **Position** pop-up menu **3**–**4**.

4. The front surface of the object is represented in the track cube by cyan, the sides by medium gray, the back by dark gray, and the top and bottom by light gray. To **rotate** the object, do any of the following:

   Drag any flat **surface** of the cube (four-way arrow pointer).

   Shift-drag to rotate the object around a fixed horizontal x- or vertical y-**axis.**

   To rotate the object on the global z-**axis,** drag inside the cyan ring that surrounds the cube.

(Continued on the following page)

Extrude & Bevel Effect

333

Extrude & Bevel Effect

To rotate the object on a **relative** axis, drag one of the edges of the cube (two-way arrow pointer). The highlight color on the edge represents the axis around which the object is rotating (red for *x*, green for *y*, and blue for *z).*

In the fields to the right of the track cube, enter how many **degrees** you want the object to be rotated from that axis.

5. To create one-point perspective (a single vanishing point), choose or enter a **Perspective** value (0–160°) **1**–**2**.

6. Change the **Extrude Depth** value (0–2000 pt) to adjust the depth of the object **3**. Try using a value below 100 at first.

    Click the **Cap On** button ● to create a solid object, or click the **Cap Off** button ● to create a hollow object.

7. To bevel the edges of the object, choose a design from the **Bevel** pop-up menu **4**–**5** and choose a **Height** value (1–100 pt) (use a low value).

    Click the **Bevel Extent Out** button ● to add the bevel onto the original shape, or the **Bevel Extent In** button ● to have Illustrator shrink the shape before applying the bevel.

8. *Optional:* To choose Surface options, click More Options, and see pages 338–339.

9. Click OK. To edit the Extrude & Bevel effect at any time, double-click the listing on the Appearance palette.

➤ You can create your own custom bevel shapes, to be listed on the Bevel pop-up menu. Open the Bevels.ai file (located in the Adobe Illustrator CS2 Plug-ins folder) and follow the instructions in the file.

➤ Separate objects can't share a common vanishing point, but you can group some 2D objects first, target the group, then apply the Extrude & Bevel effect, choosing a Perspective setting for the group.

1 *Perspective 30°*

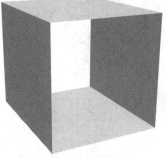

2 *Perspective 125°*

3 *Position: Custom Rotation, Extrude Depth 65 pt, Cap Off*

4 *The original editable type character*

5 *Position: Off-Axis Front, **Bevel**: Tall-Round, Bevel Extent In*

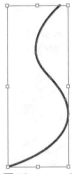

1 *The original object*

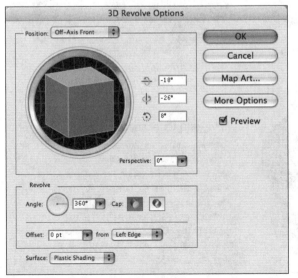

2 *After **revolving** the object around its Left Edge, Surface: Plastic Shading*

Applying the Revolve effect

The **Revolve** effect spins a path in a circular direction around a *y* (vertical) axis, and is useful for creating cylindrical shapes, such as spheres, chess pieces, vases, bottles, etc.

To apply the Revolve effect:

1. Select a closed object that has a fill color and a stroke of None, or an open path that has a stroke color and a fill of None **1**. The object will define the contour of the resulting symmetrical shape, and its stroke color will become the surface color of the 3D object. **2**.

2. Choose Effect > 3D > **Revolve.** The 3D Revolve Options dialog box opens **3**.

3. Check Preview.

4. Do any of the following:

   To rotate the track cube, follow step 4 on pages 333–334 **4**.

   Choose an **Angle** for the revolution (0–360°) by moving the dial or by entering a value.

   Click the **Cap On** button ⬡ to create a solid object or the **Cap Off** button ⬡ to

(Continued on the following page)

3 *The 3D Revolve Options dialog box*

4 *This diagram shows the relative x-y-z axes on the **track cube** that you see in all the 3D effect dialog boxes.*

Revolve Effect

create a hollow object (if it doesn't look hollow, try changing the Angle or Offset).

Choose an **Offset** value (0–1000 pt) to change the radius of revolution and thus widen (or narrow) the 3D object, and from the pop-up menu, choose whether the offset is measured from the **Left Edge** or **Right Edge** of the original object. For example, an elliptical path **1** revolved 360° around a *y*-axis along its left edge results in a doughnut, or torus shape **2**.

Optional: Choose a different Position preset. To choose Surface options, click More Options, and see pages 338–339.

5. Click OK.

➤ To revolve multiple objects around a common *y*–axis, you must group them first, then target the group. To learn how to apply effects to groups and layers, see page 310.

➤ If you revolve an open path that contains a fill color, the resulting object may be painted in unpredictable ways.

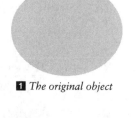

1 *The original object*

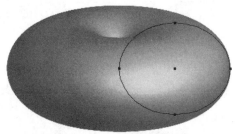

2 *After applying the Revolve effect, Offset from: Left Edge*

3 *A 3D Revolve object, with transparency*

Save your effects

Once a 3D effect is applied, it's listed as an attribute on the **Appearance** palette. Double-click the listing to reopen the dialog box and change the 3D settings. Effects are listed in the order in which they were applied, and can be restacked, edited, duplicated, or deleted. To save all the attribute(s) currently on the Appearance palette as a style, drag the icon from the top of the Appearance palette into the Graphic Styles palette (see pages 300–301).

Fresh start

To reset the settings in a 3D effect dialog box, hold down Option/Alt and click **Reset** (the Cancel button changes to Reset).

Revealing inner shapes

To create transparent surfaces through which hidden planes are visible, such as in the revolved object shown in **3**, create a two-dimensional object, then adjust its transparency by using the **Transparency** palette. Choose Object > Group, then apply the 3D Revolve effect to the targeted group. In the 3D Revolve Options dialog box, click More Options and check **Draw Hidden Faces** (see step 7 on page 339).

Building blocks

You can't merge 3D objects with one another (you can't, say, put a sphere partially inside a cube). You can, however, let 3D objects share the same axes of **revolution, lighting sources,** or **perspective** vanishing points. First group them or put them on the same layer, then apply the 3D effect to the targeted group or layer. Or to create intricate constructions, you could **stack** 3D shapes such as cylinders, cones, cubes, and spheres on the artboard like building blocks.

Applying the Rotate effect

You can use the **Rotate** effect to alter the perspective of a two-dimensional object in 3D space, as you might tilt a piece of paper. In other words, the object remains two-dimensional but is thrust into 3D space.

To apply the Rotate effect:

1. Select the object to be rotated **1**.

2. Choose Effect > 3D > **Rotate.** The 3D Rotate Options dialog box opens **2**.

3. Check Preview.

4. To rotate the track cube, follow step 4 on pages 333–334.

5. *Optional:* To preserve spot colors, click More Options, then check Preserve Spot Colors.

6. Click OK **3**. To edit the Rotate effect at any time, double-click the listing on the Appearance palette.

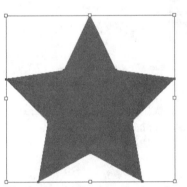

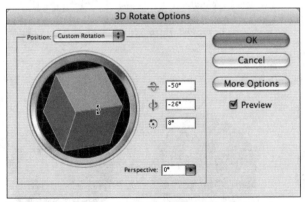

1 *The original object: a star-shaped path with a gray fill and no stroke*

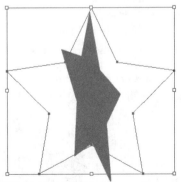

3 *After applying the **Rotate** effect, using the preset Off-Axis Right position*

2 *In the **Position** area of all the 3D effects dialog boxes, you can choose a Position preset, fiddle with the track cube, enter rotation values for each axis, and add one-point Perspective.*

Rotate Effect

Using the 3D Surface options

In the **Surface** area of the 3D Extrude & Bevel Options and 3D Revolve Options dialog boxes, you can choose a surface preset, edit lights on the lighting sphere, make lighting and surface texture adjustments, and adjust the shading color behavior and other options to change an object's appearance. For the Rotate effect, you can choose from a more limited number of surface options.

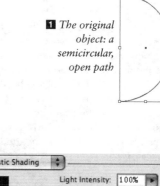

1 *The original object: a semicircular, open path*

To use the Surface options:

1. Select an object **1**, then apply an effect from the Effect > 3D submenu or double-click an existing 3D effect on the Appearance palette to reopen the dialog box. If the Surface options aren't showing in the dialog box, click **More Options**.

2. From the **Surface** pop-up menu, choose a rendering setting **2**: **Wireframe 3** shows the object's edges only; **No Shading 4** uses only the surface properties of the original 2D object; **Diffuse Shading 5** creates a soft light reflection; and **Plastic Shading 6** creates a highly reflective, glossy surface. In the 3D Rotate Options dialog box, you can choose only No Shading or Diffuse Shading.

2 *Choose **Surface** options in the 3D Extrude & Bevel Options and 3D Revolve Options dialog boxes.*

3. For the Diffuse Shading and Plastic Shading settings, you can change the lighting. Each light source appears on the **lighting sphere** as a white circle, changing to a circle in a black square when selected. Do any of the following:

   Drag a light to a new location.

   To move a selected light source to the back, click the **Move Selected Light to Back of Object** button. Click the button again to move the light to the front.

3 *This is after applying the **3D Revolve** effect using the Surface: Wireframe option (the object was revolved around its left edge).*

4 *Surface: No Shading*

5 *Surface: Diffuse Shading*

6 *Surface: Plastic Shading*

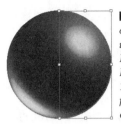

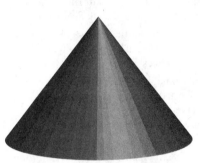

This is the last figure on the previous page after we lowered the Ambient Light to 20%, raised the Highlight Intensity to 100%, repositioned the first light, and added a second light in the lower rear.

*A revolved cone with a **Blend Steps** setting of 8*

*A revolved cone with a **Blend Steps** setting of 256*

To add a light source, click the **New Light** button.  Objects must have a minimum of one light source.

To delete a light, click on it, then click the **Delete Light** button.

4. On the right side of the dialog box, you can choose :

    A **Light Intensity** percentage to control the brightness of the currently selected light.

    An **Ambient Light** percentage to control the uniform brightness of all the surfaces.

    A **Highlight Intensity** percentage to control the object's reflectivity (not available for the Diffuse Shading setting).

    A **Highlight Size** percentage to control the size of all the highlight areas (not available for the Diffuse Shading setting).

5. Change the **Blend Steps** value (1–256) to control the shading on the object. Higher settings produce smoother shading and longer rendering times.

6. Choose a **Shading Color** option:

    None to use the object color for shading. Spot colors aren't affected.

    Black to apply only black ink over the original color for shading. This option preserves spot colors in objects and mapped artwork.

    Custom, click the swatch, then choose a shading color in the Color Picker.

7. Check **Preserve Spot Colors** to prevent spot colors in the object from being converted to process colors. This option disables the Custom shading option. Gradients in the object will be rasterized.

    Check **Draw Hidden Faces** to enable rendering of surfaces that, though normally hidden from view, may become visible in transparent or expanded objects (not available for the Wireframe setting).

8. Click OK.

Recolor the wireframe

To display a 3D object's wireframe outline in a color other than black, apply the 3D effect with Surface set to Wireframe, choose Object > **Expand Appearance,** then change the **stroke** color. The 3D effect will no longer be editable.

3D Surface Options

Mapping artwork to a 3D object

You can **map** any **artwork**—object, path, text, image, mesh object, or group that you've saved as a symbol—onto the surface of a **3D object**. The symbol instances remain editable and automatically update on the surfaces they're mapped to.

To map artwork to a 3D object:

1. Create and select a 3D object 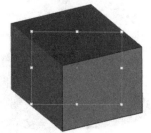, then double-click a 3D Extrude & Bevel or 3D Revolve effect on the Appearance palette to reopen the dialog box for that effect.

2. Click **Map Art.** The Map Art dialog box opens 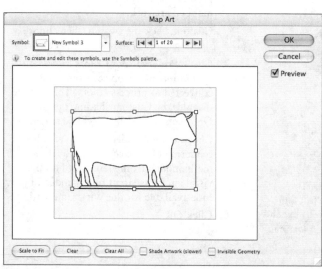. Check Preview.

3. Using the **Surface** arrow buttons or field, choose which surface of the object you want to map the symbol onto. Currently visible surfaces display as light gray, hidden surfaces as dark gray. If Preview is checked, the surface you chose will have a red wireframe in the document window. If you want to hide the object's fill, check **Invisible Geometry.**

4. From the **Symbol** pop-up menu, choose the artwork to be mapped. The symbols that are currently on the Symbols palette will be listed on the menu. (To learn how to create symbols, see page 420.)

5. *Do any of the following optional steps:*

   Reposition the symbol by dragging inside its bounding box.

   Scale the symbol by dragging a corner or side handle.

   Rotate the symbol by dragging outside its bounding box.

   To have the artwork conform to the shape of the surface, click **Scale to Fit.**

   To match the lighting and shading of the artwork to the surface onto which it's mapped, check **Shade Artwork (slower).**

   At any time, you can click Clear to remove artwork from the currently displayed surface or click Clear All to remove artwork from all surfaces.

6. Repeat steps 3–5 for any other surfaces. Click OK, then click OK again . *Note:* If you reshape a 3D object, any mapped artwork will be repositioned relative to the object's new center point. If you delete a side from the object, any artwork that was mapped to it will also be discarded.

1 *3D Extrude & Bevel applied to a rectangle*

2 *In the Map Art dialog box, choose a Symbol and a Surface*

3 *After using Map Art to apply symbols to the rectangle*

LIVE TRACING **21**

In this chapter you'll learn how use Illustrator's live tracing features to convert raster images into editable vector art, apply custom tracing settings before and after tracing, create tracing presets, release a tracing, expand a live tracing into separate paths, and convert a live tracing into a live paint group. A practice exercise is also included.

New chapter!

1 *The original **raster** image*

2 *After **tracing** the image*

3 *After **expanding** the tracing into separate objects (shown in Outline view)*

Using the live tracing features ⟨NEW⟩

Until now, if you wanted to convert a raster image (such as a Photoshop EPS, TIFF, JPEG, or PSD file) into editable path objects, you had to use a standalone tracing program, such as Adobe Streamline (which was long overdue for an overhaul) or use Illustrator's anemic Auto Trace tool. With the **Live Trace** command, you can perform usable tracings right in Illustrator.

You can choose custom tracing options prior to tracing, or because traced objects are "live," fine-tune your tracing afterward via the **Tracing Options** dialog box. You can use a built-in preset (set of presaved settings) as a starting point, or create and save your own presets. Among the numerous settings that you can specify are the number of anchor points used to define the image, the stroke weight and length, the number of colors, and a color palette for the resulting artwork. When you're done tracing an image, you can convert the results into editable paths or a live paint group **1**–**3**.

With such a wide range of tracing controls at your fingertips, you can produce everything from a close simulation of your original art-work (such as a logo) to a dramatic meta-morphosis (from a photograph). Regardless of the type of imagery you trace, the end result will be paths that contain a restricted range of fill colors, or just strokes, or both.

Tracing a raster image

In these instructions, you'll **trace** a raster **image** using **preset** settings. In the instructions that begin on the next page, you'll learn how to trace an image using custom settings, or apply custom settings to an existing live tracing.

After tracing the image, you can either convert the results into editable paths via the Expand command (see page 347) or convert the artwork to a live paint group (see page 348).

To trace a raster image:

1. Using File > **Open,** open a raster image, such as a TIFF, JPG, or PSD file; or with an Illustrator document open, use File > **Place** to place a raster image . *Note:* If you open or place a PSD (Photoshop) file that contains layers, the Photoshop Import Options dialog box will open. Click "Convert Photoshop layers to objects" to trace a particular layer, or "Flatten Photoshop layers to a single image" to trace the whole image.

2. Select the image that you want to trace.

3. To trace the object using preset settings, from the **Tracing presets and options** pop-up menu on the Control palette ▼ **2**–**3**, choose a preset based on how complex you want the end result to be. *or* To trace the object using the last-used (or default) settings, click **Live Trace** on the Control palette (or choose Object > Live Trace > Make). If an alert dialog box appears, click OK (some presets take much longer to process than others). A progress bar will appear onscreen as Illustrator traces the object.

   New options will appear on the Control palette.

4. *Optional:* To customize the tracing, follow the instructions on the next page.

1 *The original raster image (placed in an Illustrator document)*

ORIGINAL IMAGE © PHOTODISC

2 *Choose a tracing preset from the Control palette.*

Custom
[Default]
Color 6
Color 16
Photo Low Fidelity
Photo High Fidelity
Grayscale
Hand Drawn Sketch
Detailed Illustration
Comic Art
Technical Drawing
Black and White Logo
Inked Drawing
Type

Tracing Options...

3 *After choosing the [Default] tracing preset*

Applying tracing options

By choosing settings in the **Tracing Options** dialog box or the Control palette, you can make your live trace object conform more closely to the original artwork or you can simplify it dramatically. You may choose these options before or after your image is traced (remember, the tracing is live).

To apply tracing options:

1. *Optional:* To have Illustrator apply colors from a custom swatch palette to the resulting vector art, open the desired library palette via the Swatches palette menu.

2. To choose custom options prior to tracing, click an image, then from the **Tracing presets and options** pop-up menu 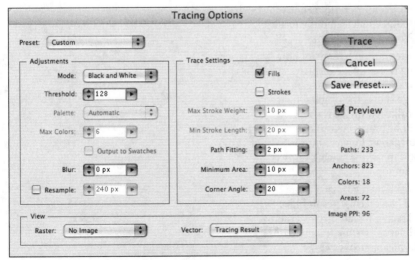 on the Control palette, choose **Tracing Options** (or choose Object > Live Trace > Tracing Options).

   or

   To apply custom options after tracing an image, with the tracing selected in your document, click the **Tracing options dialog** button on the Control palette.

   The Tracing Options dialog box opens **1**. Check Preview, then do any of the following steps.

3. Choose a different **Preset** (the same choices as on the Control palette).

4. Choose **Adjustments** options to control how Illustrator preps the image for tracing:

   From the **Mode** pop-up menu, choose Color, Grayscale, or Black and White, depending on how many colors you want the final tracing to contain.

   For Black and White mode only, choose a **Threshold** value (0–255; the default is 128). All pixels darker than this value will be converted to black; all pixels lighter than this value will be converted to white. You can also choose a Threshold value on the Control palette.

   For Grayscale or Color mode, from the **Palette** pop-up menu, choose Automatic

   (Continued on the following page)

1 *Choose custom settings in the **Tracing Options** dialog box.*

to have Illustrator use colors from the image for the tracing, or choose the name of any open swatch library to have the final tracing contain only colors from that library.

For Grayscale or Color mode only and for the Palette choice of Automatic, choose a **Max Colors** value for the maximum number of colors the final tracing may contain (2–256; the default is 6). Reducing the number of colors will speed up the tracing process and produce fewer fill areas. (You can also change the Max Colors value on the Control palette after exiting the dialog box.)

Click **Output to Swatches** to save the colors in the resulting tracing as new global swatches on the Swatches palette.

Choose a **Blur** value (0–20 pixels) to reduce artifacts, noise, and extraneous marks, and thus simplify the image for tracing.

Click **Resample** and change the resolution for tracing. A lower resolution will speed up the tracing process but also provide fewer image details, resulting in less precise outlines. Choose Vector: Tracing Result (see the next step) to verify the result.

5. In the **View** area, make choices from the Raster and Vector pop-up menus to compare the source image and the result (make sure **Preview** is checked!):

Choose a **Raster** option to control how the underlying raster image displays: **No Image** hides the original image; **Original Image** shows the original image unchanged; **Adjusted Image** shows how the image will be preprocessed for tracing; and **Transparent Image** dims the image so you can see the tracing results more clearly on top.

Vector controls how the tracing results are displayed: **No Tracing Result** hides the tracing; **Tracing Result** displays the tracing; **Outlines** shows the tracing paths only, without fills or strokes **1**–**2**;

1 *View choices of* **Raster: Original Image** *and* **Vector: Outlines**

2 *View choices of* **Raster: No Image** *and* **Vector: Outlines**

Tracing Options

and **Outlines with Tracing** displays the resulting paths on top of a dimmed version of the resulting fills and strokes.

View settings can also be chosen via the **Preview different views of the raster image** ▲ and **Preview different view of the vector result** △ pop-up menus on the Control palette ❶, and from the Object > **Live Trace** submenu.

➤ To see how Illustrator will lower the number of tonal values in an image for tracing, choose Raster: Adjusted Image and Vector: No Tracing Result.

6. Use the **Trace Settings** options to control how the image will be converted into vector art:

➤ As you choose Adjustments and Trace Settings, monitor the number of Paths, Anchors, Colors, Areas, and Image PPI (pixels per inch) in the resulting art-work via the readouts in the lower right corner of the dialog box.

For Black and White mode only, check **Fills** to create filled paths and/or **Strokes** to create stroked paths.

If Strokes is checked, specify a **Max Stroke Weight** value (0–100 px; the default is 10). Areas at or below this width will become strokes; areas wider than this value will become outlined areas.

If Strokes is checked, specify a **Min Stroke Length** value (0–200 px; the default is 20). Areas this length or longer will be converted to strokes; areas shorter than this length will be ignored.

Specify a **Path Fitting** value to control how closely traced paths will follow the edges of shapes in the image (0–10 px; the default is 2). A low Path Fitting value will yield a more accurate fit but will also produce more anchor points.

Change the **Minimum Area** setting to minimize the number of extraneous small path objects. Specify the smallest area that you will permit the program to trace (0–3000 pixels squared). For example, a 5 x 5 pixel object would occupy a 25-pixel area. (You can also change the **Min Area** value on the Control palette after exiting the dialog box.)

Choose a **Corner Angle** for the minimum angle a path must have to be defined by a corner anchor point (rather than a smooth anchor point) (0–180°; the default is 20°) .

7. *Optional:* If you save your settings as a preset, you'll be able to apply them to any image or use them as a starting point when choosing custom settings. Click **Save Preset,** type a name for the preset, then click OK. (Views and Resampling settings aren't saved.) Saved presets can be chosen from the Preset pop-up menu on the Control palette when a raster image or live trace object is selected, and from the Preset pop-up menu in the Tracing Options dialog box.

8. Click **Trace.** A progress bar will appear onscreen as Illustrator traces the image, then a single Tracing listing will appear on the Layers palette. If you're happy with the results, you can either expand the tracing into editable paths (see page 347), or convert it into a live paint group (see page 348).

❸ *The **Control** palette when a traced image is selected (with the Tracing Options dialog box closed)*

Managing tracing presets

You can use the **Tracing Presets** dialog box to create, edit, delete, import, or export custom tracing presets.

To create, delete, edit, import, or export a tracing preset:

1. Choose Edit > **Tracing Presets.** The Tracing Presets dialog box opens 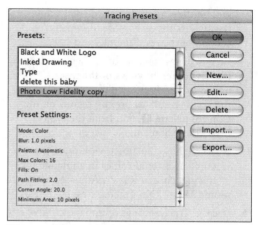.

2. To create a new preset based on the default settings, click **New.** The Tracing Options dialog box opens. Enter a name, choose settings, then click Done.

   To create a new preset based on an existing one, click a preset on the **Presets** scroll list, click **New,** enter a name, choose settings, then click Done.

   To edit the preset, click **Edit.** The Tracing Options dialog box opens. Choose settings, then click Done.

   To import preset settings, click **Import,** locate the desired presets file, then click Open.

   To export the current settings to a file, click **Export,** choose a location, then click Save.

3. Click OK.

1 *Use the* **Tracing Presets** *dialog box to create, edit, delete, import, or export tracing presets (settings).*

Releasing a live tracing

Clicking Cancel in the Tracing Options dialog box cancels only changes made in that dialog box. To restore a tracing to its virgin bitmap state, use the **Release** command as per the instructions below.

To release a live trace object:

1. Select the live trace object.

2. Choose Object > Live Trace > **Release.** The listing on the Layers palette will change from Tracing to Image.

Tracing Presets; Release Live Tracing

1 *The tracing* **expanded** *(shown in Outline view)*

2 *The* **expanded** *objects (shown in Preview view)*

3 *After* **recoloring** *some of the expanded objects*

Expanding a live tracing

The **Expand** command converts a live tracing into standard paths that can be selected via the Layers palette and recolored, reshaped, transformed, etc. You can use the Expand command after tracing, or you can trace and expand an image in one quick step (see the next set of instructions). Once you expand a tracing, it's no longer "live," meaning you can't adjust its Tracing Options settings.

To expand a live trace object:

1. Select the live trace object.

2. To expand the tracing, on the Control palette, click **Expand** (or choose Object > Live Trace > Expand) **1**–**3**.
   or
   To convert the tracing to paths based on the current view options, choose Object > Live Trace > **Expand as Viewed.** For example, if the current view choice is Vector: Outlines with Tracing, the resulting paths will have a fill and stroke of None. In any case, the result will be a group of paths from the tracing outlines, separate from the original placed image.

   On the Layers palette, you'll see a group containing a gazillion paths (or maybe fewer, depending on the tracing settings used).

When you **trace and expand** an image in one step, the default tracing settings are applied.

To trace and expand an image in one step:

1. Open a raster image via File > Open, or use File > Place to place a raster image into an Illustrator document, then select the image.

2. Choose Object > Live Trace > **Make and Expand.**

Trace and Expand

Converting a tracing to a live paint group

Follow these instructions to **convert** a live trace object to a **live paint group** (see Chapter 13). This is a good route to take if your tracing is relatively simple and you want to utilize such live paint features as the ability to hide or recolor edges or the ability to quickly recolor faces (fill areas).

To convert a live trace object to a live paint group:

1. Select the live trace object.

2. On the Control palette, click **Live Paint** (or choose Object > Live Trace > Convert to Live Paint).

To trace and convert an image to a live paint group in one step:

1. Open a raster image via File > Open, or use File > Place to place a raster image into an Illustrator document, and select the image 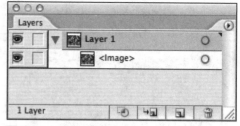.

2. Choose Object > Live Trace > **Make and Convert to Live Paint**.

1 *The original raster image*

Paleolithic tracing

If you want to trace an image manually, first place it into your Illustrator document. Double-click the new layer, and in the Layer Options dialog box, click **Template** to dim the placed image on the layer and make it uneditable. Create a new layer above the template layer, then with any drawing tool, such as the Pencil or Pen, trace the image.

(side tab) Tracing to Live Paint Group

ORIGINAL IMAGE © PHOTODISC

1 *The original placed image*

2 *The image traced using the **Photo Low Fidelity** preset (Max Colors 28; Minimum Area 87)*

Exercise

In this practice exercise, you'll trace a photograph of an object on a blank background.

Trace an object

1. Place a bitmap image into an Illustrator document **1**, and keep it selected (a product shot would be a good choice for this exercise).

2. From the **Tracing presets and options** pop-up menu on the Control palette, choose **Tracing Options.** The Tracing Options dialog box opens.

3. From the **Preset** pop-up menu, choose **Photo Low Fidelity.**

4. Set the **Max Colors** value to 30. The lower the Max Colors value, the fewer the number of areas and the simpler the trace. Check Preview.

5. To preview the tracing lines, choose **Outlines** from the **Vector** pop-up menu.

6. To add more tracing lines, raise the **Max Colors** value to 50 and lower the **Minimum Area** value to 4. Or to remove tracing lines, lower the Max Colors value to 10–16 and raise the Minimum Area value to 100.

7. Click **Trace 2**.

8. On the Control palette, click **Expand.**

9. *Optional:* To remove the fill colors and produce a line art tracing, keep the expanded objects selected. Via the Control palette, choose a Fill of None, a Stroke of black, and a Stroke Weight of .5 or .3 pt (**1**, next page). Also, zoom in and delete any stray or extraneous paths.

(Continued on the following page)

Exercise: Trace an Object

Simple or complex?

One way to control the complexity of a color tracing is by adjusting the **Max Colors, Path Fitting,** and **Minimum Area** options in the **Tracing Options** dialog box.

To produce a simple tracing, in the Tracing Options dialog box, check Resample and enter a value of 72 px, and choose Mode: Color, Max Colors 10–16, Path Fitting 4–6, and Minimum Area 200–300.

For a more complex color tracing, place a 150–200 ppi color image (or in the Tracing Options dialog box, check Resample and enter a value of 150–200 px). Choose Mode: Color, Max Colors 50–64, Path Fitting 1–2, and Minimum Area 5–10.

1 *The same tracing after applying a Fill of None and a Stroke of black*

➤ To produce **2**–**3**, from the Preset pop-up menu in the Tracing Options dialog box, we chose Technical Drawing, then adjusted the Threshold value (you could lower the Threshold value to trace dark shapes or raise it to trace lighter shapes). We think the method on the previous page produced superior results.

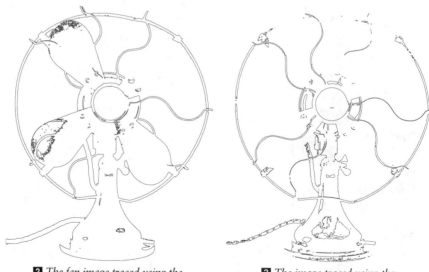

2 *The fan image traced using the* ***Technical Drawing*** *preset at a* ***Threshold*** *value of 170*

3 *The image traced using the same preset at a* ***Threshold*** *value of 78*

In this chapter you'll learn how to use the Paintbrush tool; embellish path edges with shapes, objects, and textures using Calligraphic, Scatter, Art, and Pattern brushes; create and edit custom brushes; add, modify, and remove brush strokes from existing paths; open and create brush libraries; and duplicate, move, and delete brushes from the Brushes palette.

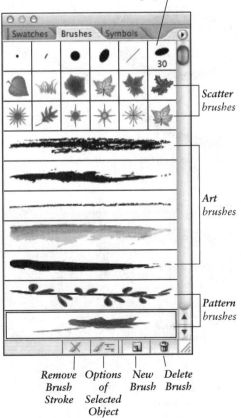

Calligraphic brushes

Scatter brushes

Art brushes

Pattern brushes

Remove Brush Stroke Options of Selected Object New Brush Delete Brush

1 To open/close the **Brushes** palette, press F5 or click the brush thumbnail or arrow-head ● ▾ on the **Control** palette. **NEW**

Using brushes

Illustrator's **brushes** let you draw variable, freehand brush strokes or apply a pattern or objects to a path with all the advantages of vector graphics—small file sizes, resizability, and crisp output.

The brushes come in four flavors: **Scatter, Calligraphic, Art,** and **Pattern,** and they're stored on and accessed from the **Brushes** palette (F5) **1**. (Note that the default Brushes palette contains only a few calligraphic and art brushes, but we'll show you how to add more.)

To apply a brush stroke, you can either choose the Paintbrush tool and a brush and draw a shape right off the bat with a brush stroke built into it, or you can apply a brush stroke to an existing path. To change the contour of a brush stroke, you reshape the path it's attached to with a tool, such as Reshape, Pencil, Smooth, Erase, Add Anchor Point, or Convert Anchor Point.

Brushes are also live, meaning that if you edit a brush being used in your document, you'll be given the option via an alert dialog box to update those paths with the revised brush. You can also create your own brushes.

To start you off, grab the Paintbrush tool, click a brush on the Brushes palette, and draw some shapes (see the instructions on the next page).

Using Brushes

Using the Paintbrush tool

If you use a stylus and a pressure-sensitive tablet, the **Paintbrush** tool will respond to pressure. The harder you press on the tablet, the wider the shape or stroke.

To draw with the Paintbrush tool:

1. Choose the **Paintbrush** tool (B), and choose a fill color of None.

2. Show the **Brushes** palette (press F5 or click the Brush thumbnail or arrowhead **NEW** on the Control palette), then click any type of brush on the palette.

3. To draw open paths, draw freehand lines **1**–**2**. Or to draw a closed path, drag to draw the path, then Option-drag/Alt-drag to close it (release Option/Alt last).

➤ To reshape the path, use the Pencil, Paintbrush, or Direct Selection tool (see Chapter 12).

Preferences you choose for the **Paintbrush** tool affect only future (not existing) brush strokes. You'll learn how to choose options for individual brushes later in this chapter.

To choose preferences for the Paintbrush tool:

1. Double-click the **Paintbrush** tool (or choose the tool, then press Return/Enter).

2. Choose a **Fidelity** value (0.5–20 pixels) **3**. A low Fidelity setting produces many anchor points and paths that accurately follow the movement of your mouse; a high setting produces fewer anchor points and smoother but less accurate paths.

3. Choose a **Smoothness** value (0–100%). The higher the Smoothness, the fewer the irregularities in the path.

4. Check any of the following **Options:**

   Fill new brush strokes to have new paths fill with the current fill color.

   Keep Selected to have paths stay selected after you draw them for immediate reshaping with the same tool.

   Edit Selected Paths, and choose a range (2–20 pixels) within which selected paths can be reshaped by the tool (see page 159).

5. Click OK.

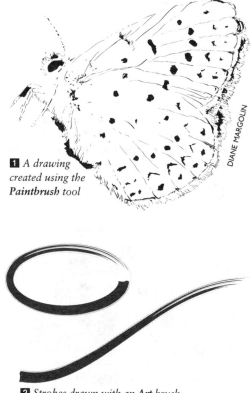

1 *A drawing created using the Paintbrush tool*

DIANE MARGOLIN

2 *Strokes drawn with an Art brush*

3 *Choose settings for the **Paintbrush** in its own preferences dialog box.*

Scatter or pattern?

On the surface, the Pattern and Scatter brushes may appear similar, but they have different reasons for being. Via the Brush Options dialog box, you can specify how random you want the size, spacing, and scatter variables to be for a **Scatter** brush, but not for a Pattern brush. **Pattern** brushes, on the other hand, are made from up to five tiles: Side, Outer Corner, Inner Corner, Start, and End, and are good for creating borders or frames because they fit more tightly on a path than Scatter brushes.

1 *Select a path...*

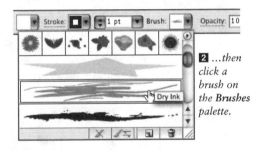

2 *...then click a brush on the* **Brushes** *palette.*

3 *The* **Calligraphic** *brush stroke appears on the path.*

Applying brushes

You'll learn how to create and modify Scatter, Calligraphic, Art, and Pattern brushes later in this chapter. In these instructions, you'll learn the first step: how to **apply** a **brush** to an existing **path**.

To apply a brush to a path:

1. Display the **Brushes** palette (press F5 or click the Brush thumbnail or arrowhead on the Control palette).

2. Select a path of any kind with any selection tool **1**, then **click** a brush on the **Brushes** palette **2**–**7**. You can apply a brush to a type path.
   or
   Drag a brush from the **Brushes** palette onto a path or type (the object doesn't have to be selected). Release the mouse when the pointer is over the object.

➤ If you scale an object that has a brush stroke and Scale Strokes & Effects is checked in the Scale dialog box (double-click the Scale tool) or in Preferences (Cmd-K/Ctrl-K) > General, the brush stroke will scale accordingly. With this option unchecked, a brush stroke will stay the same size when an object is scaled.

➤ To select all the paths in your document that have brush strokes (except type paths, for some reason), choose Select > Object > Brush Strokes. If you then click a brush on the Brushes palette, it will be applied to all the selected objects.

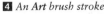

4 *An Art brush stroke*

6 *Another* **Scatter** *brush stroke (made from five birds)*

5 *A Scatter brush stroke*

7 *A Pattern brush stroke*

Using the Brushes palette

Once you open a brush library, you can apply a brush from that library directly to any path, or you can **add brushes** from the **library** to the **Brushes palette** so they'll save with your document.

You can use any brush from a library as the starting point for creating a custom brush. After adding it to your document's Brushes palette (instructions below), you can duplicate it, if desired, and then customize it.

To add brushes from other libraries:

1. From the **Open Brush Library** submenu on the Brushes palette menu, choose a library name.
   or
   Choose a library name from the Window > **Brush Libraries** submenu.
   or
   To open a library that isn't in the Adobe Illustrator CS2/Presets/Brushes folder, from the bottom of the Brushes palette menu, choose Open Brush Library > **Other Library,** locate and highlight the desired library, then click Open.

2. Deselect all the objects in your document (Cmd-Shift-A/Ctrl-Shift-A).

3. **Click** a brush in the library; it will appear on the Brushes palette.
   or
   Shift-click or Cmd-click/Ctrl-click multiple brushes in the library, then choose **Add To Brushes** from the library menu **1**–**2**.
   or
   Drag a brush directly from the library onto any object in the document window (the object doesn't have to be selected). The brush stroke will appear on the object and the brush will appear on the Brushes palette.

➤ To delete brushes from the Brushes palette, see page 368.

➤ To close a library that isn't in a palette group, click its close box. To close a library in a group, drag its tab out of the group, then click its close box.

Be persistent

Normally, open libraries don't reopen when you relaunch Illustrator, which can be irritating when you want to keep a library readily accessible. To force a particular library to reopen when you relaunch the program, choose **Persistent** from the library menu. To save brushes with your document, follow the instructions at left.

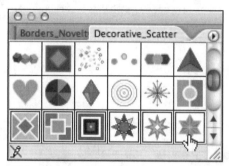

1 To append multiple brushes, select them, then choose **Add To Brushes** from the library menu.

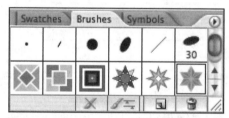

2 The brushes appear on the **Brushes** palette in the current document.

Where are they?

Type	Library
Calligraphic	Artistic_Calligraphic
Scatter	Arrow_Standard, Artistic_Ink, Decorative_Scatter
Art	Arrow_Standard, all the "Artistic" libraries except _Calligraphic, Decorative_Banners and Seals, Decorative_Text Dividers
Pattern	All the "Borders" libraries

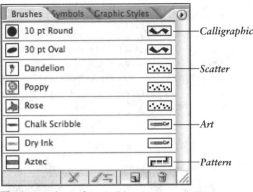

─Calligraphic

─Scatter

─Art

─Pattern

1 *The Brushes palette in* **List** *view*

2 *The original object with a* **brush stroke**

3 *The brush stroke is* **removed** *from the object.*

4 *The original* **brush stroke** *on an object*

5 *The* **Expand Appearance** *command converted the brush stroke into an object, which is now separate from the original path (we ungrouped the stroke and object and moved them apart).*

To choose Brushes palette display options:

From the **Brushes** palette menu:

Choose **List View** to have a small thumbnail, brush name, and icon for the brush type (Calligraphic, Scatter, Art, or Pattern) display for each brush on the palette **1**; or **Thumbnail View** to display larger thumbnails with no name or icon.

To control which **brush types** (categories) display on the palette, choose a brush type (Show...) to check or uncheck that option.

➤ You can drag any brush upward or downward on the palette to a different location within its category. To move multiple brushes, select them first (click, then Shift-click consecutive brushes or Cmd-click/Ctrl-click individual brushes; you can't do this if you open the Brushes palette via the Control palette).

Removing brush strokes

When you **remove a brush stroke** from a path, you're left with a plain vanilla path.

To remove a brush stroke from an object:

1. Select the object or objects from which you want to remove a brush stroke **2**.
2. Click the **Remove Brush Stroke** button ✗ at the bottom of the Brushes palette **3**.

Expanding brush strokes

When you **expand a brush stroke,** it's converted into editable outlined paths—a brush stroke-like shape that you can reshape as you would a normal path. It will no longer function as a live brush stroke, though, meaning you won't be able to switch it to another brush via the Brushes palette or update its shape by editing the brush.

To expand a brush stroke into outlined paths:

1. Select an object that has a brush stroke **4**.
2. Choose Object > **Expand Appearance.** The brush stroke is now a separate object or objects **5**. The paths will be nested (or double- or triple-nested) in a group sublayer on the Layers palette.

Creating and editing Scatter brushes

In this section, we'll show you how to modify each type of brush, starting with Scatter brushes.

Objects from a Scatter brush are placed evenly or randomly along the contour of a path. You can **create** a **Scatter brush** from an open or closed path, type character, type outline, blend, or compound path, but not from a gradient, bitmap image (placed or rasterized), mesh, or clipping mask.

To create or edit a Scatter brush:

1. To create a new brush, select one or more objects **1**, click the **New Brush** button on the Brushes palette, click **New Scatter Brush,** then click OK.
    or
    To modify, or create a variation on, an existing Scatter brush, deselect, then **double-click** the brush on the Brushes palette. Or click a brush, then choose Brush Options from the palette menu.

2. The Scatter Brush Options dialog box opens **2**. If you're creating a new brush or a variation on an existing brush, enter a new name. To edit an existing brush, leave the name as is.

3. Check Preview (available only for existing brushes) to view changes on any paths where the brush is currently being used.

4. For Size, Spacing, Scatter, and Rotation, from the pop-up menu, choose one of the following variations:

    Fixed to use a single, fixed value.

    Random, then move the sliders (or enter different values in the two fields) to define a range within which that property can vary.

NEW If you're using a graphics tablet, choose **Pressure, Stylus Wheel Tilt, Bearing, or Rotation.** Move the sliders (or enter different values in the two fields) to define a range within which that property can respond to stylus pressure. Light pressure uses the minimum property value from

Duped again

To create a variation of an existing brush of any type, either change the **name** in the Options dialog box (step 2 at left), or **duplicate** it first by following the instructions on page 361. To create a variation of a brush in a library, add the brush to the Brushes palette first.

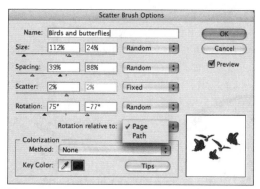

DIANE MARGOLIN

1 *The original objects*

2 *Preview is available in the* **Scatter Brush Options** *dialog box only if the brush is currently being used in your document.*

1 *The new Scatter brush applied to a path*

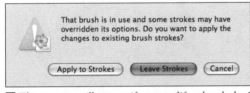

2 *The same Scatter brush after moving the Size sliders apart (Random setting)*

3 *This prompt will appear if you modify a brush that's currently in use on objects in your file.*

4 *The "Confetti" Scatter brush, from the Decorative_Scatter brush library, applied to a path*

5 *After raising the Size, Spacing, and Rotation values in the Scatter Brush Options dialog box*

the left field; heavy pressure uses the maximum property value from the right field.

The following is a description of the **properties:**

Size controls the size of the scatter objects.

Spacing controls the spacing between the scatter objects.

Scatter controls the distance between the objects and the path. When Fixed is chosen as the Scatter setting, a positive value places all the objects on one side of the path, and a negative value places all the objects on the opposite side of the path. The further the Scatter value is from 0%, the less closely the objects will adhere to the path shape.

Rotation controls how much objects can rotate relative to the page or the path. Choose **Page** or **Path** from the **Rotation relative to** pop-up menu for the axis of rotation.

5. For the **Colorization** options, see the sidebar on page 361.

6. Click OK **1**–**2**. If the brush is being used in the document, an alert dialog box will appear **3**. Click **Apply to Strokes** to update those objects with the revised brush, or click **Leave Strokes** to leave the existing objects unchanged.

➤ Shift-drag a slider in the Scatter Brush Options dialog box to move its counterpart gradually along with it. Option-drag/Alt-drag a slider to simultaneously move it and its counterpart toward or away from each other from the center.

➤ To orient the scatter objects uniformly along a path, set Scatter and Rotation to Fixed, set Scatter to 0°, and choose Rotation relative to: Path **4**–**5**.

Create, Edit Scatter Brush

Creating and editing Calligraphic brushes

Calligraphic brush strokes vary in thickness as you draw, as in traditional calligraphy.

To create or edit a Calligraphic brush:

1. To create a new Calligraphic brush, click the **New Brush** button ⬛ on the Brushes palette, click **New Calligraphic Brush** (the default setting), then click OK.
   or
   To modify or create a variation on an existing brush, deselect all objects, then **double-click** the brush on the Brushes palette **1**.

2. The Calligraphic Brush Options dialog box opens **2**. If you're creating a new brush or a variation on an existing brush, enter a new name. To edit an existing brush, leave the name as is.

3. Check Preview (available only for existing brushes) to view changes on any paths where the brush is being used. The brush shape will also preview in the dialog box.

4. For **Angle, Roundness,** and **Diameter,** from the pop-up menu, choose one of the following variations:

   Fixed to keep the value constant.

1 *Double-click a brush on the Brushes palette.*

2 *Use the Calligraphic Brush Options dialog box to adjust the settings for a new or existing brush.*

Create, Edit Calligraphic Brush

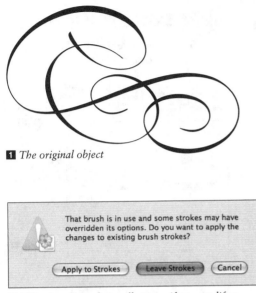

1 *The original object*

That brush is in use and some strokes may have overridden its options. Do you want to apply the changes to existing brush strokes?

Apply to Strokes   Leave Strokes   Cancel

2 *This alert dialog box will appear if you modify a brush that's currently in use.*

3 *The brush Angle and Diameter were edited in the Calligraphic Brush Options dialog box, then **Apply to Strokes** was clicked when the prompt appeared, causing the brush strokes to update on the object.*

Random, then move the Variation slider to define a range within which that brush attribute value can vary. A stroke can range between the value specified for angle, roundness, or diameter, plus or minus the Variation value. For example, a 50° angle with a Random Variation value of 10 could have an angle anywhere between 40° and 60°.

If you're using a graphics tablet, choose **Pressure, Stylus Wheel, Tilt, Bearing, NEW** or **Rotation.** Move the Variation slider to define a range within which the brush attribute can respond to pressure from a stylus. Light pressure produces a brush attribute based on the angle, roundness, or diameter value minus the Variation value; heavy pressure produces a brush attribute based on the specified value plus the Variation value.

5. Enter an **Angle** (−180° to 180°) or drag the gray arrowhead in the preview box to control the thickness of the horizontals and verticals in the stroke. A 0° angle will produce a thin horizontal stroke and a thick vertical stroke; a 90° angle will produce the opposite result.

6. Enter a **Roundness** value (0–100%), or reshape the tip by dragging either black dot inward or outward on the ellipse.

7. For the brush size, enter a **Diameter** value (0–1296 pt) or drag the slider.

8. Click OK. If the brush is already in use in the document, an alert dialog box will appear **1**–**2**. Click **Apply to Strokes** to update the existing strokes with the revised brush **3**, or click **Leave Strokes** to leave existing strokes unchanged.

Create, Edit Calligraphic Brush

Creating and editing Art brushes

An **Art brush** can be made from one or more objects, even a compound path, but not from a gradient, mask, mesh, or bitmap image. When applied to a path, an Art brush stroke will conform to the path. If you reshape the path, the Art brush stroke will stretch or bend to fit the new path contour (fun!).

To create or edit an Art brush:

1. To create a new brush, select one or more objects 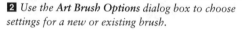, click the **New Brush** button 🔲 on the Brushes palette, click **New Art Brush** in the New Brush dialog box, then click OK.
   or
   To modify, or create a variation on, an existing brush, deselect all objects, then **double-click** the brush on the Brushes palette. Or click an Art brush, then choose **Brush Options** from the palette menu.

2. The Art Brush Options dialog box opens **2**. If you're creating a new brush or a variation on an existing brush, enter a new name. Or to edit an existing brush, leave the name as is.

3. Check Preview (available only for existing brushes) to view changes on any paths where the brush is being used.

4. Click a **Direction** button to control the orientation of the object on the path. The object will be drawn in the direction the arrow is pointing. The direction will be more obvious for objects that have a distinct directional orientation, such as text outlines, or for recognizable objects, such as a tree or building.

5. Enter a **Size: Width** to scale the brush. Check **Proportional** to preserve the proportions of the original object as you change its size.

6. *Optional:* Check Flip Along to reverse the object on the path (left to right) and/or check Flip Across to reverse the object across the path (up and down).

7. Choose a **Colorization** option (see the sidebar on the following page).

8. Click OK **3**–**4**.

1 *To create an **Art** brush, select an object (or objects).*

2 *Use the **Art Brush Options** dialog box to choose settings for a new or existing brush.*

3 *The original object*

4 *After applying the new Art brush*

Create, Edit Art Brush

The Colorization options

From the **Colorization: Method** pop-up menu (available for all brush types except Calligraphic), you can choose any of these options to change the colors the brush will paint with:

None to leave the colors unchanged.

Tints to change black areas in the brush stroke to the current stroke color at 100% and non-black areas to tints of the current stroke color. White areas stay white. Use for grayscale or spot colors.

Tints and Shades to change colors in the brush stroke to tints of the current stroke color. Black and white areas stay the same.

Hue Shift to apply the current stroke color to areas that contain the most frequently used color on the object (called the key color) and to change other colors in the brush stroke to related hues. Use for multicolored brushes.

If you're editing the brush itself (not a brush stroke), you can click the **Key Color** eyedropper, then click a color in the preview area of the dialog box to change the key color.

To learn more, click **Tips** in the Stroke Options dialog box **1**.

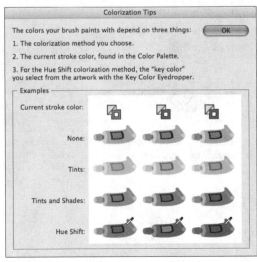

1 *Click Tips in any Brush Options dialog box to open this* **Colorization Tips** *dialog box.*

Duplicating brushes

Using the **Duplicate Brush** command, you can create a variation of an existing brush—a slimmer or fatter version, for example.

To duplicate a brush:

1. Deselect all objects, then click the brush you want to duplicate **2**. (To create a variation from a brush in a library, first add the brush to the Brushes palette.)

2. Choose **Duplicate Brush** from the palette menu.
or
Drag the selected brush over the **New Brush** button. **▣**

The word "copy" will be appended to the brush name **3**. To modify the brush, see the individual instructions for that brush type later in this chapter.

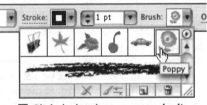

2 *Click the brush you want to* **duplicate.**

3 *The duplicate brush appears after the last brush icon in the same category.*

Creating and editing Pattern brushes

Pattern brushes render patterns along the edge of a closed or open path, and are good for creating custom frames and borders. You can use up to five different-shaped tile pieces when you create a path pattern: a side tile, an outer corner tile, an inner corner tile, a start tile, and an end tile. Each type of tile adapts to fit its assigned location on the path.

The first step is to **draw shapes** to be used for the **five different types of tiles** and save them to the Swatches palette. Then, in the instructions on the next page, you'll turn your swatches into pattern tiles.

To create swatches for a Pattern brush:

1. Draw path shapes for the side pattern tile (no gradients, meshes, bitmap images, type, or masks). Try to limit the overall design to approximately 1 inch wide, 2 inches at the most. You can resize the tile later via the Pattern Brush Options dialog box.

2. Because side tiles in Pattern brushes are placed perpendicular to the path, you should rotate any design that's taller than it is wide. To do this, choose the Selection tool, select the shapes for the side tile, double-click the Rotate tool, enter 90° for the Angle, then click OK.

3. Draw separate shapes for the outer corner, inner corner, start, and end tiles **1**, if necessary, to complete the overall pattern. The corner tile design should form a square, and should be exactly the same height as the side tile design.

4. Choose the **Selection** tool, then select one of the designs that you created in the previous step. Group the shapes, if desired.

5. Drag the selection onto the **Swatches** palette **2** (not the Brushes palette!), then deselect the objects.

6. Double-click the new swatch. The Swatch Options dialog box opens **3**. Enter a **Swatch Name.** We recommend typing words such as "side," "outer," "start," and "end" after the swatch name to help you remember its function. Click OK.

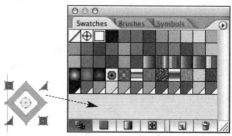

Start tile   *Side tile*   *Outer corner tile*

1 *Four tiles for a Pattern brush*

End tile

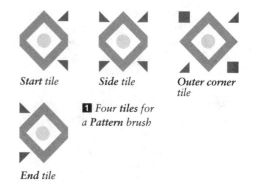

2 *Drag the tile shapes onto the Swatches palette.*

Swatch Options

Swatch Name: zag border.side

Color Type: Process Color

☐ Global

Color Mode:

C ——— 0 %
M ——— 0 %
Y ——— 0 %
K ——— 0 %

☐ Preview

OK   Cancel

3 *Use the Swatch Options dialog box to name the swatch that will be used as a pattern tile.*

Speedy recoloring

Apply **global** process fill and stroke colors to your pattern tile shapes, and name the colors appropriately so they can be readily associated with each tile. Then, to recolor the tiles, all you have to do is modify the global process colors.

Side tile *Outer corner tile* *Inner corner tile* *Start tile* *End tile*

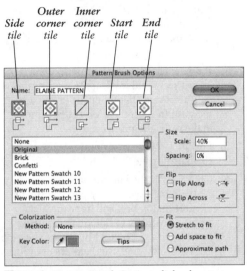

1 *Use the* **Pattern Brush Options** *dialog box to turn swatches into* **tiles**.

2 *The pattern tiles made into a Pattern brush and then applied to an oval path*

7. Repeat steps 4 through 6 for the other four tile types.

8. Follow the next set of instructions to turn the new swatches into a Pattern brush.

➤ When applied to a path, corner tiles will be rotated 90° to follow the path at each point where the path direction changes, starting after the one in the upper left corner.

➤ To make geometric shapes look more hand-drawn, before turning shapes into a Pattern brush, apply Effect > Distort & Transform > Roughen at low Size and Detail settings.

To create a Pattern brush:

1. Create tiles for the Pattern brush by following the previous set of instructions.

2. Click the **New Brush** button ▣ on the Brushes palette, click **New Pattern Brush** in the New Brush dialog box, then click OK.

3. Enter a **Name** for the pattern.

4. At the top of the dialog box, click a **tile** button (e.g., Side tile, Outer corner tile), then click a pattern name on the scroll list below **1**. All the pattern tiles on the Swatches palette will be listed there.

Repeat for any other tiles that you want to create. To distinguish one tile type from another, either look at the icons under the buttons or use tool tips. To assign no pattern for a tile type, click the tile button, then click None. When designing a pattern for an elliptical path, you need to assign only a side tile.

5. Click OK. Now, via the Brushes palette, you can apply the brush to a path **2**. To edit a Pattern brush, follow the instructions on the next page.

➤ If you reshape a path that has a Pattern brush stroke, the pattern will reshape along with the path, and corner and side tiles will be added or removed as needed.

➤ Effect menu commands can be applied to objects that have Pattern brush strokes. You can have some fun with this.

To edit a Pattern brush:

1. Deselect all objects. Then, on the **Brushes** palette, double-click the **Pattern** brush you want to modify (or click a Pattern brush, then choose Brush Options from the palette menu). The Pattern Brush Options dialog box opens **1**.

2. Check Preview, if available, to preview changes on paths where the Pattern brush is currently being used.

3. To assign a different swatch pattern to a tile, click a **tile** button, then click a name on the scroll list (this change won't preview). Repeat for other tile buttons, if desired. To assign no pattern for a tile type, click None. When designing a pattern for an elliptical path, only one tile is needed.

   ➤ To restore the original pattern choice to the currently selected tile button, click Original on the scroll list.

4. The settings discussed next affect all the tiles in the pattern. Press Tab to move from one field to the next as you do any of the following:

   To scale the tiles, change the Size: **Scale** percentage (1–10000%).

   To adjust the spacing between pattern tiles, change the Size: **Spacing** percentage (0–10000%).

To change the orientation of pattern tiles on the path, check **Flip Along** and/or **Flip Across**. Be sure to preview this—you may not like the results.

In the Fit area, click **Stretch to fit** to have Illustrator shorten or lengthen the tiles, where necessary, to fit the path. Or click **Add space to fit** to have Illustrator add blank space between tiles, where necessary, to fit the pattern along the path, factoring in the Spacing percentage, if one was entered.

If you click **Approximate path,** on a closed rectangular path, the pattern tiles will be placed slightly inside or outside the path (not centered on the path) to make the tiling more even.

5. For the **Colorization** option, see the sidebar on page 361.

6. Click OK. If the Pattern brush is currently being used on any paths in the file, an alert dialog box will appear. Click **Apply to Strokes** to update the existing strokes with the revised brush, or click **Leave Strokes** to leave them unchanged.

1 Via the **Pattern Brush Options** dialog box, you can reassign tile patterns and adjust the size, spacing, orientation, fit, and color settings.

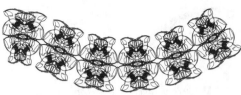

1 *The original* **Pattern** *brush stroke*

2 *Drag the brush from the Brushes palette onto the artboard. (On the palette, pattern tiles are arranged from left to right in this order: outer corner, side(s), inner corner, start, and end.) Multiple side tiles may display, depending on the current width of the palette.*

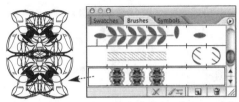

3 *Edit the pattern manually...* **4** *...and then update the brush on the* **Brushes** *palette.*

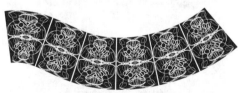

5 *The* **edited** *Pattern brush stroke*

Editing brushes manually

On the previous page you learned how to edit a brush via its options dialog box. Now you'll learn how to edit a brush manually.

To edit a Scatter, Art, or Pattern brush manually:

1. Deselect all objects, then drag a brush from the **Brushes** palette onto a blank area of the artboard **1**–**2**.

2. To recolor or transform the entire brush, select it first using the Selection tool, then perform your edits **3**. Or to recolor or transform individual objects within the brush or individual Pattern brush tiles, select them first using the Direct Selection tool or the Layers palette. For a Pattern brush, ungroup it before editing it. To isolate a group for editing, double-click it.

3. For a **Scatter** or **Art** brush, choose the Selection tool (V), and select the new or modified brush object or objects. Start dragging the objects onto the Brushes palette, hold down Option/Alt when you pass over the Brushes palette, then release the mouse when the pointer is over the original brush icon and the icon is highlighted. The options dialog box will open for that brush. Click OK (see step 4).

   ➤ To make the revised object(s) into a new brush, separate from the original, drag it (or them) into the palette without holding down Option/Alt.

   For a **Pattern** brush, start dragging each new or modified pattern tile shape (e.g., corner, side, end), hold down Option/Alt as you pass over the Brushes palette, and release the mouse when the new tile is over a specific tile slot to replace that tile **4**. The tile slots are arranged in the following order: outer corner, side(s), inner corner, start, and end. The Pattern Brush Options dialog box will open with the new tile in the chosen tile position.

4. Click OK. If the brush is currently in use on paths in the file, an alert dialog box will appear. Click **Apply to Strokes** to update the paths with the revised brush, or click **Leave Strokes** to leave them as is **5**.

Edit Brush Manually

Editing brush strokes on objects

If you edit a brush, all objects on which that brush is being used will update to reflect the changes. If you want to **edit** a **brush stroke** on a **selected object** or objects without editing the brush itself, follow these instructions instead.

To change the stroke options for an individual object:

1. Select one or more objects to which the same brush is currently applied **1**.

2. If you want to recolor the brush stroke, choose a stroke color now.

3. Click the **Options of Selected Object** button **/≡** on the Brushes palette.

4. Check Preview.

5. For a **Calligraphic** brush stroke **2**, follow steps 4–7 on pages 358–359.

   For an **Art** brush stroke **3**, follow steps 4–6 on page 360.

   For a **Scatter** brush stroke **4**, follow step 4 starting on page 356.

   For a **Pattern** brush stroke (**2**–**3**, next page), follow step 4 on page 364.

6. From the **Colorization** pop-up menu (not available for Calligraphic brushes), choose:

   None to leave the colors unchanged.

   Tints to change black areas in the brush stroke to the stroke color at 100% and nonblack areas to tints of the current stroke color. White areas stay white.

   Tints and Shades to change colors in the brush stroke to tints of the current stroke color. Black and white stay the same.

   Hue Shift to apply the current stroke color to areas containing the most frequently used color on the object (the key color) and to change other colors in the brush stroke to related hues.

   Click Tips if you want to see an illustration of the **Colorization** options.

Edit Brush Stroke on Object

1 *Select an object or objects to which a brush has been applied.*

2 *Stroke Options for a Calligraphic brush stroke*

3 *Stroke Options for an art brush stroke*

4 *Stroke Options for a Scatter brush stroke*

7. Click OK . Only the selected object or objects will change, not the brush itself on the Brushes palette.

➤ To restore the original brush stroke to the object, select the object, click the Remove Brush Stroke button ✖ on the Brushes palette, then click the original brush.

 *The* **brush stroke** *is altered on the* **object.**

2 *For this pattern, Diane Margolin turned on the* **Stretch to fit** *option. This pattern has side, outer corner, and inner corner tiles.*

3 *The pattern applied to an oval*

Creating brush libraries

By **saving brushes** in a **library,** you'll be able to find them easily and use them in any file.

To create a brush library:

1. Create brushes in a document, or move them to the Brushes palette in the current document from other libraries.

2. From the Brushes palette menu, choose **Save Brush Library.**

3. Enter a name. In Mac, leave the location as Applications/Adobe Illustrator CS2/ Presets/Brushes. In Windows, leave the location as Program Files\Adobe\Adobe Illustrator CS2\Presets\Brushes.

4. Click Save. The library can be opened from the Open Brush Library > **Other Library** submenu on the Brushes palette menu.

Deleting brushes

When you **delete** a **brush** that's being used in your document, you can choose whether to expand or remove the brush strokes.

To delete a brush from the Brushes palette:

1. Deselect all objects in your document.

2. On the Brushes palette, **click** the brush you want to delete.
   or
   To delete all the brushes that aren't being used in the file, choose **Select All Unused** from the Brushes palette menu.

3. Click the **Delete Brush** button 🗑 on the Brushes palette.

4. If the brush isn't currently being used in the document, an alert dialog box will appear **1**; click Yes.

   If the brush **is** currently being used in the document, click **Expand Strokes** in the alert dialog box **2** to expand the brush strokes (they'll be converted into standard paths and will no longer be "live"), or click **Remove Strokes** to remove them from the objects.

➤ To restore a deleted brush to the palette, choose Undo immediately. Or if the brush is in a library, you can add it again (see page 354).

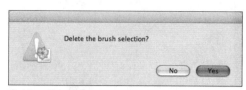

1 *This alert dialog box will appear if you **delete** a brush that isn't being used in the document.*

2 *If the brush you're deleting is being **used** in the document, this alert dialog box will appear.*

BLENDS 23

In this chapter, you'll learn how to use the Make Blend command and the Blend tool to create live (editable), multistep color and shape progressions between two or more objects; edit, change blend options for, and release a blend; and perform an easy practice exercise.

Process or spot?

➤ If you blend an object that contains a **process** color with an object that contains a **spot** color, the intermediate objects will be painted with **process** colors.

➤ If the objects you blend contain different **spot** colors, the intermediate objects will be painted with **process** colors.

➤ If the objects you blend contain different **tints** of the **same spot** color, the intermediate objects will be painted with graduated **tints** of that spot color. To blend a spot color with white, change the white fill to 0% of the spot color.

Daniel Pelavin blended two lines to create the shading on this lighthouse.

Blends are live!

Both the **Make Blend** command and the **Blend** tool create a multistep color and shape progression between two or more objects. Using the Blend tool, you can control which parts of the objects are used for calculating the blend, whereas the Make Blend command controls this function automatically.

Although you can't alter the transitional objects in a blend directly, a whole blend will update instantly if you edit the original blend objects or reshape or replace the nonprinting spine that the objects adhere to. You can also select a blend and change the number of steps (transitional objects) it contains via the Blend Options dialog box, as well as transform, recolor, or move any of the original objects.

When you create blends, bear in mind:

➤ You can blend similar shapes or nonmatching shapes, and they can have different fill and stroke attributes or brush strokes.

➤ You can blend editable type, gradients, or blends, but not mesh objects.

➤ You can blend two open paths, two closed paths, or a closed path and an open path.

➤ You can blend symbol instances, but to prevent printing errors, we don't recommend blending symbol sets.

Note: To blend colors between objects without blending their shapes, use a Blend filter (see page 132).

Blending objects via a command
To blend objects via a command:

1. Position two or more objects or groups, allowing room for the transition shapes that will be created between them, and select all the objects using the Selection tool, Lasso tool, or Layers palette 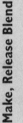.

   ➤ Try blending two different sizes of the same object, with the same or different fill colors but no stroke colors.

2. Choose Object > Blend > **Make** (Cmd-Option-B/Ctrl-Alt-B) **2**–**3**.

3. To change the appearance of the blend, read the instructions on the following three pages.

   ➤ If you don't like the blend, you can Undo it, or you can release it (instructions below).

   ➤ To prevent banding when printing a blend, see page 373.

Releasing a blend
To release a blend:

1. Select the blend.

2. Choose Object > Blend > **Release** (Cmd-Option-Shift-B/Ctrl-Alt-Shift-B). The original objects and the path that was created by the blend will remain; the transitional objects will be deleted.

1 *The original objects*

2 *After choosing Object > **Blend** > **Make**, with Spacing: **Smooth Color** chosen in the Blend Options dialog box (see the following page)*

3 *The original objects after choosing Object > **Blend** > **Make**, with Spacing: **Specified Steps** (2) chosen in the Blend Options dialog box (see the following page)*

DANIEL PELAVIN

370

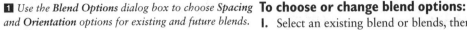

1 *Use the Blend Options dialog box to choose Spacing and Orientation options for existing and future blends.*

2 *Spacing: Smooth Color*

3 *Spacing: Specified Steps (7)*

4 *Orientation: Align to Page*

5 *Orientation: Align to Path*

Choosing blend options

If you change the settings in the **Blend Options** dialog box, the new settings will be applied automatically to all currently selected and subsequently created blends.

To choose or change blend options:

1. Select an existing blend or blends, then choose Object > Blend > **Blend Options.**
   or
   To choose options only for future blends, deselect, then double-click the **Blend** tool (W) (not the Gradient tool!).

   The Blend Options dialog box opens **1**. Check Preview, if available (if a blend is selected).

2. From the **Spacing** pop-up menu, choose one of the following:

   Smooth Color to have Illustrator automatically calculate the necessary number of blend steps (transition shapes) to produce smooth, nonbanding color transitions **2**. This option may take a moment to preview.

   Specified Steps, enter the desired number of transition steps for the blend (1–1000), then press Tab to preview. Use this option if you want to create distinct, discernible transition shapes **3**.

   Specified Distance, then enter the desired distance (.1–1000 pt) between the transition shapes in the blend. The Specified Distance has no effect on the overall length of the blend.

3. Click an **Orientation** button:

   Align to Page to keep the blend objects perpendicular to the horizontal axis **4**.
   or
   Align to Path to keep the blend objects perpendicular to the blend path **5**. (To place blend objects on a user-drawn spine, see page 375.)

4. Click OK.

Blend Options

Editing blend objects

You can use any of the following methods to **edit a blend.** As you do so, the blend will update instantly **1**–**2**.

➤ To **recolor, move,** or **transform** the original blend objects, select them with the **Direct Selection** tool, or double-click the blend with the **Selection** tool to **isolate** it. To perform a transformation, you can use the Free Transform tool, an individual transformation tool, or the object's bounding box. (When you're done, double-click outside the gray frame or click the Exit Isolate Group button ⊞ on the Control palette.)

NEW

➤ You **can't** select or edit the transitional objects individually—no way, no how.

➤ To **recolor all** the objects in a blend, select it via the Selection tool or the Layers palette, then use a filter on the Filter > **Colors** submenu, such as Adjust Colors.

➤ Apply a **stroke** color to the blend objects if you want the transitional shapes to be clearly delineated. To do this after the blend is created, choose the Selection tool, click the blend, then apply a stroke.

➤ To **transform** an **entire** blend, select it with the Selection tool, then manipulate the bounding box or use a transformation tool.

➤ To **reshape** a blend **path,** move one of the original objects with the Direct Selection tool or use any of the path-reshaping tools, such as the Reshape, Direct Selection, Add Anchor Point, or Convert Anchor Point tool.

➤ To reshape a blend object or blend path dramatically, use the **liquify** tools (see Chapter 28).

➤ **Effects** and other appearance attributes can be applied to blend objects, either before or after the blend is created (see page 296).

➤ To recolor a blend between symbols, use the **Symbol Stainer** tool on a selected instance (see pages 432–433).

Edit Blend Objects

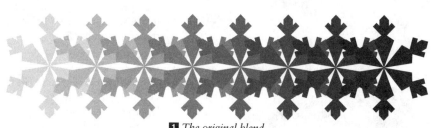

1 *The original blend*

2 *The same blend after **recoloring** the rightmost snowflake, **adding points** to the blend path, and **reshaping** the path*

The 39 steps

When printing a blend created using the **Smooth Color** option, Illustrator calculates the number of steps needed to make the blend look smooth based on the percentage differences for each CMYK color component in the blend objects (e.g., changes in the percentage of magenta between each object), and based on the assumption that the blend will be output on a high-resolution device (1200 dpi or higher).

To specify the number of steps for a selected blend, choose Object > Blend > **Blend Options,** choose Spacing: **Specified Steps,** then enter the desired number of steps (1–1000). Banding is most likely to occur in blends that span a wide distance (say, wider than 7 inches). We recommend rasterizing a wide blend by using Object > Rasterize, then applying Filter > Blur > Smart Blur at low settings to soften the color transitions. (Outputting blends to the Web is a different story. See pages 520 and 522.)

Reversing blend components

The **Reverse Front to Back** command changes the stacking order of the blend objects without changing their *x/y* locations.

To reverse the stacking position of objects in a blend:

1. Select a blend **1**.

2. Choose Object > Blend > **Reverse Front to Back 2**. The original and transitional objects will now be in reverse stacking order (what was originally the backmost object will now be the frontmost object, and vice versa).

The **Reverse Spine** command swaps the *x/y* location of all the blend objects without changing their stacking positions.

To reverse the location of objects in a blend:

1. Select a blend **1**.

2. Choose Object > Blend > **Reverse Spine**. The blend objects will swap locations **3**.

1 *The original blend*

2 *After applying the* **Reverse Front to Back** *command*

3 *After applying the* **Reverse Spine** *command to the original objects*

Reverse Front to Back, Spine

Using the Blend tool

To blend objects using the Blend tool:

1. Position two or more different-shaped open or closed paths, allowing room for the transition shapes that will be created between them. You can apply different colors or gradients to each object.

2. Choose the **Blend** tool (W).

3. To let Illustrator decide which anchor points to use for the blend, click the **fill** of the first object (not the center point!).
   or
   If you want to control which anchor point will be used, click an **anchor point** on the first object **1**. The little square on the Blend tool pointer will change from hollow to filled when it's over an anchor point.

4. Click either the fill or an anchor point on the next object **2**. If the path is open, click an endpoint. For the smoothest shape transitions, click corresponding points on all the objects (say, the top left corner point of all the objects, not the top left corner point of one object and the lower right corner point of another object). You can add points in advance so the objects have a similar number of points. The blend will appear **3**–**4**.

   Repeat this step for any other objects that you want to include in the blend. The blend will update automatically!

5. To edit the blend, see the previous three pages.

➤ If you don't like the blend, use Undo or choose Object > Blend > Release.

➤ If the original objects contain different pattern fills, the transition shapes will be filled with the pattern from the topmost object.

1 *With the **Blend tool**, click the fill or an anchor point of one object...*

2 *...then click the fill or an anchor point of another object.*

3 *The blend appears.*

4 *This is the kind of thing that happens if you click noncorresponding points. Who knew?!*

1 *The original user-drawn path and blend*

2 *After **Replace Spine** is chosen, the blend flows along the user-drawn path.*

Replacing the blend spine

You can use any path as a **replacement spine** for the original blend and transitional objects to adhere to, in lieu of the one that Illustrator created automatically.

To replace a blend spine:

1. Create a blend, then draw a separate path to become the new spine. The path can be closed or open, but an open one will probably work better.

2. With the Selection tool or the Lasso tool, select both the blend and the path **1**.

3. Choose Object > Blend > **Replace Spine.** The blend will adhere to the new path **2**.

➤ If you release a blend that has a replacement spine, the path (turned spine) will have a stroke color of None. You can locate it in Outline view or by using smart guides with Object Highlighting.

➤ To change the orientation of the blend objects relative to the path, select the blend, choose Object > Blend > Blend Options, then click whichever Orientation icon isn't currently highlighted (see the last two figures on page 371).

Replace Spine

375

Exercise

Use a blend to apply shading

1. Select an object, then apply a fill color and a stroke of None.

2. Double-click the **Scale** tool.

3. Click **Uniform**, enter a number between 60 and 80 in the **Scale** field, then click **Copy**.

4. With the copy still selected, choose a lighter or darker variation of the original fill color (or black or white). For a process color, you can Shift-drag a process color slider on the Color palette to lighten or darken the color.

5. Make sure the smaller object is in front of the larger one, then select both objects with the Selection tool or Lasso tool **1**.

6. Choose Object > Blend > **Make** (Cmd-Option-B/Ctrl-Alt-B) **2**. If the resulting blend doesn't look smooth, select it, double-click the Blend tool, choose Smooth Color from the Spacing pop-up menu, then click OK.

➤ For even more flexible and editable color gradations, use the mesh features (see pages 384–389).

1 *Select two objects*

1 *After choosing Object > Blend > Make.*

GRADIENTS 24

A gradient fill is a gradual blend between two or more colors. In this chapter you'll learn how to fill an object or objects with a gradient; create and save gradients; edit a gradient using the Gradient palette; and change the way a gradient fills an object or objects by using the Gradient tool. You'll also learn how to use the Mesh tool, the Create Gradient Mesh command, and the Expand command to create painterly mesh objects, and how to modify mesh objects by adding, moving, deleting, and recoloring mesh points and lines.

DANIEL PELAVIN

Blend or gradient?

A **blend** consists of two or more objects with transitional shapes and colors between them.

A **gradient** is a smooth transition between two or more colors inside an object, with no transitional shapes to other objects.

A **mesh** is an object with a flexible armature, to which you can apply multiple smoothly blended fill colors.

Applying gradients

If you want to soften some abstract shapes or add shading or volume to realistic or geometric objects, use **gradients.** A gradient can be a simple transition between two colors—a starting and ending color—or it can contain multiple colors. It can spread from one side of an object to another (linear) or spread outward from the center of an object (radial), and it can be applied to one object or across many objects. A set of predefined gradients is supplied with Illustrator, but you can also create custom gradients by using the **Gradient palette** (Cmd-F9/Ctrl-F9). **NEW**

Once an object is filled with a gradient, you can use the **Gradient tool** to change the direction of the gradient or change how quickly one color blends into another.

You'll be using the Color, Swatches, and Gradient palettes for the instructions in this chapter. The Color and Swatches palettes can be opened via the Window menu or displayed temporarily via the Control palette. **NEW**

You can apply any of the gradients that are supplied with Illustrator or, even better, create your own. Follow these instructions to **apply** an **existing gradient** to an **object.** In the next set of instructions, you'll create your own gradients.

To fill an object with a gradient:

1. Select an object 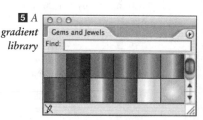, then click a gradient swatch on the **Swatches** palette **2**–**3**

   NEW (access it via the Control palette, if you like), or on any open gradient **library** (see the sidebar).

   or

   Drag a gradient swatch from the **Swatches**

   NEW palette (access it via the Control palette, if you like), or from any open gradient **library,** or from the Gradient Fill box on the **Gradient** palette (Cmd-F9/Ctrl-F9) **4** over a selected or unselected object.

2. *Optional:* If the object contains a Linear gradient, you can select the object and change the Angle on the Gradient palette.

➤ If a selected object has a solid-color or pattern fill, but it previously had a gradient fill, you can reapply the gradient by clicking the Gradient Fill box on the Gradient palette, or by clicking the Gradient button on the Toolbox, ■ or by pressing "." (period).

➤ You can't apply a gradient to a stroke, but here's a workaround: Make the stroke the desired width, apply Object > Path > Outline Stroke to convert the stroke into a closed object (see page 395), then apply the gradient.

➤ To fill type with a gradient, first convert it into outlines (Type > Create Outlines). Or select the type, choose Add New Fill from the Appearance palette menu, then apply a gradient.

1 *The original object*

2 *Click a gradient on the Swatches palette.*

3 *The object filled with a radial gradient*

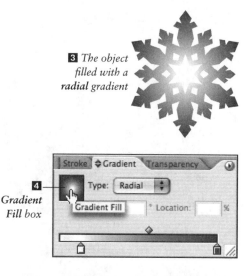

Gradient Fill box

5 *A gradient library*

More gradients

To access the other gradient libraries that are supplied with Illustrator, from the bottom of the Swatches palette menu, choose **Open Swatch Library > Other Library,** open the Adobe Illustrator CS2/Presets/Gradients folder (Mac) or the Adobe\Adobe Illustrator CS2\Presets\Gradients folder (Windows), click the library you want to open, then click Open **5**. Any gradient that you click in a library palette will appear at the bottom of the Swatches palette.

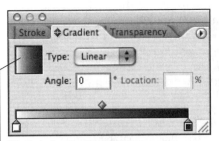

1 *Click the Gradient Fill box on the Gradient palette.*

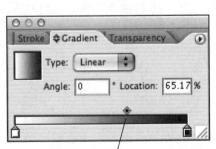

2 *Choose a color for the left gradient stop...*   *...and the right gradient stop.*

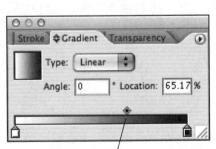

3 *Move the midpoint diamond to adjust the amount of each color.*

Creating gradients

A **custom gradient** can be composed of all CMYK colors, all RGB process colors, tints of the same spot color, or multiple spot colors.

To create and save a two-color gradient:

1. Display the full Gradient palette (Cmd-F9/Ctrl-F9), with its options panel.

2. Click the **Gradient Fill** box on the Gradient palette **1**. *Note:* If you previously applied a gradient in the same work session, click the "White, Black" gradient on the Swatches palette instead.

3. Drag a solid-color swatch from the **Swatches** palette over the left gradient stop on the Gradient palette **2**.
   or
   Click the left gradient stop on the Gradient palette. Then use the **Color** palette to mix a solid color; or Option-click/Alt-click a solid-color swatch on the **Swatches** palette; or choose the **Eyedropper** tool and Shift-click a color anywhere in the document window.

4. Repeat the previous step to choose a solid color for the right gradient stop.

5. From the **Type** pop-up menu on the Gradient palette, choose **Radial** or **Linear**.

6. *Optional:* Move the midpoint diamond to the right to produce more of the starting color than the ending color, or to the left to produce more of the ending color than the starting color **3**. Or click the diamond, then change the Location value.

7. *Optional:* For a Linear gradient, you can change the Angle.

8. If you select another object or swatch now, the new gradient will be lost—unless you save it (and then save your document). To save the gradient:

   Drag the Gradient Fill box from the Gradient palette onto the **Swatches** palette.
   or
   Click the Gradient Fill box on the Gradient palette, then click the **New**

(Continued on the following page)

Create, Save Two-Color Gradient

Swatch button ▣ at the bottom of the Swatches palette.

or

To name the gradient as you save it, click the Gradient Fill box on the **Gradient** palette, Option-click/Alt-click the **New Swatch** button on the Swatches palette, enter a name, then click OK.

➤ To swap the starting and ending colors or any other two colors in a radial or linear gradient, Option-drag/Alt-drag one stop on top of the other.

➤ To delete a gradient swatch from the Swatches palette, drag it over the Delete Swatch button. 🗑

Editing gradients

It's hard to tell whether a gradient is going to look good until it's been applied to an object. Luckily, gradients are easy to edit. You can recolor existing stops, add new ones, move or remove stops, change the location of any stop, or change the overall gradient type or angle at any time.

You can either **edit** a **gradient** in an object and leave the swatch alone, or you can edit the gradient swatch, with or without recoloring any objects that the gradient is currently applied to. For steps 2–5, you can pick and choose which aspects of the gradient you want to edit.

To edit a gradient:

1. Choose the **Selection** tool (V), then click an object that contains the gradient you want to edit. For editable type, click the type, then click the Fill attribute on the Appearance palette that has a gradient icon.

or

On the **Swatches** palette, click the gradient swatch that you want to edit. In addition, you may also select any objects that contain that gradient.

2. To **recolor** any existing gradient **stop:**

On the **Gradient** palette (Cmd-F9/Ctrl-F9), click a stop that you want to recolor, then choose a color from the **Color**

Start from something

To use an existing gradient as a starting point for a new gradient, click a gradient swatch on the Swatches palette, choose **Duplicate Swatch** from the palette menu, click the duplicate swatch, then edit the gradient as per the instructions on this page. To use a gradient in a gradient library as a starting point, click the swatch in the library before following the instructions above.

Color-separating gradients

➤ To color-separate a gradient that changes from a spot color to white onto one plate, create a gradient with the spot color as the starting color and a **0%** tint of the **same spot color** as the ending color.

➤ If you're going to color-separate a gradient that contains **more than one** spot color, get some advice from your prepress specialist. He or she may tell you to assign a different screen angle to each color using File > Print > Output Panel (Convert All Spot Colors to Process should be unchecked). See pages 488–489.

➤ To convert spot colors in a gradient to **process** colors, click a color stop on the Gradient palette, then on the Color palette, click the **Spot Color** button. ▣ The color will convert to the current document color mode (RGB or CMYK). Repeat for the other stops.

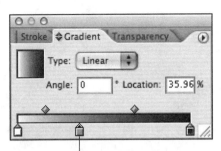

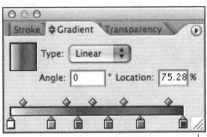

1 *Click below the **gradient slider** to add a new stop, then choose a color.*

2 *Four shades of gray were **added** to this gradient.*

*You can drag the **resize** box to widen the palette.*

3 *Multicolored gradients*

palette or Option-click/Alt-click a solid color on the **Swatches** palette.
or
Drag a solid-color swatch from the **Swatches** palette over a gradient stop on the Gradient palette.

3. To **add** gradient **stops:**

   On the **Gradient** palette, click below the gradient slider to add a stop **1**, then use the **Color** palette to mix a color or Option-click/Alt-click a swatch on the **Swatches** palette.
   or
   Drag a solid-color swatch from the **Swatches** palette to the gradient bar (but not on top of an existing stop) on the **Gradient** palette. A new stop will be created.

   Repeat to add more colors **2**–**3**.

4. **Move** a **stop** to the left or the right to change how abruptly that color spreads into adjacent colors.

   Move any **midpoint** diamond (above the gradient bar) to the left or right to adjust the amount of that color; or click the diamond, then change the Location value.

   To **duplicate** a **stop,** Option-drag/Alt-drag it.

   To **remove** a **stop,** drag it downward out of the Gradient palette.

5. Choose a different gradient **Type** (Radial or Linear), or for a Linear gradient, change the **Angle.**

6. To **resave** the edited swatch, Option-drag/Alt-drag from the Gradient Fill box on the Gradient palette over the swatch on the Swatches palette.
   or
   If you want to save your modified gradient as a **new** swatch instead of saving over the original, drag it to the Swatches palette without holding down Option/Alt.

   Also remember to save your document!

➤ To make a gradient appear in every new Illustrator document, save it in either or both of the two Illustrator Startup files (see page 469).

Using the Gradient tool

You've already learned how to edit a gradient swatch. Now you'll learn how to use the **Gradient tool** on an object to quickly change how abruptly the gradient colors blend, change the angle of a linear gradient, or change the location of the center in a radial gradient. On the next page, you'll learn how to use this tool to spread a gradient across multiple objects.

To use the Gradient tool:

1. Apply a gradient fill to an object , and keep the object selected.

2. Choose the **Gradient** tool (G).

3. Drag across the object in any direction, such as from right to left or diagonally:

   To blend the colors abruptly, drag a short distance **2**–**3**. To blend the colors more gradually across a wider span, drag a longer distance.

   To reverse the order of the colors in a linear gradient, drag in the opposite direction.

   For a radial gradient, position the pointer where you want the center of the fill to be, then click or drag.

   ➤ You can start dragging or finish dragging with the pointer outside the object. In this case, the colors at the beginning or end of the gradient won't appear in the object.

4. If you don't like the results, drag in a different direction. Keep trying until you're satisfied with the results **4**.

➤ If you use the Gradient tool on an object and then apply a different gradient of the same type (radial or linear) to the same object, the effect of the Gradient tool will be applied to the new gradient.

➤ To restore the original gradient to the object, select the object, then click the swatch on the Swatches palette.

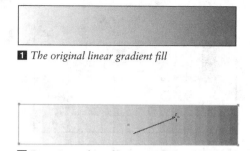

1 *The original linear gradient fill*

2 *Dragging a short distance with the **Gradient** tool*

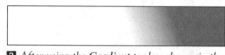

3 *After using the **Gradient** tool as shown in the previous figure*

4 *The same linear gradient fill, three different ways, thanks to the **Gradient** tool*

To spread a gradient across multiple objects:

1. Select several objects, fill all of them with the same gradient **1**, and keep them selected.

2. Choose the **Gradient** tool (G).

3. Drag across all the objects in one pass **2**. Shift-drag to constrain the angle to a multiple of 45° (actually, to a multiple of the current Constrain Angle in Preferences > General).

➤ Once multiple objects are filled with the same gradient, don't combine them into a compound path (doing so could change how the gradient looks or cause a printing error).

1 *In the original gradient fill, the gradient starts **anew** in **each** type outline.*

2 *After we dragged across all the objects using the **Gradient tool** in the direction shown by the arrow, the gradient starts in the **first** type outline and ends in the **last** type outline.*

Creating meshes

What is a mesh?

A **mesh** object is a flexible, editable armature with interior mesh points, patches, and intersecting lines. Colors that you assign to the points and patches blend seamlessly into one another. This feature is ideal for rendering photorealistic objects, painterly graphics, complex modeled surfaces, skin tones, or objects of nature **1**.

Both the **Mesh tool** and the **Create Gradient Mesh command** (a bit of legacy terminology) convert a standard object into a mesh object with lines and intersecting points. A mesh can be produced from any path object or bitmapped image, even a radial or linear blend. To produce a mesh from a compound path, text object, or linked image, you must rasterize it first.

After you create a mesh object, you'll assign colors to mesh points or mesh patches. Then you can add or delete colors or sharpen or soften color transitions by manipulating the points and lines. A mesh is like a watercolor or airbrush drawing inside a flexible armature. Reconfigure the armature, and the colors shift accordingly.

Mesh building blocks

A mesh object consists of anchor points, mesh points, mesh lines, and mesh patches **2**. The mesh can be reshaped by manipulating its anchor points, mesh points, or mesh lines.

➤ **Anchor points** are square. You can add, delete, or move them or pull on their direction lines in order to reshape the object, as in nonmesh objects.

➤ **Mesh points** are diamond shaped and are located where two mesh lines intersect. You'll use them to assign colors to the mesh. Like anchor points, they can be added, deleted, and moved.

➤ **Mesh lines** crisscross the object to connect the mesh points, and act as guides for placing and moving points.

➤ **Mesh patches** are the areas inside the mesh lines, which can also be moved.

Mesh another way

The Object > Envelope Distort > **Make with Mesh** command can also be used to produce a mesh. It will have the same components, and can be edited using the same techniques, as a mesh created by using the Mesh tool or the Create Gradient Mesh command. See pages 385–386.

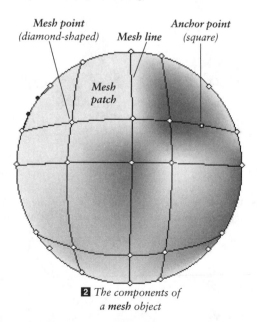

1 *Danny Pelavin used* **gradient meshes** *to render the glossy surfaces and complex shading in this illustration.*

2 *The components of a* **mesh** *object*

Mesh Building Blocks

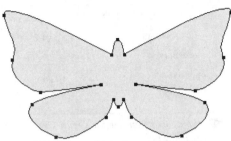

1 *Select an object that contains a fill.*

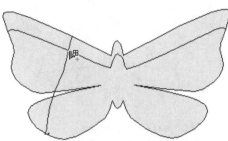

2 *Click the object with the Mesh tool to convert it to a **mesh** object.*

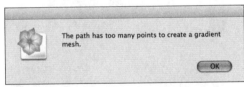

The path has too many points to create a gradient mesh.

OK

3 *If you get this alert dialog box, remove some points from the path, then try converting it again.*

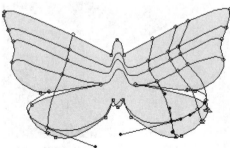

4 *Continue to click to add more mesh lines.*

You can **convert** a standard **object** into a **mesh** by using either the **Mesh** tool or the **Create Gradient Mesh** command. To convert a complex object or bitmap image into a mesh, you're better off using the Create Gradient Mesh command. To convert simpler objects, you can use either the Create Gradient Mesh command or the Mesh tool. The Create Gradient Mesh command creates more regularly spaced mesh points and lines than does the Mesh tool.

Beware! The only way to convert a mesh object back to a path object is by choosing Undo.

To convert an object into a mesh with the Mesh tool:

1. Select an object (not a text object, compound path, or linked image) and apply a solid-color fill to the object if it doesn't already have one **1**. The object can have a brush stroke, but the Mesh tool will remove it.

   ➤ To preserve a nonmesh version of the object, copy it before proceeding.

2. Choose the **Mesh** tool (U).

3. Click the object to place a mesh point. The object will be converted into a mesh object containing the minimum number of mesh lines **2**.

   If an alert dialog box appears **3**, it means you must remove points from the path before it can be converted into a mesh. You can do this with the Delete Anchor Point tool or the Smooth tool.

4. Granted, the mesh doesn't look very interesting yet. To start building up the mesh, click in the object to create a few additional sets of mesh lines **4**, then see pages 387–388 to learn how to apply colors to the mesh.

In these instructions, you'll learn how to create a mesh using the **Create Gradient Mesh** command.

Note: Complex meshes (messes!) will increase your file size, require a significant amount of computation, and may also cause printing errors. Try to keep things simple by, say, creating a few smaller mesh objects instead of an overly large, complex one.

To convert an object into a mesh via a command:

1. Choose the **Selection** tool (V), select an object (not a text object, compound path, or linked image), and apply a solid-color fill to the object, if it doesn't already have one. The object can have a brush stroke, but the Create Gradient Mesh command will remove it. You can use an embedded bitmap image.

   ➤ To preserve a nonmesh version of the object, copy it before proceeding.

2. Choose Object > **Create Gradient Mesh.**

3. Check Preview **1**.

4. Enter the desired number of horizontal **Rows** and vertical **Columns** for the mesh grid.

5. From the **Appearance** pop-up menu, choose **Flat** for a uniform surface with no highlight; **To Center** for a highlight at the center of the object; or **To Edge** for a highlight at the edges of the object.

6. If you chose To Center or To Edge in the previous step, enter an intensity percentage (0–100%) for the white **Highlight.**

7. Click OK **2**–**4**. To apply colors to the mesh, follow the instructions beginning on the following page.

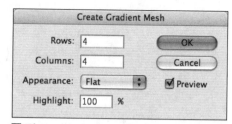

1 *Choose parameters in the **Create Gradient Mesh** dialog box.*

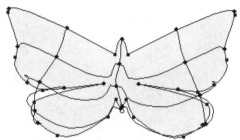

2 ***Create Gradient Mesh** command, Appearance: Flat*

3 ***Create Gradient Mesh** command, Appearance: To Center*

4 ***Create Gradient Mesh** command, **Appearance: To Edge** (shown here on a dark background so you can see the highlight on the edge)*

Create Gradient Mesh Command

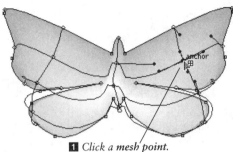

1 *Click a mesh point.*

2 *The point is recolored.*

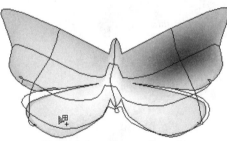

3 *Or click inside a mesh patch...*

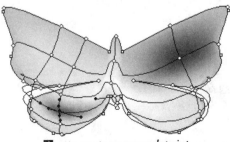

4 *...to create a new mesh point.*

Recoloring meshes

Each mesh **point** and mesh **patch** can be assigned a different **color,** and each color will blend into its surrounding colors. Click a mesh point to assign a color to a small area, or click a mesh patch to spread a color across a wider area.

To recolor a mesh:

1. Zoom in on a mesh object (you should still be able to see the entire object in the document window, though) and deselect it.

2. Choose the **Direct Selection** tool (A), then click the edge of the mesh object.

3. Do any of the following:

   Click a mesh **point 1** or Shift-click multiple points, then choose a fill color from the Color palette or Swatches palette **2**.

   Drag a color from the Swatches palette over a mesh **point** or mesh **patch.**

   Click a mesh **patch,** then choose a fill color from the Color or Swatches palette. The four mesh points that surround the patch will be recolored.

➤ You can also recolor mesh points by selecting the object using the Direct Selection tool, then using the Mesh tool (U) for recoloring. To select a mesh patch with the Mesh tool without adding a mesh point, Cmd-click/Ctrl-click the patch.

You can use the Mesh tool to **add mesh points** or **lines,** and thus more colors.

To add mesh points or lines:

1. Deselect all.

2. Choose the **Mesh** tool (U).

3. Choose a color from the Swatches palette or Color palette, then click inside the mesh **3**–**4**. A new mesh **point** with connecting mesh lines will appear, and the current fill color will be applied to that point.
   or

(Continued on the following page)

Choose a fill color, then click an existing mesh **line** to add a line that runs perpendicular to it **1**–**2**.

or

Shift-click a mesh **line** to add a mesh point using the existing color from that line.

4. *Optional:* To recolor a new mesh point with a color from elsewhere in the same object, keep the point selected, choose the Eyedropper tool (I), *✎* then Shift-click the desired color.

➤ You can also recolor an entire mesh by using Filter > Colors > Adjust Colors, Convert to CMYK (or Convert to RGB), Invert Colors, or Saturate.

Reshaping meshes

In these instructions, you'll **add** or **remove** square-shaped **anchor points** in order to reshape the overall mesh object—not to add colors or push colors around on the mesh. (To add diamond-shaped mesh points to the interior of the mesh, follow the previous set of instructions instead.)

To reshape the overall mesh path:

1. Choose the **Direct Selection** tool (A), then click the edge of a mesh object. Zoom in on it, if you need to.

2. To add an anchor point, choose the **Add Anchor Point** tool (+), *✎* then click the outer edge of the mesh object or click a mesh line inside the object **3**.

   or

   To delete a user-created anchor point, choose the **Delete Anchor Point** tool (-), *✎* then click the point **4**.

➤ Hold down Option/Alt to toggle to the Add Anchor Point tool if the Delete Anchor Point tool is selected, or vice versa.

Recoloring tips

To select and change multiple instances of the same color, choose the Direct Selection tool, click a mesh point or patch, choose Select > Same > **Fill Color,** then choose a new color from the Color palette or the Swatches palette.

To make a color area **smaller,** add more mesh lines around it in a different color. To **spread** a color, delete mesh points from around it or assign the same color to adjacent mesh points.

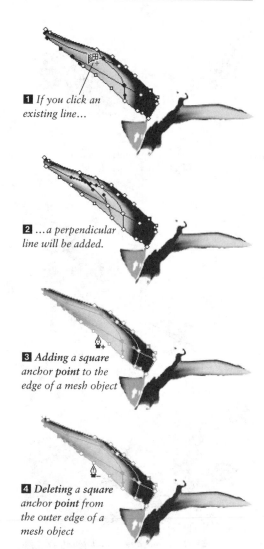

1 *If you click an existing line...*

2 *...a perpendicular line will be added.*

3 *Adding a square anchor point to the edge of a mesh object*

4 *Deleting a square anchor point from the outer edge of a mesh object*

Reshape Mesh Path

1 *Option-click/Alt-click a mesh point to delete it.*

When a **mesh point** is **deleted,** the mesh lines that cross through that point are deleted, too.

To delete mesh points:

1. Choose the **Direct Selection** tool (A), then click the edge of the mesh object.

2. Click the mesh **point** that you want to delete, then press Delete/Backspace.
   or
   Choose the **Mesh** tool (U), then Option-click/Alt-click the **point** that you want to delete (a minus sign will appear next to the pointer) **1**–**2**.

Next, you'll learn how to **push mesh colors around**—like electronic sculpting!

To reshape the interior mesh:

1. Choose the **Direct Selection** tool (A), then click the edge of the mesh object.

2. Click a **mesh point** or **anchor point.**

3. Do any of the following:

   Lengthen or rotate either of the point's **direction lines** to reshape its adjacent mesh lines **3**. To constrain the line angle to a multiple of 45° (or to the current Constrain Angle in Preferences > General), start dragging the line, then Shift-drag. If the direction lines are hard to see on the mesh, double-click the layer name, and change the Color.

   Drag a mesh **point 4**, mesh **patch 5**, or anchor point (even outside the object!).

   Shift-drag a mesh **point** to drag it along an existing mesh line.

   To convert a mesh point into a corner point, select the point, choose the **Convert Anchor Point** tool (Shift-C), click the point, then drag one of its direction lines.

2 *The point is deleted.*

3 *Drag a direction line.*

Delete Mesh Points; Reshape Mesh

4 *Drag a mesh point.*

5 *Drag a mesh patch.*

Using the Expand command

To expand a standard gradient into separate objects:

1. Select an object that contains a gradient fill (not a mesh) .

2. Choose Object > **Expand.**

3. Click **Expand Gradient To: Specify,** then enter the desired number of objects to be created **2**. To print a gradient successfully, this number must be high enough to produce smooth color transitions.

4. Click OK **3**. *Note:* The resulting number of objects may not match the specified number of objects if there were too few color changes in the original gradient.

➤ You can also use the Expand command to simplify a gradient fill that won't print.

➤ To expand a gradient using the last-used "Specify [ ] Objects" setting, hold down Option/Alt as you choose Object > Expand.

You can also use the **Expand** command to create a **mesh.**

To expand a radial or linear gradient into a mesh:

1. Select an object that contains a radial or linear gradient fill **1**.

2. Choose Object > **Expand.**

3. Click **Expand Gradient To: Gradient Mesh.**

4. Click OK **4**. The resulting expanded objects might be a bit confusing: a clipping path object that limits the gradient color area above the mesh object. Use the Layers palette to view the nested groups, clipping path, and mesh.

1 *The original object contains a **linear** gradient.*

2 *In the **Expand** dialog box, specify the number of objects to expand the gradient to.*

3 *The **Expand** command converted the gradient into a series of separate rectangles in different shades, grouped with a clipping mask.*

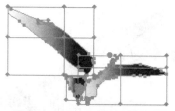

4 *This is the original object after expanding it into a **mesh.***

Expand Command

BIRD BY DIANE MARGOLIN

COMBINE PATHS 25

In this chapter, you'll first learn about the Shape Mode commands, which create editable compound shapes. Second, you'll learn about the Pathfinder commands, which divide, trim, merge, crop, outline, or subtract from multiple overlapping paths, producing a flattened, closed object or compound path. Finally, you'll learn how to join two or more objects into a compound path, then add objects to, reverse an object's fill in, and release compound paths.

Shop and compare

For a comparison between **compound shapes** and **compound paths,** see page 396. Also remember that you can recolor intersecting shapes in a live paint group without having to use any Pathfinder commands (see Chapter 13).

Add to   Subtract   *Exclude*
Shape   from   *Intersect*   *Overlapping*
—Area   Shape Area   Shape Areas   Shape Areas

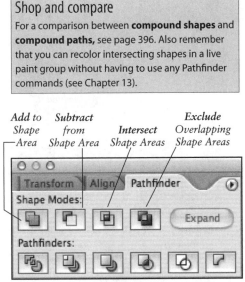

1 *The Shape Mode buttons,* **Pathfinder** *palette*

DANIEL PELAVIN

Applying Shape Mode commands

The **Shape Mode** commands **1** on the **Pathfinder** palette produce a compound shape from selected, overlapping objects. Like appearances, compound shapes are fully editable and reversible. On the Layers palette, the objects are nested individually under a compound shape listing, making it easy to select them for editing. When individual objects within a compound shape are moved, restacked, or reshaped, the overall compound shape adjusts accordingly. And finally, if a compound shape is released, the objects' original attributes are restored.

A few rules to keep in mind:

➤ Shape Modes can be applied to multiple paths, compound paths and shapes, blends, envelopes, editable type, or to a live paint group in combination with other paths.

➤ Shape Modes can't be applied to a single group, but they can be applied to a group in combination with other paths.

➤ Shape Modes can't be applied to placed images, rasterized images, or mesh objects.

➤ Except for the Subtract from Shape Area command, which preserves the color attributes of the backmost selected object, the Shape Mode commands apply the color attributes of the topmost object and hide other color attributes.

➤ Distort and warp effects remain visible; other effects are hidden.

To apply the Shape Mode commands:

1. Select two or more overlapping objects.

2. Click one of the following Shape Mode buttons on the **Pathfinder** palette:

   Add to Shape Area joins the outer edges of selected objects into one compound shape, hides interior object edges (see also page 167), and closes open paths .

   Subtract from Shape Area subtracts the objects in front from the backmost object, preserving the paint attributes of only the backmost object **2**.

   Intersect Shape Areas preserves areas that overlap and hides areas that don't **3**. Use it on objects that partially overlap.

   Exclude Overlapping Shape Areas makes areas where objects overlap transparent, revealing underlying objects **4**.

➤ You can apply the Shape Mode commands to an object in a compound shape (select the object with the Direct Selection tool first). Try clicking, say, Subtract from Shape Area to make an object in a compound disappear.

➤ A compound shape that's copied from Illustrator and pasted into Adobe Photoshop (click Shape Layer in the Paste dialog box) will show up as multiple paths on a shape layer. You can also copy a shape layer containing two or more paths from Photoshop into Illustrator as a compound shape.

When you **expand** a **compound shape,** the result is a single path, unless the compound shape has interior cutouts, in which case the result is a compound path. Compare with the Release Compound Shape command, which is discussed on the next page.

To expand a compound shape:

1. Select the compound shape with the **Selection** tool.

2. Click the **Expand** button on the Pathfinder palette (or choose Expand Compound Shape from the Pathfinder palette menu).

1 *The original objects: The leaf is the topmost object.*

Add to Shape Area

2 *The original objects*

Subtract from Shape Area *uses the frontmost object like a cookie cutter on the object(s) behind it.*

3 *The original objects*

Intersect Shape Areas: *Only areas that originally overlapped other objects remain.*

4 *The original objects*

Exclude Overlapping Shape Areas: *Areas where the objects overlapped become a cutout.*

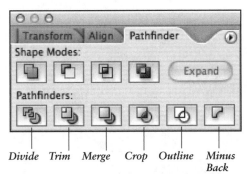

Divide Trim Merge Crop Outline Minus Back

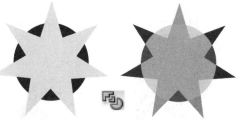

2 *The original objects*

After applying the **Divide** *command, then recoloring the resulting shapes*

Pathfinder Options

Options
Precision: 0.028 points

☐ Remove Redundant Points
☐ Divide and Outline Will Remove Unpainted Artwork

OK
Cancel
Defaults

3 *Use the* **Pathfinder Options** *dialog box to choose preferences for the Pathfinder commands.*

Pathfinder options

To open the **Pathfinder Options** dialog box **3**, choose **Pathfinder Options** from the Pathfinder palette menu.

The higher the **Precision** value (.001–100 pt), the more precisely commands are applied, and the longer they take to process.

With **Remove Redundant Points** checked, duplicate anchor points in the same location will be deleted.

With **Divide and Outline Will Remove Unpainted Artwork** checked, the Divide and Outline commands will delete overlapping areas of selected paths that have a fill of None.

When you **release** a **compound shape**, the objects' original attributes are restored.

To release a compound shape:

1. Select the compound shape with the **Selection** tool (V).

2. Choose **Release Compound Shape** from the Pathfinder palette menu.

Applying the Pathfinder commands

The **Pathfinder** commands divide, trim, merge, crop, outline, or subtract areas where selected paths overlap to produce separate, nonoverlapping closed paths or lines. Object colors and appearances are preserved, and the resulting paths are put into a group. The Pathfinder commands can be applied using the Pathfinder palette **1** or as removable effects (for the latter, see page 312).

Here are a few guidelines:

➤ Unfortunately, the original objects can't be restored after applying a Pathfinder command, except by choosing Undo, so duplicate your objects first!

➤ We recommend applying the Pathfinder commands to closed paths, as Illustrator may take the liberty of closing open paths for you as it performs the command. To close paths first, see page 395.

➤ Pathfinder commands can be applied to objects that contain a pattern fill, brush stroke, or applied effect, or to a live paint group in combination with other paths.

➤ To apply Pathfinder commands to type, convert it into outlines first.

To apply the Pathfinder commands:

1. Select two or more overlapping objects.

2. Click one of the following Pathfinder buttons on the **Pathfinder** palette:

   Note: See the sidebar at left for a description of Divide and Outline.

   Divide: Each overlapping area becomes a separate, nonoverlapping object **2**.

   ➤ After applying the Divide command, deselect all the objects, choose the

   (Continued on the following page)

Direct Selection tool, click any of the objects, then apply new fill colors or effects; or apply a fill of None; or lower an object's transparency; or remove an object to create a cutout effect.

Trim ▮: The frontmost object shape is preserved; sections of objects behind and overlapping it are deleted. Adjacent or overlapping objects of the same color or shade remain separate (unlike the Merge command). Stroke colors are deleted, unless they contain effects.

Merge ▮: Adjacent or overlapping objects with the same fill attributes are united. Stroke colors are deleted, unless they contain effects.

Crop ▮: Areas of objects that extend beyond the edges of the frontmost object are cropped away, and the frontmost object loses its fill and stroke. Stroke colors are removed (unless effects were applied to the original strokes). Crop works like a clipping mask, but in this case, you can't restore the original objects except by choosing Undo.

Outline ▮: All the objects turn into 0-pt. strokes, and the original fill colors are applied as stroke colors. Transparency settings are preserved; fill colors are removed. The resulting strokes can be scaled and recolored individually.

Minus Back ▮: Objects in back are subtracted from the frontmost object, leaving only portions of the frontmost object. The paint attributes and appearances of the frontmost object are applied to the new path. The objects must overlap (at least partially) for this command to produce a result.

Pathfinder shortcuts

Apply **last-used Pathfinder** command to any objects	Cmd-4/Ctrl-4
Turn **Shape Mode** command into **Pathfinder** command	Option-click/Alt-click the button

▮ *The original objects*

Trim (pulled apart afterward)

▮ *The original objects*

Merge (pulled apart afterward)

▮ *The original objects*

Crop

▮ *The original objects*

Outline (pulled apart afterward)

▮ *The original objects*

Minus Back (the objects in back cut through the topmost object)

1 *Select an object that has a stroke in the desired width (this object has gradient fill and a stroke color.)*

2 *The **Outline Stroke** command converted the stroke into a compound path. (We selected the outer ring, applied a gradient fill, then dragged downward with the Gradient tool to make the ring contrast more with the inner circle.)*

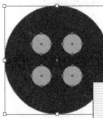

3 *Place smaller objects on top of a larger object, make sure all the objects are selected,...*

4 *...then Control-click/right-click and choose **Make Compound Path** from the context menu.*

Instead of letting a Pathfinder command close your open paths for you, you can use the **Outline Stroke** command to turn the path's stroke into a filled object first. (You can also use this command to convert a line or a stroke into a closed path so it can be filled with a gradient, or to prepare it for trapping.)

To convert a stroke or an open path into a filled object:

1. Select an object that has a stroke color in the desired width **1**.

2. Choose Object > Path > **Outline Stroke.** The new object **2** will have the same width as the original stroke, and the original fill color, if any, will be preserved as a separate object.

Creating compound paths

The **Make Compound Path** command joins two or more objects into one (until or unless the compound path is released). A transparent hole is created where the objects originally overlapped, through which shapes or patterns behind the object are revealed. Regardless of their original paint attributes, all the objects in a compound path are painted with the attributes of the backmost object, and form one unit.

To create a compound path:

1. Arrange the objects you want to make see-through in front of a larger shape **3**. Closed paths work best, and they may have brush strokes.

2. Select all the objects.

3. Choose Object > Compound Path > **Make** (Cmd-8/Ctrl-8).
   or
   If the objects aren't grouped, you can Control-click/right-click on the artboard and choose **Make Compound Path** from the context menu **4**.

(Continued on the following page)

Outline Stroke; Create Compound Path

The frontmost objects will cut through the backmost object like a cookie cutter **1**–**2**. A Compound Path listing will appear on the Layers palette, but the original objects will no longer be listed separately. (Compound shapes, in contrast, are preserved as individual objects within a Compound Shape listing on the Layers palette.)

The fill and stroke attributes of the backmost object will be applied to areas of objects that overlap it or that extend beyond its edges.

If the see-through holes don't result, follow the second set of instructions on the next page.

➤ All objects in a compound path are placed onto the layer of the frontmost object.

➤ Don't overdo it. To avoid printing errors, don't make compound paths from very complex shapes or create a lot of compound paths in one file.

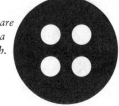

1 *The objects are converted into a* **compound path.**

2 *We placed a background object behind the compound path and applied a white stroke to the black compound path.*

Compound shapes...	versus compound paths	How they're alike
Subpaths are nested as **separate** objects within a **Compound Shape** listing on the Layers palette.	Subpaths are part of a **Compound Path** object.	Use the **Selection** tool to select or move a whole compound shape or compound path.
Click with the **Direct Selection** tool to select a whole subpath within a compound shape.	**Option-click/Alt-click** with the **Direct Selection** tool to select a whole subpath within a compound path.	**Reshape** any subpath within a compound shape or compound path by the usual methods (e.g., add points, delete points, move points).
There are **four** Shape Mode buttons to choose from. And after a compound shape is created, Shape Mode commands can also be applied to individual objects within it.	There is only **one** kind of compound path: Overlapping areas are subtracted from the backmost object, period.	Only one **fill color** can be applied to a compound shape or compound path at a time.
When released, the objects' **original** appearances (e.g., effects, opacity, blending modes) are restored.	Released objects adopt the appearances of the **compound path**, not their original appearances.	

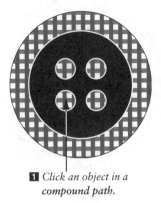

1 *Click an object in a compound path.*

Use Even-Odd Fill Rule

Use Non-Zero Winding Fill Rule

2 *Click the Reverse Path Direction On or Reverse Path Direction Off button on the Attributes palette.*

To add an object to a compound path:

1. Move the object you want to add in front of the compound path. If it's in the back, its attributes will be applied to the compound path. Using the Selection tool or the Lasso tool, select both the compound path and the object you want to add to it.

2. Choose Object > Compound Paths > **Make** (Cmd-8/Ctrl-8).

You can remove the fill color of any shape in a compound path, making the object transparent, or vice versa, by flipping the **Reverse Path Direction** switch on the Attributes palette.

To reverse an object's fill in a compound path:

1. Deselect the compound path.

2. Choose the **Direct Selection** tool (A).

3. Click the edge of the object in the compound path that you want to reverse the color of **1**.

4. Show the **Attributes** palette (Cmd-F11/ Ctrl-F11). **NEW**

5. Click the **Reverse Path Direction Off** button or **Reverse Path Direction On** button—whichever one isn't currently highlighted **2**–**3**.

Note: If the Reverse Path Direction buttons have no effect, you have selected the whole compound path. Select only one path in the compound and try again. If the buttons are dimmed, click the **Use Non-Zero Winding Fill Rule** button, which is Illustrator's default rule for combined paths.

The **Use Even-Odd Fill Rule** makes every other overlapping shape within a compound transparent. It produces more cutouts than the Use Non-Zero Winding Fill Rule (try it on a compound path made from overlapping objects).

3 *The color of two of the holes is reversed.*

Add to, Reverse Fill in Compound Path

397

You can **release** a **compound path** back into its individual objects at any time.

To release a compound path:

1. Choose the **Selection** tool, then click the compound path .

2. Choose Object > Compound Path > **Release** (Cmd-Option-Shift-8/Ctrl-Alt-Shift-8).
   or
   Control-click/right-click the artboard and choose **Release Compound Path** from the context menu.

   All the objects will be selected and will be painted with the attributes, effects, and appearances from the compound path—not their original, precompound appearances . You can use smart guides (Object Highlighting on) to figure out which shape is which.

➤ All the released objects will be nested within the same top-level layer that originally contained the compound path.

➤ When the Type > Create Outlines command is used on any type character, the result is a compound path. If the original character had a counter (interior shape) and you release the compound path, the counter will be a separate path, with the same paint attributes and appearances as the outer part of the letterform –.

1 *Click a compound path.*

2 *The **compound path** is **released**. The holes are no longer transparent.*

3 *Type outlines (a compound path)*

4 *The **compound path** is **released** into separate objects. (We moved the counter of the "P.")*

*A **compound path** by Daniel Pelavin. The holes in the center were originally separate paths.*

MASKS & TRANSPARENCY | 26

In this chapter you'll learn the art of illusion: how to create a clipping set, in which a masking object crops objects or images below it like a picture frame; how to choose opacity levels and blending modes to create an appearance of transparency; and how to partially conceal objects based on shapes and luminosity levels in an opacity mask.

DANIEL PELAVIN (ICON APPEARS COURTESY DFS GROUP, LTD.)

*The rectangular masking object is masking (cropping) parts of objects that extend beyond its border. Together, the objects form a **clipping set**.*

The **masking** object   A **masked** object

*The same image in **Outline** view*

Using clipping sets

In Illustrator, a clipping path works like a picture frame or mat, clipping objects outside its borders and revealing objects within. Masked objects can be moved, restacked, reshaped, or repainted. A clipping path and the objects it masks are referred to collectively as a **clipping set.**

To create a clipping set:

1. Arrange the object or objects to be masked **1**. They can be grouped or not. To avoid a printing error, don't use very intricate objects.

2. Put the masking object (called the **clipping path**) in front of the objects it will be masking. If you need to restack it, on the Layers palette, drag its name upward on the list. It can be an open or closed path, editable type, or a compound shape, and it can have a brush stroke (the path itself—not the brush stroke—will do the clipping).

3. Choose the **Selection** tool (V).

4. Select the clipping path and the object or objects behind it that are to be masked.

5. Control-click/right-click and choose **Make Clipping Mask,** or choose Object > Clipping Mask > **Make** (Cmd-7/Ctrl-7) **2**. The clipping path will now have a stroke and fill of None, and all the objects will remain selected. The words "<Clipping Path>" (underlined) will appear on the Layers palette (unless editable type was used as the clipping path, in which case the type characters will be underlined instead). Also, the clipping path and masked objects will be moved into a clipping set <Group> in the top-level layer of the original clipping path object.

Note: To recolor the clipping path, see page 403.

Click the button

The **Make/Release Clipping Mask** button at the bottom of the Layers palette clips all the objects and groups on the currently active layer, sublayer, or group (whether objects are selected or not), using the topmost object of the layer or group as the clipping path. If a layer is active, the resulting clipping set won't be in a group. The instructions for using clipping sets on pages 400–404 in this chapter also apply to clipping sets made using the Layers palette, but instead of working with a group you'll be working with a layer.

Exporting clipping sets

If you use File > **Export** to export your file in the Photoshop (psd) format, a clipping set in a layer or within a group will export as a layer group with a layer mask, and the clipping effect will be applied to the group.

ORIGINAL IMAGE © PHOTOSPIN

1 *Two objects are selected: a standard type character and a placed raster image.*

2 *After choosing Object > Clipping Mask > Make*

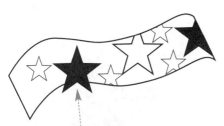

1 *The object to be added (the star) is moved over the clipping set (the banner) to the desired x/y location.*

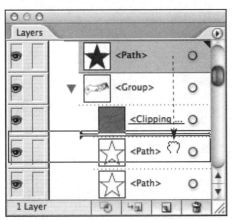

2 *A path is moved downward into the **clipping set** <Group>.*

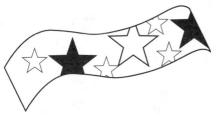

3 *The object is now part of the **clipping set**.*

A **clipping set** contains a clipping path and the objects it's masking.

To select a whole clipping set:

On the **Layers** palette (F7), click the selection area for the layer or group containing the clipping set.
or
Choose the **Selection** tool (V), then click the clipping path or one of the masked objects in the document window.

To select an individual clipping path or masked object:

On the **Layers** palette, click the selection area for the clipping path or a masked object.
or
Choose the **Direct Selection** tool (A), then click the clipping path or a masked object in the document window. You can use smart guides to help you locate the objects (check Object Highlighting in Preferences > Smart Guides & Slices).
or
Choose the **Selection** tool, double-click a **clipping set group** (not a layer) to isolate it, then select a masked object.

To select all the clipping masks in a document:

Deselect all objects, then choose Select > Object > **Clipping Masks.** (With the Selection tool, Shift-click the edge of any masking object you don't want selected.)
Note: This command won't select type if the type is being used as a clipping mask.

To add an object to a clipping set:

1. Choose the **Selection** tool (V).

2. In the document window, move the object to be added over the clipping set **1**.

3. On the Layers palette, expand the list for the clipping set <Group> or layer.

4. Drag the name of the object to be added to the set upward or downward into the <Group> **2** or layer, and release when the object name is in the desired position **3**.

Basic **stacking** techniques are explained on pages 208–209. Here's just a simple rehash.

To restack a masked object within its clipping set:

On the **Layers** palette (F7), drag the object name upward or downward to a new position within the group or layer **1**–**4**.

To copy a masked object:

1. On the Layers palette, click the selection area for the object you want to copy.

2. Option-drag/Alt-drag the selection square upward or downward, and release it somewhere within the same clipping set <Group> or layer.

3. The copy will be in the same *x/y* location as the original object, so you'll probably want to reposition it. You can use the Direct Selection tool to do this, or select the masked object via the Layers palette, then move it using the Selection tool.

➤ If you drag an object's selection square or name outside its group or layer, it will no longer be in the clipping set.

➤ Using the Layers palette, you can lock any object within a clipping set or lock a whole set (see page 214).

1 The original *clipping set, masked by* a rectangle

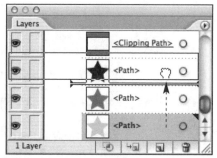

2 The lightest star <Path> is dragged **upward**...

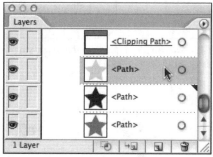

3 ...to the **top** of its clipping set.

4 The lightest star is now in **front** of the other masked objects.

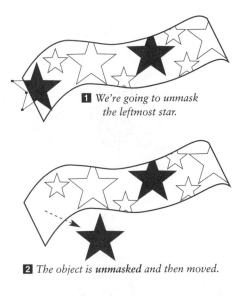

1 *We're going to unmask the leftmost star.*

2 *The object is **unmasked** and then moved.*

3 *The original clipping mask*

4 *After applying a black **fill** to the clipping mask object and recoloring the masked objects*

5 *The original clipping mask object (zebra) and masked objects (stripes)*

6 *The **recolored** clipping mask object and masked objects*

To take an **object out** of a **clipping set,** all you have to do is drag it outside its group or top-level layer on the Layers palette.

To take an object out of a clipping set:

1. Expand the clipping set list on the Layers palette.
2. On the Layers palette, drag the nested object upward or downward out of the group or layer **1**–**2**.
➤ To simultaneously take an object out of a clipping set and delete it from the document, select it, then press Delete/Backspace. Adios.

To recolor a clipping path:

1. Select the clipping path by clicking in its selection area on the Layers palette.
2. Apply color as you would to any object **3**–**6**. The fill and stroke will be listed as attributes on the Appearance palette. The fill will be visible only if there are gaps between the masked objects.
➤ Don't apply a brush stroke to a clipping path—the path will clip the brush stroke.

Take Object Out of Set; Recolor Clipping Path

403

If you **release** a **clipping set,** the complete, original objects will redisplay, and the former clipping path will be listed as a standard path on the Layers palette. If you created the clipping set via Object > Clipping Mask, you can use Method 1 or 2 below; if you created the clipping set via the Layers palette, use only Method 2.

To release a clipping set:

Method 1 (command)

1. Choose the **Selection** tool (V).

2. In the document window, click any part of the clipping set .
   or
   On the Layers palette, click the selection area for the clipping set <Group> you want to release.

3. Control-click/right-click in the document window and choose **Release Clipping Mask,** or choose Object > Clipping Mask > **Release** (Cmd-Option-7/Ctrl-Alt-7) . The <Group> listing for the clipping set will disappear from the Layers palette.

Method 2 (Layers palette)

1. On the Layers palette (F7), click the name of, or click the selection area for, the layer or group that contains a clipping set.

2. Click the **Make/Release Clipping Mask** button 🕐 at the bottom of the Layers palette. If you release a clipping set in a group, the released objects will remain in the group.

   Note: A whole clipping set, if created within a layer via the Layers palette, can't be selected using the Selection tool; you have to use the Layers palette.

➤ The stroke and fill were removed from the clipping path when the mask was created, so unless you recolored it, it will still have a stroke and fill of None. To recolor it, you can use the Layers palette to select it first.

1 *The original **clipping set***

Former clipping path

2 *After choosing Object > Clipping Mask > Release*

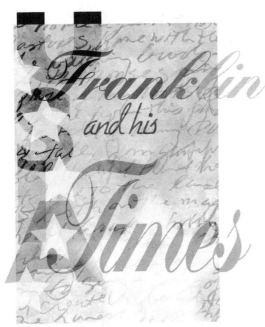

1 *A variety of **opacities** and **blending modes** were applied to the objects in this illustration.*

Using transparency

Using Illustrator's **transparency** controls **1**, you can add a touch of realism to your drawings. Study an object on your desk for a minute, such as a lamp or a beverage in a glass. You might say "The shade is white" when you describe it, but on closer inspection, you'll see that rather than being a dense, uniform color, it contains various permutations of white. And if the lamp is on and light is projecting through it, the shade will look semitransparent rather than opaque. Real objects have different densities, depending on what material they're made of.

By rendering light filtering through various materials or reflecting from various surfaces, you can create a sense of realism. If you draw a window, for example, you can then draw a tinted, semisheer, diaphanous curtain on top of it. If you draw a vase on a table, you can create a shadow for the vase that feathers softly into the table.

In Illustrator, the **opacity** of any kind of object, even editable type, can be changed at any time. You can also choose a **blending mode** for any object to control how it blends with objects below it.

Another way to work with transparency in Illustrator is to turn an object into an **opacity mask.** In this scenario, lights and darks in the topmost object mask control the visiblity of the objects below it.

We'll start by showing you how to change an object's opacity and blending mode. The instructions in this section use the **Transparency** palette. To open it, press Cmd-Shift-F10/Ctrl-Shift-F10; or select an object or objects, then click the blue underlined word "Opacity" on the Control palette. **NEW**

➤ Exporting a file that contains transparency to another application involves choosing options in the File > Export dialog boxes and in the Document Setup dialog box— and can be very problematic. Read about these options on pages 494–498.

Using Transparency

Choosing opacity and blending modes

The **Opacity** setting controls the transparency of each object; the **blending modes** control how object colors are affected by the colors in underlying objects. Objects added to a group or layer adopt the transparency settings of that group or layer.

To change the opacity or blending mode of an object, group, or layer:

1. Do one of the following:

   On the Layers palette (F7), select (or click the target circle for) the **object** or image you want to choose opacity or blending mode settings for **1**.

   To edit the appearance of all the objects on a **group** or **layer,** click the target circle for the group or layer.

   Select an **object** or objects in the document window.

   Select some **type** characters with a type tool, or select a whole type object using the Selection tool.

2. To change just the opacity, on the Control palette, enter or choose an **NEW** **Opacity** percentage (0–100%).
   or
   To change the opacity and/or blending **NEW** mode, click the word **Opacity** on the Control palette or press Cmd-Shift-F10/ Ctrl-Shift-F10. A thumbnail for the selected or targeted layer, group, or object will display on the **Transparency** palette **2**. Move the **Opacity** slider and/or choose a different **blending mode** **3** from the pop-up menu (see the next page).

To change the opacity or blending mode of only an object's fill or stroke:

1. On the Layers palette, click the target circle for an object. (For a type object, see the sidebar on page 408.)

2. On the Appearance palette (Shift-F6), click **Fill** or **Stroke.**

3. On the Transparency or Control palette, **NEW** move the **Opacity** slider **4**; or choose

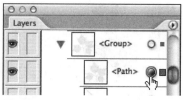

1 *On the Layers palette, click the **target** circle for an object, group, or layer.*

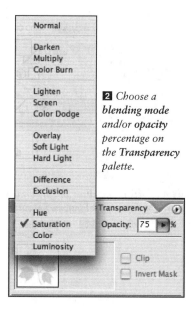

2 *Choose a **blending mode** and/or **opacity** percentage on the **Transparency** palette.*

3 *The **opacity** of the **entire** type character is lowered to 29%.*

4 *The type **Fill opacity** is lowered to 29%; the Stroke opacity is left at 100%.*

Change Opacity, Blending Mode

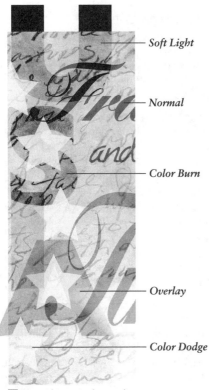

— Soft Light

— Normal

— Color Burn

— Overlay

— Color Dodge

1 *Text objects in front of an image object, with five different blending modes used*

a **blending mode** on the Transparency palette. Attribute changes will be nested in the Fill or Stroke attribute of the targeted object on the Appearance palette.

The blending modes

You can choose from 16 **blending modes** on the Transparency palette **1** (if you use Adobe Photoshop, you're already familiar with them). The blending mode controls how the color of an object (called the **object color** in the descriptions below) blends with underlying colors (the **base color**).

NORMAL
All base colors are modified equally. At 100% opacity, the object color will be opaque.

DARKEN
The object color darkens light colors in the base color; darker colors remain unchanged; contrast in the object color is lowered.

MULTIPLY
A dark object color produces a darker base color, whereas a light object color merely tints the base color. Good for creating semi-transparent shadows.

COLOR BURN
Increases contrast in the base color by making dark colors darker.

LIGHTEN
Base colors that are darker than the object color are modified; base colors that are lighter than the object color are not. Choose for an object color that's lighter than the base colors you want to modify.

SCREEN
A light object color produces a lighter, bleached base color; a dark object lightens the base color less.

COLOR DODGE
A light object color lightens the base color by decreasing the contrast; a dark object color tints the base color less.

(Continued on the following page)

Blending Modes

OVERLAY

Multiplies (darkens) dark base colors and screens (lightens) light base colors while preserving luminosity (light and dark) values. Black and white areas aren't changed, so details are preserved.

SOFT LIGHT

Lowers contrast in the object color, producing a softening and fading effect; preserves luminosity values in the base color.

HARD LIGHT

Screens (lightens) the base color if the object color is light; multiplies (darkens) the base color if the object color is dark. Contrast is increased in the blended color areas. Good for creating glowing highlights.

DIFFERENCE

Produces marked color changes by inverting the base and object colors. The lighter the object color, the more saturated the inverted color.

EXCLUSION

Grays out the base color where the object color is dark; inverts the base color where the object color is light.

HUE

The object color's hue is applied. Saturation and luminosity values aren't changed in the base color.

SATURATION

The object color's saturation is applied. Hue and luminosity values aren't changed in the base color.

COLOR

The object color's saturation and hue are applied. The base color's light and dark (luminosity) values aren't changed, so details are preserved. Good for tinting.

LUMINOSITY

The base color's luminosity values are replaced by luminosity values from the object color. Preserves hue and saturation values in the base color.

Stroke or fill opacity in type

Before you can change the opacity of the stroke on a type object separately from the fill, or vice versa, you must either convert the type to outlines or, to keep the type editable, do the following:

1. Select the type object using the Selection tool.

2. Choose **Add New Fill** or **Add New Stroke** from the Appearance palette menu, then choose a fill color, stroke color, and stroke weight. Make sure the type is large enough for both the fill and stroke to be visible.

3. Double-click the word "Characters" on the Appearance palette. All the characters in the object, plus a type tool, will become selected.

4. Click Fill on the Appearance palette, then click the Delete Selected Item button 🗑 on the palette; do the same for the Stroke attribute.

5. Click the word "Type" at the top of the Appearance palette, then click the Fill or Stroke attribute.

6. Now you can modify the Fill or Stroke attribute by moving the Opacity slider and/or choosing a different blending mode on the Transparency palette.

1 *The original objects (an image and a group of squares): the blending mode and opacity for each square interacts with **all** the underlying layers.*

2 *With **Isolate Blending** on for the group of nested squares, the blending modes affect only objects **within** the group. (Where the objects in the group don't overlap one another, though, you can still see through to the globe below the group.)*

Restricting transparency effects

If you apply a blending mode to multiple selected objects, that mode will become an appearance for each object. In other words, the objects will blend with one another and with underlying objects below them. Checking the **Isolate Blending** option, as per the instructions below, seals a collection of objects so the blending modes affect only those objects, but not the underlying objects.

Note: The Isolate Blending option has no effect on opacity settings; underlying objects will still show through objects that aren't fully opaque.

To restrict a blending mode effect to specific objects:

1. On the Layers palette (F7), click the target circle for a group or layer that contains nested objects to which a blending mode or modes are applied **1**.

2. On the Transparency palette, check **Isolate Blending 2**. (If this option isn't visible, double-click the double arrowhead on the palette tab.) Nested objects within the targeted group or layer will blend with one another, but not with any underlying objects outside the layer or group.

   Note: To reverse the effect, retarget the group or layer, then uncheck Isolate Blending.

➤ Isolate Blending can also be used on individual objects that have overlapping strokes and/or fills. Each stroke or fill can have a different blending mode.

➤ If Isolate Blending is checked for objects nested within a group or layer and the Illustrator file is exported to Photoshop (via File > Export, with the Photoshop .psd format chosen), the group will be preserved as separate layers within a layer group and each layer will keep its blending mode setting from Illustrator.

Isolate Blending

The **Knockout Group** option on the Transparency palette controls whether objects nested in a group or layer will show through each other (knock out) where they overlap. This option affects only objects within the currently targeted group or layer.

To knock out objects:

1. Nest objects in the same group or layer and arrange them so they partially overlap one another. In order to see how the Knockout Group option works, to some or all of the nested objects, apply opacity values below 100% and/or different blending modes (not Normal mode).
2. On the Layers palette (F7), target the group or layer that the objects are nested within **1**.
3. On the Transparency palette, keep clicking the **Knockout Group** box until a check mark displays **2**. With this option checked, objects won't show through each other, but you'll still be able to see through any semitransparent objects to underlying objects.

   Note: To turn off the Knockout Group option at any time, target the group or layer to which the option is applied, then keep clicking the Knockout Group box until the check mark disappears.

➤ If both Knockout Group and Isolate Blending are checked, nested objects will look as though they have a blending mode of Normal, regardless of their actual blending mode.

➤ Let's say you lower the opacity of a stroke attribute for an object or type outline via the Appearance palette. If you want the stroke to be opaque just where it overlaps the fill, select the object, click the Default Transparency listing on the Appearance palette to target the whole object, then check Knockout Group on the Transparency palette **3**–**4**.

When to put it in neutral

Objects that have an opacity below 100% will show through one another, whether the **Knockout Group** icon is blank (unchecked) or **neutral.** Neutral is represented by a dash in Mac and by a green square in Windows. If you choose the neutral setting for a group of objects nested within a larger group, the nested group will adopt the Knockout Group setting of the larger group.

1 *The original group of nested objects on top of an image, with* ***Knockout Group off***

2 *With* ***Knockout Group on,*** *objects are no longer transparent to each other and no longer blend with each other.*

3 ***Knockout Group off:*** *The stroke is transparent, revealing the object's fill.*

4 ***Knockout Group on:*** *The stroke knocks out the object's fill.*

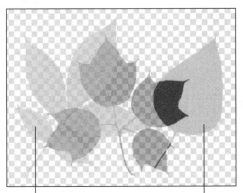

Semitransparent object   Light-colored,
                                opaque object

1 With the **transparency grid** showing, you can more easily see which objects are opaque and which are not.

Using the transparency grid

Once you start working with semitransparent objects, you may find it hard to distinguish between objects that have a light but solid tint and those that are semitransparent. With the **transparency grid** on, you'll be able to see the gray and white checkerboard behind any object whose opacity is lower than 100%.

To show/hide the transparency grid:

Choose View > **Show Transparency Grid** (Cmd-Shift-D/Ctrl-Shift-D) **1**. To turn this feature off, choose View > Hide Transparency Grid or press the shortcut again.

Flatten selectively?

You can use the Object > **Flatten Transparency** command to prepare overlapping, semitransparent **objects** for print output by flattening (dividing) the overlapping areas into separate, nonoverlapping objects **2**–**3**. The semitransparent look is preserved, but the transparency is no longer editable. Select the objects, then choose the command.

Transparency Flattener settings chosen in File > Document Setup and in File > Print (Advanced panel) affect the whole **document,** not individual objects. Read more about printing and exporting transparency on pages 494–498.

Transparency Grid

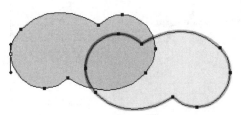

2 Two objects are selected. The object on the right has a semitransparent fill and a stroke color; the object behind on the left it has a fill color and a stroke of None.

3 After the **Flatten Transparency** command is applied, the paths now number five instead of two. (We pulled the paths apart to show you.)

You can change the **colors** or **size** of the **transparency grid** to make it contrast better with colors in your artwork.

To choose preferences for the transparency grid:

1. Choose File > **Document Setup** (Cmd-Option-P/Ctrl-Alt-P) **1**.

2. Choose **Transparency** from the topmost pop-up menu.

3. Choose the desired **Grid Size: Small, Medium,** or **Large.**

4. From the **Grid Colors** pop-up menu, choose **Light, Medium,** or **Dark** for a grayscale grid, or choose a preset color.
or
To choose custom grid colors, click the top color swatch (this color will also be the artboard color when no transparency grid is showing), choose a color from the **Colors** dialog box, then click OK. Click the second swatch, click a second color, then click OK again.

5. *Optional:* Check Simulate Colored Paper if you want objects and placed images in the document to look as though they're printed on colored paper. The object color will blend with the "colored paper" (the top color swatch is used as the paper color). Hide the transparency grid to see the full effect.

6. Click OK.

1 *In the* **Transparency** *panel of the* **Document Setup** *dialog box, choose preferences for the transparency grid.*

Transparency Grid Preferences

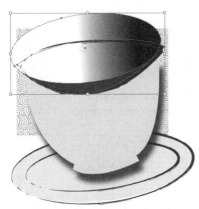

1 *Two objects are selected: the top of the cup and a gradient oval directly above it.*

2 *After applying the Make Opacity Mask command*

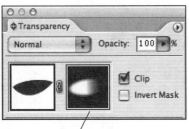

3 *The Mask thumbnail*

Using opacity masks

When you create an **opacity mask,** the shape and value levels of the topmost object (the **masking object**) control the opacity (transparency) of the objects below it. Black or dark values in the mask make the underlying masked objects totally transparent (see-through); white or very light values make the underlying masked objects opaque; and shades of gray (mid-range values) make the underlying masked objects semitransparent.

To create an opacity mask:

1. Place the object to be used as the mask above the object or objects to be masked, then select them all **1**. As the mask, you may use editable type, a placed (linked or embedded) image, an object containing a pattern or gradient, or a mesh.

2. From the Transparency palette menu, choose **Make Opacity Mask 2** to link the object(s) and mask. On the Transparency palette, a thumbnail of the objects being masked will appear on the left and a thumbnail for the mask will appear on the right, with the link icon between them **3**. (If the thumbnails aren't visible, choose Show Thumbnails from the Transparency palette menu.)

   If you used only two objects in step 1, those objects will be combined into one; if you used more than two objects, they'll be nested within a <Group> on the Layers palette. The new object or <Group> name will have a dashed underline, indicating the presence of an opacity mask.

➤ The object/mask combination can be transformed, recolored, or assigned transparency attributes, effects, or graphic styles—like any object or group.

➤ If you place a Photoshop (psd) file into Illustrator and convert its layers into objects, any layer mask from the Photoshop file will be converted into an opacity mask (see pages 280–281).

Create Opacity Mask

You can control whether or not an opacity mask clips parts of objects that extend beyond its edges. Regardless of the current **Clip** setting, the mask will still affect the objects it's grouped with.

To turn clipping on or off for an opacity mask:

1. Choose a selection tool, then select an opacity mask group via the Layers palette **1**.

2. On the Transparency palette, check or uncheck **Clip 2**–**3**.

➤ To have future opacity masks be clipped by default, make sure the New Opacity Masks Are Clipping command on the Transparency palette menu has a check mark.

The **Invert Mask** option reverses the value levels in the masking object, and thus reverses the masking effect.

To invert an opacity mask:

1. Choose a selection tool, then select the opacity mask object **4** via the Layers palette.

2. Check **Invert Mask** on the Transparency palette **5**–**6** (uncheck the box to restore the original effect).

➤ To have future opacity masks be inverted by default, make sure the New Opacity Masks Are Inverted command on the Transparency palette menu has a check mark.

1 *The original objects. (The round object will serve as the opacity mask.)*

2 *After choosing **Make Opacity Mask** with the **Clip** option on...*

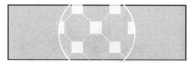

3 *...and with the **Clip** option off*

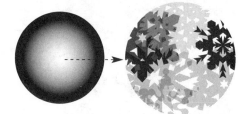

4 *A circle with a radial gradient fill is moved over a group of snowflake shapes...*

5 *...then turned into an **opacity mask**. Where the gradient is white (in the center), shapes are revealed.*

6 *The opacity mask is **inverted** (the center of the gradient is now black); the shapes in the center are masked.*

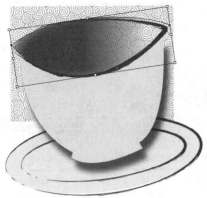

1 *An opacity mask, positioned at the top of a cup, is selected for editing.*

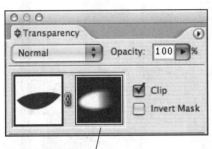

2 *Opacity mask thumbnail*

Follow these instructions to edit a **masking object** separately from the masked objects.

To reshape or edit an opacity masking object:

1. On the **Layers** palette, select the opacity mask object or group by clicking its target circle **1**.

2. On the **Transparency** palette, click the opacity mask thumbnail (on the right) **2**.

   When an opacity mask thumbnail is active, all you'll see on the Layers palette is an <Opacity Mask> layer containing a nested object or objects. For editing or appearance changes, you can target this layer or the individual objects or click the object in the document window.

3. Do any of the following: Use any path reshaping tool to change the contour of the mask; transform the object; change its color, pattern, or gradient fill; change its opacity; or apply an effect or graphic style to it.

4. When you're done, be sure to click the object thumbnail on the Transparency palette. The Layers palette will now list all the layers and objects in the document again.

➤ Option-click/Alt-click the opacity mask thumbnail on the Transparency palette to toggle between viewing just the masking object and viewing the artwork in the document window.

Reshape, Edit Opacity Mask

In order to **move** a **masking object** separately from the masked objects, you have to unlink them.

To move a mask object independently:

1. Choose a selection tool, then select the opacity mask object.

2. On the Transparency palette, click the **link** icon between the object thumbnail and the mask thumbnail **1** (or choose Unlink Opacity Mask from the Transparency palette menu), then click the mask thumbnail.

3. Move the masking object in the document window **2**–**3**.

4. To relink the mask, make sure the object thumbnail is selected on the Transparency palette, then click between the thumbnails; the link icon will reappear. The link icon is accessible only when the object thumbnail is selected.

To deactivate a mask:

1. Select the opacity mask object via the Layers palette.

2. Shift-click the **mask thumbnail** on the Transparency palette. A red "X" will appear over the thumbnail, and the mask effect will disappear from view.

3. To reactivate the mask, Shift-click the mask thumbnail again.

If an **opacity mask** is **released,** the masked objects and masking object will become separate objects. Any modifications that were made to the mask will be preserved, however, along with the objects' original appearances.

To release an opacity mask:

1. Select the opacity mask object via the Layers palette.

2. From the Transparency palette menu, choose **Release Opacity Mask.** The opacity mask thumbnail will disappear from the Transparency palette.

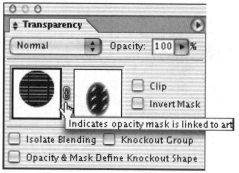

1 *Click the* **link** *icon to unlink (not unmask!) the masking and masked objects.*

Mask

2 *The masking object is selected (it contains a gradient, to produce a reflection)...*

3 *...and then moved to the left.*

SYMBOLS 27

In this chapter you'll learn how to work with symbols—Illustrator objects that are stored on the Symbols palette and can be placed in any document. You'll learn how to place symbol instances into a document, either by dragging or by using the Symbol Sprayer tool; edit those instances using the Symbol Shifter, Scruncher, Sizer, Spinner, Stainer, Screener, and Styler tools; and use the Symbols palette to create, rename, duplicate, edit, and delete symbols.

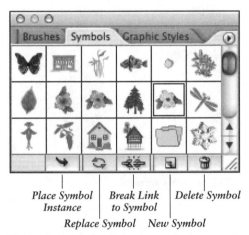

Place Symbol Instance · Break Link to Symbol · Delete Symbol

Replace Symbol · New Symbol

1 Use the Symbols palette to store, duplicate, replace, and delete symbols, and to place symbol instances.

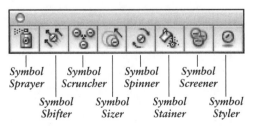

Symbol Sprayer · Symbol Scruncher · Symbol Spinner · Symbol Screener

Symbol Shifter · Symbol Sizer · Symbol Stainer · Symbol Styler

2 The symbolism tools

Using the Symbols palette

Any object that you can create in Illustrator can be stored on the **Symbols** palette (Cmd-Shift-F11/Ctrl-Shift-F11) **1** and placed into any document. To place an **instance** of a symbol onto the artboard, you simply drag it out of the Symbols palette. To place multiple instances of a symbol, you drag or hold the **Symbol Sprayer** tool in one spot. A collection of instances in its own bounding box is called a **symbol set**. With symbols, you can create complex art quickly and easily. Spray a tree symbol, spray a grass symbol, then spray a flower symbol to create a flowering forest meadow with just a few mouse clicks.

Using the other symbolism tools (**Symbol Shifter, Scruncher, Sizer, Spinner, Stainer, Screener,** and **Styler**) **2**, you can change the density, position, stacking order, size, rotation, transparency, color tint, or style of multiple symbol instances in a selected symbol set, while still maintaining the link to the original symbol. Because of this link, if you edit the original symbol, any instances of that symbol in the document will update automatically. Also, you can apply graphic styles, effects, and tranformations to individual instances or whole sets.

Another advantage of using symbols is that each time you create an instance, Illustrator uses the original symbol instead of creating

(Continued on the following page)

individual objects multiple times. For example, say you draw a boat, save it as a symbol in the Symbols palette, then drag with the Symbol Sprayer to create multiple instances in a symbol set. Even though 50 instances of the boat may appear in the symbol set, Illustrator defines the object in the document code only once. This not only saves you time, it also keeps the file size down. File size is especially critical when outputting to the Web in SVG (Scalable Vector Graphics) or Flash (swf) format. Because each symbol is defined only once in the exported SVG image or Flash animation, the size of the export file is kept small, and thus its download time is significantly reduced.

When you **drag** a **symbol** out of the **Symbols palette,** an **instance** of the symbol is made automatically; the original symbol remains on the palette. To begin with, you can use the default symbols on the Symbols palette. On page 420, you'll learn how to create symbols of your own.

To create individual symbol instances:

Drag a symbol from the **Symbols** palette onto the artboard **1**–**2** (Cmd-Shift-F11/ **NEW** Ctrl-Shift-F11 opens and closes the palette).
or
Click a symbol on the Symbols palette, then click the **Place Symbol Instance** button ➥ on the palette. The instance will appear in the center of the document window.

Repeat to add more instances. Each instance is automatically linked to its original symbol. To demonstrate this point, select an instance on the artboard, then look at the Symbols palette; the symbol on the palette will be selected automatically. You'll learn how to preserve or break this link later in this chapter.

➤ To duplicate an instance, Option-drag/ Alt-drag the instance on the artboard. To place many instances of a symbol quickly, it's much more efficient (and fun) to use the Symbol Sprayer tool (see page 424).

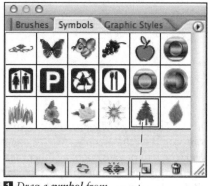

1 *Drag a symbol from the Symbols palette...*

2 *...onto the artboard.*

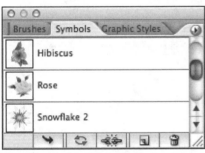
1 *The Symbols palette in* **Thumbnail view**

(The Symbols palette in Small List view)

2 *The Symbols palette in* **Small List view**

(The Symbols palette in Large List view)

3 *The Symbols palette in* **Large List view**

4 *Part of the Adobe Illustrator* **Maps** *symbol library*

To change the Symbols palette display:

From the Symbols palette menu, choose one of the following:

Thumbnail View 1 to display symbols as swatches. Use tool tips to learn the names.

Small List View 2 to display symbols as small swatches with their names listed.

Large List View 3 to display symbols as large swatches with their names listed.

➤ Choose Sort by Name from the palette menu to sort the symbols alphabetically by name.

Opening symbol libraries

Already bored with the default choices on the Symbols palette? Take a peek at some of the **Adobe symbol libraries.**

To use symbols from other libraries:

1. From the **Open Symbol Library** submenu on the Symbols palette menu (or the Window > Symbol Libraries submenu), choose a library. A library palette will open **4**–**5**.

2. Click a symbol on the library palette to add it to the Symbols palette. Or to add multiple symbols, click the first symbol in a series of consecutive symbols, then Shift-click the last symbol in the series (or Cmd-click/Ctrl-click nonconsecutive symbols), then drag them to the Symbols palette.

➤ If you drag a symbol from a library into your document, the symbol will appear on the Symbols palette automatically.

➤ To save a symbol library, see page 421.

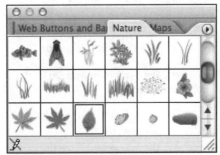
5 *Part of the Adobe Illustrator* **Nature** *symbol library*

419

Replacing symbols

When you **replace** a **symbol in an instance** with a different symbol, any transformations, transparency settings, or effects that were applied to the original instance will also be applied to the replacement.

To replace the symbol in an instance:

1. Choose the **Selection** tool (V), then click an instance in your document **1**.

2. On the Symbols palette, click the desired symbol.

3. Click the **Replace Symbol** button ⟳ on the palette **2** (or choose Replace Symbol from the palette menu).

Creating symbols

Now that you're acquainted with the Symbols palette, it's time to get personal and **create your own symbols.** Any Illustrator object—path, compound path, mesh, embedded raster image, text, group of objects, or even another symbol—can be made into a new symbol. Within reason, that is. If you're going to use the Symbol Sprayer to spray a gazillion instances of a symbol, you'd be wise to keep it relatively simple.

Note: If the object (to become a symbol) contains a brush stroke, blend, effect, style, or other symbols, those attributes will become fixed parts of the new symbol, which means they can't be edited in a linked instance of that symbol (see page 422).

To create a symbol from an object in your artwork:

1. Create one or more objects (or a group) to become a symbol, scale it to the desired size, and keep it selected **3**.

2. Choose the **Selection** tool (V), then drag the object onto the **Symbols** palette **4**.
   or
   Click the **New Symbol** button ⬚ at the bottom of the palette.
   or
   Choose **New Symbol** from the palette menu, type a name, then click OK.

   To rename the new symbol, see the sidebar on the next page.

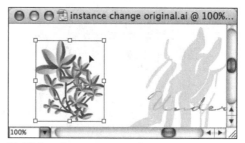

1 *Click an **instance** in your document,...*

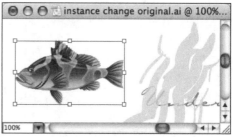

2 *...click a different symbol on the Symbols palette, then click the **Replace Symbol** button on the palette. Here, the plant is replaced with a fish.*

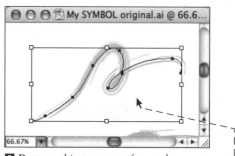

3 *Drag an object or group from a document...*

4 *...onto the **Symbols** palette.*

This alert dialog box will appear if you reopen a document that contains a symbol whose color mode doesn't match the mode of the current document.

Saving symbol libraries

You can **save** the **symbols** currently on the Symbols palette into a **library**.

To save a symbol library:

1. Choose **Save Symbol Library** from the bottom of the Symbol palette menu.

2. Type a new name for the library in the Save As field, choose a location (the default location is fine), then click **Save**.

3. To open the new library or any other custom library, from the Symbols palette menu, choose Open Symbol Library > **Other Library** (or choose Window > Symbol Libraries > Other Library), locate and click the desired library, then click **Open**.

Deleting symbols

If you try to **delete** a **symbol** from the **Symbols** palette that's being used in your document, an alert dialog box will appear. You can expand the instances, delete the instances, or cancel the deletion.

To delete a symbol:

1. Drag the symbol you want to delete over the **Delete Symbol** button 🗑 at the bottom of the palette.
   or
   Click a symbol on the Symbols palette, click the **Delete Symbol** button 🗑 at the bottom of the palette, then click **Yes**.

2. An alert dialog box will appear if the document contains any linked instances of the symbol being deleted **2**. Click **Expand Instances** to expand the linked instances into standard, nonlinked objects, or click **Delete** Instances to delete the linked instances (or click Cancel to call the whole thing off).

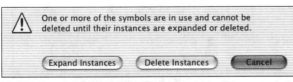

2 *This alert dialog box will appear if you try to **delete** a symbol that's **linked** to **instances** in the document.*

Modifying symbol instances

To modify symbol instances:

Modifications that are made to an instance or set don't affect the original symbol or the link to it. You can **modify** an instance or set in the following ways **1**–**2**: **move** it; change its **opacity**; change its **blending mode**; apply **graphic styles** or **effects** to it; or **transform** it (via the Transform palette, by dragging the handles on its box, or via an Object menu > Transform command).

To modify any **effect** that was applied to an instance or set after it was placed into the artwork, double-click the effect listing on the **Appearance** palette, then change the settings.

You can also use the **Symbol Shifter, Symbol Scruncher, Symbol Sizer, Symbol Spinner, Symbol Stainer, Symbol Screener,** or **Symbol Styler** tool to modify instances or sets. Instances can be recolored via the Symbol Stainer tool, but not via the Swatches or Color palette or via filters. You'll learn about these tools later in this chapter.

➤ When an instance is expanded, the link between the instance and the original symbol is broken (see page 436).

Duplicating symbols

On the next page you'll learn how to edit a symbol (the original symbol—not an instance). Before you do this, you may want to **duplicate** the **symbol,** as per the following instructions.

To duplicate a symbol:

On the Symbols palette, drag a symbol over the **New Symbol** button ▣ at the bottom of the palette **3**–**4**.
or
Click a symbol, then choose **Duplicate Symbol** from the palette menu.

The duplicate symbol will appear after the last symbol.

➤ You can drag any symbol thumbnail or listing to a new position on the palette.

➤ Option-drag/Alt-drag one symbol over another to copy the first symbol and remove the second one.

1 *The original **instance** of a symbol*

2 *After **enlarging** the instance, lowering its **opacity**, and applying the Drop Shadow **effect** to it*

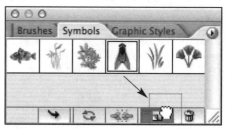

3 *Drag a symbol over the **New Symbol** button.*

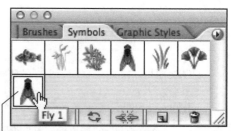

4 *A **duplicate** of the symbol appears on the palette.*

Modify Instances; Duplicate Symbol

1 *The original* **instance**

2 *We* **broke** *the* **link** *between the instance and the original symbol, edited the former instance (recolored it), then Option-dragged/ Alt-dragged it over the original symbol.*

3 *The newly* **redefined** *symbol*

Redefining symbols

To edit a symbol, the first step is to break the link between the symbol and one of its instances. Next, you'll modify the former instance. And finally, you'll use that object to **redefine** the **original symbol.**

Beware! Every instance is linked to its original symbol. If you redefine a symbol, those changes will be applied to any and all instances in the document that originated from that symbol. This makes for efficient document editing, of course, but it can also wreak havoc if you don't keep it in mind.

To redefine a symbol:

1. Create an instance of a symbol (or a duplicate of a symbol) in your document **1** and keep it selected. To duplicate a symbol, see the previous set of instructions.

2. Click the **Break Link** button 🔗 at the bottom of the Symbols palette.

3. Modify the resulting object (former instance) to your liking, as you would any object.

4. With the object still selected:

    Option-drag/Alt-drag the object over the symbol on the **Symbols** palette that you want to redefine **2**–**3**.
    or
    Click a symbol on the palette, then choose **Redefine Symbol** from the palette menu.

    All instances that are currently linked to the now redefined symbol will automatically update to reflect the changes that were made to the symbol, but any transformations, effects, opacity values, etc. that were applied to those instances before the symbol was redefined will be preserved.

➤ To create a new symbol instead of redefining an existing one, drag the object onto a blank area of the Symbols palette.

Using the Symbol Sprayer tool

There are eight symbolism tools 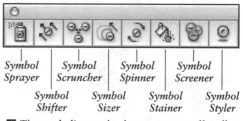. The **Symbol Sprayer** tool sprays multiple instances of a symbol onto the artboard. Each time you use it, the objects that result are grouped together into what is called a **symbol set.** You can also use this tool to delete instances from a set.

1 *The symbolism tools, shown on a tearoff toolbar*

You'll use the other symbolism tools—Symbol Shifter, Symbol Scruncher, Symbol Sizer, Symbol Spinner, Symbol Stainer, Symbol Screener, and Symbol Styler—to modify the position, size, orientation, color, transparency, or style of a symbol instance or symbol set while preserving the link to the original symbol. (If the folks at Adobe couldn't think of a tool name beginning with the letter "S," the tool got scrapped!)

First, the Symbol Sprayer. You can choose from a slew of options for this tool, but before you get into that, do a bit of spraying.

To use the Symbol Sprayer tool:

1. Choose the **Symbol Sprayer** tool (Shift-S).

2. Click a symbol on the **Symbols** palette.

3. To create **instances,** click once; or click and hold the mouse in the same spot **2**–**3**; or drag.

   To **add** more instances to a set, select the set via a Selection tool or the Layers palette, click a symbol on the Symbols palette, then use the Symbol Sprayer tool.

   To create a **new set,** Cmd-click/Ctrl-click outside the bounding box for the current set first.

   To **remove** symbol instances, select the set via a Selection tool or the Layers palette, click the symbol on the Symbols palette, then with the Symbol Sprayer tool, Option-click/Alt-click or Option-drag/Alt-drag inside the set.

➤ To move a whole symbol set on the artboard, drag one of the objects in the set with the Selection tool. To transform all the instances in a set, use the handles on its bounding box (see page 139).

2 *Multiple instances created by holding down the Symbol Sprayer tool in one spot (the original symbol had an opacity of 50%)*

3 *Symbols placed by using the Symbol Sprayer tool*

Choosing symbolism tool options

The **Symbolism Tools Options** dialog box lets you choose global settings that apply to all the symbolism tools, as well as settings that apply just to individual tools. First, we'll discuss the global settings.

To choose global properties for the symbolism tools:

1. If you're going to adjust the Density for the Symbol Sprayer, you may want to select a symbol set in your document now so you'll be able to preview Density changes with the dialog box open.

2. Double-click any symbolism tool. The Symbolism Tools Options dialog box opens **1**.

3. To specify a default size for all the symbolism tools, choose or enter a **Diameter** value (1–999).

4. To adjust the rate at which the tools apply their effect (or the sprayer creates instances), choose an **Intensity** value (1–10). The higher the Intensity, the more quickly an effect is applied. Or to have a stylus control this option instead, choose any option from the pop-up menu other **NEW** than Fixed.

5. To specify how close instances will be to one another when applied with the Symbol Sprayer tool, choose a **Symbol Set Density** value (1–10) **2**–**3**. The higher the Symbol Set Density, the more tightly the instances will be packed within each set. Changes in this value will preview in any currently selected sets.

6. Check **Show Brush Size and Intensity** to have the current Diameter setting be reflected in the brush cursor size, and the Intensity setting be expressed as a shade on the ring of the brush cursor—black for high intensity **4**, gray for medium intensity, and light gray for low intensity **5**. With this option off, the tool icon cursors will be used instead.

7. Click OK.

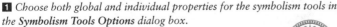

 High intensity cursor

5 *Low intensity* cursor

1 *Choose both global and individual properties for the symbolism tools in the Symbolism Tools Options dialog box.*

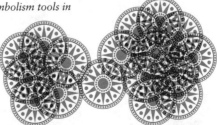

2 *The Symbol Sprayer tool used with low Intensity and Symbol Set Density values*

3 *The Symbol Sprayer tool used with high Intensity and Symbol Set Density values*

To choose Symbol Sprayer tool options:

1. Double-click the **Symbol Sprayer** tool (Shift-S).
   or
   Double-click a symbolism tool, then click the **Symbol Sprayer** button in the Symbolism Tools Options dialog box.

2. Choose **Diameter, Intensity,** and **Symbol Set Density** settings **1** (see the previous page for definitions).

3. The **Scrunch, Size, Spin, Screen, Stain,** and **Style** pop-up menus define the parameters for instances that are created by the Symbol Sprayer tool. Choose **Average** from a property pop-up menu to add instances based on an average sampling from neighboring instances in the set within the diameter of the brush cursor in its current location. Or choose **User Defined** to add instances based on a predetermined value (see the sidebar).

   Note: The settings chosen from the six individual tool pop-up menus bear no relationship to the Method setting, which applies to the other symbolism tools.

4. Click OK.

User Defined defined

For the **Symbol Sprayer** tool, you can choose either Average or User Defined for each property. If you choose **User Defined,** the properties will be based on the following variables:

Scrunch (density) and **Size** are based on the original symbol size.

Spin is based on the direction the mouse is moved.

Screen is based on 100% opacity.

Stain is based on the current Fill color at a 100% tint.

Style is based on whichever graphic style is currently selected on the Graphic Styles palette.

➤ For more information, read about the individual tools on the following pages.

➤ When you use a symbolism tool (such as the Symbol Shifter, Scruncher, or Sizer) to modify instances in a symbol set, keep these two seemingly conflicting tendencies in mind: Instances try to stay as close as possible to their original position in the set in order to maintain their original set density, yet also try to stay apart.

1 *The pop-up menus in the lower portion of the Symbolism Tools Options dialog box appear only when the Symbol Sprayer tool is chosen.*

Interactive brush cursor

When you use a symbolism tool, you can maximize your control by interactively readjusting the brush size and intensity (e.g., a small brush will affect a handful of instances; a large brush will affect a larger number of instances).

To **increase** the brush **intensity** interactively as you use a symbolism tool, press or hold down Shift-] (right bracket); or to **decrease** the brush intensity, press or hold down Shift-[(left bracket).

To **enlarge** a brush interactively as you use a symbolism tool, press or hold down]; or to **shrink** it, press or hold down [.

The effect of the symbolism tools is strongest in the center of the brush cursor and diminishes gradually toward the edge of the cursor. The longer you hold the mouse button down, the stronger the effect.

Adding symbol instances to a set

To **add symbols** to an **existing set,** you must use the Symbol Sprayer tool (not the Place Symbol command). Similarly, you can't select or delete instances in a set using a selection tool, but as we showed you on page 424, you can delete instances by Option/Alt clicking or dragging with the Symbol Sprayer tool.

To add symbol instances to a set:

1. Select a symbol set in your document via the Selection tool or the Layers palette.

2. Choose the **Symbol Sprayer** tool. 🔲

3. The icon for the symbol that was last sprayed into a symbol set will become selected on the Symbols palette when the set is reselected. You can either continue to spray with that symbol or click a different symbol on the palette.

4. Drag inside the selected set **1**.

➤ If a selected set contains two or more different symbols and you want to remove symbols of one type, on the Symbols palette, click the symbol to be removed, then Option-drag/Alt-drag in the set with the Symbol Sprayer tool.

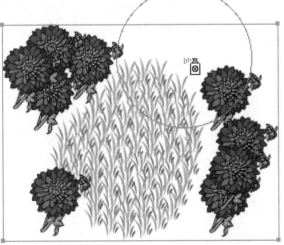

1 *To add instances of a **different** symbol to a set, select the set, choose the **Symbol Sprayer** tool, click a **symbol** on the Symbols palette, then **drag** inside the set.*

Add Instances to Set

427

Using the Symbol Shifter tool

With the exception of the Symbol Sprayer, the symbolism tools—Shifter, Scruncher, Sizer, Spinner, Stainer, Screener, and Styler—modify existing instances (they don't create them). Each tool has a different function (e.g., the Stainer recolors, the Sizer scales, the Styler applies a graphic style); we'll explore each one individually. Keep in mind that you can change the intensity and brush size for each tool interactively via the shortcuts listed on the previous page.

The **Symbol Shifter** tool has two functions. It either shifts instances in a set sideways, based on the direction you drag the cursor, or changes their stacking order (front-to-back position). Being able to bring instances forward or behind other instances would be useful, say, in a set in which trees are obscuring some figures. You could use the Symbol Shifter tool to move the trees closer together to create a forest, then bring the figures forward, in front of the trees.

To use the Symbol Shifter tool:

1. Select a symbol set in your document.

2. Choose the **Symbol Shifter** tool. 🖐

3. Drag in the direction you want the instances to **shift.** The tool will try to preserve the current density and arrangement of instances as it performs its job.
   or
   Shift-click an instance to bring it in **front** of adjacent instances ◼1–◼2.
   or
   Option-Shift/Alt-Shift click an instance to send it **behind** adjacent instances.

To choose Symbol Shifter tool options:

1. Double-click the **Symbol Shifter** tool.

2. Choose a brush **Diameter** ◼3.

3. Choose an **Intensity** value for the rate of shifting and thus the amount of space the tool creates between shifted instances.

4. Choose a **Symbol Set Density** value (see page 425).

5. Click OK.

Why aren't all the instances changing?

If a selected set contains instances from more than one symbol and one of those symbols happens to be **selected** on the Symbols palette, modifications made by a symbolism tool will be limited to only the instances from the currently selected symbol. If you want to modify instances of more than one type of symbol in a set, **deselect all** symbols by clicking an empty area of the Symbols palette first.

◼1 *The Symbol Shifter tool is used (with Shift held down, in this case) on this symbol set…*

◼2 *…to shift the plovers into a more believable front-to-back order.*

◼3 *Options for the Symbol Shifter tool*

Symbolism Tools Options

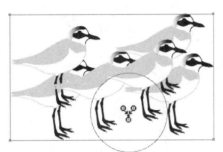

1 *Option-drag/Alt drag across a symbol set with the Symbol Scruncher tool.*

2 *After moving the plovers apart*

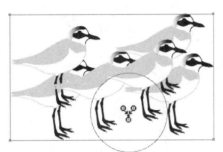

3 *Options for the Symbol Scruncher tool*

Using the Symbol Scruncher tool

The **Symbol Scruncher** tool pulls symbol instances closer together or spreads them apart. A symbol set of clouds or fish, for example, could be contracted (scrunched) to bring the instances closer together or expanded to spread them out. You can either drag the mouse with the tool or hold the mouse button down in one spot.

To use the Symbol Scruncher tool:

1. Select a symbol set in your document.
2. Choose the **Symbol Scruncher** tool.
3. To move instances closer **together,** either click and hold in one spot or drag inside the set.
   or
   To push symbol instances **away** from one another, Option-click/Alt-click or Option-drag/Alt-drag **1**–**2**.

To choose Symbol Scruncher tool options:

1. Double-click the **Symbol Scruncher** tool.
   or
   To change the density in an existing set, click the set, then double-click the **Symbol Scruncher** tool.
2. Choose a brush **Diameter** and choose a **Symbol Set Density** (see page 425) **3**.
3. Choose an **Intensity** value to control how much the tool changes the density, and how quickly it produces the change.
4. Choose a **Method:**

   User Defined to gradually increase or decrease the amount of space between symbol instances based on how you click or drag.

   Average to even out and make more uniform the amount of space between instances based on an average of the existing density of instances. This method will produce a minor effect if the spacing is already averaged.

   Random to randomize the spacing between instances.

5. Click OK.

Symbol Scruncher Tool

Using the Symbol Sizer tool

The **Symbol Sizer** tool reduces or enlarges instances in a symbol set. Because the Symbol Sprayer tool creates instances only of a uniform size, the Symbol Sizer tool is useful for producing scale variations within a set.

To use the Symbol Sizer tool:

1. Click a symbol set in your document.
2. Choose the **Symbol Sizer** tool.
3. Click on or drag over instances to **enlarge** them **1**.
   or
   Option-click/Alt-click or Option-drag/Alt-drag over instances to **shrink** them.

   The instances closest to the cursor will scale the most.

   Note: If very little happens when you use this tool, change the Method to User Defined or Random (see step 6, below).

➤ Use a small brush Diameter to scale instances with more precision.

To choose Symbol Sizer tool options:

1. Double-click the **Symbol Sizer** tool.
2. Choose brush **Diameter** and **Symbol Set Density** values **2**.
3. Choose an **Intensity** value for the rate and amount of resizing. The higher the Intensity, the wider the range of scale changes.
4. *Optional:* Check Proportional Resizing to resize instances without distortion.
5. *Optional:* Check Resizing Affects Density to force instances to move away from each other when they're enlarged or move closer together when they're scaled down, while maintaining the current set density. With this option unchecked, instances may overlap more.
6. Choose a **Method:**

   User Defined to gradually increase or scale the instances based on the way you click or drag.
   or
   Average to make the instances more uniform in size. If the sizes are already near

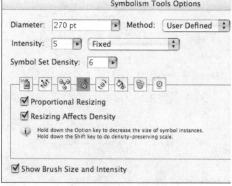

1 *Instances scaled using the Symbol Sizer tool*

2 *Options for the Symbol Sizer tool*

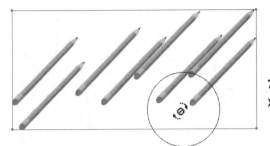

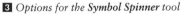

1 *Dragging across a symbol set with the Symbol Spinner tool, Method: Random chosen*

2 *The pencils are rotated randomly.*

3 *Options for the Symbol Spinner tool*

uniform, this method will produce little effect.

or

Random to randomize scale changes within the brush diameter.

7. Click OK.

➤ With Average or Random chosen as the brush Method, Shift-click or Shift-drag to scale instances while maintaining (if possible) the current density.

Using the Symbol Spinner tool

The **Symbol Spinner** tool changes the orientation of instances within a symbol set.

To use the Symbol Spinner tool:

1. Click a symbol set in your document.

2. Choose the **Symbol Spinner** tool.

3. Drag a symbol instance or instances in the direction you want them to rotate, using the arrows as an orientation guide **1**–**2**. Clicking and holding has no effect.

➤ If the arrows are hard to see, change the selection color for the layer that the set resides in.

➤ The smaller the brush diameter, the easier it will be to isolate individual symbol instances for rotation.

To choose Symbol Spinner tool options:

1. Double-click the **Symbol Spinner** tool.

2. Choose brush **Diameter** and **Symbol Set Density** values **3**.

3. Choose an **Intensity** value for the rate and amount the instances can be rotated. The higher the Intensity, the sharper the angles of rotation using the least amount of mouse action.

4. Choose a **Method:**

User Defined to rotate symbol instances in the direction of the cursor.

Average to gradually even out and make uniform the orientation of all instances within the brush diameter.

Random to randomize the orientation of instances.

5. Click OK.

Using the Symbol Stainer tool

Like the Colorization (Tints and Shades) option for brushes, the **Symbol Stainer** tool colorizes symbol instances. It recolors solid fills, patterns, and gradients with varied tints of the current fill color. Use it to vary the shades of green in foliage, the shades of brown in buildings, and so on.

Note: The Symbol Stainer tool increases the file size and diminishes performance, so don't use it if you're going to export your file in the Flash (swf) format or if memory is a concern.

To use the Symbol Stainer tool:

1. Select a symbol set in your document.
2. Choose the **Symbol Stainer** tool.
3. Choose a fill color to be used for staining.
4. **Click** an instance to apply a tint of the current fill color. Continue clicking to increase the amount of colorization, up to the maximum amount.
   or
   Drag across the symbol set to colorize any instances within the brush diameter **1**–**2**. Drag again to intensify the effect.

➤ Option-click/Alt-click or Option-drag/ Alt-drag to decrease the amount of colorization and restore more of the original symbol color.

➤ Shift-click or Shift-drag to tint only instances that have already been stained, while leaving instances that haven't been stained unchanged.

➤ To recolor black-and-white instances, use the Symbol Styler tool with a graphic style that contains the desired color.

To choose Symbol Stainer tool options:

1. Double-click the **Symbol Stainer** tool.
2. Choose brush **Diameter** and **Symbol Set Density** values **3**.
3. Choose an **Intensity** value for the rate and amount of tint the Stainer applies.
4. Chose a **Method:**
   User Defined to gradually tint symbol instances with the current fill color.

1 *Dragging across a symbol set with the Symbol Stainer tool*

2 *The fireworks are **tinted** gradually.*

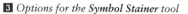

3 *Options for the Symbol Stainer tool*

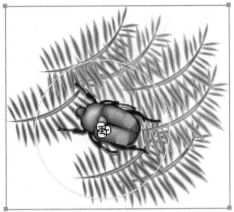

1 *Holding the mouse down on an instance (the beetle) with the* **Symbol Screener** *tool*

2 *The beetle is* **screened**.

Average to even out the amount of existing colorization among selected instances without applying a new tint.

Random to randomize the colorization for a more naturalistic effect.

5. Click OK.

Using the Symbol Screener tool

The **Symbol Screener** tool increases or decreases the opacity of instances within the brush diameter. Use this tool to fade instances and make them more transparent.

To use the Symbol Screener tool:

1. Select a symbol set in your document.

2. Choose the **Symbol Screener** tool.

3. Click and hold on or drag across instances to make them more **transparent** **1**–**2**.
   or
   Option-click/Alt-click on or Option-drag/Alt-drag across instances to make them more **opaque.**

   Note: If nothing happens when you use this tool, change the Method to User Defined or Random (see step 4, below).

To choose Symbol Screener tool options:

1. Double-click the **Symbol Screener** tool.

2. Choose brush **Diameter** and **Symbol Set Density** values **3**.

3. Choose an **Intensity** value for the rate and amount of transparency that is applied. The higher the Intensity, the more quickly and intensely instances will fade.

4. Choose a **Method:**

   User Defined to have transparency increase or decrease gradually.

   Average to even out and make more uniform the amount of transparency among instances within the brush's diameter.

   Random to gradually introduce transparency in a random fashion.

5. Click OK.

Symbolism Tools Options

Diameter: 87 pt   Method: Average

Intensity: 10   Fixed

Symbol Set Density: 4

ⓘ Hold down the Option key to decrease the amount of colorization.
Hold down the Shift key to keep the amount of colorization constant.

☑ Show Brush Size and Intensity

3 *Options for the* **Symbol Screener** *tool*

Using the Symbol Styler tool

The **Symbol Styler** tool applies the graphic style currently selected on the Graphic Styles palette to instances in a set. By selecting different styles on the Graphic Styles palette, you can apply multiple styles to a symbol set. Logically, the tool can also be used to remove styling.

To use the Symbol Styler tool:

1. Select a symbol set in your document.
2. Choose the **Symbol Styler** tool.
3. Click a graphic style on the Graphic Styles palette (you can access it via the NEW Control palette) **1**. *Note:* Be sure to choose the symbolism tool first. If you choose a style while a nonsymbolism tool is selected, the style will be applied to the whole symbol set.
4. Click and hold on or drag across an instance or instances to **apply** the selected style within the brush diameter **2** (and **1**, next page). The longer you hold the mouse down, the more intensely the style will be applied. Pause for the screen to redraw. This can take some time even on a fast machine.
   or
   Option-click/Alt-click or Option-drag/Alt-drag to **undo** the styling.

➤ Shift-click or Shift-drag to gradually apply the currently selected graphic style only to instances that have already been styled, while keeping unstyled instances unchanged.

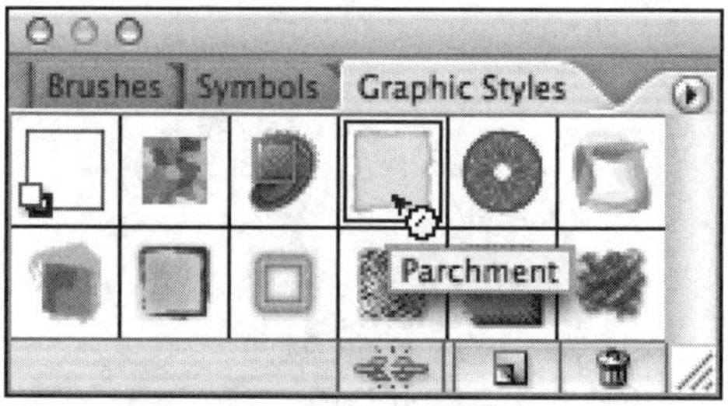

1 *Choose the **Symbol Styler** tool, then click a style on the **Graphic Styles** palette.*

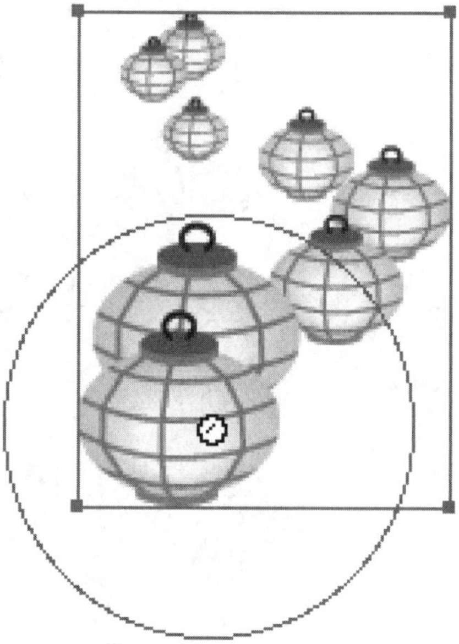

2 *Clicking an instance with the **Symbol Styler** tool*

To choose Symbol Styler tool options:

1. Double-click the **Symbol Styler** tool.
2. Choose brush **Diameter** and **Symbol Set Density** values.
3. Choose an **Intensity** value for the rate and amount of attributes in a graphic style that are applied. The higher the Intensity, the more intense and quick the styling.
4. Choose a **Method:**

   User Defined to gradually increase or decrease the amount of styling.

Symbol Styler Tool

1 *To produce this graphic, different **graphic styles** were applied to **different** instances. Compare with **2** on the previous page.*

Average to even out the amount of styling already applied to instances within the brush diameter, without applying new styling.

Random to apply styling gradually and randomly.

5. Click OK.

➤ If you want to view the attributes used in an applied graphic but you don't know which style was applied, click the symbol set, choose Object > Expand, check Fill and Stroke, then click OK. On the Layers palette, click the gray target circle for one of the expanded instances, then look at the appearance listings on the Appearance palette. Undo to restore the symbol set.

Symbol Styler Tool

435

Expanding symbol instances

Vis-a-vis symbols, the **Expand** command can be used for two different purposes. When applied to a **symbol set,** it breaks the set apart without disturbing the instances themselves or their link to the original symbol. The instances will be nested inside a group on the Layers palette.

When applied to an **individual instance** (not in a set), the Expand command does break the link to the original symbol. In this case, the individual paths from the former instance will be nested inside a group on the Layers palette.

To expand an instance or a symbol set:

1. Select a symbol instance, multiple instances, or symbol set.

2. Choose Object > **Expand** (or choose Object > **Expand Appearance** if the instance has an effect applied to it).

3. Check **Object** and **Fill** █, then click OK.

4. If you expanded a symbol set █–█, you can now use the **Direct Selection** tool to move the individual instances apart, if desired, or double-click the group with the **Selection** tool to isolate the group, then use the Selection tool to modify the instances. In either case, they'll remain linked to the original symbol.

   If you expanded an individual instance █–█, it will now be a group of paths. To modify any path, select it via the Layers palette.

➤ If the original symbol artwork contained any live appearances or effects, they'll be editable once an individual instance of that symbol (not in a set) is expanded. Use the Layers palette to select any individual path or group. The applied effects will be listed on the palette, and are editable. To use the edited object to redefine the symbol, see page 423.

➤ If you use the Symbol Stainer tool on a symbol set and then expand the set, the instances affected by the tool will have a numeric listing on the Layers palette but will remain linked to the symbol.

Select all instances

To select all the solo instances of a particular symbol in your document that don't belong to a set, click the symbol on the Symbols palette, then choose **Select All Instances** from the palette menu.

█ Check **Object** and **Fill** in the **Expand** dialog box.

█ The original symbol **set**

█ After using the **Expand** command

█ The original symbol **instance**

█ After using the **Expand** command, and moving paths apart

In this chapter, you'll learn about the tools that do strange things—
Warp, Pucker, Bloat, Twirl, Scallop, Crystallize, and Wrinkle—
and about envelopes, which allow you to sculpt whole objects.

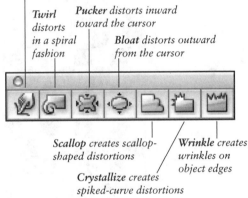

Warp (Shift-R) distorts by
pushing or pulling an edge

Twirl
distorts
in a spiral
fashion

Pucker *distorts inward*
toward the cursor

Bloat *distorts outward*
from the cursor

Scallop *creates scallop-*
shaped distortions

Wrinkle *creates*
wrinkles on
object edges

Crystallize *creates*
spiked-curve distortions

1 *The tearoff toolbar for the seven* **liquify** *tools*

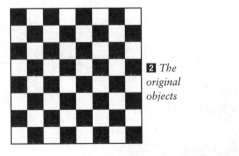

2 *The*
original
objects

3 *Warp*

Using the liquify tools

The seven **liquify** tools—Warp, Twirl, Pucker, Bloat, Scallop, Crystallize, and Wrinkle—distort the edges of individual objects or groups of objects **1**–**3**. You push and pull on an object's edges with the brush's circular cursor, much as you would sculpt a piece of clay by pushing and pulling. Each tool offers different sculpting controls, and each can be customized. For the instructions in this chapter, we recommend that you create a tearoff toolbar for the liquify tools.

To use one of the liquify tools, first you specify option settings for the particular tool, then you drag across an object. You don't have to select the object or group of objects first, but doing so will help prevent other nearby objects from becoming distorted.

The distortions produced by the liquify tools depend on three factors:

➤ The **size** and **angle** of the tool cursor

➤ The tool's **Intensity** setting

➤ The length of **time** the cursor is clicked and held over an object and/or the **distance** the cursor is dragged

As with any feature that offers a lot of options, you'll need to spend some time working with the liquify tools in order to discover how they can be of service to you or how you can achieve the desired effect—or degree of effect. Feel free to experiment with different global brush dimensions and individual tool options settings.

(Continued on the following page)

Liquify Tools

To start, we'll give you a few ground rules so you can get your bearings:

➤ The liquify tools can be used on an individual object, a multiobject selection **1**–**3**, a group, or any combination thereof.

➤ The liquify tools can be used on an object that contains appearances, effects, brush strokes, graphic styles, a pattern, or a mesh.

➤ To use a liquify tool on type, the type must be converted to outlines first (Type > Create Outlines).

➤ To use a liquify tool on a symbol instance or set, the instance or set must be unlinked from the original symbol first (click the Break Link to Symbol button ⚙ on the Symbols palette).

1 *Twirl*

Choosing liquify tool options

Every liquify tool has an options dialog box in which you can choose **Global Brush Dimensions** settings **4**, among other options. The global settings—the dimensions and angle of the cursor and the intensity of the liquify effect—apply to all the liquify tools and remain in effect until they're changed in any of the tool option dialog boxes. (To choose nonglobal settings for an individual liquify tool, see page 440.)

2 *Pucker*

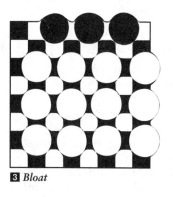

3 *Bloat*

4 *The **Global Brush Dimensions** and **Show Brush Size** options, shown here in the **Warp Tool Options** dialog box, are available in the options dialog box for all the liquify tools.*

(sidebar) **Global Brush Dimensions**

	Click	Shift-Click*
Points	±1 pt	±6 pt
Picas	±p3	±1p
Inches	±1/8"	±1"
Millimeters	±1 mm	±10 mm
Centimeters	±0.1 cm	±1 cm
Pixels	±1 px	±10 px

1 *The* **nudge** *value changes for a cursor's Width and Height*

* The first click rounds off the value in the current meaurement units, then the next click or Shift-click raises or lowers the value by the quantity shown above.

2 *Two liquify tool* **cursors:** *The cursor on the left is ½ in. x ½ in.; the cursor on the right is 1 in. x ½ in. at a −30° angle.*

To choose global brush dimensions:

1. Double-click any **liquify** tool to open its options dialog box. When choosing values, you can use the field or pop-up menu or click the up or down arrowhead. Each click on an arrowhead nudges that value up or down; Shift-click to change the value by a larger increment **1**.

2. Enter **Width** and/or **Height** values in any unit of measure.

3. Choose the cursor **Angle 2**, as measured counterclockwise from the vertical axis.

4. Choose an **Intensity** (1–100%) for the rate of change and amount of pull or push the tool exerts on the edges of an object. At 5%, edges will barely be distorted; at 100%, edges will be distorted exactly as the cursor is dragged **3**.

5. To have a pen or graphics tablet control the Intensity, check **Use Pressure Pen.**

6. Click OK. To choose options for the individual liquify tools, see the following page.

➤ Press a keyboard arrow, alone or in combination with Shift, to nudge the value in the currently active field upward or downward.

➤ Click Reset to restore the options settings for the current tool, as well as all global dimensions, to their default values.

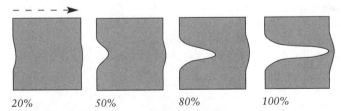

20%   50%   80%   100%

3 *The* **Warp** *tool was used with increasing* **Intensity** *on a square. In each case, the cursor was dragged from the left to the right edge of the square. At 20% Intensity, distortion was minimal; at 100%, the distortion followed the cursor almost all the way to the right edge.*

Global Brush Dimensions

In contrast to the Global Brush Dimensions discussed on the previous page, the options in the lower portion of a liquify tool's options dialog box affect only that tool. That is, you can choose different Detail and Simplify settings, say, for the Warp tool than for the Bloat tool.

The **options** that are present in all or most of the options dialog boxes (**Detail, Simplify,** and **Show Brush Size**) are discussed below. Some tools also have additional options, such as the Complexity setting for the Scallop tool. These options are mentioned, where applicable, in the instructions for the individual tools, which begin on the next page.

To choose options for an individual liquify tool:

1. Double-click a **liquify** tool to open its options dialog box.

2. All the liquify tools have a **Detail** option **1**–**2**, which controls the spacing of points that are added in order to produce distortion. To use this option, check the box, then enter a value (1–10) or drag the slider. The higher the Detail value, the closer the added points will be to one another. With Detail unchecked, distortion will be produced using only the existing points on the path, and no new anchor points will be added.

3. The **Simplify** option **3**–**4**, which is available only for the Warp, Twirl, Pucker, and Bloat tools, smooths the distorted path by reducing extraneous points. Enter a value (0.2–100) or drag the slider. The higher the Simplify value, the smoother the curve. With Simplify unchecked, the resulting distortion will have many more anchor points than are necessary or desirable.

4. Check **Show Brush Size** to have the cursor display as an ellipse using the current Global Brush Dimensions (width, height, and angle) so you can see the cursor dimensions relative to the object(s) you're distorting. If unchecked, the familiar crosshairs cursor will be used instead.

5. Click OK.

1 Use the **Detail** and **Simplify** options in any liquify tool options dialog box to control the spacing of added points and the smoothness of the distortion.

2 At left, the **Detail** for the **Twirl** tool was set to 1; at right, to 10 (with Simplify unchecked for both). Note how many points were added and how close together they are.

3 Here the **Twirl** tool is used at the minimum **Simplify** setting (0.2), resulting in rough bumps along the edge of the object.

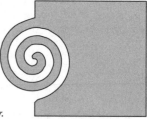

4 Here the **Twirl** tool is used at the maximum **Simplify** setting (100). The edges look smoother.

1 *Distortion produced by the Warp tool*

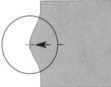

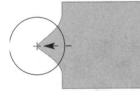

2 *First the cursor for the Pucker tool is positioned along one side of the square. Then it's dragged to the left, causing that side of the square to pucker outward.*

3 *The original object*

4 *After dragging toward the middle of the screw with the Pucker tool*

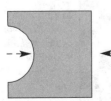

5 *After dragging into a square with the Bloat tool*

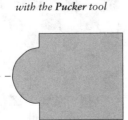

6 *After dragging away from the square with the Bloat tool*

Using the Warp, Pucker, and Bloat tools

The **Warp** tool **1** produces distortion by pushing a portion of an object's edge in the direction the cursor is dragged.

The **Pucker** tool acts like a magnet to squeeze an object's contour. As the tool nears the edge of an object, a point on the path moves toward the center of the brush cursor **2**–**4**.

The **Bloat** tool expands the edge of an object outward from the center of the cursor, filling the cursor's circumference. If you drag the tool into an object, it will look as though the cursor cut a chunk out of it **5**. If you drag the tool away from an object, it will bulge out and look as though the cursor shape was added to it **6**. You can also click and hold with this tool.

To use the Warp, Pucker, or Bloat tool:

1. Double-click the **Warp** (Shift-R) 🖉, **Pucker** 🖾, or **Bloat** 🔾 tool.

2. Choose **Detail** and/or **Simplify** options (see the previous page). *Note:* The Detail setting seems to make little difference for the Pucker or Bloat tool.

3. Click OK.

4. *Optional:* Select an object or group to prevent the tool from editing other objects nearby.

5. Click and hold, or drag, the tool over an object or objects.

➤ A bulge or indentation produced by the Bloat tool won't extend beyond the circumference of the tool cursor.

Resize/reshape cursor interactively

To **resize and reshape** the cursor interactively, check **Show Brush Size** in the tool options dialog box, then Option-drag/Alt-drag away from the cursor to enlarge it, or drag diagonally toward the lower left to reduce it. To **resize** the cursor **proportionally,** Option-Shift-drag/Alt-Shift-drag away from or toward the center of the cursor. Beware! Both shortcuts establish a new global cursor size for all the liquify tools!

Warp, Pucker, Bloat Tools

Using the Twirl tool

If used with a large brush cursor, the **Twirl** tool twirls a whole object from its center. If used with a small brush cursor, the tool twirls each edge of an object separately.

To use the Twirl tool:

1. Double-click the **Twirl** tool.

1 *The original object*

2. Under Twirl Options, choose or enter a **Twirl Rate** (–180° to 180°) to control the speed at which the spiral is created and the amount of twirl. A positive value will produce a counterclockwise twirl; a negative value will produce a clockwise twirl. The higher the value (the further the slider is moved from 0°), the greater the distortion.

3. Choose **Detail** and/or **Simplify** options (see page 440).

4. Click OK.

5. *Optional:* Select an object, group, or combination thereof.

6. Click, click and hold, or drag, the tool over an object or objects **1**–**2**. You can use smart guides, or hold down Shift to drag in a straight line.

➤ To decelerate the rate of distortion, lower the Intensity setting.

➤ Hold down Option/Alt after you start dragging to reverse the direction of the twirl. Lava lamp, here we come!

2 *After using the Twirl tool at 50% Intensity, Twirl Rate –59°, Detail 5, and Simplify 60*

Using the Scallop, Crystallize, and Wrinkle tools

The **Scallop** tool produces curves or spikes that move toward the center of the cursor. Try using it to produce soft folds or gathers **3**. For a sharper-edged distortion, try using the **Crystallize** tool. It produces spiked curves that move away from the center of the cursor **4**. Or for a more random, wrinkled-edge distortion, try using the **Wrinkle** tool (**1**, next page). As with the Twirl tool, the longer the Wrinkle tool is clicked and held over an edge, the stronger the effect.

3 *The Scallop tool was dragged along the edges of a checkerboard with Shift held down.*

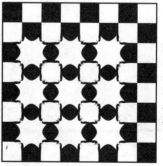

4 *The Crystallize tool was clicked in the middle of several white squares.*

1 *The Wrinkle tool was dragged quickly vertically and horizontally.*

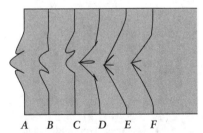

2 *The Scallop Tool Options dialog box*

3 *How the different "Brush Affects" check boxes affect the distortion produced by the Scallop tool:*

A: Brush Affects In Tangent Handles and Brush Affects Out Tangent Handles checked

B: Brush Affects In Tangent Handles checked

C: Brush Affects Out Tangent Handles checked: note the reflected direction of distortion between B and C

D: Brush Affects Anchor Points checked

E: Brush Affects Anchor Points and Brush Affects In Tangent Handles checked

F: Brush Affects Anchor Points and Brush Affects Out Tangent Handles checked

To use the Scallop, Crystallize, or Wrinkle tool:

1. Double-click the Scallop, Crystallize, or Wrinkle tool **1**.

2. Choose a **Complexity** value (0–15) **2**. The higher the Complexity, the more curves or spikes will be generated. At a Complexity setting of 0, only existing anchor points will be modified; no new points will be created.

3. Choose a **Detail** setting (1–10). In addition to controlling the spacing between points, this option controls the number of curves or spikes the tool generates.

4. For the Scallop or Crystallize tool, check one or two of the available **Brush Affects** options. For the Wrinkle tool, you can check one, two, or all three of these options. Brush Affects Anchor Points repositions anchor points; Brush Affects In Tangent Handles and Brush Affects Out Tangent Handles change the control handles of added points **3**.

   Note: To preserve the current position of the anchor points on the path, don't check Brush Affects Anchor Points.

   ➤ When using the Scallop tool, if only one Brush Affects Tangent Handles option is checked and Brush Affects Anchor Points is unchecked, distortion won't be pulled to the center of the cursor, and the effect will be more subtle (fingerlike).

5. Click OK.

6. *Optional:* Select an object, group, or combination thereof.

7. Click and hold, or drag, the tool over an object or objects.

Scallop, Crystallize, Wrinkle Tools

Creating envelopes

To use the **Envelope Distort** commands, first you create a container, called an **envelope,** for one or more objects. Then you distort the envelope shape, and the object within the envelope conforms to the distortion. Envelopes can be created by using any of the following three commands on the Object > Envelope Distort submenu:

➤ The **Make with Warp** command uses a preset, but editable, warp **1**–**3**.

➤ The **Make with Mesh** command creates a mesh, which you manipulate **4**.

➤ The **Make with Top Object** command converts a user-drawn path into an envelope (**1**–**2**, next page).

Regardless of which method you use to create an envelope, both the envelope and the object will remain fully **editable,** both while the object is contained in the envelope and after it's expanded. If you're familiar with using gradient meshes, you'll be ahead of the game here because envelopes are really meshes, and they work the same way. The primary difference between them is that envelope meshes are used for distorting shapes, whereas gradient meshes are used for applying color gradations.

Envelopes can be applied to most types of Illustrator objects, including paths (simple and compound); placed (embedded) images; images rasterized in Illustrator; type; clipping masks; objects with applied effects, graphic styles, or brush strokes; and symbol instances.

When you're done using an envelope to distort an object, you can **expand** the result, leaving the distorted object but deleting the envelope, or you can **release** the result, thus creating two separate objects—the envelope shape on top of the original, undistorted object.

➤ Envelopes can be used with type, which will remain editable (see page 449). Note, however, that if you expand an envelope that contains type, the type will be converted to outline paths.

Another way to warp

You can also create envelopes via the commands on the **Effect > Warp** submenu, but with one notable disadvantage. When an envelope is applied via an effect, the only way to edit the envelope is via the Warp Options dialog box, which you can reopen by double-clicking the Warp effect listing on the Appearance palette. You won't be able to manipulate the points or segments on the warp shape itself. If you use the **Envelope Distort** commands, on the other hand (discussed at left), you can readjust the mesh points and segments at any time.

1 *The original object*

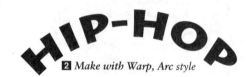

2 *Make with Warp, Arc style*

3 *Make with Warp, Bulge style*

4 *Make with Mesh using a 4x4 grid, distorted manually*

(sidebar label) **Create Envelope**

1 *Two objects are selected.*

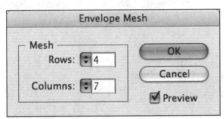

2 *After choosing the Make with Top Object command*

Envelope Mesh

Mesh
Rows: 4
Columns: 7

OK
Cancel
☑ Preview

3 *Choose Rows and Columns values for an envelope mesh in the Envelope Mesh dialog box.*

4 *A 4x7 mesh envelope*

5 *After moving handles on the mesh envelope*

➤ In order to create an envelope around a placed image, it must be embedded into your file first (to embed images, see pages 279 and 286).

➤ An envelope for a clipping path will be scaled automatically in order to cover both the visible and clipped parts of the objects.

In the following instructions you'll **create** an **envelope** as a **mesh**. Because all envelopes essentially are meshes, we think working with a mesh first will help you get a handle, in visual terms, on how the distortion process works.

To create a mesh envelope:

1. Select an object or group.
2. Choose Object > Envelope Distort > **Make with Mesh** (Cmd-Option-M/ Ctrl-Alt-M).
3. Check Preview **3**.
4. Choose the desired number of **Rows** and **Columns.**
5. Click OK. An envelope will be created in a grid, using your specifications, overlaying the object **4**. To edit the envelope mesh, see page 448 **5**.

➤ In the Envelope Mesh dialog box, clicking an up or down arrowhead changes that value by ±1; Shift-clicking changes the value by ±10.

Mesh Envelope

Another way to create an envelope is by using a preset shape, such as an arc, arch, shell, fish, or fisheye, to produce the distortion. You're not limited to the preset shape, though. With the **Warp Options** dialog box open, you can apply distortion to the envelope, then further customize it after closing the dialog box.

To create a warp envelope:

I. Select one or more objects ■.

2. Choose Object > Envelope Distort > **Make with Warp** (Cmd-Option-Shift-W/ Ctrl-Alt-Shift-W). The Warp Options dialog box opens ■.

3. Check Preview.

4. Choose a preset **Style** ■–■.

5. Click **Horizontal** or **Vertical** for the warp orientation.

6. Choose or enter a **Bend** value (–100 to 100) to control the degree of warpage ■.

7. Choose or enter Horizontal and Vertical **Distortion** values (–100 to 100) for additional horizontal and/or vertical distortion.

8. Click OK. A warp grid will now overlay the object(s), using the specifications from the Warp Options dialog box. To edit the envelope path, see page 448.

➤ To change the current warp style used for the envelope, select the envelope, then choose Object > Envelope Distort > Reset with Warp again.

HIP-HOP

■ *The original type object*

■ *In the **Warp Options** dialog box, the first step is to choose a preset **Style**. Then, if you like, you can customize the distortion by changing settings in the dialog box and/or by manipulating the mesh after closing the dialog box.*

■ *Make with Warp, Flag style*

■ *Make with Warp, Fish style*

■ *Make with Warp, Arc Lower style*

–75%

75%

20%

■ *Assorted Bend settings*

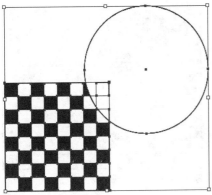

1 *The original objects*

2 *After choosing the Make with Top Object command*

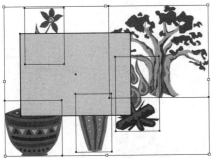

3 *A rectangle on top of five symbol instances*

And finally, a third way to create an envelope is to produce it from your own path by using the **Make with Top Object** command. Be creative!

To create an envelope from a user-created path:

1. Create a path to use for the envelope. The path can be open or closed (the Make with Top Object command will close an open path). And don't worry about whether the path has a fill or stroke; both will be removed automatically.

2. Make sure the path to be used as the envelope is on top of the objects to be put into the envelope (it makes a difference!). If necessary, Control-click/right-click and choose Arrange > Bring to Front (Cmd-Shift-]/Ctrl-Shift-]) or restack the object via the Layers palette.

3. Select the path and the object(s) to be enveloped **1**. They can overlap each other, but they don't have to. When you choose the Make with Top Object command (the next step), the objects will be sucked into the envelope like a vacuum cleaner.

4. Choose Object > Envelope Distort > **Make with Top Object** (Cmd-Option-C/Ctrl-Alt-C). The objects will be moved into, and will be scaled automatically to fit, the envelope **2**–**5**. To edit the envelope, see the next page.

➤ You can use a type character as the envelope, but only one character at a time, and it has to be converted to outlines and released from its compound path first. You can put type inside an envelope.

Envelope from Path

4 *After choosing the Make with Top Object command*

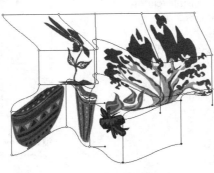

5 *After adding points to the mesh with the Mesh tool, then moving mesh patches with the Direct Selection tool*

Editing envelopes

As we said before, envelope meshes work like gradient meshes (a mesh is a mesh is a mesh). If you're not familiar with meshes yet, no big deal; they're easy to work with. The techniques for **editing mesh envelopes** are summarized in the following instructions. For more detailed instructions on editing meshes, see pages 387–389.

To edit an envelope:

1. Make sure smart guides are showing so you'll be able to see the envelope and anchor points without having to select the envelope (View > Smart Guides or Cmd-U/Ctrl-U).

2. The envelope will be listed as Envelope on the Layers palette 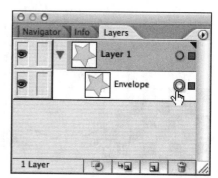. To select it, click its target circle.

3. Do any of the following (have some fun!):

   Use the **Add Anchor Point** tool (+) to add mesh points to existing mesh lines. Option-click/Alt-click with the Add Anchor Point tool to delete any mesh points that don't have lines crisscrossing through them.

   Use the **Mesh** tool (U) to add mesh points with mesh lines that crisscross through them 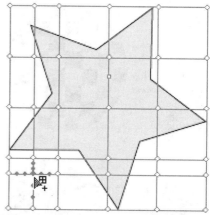. Option-click/Alt-click with the Mesh tool to delete mesh lines or points. Or drag with the tool to move mesh points.

   Use the **Direct Selection** tool (A) to move mesh points or mesh patches 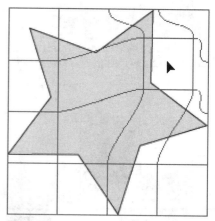.

   Modify the whole envelope by choosing the **Selection** tool, then dragging any of the handles on the bounding box. (If the bounding box isn't visible, choose View > Show Bounding Box or press Cmd-Shift-B/Ctrl-Shift-B).

   Use a **liquify** tool on the mesh (try using the Warp, Bloat, or Wrinkle tool).

➤ To edit the contents of an envelope but not the envelope itself, follow the instructions on the next page.

1 An **envelope** listing on the Layers palette

2 *Adding mesh points with the Mesh tool*

3 *Moving a mesh patch with the Direct Selection tool*

Edit Envelope

Keeping up with appearances

The **Appearance** palette lists different attributes depending on which part of an envelope is currently being edited. If you edit the envelope itself, attributes or applied effects for the envelope, if any, will be listed; if you edit the contents, attributes for the object will be listed. To avoid confusion, before adding or editing appearances, be sure to target the correct object—don't just toggle between the Edit Contents and Edit Envelope commands.

1 *An edited mesh envelope.*

2 *Use the **Reset Envelope Mesh** dialog box to restore an envelope to its preedited state.*

3 *After using the **Reset with Mesh** command, **Maintain Envelope Shape** unchecked*

In these instructions, you'll learn how to **edit objects** within an **envelope** without editing the envelope itself. You can toggle back and forth between editing objects and editing the envelope whenever you need to. With the envelope selected, you can switch to editing the object's contents; with an object selected, you can switch back to editing the envelope.

To edit objects in an envelope:

1. With an envelope selected, choose Object > Envelope Distort > **Edit Contents** (Cmd-Shift-V/Ctrl-Shift-V).

2. An expand arrowhead will appear next to the Envelope listing on the Layers palette. Click the arrowhead to expand the list, then click the target circle for an individual path to target the path for editing. You can edit the object contents as you would any nonenveloped object. The Appearance palette will update.

3. When you're done editing the objects, choose Object > Envelope Distort > **Edit Envelope** (Cmd-Shift-V/Ctrl-Shift-V). The envelope will recenter itself on the edited object automatically. If you click the target circle for the Envelope listing, any appearances you apply will affect the envelope—not its contents.

You can **reset** a **warp** or **mesh envelope** back to its preedited state.

To reset an envelope:

1. Select an envelope **1**.

2. To reset an edited warp envelope, choose Object > Envelope Distort > **Reset with Warp** (Cmd-Option-Shift-W/Ctrl-Alt-Shift-W). The Warp Options dialog box opens, listing the original warp settings.

To reset an edited mesh envelope, choose Object > Envelope Distort > **Reset with Mesh** (Cmd-Option-M/Ctrl-Alt-M), then choose options in the Reset Envelope Mesh dialog box, if desired **2**. Check **Maintain Envelope Shape** to reset the inner mesh points while preserving the envelope's outer shape, or uncheck this option to reset the whole envelope to a rectangular mesh **3**.

3. Click OK.

Releasing and expanding envelopes

Once you're done editing the object and envelope, you can use either the Release command or the Expand command.

The **Release** command is useful if you have an envelope that you like, and you think you might want to use it again. If you've taken a preset warp style and fiddled with it, for example, you can release the envelope and preserve it as a separate object so it can be used as an envelope for other objects (with the Make with Top Object command).

To release an envelope:

1. Select an envelope with a selection tool.

2. Choose Object > Envelope Distort > **Release.** The original object(s) will be unaltered, with the former envelope object above it . On the Layers palette, you'll see a <Mesh> listing for the former envelope and one or more <Path> listings for the objects 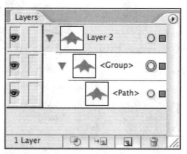.

Use the **Expand** command as a final step once you're satisfied with the distortion. To choose expand options for both raster images and vector objects, see the following page.

To expand an envelope:

1. Select an envelope. The Expand command will delete the envelope, so copy it for safekeeping, if desired.

2. Choose Object > Envelope Distort > **Expand.** The distortion will be applied to the object . The envelope will be discarded and can't be retrieved, except by choosing Undo. A <Group> containing the distorted object(s) will be created 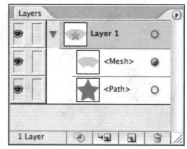. To learn more about the Expand command, see the following page.

➤ If an envelope containing a mesh object is expanded, the mesh remains a mesh. If an envelope containing a symbol or brush stroke is expanded, the symbol or brush stroke is converted to standard paths. And if type is expanded, it's converted to outline paths.

1 *The Object > Envelope Distort > Release command placed the envelope on top of the object; the object is unchanged. (We then changed the opacity of the envelope to 75%.)*

2 *The Layers palette after choosing the* **Release** *command*

3 *The* **Expand** *command applied the envelope distortion to the star and discarded the envelope.*

4 *The Layers palette after applying the* **Expand** *command*

1 *The **Envelope Options** control both the initial distortion and the final expansion.*

2 *A five-pointed star with effects is distorted by using the Arc warp style (70% Bend value, Horizontal), with **Distort Appearance checked** in Envelope Options.*

3 *The same five-pointed star with **Distort Appearance unchecked** in Envelope Options*

Choosing envelope options

Settings in the **Envelope Options** dialog box control how content (appearances, gradients, and patterns) is distorted, as well as what happens to that content when the envelope is expanded.

To choose envelope options:

1. To change the settings for an existing envelope, select it now (or select multiple envelopes).
   or
   To choose settings for future envelopes, deselect all.

2. Choose Object > Envelope Distort > **Envelope Options.** The Envelope Options dialog box opens **1**.

3. If an envelope is selected, check Preview.

4. For **Rasters** (placed images or rasterized objects), check **Anti-Alias** to smooth their edges. This option may increase the processing time.

5. For **Preserve Shape Using:**
   Click **Clipping Mask** to place a raster image in a clipping mask if it's expanded.
   or
   Click **Transparency** to make the background of the expanded raster image transparent.

6. Enter a **Fidelity** value (0–100) for the number of new anchor points to be added to a path in order to make it fit the envelope shape. The higher the Fidelity value, the more points will be added.

7. Check **Distort Appearance** to allow an object's appearance attributes (live effects, brushes, graphic styles, etc.) to be distorted by the envelope **2**. If the envelope is expanded, each appearance will also be expanded into a plain path or group, which will become a separate listing on the Layers palette. For example, if an appearance consisting of two strokes was applied to the object, when the envelope is expanded, each stroke will become a separate listing on the Layers palette.

(Continued on the following page)

Envelope Options

Uncheck Distort Appearance to distort the object, but not any appearance attributes. Any appearances will be applied after distortion (**3**, previous page). If you then expand the envelope, the appearance attributes will remain applied to the object and the resulting group will contain only one object.

Note: If appearance attributes are applied to an envelope, they won't be applied to objects within the envelope. However, if the envelope is expanded, the appearances will be applied to the resulting group (not to the individual objects).

8. When Distort Appearance is checked, these two additional options become available:

   Check **Distort Linear Gradients** to have a linear gradient fill be affected by an envelope distortion. If the envelope is then expanded, the gradient will become a mesh nested within a sequence of nested groups. If Distort Linear Gradients is off and the envelope is expanded, the linear gradient will be part of the resulting <Path>.
   and/or
   Check **Distort Pattern Fills** to have pattern fills be affected by an envelope distortion **1**–**2**. If the envelope is then expanded, the pattern will become a sequence of nested groups containing components of the pattern. If Distort Pattern Fills is off and the envelope is expanded, pattern fills will remain undistorted and will be a part of the resulting <Path>.

9. Click OK.

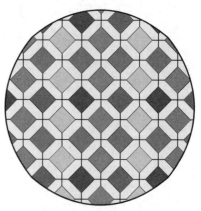

1 *The original envelope*

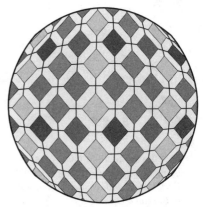

2 *After checking **Distort Appearance** and **Distort Pattern Fills** in the Envelope Options dialog box, the pattern conforms to the envelope distortion.*

RULERS, GUIDES & GRID 29

There are many tools you can use to help you position objects precisely. In Chaper 9 you learned how to use smart guides and the Align and Distribute buttons. In this chapter you'll learn how to use rulers, guides, and the grid to align objects, change the Constrain Angle to align objects at custom angles, and use the Measure tool to calculate distances between objects.

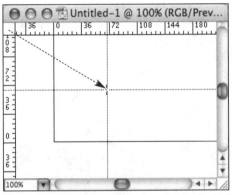

1 To change the **ruler origin,** drag diagonally from the intersection of the rulers.

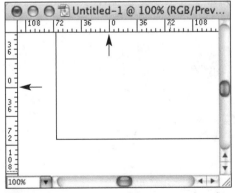

2 Note the new position of the zeros on the rulers.

Changing the ruler origin

When displayed, the rulers are located at the top and left edges of the document window. Location measurements (the X and Y readouts on the Transform, Info, and Control palettes) are calculated from the ruler origin, which is the point where the two rulers intersect. By default, the **ruler origin** is positioned at the lower left corner of the page, but it can be **moved** to a different location in any individual document where you might want to measure or position objects.

To move the ruler origin:

1. If the rulers aren't displayed, choose View > **Show Rulers** (Cmd-R/Ctrl-R); or deselect all objects, then Control-click/right-click the artboard and choose **Show Rulers** from the context menu.

2. Drag the square (where the two rulers intersect) to a new position **1**–**2**. The ruler origin will stay in the new location, even if you save, close, and reopen the file.

   The current pointer location is indicated by a mark on each ruler. Keep your eye on either ruler as you move your pointer around onscreen, and you'll see what we mean.

   Note: If you move the ruler origin, pattern fills in any existing objects may shift position.

To restore the ruler origin to its default location:

Double-click where the two rulers **intersect** at the upper left corner of the document window.

➤ Control-click/right-click either ruler to open a context menu from which you can choose a different unit of measure for the document. This setting will override the Units: General setting in Preferences > Units & Display Performance.

Creating ruler guides

For most purposes, smart guides work quite well for arranging objects (see pages 100–101). If you need **ruler guides,** which stay onscreen, follow the instructions on this page or the next page. Ruler guides don't print.

To create ruler guides:

1. Choose View > Guides > **Show Guides** (Cmd-;/Ctrl-;), or if the command is Hide Guides, leave it as is.

2. *Optional:* Create a new top-level layer expressly for the guides, label it "Guides," and keep it active.

3. If the rulers aren't showing, choose View > **Show Rulers** (Cmd-R/Ctrl-R).

4. Drag one or more guides from the horizontal or vertical ruler onto your page **1**. The guide will be locked. (If unlocked, guides are listed on the Layers palette as <Guide> in the currently active layer.)

    If View > **Snap to Grid** is on, as you create or move a guide, it will snap to the nearest subdivision as set in Preferences > Guides & Grid. (*Note:* If Pixel Preview is on, Snap to Grid won't be available.)

    If View > **Snap to Point** is on, as you drag an object near a guide or anchor point, the black pointer will turn white and the part of the object that's under the pointer will snap to that guide or point (see also the sidebar). You can change the Snapping Tolerance (the maximum distance between object and target) in Preferences > Smart Guides & Slices.

➤ Option-drag/Alt-drag from the horizontal ruler to create a vertical guide, or from the vertical ruler to create a horizontal guide.

Snap to pixel

If View > **Pixel Preview** is on, View > Snap to Grid becomes View > **Snap to Pixel,** and Snap to Pixel is automatically turned on. With Snap to Pixel on, any new objects you create or any existing objects you drag will snap to the pixel grid, and anti-aliasing will be removed from any horizontal or vertical edges on those objects.

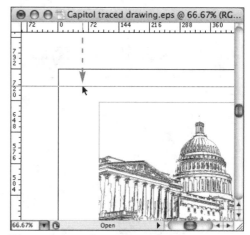

1 A **guide** being dragged from the horizontal **ruler.**

Restore Ruler Origin; Create Ruler Guides

1 *An object is selected, then View > Guides > **Make Guides** is chosen.*

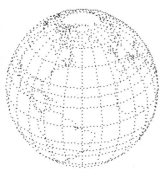

2 *The object is now a guide. The former "path" object is now listed as "<Guide>" on the Layers palette.*

Creating object guides

So far we've shown you how to work with two kinds of guides: smart guides and ruler guides. Now you'll learn how to convert standard Illustrator paths into guides. **Object guides** are reversible, meaning they can be converted back into standard objects at any time.

To turn an object into a guide:

1. Select an object, a group of objects, or an object within a group (not a symbol, an object in a blend, a mesh, or a live paint group) **1**. You can copy the object and work off the copy, if you like. *Note:* If the object you turn into a guide is part of a group, the guide will also be part of that group.

2. Choose View > Guides > **Make Guides** (Cmd-5/Ctrl-5) **2**.
   or
   Control-click/right-click and choose **Make Guides** from the context menu.

➤ You can transform or reshape a guide object, provided guides aren't locked (see the following page). Object guides can be selected using the Layers palette (look for <Guide>). Relock them when you're done.

When you **release** a **guide,** the object's former fill and stroke attributes are restored.

To turn an object guide back into an object:

1. If guides are locked, Control-click/right-click and choose **Lock Guides** from the context menu to uncheck that option.

2. On the Layers palette, make sure none of the guides to be released have a lock icon.

3. To release **one** guide, in the document window, Cmd-Shift-double-click/Ctrl-Shift-double-click the edge of the guide.

   To release **multiple** guides, choose the **Selection** tool (V), Shift-click or marquee the guides that you want to release, then Control-click/right-click and choose **Release Guides** from the context menu or choose View > Guides > **Release Guides** (Cmd-Option-5/Ctrl-Alt-5).

Object Guides

Locking/unlocking guides

To select or move ruler or object guides, you must unlock them first. By default, the **Lock Guides** command is on.

To lock or unlock all guides:

Deselect all objects, then Control-click/right-click in the document window and choose **Lock Guides** from the context menu.
or
Choose View > Guides > **Lock Guides** (Cmd-Option-;/Ctrl-Alt-;) to check or uncheck the command.

➤ To hide/show guides, choose Hide Guides from the context menu.

You can **lock/unlock** (or hide/show) ruler and object guides **individually,** because each one has a separate <Guide> listing on the Layers palette.

To lock or unlock one guide:

1. Make sure the Lock Guides command is disabled (see the previous set of instructions).

2. On the Layers palette, click in the **lock** column for any guide you want to lock or unlock.

Removing guides

To remove one guide:

1. Make sure either all guides are unlocked or the guide you want to remove is unlocked.

2. Choose the **Selection** tool (V), then click the ruler or object guide to be removed.

3. On the Mac, press Delete. In Windows, press Backspace or Del.

4. To relock all the remaining guides, deselect all objects, then Control-click/right-click in the document window and choose **Lock Guides.**

The **Clear Guides** command removes all ruler and object guides.

To remove all guides:

Choose View > Guides > **Clear Guides.**

Collect 'em all!

If you drag all your guides into **one layer** or **sublayer,** you'll be able to lock or unlock all of them at once by clicking the lock icon for that layer, and still be able to lock/unlock them individually.

While you're at it, to make it easier to tell when your guides are selected, make the selection color for the layer that contains the <Guide> listings different from the guide color. Double-click the layer name, then in the **Layer Options** dialog box, choose a Color. To change the guide color, choose Preferences (Cmd-K/Ctrl-K) > **Guides & Grid,** then change the Guides: Color.

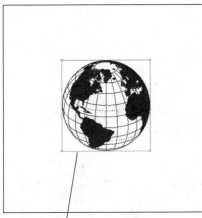

1 *Drag a rectangle around an object to define the guide area.*

Creating guides via a command
To place guides around an object or create evenly spaced guides:

1. Choose the **Selection** tool (V), then select a rectangular object. Make sure the rectangle is on the printable page. *Beware!* If you use a nonrectangular shape, the shape will be converted to a rectangle.
   or
   Choose the **Rectangle** tool, ▢ then drag a rectangle to define a guide area **1**.

2. Make sure the ruler origin is in the default location.

3. Choose Object > Path > **Split Into Grid.**

4. Check **Add Guides** and check Preview **2**.

5. To encircle the object with **guides without dividing** the object, leave the Number and Total for Rows and Columns as 1.
   or
   To **divide** the object and create **guides** around each section, choose a Number greater than 1 for the Rows and/or Columns, and enter Height/Width and Gutter values.

6. Click OK **3**.

7. The guides will be listed in a <Group> on the Layers palette. Click the <Group>, then choose View > Guides > **Make Guides 4**.

8. *Optional:* If you drew a rectangle for step 1, you may delete it now.

2 *Choose options in the **Split Into Grid** dialog box.*

Split Into Grid

Rows
Number: 1
Height: 140 pt
Gutter: 12 pt
Total: 140 pt

Columns
Number: 1
Width: 179.1 pt
Gutter: 12 pt
Total: 140 pt

OK
Cancel
☑ Preview

☑ Add Guides

Split into Grid

3 *Lines appear around the rectangle.*

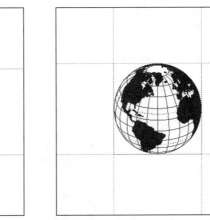

4 *The lines are **converted** into **guides**.*

Using the grid

The grid is like nonprinting graph paper. You can use it as a framework to help you arrange objects, either by eye or by using Snap to Grid. Start by showing the grid.

To show/hide the grid:

Choose View > **Show Grid** (or Hide Grid) (Cmd-"/Ctrl-") 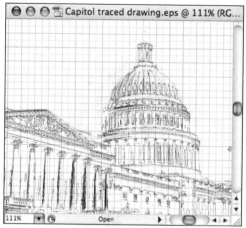.

or

Deselect, then Control-click/right-click and choose **Show Grid** (or Hide Grid) from the context menu.

You can change the grid style (lines or dots), color, or spacing in Preferences > **Guides & Grid** (see page 474). Check Grids In Back in that dialog box to have the grid appear in back of all objects instead of in front.

To use Snap to Grid:

Choose View > **Snap to Grid** (Cmd-Shift-"/ Ctrl-Shift-") to make the check mark appear. Now if you move an object near a gridline, the edge of the object will snap to the gridline. This works whether the grid is displayed or not.

1 *The Grid displayed*

What the Constrain Angle affects

➤ Type objects

➤ Rectangle, Ellipse, and Graph tools

➤ Some transformation tool dialog boxes (Scale, Reflect, and Shear, but not Rotate or Blend)

➤ Gradient tool and Pen tool when used with Shift held down

➤ Moving objects with Shift held down or by pressing an arrow key

➤ Grid

➤ Smart guides

➤ Info palette readouts

1 *Drawing* an object with 25° as the **Constrain Angle**

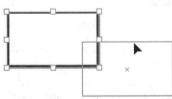

2 *Shift-dragging* an object with 25° as the **Constrain Angle**

Changing the Constrain Angle

The default **Constrain Angle** is 0°—the horizontal/vertical (*x/y*) axes. When you change the Constrain Angle, any new object that you draw will rest on the new axes, and any new object that you move or transform with Shift held down will snap to the new axes. The Constrain Angle setting affects the whole application, both existing and future documents—regardless of whether any documents are open when you change it.

To change the Constrain Angle:

Choose Preferences (Cmd-K/Ctrl-K) > General, change the **Constrain Angle** (–360 to 360), then click OK **1**–**2**. The grid will change to conform to the new Constrain Angle (display it to see what we mean).

➤ To establish a Constrain Angle based on an object that was rotated using the Rotate tool, select the object, then enter the Angle readout ⌂ from the Info palette as the Constrain Angle.

459

Using the Measure tool

You can use the **Measure tool** to calculate the distance and angle between two locations in a document. When you use this tool, its calculations are displayed on the Info palette, which opens automatically.

The distance and angle calculated using the Measure tool also become the current values in the Move dialog box, which means you can use the Measure tool as a guide to mark a distance and direction, then use the Transform Again shortcut to move any selected object.

To measure a distance using the Measure tool:

1. Choose the **Measure** tool ✎ (it's on the same pop-out menu as the Eyedropper tool).

2. **Click** the starting and ending points that span the distance and angle you want to measure.
   or
   Drag from the first point to the second point **1**.

   Distance (D), **angle,** and other readouts will display on the Info palette **2**.

3. *Optional:* To move any object the distance and angle you just measured (until you change those values), select the object, then press Cmd-D/Ctrl-D.

➤ Shift-click or Shift-drag with the Measure tool to constrain the tool to a multiple of 45° or the current Constrain Angle.

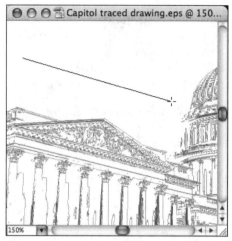

1 *Drag (or click) with the Measure tool. The distance you drag (or the distance between clicks) will be listed on the Info palette.*

Location of starting point on x axis — *Horizontal distance from starting point*

Navigator ‖ ⬦ Info		►
X : -97.783 pt	W : 89.565 pt	
Y : 536.696 pt	H : 12.174 pt	
D : 90.389 pt	∠ : 7.74°	

Location of starting point on y axis — *Total distance from starting point* — *Angle from starting point* — *Vertical distance from starting point*

2 *After a starting and ending point are clicked with the Measure tool, distance and angle values display on the Info palette. The X and Y positions are measured from the ruler origin.*

ACTIONS 30

In this chapter you'll learn how to record a sequence of edits and commands in an action, edit an action in various ways, and replay an action on one document or on a whole batch of documents.

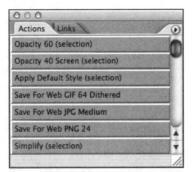

1 *The Actions palette in Button mode*

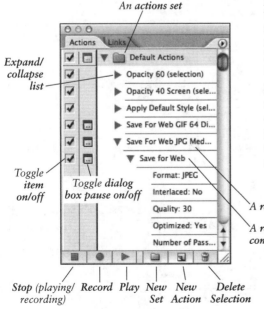

An actions set

Expand/ collapse list

Toggle item on/off

Toggle dialog box pause on/off

A recorded action

A recorded command

Stop (playing/ recording) *Record* *Play* *New Set* *New Action* *Delete Selection*

2 *The Actions palette in List mode*

Using the Actions palette

An **action** is a recorded sequence of tool and menu events. When an action is replayed, the recorded commands are executed in exactly the same sequence in which they were recorded. Actions can be simple (as short as a single command) or complex—whatever your work demands. They can be replayed on any Illustrator document, and can be edited, reorganized, and traded around among Illustrator users.

Actions are recorded, played back, edited, saved, and deleted by using the Actions palette (Window > Actions). The palette has two modes: Button and List. Only the action name is listed in **Button mode 1**, so this mode is used only for playback. To turn Button mode on or off, choose Button Mode from the Actions palette menu.

In **List mode** (the Button Mode option unchecked), the commands that the action contains are displayed in sequence on the palette **2**. Use this mode to record, play, edit, save, and load actions. Actions can be assigned keyboard shortcuts for fast access.

Creating an actions set

Note: For the instructions in this chapter, put your Actions palette into List mode (uncheck the Button Mode option on the palette menu).

Actions are organized in **sets,** which are represented by folder icons on the Actions palette.

To create an actions set:

1. Click the **New Set** button 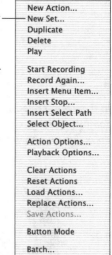 at the bottom of the Actions palette (or choose **New Set** from the palette menu **1**).

2. Enter a **Name** for the set **2**.

3. Click OK. A new folder icon and set name will appear on the palette **3**. (To save the set, see page 467.)

Recording an action

Until you become accustomed to using actions, practice **recording** them on a duplicate file. Figure out beforehand what the action is supposed to accomplish, and run through the command sequence a few times before you actually record it.

To record an action:

1. Open an existing file, or create a new one.

2. On the Actions palette, click the name of the actions set that you want the new action to belong to. (To create a set, see the previous set of instructions on this page).

3. Click the **New Action** button 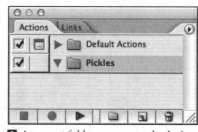 at the bottom of the Actions palette.

4. Enter a **Name** for the action **4**.

5. *Optional:* To assign a keyboard shortcut to the action, choose a Function Key from the pop-up menu, and if a modifier key is desired, also check Shift and/or Command/Control. From the Color pop-up menu, choose a new display color for the action name (for Button mode).

6. Click **Record.**

7. Create and edit objects as you would normally. Recordable tool and menu commands will appear on the action command list; not all edits are recordable.

8. Click the **Stop** button ■ to end recording.

1 *Choose New Set from the Actions palette menu (or click the New Set button at the bottom of the Actions palette).*

2 *Enter a Name for the new set.*

3 *A new set folder appears on the Actions palette.*

4 *Use the New Action dialog box to assign a name or keyboard shortcut to an action, or to assign a new display color to the action name for Button mode.*

1 *Click in the first column to exclude/include a command from playback. Note: A dimmed check mark signifies that at least one of the commands in the action is off.*

2 *Click the command that you want the new command to follow.*

3 *After opening the Insert Menu Item dialog box, we chose Object > Transform > Reflect.*

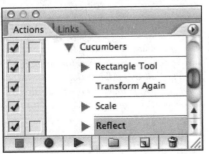

4 *The new command appears on the palette.*

Playing back actions

The first time you **play back** a new **action,** do it on a duplicate file or on a file that you don't care about preserving.

To play back an action on an image:

1. Open the Illustrator file on which you want to play the action, and select any objects, if the action requires it.

2. If the Actions palette is in List mode, make sure the check mark is present for the action that you want to play back. Click the name of the action you want to play back, then click the **Play** button. ▶

To temporarily exclude a command from playing back:

Click the check mark ✔ in the leftmost column to disable a command **1**, or click in the blank spot to reenable it.

Inserting menu commands

You may find that an action needs to be enhanced or modified from its original recorded version. There are several techniques you can use to edit actions, starting with inserting a menu item.

To insert a menu command in an action:

1. Put the Actions palette in List mode (uncheck the Button Mode option).

2. If the list for the action into which you want to insert the menu item isn't expanded, click the expand/collapse arrowhead.

3. Click the command on the action list that you want the new command to follow **2**.

4. Choose **Insert Menu Item** from the Actions palette menu.

5. Choose the desired menu command from the **menu bar.** The command name will appear in the dialog box **3**.
   or
   Type the command name into the **Find** field, then click the **Find** button.

6. Click OK **4**. The command you added will appear on the action list.

Inserting stops

By **inserting a stop into** an existing **action,** you allow the user to perform manual, non-recordable operations, such as entering type or selecting an object, during the course of playing back the action. After the pause, the user clicks the Play button to resume the playback.

To insert a stop in an action:

1. Put the Actions palette in List mode, and expand the action into which you want to insert a stop.

2. Click the command after which you want the stop to be inserted **1**.

3. Choose **Insert Stop** from the Actions palette menu. The Record Stop dialog box opens.

4. Type an instructional message to tell the user which operation(s) to perform during the stop. As a helpful reminder, at the end of the message, tell users to click the Play button on the Actions palette when they're ready to resume playback (e.g., "Click the Play button to resume") **2**.

5. *Optional:* Check Allow Continue to permit the user to bypass the pause (by clicking Continue in the alert dialog box during playback).

6. Click OK **3**. A Stop listing will appear below the chosen insertion point on the Actions palette.

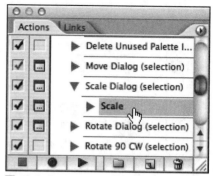

1 *Click the command that you want the stop to appear after.*

2 *Type an instructional message.*

3 *In this example of a pause dialog box, the user is instructed to click Stop, select two objects for blending, and then click the Play button on the Actions palette to resume the action playback. If the two objects are already selected, the user could click Continue instead of Stop.*

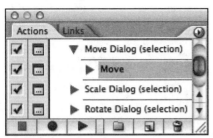

1 *Click the command that you want new commands to appear after.*

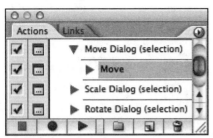

2 *Two new commands are added.*

Recording commands into actions

It's easy to record additional commands into an existing action.

To record commands into an existing action:

1. Put the Actions palette in List mode, and expand the action into which you want to insert a command or commands.

2. Choose the command you want the new command(s) to follow **1**.

3. Click the **Record** button. ●

4. Make modifications to the file as you would normally, using the commands you want inserted in the action.

5. Click the **Stop** button ■ when you're ready to stop recording. The command(s) you just recorded will be listed below the chosen insertion point on the Actions palette **2**.

Adding modal controls

Some commands or tools cause a dialog box to open in which the user must press Return/Enter (this is known as a "modal control"). By enabling a **pause for a recorded command,** you give the user the chance to change any of the dialog box settings for that command during playback.

To turn the dialog box pause for a command off or on:

On the Actions palette, click the **pause** icon ▣ for any recorded command to disable its dialog box pause and have the prerecorded settings be used during playback, or click the blank space to make the pause icon reappear to allow the user to choose settings during playback.

A red pause icon next to an action name signifies that at least one dialog box pause within that action has been turned off.

Add to Action; Modal Controls

Rerecording commands

To rerecord a command that uses a dialog box:

1. Put the Actions palette into List mode.

2. Expand the list for the action that contains the command you want to rerecord.

3. Select an object in your document, then double-click the command you want to rerecord ◼. It must have a dialog box icon (or a blank box for the icon).

4. Change any of the dialog box settings, then click OK. The next time this action is played back, your new settings will be used.

Deleting action commands

To delete an action or command:

Click the action or command that you want to delete, click the **Delete Selection** button 🗑 at the bottom of the Actions palette, then click Yes.

or

To bypass the prompt, drag the action or command over the **Delete Selection** button; or click the command, then Option-click/Alt-click the button. You can undo this. **NEW**

➤ Beware of the Clear Actions command on the palette menu, which clears all actions from the palette (you'll get a warning prompt, and you can also use the Undo command immediately afterward, if you need to). Only slightly less perilous is the Reset Actions command, which lets you either replace all the existing actions with the default actions or append the default actions to the palette.

Restacking action commands

You can **restack** and **move action commands,** just as you would restack layers on the Layers palette. *Note:* Before proceeding, you should save the actions set that contains the actions you're working on (see the next page).

To restack a command or move it to another action:

In List mode, drag any command upward or downward to a new location in the same action, or into another action.

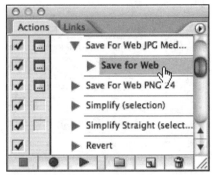

◼ *Double-click the command that you want to rerecord.*

1 *The* **duplicate** *command appears.*

2 *Enter a* **Name** *in the* **Save Set To** *dialog box.*

Copying action commands
To copy an action command:
1. In List mode, click the action command that you want to copy.
2. Option-drag/Alt-drag the command upward or downward in the same action or into another action list.
   or
   Drag the command name over the **New Action** button at the bottom of the Actions palette **1**, **2** then drag the duplicate command to any location on the palette.

Managing actions sets
One of the handiest things about actions is that you can share them with other Illustrator users. To do this, you must **save the set** that contains them. Try to keep your actions and actions sets well organized—and perform frequent backups!

To save an actions set:
1. Click the actions set that you want to save.
2. Choose **Save Actions** from the Actions palette menu.
3. If desired, change the name in the **Save As** field (but keep the .aia extension) **2**, and choose a location in which to save the set, such as in the Adobe Illustrator CS2\Presets\Actions folder.
4. Click **Save**.

To load an actions set:
1. Choose **Load Actions** from the Actions palette menu.
2. Locate and click the actions set that you want to load, then click **Open**. The actions set will appear on the palette.

Batch-processing files with actions

Actions are a great way to optimize your workflow, and being able to **play back** an **action** on a **folder full of files** instead of just one file at a time gives you extra power.

Note: Batch processing will end if it encounters a stop command in an action. You should remove any inserted stops from an action that you're going to use for batch processing.

To batch-process files with actions:

1. Make sure all the files to be batch-processed are in one folder. The folder can contain subfolders, but only one top-level folder can be chosen at a time.

2. From the Actions palette menu, choose **Batch.**

3. Choose a set from the **Set** pop-up menu **1**, and from the **Action** pop-up menu, choose the action you want to use.

4. Choose **Source:** Folder, click Choose, locate the folder that contains the files you want to process, then click Choose.

   Check **Override Action "Open" Commands** to open files from the chosen folder, thus ignoring any Open commands in the recorded action.

   Check **Include All Subdirectories** if you also want to process files within folders in the chosen folder.

(For information about working with data sets as a source, see Illustrator Help.)

5. Choose **Destination: None** to have Illustrator keep the files open after processing; or **Save and Close** to save over and close the edited files; or **Folder** to save the files to a new folder (click Choose to specify the destination folder).

6. *Do any of the following optional steps:*

   If you chose Folder as the Destination, check **Override Action "Save" Commands** to have Illustrator save the files to the designated folder, should a Save command occur in the action.

   Check **Override Action "Export" Commands** to override any Export command destination used in the action (click Choose to specify the new destination folder).

   By default, Illustrator halts batch processing if it encounters an error. If you choose **Errors: Log Errors to File,** the batch processing will continue instead, and error messages will be sent to a text file. Click Save As, then give the error log file a name and destination. If this option is chosen, an alert message will inform you of any errors encountered.

7. Click OK.

1 *Choose Play, Source, and Destination options in the Batch dialog box.*

Batch Process With Actions

PREFERENCES 31

The first task you'll learn in this chapter is to customize your startup file. Then you'll learn how to choose dozens of default command, tool, and palette settings for current and future documents in the nine panels of the Preferences dialog box: General, Type, Units & Display, Guides & Grid, Smart Guides & Slices, Hyphenation, Plug-ins & Scratch Disks, File Handling & Clipboard, and Appearance of Black.

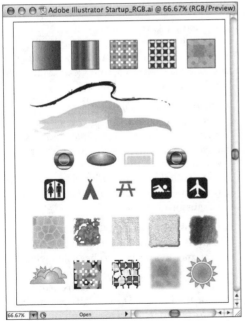

1 *The Adobe Illustrator* **Startup** *file will be blank until you add stuff to it. To this startup file, we've added objects that contain gradients, patterns, brush strokes, symbols, graphic styles, and effects.*

Creating a custom startup file

By creating a **custom CMYK** and/or **RGB startup file** containing the colors, patterns, gradients, and document settings that you work with regularly, you can have those elements be part of every new document.

To create a custom startup file:

1. For safekeeping, duplicate the existing startup file, and move the copy to a different folder (see the sidebar at left).

2. Double-click either of the two **Adobe Illustrator Startup** file icons.

3. Do any of the following **1**:

    Create colors, patterns, or gradients, and add these new items to the Swatches palette. For a visual reminder, apply swatches to separate objects in the file.

    Drag-copy swatches from any open swatch libraries to the Swatches palette.

    Create custom brushes, symbols, or graphic styles, and apply them to objects as a visual reminder.

    Choose Document Setup and Print settings.

    Choose ruler and page origins.

    Choose a document window size, scroll positions, and View menu settings.

4. To help Illustrator launch quickly, delete any items you don't need in the startup file (e.g., delete unnecessary brushes from the Brushes palette).

5. Choose File > Save As and save over the file in the **Plug-ins** folder, using the same name, as listed in the sidebar at left.

Custom Startup File

General Preferences

Choose Illustrator (Edit, in Windows) > Preferences > General (Cmd-K/Ctrl-K).

Keyboard Increment
This value is the distance (0–1296 pt) a selected object moves when an arrow key is pressed on the keyboard. To move a selected object 10 times the current Keyboard Increment, press Shift-arrow.

Constrain Angle
This is the angle (–360 to 360°) for the *x* and *y* axes. The default setting is 0° (parallel to the edges of the document window). Tool operations, dialog box measurements, and the grid, etc. are calculated relative to the current Constrain Angle (see page 459).

Corner Radius
This value (0–1296 pt) controls the amount of curvature in the corners of objects drawn with the Rounded Rectangle tool. 0 produces a right angle. Changing this value updates the Corner Radius field in the Rounded Rectangle dialog box, and vice versa.

Object Selection by Path Only
With this option checked, in order to select an object with the Selection or Direct Selection tool, you must click a path segment or anchor point. With this option unchecked, you can select a filled object in Preview view by clicking with a selection tool anywhere within the object's bounding box.

Use Precise Cursors
When this option is checked, the drawing and editing tool pointers display as cross-hairs instead of as the tool icon. To turn this option on temporarily for your tool when the preference is off, press Caps Lock.

Show Tool Tips
When this option is checked and you rest the pointer on a palette button, tool, swatch, icon, or other option, a short description of that feature pops up onscreen.

Anti-aliased Artwork
When this option is checked, edges of existing and future vector objects (not placed images) look smoother onscreen. It doesn't affect print output.

Select Same Tint %
When this option is checked, the Select > Same > Fill Color and Stroke Color commands select only objects with the same spot (not process) color and tint percentage as the selected object. When this option is off, the tint percentage is ignored as a criterion.

Append [Converted] Upon Opening Legacy Files
With this option checked, when updating text in a file that was created in a previous version of Illustrator, Illustrator appends the word "[Converted]" to the file name. See "Legacy files" on the following page.

Disable Auto Add/Delete
Checking this option disables the Pen tool's ability to change to the Add Anchor Point tool when the pointer passes over a path segment, or to the Delete Anchor Point tool when the pointer passes over an anchor point.

Use Japanese Crop Marks
Check this box to use Japanese-style crop marks when printing separations. (Preview this style via Object > Crop Area > Make or Filter > Create > Crop Marks.)

Transform Pattern Tiles
If this option is checked and you use a transformation tool on an object that contains a pattern fill, the pattern will also transform. You can also turn this option on or off for any individual transformation tool in its own dialog box, in the Move dialog box, or via the Transform palette menu.

Scale Strokes & Effects
Check this box to allow an object's stroke weight and appearances to be scaled when you scale an object by using its bounding box, the Scale tool, the Free Transform tool, or the Effect > Distort & Transform > Transform command. This option can also be turned on or off in the Scale dialog box or via the Transform palette menu.

Use Preview Bounds

If this option is checked, an object's stroke weight and any effects are factored in when an object's height and width dimensions are calculated or the Align palette is used. This option changes the dimensions of the bounding box.

Reset All Warning Dialogs

Click this button to allow warnings in which you checked "Don't Show Again" to redisplay when editing operations cause them to appear.

For the Pencil tool preferences, see page 175.

Fast track to the Preferences

Use the shortcut that opens the General Preferences dialog box (**Cmd-K/Ctrl-K**), then choose from the pop-up menu at the top of the dialog box.

Legacy files

Because Illustrator CS and CS2 provide support for such type features as Unicode, OpenType, and character and paragraph styles, text from earlier versions of Illustrator must be updated before they can be edited. When you open a file containing text from a pre-CS version of Illustrator, you can opt to have Illustrator update the text immediately or update it later.

When text is updated, some changes may occur in leading, tracking, and kerning; and in an area type object, words may shift to the next line or may overflow to the next object it's threaded to.

If you opt not to update the legacy text, you'll be able to view, move, and print it, but not edit it. **Legacy text** has an "x" in its bounding box when selected, and is listed as "Legacy Text" on the Layers and Appearance palettes.

General Preferences

Preferences

General

Keyboard Increment: 1 pt
Constrain Angle: 0 °
Corner Radius: 12 pt

OK
Cancel
Previous
Next

☐ Object Selection by Path Only ☐ Disable Auto Add/Delete
☐ Use Precise Cursors ☐ Use Japanese Crop Marks
☑ Show Tool Tips ☐ Transform Pattern Tiles
☑ Anti-aliased Artwork ☐ Scale Strokes & Effects
☐ Select Same Tint % ☐ Use Preview Bounds
☑ Append [Converted] Upon Opening Legacy Files

Reset All Warning Dialogs

Type Preferences

Choose Illustrator (Edit, in Windows) > Preferences > Type.

Type Options

Size/Leading; Baseline Shift; Tracking
Selected text is modified by this increment each time a keyboard shortcut is executed for the respective command.

Greeking
This value is the point size at or below which type displays onscreen as gray bars (greeked) rather than as readable characters in order to speed up screen redraw. Greeking has no effect on how a document prints.

Type Object Selection by Path Only
With this option checked, to select type you have to click right on a type path. With this option unchecked, you can select type by clicking with a selection tool anywhere within the type bounding box.

Show Asian Options
Check this option to access options for Chinese, Japanese, and Korean type on the Character palette, Paragraph palette, and Font menu.

Show Font Names in English
When this option is checked, Chinese, Japanese, or Korean font names display in English on the font pop-up menu. When this option is unchecked, two-byte font names display in the native language.

Number of Recent Fonts
Choose the maximum number of fonts (1–15) to be listed on the Type > Recent Fonts submenu.

Font Preview
Check this option to have font family names display in their actual fonts, for easy identification on the Type > Font menu and in the Find Font dialog box (and also on the Character and Control palettes in Mac). Also choose a Size for the font display: Small, Medium, or Large.

Units & Display Performance Preferences

Choose Illustrator (Edit, in Windows) > Preferences > Units & Display Performance.

Units

General
This unit of measure is used for the rulers, dialog boxes, and the Transform, Control, and Info palettes in the current and future documents.

➤ For the current document, the Units chosen in File > Document Setup (under Artboard: Setup) override the Units chosen in this preference panel.

Stroke
This unit of measure is used on the Stroke palette and in the Stroke Weight field on the Control palette.

Type
This unit of measure is used on the Character and Paragraph palettes. (We use points.)

Asian Type
This unit of measure is used for Asian type.

Numbers Without Units Are Points
If this option is checked, Picas is chosen for Units: General, and you enter a value in points in a field, the value won't be converted into picas. For example, if you enter "99," instead of being converted into "8p3," it will stay as "99."

Identify Objects By
When creating dynamic objects associated with variables, you can specify whether variables are assigned the Object Name or an XML ID number. Consult with your Web developer regarding this option.

Display Performance

Hand Tool
Drag the Hand Tool slider to the left toward Full Quality for better onscreen display when you move the artwork in the document window with the Hand tool; or move the slider to the right toward Faster Updates to move the artwork more quickly, but at a lower display quality.

Guides & Grid Preferences

*Choose Illustrator (Edit, in Windows) > Preferences > **Guides & Grid**.*

Guides

Color

For Guides, choose a color from the Color pop-up menu. Or choose Other or double-click the color square to open the System color picker and mix your own color.

Style

Choose Style: Lines or Dots for the guides.

➤ To help differentiate between guides and gridlines, choose the Dots style for guides.

Grid

Color

For the Grid, choose a color from the Color pop-up menu. Or choose Other or double-click the color square to open the System color picker and mix your own color.

➤ If View > Snap to Grid is on, guides and objects will snap to gridlines as you create or move them.

Style

Choose Style: Lines or Dots for the Grid. Subdivision lines won't display if the Dots Style is chosen.

Gridline every

Enter the distance (.01–1000 pt) between gridlines.

Subdivisions

Enter the number of Subdivision lines **1**–**2** (1–1000) to be drawn between the gridlines when the Lines Style is chosen for the grid.

Grids In Back

Check Grids In Back (the default setting) to have the grid display behind all objects, or uncheck this option to have the grid display in front of all objects.

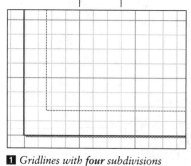

1 *Gridlines with **four** subdivisions*

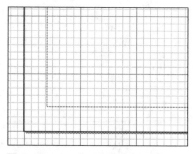

2 *Gridlines with **eight** subdivisions*

Smart Guides & Slices Preferences

Choose Illustrator (Edit, in Windows) > Preferences > Smart Guides & Slices.
To activate smart guides, choose View > Smart Guides (Cmd-U/Ctrl-U).

Display Options

Text Label Hints

These labels display as you pass the pointer over an object, anchor point, etc.

Construction Guides

Check this option to have angle lines display as you draw or drag an object **1**. Choose or create an angles set in the Angles area (see below).

Transform Tools

Check this option to have angle lines display as you transform an object via a transformation tool or the object's bounding box **2**. Choose or create an angles set in the Angles area (see below).

Object Highlighting

Check this option to have an object's path display as you pass the pointer over it **3**—helpful for locating unpainted paths, such as clipping masks, or paths hidden behind other paths. Paths for which the eye icon is off on the Layers palette won't highlight.

Angles

If Smart Guides are on and you drag an object or move the pointer, temporary angle lines will display relative to other objects in the document. Choose a preset angles set from the Angles pop-up menu or enter custom angles in any or all of the fields (press Tab to update the preview). If you enter custom angles, "Custom Angles" will appear on the pop-up menu. If you switch from Custom Angles to a predefined set and then later switch back to Custom Angles, the last-used custom angles will reappear in the fields.

Snapping Tolerance

This is the distance (0–10 pt) within which the pointer must be from an object for smart guides to display. The default is 4 pt.

Slicing

Show Slice Numbers

Check this option to have slice numbers display onscreen. From the **Line Color** pop-up menu, choose a color for those numbers and for the lines that surround each slice.

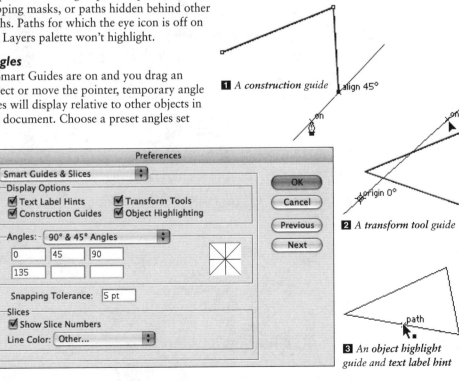

1 *A construction guide*

2 *A transform tool guide*

3 *An object highlight guide and text label hint*

Hyphenation Preferences

*Choose Illustrator (Edit, in Windows) >
Preferences > Hyphenation.*

Default Language

Choose the language dictionary for
Illustrator to refer to when it inserts hyphen
breaks. You can choose a different hyphenation language dictionary for the current
document from the Language pop-up menu
on the Character palette.

Exceptions

Enter words that you want hyphenated in a
particular way. Type the word in the New
Entry field, inserting hyphens where you
would want them to appear (or enter a word
with no hyphens to prevent Illustrator from
hyphenating it), then click Add. To remove a
word from the list, click it, then click Delete.

Plug-ins & Scratch Disks Preferences

*Choose Illustrator (Edit, in Windows) > Preferences > **Plug-ins & Scratch Disks.***
For changes made in this dialog box to take effect, you must quit/exit and relaunch Illustrator.

Plug-ins Folder

The core and add-on plug-in files that come with Illustrator provide additional functionality to the main application, and are placed in the Plug-ins folder inside the Adobe Illustrator CS2 folder.

If you need to move the Plug-ins folder (maybe another application that you want to share the plug-ins with requires them to be in a different location), you must use this Preferences dialog box to tell Illustrator where that folder is now located.

The current Plug-ins folder location is listed in the Plug-ins Folder area. To change this location, click Choose, locate and click the plug-ins folder name, then click Choose. The new location will now be listed.

Scratch Disks

Primary

The Primary scratch disk is used as virtual memory when available RAM is insufficient for image processing. Choose an available hard drive—preferably your largest and fastest—from the Primary pop-up menu. Startup is the default.

Secondary

As an optional step, choose an alternate Secondary hard drive to be used as extra virtual memory when needed. If you have only one hard drive, of course you can have only one scratch disk.

Plug-ins & Scratch Disks Preferences

Preferences

Plug-ins & Scratch Disks

Plug-ins Folder

/Applications/Adobe Illustrator CS2/Plug-ins   Choose...

Scratch Disks

Primary: Startup

Secondary: None

OK
Cancel
Previous
Next

File Handling & Clipboard Preferences

Choose Illustrator (Edit, in Windows) > Preferences > File Handling & Clipboard.

Version Cue

If you have Adobe Creative Suite 2 installed (or someone on your network has the suite installed and has given you access to a shared project), with **Enable Version Cue** checked, you'll be able to utilize the Adobe Version Cue Workspace features to control file security, organize files into private or shared projects, and search and review file information and file statuses among the suite applications, such as GoLive and Photoshop. For more information, read the Adobe Version Cue section in Illustrator Help, or the Understanding Adobe Version Cue CS2.pdf file in the Technical Information > Creative Suite 2 folder on the Extras CD-ROM.

Files

If you're working with a lot of linked files, you can enhance performance by checking **Use Low Resolution Proxy for Linked EPS;** placed images will then display as bitmap proxies. With this option unchecked, raster images will display at full resolution and vector objects will display in full color.

To specify how linked images are updated when the original files are modifed, from the **Update Links** pop-up menu, choose:

Automatically to have Illustrator update linked images automatically, with no dialog box opening, when you edit a file and then click back in Illustrator.

Manually to leave linked images unchanged when the original files are modified. You can use the Links palette to update links at any time.

Ask When Modified to display a dialog box when the original files are modified. (In the dialog box, click Yes to update the linked image, or click No to leave it unchanged.)

Clipboard on Quit

The Clipboard can be used to transfer selections between Illustrator and other programs in the Adobe Creative Suite, such as Photoshop, GoLive, and InDesign. When a selection is copied to the Clipboard, it's copied as a PDF and/or AICB, depending on which of the following **Copy As** options you choose:

PDF preserves transparency information in the Clipboard contents, and is designed for use with Photoshop, InDesign, and possibly future Adobe applications.

AICB (no transparency support), a PostScript format, breaks objects into smaller opaque objects, preserving the appearance of transparency through flattening. Check **Preserve Paths** to copy a selection as a set of detailed paths, or check **Preserve Appearance and Overprints** to preserve the appearance of the selection and any overprinting objects.

Note: If you check both PDF and AICB, the receiving application will choose its preferred format. Fills and effects will copy and paste more accurately, but the copying time will be longer and the memory requirements higher.

➤ If you're unable to paste a selection into Illustrator, try using drag-and-drop to acquire the selection instead.

➤ In Mac, if you plan to drag-and-drop or paste an Illustrator object that contains gradients, blends, patterns, or transparency into InDesign CS2, you must first uncheck the Copy as: AICB option and check the PDF option. InDesign CS2 won't read the PDF data if AICB data is also present. You can leave both options checked if you drag or paste an Illustrator object with a solid, opaque fill.

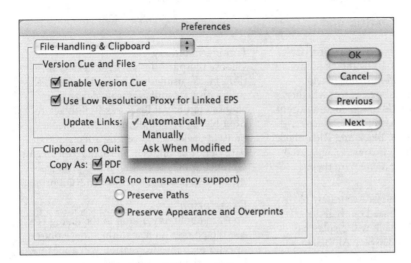

Resetting preferences

To restore all the default Illustrator preferences, trash the Adobe Illustrator **Prefs/AIPrefs** file:

➤ In Mac, it's stored in Startup drive/Users/[user name]/ Library/Preferences/Adobe Illustrator CS2 Settings.

➤ In Windows, it's stored in C:\Documents and Settings\[username]\Application Data\Adobe\Adobe Illustrator CS2 Settings\AIPrefs.

Whatever you do, don't delete the whole Preferences folder! You need the other items in that folder in order to run other applications and utilities.

🆕 Appearance of Black Preferences

Choose Illustrator (Edit, in Windows) > Preferences > Appearance of Black.

Options for Black on RGB and Grayscale Devices

Sometimes printers use a combination of CMYK inks instead of 100K (black alone) to produce richer, more lustrous blacks. Options in this dialog box control whether blacks will be displayed onscreen and output using their actual values or as rich blacks. The examples of 100K Black and Rich Black as shown in the dialog box are exaggerated intentionally so you can compare them.

On Screen

Choose Display All Blacks Accurately to display blacks onscreen based on their actual values (pure CMYK black will display as dark gray), or choose Display All Blacks as Rich Black to display all blacks as rich black regardless of their actual CMYK values.

Printing/Exporting

Choose Output All Blacks Accurately to print blacks using their actual K or CMYK values on RGB and grayscale devices, or choose Output All Blacks as Rich Black to print blacks as a mixture of CMYK values on RGB devices. This setting affects output data only, not values in the actual document. Output All Blacks as Rich Black produces the darkest possible black on an RGB printer.

Description

To learn about any option in the dialog box, rest the pointer on it with the mouse button up, and relevant information will appear below in the Description area.

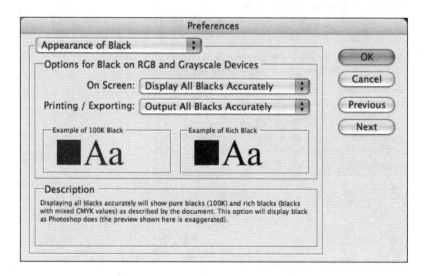

Appearance of Black Preferences

PRINT | 32

Although Illustrator objects are described and stored as mathematical commands, when they're printed, they're rendered as dots. The higher the resolution of the output device, the more smoothly and sharply lines, curves, gradients, and continuous-tone images are rendered. In this chapter you'll learn to print a document on a PostScript black-and-white or composite color printer; tile an oversized document; create printer's marks, crop marks, and bleeds; print color separations; choose flatness settings; download fonts; print to a PostScript file; print using color management; and create and edit presets—among other topics. In the next chapter, you'll learn how to save files for export to other applications; for Web output, see Chapter 34.

for Web output, see Chapter 34.

CHARLES, NANCY STAHL

NORAH, NANCY STAHL

Pirnt

Print dialog box: General and Setup panels

You'll use the **Print** dialog box to choose print settings, such as tiling, page size, printer marks, color management profiles, and flattening. The dialog box has seven panels, which we cover individually. First, we'll take a look at the **General** and **Setup** panels.

To print to a black-and-white or color PostScript printer:

1. Before outputting to a color printer, from the File > Document Color Mode submenu, choose the correct color mode for your printer.

2. Choose File > **Print** (Cmd-P/Ctrl-P).

3. From the **Printer** pop-up menu **1**, choose from the list of printers that are available in your system. The PPD pop-up menu will automatically display the PPD (PostScript printer description file) for the chosen printer. If it doesn't, choose the appropriate PPD from the pop-up menu.

4. Click **General** on the options list on the left side of the dialog box to display that panel.

5. In the **Copies** field, enter the desired number of print copies.

   For **Media,** from the **Size** pop-up menu, choose Defined by Driver or a paper size.

   Click an **Orientation** button to print vertically or horizontally on the paper.

6. In the Options area, from the **Print Layers** pop-up menu, choose which layers will print:

   Visible & Printable Layers to print only the visible layers for which the Print option is checked in the Layer Options dialog box. (To prevent any individual object from printing, uncheck the Print option for its layer before choosing File > Print.)

   Visible Layers to print only those layers that aren't hidden.

1 *The Print dialog box, General panel*

Options list

Preview window

Save your print settings!

Considering the number of options in the Print dialog box, why not save your settings as a preset so you don't have to reenter them each time you print to a particular output device? To create a print preset of the current print settings, click **Save Preset** at the bottom of the Print dialog box, enter a name for the preset, then click OK.

Saved presets can be chosen from the **Print Preset** pop-up menu at the top of the Print dialog box. To edit a print preset, see pages 497–498.

All Layers to print all layers, regardless of the current Layers palette settings.

7. Click **Do Not Scale** to print the document at its current size; or click **Fit to Page** to scale the document to fit the current paper size; or click **Custom Scale,** then enter a Width or Height value to scale the document proportionally. Or to scale nonproportionally, deselect the Constrain Proportions button, ▦ then enter separate Width and Height values.

8. Click **Setup** on the options list on the left side of the dialog box to display that panel (▮, next page).

9. From the **Crop Artwork to** pop-up menu, choose Artboard.

10. Leave the **Tiling** choice as Single Full Page. If the document is large and needs to be tiled onto multiple pieces of paper, see the next page.

11. Click a corner or side point on the **Placement** icon to position the artwork on that corresponding part of the paper; or click the center point to recenter the artwork on the paper.
or
Enter **Origin X** and **Origin Y** values to specify the position of the upper left corner of the artwork on the paper.
or
Place the pointer over the **preview** window and drag to reposition the artwork on the paper. Only the parts of the artwork that are visible in the preview window will print. Dragging the preview actually repositions the page borders on the artboard.

12. Click **Print** to print the document, or click **Done** to save the current settings with the document without printing.

➤ Although you can access the system's printer driver dialog boxes from the Print dialog box by clicking the Page Setup or Printer button in Mac or the Setup button in Windows, we recommend ignoring those buttons and choosing all your print settings from within the Print dialog box so you can utilize Illustrator's print capabilities when outputting your file.

Options in the **Setup** panel of the Print dialog box control the position of the document on the printable page. You can use this panel to tile a large document onto multiple pages or, via cropping, control which objects will print.

To print (tile) a document that's larger than the paper size:

1. Choose File > **Print** (Cmd-P/Ctrl-P), then click **General** on the options list.

2. Choose **Media** (page) **Size** and **Orientation** settings, and under Options, click **Do Not Scale.** (If you choose Fit to Page, the Tiling pop-up menu that you'll choose from in step 5 won't be accessible.)

3. Click **Setup** on the options list ■.

4. From the **Crop Artwork to** pop-up menu:

   If all the objects to be printed lie within the artboard, choose **Artboard.**
   or

Honey, I shrunk the...

Another solution for printing a document that's larger than the paper size for your printer is to reduce the output size. Go to the General panel in the Print dialog box, and in the Options area, click **Fit to Page.** In this case, the Tiling pop-up menu options won't apply.

If you want to print all the objects in the document, even objects that extend beyond the edge of the artboard, choose **Artwork Bounding Box.** A bounding box will surround all the objects in the document (see also the tiling option, step 5).
or
If you've already created crop marks in the document to limit which objects will print, choose **Crop Area** (■, next page). To create a crop area, see page 499.

■ *The* **Print** *dialog box,* **Setup** *panel*

Tile Oversized Document

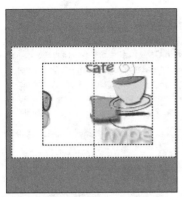

1 *Tile Imageable Areas with the Crop Artwork to: Crop Area setting, as viewed in the preview window*

2 *Tile Full Pages setting, as viewed in the preview window*

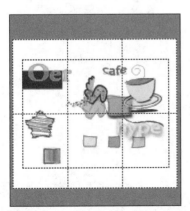

3 *Tile Imageable Areas setting, as viewed in the preview window*

5. From the **Tiling** pop-up menu, choose:
   Tile Full Pages 2 to divide the artwork into whole pages, as per the media size you chose in step 2.
   or
   Tile Imageable Areas 3 to divide the artwork into a grid of pages as per the printer media size.

   Note: These two options may produce similar tiling previews, depending on the current setting on the "Crop Artwork to" pop-up menu.

6. Click a point on the **Placement** icon to position the artwork on that corresponding part of the paper or grid of pages; click the center point if you need to recenter the artwork.
   or
   Enter **Origin** X and **Origin** Y values to specify the position of the upper left corner of the artwork on the paper.
   or
   Place the pointer over the preview window and drag to **reposition** the artwork on the grid of pages. Dragging the preview will reposition the page borders on the artboard (just as the Page tool does).

   Optional: If you chose Tile Full Pages from the Tiling pop-up menu, you can change the Overlap value for the amount of overlap between pages. **(NEW)**

7. To print all the tiled pages, in the General panel, leave the **Pages: All** button chosen and check **Skip Blank Pages** to prevent any blank tiled pages from printing. Or to print select tiled pages, click **Range**, then enter the range of pages in the field, separated by a hyphen.

8. Choose any other print settings. Click **Print** to print the document, or click **Done** to save the current settings with the document without printing.

Tile Oversized Document

Marks and Bleed panel

Use the **Marks and Bleed** panel of the Print dialog box to create printer's marks at the edge of the printable area, or to set up bleed parameters for objects that extend beyond that area. Commercial printers use crop marks to trim the final printout, registration marks to align printing plates, and color bars to help them evaluate the print colors.

To include printer's marks in your printout:

1. In the **Print** dialog box, click **Marks and Bleed** on the options list (**1**, next page).

2. Check **All Printer's Marks** to include trim marks, registration marks, color bars, and page information.
   or
   Check any of the following individual options:

   Trim Marks to add thin lines to designate where the printout is to be trimmed. The lines will align with the horizontal and vertical edges of the printable area, which is controlled by the current setting on the "Crop Artwork to" pop-up menu in the Setup panel.

   Registration Marks to add a small circle outside each corner of the bounding box.

   Color Bars to add color swatches outside the bounding box.

   Page Information to add a text label above the top edge of the printout containing specs for the commercial printer.

3. Choose a printer mark style from the **Printer Mark Type** pop-up menu: Roman or Japanese.

4. Choose a thickness for trim marks from the **Trim Mark Weight** pop-up menu.

5. Enter or choose an **Offset** value (0–72 pt) for the distance between trim marks and the bounding box (see the sidebar).

➤ The Object > Crop Area command creates nonprinting trim marks. If you use this command, you'll still need to check Trim Marks in the Print dialog box to create trim marks on the actual printout.

Setting up bleeds

If you're setting up a bleed (see the following page), enter an **Offset** value greater than the bleed width to ensure that any printer's marks won't be obscured by the bleed objects. The Offset increases the distance between the printable page size and the trim marks, but doesn't increase the printable page size.

1 *The* **Print** *dialog box,* **Marks and Bleed** *panel*

The **bleed** area is the area just outside the edge of a printed document. You can position objects in a document so they extend into the bleed area, thus ensuring that they'll print to the very edge of the final trimmed page. Have your commercial printer advise you as to what bleed values are required for their specific print setting.

To choose bleed values:

1. In the **Print** dialog box, click **Marks and Bleed** on the options list.

2. In the **Bleeds** area **1**:

   For asymmetrical bleed values, deselect the link icon, then enter **Top, Left, Bottom,** and **Right** values (0–1 inch, or 0–72 pt). Enter a low bleed value to

move the trim marks closer to the edges of the printed artwork, or a higher bleed value to move them farther away and thus print more of any object that extends into the bleed area.

Or click the link icon, then enter a single bleed value to be used for all four sides of the document.

➤ The bleed settings have no effect on the size of the final output.

➤ Click Save Preset to save the current settings as a print preset (see the sidebar on page 483). Click Done to exit the dialog box and save the current printer settings with the document without printing.

Output panel

In the **Output** panel of the Print dialog box, you can choose options for printing a document either as a **composite** print or as **color separations**.

To output a composite print or color separations:

1. Make sure your file is in CMYK Color mode, choose File > **Print**, then click **Output** on the options list **1**.

2. From the **Printer** pop-up menu, choose an output device that's available to your system.

   For steps 3–6, ask your print shop for advice.

3. From the **Mode** pop-up menu:

   To print the artwork on one sheet, choose **Composite**.
   or

To print each color on a separate sheet, choose **Separations (Host-Based)** to have Illustrator prepare the separation information and send the data to the printing device, or choose **In-RIP Separations** to have Illustrator send PostScript data to the printer's RIP to have that device perform the separation.

Available options will vary depending on the type of printer you chose in step 2.

4. Choose **Emulsion:** Up (Right Reading) or Down (Right Reading).

5. Choose **Image:** Positive or Negative.

6. From the **Printer Resolution** pop-up menu, choose a combined halftone screen ruling (lpi)/device resolution (dpi).

   For more Output panel options, see the next page.

1 *The Print dialog box, Output panel*

Overprinting

Normally, Illustrator automatically knocks out any color below an object so the object color won't mix with any underlying colors on press. If you check **Overprint Fill** and/or **Overprint Stroke** on the Attributes palette for a selected object, its fill and/or stroke colors will print on top of underlying colors instead. Where colors overlap, the inks mix and a combination color is produced. *Notes:* In RGB Color mode, only spot colors can be set to overprint. Colors overprint on a printing press, but not on a PostScript color composite printer.

To simulate overprinting, check Overprint Fill or Overprint Stroke for a selected object, then choose View > Overprint Preview ("Overprint Preview" will be listed in the document window title bar) **1**–**2**.

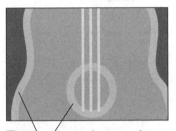

1 *The strokes on these two objects are set to overprint.*

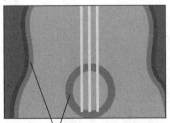

2 *With* Overprint Preview *checked, the overprint strokes simulate ink mixing with colors in underlying objects.*

If you choose a Separations option from the Mode menu in the Output panel, Illustrator will create and print a separate plate for each process and spot color used in the document. You can also use this panel to turn **printing** on or off **for individual colors** or to **convert** individual **spot colors into process colors.**

To set colors to print and/or convert colors to process:

1. Choose File > **Print,** click **Output** on the left side, then choose a Separation mode.

2. In the **Document Ink Options** area **3**, you'll see a listing for each color used in the document. For each process or spot color you don't want to print, click the printer icon 🖨 next to the color name. (Click again to redisplay the icon.)

3. Check **Convert All Spot Colors to Process** to convert all spot colors in the document to process colors.
   or
   For each spot color you want to convert to a process color, uncheck Convert All Spot Colors to Process, then click the spot color icon.⦿ The process color icon ☒ will display.

4. Choose other print settings, then click **Print.**

➤ Don't change the Frequency, Angle, or Dot Shape settings unless your commercial printer advises you to do so. If need be, you can click Reset to Defaults to restore all the default ink settings.

➤ To have black fills and strokes overprint background colors, check Overprint Black (see also the sidebar at left).

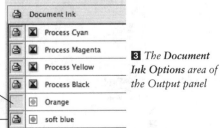

This spot color won't print at all.

This spot color will print as a spot color.

3 *The Document Ink Options area of the Output panel*

Graphics panel

The **Flatness** setting in the **Graphics** panel of the Print dialog box controls how precisely all the objects in a document print on a PostScript printer from Illustrator. If your document doesn't print, raise the Flatness setting, then trying printing again.

To change a document's flatness setting to facilitate PostScript printing:

1. Open the file that stubbornly refuses to print, choose File > **Print,** then choose **Graphics** from the options list **1**.

2. Drag the **Flatness** slider slightly to the right, then click Print. If the document prints, but with noticeably jagged curve segments, you've raised the Flatness setting too much. Lower the setting by dragging the slider to the left, and try printing again.
   or
   Check **Automatic** to have Illustrator choose an optimal Flatness value for the chosen printing device.

➤ A Flatness setting of 2 is appropriate for most printers. To see a numeric display (tool tip) of the current Flatness settings, rest the pointer on the slider.

1 *The **Print** dialog box, **Graphics** panel*

Flatten versus flatness

On output, Illustrator flattens overlapping shapes automatically in order to preserve the look of transparency—an altogether different process from the **Flatness** setting, which controls how precisely curve segments print. To arrive at this setting, Illustrator divides the printing device resolution by the output resolution. For any given printer, raising the Flatness value lowers the output resolution. The higher the Flatness value (or the lower the output resolution), the less precisely curve segments will print.

Graphics choices

Normally, you don't need to choose **PostScript LanguageLevel** or **Data Format** options in the Print dialog box (Graphics panel), because Illustrator sets these options for you automatically based on the chosen printer. However, if your printer supports more than one option in the above-mentioned categories, the settings become available, and you'll need to choose one (decisions, decisions!).

To download fonts and print meshes:

1. To manage how fonts are downloaded to the printer, in the **Fonts** area of the **Graphics** panel, from the **Download** pop-up menu, choose one of these options:

   None to have no fonts download. This is the preferred setting when fonts are permanently stored in the printer.

   Subset to download only the characters (glyphs) used in the document.

   Complete to have all the fonts used in the document download at the beginning of the print job. This is effective when printing multiple pages that use the same fonts (Illustrator files are usually single pages, though).

2. To improve gradient fill printing on an older PostScript imagesetter or printer, check **Compatible Gradient and Gradient Mesh Printing.** Any mesh objects will be converted to the JPEG format. Don't check this option if your gradients are printing well, as it may slow down printing.

3. Click Print or click Done.

PostScript is a language that describes objects and images for output to printers and other output devices. PostScript Level 2 can process grayscale vector graphics and grayscale bitmap images; it supports RGB, CMYK, and CIE color and offers compression techniques for bitmap images. Level 3 adds the ability to print mesh objects from PostScript 3 printers.

To print to a PostScript file:

1. Choose File > **Print.**

2. From the **Printer** pop-up menu, choose **Adobe PostScript® File.**

3. Click **Graphics** on the options list. If necessary, choose the desired **LanguageLevel** from the **PostScript** pop-up menu and/or a format from the **Data Format** pop-up menu (**1**, previous page). See also "Graphics choices" in the sidebar.

4. Choose other printer settings, then click **Save** to open the Save dialog box. Choose a location, enter a file name, then click **Save.**

Print: Graphics Panel

Color Management panel

Use the **Color Management** panel of the Print dialog box to control how color conversion will be handled. (*Note:* If you haven't learned about profiles and color settings yet, read Chapter 5 first.

To print using color management:

1. Choose File > **Print,** then click **Color Management** on the options list **1**.

NEW 2. Follow one of these two procedures:

From the **Color Handling** pop-up menu, choose **Let Illustrator determine colors** to let Illustrator convert document colors to the printer gamut based on the chosen printer profile and send the converted data to the printer. The quality of the conversion depends on the accuracy of the chosen printer profile. From the **Printer Profile** pop-up menu, be sure to choose the appropriate ICC profile for your printer, ink, and paper. Click **Printer/Setup,** then locate and turn off color management for the printer driver.
or

From the **Color Handling** pop-up menu, choose **Let PostScript® printer determine colors** to send the color data to a PostScript printer and let the printer convert the colors to its gamut. Click **Printer/Setup,** then locate and turn on color management for the printer driver.

3. For a CMYK document (when Let PostScript® printer determine colors is

NEW chosen), check **Preserve CMYK Numbers** to hold off any color conversion of artwork (including imported images without embedded profiles) until the color data reaches the printer. Adobe recommends leaving this option unchecked for RGB documents.

4. Leave the **Rendering Intent** on the default setting of Relative Colorimetric unless you or your output specialist have a specific reason to change it. For more about the intents, see page 62.

5. Choose other print options. Click **Print** to print the document, or click Done to save the current settings without printing.

1 *The Print dialog box,* **Color Management** *panel*

Got a non-PostScript printer?

If your document contains complex objects (such as gradients, meshes, or soft-edge effects) and you get a printing error from a non-PostScript or low-resolution printer, instead of printing the file as vectors, check **Print as Bitmap** in the Advanced panel in the Print dialog box. Note that the driver for the chosen printer controls whether this option is available, and most Mac printer drivers don't include it.

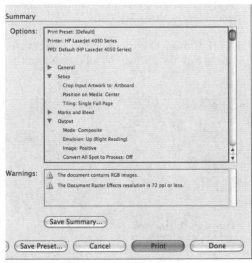

1 *The Print dialog box, **Advanced** panel*

2 *The Print dialog box, **Summary** panel*

Advanced panel

The **Advanced** panel of the Print dialog box lets you choose overprint options for fills and strokes for color separations or composite printing.

To choose overprint and flattening options for output:

1. In the **Print** dialog box, click **Advanced** on the options list.
2. Choose an option from the **Overprints** pop-up menu **1**:

   Preserve to maintain the file's overprint settings in printers that support overprinting (usually separation printers).

   Discard to ignore a file's overprint settings in the printout.

   Simulate to create the visual effect of overprinting in the composite printout. When printing a composite, Illustrator always flattens areas that are set to overprint.

   Note: The Overprints setting doesn't override Overprint Fill or Stroke settings chosen via the Attributes palette.

3. To specify how transparent objects are flattened for printing, choose a preset from the **Preset** pop-up menu (see the sidebar on the next page), or click **Custom** to create and save a custom preset that saves with the file (see page 495).
4. Choose other print settings, then click Print or click Done.

Summary panel

Use the **Summary** panel to view a summary of the current Print dialog box settings.

To view a summary of the current print settings:

1. In the **Print** dialog box, click **Summary** on the options list **2**.
2. Scroll down the **Options** window to view the settings, and read any alerts in the **Warnings** window.
3. *Optional:* Click Save Summary to save the current settings to a file.

Printing and exporting transparency

Transparency settings (nondefault blending modes and opacity levels) in objects, groups, or layers are preserved when a document is saved in either of the native Illustrator formats: Adobe Illustrator CS or CS2 or Adobe PDF (Compatibility: Acrobat 5, 6 or 7).

When a file that contains Transparency palette settings is exported in a nonnative format or is printed, Illustrator uses the current transparency flattener settings to determine how objects will be flattened and rasterized in order to preserve the document's appearance.

When flattening, Illustrator breaks up overlapping objects that contain transparency and converts each overlapping and nonoverlapping area into a separate, nonoverlapping, opaque shape.

Illustrator tries to keep flattened shapes as vector objects. However, if the look of transparency settings can't be preserved in a flattened shape as a vector object, Illustrator will rasterize the shape instead. This will happen, for example, where two gradient objects with nondefault transparency settings overlap. The resulting flattened shape would be rasterized in order to keep the complex appearance of transparency.

Print and Export Transparency

Default transparency flattener presets

[High Resolution] is suitable for high-quality color separations and film-based color proofs.

[Medium Resolution] is suitable for desktop PostScript color prints and proofs.

[Low Resolution] is suitable for black-and-white desktop printers.

Transparency to InDesign

When saving your artwork for **InDesign CS2,** use the native Illustrator CS2 (.ai) format, which preserves live transparency. Illustrator objects containing transparency will interact correctly with the content of, and any transparency in, the InDesign layout. InDesign will perform any needed transparency flattening at the time of printing.

To determine how transparency is flattened for exported files:

Choose File > **Document Setup,** then choose **Transparency** from the topmost pop-up menu **1**. In the **Export and Clipboard Transparency Flattener Settings** area, choose a preset from the **Preset** pop-up menu (see the sidebar), then click OK.

or

Click **Custom** to create a custom preset that saves with the file (see the following page).

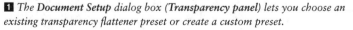

1 *The* **Document Setup** *dialog box (***Transparency** *panel) lets you choose an existing transparency flattener preset or create a custom preset.*

To choose custom transparency flattener options:

1. If you click Custom in either the Document Setup dialog box (Transparency panel) or the Print dialog box (Advanced panel), the Custom Transparency Flattener Options dialog box will open **1**. Perform any of the following steps.

2. Move the **Raster/Vector Balance** slider to control the percentage of flattened shapes that will remain as vectors versus the percentage of shapes that will be rasterized. The Raster/Vector Balance settings apply only to flattened shapes that represent transparency. Vector shapes print with cleaner, higher-quality color and crisper edges as compared with rasterized shapes.

   Higher values (to the right) produce a higher percentage of flattened shapes as vectors, though complex flattened areas may still be rasterized. A higher percentage of vector shapes will result in higher-quality output, but at the expense of slower, more memory-demanding output processing.

   The lowest value (to the left) won't necessarily produce poor output quality. In fact, if a document is very complex and contains a lot of transparency effects, this may be the only setting that produces acceptable output. Low settings produce fast output at a low resolution.

3. The rasterization process uses resolution settings to determine output quality. To specify the resolution for rasterized line art and text, enter a **Line Art and Text Resolution** value. For most purposes, the default resolution setting of 300 ppi is adequate, but for small text or thin lines, you should increase it to 600 ppi. Transparent text is flattened and preserved as text objects; clipping and masking are used to preserve the look of transparency.

4. When printed on a PostScript level 3 printer, mesh objects print as vectors. When mesh objects are printed to a PostScript level 2 printer or saved in an EPS format that is PostScript Level 2 compatible, both vector data and rasterized data are saved in the file, allowing the output device to choose which set of data to use. Specify the resolution for the rasterized mesh object in the **Gradient and Mesh Resolution** field. The default value is 150 ppi; 300 ppi would be considered a high value.

   When the Raster/Vector Balance slider is below 100, due to transparency flattening, Illustrator may rasterize placed or embedded images at the resolution specified in the Gradient and Mesh Resolution field. This value will be used only for portions of an image that are overlapped by a transparent object; the remainder of the image will print at the original image resolution. To keep things simple, always

(Continued on the following page)

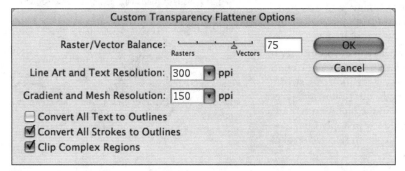

1 *Use the **Custom Transparency Flattener Options** dialog box to choose custom settings for the current file.*

Custom Transparency Flattener Options

make the Gradient and Mesh Resolution value equal to or higher than the original resolution of the placed or embedded image.

For an EPS image that overlaps an object containing transparency, embed the image into the Illustrator document via the Embed Image command on the Links palette menu. This will ensure an accurate printout of the image and the transparency effect.

5. When path strokes are converted to outlines, the filled "strokes" may be wider than the original stroke by one or two pixels. To prevent this thickening, move the Raster/Vector Balance slider to 100 (far right) or 0 (far left). At 100, all strokes will be converted to outlines and thickening will be uniform; at 0, all objects will be rasterized. Another option is to check **Convert All Text to Outlines,** which makes all the text within a given font print in the same width.

6. Strokes are converted into filled objects. The width of the object will equal the weight of the original stroke. With the Raster/Vector Balance slider at 0, all strokes (and all objects, for that matter) will be rasterized. A high Line Art and Text Resolution setting ensures high-quality output.

With the Raster/Vector Balance slider between 10 and 90, any strokes that overlap an object with transparency will be converted to outlines. Very thin strokes may be thickened slightly and may look noticeably different from parts of strokes that don't overlap transparency.

Check **Convert All Strokes to Outlines** to convert all strokes in a document to outlines. This preserves the look of a stroke for its entire length, but results in a larger number of paths in the file. An alternative to using this option is to apply Object > Path > Outline Stroke to selected strokes in the artwork.

7. When a file is sent to print, any areas of semitransparent objects that overlap other objects will be flattened and rasterized. The new flattened areas, however, won't match the exact path shapes of the objects. Also, the resulting flattened object may contain a combination of pixel and vector areas, and color discrepancies ("stitching") between adjacent pixel and vector areas may result. (*Note:* If the entire document is rasterized, no stitching occurs.) If you check **Clip Complex Regions,** boundaries between raster and vector flattened shapes will fall exactly on object paths. This helps eliminate the signs of stitching, but also slows down printing because of the complexity of the resulting paths.

8. Click OK.

Flatten a selection

To control the flattening of a selected object, choose Object > **Flatten Transparency,** then adjust the Raster/Vector Balance slider, the Line Art and Text Resolution value, and the Gradient and Mesh Resolution value.

Don't stop here

You can use the **Flattener Preview** palette to see which transparent areas of a document will be flattened. Open the Flattener Preview palette and click Refresh. Choose Show Options from the palette menu; move the Raster/Vector Balance slider, if desired; check Options; then click Refresh again. You can save your settings as a preset by choosing Save Transparency Flattener Preset from the Flattener Preview palette menu. For more information about flattening and the Flattener Preview palette, see Illustrator Help. Or if you're using the Adobe CS2 Creative Suite, on the **NEW** Resources and Extras CD-ROM, check out Technical Information > Creative Suite 2 > Designer's Guide to Transparency.pdf.

Creating and editing presets

You can create a **preset** for your custom **transparency flattener** and **Print** dialog box **settings.** Presets help ensure consistency when applying flattening to a series of documents or when outputting a series of documents to the same printer, and can also be exported as files for use by other users.

Custom flattener settings that you choose via the Print dialog box (Advanced panel) and Document Setup dialog box (Transparency panel) apply only to the current file. To create flattener presets for display on the Preset pop-up menus in the Document Setup dialog box (Transparency panel) and in the Print dialog box (Advanced panel) for any file, use one of the "…Presets" commands found on the Edit menu instead.

Printing presets saved using the Print dialog box can be edited using the Print Presets command. You can also use this command to create a new print preset.

To create a transparency flattener, tracing, print, or PDF preset:

1. From the Edit menu, choose one of **NEW** the following: **Transparency Flattener Presets, Tracing Presets, Print Presets,** or **PDF Presets.** A preset dialog box will open.

2. *Optional:* Click New to create a new preset; or click an existing preset, then click New to create a variation (copy) of that preset.

3. In the **Transparency Flattener Preset Options** dialog box **1**, enter a Name,

(Continued on the following page)

1 *The Transparency Flattener Preset Options dialog box*

choose settings for the various options (see pages 495–496), then click OK.

NEW In the **Tracing Options** dialog box, enter a Name, and choose settings as you would when creating a live tracing (see pages 341–345).

In the **Print Presets Options** dialog box, enter a name, choose settings as you would in the Print dialog box (see pages 482–493), then click OK.

In the **New PDF Presets** dialog box, enter a name, choose settings as you would in the Save Adobe PDF dialog box (see pages 506–510), then click OK.

4. *Do any of the following optional steps:*

For a summary of the current settings, click a preset name, then look in the **Preset Settings** window.

Click a user-created preset name or a name not in brackets, click **Edit,** modify any of the settings, then click OK.

Click **Delete** to delete a user-created preset.

Click **Export** to save the settings as a separate file.

Click **Import** to locate and open an exported settings file.

Note: You can edit the [Default] print preset, but you can't edit any of the default transparency flattener presets or default PDF presets.

5. Click OK. *Note:* If your artwork contains transparency, when saving it in the Adobe PDF format with compatibility set to Acrobat 4 (PDF 1.3), you must choose transparency flattener options.

1 *A rectangle is drawn.*

2 *After choosing the Crop Area > Make command*

Creating custom crop marks

Crop marks are short perpendicular lines around the edge of a page that a commercial printer uses as guides to trim the paper. Illustrator's **Crop Area** command creates visible, nonprinting crop marks around a rectangle that you draw.

To create a crop area:

1. Choose the **Rectangle** tool (M).

2. Carefully draw a rectangle that encompasses some or all of the artwork in the document **1**.

3. With the rectangle still selected, choose Object > Crop Area > **Make 2**. The rectangle will disappear, and crop marks will appear where the corners of the rectangle were.

➤ If you don't create a rectangle before choosing Object > Crop Area > Make, crop marks will be placed around the entire artboard.

➤ You can create only one set of crop marks per document by using the Crop Area command. If you apply Object > Crop Area > Make a second time, new marks will replace the existing ones. To create more than one set of crop marks in a document, use the Crop Marks filter instead (see the following page).

Crop marks that are created via the Crop Area command **limit** what part of the document will **print**.

To limit the printout to the crop area:

1. Follow the steps in the previous set of instructions to create crop marks in the document.

2. Choose File > **Print,** then click **Setup** on the options list.

3. From the **Crop Artwork to** pop-up menu, choose **Crop Area.** The crop area will display in the preview window.

4. Choose any other print settings, then click Print to print the document.

To remove crop marks created with the Crop Area command:

Choose Object > Crop Area > **Release.** The selected rectangle will reappear, with a fill and stroke of None. Toggle to Outline view or use smart guides (with Object Highlighting option checked in Preferences > Smart Guides & Slices) to locate it. You can recolor it or delete it.

➤ If crop marks were created for the entire page, the released rectangle will have the same dimensions as the artboard.

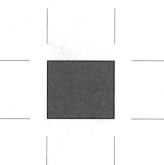

1 *After applying the Crop Marks filter to a rectangle*

The **Crop Marks** filter places eight crop marks around a selected object or objects. You can create more than one set of crop marks in a document using this filter.

To create crop marks for an object:

1. Select the object or objects that you want to create crop marks for.

2. Choose Filter > Create > **Crop Marks.** Crop marks will surround the smallest rectangle that could be drawn around the selection **1**.

➤ Group the crop marks with the objects they surround so you can move them in unison. On the Layers palette, the crop marks are listed as nested objects within a group.

➤ To move or delete crop marks, select them first with the Selection tool or via the Layers palette.

➤ The "Crop Artwork to" pop-up menu in the Print dialog box (Setup panel) doesn't recognize crop marks that are generated via the Crop Marks filter. Illustrator treats such crop marks as artwork.

➤ Similarly, the Marks and Bleed panel trim marks are aligned with the edge of the entire printed document and are independent of any marks created by the Crop Marks filter.

Remove Crop Area; Create Crop Marks

What gets rasterized

All the Photoshop effects in the lower half of the **Effect** menu will **rasterize** upon export or output. The following effects on the Stylize submenu will also rasterize: Drop Shadow (if the Blur value is greater than 0), Inner Glow, Outer Glow, and Feather.

Spot colors on raster effects **NEW**

You can specify **spot colors** for the four Illustrator **effects** mentioned above. In the effect dialog box, click the color square. The Color Picker opens; you can click the Color Swatches button to access and choose from a list of spot and process colors currently on the Swatches palette.

The Adobe Illustrator, Illustrator EPS, and Adobe PDF formats preserve spot colors. Spot colors applied to objects, raster effects, and grayscale images will generate separate plates, whether you output the file from a layout program or directly from Illustrator.

(To colorize an embedded grayscale TIFF image with a spot color, see page 133.)

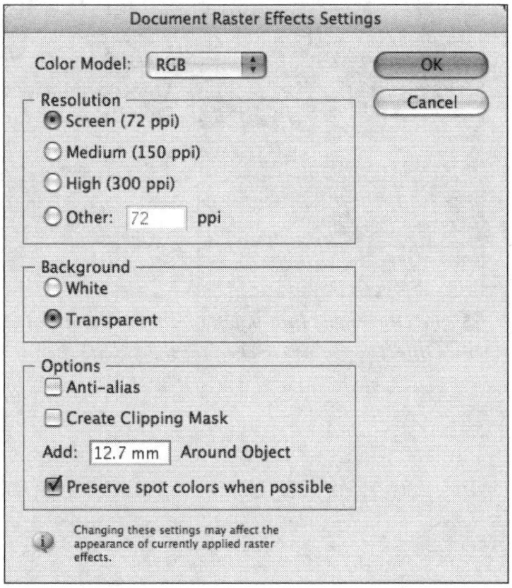

Choosing raster settings for effects

Some Effect menu commands are rasterized when output or exported. The default resolution setting is 72 ppi, a rather low setting that's suitable only for onscreen output.

To choose a higher resolution, choose Effect > **Document Raster Effects Settings** 1, then click another resolution option, or click Other and enter a custom resolution value. The higher the resolution, the slower the output processing time.

➤ Leave the resolution for effects at the default 72 ppi while editing your document, then increase the resolution before printing or exporting the file. A new resolution setting will affect all objects with applied effects that are rasterized, as well as resolution-dependent filters, such as Crystallize and Pointillize.

➤ For information about the options in the Document Raster Effects Settings dialog box, see pages 319–320.

➤ The current Resolution setting in the Document Raster Effects Settings dialog box is also listed in the Graphics panel of the Print dialog box.

➤ See the sidebar for information about spot colors in raster effects.

1 The **Document Raster Effects Settings** dialog box

Using the Document Info palette

To display information about an object or a document:

1. *Optional:* Select the object (or objects) about which you want to read info.

2. Display the **Document Info** palette (Window > Document Info) 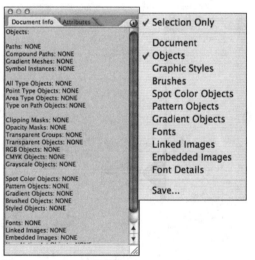.

3. To display information about a currently selected object, on the palette menu, make sure **Selection Only** has a check mark **2**, or uncheck it to display information pertaining to all the objects in the document.

4. Choose **Objects** from the palette menu to list the number of paths, clipping masks, compounds, opacity masks, transparent groups, transparent objects, objects with graphic styles, meshes, and objects that contain brush strokes, as well as color, font, and linking info.

   or

   Choose another category from the palette menu to see a listing of graphic styles; brushes; objects containing spot colors, patterns, or gradients; fonts; linked or embedded images; or font details (PostScript name, font file name, language, etc.).

5. *Optional:* If the Selection Only option is checked on the palette menu, you can click any other object in the document to see info for that object in the currently chosen category.

6. *Optional:* Choose Save from the palette menu to save the currently displayed information as a text document. Choose a location in which to save the text file, rename the file, if desired, then click Save. Use the system's default text editor to open the text document. You can print this file and refer to it when preparing your document for high-resolution printing.

1 *The **Document Info** palette, with **Document** information displayed: this information is always available—whether the Selection Only option is on or off.*

2 *The **Document Info** palette with the **Selection Only** and **Objects** options checked on the palette menu*

Document Info Palette

EXPORT 33

In this chapter you'll learn how to save files in the EPS and PDF formats; export files in the Flash (swf), JPEG, and other formats; and learn about options for exporting Illustrator files to Photoshop.

Legacy EPS **NEW**

If you need to save a file to an earlier EPS format than Illustrator CS2 EPS, in the Save As dialog box, choose that format from among the **Legacy Formats** on the **Version** pop-up menu, and also be sure to read any messages in the Warnings area at the bottom of the EPS Options dialog box. Live features from Illustrator CS2 won't be preserved.

When saving to Illustrator 8...

...you'll need to choose one of these **Transparency** options in the EPS Options dialog box:

Preserve Paths (discard transparency) to preserve object paths and eliminate all transparency effects, such as blending modes and opacity masks.

Preserve Appearance and Overprints to preserve the appearance of transparency and overprints by rasterizing objects that contain such attributes.

1 *This prompt will appear if you save a file in Illustrator EPS format and the file contains spot colors that interact with transparency.*

Not all applications can read files in the native Illustrator Document (.ai) format, and no preview options are available for this format. To prepare an Illustrator file for export to a page layout application or another drawing application, you need to save it in either the Illustrator **EPS** format or the **PDF** format. We'll discuss EPS first.

Saving as EPS

The **EPS** (Encapsulated PostScript) format saves both vector and bitmap objects and is supported by most illustration and page layout programs. Also, EPS files can be reopened and edited in Illustrator.

Note: When exporting artwork containing transparency to InDesign CS2, don't use the Illustrator EPS format, as InDesign will be able to read only the flattened part of the EPS file—not the live transparency. Use the native Illustrator CS2 format (.ai) instead.

To save a file as EPS:

1. With the file open in Illustrator, choose File > **Save As** or **Save a Copy.**

2. Choose **Format/Save as Type: Illustrator EPS (eps)**, choose a location for the file, then click Save.

   If your Illustrator file contains spot colors that interact with transparency and you save it in the Illustrator EPS format, an alert dialog box will appear **1**. If you allow those spot colors to be converted to process colors in another application, the results may be unpredictable. Click Cancel and convert the spot colors in Illustrator (or click Continue if you know

(Continued on the following page)

EPS Format

the spot colors won't be an issue). The EPS Options dialog box opens **1**.

NEW 3. Keep the Version as **Illustrator CS2 EPS.** (Or to save to an earlier version, see the sidebar on the previous page.)

4. Choose a Preview **Format:**

None for no preview. The image won't display onscreen in any other application, but it will print.

TIFF (Black & White) for a black-and-white preview.

TIFF (8-bit Color) for a color preview.

In Mac, you can also choose **Macintosh (Black & White)** for a black-and-white PICT preview, or **Macintosh (8-bit Color)** for a color preview in the PICT format.

Note: Regardless of which preview option you choose, color information will be

saved with the file, and the file will print normally from Illustrator or any other application into which it's imported.

If you chose the TIFF (8-bit Color) format, click **Transparent** to save the file with a transparent background, or click **Opaque** to save it with a solid background. If you're going to import the file into a Microsoft Office application, choose Opaque.

5. If the artwork contains overprints, from the Transparency: **Overprints** pop-up menu, choose **Preserve** to record any overprint information in the EPS file, or **Discard** to save the EPS file without overprint information.

If the artwork contains transparency, from the **Preset** pop-up menu, choose **[High Resolution], [Medium Resolution],**

1 *Choose Preview, Transparency, Font, and other options in the EPS Options dialog box.*

or [Low Resolution] as the transparency flattening preset to be used when flattening is necessary (see page 494).

Take a moment to read any information **NEW** messages 🔆 that you see in the Warnings area. For example, you may learn that the document contains transparency that will require flattening, or how overprinting in transparent areas will be handled.

6. Under Fonts, check **Embed Fonts (for other applications)** to save any fonts being used as a part of the file so they'll display and print properly on any system, even where they aren't installed. Check this option if your Illustrator file contains type and you're going to import it into a layout application.

7. *Check any of these optional boxes:*

   Include Linked Files to embed a copy of any linked, placed files with the Illustrator EPS file, so you won't need the original EPS image to print the file from another program, such as InDesign. Don't discard the original EPS image, though—you'll still need it to print the file from Illustrator. Note also that this option increases the file storage size.

Include Document Thumbnails to save a thumbnail of the file for previewing in the Open or Place dialog box in Illustrator.

Include CMYK PostScript in RGB Files to enable RGB files to print from programs that output only CMYK color. (RGB colors will be preserved as RGB if the EPS file is reopened in Illustrator.)

Compatible Gradient and Gradient Mesh Printing to include instructions to help older PostScript printers print gradients and meshes. If your printer isn't having problems printing gradients or meshes, leave this option unchecked.

8. Choose the **Adobe PostScript®** option that conforms to your printing device: **LanguageLevel 2** or **LanguageLevel 3**. Choose LanguageLevel 3 if the file contains meshes and will be output to a Level 3 printer.

9. Click OK. If you didn't check Include Linked Files and your file contains placed, linked images, an alert dialog box will appear ■; click **Embed Files** or **NEW** **Preserve Links.**

■ *This prompt will appear if you **didn't** check Include Linked Files in the EPS Format Options dialog box and your file contains placed, linked images. Here's a second chance to include those placed files.*

EPS Format

Saving as PDF

The versatile **Adobe PDF** (Portable Document Format) is a good choice for Web output and for transferring files to other applications or platforms that read PostScript-based Adobe PDF files. The only software users need in order to view a PDF file is Acrobat Reader or Adobe Reader 6 or later (both free of charge) or, in Mac OSX, the Preview application; they don't need the Illustrator application. Plus, your artwork will look as it was originally designed, as this format preserves all object attributes, groups, fonts, and text; the Acrobat 6 and 7 formats also preserve layers. PDF files can also be viewed in Adobe Acrobat, where edits and comments can be applied. The PDF format also supports document text search and navigation features.

If you save an Illustrator file as PDF (using any non-PDF/X preset), and then reopen or place it in Illustrator, the document will be fully editable.

To save a file as Adobe PDF:

1. With the file open in Illustrator, choose File > **Save As** or **Save a Copy.**

2. Type a name in **Save As/File Name** field, choose a location for the file, choose **Format/Save as Type: Adobe PDF (pdf),** then click Save. The Save Adobe PDF dialog box opens **1**.

3. *Optional:* From the **Adobe PDF Preset** **NEW** pop-up menu, choose a preset that best suits the intended output:

   Illustrator Default creates a PDF file that can be reedited in Illustrator or placed into InDesign or QuarkXPress. The file is Acrobat 5-compatible, and fonts are embedded. Bitmap images aren't down-sampled or compressed.

   NEW **High Quality Print** creates PDF files for desktop printers and proofers. Files can be opened in Adobe Acrobat 5 and later.

   NEW **PDFX1a** and **PDFX3** create Acrobat 4-compatible PDF files that will be checked for compliance with specific printing standards, thus helping to prevent printing problems. Note, however, that PDF/X files can't be reopened or

1 *The [Illustrator Default] settings in the **General** panel of the Save Adobe PDF dialog box*

reedited in Illustrator, and transparency settings aren't preserved.

Press Quality is for high-quality prepress output. The files are compatible with Adobe Acrobat 5 and later, all fonts are automatically embedded, compression is JPEG, the quality is Maximum, and custom color and high-end image options are preserved. To accommodate all this data, the resulting file size is large.

Smallest File Size creates compact PDF **NEW** files for output to the Web, e-mail, or other onscreen purposes; fonts aren't embedded.

➤ You can read about the presets in the Description window.

If you're satisfied with the settings in the chosen preset, click Save PDF, or if you want to customize the preset, proceed with any or all of the remaining steps.

4. Choose a PDF/X standard from the **NEW** **Standard** pop-up menu (see Illustrator Help or the Acrobat User Guide).

   or

   Choose Standard: **None,** then choose from the **Compatibility** pop-up menu: Acrobat 4, Acrobat 5, Acrobat 6, or Acrobat 7. Acrobat 6 and 7 preserve layers; Acrobat 5, 6, and 7 preserve transparency. (Not all applications can read Acrobat 7 files yet.)

   If you changd any settings from the preset defaults, "[Chosen Preset] (Modified)" will appear on the Adobe PDF Preset pop-up menu.

   If you want to further alter the preset, click a category at the left of the dialog box to display that panel.

5. Under **Options,** check any of the following:

   Preserve Illustrator Editing Capabilities to enable the PDF file to be reopened and edited in Illustrator. This option limits how much the file can be compressed.

   Embed Page Thumbnails to save a thumbnail of the file (or page) that will display in the Open and Place dialog boxes.

   Optimize for Fast Web View to enable the file to display quickly in a Web browser.

   View PDF after Saving to automatically launch your system's default PDF viewer (usually Adobe Reader or Acrobat) and display the newly saved file.

   For the Acrobat 6 or 7 Compatibility option, check **Create Acrobat Layers from Top-Level Layers** to preserve the ability to work with layers when the file is opened in Acrobat 6 or 7.

   Create Multi-page PDF from Page Tiles **NEW** to have each tiled area in your artwork become a separate page in the PDF file (see the sidebar on page 510).

6. The **Compression** panel (**1**, next page) lets you control how imagery will be compressed in the PDF, which in turn will affect the overall file size. Downsampling reduces the total number of pixels in an image. Downsampling isn't recommended for print output, but it is recommended for online output, as it decreases the file size. Choose an interpolation method from the pop-up menus for **Color Bitmap Images, Grayscale Bitmap Images,** and **Monochrome Bitmap Images:**

   Do Not Downsample keeps the image at the size it was created.

   Average Downsampling To divides the image into sample areas, averages the pixels in each area, and substitutes the average values for the original values.

   Subsampling To replaces a sampled area with pixel data taken from the middle of that area, producing smaller but not necessarily accurate files.

   Bicubic Downsampling To replaces the sampled area with an average of the area's values, and often is more accurate than average downsampling.

   If you chose an interpolation method, enter a **ppi** resolution to downsample to and a resolution threshold above which images will be downsampled.

(Continued on the following page)

PDF Format

Other options in the Compression panel:

Choose a compression type from the **Compression** pop-up menu: **None, ZIP, JPEG,** or **JPEG2000,** or an Automatic option to let Illustrator choose compression settings for the artwork: **Automatic (JPEG)** for the widest compatibility, or **Automatic (JPEG2000)** for the best compression. ZIP and JPEG2000 can be lossy or lossless; JPEG is lossy. Options on the Image Quality pop-up menu vary depending on which compression type you choose. For JPEG2000, you also can choose a **Tile Size.**

7. For information about the **Marks and Bleeds** panel, see pages 486–487.

NEW 8. The **Output** panel lets you control color conversion and profile inclusion in the PDF file. The panel contains two areas:

Use the **Color** area to specify color conversions. From the **Color Conversion** pop-up menu, choose **No Conversion** or **Convert to Destination,** depending on whether you want Illustrator or the

> ## Save your preset
>
> Once you've chosen Adobe PDF settings, you can save them in your own user-created preset by clicking **Save Preset** in the lower left corner of the Save Adobe PDF dialog box. Your newly saved settings will be listed on the Adobe PDF Preset pop-up menu and can be chosen as a preset when saving other files as PDF.
>
> To edit a user-created preset, choose Edit > Adobe PDF Presets, click your user-created preset on the Presets scroll list, then click **Edit.**

output device to convert colors to a destination profile. Choose **Convert to Destination (Preserve Numbers)** if the file has the same color space as the destination profile (e.g., when converting a CMYK file to a CMYK profile). If you opt for conversion, choose a destination profile from the **Destination** pop-up menu. For No Conversion, you can include or exclude the destination profile by choosing an option from the **Profile Inclusion Policy** pop-up menu.

1 *The Compression panel in the Save Adobe PDF dialog box*

The **PDF/X** options will be available if you chose a PDF/X Standard:

Choose a profile to embed from the **Output Intent Profile Name** pop-up menu.

Type your own description in the **Output Condition Name** field, to be saved with the file.

Output Condition Identifier is a pointer to more information about that profile.

Registry Name lists the Web site for more information about that registry. For some profiles, both of these will be filled in. If not, enter the information yourself.

9. The **Advanced** panel lets you control font, overprint, and flattening options.

For the **Fonts** option, the included default PDF presets automatically embed all the characters in each font used in the file. If not all the characters in those fonts were used in your artwork, you can choose to embed just a subset of characters by entering a percentage in the **Subset fonts when percentage of characters used is less than** field. If you enter 50%, for example, the entire font will be embedded if you use more than 50% of its characters in the file, and the Subset option will be used if you use fewer than 50% of its characters. This helps reduce the file size of the PDF.

When Acrobat 4 is chosen as the Compatibility option, you also need to choose **Overprint** and **Transparency Flattener** options (if those features were used). Choose to preserve or discard overprint areas in the PDF file. For information on the Transparency Flattener feature, see pages 494–498. Acrobat 5, 6, and 7 automatically preserve overprinting and transparency.

10. The **Security** panel lets you restrict user access to the PDF. The following options are available to only non-PDF/X-compliant files:

Check **Require a password to open the document** if you want the file to be password protected. Type a password in the Document Open Password field.

Note: Passwords can't be recovered from the document, so keep a copy of them in a separate location.

Check **Use a password to restrict editing Security and Permissions settings** if you want to maintain control over these options. Type a password in the Permissions Password field. The following options become available:

The **Printing Allowed** pop-up menu lets you control whether users can print the file. Options are None, Low Resolution (150 dpi), and High Resolution.

The **Changes Allowed** pop-up menu lets you specify precisely what users can and cannot alter.

Check **Enable copying of text, images and other content** to permit users to alter text or images.

(Continued on the following page)

Ready to convert?

Choices made in the **Output** panel of the **Save Adobe PDF** dialog box control whether the output device or Illustrator converts colors in the file.

➤ To have the **output device** (not Illustrator) convert colors to the profile you include in the PDF file, choose Output settings of Color Conversion: No Conversion, and Profile Inclusion Policy: Include Destination Profile.

➤ To have **Illustrator** convert the colors to the destination (output) profile and save the converted colors in the PDF file, choose Output settings of Color Conversion: Convert to Destination, Destination: [the profile for your output device], and Profile Inclusion Policy: Don't Include Profile.

➤ When in doubt, leave the **default** PDF presets settings as is. To learn about an option, rest the pointer on it and read the info in the Description area.

PDF Format

Check **Enable text access of screen reader devices for the visually impaired** to let screen readers view and read the file.

11. Check **Enable plaintext metadata** if you want the file metadata to be searchable by other applications (available only for Acrobat 6 and 7).

The **Summary** panel lists the settings you've chosen for each category, for your perusing pleasure. Expand any category to view its settings.

12. Click Save PDF, then give yourself a pat on the back.

Using the Export command

In the remaining pages of this chapter, we'll discuss some of the formats that you can use for **exporting** your Illustrator files to **other** applications.

To export a file:

1. With the file open, choose File > **Export**. The Export dialog box opens.

2. *Optional:* Enter a new name in the **Save As/File Name** field.

Illustrator will append the proper file extension to the name for the chosen file format automatically (e.g., .ai, .eps, .tif).

3. Choose a file format **1**–**2** from the **Format/Save as type** pop-up menu.

4. Choose a location for the new file.

   ➤ To create a new folder for the file in Mac, click New Folder, enter a name, then click Create; in Windows, click Create New Folder, then enter a name.

5. Click **Export/Save.** Choose settings in any additional dialog box that opens, then click OK. Some file formats are discussed in brief on the next page; then Flash, JPEG, and options for exporting to Photoshop are discussed in depth.

Attention Web designers! NEW

To have each graphic or large block of text become a **separate Web page** of PDF art or text, do the following: In a new Illustrator file, choose File > Print. Click Setup; from the Tiling menu, choose Tile Full Pages or Tile Imageable Areas; then click Done. Choose View > Show Page Tiling. Create your art and/or text in the page tiles, and save the file as Adobe PDF, making sure to check Create Multipage PDF from Page Tiles in the General panel.

BMP (bmp)
Targa (tga)
PNG (png)
AutoCAD Drawing (dwg)
AutoCAD Interchange File (dxf)
Enhanced Metafile (emf)
Macromedia Flash (swf)
JPEG (jpg)
Macintosh PICT (pct)
Photoshop (psd)
TIFF (tif)
Text Format (txt)
✓ Windows Metafile (wmf)

1 *Choices on the **Format** pop-up menu in Mac*

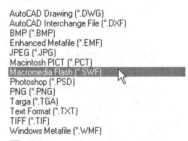

AutoCAD Drawing (*.DWG)
AutoCAD Interchange File (*.DXF)
BMP (*.BMP)
Enhanced Metafile (*.EMF)
JPEG (*.JPG)
Macintosh PICT (*.PCT)
Macromedia Flash (*.SWF)
Photoshop (*.PSD)
PNG (*.PNG)
Targa (*.TGA)
Text Format (*.TXT)
TIFF (*.TIF)
Windows Metafile (*.WMF)

2 *Choices on the **Format** pop-up menu in Windows*

A few formats in brief

Rasterize

When exporting a file, if you choose a raster (bitmap) file format, such as **BMP,** the **Rasterize Options** dialog box will open **1**. Choose a Color Model for the resulting file color. For file Resolution, choose Screen (72 dpi), Medium (150 dpi), or High (300 dpi), or enter a custom resolution (Other). Check Anti-Alias to smooth the edges of objects (pixels will be added along object edges).

BMP (bmp)

BMP is the standard bitmap image format on Windows and DOS computers. When you choose rasterization settings and click OK, the **BMP Options** dialog box opens. Choose the Windows or OS/2 format for the desired operating system, specify a bit depth, and choose whether you want to include RLE compression.

TIFF (tif)

TIFF, a bitmap image format, is supported by virtually all paint, image-editing, and page-layout applications. It supports RGB, CMYK, and grayscale color schemes, as well as the lossless LZW compression model.

If you choose the TIFF file format in the Export dialog box, the **TIFF Options** dialog box will open **2**. Choose a Color Model; choose a Resolution of Screen (72 dpi), Medium (150 dpi), or High (300 dpi) or

enter a custom resolution; and turn Anti-Alias on or off. Check LZW Compression to compress the file—a lossless method that doesn't discard or degrade image data. Choose your target platform in the Byte Order area, and check Embed ICC Profile if you've assigned such a profile to your file.

Windows metafile (wmf) and Enhanced metafile (emf)

A metafile describes a file and functions as a list of commands for drawing a graphic. Typically, a metafile is made up of commands for drawing objects such as lines, polygons, and text, and commands to control the style of the objects.

WMF, a 16-bit metafile format, is used on Windows platforms; **EMF,** a 32-bit metafile format used on Windows platforms, can contain a wider variety of commands than WMF.

Microsoft Office

Choose File > **Save for Microsoft Office** to save your document in a PNG format that will be readable in Microsoft Word, PowerPoint, and Excel. The Save for Microsoft Office dialog box opens. Choose a location, enter a file name, then click Save. *Note:* Any transparent areas in your file will become opaque when saved in this format.

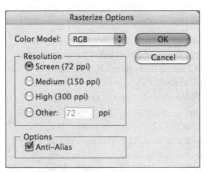

1 *The Rasterize Options dialog box opens if you choose a raster format in the Export dialog box.*

2 *The TIFF Options dialog box*

Exporting as Flash (swf)

The **Macromedia Flash** (swf) format, a vector graphics format, is used for Web animations, as SWF files are compact and scale well. In Illustrator, you can create frames for an animation on separate layers and then export the layers as a Flash file.

Note that the Flash format doesn't support such transparency appearances as blending modes and opacity masks. Also, gradients that encompass a wide range of colors will appear as rasterized shapes, and patterns will be rasterized. And finally, Flash supports only some kinds of joins. For example, beveled or square joins and caps will be converted to rounded joins.

NEW To create a Flash (swf) file:

1. *Optional:* Choose Release to Layers from the Layers palette menu to put nested objects onto their own layers before exporting them to the Flash format.

2. Choose File > **Export.** The Export dialog box opens.

3. Type a name and choose a location for your file, choose **Format/File Type: Macromedia Flash (swf),** then click Export/ Save. The Macromedia® Flash™ (SWF) Format Options dialog box opens (**1**, next page).

4. From the **Export As** pop-up menu, choose **AI File to SWF File** to export your entire Illustrator file as one Flash frame; or **AI Layers to SWF Frames** to export each layer in your Illustrator file as a separate Flash frame within a Flash document; or **AI Layers to SWF Files** to export each Illustrator layer as a separate Flash file consisting of one frame.

5. *Check any of the following options:*

   Generate HTML to create an HTML file for the exported SWF file so the SWF file can be used on a Web page. The HTML and SWF files will be saved in the same location.

   Protect from Import to prevent users from editing the exported SWF file.

Clip to Artboard Size to export only the artwork within the artboard bounds.

Export Text as Outlines to convert type to vector paths in order to preserve its appearance.

Compress File to compress the SWF data to reduce the file size. Note that Flash Player version 6 and earlier can't read compressed files.

To change the **Background Color** for the SWF file, click the color swatch, then choose a color from the Color Picker.

Choose a **Curve Quality** value (0–10) to control how accurate the vector curves will be in your Flash file. The higher the Curve Quality value, the more accurate the curves (and the larger the file size).

6. In the **Animation** area:

   If you chose AI Layers to SWF Frames in step 4, choose a **Frame Rate** (in frames per second) for the rate at which your animation will play, then choose any of the following options:

   Looping to have the animation loop continuously, or leave it unchecked to have the animation play once and then stop.

   Use as Background, then click a layer or sublayer to be used as a stationary background in all the SWF frames.

   Layer Order: Bottom Up or **Top Down** to determine the order in which layers are exported as animation frames.

   Animate Blends to have each step in a blend become an animation frame (you don't need to expand the blend in Illustrator). Click an export method: **In Sequence** to export each object in a blend to a separate animation frame, or **In Build** to have the first step become the first frame, the first and second steps become the second frame, and so on (the last frame will contain all the steps).

7. For **Method,** click **Preserve Appearance** to flatten objects and maintain the look of effects and opacity, or **Preserve**

Editability Where Possible to keep as much of the object's live, editable attributes as possible.

8. In the Image area, for **Image Format,** click **Lossless** for images that contain large solid-color areas or are to be edited in Flash, or click **Lossy (JPEG)** to apply greater compression to images and objects that must be rasterized, with a resulting reduction in image quality.

   If you clicked Lossy (JPEG), choose a **JPEG Quality** to control the amount of compression in images and objects that are rasterized. As quality increases, so does file size. Also click a compression **Method: Baseline (Standard)** for standard compression, or **Baseline Optimized** for standard plus additional compression.

   Enter a screen **Resolution** value (72–600 ppi) for bitmap images in the file. As the resolution increases, so does the file size. If you're planning to export any rasterized images and scale them up in Flash, choose a resolution greater than 72 ppi so the scaled images won't look pixelated.

9. Click OK.

■ *The Macromedia® Flash™ (SWF) Format Options dialog box*

Flash Format

Exporting as JPEG

The **JPEG** format is a good choice for exporting files that contain placed, continuous-tone bitmap images or objects with gradient fills, and for viewing 24-bit images on the Web. (For more about this format for Web output, see pages 520–521 and 535–536).

When you make an image Quality choice in the JPEG Options dialog box (step 3, below), bear in mind that the greater the compression, the greater the loss of image data and the lower the image quality. To experiment with this tradeoff, export multiple copies of a file, using a different compression setting for each copy, then view the results in the target application. You can also use the Save for Web command to preview different compression settings (see page 517).

To create a JPEG file:

1. Choose File > **Export**. The Export dialog box opens.

2. Type a name and choose a location for your file, choose **Format/File Type: JPEG (jpg)**, then click **Export/Save**. The JPEG Options dialog box opens (**1**, next page).

3. Choose an image **Quality:** Enter a numeric value (0–10); or move the slider; or choose **Low, Medium, High,** or **Maximum** from the pop-up menu.

4. Choose a **Color Model: RGB, CMYK,** or **Grayscale.**

5. Choose a Format **Method: Baseline (Standard);** or **Baseline Optimized** to optimize color and slightly reduce the file size; or **Progressive** to display the file at increasingly higher resolutions as it downloads on the Web. For the Progressive option, choose the number of **Scans** (iterations) to display before the final image appears. This type of JPEG isn't supported by all Web browsers and

requires additional RAM in order to be viewed.

6. Choose a Resolution **Depth: Screen, Medium,** or **High.** Or choose **Custom** and enter a Custom resolution (dpi).

7. In the **Options** area:

   Check **Anti-Alias** if you want your image to have smooth edges.

   If any objects in the file are linked to URLs, check **Imagemap,** then click **Client-side** or **Server-side.** For Client-side, Illustrator saves the JPEG file with an accompanying HTML file to hold the link information; both files are required by your Web layout program in order to interpret the links correctly. For Server-side, Illustrator saves the file for use on a Web server.

   Check **Embed ICC Profile** to embed the file's current Color Settings profile.

8. Click OK.

JPEG Format

1 *The JPEG Options dialog box lets you tailor your file for a number of uses, whether it's optimizing it for fast downloading on the Web or preserving enough resolution to output a crisp print.*

Photoshop (psd) format

➤ The **Photoshop (psd)** export format preserves opacity masks and layers, and editable type that doesn't have a stroke or effects. Blending modes and transparency will look the same in Photoshop, although on the Layers palette the imported layers will have a blending mode of Normal and an Opacity of 100%.

➤ If an Illustrator layer contains an object that Photoshop can't import as is (e.g., a stroke and effects), that layer and any layers below it will be **merged** into one layer in Photoshop.

➤ **Opacity masks** from Illustrator are converted to layer masks in Photoshop (whereas a layer mask in a Photoshop file would be converted to an opacity mask in Illustrator).

➤ **Compound shapes** translate easily between the two programs.

To learn more about importing Photoshop files into Illustrator, see pages 280–281.

Exporting to Photoshop

There are a number of ways to get **Illustrator** files into **Photoshop.**

Illustrator objects can be brought into Photoshop CS2 as fully editable vector art on a **smart object layer.** When you double-click a smart object layer in Photoshop, the Illustrator artwork opens in Illustrator for editing. Save the temporary file, and the smart object layer updates in Photoshop. Smart object layers are created when you use Photoshop or Bridge to place an Illustrator .ai file into Photoshop; drag an object from Illustrator into Photoshop; or copy/paste an object into Photoshop and choose Smart Object in the Paste dialog box.

You can also **copy and paste** an object into Photoshop as pixels, as a path, or as a shape layer, choosing an option in the Paste dialog

box. To ensure that the Paste dialog box will display in Photoshop, in Illustrator, go to Preferences > File Handling & Clipboard and for Copy As, check the PDF and AICB options.

You can also **drag and drop** an Illustrator object into Photoshop. If you want to preserve it as a path outline, Cmd-drag/Ctrl-drag.

And last but not least, the **Photoshop (psd)** export format converts Illustrator objects into pixels, and preserves layers and transparency (see the sidebar above).

To create a Photoshop (psd) file:

1. Choose File > **Export.** The Export dialog box opens.

2. Type a name and choose a location for your file, choose **Format/File Type: Photoshop (psd),** then click **Export/Save.**

(Continued on the following page)

Exporting to Photoshop

The **Photoshop Export Options** dialog box opens **1**.

3. Choose a **Color Model.**

4. Choose a preset or custom **Resolution.**

5. In the **Options** area, do any of the following:

NEW Leave the **Export As** choice as **Photoshop CS2,** unless you have a specific reason to change it.

Click **Flat Image** to flatten layers and have the artwork appear as one layer in Photoshop. Or to export the Illustrator layers to Photoshop, click **Write Layers** and check **Maximum Editability.** If the Illustrator file contains text that doesn't have a stroke or effects applied to it, you can check **Preserve Text Editability** to keep the text editable in Photoshop. *Note:* The Write Layers option preserves the stacking appearance of objects nested within a layer, but only top-level layers will become layers in Photoshop. Hidden layers in the Illustrator file will become hidden layers in Photoshop.

Check/uncheck **Anti-alias.**

Check **Embed ICC Profile** to embed the current profile in the file, if one was assigned.

6. Click OK.

Smart type **NEW**

If you create type in Adobe Illustrator CS2 and import it into Photoshop by using either of the two methods outlined below, it becomes a **smart object** layer in Photoshop. The contents of the smart object layer can be edited easily at any time in the original application.

AI format

In Illustrator, make sure the type is on its own layer, then save the file in the **Illustrator Document (.ai)** format. With a file open in Photoshop, use File > Place in Photoshop or Bridge to import the type file as a new smart object layer; it will appear on the Layers palette. If you double-click the smart object layer, a temporary file will open in Illustrator. Edit and resave it, and the type will update in the Photoshop document.

PSD format

To create a smart object layer that can be edited as a separate Photoshop file, in Illustrator, choose File > Export, choose Format: **Photoshop (psd);** click Write Layers; check Preserve Text Editability, Maximum Editability, and Anti-alias; then click OK. Open a Photoshop file, then use File > Place in Photoshop or Bridge to place the type file as a new smart object layer. If you double-click the smart object layer, a separate Photoshop file will appear onscreen, with the editable type in a layer group. Edit and resave the file, and the type will update in the original Photoshop document.

1 *The Photoshop Export Options dialog box*

This chapter covers the preparation of Illustrator files for the Web. You'll learn how to choose an appropriate export format, create and use slices to achieve faster download speeds, choose optimization settings via the Save for Web dialog box, save a file as SVG, and export as CSS layers.

Illustrator's Save for Web dialog box

In Illustrator, optimization settings are chosen in the File > **Save for Web** dialog box **1**. There, you'll find Original, Optimized, 2-Up, and 4-Up preview tabs at the top of the main window; a Color Table palette; format, matte, quality, and other options; a Preview in [default browser] button; and a Select Browser menu.

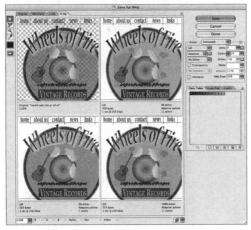

1 *The Save for Web dialog box in Illustrator*

Exporting Web graphics

Illustrator is an ideal program for creating crisp, sharp graphics—the kind of graphics that are well suited for **online display.** Thankfully, the program also boasts a number of tools that streamline the preparation of graphics for the Web.

The basic formula for outputting a file for online viewing may seem straightforward: Design your vector artwork in RGB color mode, then rasterize it by saving it in the **GIF, JPEG,** or **PNG** bitmap file format for display in a Web browser (the application that combines text, images, and HTML code into a viewable page on the Web). However, when you load and view your bitmap artwork via a Web browser, you may be disappointed to find that not all colors, blends, gradients, or other elements of your artwork display well on the Web.

What's more, a document that contains a large, placed image may take an unacceptably long time to download and render, due to its large file size. If your artwork looks overly dithered (grainy), was subject to unexpected color substitutions, or takes too long to view on a Web page, it means it isn't outputting well.

Some key issues that you'll need to address for online output are discussed in the sections that follow, such as image size, compression, file formats (GIF, JPEG, PNG, Flash, and SVG), dithering, anti-aliasing, transparency, and matte color.

Image size

Your first task when designing Web graphics is to calculate the appropriate **artboard size,** and it's not hard to figure out. Normally, you'll be designing for an 800 x 600-pixel viewing area, the most common browser window size, and for a 56 Kbps modem—although most users now have faster broadband access. Your maximum artboard size will occupy only a portion of the browser window—about 10 inches wide (740 pixels) by 7.5 inches high (550 pixels).

To determine a file's actual storage size, in Mac, highlight the file name in the Finder, then choose File > Get Info. In Windows, right-click the file in Windows Explorer and choose Properties from the context menu. Saving your file in the GIF, JPEG, or PNG file format will reduce its storage size significantly, as these formats have built-in compression schemes and rasterize all artwork to a resolution of 72 ppi. We'll discuss them in depth shortly.

Compression

If you know the exact file size of a **compressed** (optimized) file, you can calculate how long it will take to transmit over the Web. Using the File > Save for Web dialog box, you can find out exactly how large your optimized JPEG, GIF, PNG-8, or PNG-24 file is and how long it will take to download **1**. To calculate the **download time** based on file size and modem speed, choose a Size/Download Time from the Preview menu ⊙ at the top of the main window (or Control-click/right-click in the main window, then choose a Size/ Download Time). A 70K file traveling on a 56 Kbps modem, for example, will take approximately 14 seconds to download.

When saved in the GIF format, such elements as continuous-tone placed images and gradients may compress less than type or path objects that contain flat colors. If you reduce the color table of a continuous-tone image down to around 8 to 16 colors, the resulting GIF file size will be similar to that of a flat-color object, but you will have lost continuous color transitions in the bargain **2**–**3**.

Browser window layer

Take a **screen shot** of your **browser window,** place the file into an Illustrator document, then drag it into the bottommost layer. Now you can design your layout for the specific dimensions of that browser window.

```
GIF
12.66K
1 sec @ 256 Kbps
```

1 *The size and download time for the current file display in the Info annotation area in the lower left corner of each preview window of the Save for Web dialog box.*

2 *A continuous-tone image, saved as a 120K GIF...*

3 *...as compared with the same image saved as a GIF with a reduced color table, which shrank the file size to 20K*

1 *GIF is a suitable optimization format for this illustration, because it contains only **flat** colors.*

Color depth	
Number of colors	**Bit depth**
256	8
128	7
64	6
32	5
16	4
8	3
4	2
2	1

JPEG is a better format choice for continuous-tone, placed images.

The compression schemes in the GIF and JPEG formats lower the image quality slightly, but the resulting smaller file sizes download more quickly on the Web, making it a worthwhile compromise.

To summarize, artwork with large dimensions (say, 500 x 400 pixels or larger) should ideally contain only a handful of large, flat-color shapes, and objects containing blends and gradients should be restricted in size to only a portion of the Web browser window.

One effective way to minimize the download time for a document is to divide it into **slices**. Each slice can be optimized separately using different settings (more about that later!).

For a design that contains repetitive elements, another way to minimize the download time is by using **symbol** instances. Create a symbol set and place it behind other Illustrator objects, use the symbolism tools to modify the symbol set, if desired, then save the entire Web page in SVG format. In fact, a symbol set could be used as a backdrop behind other elements on a page, instead of the more common technique of background tiling.

GIF

GIF is an 8-bit file format, meaning that it can save up to 256 colors. It's suitable for artwork that contains flat-color vector objects or type in which color fidelity is a priority **1**. As this type of artwork contains fewer colors to begin with than continuous-tone images or gradients, a color restriction won't have a negative impact.

Your choice to use the GIF format should be influenced partially by the equipment used by your Web viewers. An 8-bit monitor can display a maxiumum of 256 colors, whereas the more prevalent 16-bit monitors can display thousands of colors, and 24-bit and 32-bit monitors can display millions of colors. Colors that a monitor can't display are simulated by dithering (see page 522). To prevent unexpected dithering, you can use the Web Snap option in the Save for Web dialog box

(Continued on the following page)

GIF

to shift some of the artwork colors to the Web-safe palette, or you can Web-shift flat-color areas manually.

By lowering the number of colors in the color table of a GIF file, you create a smaller file size that downloads faster on the Web, although the image may be dithered (grainy) and the colors duller.

In the Save for Web dialog box, not only can you reduce the number of colors in an 8-bit image from its original 256 colors, you can also preview how it will look with fewer available colors. To evaluate the color quality, choose a zoom level of 100% for the preview in the Save for Web dialog box.

➤ If you want to apply a gradient fill to a large area of a document and you're going to use the GIF format, create a top-to-bottom gradient. Top-to-bottom gradients produce smaller file sizes than left-to-right or diagonal gradients. We kid you not.

➤ Consider also creating a slice area around a gradient object, then optimizing the slice in the JPEG or SVG format  (see pages 535–536 and pages 539–540).

To optimize and preview a file as GIF, see pages 532–533.

JPEG

If your artwork contains gradients, placed images, or other continuous-tone elements and will be viewed on 24-bit monitors (which can display millions of colors), the JPEG format is a good choice. In this scenario, JPEG will preserve color fidelity better than GIF ❷–❸ (and ❶–❷, next page).

Another of JPEG's strengths is its compression power: It can shrink objects that contain color gradations significantly without noticeably lowering their quality.

The JPEG format does have some shortcomings, however. Unlike GIF files, JPEG files are decompressed as they're downloaded onto a Web page, which takes time. Second, the JPEG compression methods tend to produce

❶ *This **hybrid** illustration, which contains both sharp-edged elements (type) and a continuous-tone element (the gradient), is a good candidate for optimization in slices. Each slice can be optimized using a format appropriate for its particular content (e.g., GIF for the type, JPEG for the gradient).*

❷ *JPEG isn't a great choice for optimizing sharp-edged graphics. Note the artifacts around the type.*

❸ *The sharp-edge type looks crisper in this **GIF**.*

1 *A gradient optimized using the GIF format with 256 colors. Even using the maximum allowable number of colors in the GIF color table, the gradient exhibits banding.*

2 *The same gradient optimized using the JPEG format with a **Quality** setting of **High** is smooth and continuous. (The resulting file sizes produced by the GIF and JPEG formats are about equal.)*

artifacts along the well-defined edges of flat-color vector objects and type, so it's not a good format choice for those types of objects.

With the Progressive option chosen for the JPEG format, a file will display in increasing detail as it downloads onto a Web page. Note that some older browsers don't support progressive JPEGs.

If you choose JPEG as your output format in the Save for Web dialog box, you can use the 4–Up option to preview versions of a slice or docment in varying degrees of compression. As you choose a compression level, weigh the file size versus the diminished image quality.

Each time artwork is optimized in the JPEG format, some data is lost; the greater the compression, the greater the loss. To minimize such data loss, finish all your edits and save your document in Illustrator, then save an optimized copy of the file as JPEG.

To optimize and preview a file as JPEG, see pages 535–536.

PNG-8 and PNG-24

There are two PNG formats, **PNG**-8 and **PNG**-24. The compression scheme used by these formats is lossless, meaning it doesn't cause data loss, and they're supported by most major Web browsers.

The PNG-8 format supports only one level of transparency and can contain a maximum of only 256 colors (similar to GIF). PNG-24, on the other hand, can save semitransparent pixels, such as soft-edged effects. Each pixel can have one of 256 levels of opacity, ranging from totally transparent to totally opaque. Like JPEG, a PNG-24 file can contain millions of colors, but PNG-24 produces larger file sizes (compresses less) than JPEG.

Neither PNG format can save animations (whereas the GIF format does).

To optimize and preview a file as PNG-8 or PNG-24, see pages 532–533 and 536.

Vector formats for the Web

There are two alternatives to the bitmap formats: The **SVG** format (see pages 539–541), and the **Flash** format (see pages 512–513).

(Continued on the following page)

PNG-8, PNG-24

Dithering

Dithering is the process by which two or more palette colors are juxtaposed to create the impression of a third color. Placed images that contain a limited number of colors (256 or fewer) benefit from dithering, as it makes them appear to contain a wider range of colors and shades.

Because continuous-tone placed imagery, blends, gradients, and meshes contain a wide range of colors, they tend to look okay on both 8-bit and 24-bit displays. However, if you reduce the number of colors in the GIF color table for such objects, you'll increase the likelihood of banding (stripes instead of smooth gradations). Banding can be prevented by applying dithering (a low value is recommended). You can choose a dither method and amount in the Optimize panel in the Save for Web dialog box. Keep in mind that the higher the dither value, the more seamless the color transitions, but the more grainy the color **1**–**2**. Also, dithering adds noise and additional colors to a file, so compression is less effective with dithering on than with it off.

Anti-aliasing

By adding pixels with progressively less opacity along the edges of nonrectangular objects, **anti-aliasing** smooths the transition between such objects and their backgrounds. This option is applied automatically to all objects when a file is optimized in any of the bitmap Web formats (GIF, JPEG, or PNG). To preview the anti-aliasing that will be applied to vector objects, use View > Pixel Preview (see page 530).

Sometimes you may want to **rasterize** individual objects before optimizing a whole file in order to control the rasterization settings. For example, you could rasterize a type object without anti-aliasing in order to preserve its sharp edges. For type, you can either use Object > Rasterize to rasterize the type object in Illustrator (and make the type noneditable), or apply Effect > Rasterize to the type object (and preserve its editability). The effect will be applied permanently when

1 *A closeup of a placed image that has a* **small** *amount of* **dithering**

2 *The same image with a* **lot** *of* **dithering**

Dressing down placed images

One way to reduce the number of pixels and lessen the color complexity of a bitmap image is to **scale** it to the actual size needed for the Web page (and also lower the image resolution to 72 ppi) in Photoshop or another image-editing program before placing it into Illustrator. You could also lower the pixel resolution of a placed image via the Rasterize command in Illustrator (but check the Anti-Alias option).

To reduce the color complexity of a continuous-tone image, try **posterizing** it down to somewhere between four and eight levels in Photoshop before placing it into Illustrator. The result will be a smaller file size—albeit with noticeable color transitions.

the type is converted to a bitmap Web format. In either Rasterize dialog box, choose None to add no anti-aliasing to the type, or choose Type Optimized to allow Illustrator to apply anti-aliasing to the type.

Transparency and matte

You can use the **Transparency** and **Matte** options on the Optimize panel in the Save for Web dialog box to control how transparent and semitransparent pixels will be treated in a bitmap GIF, PNG-8, or JPEG file. Using transparent pixels, a nonrectangular object can display on a Web page without an opaque rectangular background behind it. Semitransparent pixels are used to create the soft edges generated by the raster effects (e.g., all the Photoshop effects, and Illustrator effects such as Drop Shadow and Outer Glow).

The GIF and PNG-8 formats support only fully transparent pixels (not semitransparent pixels). Soft-edged shapes can be optimized in these formats by checking Transparency and choosing a matte color. The matte color will be applied to semitransparent pixels to create a soft transition to full transparency. You will need to use a large number of colors in the color table to enhance the effect. If you uncheck Transparency, the matte color will be applied to fully transparent background pixels instead, and the semitransparent pixels will blend into the matte color.

In the JPEG format, which doesn't support transparency, any matte color will also be applied to fully transparent pixels, and semitransparent pixels will blend into the matte color.

PNG-24 supports fully transparent and semitransparent pixels, so the matte color isn't applicable to this format.

Transparency and Matte

Slicing a document

If you divide a document into **slices** , you can choose different optimization formats and settings for each slice in order to achieve faster download speeds. A separate export file is generated for each slice, containing the object or objects within the slice area. Slices also control how an exported document is translated into a valid HTML table for display as a Web page within a browser. Slices created in Illustrator can be edited in Adobe Photoshop and read by Adobe GoLive. In Illustrator, you'll work with four types of slices: image, HTML text, "user," and auto.

An **image** slice is defined by the smallest rectangle that could completely enclose an object. If the object is moved or resized, or an effect is applied to it, the slice resizes automatically to accommodate the modified object. If you move an image slice, the slice content moves with it. A group can also be made into an image slice and, as with a single object, the slice will resize to accommodate changes made to the group.

An HTML **text** slice is based on the bounding box of selected text. When an HTML text slice is exported, the text is converted to HTML text with all its format and character settings intact.

Each **"user"** slice that's created manually with the **Slice tool** is an independent object, with a separate <Slice> listing on the Layers palette, and can be moved and resized using the Slice Select tool.

Auto slices are described in the sidebar on this page.

When you create a text or user slice, all slices display automatically. To control the **display of slices** manually, do the following.

To show/hide slices:

Choose View > **Show Slices.** (To hide slices, choose View > Hide Slices.)

➤ To view slices in the Save for Web dialog box, click the Toggle Slice Visibility button in the upper left corner. To hide slices, click the button again.

Automatic slices

Illustrator divides up the rectangular areas around any image or user slices into **automatic ("auto")** slices. Auto slices can't be selected or edited directly in the document window, but they can be selected en masse for optimization in the Save for Web dialog box; all the auto slices in a document use the same optimization settings. Auto slices are redrawn and renumbered automatically whenever an image or user slice is edited, enabling a valid HTML table to be created for the exported file. Auto slices have lighter borders and a vertical link symbol (indicating that they're linked together) to the right of the slice number icon in the upper left corner.

1 *This Illustrator document contains* **slices.**

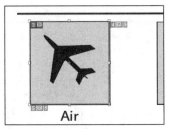

1 An **image slice** is created for a selected rectangular object.

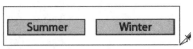

2 Drag with the **Slice** tool over the area to be **defined** as a slice.

Image slice

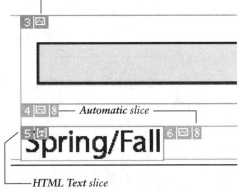

Automatic slice

HTML Text slice

3 A **sequence number** displays on each slice. An icon also displays next to the number to signify what type of slice it is.

4 A selected **user slice**

To create an image or HTML text slice:

1. On the artboard, select an object, multiple objects, or a group.

2. Choose Object > Slice > **Make** ■. A rectangle will snap to the boundaries of the object to define the new slice.

3. *Optional:* To create an HTML text slice, follow the previous two steps, select the object, choose Object > Slice > Slice Options, then choose HTML Text from the Slice Type pop-up menu (read about the Slice Options on pages 528–529).

User slices (created with the **Slice** tool) can be selected, moved, resized, divided, combined, duplicated, and aligned by way of slice commands, the Slice Select tool, and the Control palette. (Image slices, by contrast, resize automatically if the object inside them is resized or moved.)

To create a user slice:

1. Choose the **Slice** tool (Shift-K).

2. **Drag** over the area of the artwork to be defined as a slice ■. A rectangle will surround the selected object or area you marqueed.

➤ Shift-drag to constrain a slice to a square. Option-drag/Alt-drag to create a slice from the center.

➤ To create slices from existing guides in the artwork, choose Object > Slice > Create from Guides. But beware: This command deletes all existing slices!

A rectangle surrounds each area or object that has been designated as a slice, and each slice has a sequence number in its upper left corner ■. The slice in the upper left corner of the document is assigned the number 1, and the remaining slices will be numbered in ascending order from left to right and top to bottom. Here's how to **select slices**.

To select a slice:

1. Choose the **Slice Select** tool (on the Slice tool pop-out menu).

2. Click a user slice or image slice ■. Shift-click to select additional slices, if desired.

Unlike image slices, user slices don't scale automatically to accommodate changes made to their contents. If you modify or move objects inside such a slice, you'll need to scale the slice afterward.

To scale a user slice:

1. Choose the Slice Select tool, then click a slice made with the Slice tool.

2. Position the pointer over a slice border or corner **1**. When the double-headed border ↔ or corner arrow ⬎ displays, drag to scale the slice **2**.

To move a user slice:

1. Choose the Slice Select tool, then click a slice.

2. Position the pointer inside the slice, then drag to reposition it.

To duplicate a user slice:

1. Choose the Slice Select tool, then select a user slice.

2. Choose Object > Slice > Duplicate Slice. A copy of the slice will appear, offset from the original slice **3**–**4**.

➤ A selected slice can also be copied and pasted within the current document or into another document.

To combine two or more user slices into one:

1. Choose the Slice Select tool, then, holding down the Shift key, select two or more user slices. The selected slices can overlap one another, but they don't have to.

2. Choose Object > Slice > Combine Slices. One larger user slice will be created that encompasses the area of the formerly selected slices **5**–**6**.

Align it

To align user slices precisely, select them, then use the **Align** buttons on the Control palette. This will streamline the overall layout of objects, eliminate any small, unnecessary slices that may have been generated automatically, and produce a simpler HTML table.

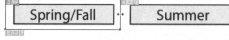

1 *Position the Slice Select tool over the border of a selected slice...*

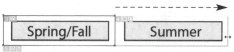

2 *...then drag with the tool to resize the slice.*

3 *A user slice is selected...*

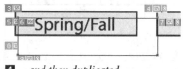

4 *...and then duplicated.*

5 *Several user slices are selected...*

6 *...and then combined into one slice.*

Scale, Move, Duplicate, Combine User Slices

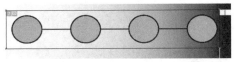

1 *A user slice is selected.*

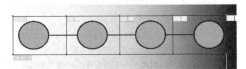

2 *Choose options in the Divide Slice dialog box.*

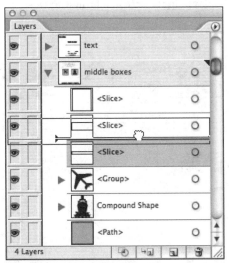

3 *The user slice is divided into four separate user slices.*

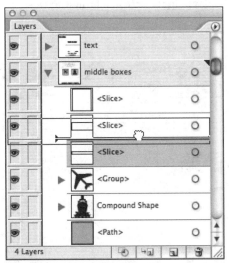

4 *A user slice is restacked via the Layers palette.*

To divide a user slice into smaller slices:

1. Choose the **Slice Select** tool, 🖰 then select a user slice **1**.

2. Choose Object > Slice > **Divide Slices 2**.

3. Check **Divide Horizontally Into** and/or **Divide Vertically Into** to specify where the division will occur, then for either or both options, click the first button and enter a value to divide the slice into equal-sized parts, or click the second button and enter an exact number of pixels for the divided parts.

4. Check Preview to preview the divisions.

5. Click OK **3**.

To restack a user slice:

1. Choose the **Slice Select** tool, 🖰 then select a user slice.

2. Locate the <Slice> you want to restack on the Layers palette, then drag it upward or downward **4**.

The **Lock Slices** and **Release** commands apply to any type of slice.

To lock all slices:

Choose View > **Lock Slices**. The Slice commands aren't available when slices are locked.

To release a slice:

1. Select any type of slice, or select an object inside an image slice.

2. Choose Object > Slice > **Release.** Any image slices will be deleted, whereas user slices will be released but not deleted. The original artwork objects will remain.

To delete a user slice:

1. Choose the **Slice Select** tool, 🖰 then select a user slice.

2. Press Delete/Backspace.

➤ To remove all slices, choose Object > Slice > Delete All.

➤ Don't delete an image slice, or the artwork inside it will also be deleted. Release it instead.

Choosing slice options

You can use the **Slice Options** dialog box to categorize the content of a slice for browser viewing and to assign a URL and Alt tag for the display of substitute text.

To choose slice options:

1. For an object that contains slices, choose Object > Slice > **Slice Options.**
   or
   In the Save for Web dialog box, choose the **Slice Select** tool (K), 🔲 then double-click a slice.

   The Slice Options dialog box opens **1**.

2. From the **Slice Type** pop-up menu, choose a category for the slice content: **No Image, Image,** or **HTML Text.**

3. Follow the steps under the appropriate category below for the chosen Slice Type:

   For the **Image** Slice Type:

   Leave the default slice name as is or enter a **Name** (with no spaces). This name will be used for the separate slice file.

   Enter a **URL** or choose a previously used URL from the pop-up menu. Viewers will be linked to this URL if they click the slice area in a browser.

   Optional: Enter a frame **Target** or choose a standard frame from the pop-up menu. Linked content will load into the chosen

frame target: _blank opens a new browser window for the link contents; _self loads the new link contents into the HTML frame for the current slice; _parent replaces the current HTML frames with the new link contents; and _top loads the new link contents into the entire browser window (this is similar to the _parent option). The Target field is available only when information is entered in the URL field.

Enter a **Message** to have text appear on the status bar at the bottom of the browser window when the user's pointer is over that slice.

Enter **Alt** text to be displayed while the actual image downloads or if a user's browser is set to display without images. This text is also spoken by browser-installed voice recognition software for visually impaired users.

Choose a **Background** color to be displayed in the slice in a browser. (This color choice won't display in Illustrator.)
or

1 *The* **Slice Options** *dialog box with* **Image** *chosen as the* **Slice Type**

For the **No Image** Slice Type **1** (a slice that will display only optional text and a background color):

Enter **text** to be displayed in the slice when viewed in a browser. (This text won't display in Illustrator.) Standard HTML formatting tags can be entered to control the text styling. The text you enter must fit within the slice area.

Under **Cell Alignment,** choose Horiz and/or Vert pop-up menu options to align the text inside the slice.

Choose a **Background** color to be displayed inside the slice in a browser. This color choice won't display in Illustrator.

or

For the **HTML Text** Slice Type **2**:

Under **Cell Alignment,** choose Horiz and/or Vert pop-up menu options to align the text within the slice.

Choose a **Background** color to be displayed in the slice in a browser. This color choice won't display in Illustrator.

4. Click OK.

➤ If text in a type object is changed, any HTML text slice made for that object will resize to reflect the changes.

Slice Options

Slice Type: No Image

Text Displayed in Cell: ☐ Text is HTML

Insert client vertical banner in left
placeholder

OK
Cancel

Cell Alignment

Horiz: Center   Vert: Top

Background: None

1 *The Slice Options dialog box with No Image chosen as the Slice Type*

Slice Options

Slice Type: HTML Text

Text Displayed in Cell: ☐ Text is HTML

<FONT SIZE=5 COLOR=#000000>Your
source for travel around the world</FONT>

OK
Cancel

Cell Alignment

Horiz: Left   Vert: Top

Background: None

2 *The Slice Options dialog box with HTML Text chosen as the Slice Type*

Slice Options

Using pixel preview view

While you're working in Illustrator, your vector drawings will appear crisp and smooth. But if you save your document in the GIF, JPEG, or PNG format, Illustrator will rasterize it at 72 ppi. The edges of any rasterized objects that don't precisely align with the pixel grid will appear jagged or blurry, due to anti-aliasing. Before optimizing your file, you can use **Pixel Preview** view to see how your artwork might look when rasterized for the Web.

To use Pixel Preview view:

Choose View > **Pixel Preview** **1**–**2**. Your artwork will display as if it's already rasterized, allowing you to see the impact of anti-aliasing.

With View > **Snap to Pixel** selected as well, any artwork you create while your document is in Pixel Preview mode will automatically snap to a pixel grid and prevent any horizontal and vertical edges in your artwork from being anti-aliased.

Optimizing using preset settings

Optimization is the process by which file format, storage size, and color parameters are chosen for a document to enable it to download quickly on the Web while preserving as much of its image quality as possible. Illustrator provides a variety of choices and options for optimization. Your overall goal is to reduce the file size until the quality of the optimized artwork reaches its reduction limit (starts to degrade). Keep this goal in mind as you choose a **preset** (as in the instructions on the next page), or as you choose a file format and palette options.

The Save for Web dialog box forces you to save an optimized file separately and keeps the original Illustrator file intact for future revision.

For general information about the GIF, JPEG, and PNG formats, see pages 519–521. To optimize a file in these formats, see pages 532–536. Or to output objects as vectors (without rasterization), use the SVG format.

1 *View > **Pixel Preview** unchecked (off)*

2 *View > **Pixel Preview** checked (on)*

Web color palette

If you've ever created a document on a monitor that can display millions of colors and then viewed it on a monitor that can display only thousands (or hundreds) of colors, you have some idea of how drastically colors can change in different onscreen settings and what **Web-safe colors** are all about.

No matter how few—or how many—colors a monitor is capable of displaying, all monitors that have at least 8 bits of color can render 256 specific colors without dithering. Subtract 40 for the colors that the Mac and Windows systems reserve for other uses, and you're left with 216 colors that you can use with confidence in your Web graphics.

But keep in mind that not even these 216 colors will display in the same way on every machine. Windows and Mac systems use different color gamma values, and each monitor may be calibrated somewhat differently. The Windows operating system uses a higher gamma value than the Macintosh operating system, so a document created on a Mac will appear darker on a Windows system than on the Mac.

Saving your settings

To **save** the current **optimization settings** to the current Illustrator file without actually exporting the file, click **Done** in the Save for Web dialog box.

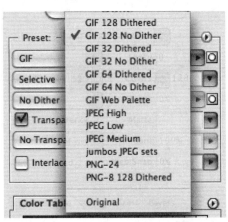

1 *Choose an optimization preset from the* **Preset** *pop-up menu in the* **Save for Web** *dialog box.*

The GIF and JPEG formats don't preserve the transparency of soft-edged effects. If you want an optimized object to fade into a solid-color background, create two objects in your Illustrator document: an object containing a solid Web-safe color (the same color as the background of the Web page, if that color is known) and an overlapping object above it containing a soft, raster effect (such as Drop Shadow or Outer Glow) that fades into the underlying object. Then create a slice that includes both objects.

For a hybrid document that contains solid-color areas or type combined with placed imagery, gradients, blends, or meshes, the best approach is to create separate slices for the different elements in the document, then use the Save for Web dialog box to assign different optimization formats and settings to each slice. This way, the solid-color areas will remain Web-safe and the continuous-tone areas will render reasonably well.

Before we delve into options for the individual file formats, remember that you can **optimize** a document or slice **using preset settings.**

To optimize a document or a slice using preset settings:

1. Save your file, then choose File > **Save for Web** (Cmd-Option-Shift-S/Ctrl-Alt-Shift-S).

2. Click the **2-Up** tab above the preview windows to display both the original and optimized previews of the image simultaneously. To optimize a slice, select it now in the preview window.

3. Choose a named preset combination of optimization settings from the **Preset** pop-up menu **1**, and don't change any of the optimization settings. Repeat for other slices.

4. Click Save. The Save Optimized As dialog box opens.

5. Choose **Format/Save as Type: HTML and Images** (change the file name, if desired), leave the extension as is, then click Save.

Optimizing as GIF or PNG-8

To optimize a file in the GIF or PNG-8 format:

1. Save your file, then choose File > **Save for Web.** The Save for Web dialog box opens **1**.

2. Click the **2-Up** or **4-Up** tab above the preview windows to display both the original and optimized previews of the image simultaneously. To optimize one or more slices, select them in the preview window.

3. From the **Optimized file format** pop-up menu, choose **GIF** or **PNG-8.**

4. For GIF only, enter or choose a **Lossy** value to allow the compression scheme to simplify pixels in the image, and thus reduce the file size. The lossy effect will display in the selected preview window. *Note:* You can't use the Lossy option with the Interlaced option, or with the Noise or Pattern Dither algorithm.

5. Choose a color reduction method from the next pop-up menu (see the sidebar on the next page), bearing in mind that the GIF and PNG-8 formats restrict a file to a maximum of 256 colors. **Perceptual, Selective,** and **Adaptive** render the optimized image using colors from the original document, whereas **Restrictive (Web)** shifts all colors to Web-safe equivalents but isn't the best choice if the document contains continuous-tone images, blends, or gradients. **Custom** optimizes colors based on a previously saved palette.

6. If you want to choose a specific number of colors, choose that value from the **Colors** pop-up menu, or enter a value in the field, or click the arrows to arrive at the desired number of colors.

7. From the next pop-up menu, choose a **dither** method: **No Dither, Diffusion** (also enter or choose a **Dither** value), **Pattern,** or **Noise.**

8. If the document contains transparency that you want to preserve, check **Transparency.** Fully transparent pixels will be preserved as transparent; semi-transparent pixels will be filled with

No halos

When creating GIF or PNG-8 files, you can create a hard-edged transparency effect in which all pixels that are more than 50% transparent become fully transparent and pixels that are less than 50% transparent become fully opaque. This type of transparency prevents a halo effect from occurring when a matte color is different from the background color in the original document.

To create hard-edged transparency:

1. Open a document that contains **transparency.**

2. Choose File > **Save for Web,** then choose **GIF or PNG-8.**

3. Check **Transparency.**

4. Choose **None** from the **Matte** pop-up menu.

5. Click **Save** to save the file.

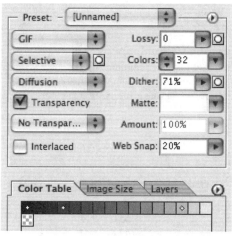

1 Use the *optimize* panel to choose custom settings for a GIF file.

Optimize as GIF or PNG-8

Color reduction methods

Perceptual

Generates a color table based on the colors currently in the document, with particular attention paid to how colors are actually perceived. This method's strength is in preserving overall color integrity.

Selective

Generates a color table based on the colors currently in the document. The Perceptual and Selective options are similar, but the Selective option leans more toward preserving solid and Web-safe colors.

Adaptive

Generates a color table based on the part of the color spectrum that represents most of the color in the document. This choice produces a slightly larger optimized file.

➤ If you switch among the Perceptual, Selective, and Adaptive methods, any Web-safe colors currently on the Color Table palette are preserved.

Restrictive (Web)

Generates a color table by shifting image colors to colors that are available on the standard Web-safe palette. This choice produces the least number of colors and thus the smallest file size, though not necessarily the best image quality.

Where exported image files go

By default, when the Save for Web dialog box saves a Web page as a set of multiple image files, it places them in a new **images** folder in the same folder as the exported HTML file. To rename this folder, click Save in the Save for Web dialog box, then choose Other from the Settings pop-up menu. The Output Settings dialog box opens. Choose Saving Files from the second pop-up menu from the top. In the Optimized Files area, change the folder name in the **Put Images in Folder** field, then click OK.

the Matte color or will be converted to fully transparent or fully opaque pixels, depending on which Matte option you choose.

If you don't check Transparency, both fully and partially transparent pixels will be filled with the Matte color.

9. To apply a color to the partially transparent pixels along soft edges of the optimized image (such as raster effect edges), if any, choose a **Matte** option.

Choose **Other** to set the Matte color to any color you wish. If you're not sure which color the graphic will be displayed against, set Matte to None (this will result in hard, jagged edges). Both options eliminate halo effects along the edges of optimized images when they're displayed on the Web. Any soft-edged effect (such as Drop Shadow or Feather) on top of transparency will blend into the current Matte color.

10. From the next pop-up menu, choose a method by which transparent pixels will be dithered with opaque pixels in order to simulate semitransparency: **No Transparency, Diffusion, Pattern,** or **Noise.** Only the Diffusion option makes use of the accompanying 0–100% Amount value.

11. *Optional:* Check **Interlaced** to have the GIF or PNG image display in successively greater detail as it downloads on the Web page.

12. *Optional:* To automatically shift colors to their closest Web-safe palette equivalents, drag the **Web Snap** slider or enter a value. The higher the Web Snap value, the more colors will be shifted.

13. Click Save. The Save Optimized As dialog box opens.

14. Choose **Format/Save as Type: HTML and Images.** This format creates all the necessary files to use the image as a Web page. Change the name, if desired (keep the file extension), then click Save. (See "Where exported image files go" at left.)

Optimize as GIF or PNG-8

Making solid colors Web-safe

Let's say you have a document that you're going to optimize in the GIF format using the Perceptual, Selective, or Adaptive palette, but the document has solid-color areas that aren't Web-safe. Before outputting the image online, you can make the **solid-color areas Web-safe.**

To make solid colors Web-safe:

1. Open the file and optimize it in the GIF format, using File > **Save for Web.** Keep the dialog box open.

2. Choose the **Eyedropper** tool.

3. Click a solid-color area in one of the optimize previews.

4. If the Color Table panel isn't showing, click the **Color Table** tab. The color you just clicked will be the highlighted swatch **1**.

5. Click the **Shift Selected Colors to the Web Palette** button at the bottom of the color table. A diamond with a diagonal line will display on the selected swatch to signify that the color was shifted to a Web-safe equivalent, and the swatch will be locked automatically (see the first tip, below).

➤ To keep a selected, unlocked swatch from being deleted, even if the number of colors in the GIF palette is reduced, click the Lock Selected Color button. A tiny square will display in the lower right corner of the swatch.

➤ Shift-click with the Eyedropper tool on multiple areas in an optimized preview to select more than one color, then Web-shift all the selected colors at once.

➤ Click a Web-shifted color swatch, then click the Shift Selected Colors to the Web Palette button again to unshift the color out of the Web-safe range.

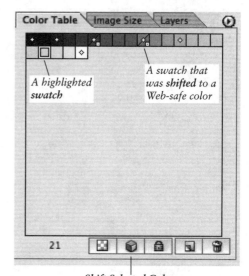

A highlighted swatch

*A swatch that was **shifted** to a Web-safe color*

Shift Selected Colors to the Web Palette

1 *The Color Table panel in the Save for Web dialog box, with a color swatch highlighted*

JPEGs and Web-safe colors

JPEG compression adds artifacts to an image and renders Web-safe colors non-Web-safe. However, this is acceptable because on the continuous-tone imagery that the JPEG format is usually chosen for, browser dither isn't objectionable. Don't try to match a color area in a JPEG file to a color area in a GIF file or to a color on the background of a Web page, though, because the JPEG compression will dither the colors.

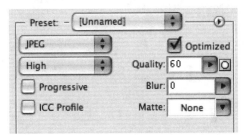

1 *The* optimize *panel of the Save for Web dialog box, with settings chosen for a JPEG export*

Optimizing as JPEG

JPEG is the format of choice for optimizing continuous-tone imagery (photographs, paintings, gradients, blends, and the like) for display on the Web. If you optimize as JPEG, the file's full color depth will be preserved, and the colors will be seen and enjoyed by any Web viewer whose monitor is set to 16-bit or 24-bit color. Keep in mind, however, that the JPEG compression method causes image data loss.

To optimize a file in the JPEG format:

1. Open the original Illustrator file, choose File > **Save for Web,** then choose one of the JPEG settings from the **Preset** pop-up menu or choose JPEG from the next pop-up menu (the tool tip says "Optimized file format") **1**.

2. Click the **2-Up** or **4-Up** tab at the top of the main window to display the original and optimized previews of the document simultaneously. To optimize a slice, select it now in the preview window.

3. In the optimize panel, choose or enter a **Quality** value for the optimized image.
   or
   Choose **Low, Medium, High, Very High,** **NEW** or **Maximum** from the compression **Quality** pop-up menu to the left. A higher setting preserves more color information but compresses less. Experiment with this setting to achieve an acceptable balance between file size and image quality.

4. *Do any of the following optional steps:*
   Check **Progressive** to have the image render in stages as it downloads onto the Web page.

   Increase the **Blur** value to lessen the visibility of JPEG artifacts that arise from the JPEG compression method and to reduce the file size. Don't overblur the image, though, or details in the artwork will soften too much. You can lower the Blur setting later to reclaim image sharpness.

   Check **ICC Profile** to embed an ICC profile in the optimized image. To utilize this

   (Continued on the following page)

Optimize as JPEG

option, the document must have had a profile assigned to it in Illustrator (see the sidebar at right).

5. Choose a **Matte** color to be substituted for areas of transparency in the original document. If you choose None, transparent areas will become white.

   Note: For the JPEG format, which doesn't support transparency, you can use the Matte color option to simulate transparency. Choose Matte: Other, then choose the solid color that matches the background color of the Web page.

6. *Optional:* Check Optimized to produce the smallest possible file size.

7. Click Save. The Save Optimized As dialog box opens.

8. Choose **Format/Save as Type: HTML and Images,** change the name, if desired (keep the file extension), then click Save.

Optimizing as PNG-24

The PNG-24 format is similar to JPEG, except PNG-24 saves both fully transparent and semitransparent pixels (e.g., along the edges of effects) and employs a nonlossy compression method. You can preserve up to 256 levels of transparency in PNG-24 files by using a feature called alpha transparency (not all browsers support this feature). PNG-24 files are also larger than equivalent JPEGs.

To optimize as PNG-24:

1. Open the Illustrator file, then choose File > **Save for Web.**

2. From the Optimized file format pop-up menu, choose **PNG-24** ■.

3. *Optional:* Check Interlaced to have the PNG image display in successively greater detail as it downloads on the Web page. This option increases the file size.

4. Check **Transparency** to preserve transparent pixels. (Semitransparent pixels are preserved regardless of this setting.)

5. Click Save. The Save Optimized As dialog box opens. Choose **Format/Save as Type: HTML and Images,** change the name, if desired (keep the file extension), then click Save.

■ *The optimize panel with PNG-24 settings chosen*

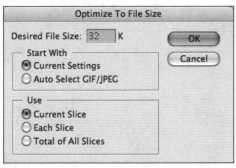

1 *Choose* **Optimize to File Size** *from the pop-up menu.*

Optimize To File Size

Desired File Size: `32` K

Start With
- ● Current Settings
- ○ Auto Select GIF/JPEG

Use
- ● Current Slice
- ○ Each Slice
- ○ Total of All Slices

OK
Cancel

2 *The* **Optimize To File Size** *dialog box*

Creating an optimization preset

By **saving** your current **optimization settings** as a **preset,** you'll be able to apply them to other files.

To create an optimization preset:

1. Choose the desired settings in the Save for Web dialog box, then from the **Optimize** pop-up menu ⊙ (next to the Preset pop-up menu), choose **Save Settings**.

2. Name the settings file. By default, it will be saved in Adobe Illustrator CS2/Presets/ Save for Web Settings/Optimize folder.

3. Click Save. If you saved the settings file in the default location, it will appear as a listing on the Preset pop-up menu.

Optimizing to a specific file size

You can let **Illustrator** pick your **optimization settings** based on the desired **file size.**

To optimize to a specific file size:

1. Open the **Save for Web** dialog box, then from the **Optimize** pop-up menu ⊙ (next to the Preset pop-up menu), choose **Optimize to File Size 1**.

2. Click a **Start With** option. **Current Settings** uses your current optimization settings; **Auto Select GIF/JPEG** uses either GIF or JPEG, depending on the program's analysis of your output image **2**. (PNG isn't available as an option.)

3. Enter a value for the **Desired File Size.**

4. Click one of the buttons in the Use area to specify whether the file size limit should be applied to the size of the current slice, each individual slice, or the combined size of all the slices.

5. Click OK.

6. In the Save for Web dialog box, click Save. The Save Optimized As dialog box opens.

7. Choose **Format/Save as Type: HTML and Images,** change the name, if desired (keep the file extension), then click Save.

Resizing an optimized image

You can **resize** an **optimized image** directly in the Save for Web dialog box. *Note:* To make the best use of this option, size your artboard to the desired final size before opening the Save for Web dialog box.

To resize an optimized image:

1. Open the File > **Save for Web** dialog box, then click the **Image Size** tab ■.

2. *Optional:* Check **Constrain Proportions** to maintain the relative width and height of your output image.

3. Enter a **Percent** value to make the new image a specific percentage of the original size.
   or
   Enter exact **Width** and/or **Height** values.

4. *Optional:* To clip the exported document to the size of the current artboard, check **Clip to Artboard.** You could, for example, clip artwork to an artboard that's been sized to the dimensions of a banner ad.

5. Click **Apply** to preview the clipping effect on the image. (If you need to undo Clip to Artboard, uncheck it, then click Apply again.)

6. *Optional:* Check the Anti-Alias option to keep the image smooth.

7. Click Done. Or click Save, choose Format/Save as Type: HTML and Images, change the name, if desired (keep the file extension), then click Save.

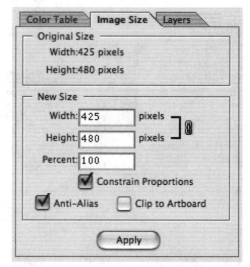

■ *The Image Size panel in the Save for Web dialog box*

Optimizing as SVG

The SVG (Scalable Vector Graphics) format lets you incorporate interactivity into an optimized image and also lets you scale objects on a Web page. Unlike the bitmap formats (GIF, JPEG, and PNG), which produce large files and require a large bandwidth for Web viewing, SVG, a vector format based on XML, lets you store shapes, paths, text, SVG filter effects, and color quality support in a small, efficient file for viewing in a browser or on a handheld device. Note that Web surfers must download an SVG plug-in in order to view graphics in this format; many people won't bother to do this and thus will miss seeing your artwork.

If you optimize a file or slice as SVG via File > Save for Web, you'll access export options that are geared specifically for Web graphics. If you save a file as SVG via File > Save or Save As, you'll access all the SVG export options. Illustrator can open and save SVG files, as SVG is a native Illustrator format.

Keep the following guidelines in mind to improve SVG performance:

➤ Each layer in the document will become a group element in the SVG file; nested layers will become nested group elements. Plan your SVG groups accordingly by organizing your Illustrator layers.

➤ Let each object have its own transparency setting; don't change the transparency value for the whole layer the objects reside in.

➤ When the SVG file is exported, any linked images used in the document that don't have an alpha channel will export in the JPEG format, and any linked images that do have an alpha channel will export in the PNG format.

➤ All of the Photoshop effects listed (on the lower half of the Effects menu) will produce a raster object in the SVG file. Mesh objects are also rasterized by the SVG format. Bear in mind that rasterization increases the file size and thus the download time of an SVG file.

Using SVG

When you use an **SVG filter effect,** you avoid the rasterization that the other Effect menu commands produce. SVG filter effects are rendered to the object in the browser, not in Illustrator, and this helps to reduce the file size and download time. In Illustrator, you'll see only a preview of the SVG filter effect.

To apply an SVG filter effect to an object:

1. Select an object.

2. Choose a filter from the Effect > **SVG Filters** submenu.

➤ To prevent an SVG effect from becoming rasterized, it must be the second-to-last listing on the Appearance palette, just above the Transparency listing. Drag it downward to move it to the correct position, if necessary.

To optimize as SVG:

The SVG format saves objects as vectors, and preserves gradients, animation, and SVG filter effects as efficient vector shapes. SVG files can be opened and displayed in Internet Explorer 5 and later or Netscape Navigator 4.6 and later (the browser requires the SVG plug-in in order to display SVG files).

You can optimize an entire file or individual slices as SVG by choosing it as the format in the File > **Save for Web** dialog box 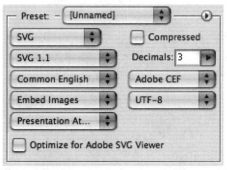. As NEW listed in top-to-bottom order, the pop-up menu options are: File Format, DTD, Font Subsetting, Image Location, CSS Properties, Font Type, and Character Encoding (the names will be visible if you use tool tips). On the right side, you'll also see the Compressed option for creating a compressed SVGZ file, as well as the Decimals option.

NEW Equivalent DTD, Font Type, Font Subsetting, and Image Location options are also found in the **SVG Options** dialog box, and the CSS Properties, Character Encoding, and Decimals options are also found in the More Options portion of the SVG Options dialog box. See the following page.

1 *The **optimize** panel in the **Save for Web** dialog box, with SVG settings chosen*

Apply SVG Filter Effect; Optimize as SVG

To save a file as SVG or SVGZ:

1. Choose File > Save or Save As, choose a location and file name for the file, choose **Format/Save as Type: SVG (svg)** or **SVG Compressed (svgz)**, then click Save. Note that a compressed SVG file can't be edited using a text editor. The SVG Options dialog box opens **1**.

2. Do the following:

   Choose a **DTD** (Document Type **NEW** Definition) option to control how much of the full SVG specification (feature list) is saved with the SVG file: **SVG 1.1** saves the full specification and is used for output to desktop computers; the **SVG Tiny** options save part of the full specification and are used for output to mobile phones; **SVG Basic 1.1** saves most of the full specification and is used for output to PDAs.

   Choose a **Fonts: Type** to control how **NEW** type is exported: **Adobe CEF** produces the best visual results but is not supported by all SVG viewers; **SVG** provides standard type support for all SVG viewers; **Convert to Outline** converts all type to outlines (the font appearance may change slightly).

   Choose a **Fonts: Subsetting** option to embed the specific characters of the fonts used in your document. **Only Glyphs Used** (the default) includes only the set of glyphs for text used in the document (excluding linked fonts); **Common English** and **Common Roman** include only English or Roman characters (these options also combine with the Glyphs Used option); **All Glyphs** includes every font character, including non-Roman characters.

   All the Subsetting choices (except for Only Glyphs Used) allow for changes in text content in dynamic text (as in data-driven graphics for the Web).

   ➤ Rest the cursor over any option or pop-up menu in the dialog box, then read information about it in the Description area below.

3. Click **Images: Location: Embed** to embed rasterized images in the file, or click **Link** to link the exported images (in either JPEG or PNG format) to the SVG file. Linking is recommended if you're going to share the image file amongst multiple SVG files, whereas embedding guarantees that the image will be available to the SVG file but also increases the file size.

4. Check **Preserve Illustrator Editing Capabilities** to include Illustrator-related data in the file. This permits the saved SVG file to be edited by designers even after a developer's code is added to it.

5. *Optional:* Click More Options to choose additional options in the SVG Advanced Options dialog box—but only if you have a thorough understanding of this format (see Illustrator Help).

6. Click OK.

➤ Click Preview to preview the SVG file in your system's default browser.

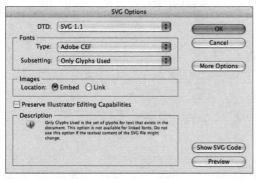

1 *The SVG Options dialog box*

Save as SVG or SVGZ

Exporting objects as CSS layers

If you build your Web page using CSS (**cascading style sheets**), the page can contain layers (similar to layers in Illustrator). Each layer is an object that is defined by HTML, and can be stacked, moved, hidden, and revealed. Layers can be used to create interactive elements on a page, such as pop-up menus. (CSS layers are equivalent to Adobe GoLive layers.)

The **Export As CSS Layers** option in the Save for Web dialog box does just what you might expect: It converts Illustrator layers to CSS layers. Each layer is exported as a separate image file.

To export Illustrator objects as CSS layers:

1. Use the Layers palette in Illustrator to arrange objects on separate layers, then choose File > **Save for Web.** The Save for Web dialog box opens **1**.

2. Click the **Layers** tab.

3. Check **Export As CSS Layers.**

4. Choose a layer from the **Layer** pop-up menu.

5. Click **Visible, Hidden,** or **Do Not Export** to control the display of the layer in the exported HTML file.

6. From the optimize panel, choose optimization settings for the objects on the currently selected layer.

7. Choose other layers from the **Layer** pop-up menu, and repeat steps 5–6 for each one.

8. *Optional:* Check Preview Only Selected Layer to preview only the layer currently chosen in step 4 in the Save for Web previews instead of the whole file.

9. Click Save. The Save Optimized As dialog box opens. Choose a location, then click Save. The files will be collected in the folder name designated in the Output Settings dialog box under the Saving Files option. The default folder name is "images" (see "Where exported image files go" in the sidebar on page 533).

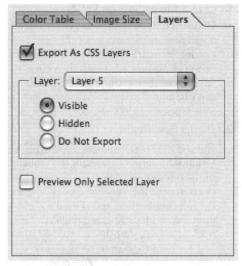

1 *The Layers panel in the Save for Web dialog box*

Export CSS Layers

1 *Select the object to which you want to assign a URL…*

Document Info ❖ Attributes

☐ Overprint Fill   ☐ Overprint Stroke

Image Map: Polygon ⬍   Browser

URL: http://www.marshlandview.org ▾

2 *…then enter the desired URL for the object on the Attributes palette.*

Creating image maps

The **Image Map** option lets you attach a URL to any **object** you create in Illustrator.

To create an image map:

1. Select the object to which you want to attach a URL **1**.

2. Show the **Attributes** palette (Cmd-F11/Ctrl-F11).

3. From the **Image Map** pop-up menu, choose **Rectangle** to create a rectangular image map around the object (the image map boundaries will be similar to the object's bounding box), or **Polygon** to create a map that follows the object's actual contour.

4. Type a **URL** into the URL field **2** or choose a URL from the pop-up menu.

5. You can verify the URL location by clicking the **Browser** button on the palette to launch your system's default Web browser (assuming you have one loaded on your system and your computer is currently connected to the Web).

6. When you're ready to export the file, use the Save for Web dialog box to optimize it. Click Save when you're done, and in the Save Optimized As dialog box, choose Format: **HTML and Images** to save the necessary HTML file, complete with the image map and URL links, then click Save.

   Note: The HTML file, the folder that contains the optimized image file, and the other images being used in the document must be kept together in the same folder when the image map is imported into your Web-page creation program. The HTML file contains the URLs, image name, dimensions, and necessary code to display the image on a Web page.

Image Map

Creating data-driven graphics

This page contains a brief synopsis of how the **Variables** palette is used. For more information, read *Real World Adobe Illustrator CS2* by Mordy Golding (Peachpit Press) or use Illustrator Help.

A Web server can connect with a database in order to download text and graphics for inclusion in a Web page. Using Illustrator, a Web page designer can control which objects in a document don't change and which objects can receive changes from a server. Each element the designer decides can be changed is assigned (bound) to a **variable** via the **Variables** palette **1**. Then, once the Illustrator object and a variable are bound together, they become dynamic and will update automatically whenever the server software accesses the database and downloads new data to the variable. Only objects that are bound to variables will change.

You can use the Variables palette to turn object attributes into four types of variables: **Graph Data, Linked File, Text String,** or **Visibility.** A Graph Data variable updates a graph with new graph data; a Linked File variable replaces one placed, linked image with another; and a Text String variable replaces text. The Visibility variable controls whether an object is visible, and can be changed for any object. The objects that are bound (to variables) serve merely as placeholders in the document, displaying whatever data the database and the server send down to that variable.

Variables and their currently displayed data can be captured into a **data set.** Each data set may contain the same variables but different object content. Sets are listed on the Data Set drop-down menu at the top of the Variables palette.

To edit the data associated with a variable, you edit the object in the artwork to which that variable is bound. A Visibility variable is edited by hiding or displaying its associated object via the Layers palette. After editing the objects that are bound to variables, you can use the Variables palette to capture those edits into a new data set. You can switch between data sets on the palette to preview how the changeable objects will look on the page.

Let's say you have a template for a Web page that displays a picture and text for a different car each week. It could contain several different data sets, with each set containing a Linked File variable bound to a picture of a car, and Text String variables that display text objects with a description of each car. If you change the car images and text descriptions and capture those changes to a new data set, as you display each data set, the image and text content will update in the artwork.

Text String variable — Variable1 — Vacation tours
Linked File variable — Variable2 — stroke effect.psd
Visibility variable — Variable3 — Cruise ship
— Variable5 — Your source for travel around the...
— Variable6 — <Group>
Graph Data variable — Variable7 — travel data
— Variable9 — Travel Getaways

Make Object/ Text Dynamic   *Make Visibility Dynamic*   *Unbind Variable*   *New Variable*

1 *The Variables palette lists variables and the objects that are bound to them within each data set.*

Variables Palette

DANIEL PELAVIN

KEYBOARD SHORTCUTS A

	Mac	Windows
FILES		
New Document dialog box	Cmd + N	Ctrl + N
New Document from Template	Cmd + Shift + N	Ctrl + Shift + N
New Document from last used settings (no dialog box opens)	Cmd + Option + N	Ctrl + Alt + N
Open dialog box	Cmd + O	Ctrl + O
Open Bridge (Browse)	Cmd + Option + O	Ctrl + Alt + O
Close	Cmd + W	Ctrl + W
Save	Cmd + S	Ctrl + S
Save As dialog box	Cmd + Shift + S	Ctrl + Shift + S
Save a Copy dialog box	Cmd + Option + S	Ctrl + Alt + S
Document Setup dialog box	Cmd + Option + P	Ctrl + Alt + P
File Info	Cmd + Option + Shift + I	Ctrl + Alt + Shift + I
Revert (to last saved version)	F12	F12
Quit/exit Illustrator	Cmd + Q	Ctrl + Q
PALETTES		
Show/hide all palettes	Tab	Tab
Show/hide all palettes except Toolbox	Shift + Tab	Shift + Tab
Apply value in palette field	Return	Enter
Apply value in field, keep field selected	Shift + Return	Shift + Enter
Highlight next field (pointer in palette)	Tab	Tab
Highlight previous field (pointer in palette)	Shift + Tab	Shift + Tab
Open/close individual palettes		
Align palette	Shift + F7	Shift + F7
Appearance palette	Shift + F6	Shift + F6
Attributes palette	Cmd + F11	Ctrl + F11
Brushes palette	F5	F5
Color palette	F6	F6
Gradient palette	Cmd + F9	Ctrl + F9
Graphic Styles palette	Shift + F5	Shift + F5

Keyboard Shortcuts

	Mac	**Windows**
Info palette	F8	F8
Layers palette	F7	F7
Pathfinder palette	Cmd + Shift + F9	Ctrl + Shift + F9
Stroke palette	Cmd + F10	Ctrl + F10
Symbols palette	Cmd + Shift + F11	Ctrl + Shift + F11
Transform palette	Shift + F8	Shift + F8
Transparency palette	Cmd + Shift + F10	Ctrl + Shift + F10

Type palettes

	Mac	**Windows**
Character palette	Cmd + T	Ctrl + T
OpenType palette	Cmd + Option + Shift + T	Ctrl + Alt + Shift + T
Paragraph palette	Cmd + Option + T	Ctrl + Alt + T
Tabs palette	Cmd + Shift + T	Ctrl + Shift + T

TOOLS

	Mac	**Windows**
Add Anchor Point	+ (plus)	+ (plus)
Blend	W	W
Column Graph	J	J
Convert Anchor Point	Shift + C	Shift + C
Delete Anchor Point	– (minus)	– (minus)
Direct Selection	A	A
Ellipse	L	L
Eyedropper	I	I
Free Transform	E	E
Gradient	G	G
Hand	H	H
Lasso	Q	Q
Line Segment	\ (backslash)	\ (backslash)
Live Paint Bucket	K	K
Live Paint Selection	Shift + L	Shift + L
Magic Wand	Y	Y
Mesh	U	U
Paintbrush	B	B
Pen	P	P
Pencil	N	N
Rectangle	M	M
Reflect	O	O
Rotate	R	R

	Mac	Windows
Scale	S	S
Scissors	C	C
Selection	V	V
Slice	Shift + K	Shift + K
Symbol Sprayer	Shift + S	Shift + S
Type	T	T
Warp	Shift + R	Shift + R
Zoom	Z	Z

DIALOG BOXES

	Mac	Windows
Highlight next field/option	Tab	Tab
Highlight previous field/option	Shift + Tab	Shift + Tab
Cancel	Cmd + . (period) or Esc	Esc
OK	Return	Enter
Convert Cancel button to Reset button	Option	Alt

Open/Save dialog boxes

	Mac	Windows
Desktop	Cmd + D	
Up one folder level	Cmd + left arrow	

MANAGE COLOR

	Mac	Windows
Color Settings dialog box	Cmd + Shift + K	Ctrl + Shift + K

WORKSPACE/VIEWS

	Mac	Windows
Preview/Outline view toggle	Cmd + Y	Ctrl + Y
Pixel Preview view on/off	Cmd + Option + Y	Ctrl + Alt + Y
Overprint Preview view on/off	Cmd + Option + Shift + Y	Ctrl + Alt + Shift + Y
Toggle crosshair pointer on/off (drawing tools)	Caps Lock	Caps Lock
Show/hide edges	Cmd + H	Ctrl + H
Display entire artboard	Double-click Hand tool	Double-click Hand tool
Fit in window	Cmd + 0	Ctrl + 0
Minimize window	Cmd + M	
Actual size	Double-click Zoom tool	Double-click Zoom tool
Actual size and center artboard in window	Cmd + 1	Ctrl + 1
Zoom out from tool position (Zoom tool selected)	Option + click	Alt + click
Zoom in at tool position (any tool selected)	Cmd + + (plus) or Cmd + Spacebar + click	Ctrl + + (plus) or Ctrl + Spacebar + click
Zoom out from tool position (any tool selected)	Cmd + – (minus) or Cmd + Option + Spacebar + click	Ctrl + – (minus) or Ctrl + Alt + Spacebar + click

	Mac	Windows
Adjust zoom marquee position	Drag with Zoom tool, then Spacebar + drag	Drag with Zoom tool, then Spacebar + drag
Zoom in on specific area of artboard	Drag Zoom tool or Cmd + drag in Navigator palette	Drag Zoom tool or Ctrl + drag in Navigator palette
Use Hand tool (any tool selected)	Spacebar	Spacebar
Hide selected objects	Cmd + 3	Ctrl + 3
Hide all unselected objects	Cmd + Option + Shift + 3	Ctrl + Alt + Shift + 3
Show all	Cmd + Option + 3	Ctrl + Alt + 3
Show/hide template(s)	Cmd + Shift + W	Ctrl + Shift + W
Show/hide transparency grid	Cmd + Shift + D	Ctrl + Shift + D
Standard screen mode/Full Screen mode with menu bar/Full Screen mode	F	F

UNDO, REDO

	Mac	Windows
Undo last operation	Cmd + Z	Ctrl + Z
Redo last undone operation	Cmd + Shift + Z	Ctrl + Shift + Z

GEOMETRIC OBJECTS

	Mac	Windows
Draw object from center using Rectangle, Rounded Rectangle, or Ellipse tool	Option + drag	Alt + drag
Draw square with Rectangle or Rounded Rectangle tool; circle with Ellipse tool	Shift + drag	Shift + drag
Move object as you draw with Rectangle, Rounded Rectangle, Ellipse, Polygon, Star, or Spiral tool	Spacebar	Spacebar
Draw multiples of an object while dragging	~ (tilde)	~ (tilde)

Polygon, Star, and Spiral tools

	Mac	Windows
Constrain orientation to horizontal and vertical axes as you draw with Polygon or Star tool, or constrain ends of Spiral to a multiple of 45° as you draw with Spiral tool	Shift	Shift
Add or subtract sides as you draw with the Polygon tool, points as you draw with the Star tool, or segments as you draw with the Spiral tool	Up or down arrow	Up or down arrow
Align shoulders as you draw with Star tool	Option	Alt
Increase or decrease outer radius as you draw with Star tool, or decay as you draw with Spiral tool	Cmd	Ctrl

SELECT

	Mac	Windows
Reselect	Cmd + 6	Ctrl + 6
Use last-used selection tool (any nonselection tool chosen)	Cmd	Ctrl
Toggle between Group Selection and Direct Selection tools	Option	Alt

	Mac	**Windows**
Select all	Cmd + A	Ctrl + A
Deselect all	Cmd + Shift + A	Ctrl + Shift + A
Select next object below	Cmd + Option + [	Ctrl + Alt + [
Select next object above	Cmd + Option +]	Ctrl + Alt +]
Add to selection with Lasso tool	Shift + drag	Shift + drag
Subtract from selection with Lasso tool	Option + drag	Alt + drag

MOVE

Open Move dialog box (object selected)	Double-click Selection tool or Cmd + Shift + M	Double-click Selection tool or Ctrl + Shift + M
Move object regardless of selected tool	Cmd + drag	Ctrl + drag
Move selected object the current Keyboard Increment (Preferences > General)	Any arrow key	Any arrow key
Move selection 10x Keyboard Increment	Shift + arrow key	Shift + arrow key
Constrain movement to multiple of 45°	Shift	Shift
Show/hide smart guides	Cmd + U	Ctrl + U

COPY

Drag copy of object with Selection or Direct Selection tool	Option + drag	Alt + drag
Drag copy of object (any tool chosen)	Cmd + Option + drag	Ctrl + Alt + drag

Clipboard

Cut	Cmd + X	Ctrl + X
Copy	Cmd + C	Ctrl + C
Paste	Cmd + V	Ctrl + V
Paste in Front	Cmd + F	Ctrl + F
Paste in Back	Cmd + B	Ctrl + B

FILL & STROKE

Default fill/stroke	D	D
Eyedropper and Paint Bucket tool toggle (either one selected)	Option	Alt
Toggle between Fill and Stroke boxes on Toolbox and Color palette	X	X
Apply last-used solid color	<	<
Apply last-used gradient	>	>
Apply fill or stroke of None	/	/

Color palette

Cycle through color models	Shift + click color spectrum bar	Shift + click color spectrum bar
Swap fill/stroke	Shift + X	Shift + X

	Mac	Windows
Swatches palette		
Set options for new swatch	Option + click New Swatch button	Alt + click New Swatch button
Create new spot color	Cmd + click New Swatch button	Ctrl + click New Swatch button
Create new global process color	Cmd + Shift + click New Swatch button	Ctrl + Shift + click New Swatch button
TRANSFORM		
Set origin, open dialog box for Rotate, Reflect, Scale, or Shear tool	Option + click	Alt + click
Transform object along multiple of 45° for Rotate, Shear tools; 90° for Reflect tool	Shift + drag	Shift + drag
Scale object uniformly (Scale tool dragged diagonally)	Shift + drag	Shift + drag
Transform again	Cmd + D	Ctrl + D
Transform pattern fill, not object, with Rotate, Reflect, or Shear tool	~ drag	~ drag
Transform copy of object with Rotate, Reflect, or Shear tool	Start dragging, then Option + drag	Start dragging, then Alt + drag
Transform copy of object (Transform palette)	Modify value, then press Option + Return	Modify value, then press Alt + Enter
Scale object uniformly (Transform palette)	Modify W or H value, then press Cmd + Return	Modify W or H value, then press Ctrl + Enter
Transform Each dialog box	Cmd + Option + Shift + D	Ctrl + Alt + Shift + D
Bounding box		
Show/hide bounding box	Cmd + Shift + B	Ctrl + Shift + B
Scale object uniformly using bounding box (Free Transform or Selection tool)	Shift + drag handle	Shift + drag handle
Scale object from center using bounding box (Free Transform or Selection tool)	Option + drag handle	Alt + drag handle
Scale object uniformly from center (Free Transform or Selection tool)	Option + Shift + drag corner handle	Alt + Shift + drag corner handle
Free Transform tool		
Transform selected object from center	Option + drag a handle	Alt + drag a handle
Distort selected object	Start dragging corner handle, then Cmd + drag	Start dragging corner handle, then Ctrl + drag
Distort selected object in perspective	Start dragging corner handle, then Cmd + Option + Shift + drag	Start dragging corner handle, then Ctrl + Alt + Shift + drag
Shear selected object along side axis	Start dragging side handle, then Cmd + drag	Start dragging side handle, then Ctrl + drag

	Mac	**Windows**
Shear selected object around center axis	Start dragging side handle, then Cmd + Option + drag	Start dragging side handle, then Ctrl + Alt + drag

LIVE PAINT

Convert to Live Paint object	Cmd + Option + X	Ctrl + Alt + X

RESHAPE

Add Anchor Point and Delete Anchor Point tool toggle (either selected)	Option	Alt
Use Add Anchor Point tool (Scissors tool chosen)	Option	Alt
Use Convert Anchor Point tool (Pen tool chosen)	Option	Alt
Constrain direction line angle to multiple of 45° with Direct Selection or Convert Anchor Point tool	Shift + drag	Shift + drag
Join two selected endpoints	Cmd + J	Ctrl + J
Average two selected endpoints	Cmd + Option + J	Ctrl + Alt + J
Average and Join two selected endpoints	Cmd + Option + Shift + J	Ctrl + Alt + Shift + J
Cut in a straight line with Knife tool	Option + drag	Alt + drag
Cut in 45° increment with Knife tool	Option + Shift	Alt + Shift

DRAWING

Temporary Smooth tool (Pencil tool chosen)	Option	Alt
Close path while drawing with Pencil or Paintbrush tool	Drag, then Option-release	Drag, then Alt-release
Add to existing open path using Pencil tool	Cmd + click to select, then drag from endpoint	Ctrl + click to select, then drag from endpoint
Move anchor point while drawing with Pen	Spacebar + drag	Spacebar + drag

LAYERS

Expand/collapse all sublayers and groups in a layer	Option + click arrowhead	Alt + click arrowhead

Grouping

Group selected objects	Cmd + G	Ctrl + G
Ungroup selected objects	Cmd + Shift + G	Ctrl + Shift + G

Restacking

Bring to front	Cmd + Shift +]	Ctrl + Shift +]
Send to back	Cmd + Shift + [	Ctrl + Shift + [
Bring forward	Cmd +]	Ctrl +]
Send backward	Cmd + [	Ctrl + [

Select

Select layer, sublayer, group, or object	Click selection area or Option + click name	Click selection area or Alt + click name
Add to selection	Shift + click selection area	Shift + click selection area
Copy selection to new layer, sublayer, group	Start dragging selection square, then Option + drag	Start dragging selection square, then Alt + drag

	Mac	**Windows**
Views		
Hide/show all other layers	Option + click eye icon	Alt + click eye icon
View a layer in Outline/Preview view	Cmd + click eye icon	Ctrl + click eye icon
View all other layers in Outline/Preview view	Cmd + Option + click eye icon	Ctrl + Alt + click eye icon
Lock/unlock all other layers	Option + click blank box in second column	Alt + click blank box in second column
Create top-level layers		
Create layer at top of layers list	Cmd + L; or Cmd + click New Layer button	Ctrl + L; or Ctrl + click New Layer button
Create layer, open Layer Options dialog box	Option + click New Layer button	Alt + click New Layer button
Create layer below currently selected layer, open Layer Options dialog box	Cmd + Option + click New Layer button	Ctrl + Alt + click New Layer button
Lock/unlock objects		
Lock selected object	Cmd + 2	Ctrl + 2
Lock all unselected objects	Cmd + Option + Shift + 2	Ctrl + Alt + Shift + 2
Unlock all	Cmd + Option + 2	Ctrl + Alt + 2
TYPE		
Show hidden characters	Cmd + Option + I	Ctrl + Alt + I
Hard return	Return or Enter	Enter
Soft return	Shift + Return or Enter	Shift + Enter
Highlight font field on Character palette	Cmd + Option + Shift + M or F	Ctrl + Alt + Shift + M or F
Create outlines from selected type	Cmd + Shift + O	Ctrl + Shift + O
Type tools		
Use Area Type tool (Type tool selected, over open path)	Option	Alt
Use Path Type tool (Type tool selected, over closed path)	Option	Alt
Switch to vertical/horizontal type tool equivalent as you create type	Shift with any type tool	Shift with any type tool
Switch to Type tool when selecting type block	Double-click with any selection tool	Double-click with any selection tool
Show/hide text threads	Cmd + Shift + Y	Ctrl + Shift + Y
Selecting type		
Select a word	Double-click	Double-click
Select a paragraph	Triple-click	Triple-click
Select all the type in a block	Cmd + A	Ctrl + A
Move insertion pointer left/right one word	Cmd + left/right arrow	Ctrl + left/right arrow

	Mac	**Windows**
Move insertion pointer up/down one line	Up/down arrow	Up/down arrow
Move insertion pointer up/down one paragraph	Cmd + up/down arrow	Ctrl + up/down arrow

Aligning
Align left	Cmd + Shift + L	Ctrl + Shift + L
Align center	Cmd + Shift + C	Ctrl + Shift + C
Align right	Cmd + Shift + R	Ctrl + Shift + R
Justify	Cmd + Shift + J	Ctrl + Shift + J
Justify all lines	Cmd + Shift + F	Ctrl + Shift + F

Point size
Increase point size of selected type	Cmd + Shift + >	Ctrl + Shift + >
Decrease point size of selected type	Cmd + Shift + <	Ctrl + Shift + <
Increase point size by 10	Cmd + Option + Shift + >	Ctrl + Alt + Shift + >
Decrease point size by 10	Cmd + Option + Shift + <	Ctrl + Alt + Shift + <

Leading
Increase leading	Option + down arrow	Alt + down arrow
Decrease leading	Option + up arrow	Alt + up arrow
Increase leading by 10	Cmd + Option + down arrow	Ctrl + Alt + down arrow
Decrease leading by 10	Cmd + Option + up arrow	Ctrl + Alt + up arrow
Set leading to current font size	Double-click leading button on Character palette	Double-click leading button on Character palette

Scaling
Reset horizontal and vertical scale to 100%	Cmd + Shift + X	Ctrl + Shift + X

Kerning and tracking
Highlight kerning field (cursor in text) or highlight tracking field (type object or text selected)	Cmd + Option + K	Ctrl + Alt + K
Increase kerning/tracking	Option + right arrow	Alt + right arrow
Decrease kerning/tracking	Option + left arrow	Alt + left arrow
Increase kerning/tracking 5x	Cmd + Option + right arrow	Ctrl + Alt + right arrow
Decrease kerning/tracking 5x	Cmd + Option + left arrow	Ctrl + Alt + left arrow
Reset kerning/tracking to 0	Cmd + Option + Q	Ctrl + Alt + Q

Baseline shift
Increase baseline shift	Option + Shift + up arrow	Alt + Shift + up arrow
Decrease baseline shift	Option + Shift + down arrow	Alt + Shift + down arrow
Increase baseline shift 5x	Cmd + Option + Shift + up arrow	Ctrl + Alt + Shift + up arrow
Decrease baseline shift 5x	Cmd + Option + Shift + down arrow	Ctrl + Alt + Shift + down arrow

	Mac	**Windows**
Smart quotes		
'	Option + Shift +]	Alt + 0146
'	Option +]	Alt + 0145
"	Option + Shift + [	Alt + 0148
"	Option + [	Alt + 0147

Numeric keypad only

Spelling		
Check spelling	Cmd + I	Ctrl + I
APPEARANCES		
Add new fill	Cmd + /	Ctrl + /
Add new stroke	Cmd + Option + /	Ctrl + Alt + /
EFFECTS & FILTERS		
Apply last filter	Cmd + E	Ctrl + E
Last filter (reopen last filter dialog box)	Cmd + Option + E	Ctrl + Alt + E
Apply last effect	Cmd + Shift + E	Ctrl + Shift + E
Last effect (reopen last effect dialog box)	Cmd + Option + Shift + E	Ctrl + Alt + Shift + E
BLENDS		
Blend > Make	Cmd + Option + B	Ctrl + Alt + B
Blend > Release	Cmd + Option + Shift + B	Ctrl + Alt + Shift + B
GRADIENTS		
Reset Gradient palette to black and white, linear, and 0° angle	Cmd + click Gradient square on palette	Ctrl + click Gradient square on palette
Duplicate color stop	Option + drag color stop	Alt + drag color stop
Apply swatch color to active color stop	Option + click swatch	Alt + click swatch
Mesh tool		
Move mesh point along one of its lines without reshaping perpendicular line	Shift + drag	Shift + drag
Add mesh point using adjacent mesh color	Shift + click	Shift + click
Remove mesh point	Option + click	Alt + click
COMBINE PATHS		
Object > Compound Path > Make	Cmd + 8	Ctrl + 8
Object > Compound Path > Release	Cmd + Option + Shift + 8	Ctrl + Alt + Shift + 8
Pathfinder commands		
Repeat last-used Pathfinder command	Cmd + 4	Ctrl + 4
Turn shape mode button into pathfinder button	Option + click button	Alt + click button
CLIPPING MASKS		
Object > Clipping Mask > Make	Cmd + 7	Ctrl + 7
Object > Clipping Mask > Release	Cmd + Option + 7	Ctrl + Alt + 7

	Mac	**Windows**
TRANSPARENCY		
View only opacity mask in mask edit mode (toggles on/off)	Option + click mask thumbnail	Alt + click mask thumbnail
Disable/enable opacity mask	Shift + click mask thumbnail	Shift + click mask thumbnail
Change opacity in increments of 10 (for increments of 1, omit Shift)	Click field, then Shift + arrow	Click field, then Shift + arrow
ENVELOPE DISTORT		
Make with warp	Cmd + Option + Shift + W	Ctrl + Alt + Shift + W
Make with mesh	Cmd + Option + M	Ctrl + Alt + M
Make with top object	Cmd + Option + C	Ctrl + Alt + C
Edit envelope contents	Cmd + Shift + V	Ctrl + Shift + V
RULERS, GRID & GUIDES		
Show/hide rulers	Cmd + R	Ctrl + R
Show/hide guides	Cmd + ;	Ctrl + ;
Make [convert selected objects to] guides	Cmd + 5	Ctrl + 5
Release [object] guides	Cmd + Shift + double-click guide	Ctrl + Shift + double-click guide
Convert ruler guide between horizontal/vertical orientation	Option + drag new guide	Alt + drag new guide
Lock/unlock guides	Cmd + Option + ;	Ctrl + Alt + ;
Show/hide grid	Cmd + "	Ctrl + "
Snap to grid if Pixel Preview is off; Snap to pixel if Pixel Preview is on	Cmd + Shift + "	Ctrl + Shift + "
Snap to point	Cmd + Option + "	Ctrl + Alt + "
Constrain Measure tool to multiple of 45°	Shift + drag with tool	Shift + drag with tool
PREFERENCES		
General Preferences dialog box	Cmd + K	Ctrl + K
PRINT		
Print dialog box	Cmd + P	Ctrl + P
WEB		
Save for Web dialog box	Cmd + Option + Shift + S	Ctrl + Alt + Shift + S
KEYBOARD SHORTCUTS		
Keyboard Shortcuts dialog box	Cmd + Option + Shift + K	Ctrl + Alt + Shift + K
HELP		
Illustrator Help (HTML Help files)	F1 or Help key	F1

	Mac	**Windows**
BRIDGE		
Browse (Go to Bridge, from Illustrator), or return to Illustrator (or last Adobe Creative Suite 2 application) from Bridge	Cmd + Option + O	Ctrl + Alt + O
FILE MENU		
New Window	Cmd + N	Ctrl + N
New Folder	Cmd + Shift + N	Ctrl + Shift + N
Open	Cmd + O	Ctrl + O
Open in Camera Raw	Cmd + R	Ctrl + R
Eject	Cmd + E	
Close Window	Cmd + W	Ctrl + W
Move to Trash/Recycle Bin	Cmd + Delete	Ctrl + Delete
File Info	Cmd + Option + Shift + I	Ctrl + Alt + Shift + I
Versions	Cmd + Option + Shift + V	Ctrl + Alt + Shift + V
EDIT MENU		
Select All	Cmd + A	Ctrl + A
Select Labeled	Cmd + Option + L	Ctrl + Alt + L
Select Unlabeled	Cmd + Option + Shift + L	Ctrl + Alt + Shift + L
Invert Selection	Cmd + Shift + I	Ctrl + Shift + I
Deselect All	Cmd + Shift + A	Ctrl + Shift + A
Find	Cmd + F	Ctrl + F
Copy Camera Raw Settings	Cmd + Option + C	Ctrl + Alt + C
Paste Camera Raw Settings	Cmd + Option + V	Ctrl + Alt + V
Rotate 90° Clockwise	Cmd +]	Ctrl +]
Rotate 90° Counterclockwise	Cmd + [	Ctrl + [
TOOLS MENU		
Batch Rename	Cmd + Shift + R	Ctrl + Shift + R
LABEL MENU		
No Rating	Cmd + 0	Ctrl + 0
Rating * (one star)	Cmd + 1	Ctrl + 1
Rating ** (two stars)	Cmd + 2	Ctrl + 2
Rating *** (three stars)	Cmd + 3	Ctrl + 3
Rating **** (four stars)	Cmd + 4	Ctrl + 4
Rating ***** (five stars)	Cmd + 5	Ctrl + 5
Decrease rating	Cmd + , (comma)	Ctrl + , (comma)
Increase rating	Cmd + . (period)	Ctrl + . (period)

Keyboard Shortcuts

	Mac	Windows
Label Red	Cmd + 6	Ctrl + 6
Label Yellow	Cmd + 7	Ctrl + 7
Label Green	Cmd + 8	Ctrl + 8
Label Blue	Cmd + 9	Ctrl + 9

VIEW MENU

Toggle between Compact and Full modes	Cmd + Return	Ctrl + Enter
Show Thumbnail Only	Cmd + T	Ctrl + T
Refresh	F5	F5

WINDOW MENU

Reset to Default Workspace	Cmd + F1	Ctrl + F1
Lightbox	Cmd + F2	Ctrl + F2
File Navigator	Cmd + F3	Ctrl + F3
Metadata Focus	Cmd + F4	Ctrl + F4
Filmstrip Focus	Cmd + F5	Ctrl + F5

BRIDGE SLIDESHOW

Slide Show	Cmd + L	Ctrl + L
Show/Hide slideshow commands	H	H
Exit Slideshow	Esc	Esc
Play/Pause	Spacebar	Spacebar
Loop on/off	L	L
Window mode on/off	W	W
Change caption mode	C	C
Change display mode	D	D
Increase/decrease slide duration	S or Shift + S	S or Shift + S
Previous page	Left arrow	Left arrow
Next page	Right arrow	Right arrow
Previous document	Cmd + Left arrow	Ctrl + Left arrow
Next document	Cmd + Right arrow	Ctrl + Right arrow
Rotate 90° clockwise	]	]
Rotate 90° counterclockwise	[	[
Set rating	1–5	1–5
Set label	6–9	6–9
Decrease rating	, (comma)	, (comma)
Increase rating	. (period)	. (period)
Clear rating	0	0
Toggle rating	' (apostrophe)	' (apostrophe)

Customizing shortcuts

If you don't like Illustrator's default shortcuts for commands and tools, or if you want to **assign a shortcut** to a command that has none, you can assign your own. Shortcuts are organized into keysets.

To assign your own shortcuts:

1. Choose Edit > **Keyboard Shortcuts** (Cmd-Option-Shift-K/Ctrl-Alt-Shift-K). The Keyboard Shortcuts dialog box opens (**1**, next page).

2. To edit an existing keyset (set of short-cuts), choose a keyset name from the Set pop-up menu. To create a new keyset, ignore this step (you'll create one later).

3. Choose **Menu Commands** or **Tools** from the next pop-up menu.

4. If you chose Menu Commands, click the arrowhead next to a menu name. To access some commands (e.g., the Type submenu under the Window menu), you'll need to click yet another arrowhead.

5. In the **Shortcut** column next to the com-mand that you want to assign a shortcut to, click in the blank area if the command doesn't have a shortcut (hand pointer), or click an existing shortcut.

6. Press the desired **shortcut** key.

   If that key is already assigned to another command or tool, an alert message will appear in the dialog box, and the short-cut will be removed from the previous command or tool. To assign a new short-cut to the command or tool from which you just removed a shortcut, click Go To, then press a shortcut.
   or
   If you change your mind, click Undo in the dialog box. The shortcut will be reas-signed to its original command or tool. To clear a shortcut altogether, click Clear.

7. *Optional:* In the Symbol column, enter the keyboard symbol you want to appear on the menu or tool tip for the command or tool.

8. Repeat steps 4–7 for any other shortcuts you want to assign.

9. As soon as one user-defined shortcut is entered in the dialog box, the word "Custom" appears on the Set pop-up menu. To create a new keyset to include your new shortcuts, click Save, type a name for the new keyset, click OK, then click OK again to exit the dialog box. The new keyset name will appear on the Set pop-up menu.

or

To save your changes to the currently chosen keyset, click OK.

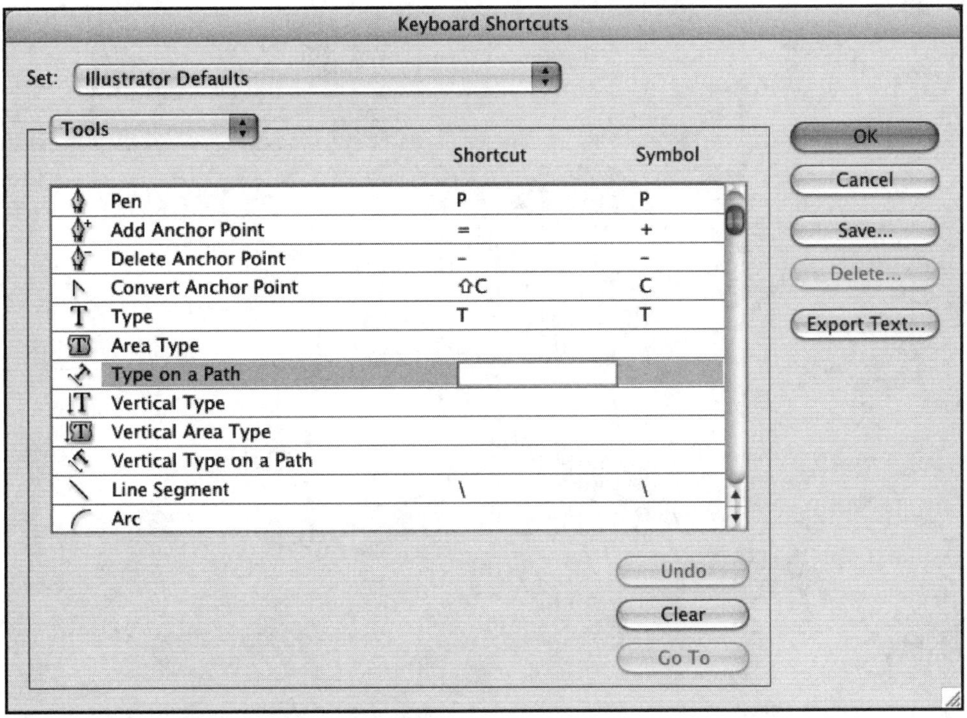

1 *The Keyboard Shortcuts dialog box*

Customize Keyboard Shortcuts

To choose, delete, or print a keyset:

1. Choose Edit > **Keyboard Shortcuts** (Cmd-Option-Shift-K/Ctrl-Alt-Shift-K).

2. Choose a keyset from the **Set** pop-up menu.

3. To **use** the chosen keyset, click OK.
   or
   To **delete** the chosen keyset, click Delete, then click OK.
   or
   To **print** the chosen keyset, click Export Text, choose a location in which to save the file, type a name for the keyset, click Save, then click OK to exit the dialog box. Open the new file in TextEdit in Mac ■ or Notepad in Win, and print it.

1 *The keyset displayed as a TextEdit document*

Choose, Delete, Print Keyset

INDEX

DANIEL PELAVIN

Index

DANIEL PELAVIN

Index

DANIEL PELAVIN

Index

Index

Index

Index

Index

Index

Index

Index

Index

Index

DANIEL PELAVIN